THE NEW NATURAL

A SURVEY OF BRITISH N

FUN

The aim of this series is to interest the general reader in the wildlife
of Britain by recapturing the enquiring spirit of the old naturalists.
The editors believe that the natural pride of the British public
in the native flora, fauna and fungi, to which must be added
concern for their conservation, is best fostered
by maintaining a high standard of accuracy
combined with clarity of exposition
in presenting the results
of modern scientific
research.

THE NEW NATURALIST LIBRARY

FUNGI

BRIAN SPOONER &
PETER ROBERTS

Collins

This edition published in 2005 by Collins,
an imprint of HarperCollins Publishers

HarperCollins Publishers
77–85 Fulham Palace Road
London W6 8JB
www.collins.co.uk

First published 2005

A cip catalogue record for this book is available
from the British Library

Set in FF Nexus by
Rowland Phototypesetting Ltd,
Bury St Edmunds, Suffolk

Printed in Thailand by Imago
Reprographics by Colourscan, Singapore

Hardback ISBN 0–00–220152–6
Paperback ISBN 0–00–220153–4

Contents

Editors' Preface

I T I S N O W more than 50 years since John Ramsbottom's *Mushrooms and Toadstools* first appeared as Volume 7 in the New Naturalist series. It fast became one of the most prominent of the early titles, running to a total of six impressions before finally going out of print in 1983. The Editors have long planned a successor which would present an up-to-date account of fungal natural history that took into account all the developments in the subject over the past half-century. Thus it is with particular satisfaction that we welcome *Fungi* as Volume 96, written by two of the country's leading mycologists.

Brian Spooner is Head of Mycology at the Royal Botanic Gardens, Kew, where he has worked since 1975, and is an authority on the British Ascomycetes. Peter Roberts also works at Kew as a Senior Mycologist with a particular interest in the non-agaricoid Basidiomycetes.

In 1953, the Editors wrote in the preface to *Mushrooms and Toadstools*, 'Dr. Ramsbottom could undoubtedly have written – in fact, did, in the first place, write – a book more than double the present length; and even then, he complained that much had to be omitted!' Honesty compels us to record that the present authors had to be no less curtailed and no doubt harbour a similar grumble about the Editors! It is now generally accepted that the original view that the living world could be conveniently divided into plants and animals, albeit with the bacteria constituting an awkward anomaly, is no longer adequate to describe the diversity of the planet. The fungi are now recognised as a separate Kingdom of their own, but back in the early 1950s, this view was only just beginning to be universally accepted. Indeed, one of the questions that John Ramsbottom rather coyly skirted around was 'What is a fungus?'.

Fungi contain some of the most beautiful, bizarre and grotesque products of evolution on the planet. Among them can be found some of the largest and long-lived organisms on earth. There is probably no corner of the globe that is without them. Most importantly, they form intimate associations with other organisms, enabling them to live in conditions from which they would otherwise be excluded. The partnerships between fungi and green algae, or cyanobacteria, that produce lichens are well known, but it is now recognised that, among the higher plants, those without a fungal partner are the exception rather than the rule. Indeed, it may well be that the invasion of the land itself was crucially facilitated by the evolution of these plant-fungal partnerships. Finally, fungi touch our own lives as causers of crop diseases and, more positively, from the yeast that provides our daily bread to the antibiotics on which modern medicine depends. Some of these aspects have already been covered in recent New Naturalist volumes such as David Ingram's and Noel Robertson's *Plant Disease* (85) and Oliver Gilbert's *Lichens* (86), but for the rest, we confidently leave the reader to discover in the following pages.

Authors' Foreword and Acknowledgements

I T I S N O W more than half a century since John Ramsbottom's classic *Mushrooms and Toadstools* was published in the New Naturalist series. It was the first of the series to deal with fungi and contained a wealth of information, focused particularly on the development of mycology and the ecology of fungi, which helped bring both subjects to the wider audience they deserve.

The succeeding 50 years has seen immense progress in the study of fungi, establishing even more firmly the major role they play in the environment and in our day-to-day lives, and highlighting the extraordinary diversity of these ancient and ubiquitous organisms. Gone are the days when fungi were treated as an obscure subset of 'lower plants' studied mainly as unwanted causers of disease. They are now understood to form intimate and beneficial partnerships with almost every form of life, from bacteria and algae to flowering plants, insects and even mammals, while also providing the vital service of decay, decomposition and nutrient recycling on which all terrestrial life depends.

So integral are fungi to the health and wealth of mankind that nobody can escape their influence even on a daily basis. It is true we still suffer the unwanted effects of fungal decay – from moulds and crop diseases to dry rot and athlete's foot – but increasingly we are discovering the many and varied benefits of fungi, in new and traditional foods and drinks, in pharmaceuticals, in forest and agricultural management, in biological pest-control and in the bioremediation of oil spills and waste pollution.

The fungi themselves have finally been recognised as forming their own kingdom distinct from animals and plants. It is no small kingdom either. The mushrooms and toadstools of Ramsbottom's book, as diverse and numerous as they are, are just a small part of the vast assemblage of fungi, probably amounting to well over a million species worldwide, the majority of which remain as yet undescribed and still unknown to science.

It is clearly impossible to cover all aspects of modern mycology in a single volume, and our aims have therefore been to look at the ecology and influence of fungi, to give some idea of their diversity and importance, and to outline their main characteristics. A lot more could be said about their structure, biology and physiology, but these topics are already well covered in student and academic texts. A lot more could also be said about recognising and identifying fungi in the field but, fortunately, today's forayers can choose from a wide selection of well-illustrated field guides – an indication of the growing popularity of fungi as a worthwhile subject to explore. We hope this new book will be a complementary volume to such field guides, giving the interested naturalist a few extra insights into what is going on behind the scenes in the fungal world.

The writing of this work has proved to be a far longer and more involved exercise than was originally envisaged, and we owe considerable thanks to our publishers for their patience in allowing it to develop over several more years than were initially planned. It has also been the source of endless surprise and learning, with many of the subjects covered proving far more complex and far-reaching than we ever imagined, leading us not only into byways but also some major highways of research of which we previously knew little. Keeping up with the constant flow of new papers, new discoveries and information has also been a challenge, albeit an exciting one, and we have tried our best to keep pace. We would like to acknowledge all the mycologists and other researchers who, through their many and various papers and books, have unwittingly helped us create this book. Our initial hope was to list all our sources and references, but when the working bibliography started heading for the 100-page mark, common-sense (and our publishers) dictated a substantial cut-back. The references that remain will, we hope, still be of use for exploring many topics further.

It is a big book, but the kingdom of the fungi is an even bigger subject. We trust that you may find at least a few new, interesting, remarkable and entertaining things inside.

The broad scope of the book has required an equally broad search for photographs and images to illustrate the many different kinds of fungi involved. The authors are indebted to the following generous individuals, who responded so promptly and positively to our requests for help in sourcing illustrations, and for kindly giving permission to use their photographs and images. Additional thanks are due to Paul Bridge and Julian Mitchell and also to Lynton Mclain who supplied further information on some specialist topics.

Mary Adler; Gordon Beakes (School of Biology, Newcastle University); Paul Bridge (British Antarctic Survey, Cambridge); Hilda Canter-Lund (Freshwater Biological Association, Ambleside); Tom Cope (Royal Botanic Gardens, Kew); Jim Cross (deceased); Rod Eaton (University of Portsmouth); David Ellis (Women's and Children's Hospital, Adelaide, Australia; Kaminski's Digital Image Library); Shelley Evans; Tony Fletcher (University of Leicester); Neil Gow (University of Aberdeen); Liz Holden; F.B. Hora (deceased); Barrie Hughes; Kevin Ingleby (Centre for Ecology and Hydrology, Edinburgh); Hans Kerp (University of Münster, Germany); Geoffrey Kibby; Paul Kirk (CABI Bioscience, Egham); Thomas Læssøe (Institute of Biology, Copenhagen); Tony Leech; Patricia Livermore; Joyce E. Longcore (University of Maine, USA); Martin Love; Andrew McRobb (Royal Botanic Gardens, Kew); Julian Mitchell (University of Portsmouth); Steve Moss (deceased); J. Palmer; Graham Piearce; Grace Prendergast (Royal Botanic Gardens, Kew); Margaret Ramsay (Royal Botanic Gardens, Kew); John Rickwood; Susan Stanley (University of Portsmouth); H. Voglmayr (Institute of Botany, University of Vienna); Alex Weir (University of Syracuse, USA); Alga Zuccaro (Technische Universität Braunschweig, Germany).

CHAPTER 1

Neither Animals nor Plants

A NIMAL, vegetable, or mineral? For centuries, this simple system of classification happily divided the natural world into three great, god-given categories. Fungi, if considered at all, were normally placed in the 'vegetable' category or occasionally (as 'excrescences of the earth') in amongst the minerals.

We now know that fungi are neither plants nor animals, and are certainly not earthy outgrowths. But if not these, then what exactly are they? The question sounds simple, but proves in fact to be a highly complex one, with many aspects still not fully understood. The enormous diversity of the fungi, not just the larger and more obvious species, but the innumerable microfungi and 'fungus-like' organisms, presents an immense challenge in clarifying their interrelationships and defining their characters. Nevertheless, remarkable progress in recent years, due not least to the advent of molecular systematics, has painted a much clearer picture and allows a fuller answer to the question 'What are fungi?'.

In this first chapter, we consider this question and say something about the distinguishing characters of fungi, their classification, and main groups.

Hyphae: the threads of fungal life

Scoop up a handful of old, damp, woodland leaf litter and you will probably find that it is bound together with a cobweb-like mat of fungal strands. The same thing can be found in the compost of a mushroom bed or in a crumbling piece of rotten wood. Under a microscope, mushrooms them-selves, the moulds on rotting food, and the hard brackets on a tree stump are all seen to be composed of these same fine strands. These are 'hyphae' (Fig. 1), the building blocks of all filamentous fungi. They are essentially hollow tubes, the living parts of which contain nuclei, mitochondria, and other organelles, just as do animal and plant cells. In most fungi, the hyphae are divided into compartments by cross-walls (septa), keeping the organelles separate in cell-like units, the septa themselves having microscopic pores, allowing movement of water and nutrients from one compartment to another.

Fungi absorb nutrients through the walls of the hyphae, 'feeding' in much the same way as plant roots. All species can absorb small molecules such as amino acids and simple sugars, particularly glucose, but many produce digestive enzymes which can attack more complex substances such as cellulose and starch, breaking them down into simpler components. Wood-rotting fungi, for example, can break down cellulose and sometimes

FIG 1. Hyphae from the agaric *Leucopaxillus giganteus* showing septa (cross-walls) and swollen clamp connections (see also Fig. 4) which are typical of basidiomycetes (RBG Kew).

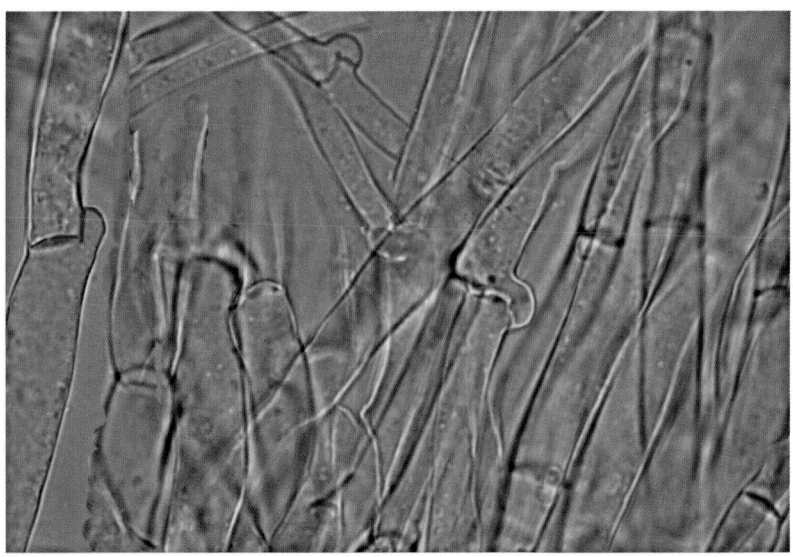

FIG 2. Mycelium of a corticioid fungus spreading over the underside of a log. The hyphae show a tendency to clump together, forming visible branches and fronds (S. Evans).

lignin, whilst others can break down keratin (found in hair and feathers), chitin (found in insects and other fungi), and various more surprising substances, including kerosene. This method of nutrition is the main reason why fungi are the principal agents of natural decay and nutrient recycling (Chapter Three).

Individual hyphae are microscopically small, typically around 5–20 μm wide (a micrometre (μm) or 'micron' is one millionth of a metre), but when branched and growing together they can easily be seen as a cobwebby, mould-like growth (Fig. 2). This is termed the 'mycelium' (or 'spawn' in cultivated mushrooms) and is how most filamentous fungi grow through a nutrient-rich substratum, be it rotten wood, dung, damp leaf litter, or a long-forgotten sandwich. Each hypha branches and grows from the tip, spreading indefinitely as long as there is a food source. Components needed to synthesise new walls are produced throughout the hypha and actively transported to the growing tip. Branching commonly occurs, usually behind a septum, by thinning of the hyphal wall and extension of a new growing tip. This method of growth can be extremely efficient in appropriate conditions, with growth rates in some fungi, such as the common ascomycete *Neurospora crassa*, as high as 6 mm per hour. This is one reason why moulds are such rapid and effective colonisers. It also explains why some fungi have become very large (the biggest living organisms on the planet, in fact) and also very old (potentially, perhaps even immortal).

Fruitbodies: from mushrooms to moulds

Hyphae become most visible when they combine to produce complex spore-bearing structures or 'fruitbodies'. These fruitbodies include the mushrooms and toadstools, brackets, puffballs, truffles, cup fungi, morels, and so on, which most people think of as 'fungi'.

Examination of sections of any fruitbody under a microscope will demonstrate that it is almost entirely composed of hyphae. In fleshy species, like mushrooms, the hyphae are generally distinct and easily visible but in many fungi the hyphae are variously modified by being swollen, thick-walled, gelatinised, compacted, pigmented, ornamented, or any combination of these. From these structural hyphae, which comprise the bulk of any fruitbody, specialised spore-bearing hyphae arise, capable of releasing the spores by which the fungus reproduces and forms new colonies.

An ordinary cultivated mushroom provides a familiar example. The fruitbodies arise from the mycelium in soil or compost, once it has reached a certain age and bulk. Their development is triggered by various factors, including temperature, humidity, aeration, nutrient availability, and the presence of physical constraints (many larger fungi fruit where mycelial growth is checked, often by compacted earth at the edge of a path). Though mushrooms famously grow in the dark, other fungi may need light to initiate fruiting. However, this can be astonishingly brief, an exposure of just 12 seconds being sufficient for *Neurospora crassa*. Blue light at the right intensity is required for this species, whilst others prefer near-ultraviolet light, or varying periods of light and darkness. The effects of light on fruitbody development can be quite complex, stimulating the development of some species but inhibiting others. In some cases, fruitbodies developed in dark conditions exhibit weird and monstrous forms (Chapter 13).

Many species of dung-inhabiting fungi are 'phototropic', actively growing towards a light source in order to discharge their spores most efficiently into the air stream.

The young mushroom fruitbody or 'primordium' initially resembles little more than a knot of hyphae, but quickly grows and differentiates below the soil surface. At the 'button' stage it is effectively fully formed and (if conditions, particularly humidity, are right) is ready to expand, breaking the surface and becoming visible as a fresh mushroom. It continues to expand and mature until the spores are released. This expansion phase, effectively using hydraulic pressure, is rapid and extremely powerful, generating a considerable force. Mushrooms developing below paving stones, for example, will readily lift the stones as they expand and mature. Buller (1931) showed that the delicate ink-cap toadstool *Coprinus sterquilinus* can raise a weight of over 200 grams during the development of its fruitbody, without breaking its stem. Spore production in the cultivated mushroom typically continues for several days (if left unpicked), after which the fruitbody collapses and rots away. A single mycelium will produce many such mushrooms, both simultaneously and in succession, during the fruiting season. In the wild state, further crops will be produced the following year, and so on indefinitely, as long as nutrients are available.

The mushroom itself has three main parts: the stem (or 'stipe'), which lifts the fertile part into the air; the cap (or 'pileus') which covers and supports the fruiting surface; and the gills (or 'lamellae'), on which the spores are produced. In addition, protective membranes (or veils) are present in many mushroom and toadstool species. These may enclose the entire developing fruitbody (a universal veil) or cover just the developing gills (a partial veil). At maturity, these veils rupture and leave either a sac-like 'volva' at the base of the stem and scale-like remnants on the cap (universal veil), or a ring on the stem (partial veil) (Fig. 3).

Though mushrooms and toadstools are ephemeral, lasting only for a few hours or at most for a few days, some of the wood-rotting bracket fungi have tough, long-lasting fruitbodies which allow a much longer period of spore release but represent a substantial investment for the fungus concerned. As a result, many brackets are perennial, some persisting for twenty years or more, producing a new spore-producing layer each year. It is often possible

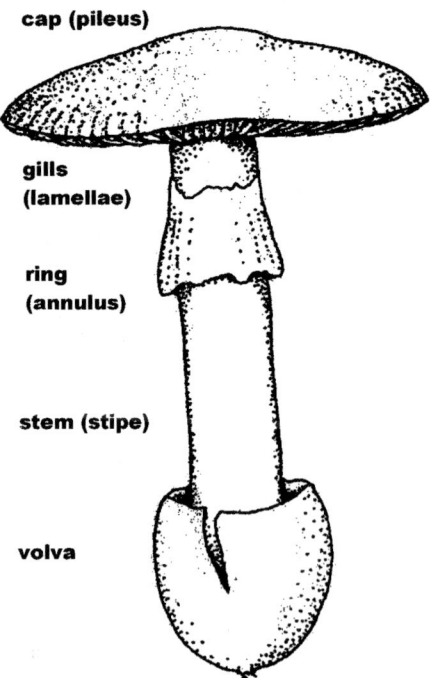

cap (pileus)

**gills
(lamellae)**

**ring
(annulus)**

stem (stipe)

volva

FIG 3. Features of a typical agaric fruitbody (*Amanita* species). The ring and volva are remnants of veils that rupture as the toadstool expands (P. Roberts).

to count these, like tree rings, if the bracket is damaged or cut through vertically. The structural hyphae in such fruitbodies are unusually thick-walled (so-called 'skeletal' hyphae) and in the toughest fruitbodies are further strengthened by being interwoven with equally thick-walled 'binding' hyphae. The result may be a bracket that feels as hard and solid as the wood on which it is growing.

Most moulds, mildews, and other microfungi produce small, often microscopic fruitbodies, or have no specialised structures. Typically, a mould produces a felty colony of modified surface hyphae which produce asexual spores (or 'conidia') on specialised cells. These conidia, often produced in vast quantities, serve to colonise new and often ephemeral substrata.

Sex and spores

Sex, as we know it, is a very different process in the fungi. Indeed, some species, mainly moulds and yeasts, manage without it, and populations are essentially clones. In others, both sexual and asexual reproductive stages occur at different points in their life cycle, each stage producing a distinct and usually independent fruitbody, known as the 'anamorph' (asexual fruitbody) and 'teleomorph' (sexual fruitbody). In addition, a mechanism termed 'heterokaryosis', which also leads to genetic diversification, may occur in asexual stages. This follows fusion of different hyphae, which results in two or more genetically slightly different nuclear types in the same mycelium, providing some genetic mixing despite the lack of sex.

In general, however, sexual reproduction is as important to fungi as to other organisms. Typically it involves the union of hyphae (or yeast cells)

FIG 4. How clamp connections are formed in basidiomycetes. Hyphae are typically dikaryotic (with two genetically distinct nuclei in each hyphal cell, represented by black and white dots). When the nuclei divide and new cells start to form, there is a danger that two of the same nuclei may enter the new cell. But the process of clamp formation, shown here in three very simplified stages, ensures that the dikaryotic condition is maintained (P. Roberts).

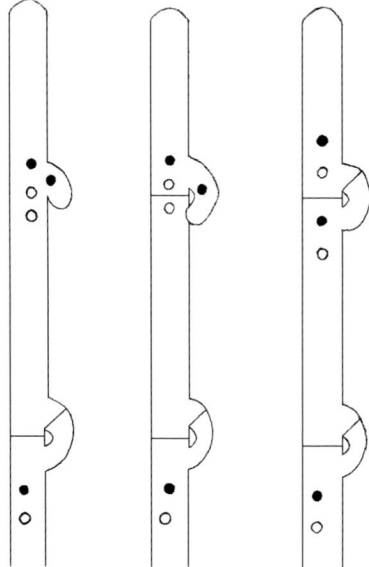

containing nuclei with a single set of chromosomes (i.e. haploid, with half the full complement), the resulting hypha (or cell) being then 'dikaryotic', containing nuclei of two different types. In basidiomycetes (the large group which includes mushrooms and toadstools) proliferation of dikaryotic hyphae usually occurs through the formation of 'clamp connections', unique structures found in no other group of fungi. After division of each nucleus, one nucleus migrates into a bulge in the wall of the hypha and, after formation of a septum, is transferred to the newly formed uninucleate adjacent cell, so maintaining the dikaryotic condition (Fig. 4). Sooner or later, the haploid nuclei in dikaryotic hyphae will fuse to produce a diploid nucleus with two sets of chromosomes. In due course, this nucleus undergoes 'meiosis', a division process which effectively restores the haploid condition, but combines in each resulting cell chromosomes from two different sources. Following meiosis, haploid spores are produced, allowing dispersal to occur (Fig. 5). A few species of fungi produce morphologically distinct reproductive cells, roughly the equivalent of sperm and ova, but since both can arise from the same parent fungus there is no real differentiation between 'male' and 'female'.

Inbreeding within a population in general decreases its adaptive potential. In many fungi, populations are therefore self-sterile and can 'mate'

FIG 5. Meiosis in typical basidiomycetes. The young basidium is dikaryotic, containing two genetically distinct haploid nuclei. These fuse to form a single diploid nucleus which then undergoes meiosis, forming four new haploid nuclei. Each of the new nuclei then migrates into a developing haploid spore (P. Roberts).

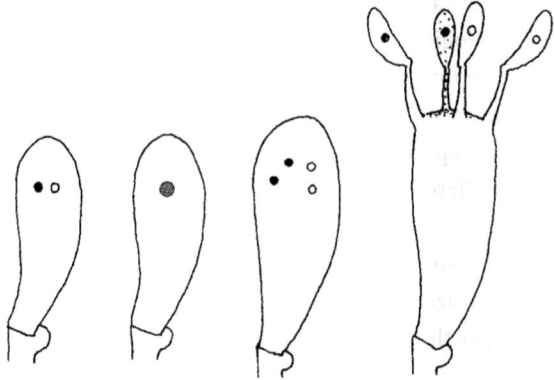

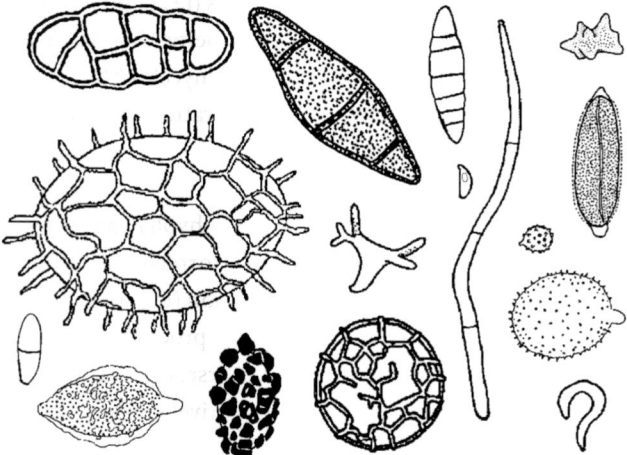

FIG 6. A selection of fungal spores to give a flavour of the enormous diversity of size, shape, pigmentation, ornamentation and septation that they exhibit. Spores may be simple or multicellular, and many bear appendages or a mucilaginous coat, all adaptations to particular ecologies. Others may have complex coils and branches, as shown in Fig. 103 depicting spores of aquatic fungi (P. Roberts & B. Spooner).

only with adjacent populations. Such fungi are termed 'heterothallic'. Others, in contrast, are self-fertile and these are known as 'homothallic'. Heterothallism is due to the existence of 'alleles' (different types of a single gene) which effectively produce different strains of the same fungus, commonly referred to as 'plus' and 'minus'. A plus strain cannot mate with another plus strain, but can do so with any minus strain. Such different mating types, morphologically indistinguishable, occur in the majority of fungi. The existence in many species of multiple alleles, present in different populations, can lead to highly complex situations with large numbers of mating types. The ink cap *Coprinus cinereus*, for example, has been shown to have at least 1,152 different mating types, whilst other fungi may have even more!

Most fungi produce some kind of spores, individually microscopic but varying enormously in size. The smallest, no more than about 2 or 3 μm across, are hardly larger than bacteria, whereas the largest may reach almost 500 μm (0.5 mm) in length (Fig. 6). In mushrooms and toadstools, spores are normally around 5–20 μm long, depending on species. They are typically produced in vast quantities, often in billions. To see them, take a mature mushroom, remove the stalk, place the cap on a piece of white paper or glass, cover with a glass to prevent drying out, and leave overnight. The result will be an attractive chocolate-brown spore deposit comprising several million spores (Fig. 7). Each spore is capable of germination, but clearly very, very few ever encounter precisely the right conditions to form a new mycelium and continue the species.

FIG 7. Spore deposit or 'print' of the commercial mushroom (*Agaricus bisporus*). As well as forming attractive patterns reflecting gill arrangement, spore deposits have scientific value in showing precise spore colour and in comprising fully mature spores (RBG Kew).

A KINGDOM APART

Fungi are clearly a very distinctive group of organisms, but just where do they fit into the grand scheme of things?

All life on Earth can be classified into a number of separate, major units known as 'kingdoms', each representing an ancient lineage that has evolved into a multiplicity of modern species. Just how many kingdoms are required to encompass this multiplicity is, however, uncertain. The simplistic view recognised just two, 'animals' and 'plants', following classical beliefs established long before the foundation of modern systematics by Linnaeus in the mid 18th century. This comfortable tradition continued almost unchallenged for close on three centuries, and not until the latter part of the 20th century has it been radically reviewed and replaced. This change has largely reflected progress in the study of micro-organisms, involving ultrastructural and biochemical characters and especially the application of molecular systematics, advances which have finally shown that a two-kingdom system is hopelessly inadequate to encompass the huge diversity of life on Earth. A several-kingdom structure of life is now not in dispute.

Although fungi, as well as protozoa and bacteria, had occasionally been considered separate kingdoms at various times since the 17th century, no consensus on this view was held until comparatively recently. Margulis & Schwartz (1982) were the first to propose the classification of living organisms into five kingdoms, following earlier suggestions by Whittaker (1969). More recently, a six kingdom system has been suggested (Cavalier-Smith, 1998), although it now seems that Woese et al. (1990) were correct in splitting one of these kingdoms (the *Prokaryota* or bacteria) into two, the *Archaea* and the *Bacteria*. Prokaryotes are single-celled structures, the most ancient of all organisms, with which life on Earth began. Their cells lack nuclei or other subcellular structures (organelles) such as mitochondria, and their DNA is dispersed. Prokaryotes probably evolved at least 4,000,000,000 years ago and were for an immense period of time the only life forms on the planet. Eventually, after at least two billion years of slow evolution, they gave rise to the more complex 'eukaryotes', organisms with sophisticated cells containing separate organelles. The most important of these are the 'nucleus', which governs the cell and in which the DNA is packaged, and the 'mitochondria', which provide energy.

All life other than bacteria is eukaryotic, highly evolved and diversified over the last two billion years into five separate kingdoms. These are the plants (kingdom *Plantae*), the animals (kingdom *Animalia*), the true fungi (kingdom *Fungi*), and the less well-known kingdoms *Chromista* and *Protozoa* which both contain some fungus-like organisms. *Protozoa* is probably the most ancient of the eukaryotic kingdoms and includes a total of thirteen 'phyla' (the next main unit (or taxon) below kingdom), a level which distinguishes human beings (phylum *Chordata*) from jellyfish (phylum *Cnidaria*). *Animalia* comprises 23 phyla, *Plantae* and *Chromista* each have five, and four phyla make up the *Fungi*. In this system, most of the organisms traditionally called 'fungi' belong within the kingdom *Fungi*, but some are placed within the *Protozoa* and *Chromista*. Although this seven-kingdom system is not yet fully accepted, it seems to be gaining favour as the current standard model. Nonetheless, significant changes are still being proposed and it seems likely that even the highest levels in the classification of life will remain in a state of flux for a long time to come.

Defining the fungi

Each of the seven kingdoms, as with all taxa, has its own unique features. In the old two-kingdom view of life, fungi were placed with plants mainly because, unlike animals, they do not move around. This is undeniably true, but is hardly a good scientific definition. The fungal mode of nutrition, for example, is quite different from that of plants. Like animals, they are 'heterotrophs', unable to make their own food and requiring organic carbon derived from plants or other organisms. Unlike animals, however, which ingest their food, fungi digest and absorb nutrients externally. Plants, in contrast, are 'autotrophs', making their food by photosynthesis, their cells containing chlorophyll and able to use sunlight to convert carbon dioxide into sugars. Fungi also differ structurally from plants, in particular lacking cellulose which is characteristic of plant cell walls. Instead, fungi are mainly composed of chitin, the same basic material that makes up insect exoskeletons.

Recognition of a separate kingdom for fungi was a major advance, although it was soon evident that the kingdom was not yet homogeneous but included organisms placed there because of similarities in their mode of nutrition, now known to have arisen independently from a different ancestor. As long ago as 1864, de Bary had proposed that slime moulds were not fungi but actually protozoa, a conclusion which, because of the fungus-like nature of their fruitbodies, only recently received acceptance. Slime moulds (*Myxomycota*) are actually 'phagotrophs', ingesting bacteria and fungi by means of amoeboid stages, typical of protozoa. Again, the filamentous nature and mode of nutrition of the 'actinomycetes' placed them with the fungi until it was realised that they were actually prokaryotic and belonged instead with the bacteria. Their fungus-like characters were evolved quite independently, and the same has been found to apply to some other fungus-like organisms. As a result, definition of the 'true fungi' cannot be simply stated but relies on characters such as mode of nutrition, chemistry of the cell wall, biosynthetic pathways and ultrastructure of the mitochondria. The taxonomic value of this last character, first suggested in the 1960s, has now become firmly established (Cavalier-Smith, 2001). Mitochondrial cristae, essentially folds of the inner membrane of the mitochondrion, are flattened in *Fungi* but tubular in other groups, providing a major (but not the only) distinction between *Fungi* and other heterotrophs. On this basis, the kingdom can be technically defined as follows:

> "*The* Fungi *comprise non-photosynthetic eukaryotes with an absorptive nutrition that do not have an amoeboid pseudopodial stage, and may occur as both single celled and multicelled organisms. The cell walls contain chitin and ß-glucans, and their mitochondria have flattened cristae.*"

FROM MOULDS TO MUSHROOMS: A GUIDE TO THE MAJOR GROUPS

The classification adopted for fungi in this book recognises the three kingdoms (*Fungi*, *Chromista*, and *Protozoa*) noted above and broadly follows that given in the most recent edition of the 'Dictionary of the Fungi' (Kirk *et al.*, 2001), with some modifications based on recent findings. However, with continued rapid development of techniques such as molecular analysis it seems unlikely that the system suggested here will yet prove a stable one. Nevertheless, the following brief guide should help place the fungi discussed throughout this book into appropriate context.

KINGDOM FUNGI: ASCOMYCOTA

The *Ascomycota*, the largest of the fungal phyla, contains not only the more visible cup-fungi, morels and truffles, but also the ubiquitous and often microscopic flask fungi, most of the lichens, and many of the asexual yeasts and moulds. Ascomycetes occur worldwide, and exhibit an enormous range of life styles and forms. Currently, the phylum is divided into seven classes, 56 orders, and well over 200 families. Total species numbers are difficult to estimate, but it seems that at least 40,000 ascomycetes are known worldwide, with several times that number yet to be described. About 5,500 ascomycetes (excluding asexual stages likely to belong within this phylum) have been recorded from Britain, including around 1,800 lichenised species.

Ascomycetes are characterised by the possession of 'asci', microscopic club-shaped cells in which sexual spores ('ascospores'), are developed. Asci themselves are extremely diverse in structure and provide the basis for the current classification of these fungi (Fig. 8). In many species, including

FIG 8. Examples of different types of asci, the cells in which the spores of ascomycetes are produced. They exhibit immense diversity in shape, size, wall structure and method of spore release, providing a basis for classification of these fungi (B. Spooner).

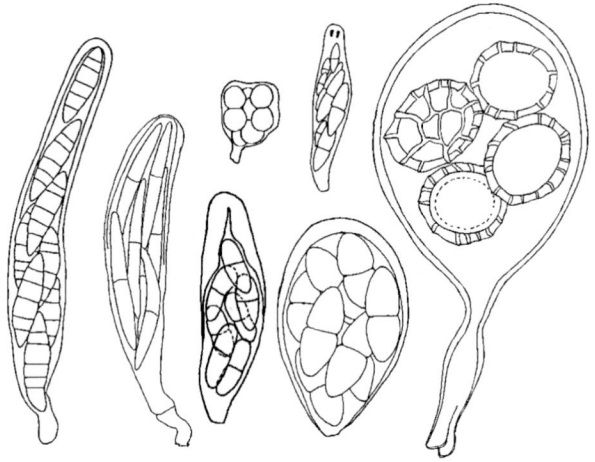

most of the larger ascomycetes, asci are simple structures which have a single, one-layer wall and are therefore referred to as 'unitunicate'. However, many other ascomycetes have asci with complex wall structures involving more than one layer. These are termed 'bitunicate' but are themselves diverse in their microanatomy and method of functioning for spore discharge. Ascomycetes are also characterised by the structure of their hyphal walls which involve two layers of differing density to electrons. It is this character which can be used to determine the ascomycetous affinities of most asexual fungi in which the ascus stage is lacking.

Two main forms of fruitbody provide convenient if artificial groupings for the bulk of species. These are the cup-fungi, or 'discomycetes', and the flask fungi, or 'pyrenomycetes'. In addition, there are the ascomycetous yeasts together with the anamorphic stages of ascomycetes, usually known as 'hyphomycetes' and 'coelomycetes'.

Cup-fungi or discomycetes

Cup-fungi are virtually cosmopolitan in distribution and occur in all habitat types. Although most are saprobes (living off dead matter), they also include mycorrhizal species (symbiotically associated with plant roots) as well as many parasites and pathogens. Some of the larger cup-fungi, particularly truffles and morels, are edible and sought after.

The term 'cup fungus' refers only to a general design and has little taxonomic value in itself. The fruitbodies (known as 'apothecia') of most species take the form of miniature cups, goblets, or discs, with the spore-bearing layer on the inner surface. However, some have diverged markedly from this basic design, and form complex, compound structures, as in the honeycomb-like morels (*Morchella* species), or have become totally enclosed and chambered, as in the truffles and other subterranean species.

Most apothecia are small, only a millimetre or so across and sometimes much smaller, but they often occur in swarms on rotting stems or leaves. Many are highly attractive, especially when examined with a lens, displaying a range of colours and often delicately ornamented with hair-like structures. Most of the smaller species have characteristic asci termed 'inoperculate' (lacking a lid) referring to their mode of spore discharge through an apical pore (as in the genus *Bisporella*, Fig. 9) . They belong mainly to the order

FIG 9. *Bisporella citrina*, one of the smaller inoperculate discomycetes, often found in swarms on dead wood and stems. The distinctive bright yellow fruitbodies are fairly common on rotten logs (B. Spooner).

Helotiales and are the most numerous of the cup-fungi with perhaps 1,500 species known from Britain and 4,000 or so worldwide.

Fundamentally distinct from the *Helotiales* are the cup-fungi that belong to the *Pezizales*. These are distinguished by their asci being 'operculate', releasing their spores through an apical lid or 'operculum'. Most *Pezizales* have easily visible fruitbodies often several centimetres across or more, and most of the larger cup fungi belong here. They include the striking orange-peel fungus *Aleuria aurantia*, the equally flamboyant scarlet elf-cups in the genus *Sarcoscypha*, and a range of variously coloured *Otidea* and *Peziza* species. More complex in form and among the largest of the *Pezizales* are the spring-fruiting morels (*Morchella* species) and autumn-fruiting saddle-fungi (*Helvella* species; Fig. 10). Though less numerous than the *Helotiales*, there are nevertheless over 300 species of *Pezizales* known in Britain and almost 1,200 worldwide. Closely related to them are the truffles (*Tuber* species) and others which have evolved underground fruitbodies adapted to their unique ecology and quite unlike typical discomycetes. They include some of the most sought after edible fungi.

Disc-like fruitbodies are also produced by many lichens, these belonging mainly in the *Lecanorales*, distinguished not just by their mode of life but by the structure of their asci. This is the largest order of ascomycetes, comprising a huge range of forms currently divided into more than 40 families and including some 5,500 species worldwide, more than 1,000 of which occur in Britain.

Although more than 11,000 cup-fungi (including lichenised species) have been described world-wide, they remain little known. New species are frequently encountered, and their ecology and life histories, physiology and chemistry are, for the most part, little-studied. Their bewildering diversity provides a seemingly endless challenge, even within the British Isles.

FIG 10. *Helvella crispa*, one of the larger operculate discomycetes which have become modified into a stalk and a saddle-shaped cap. This whitish species is common in woodlands (B. Spooner).

Flask fungi or pyrenomycetes

The second big group of ascomycetes has flask-shaped fruitbodies ('perithecia'), fully enclosing the asci except, in most cases, for an apical pore ('ostiole') through which the spores are liberated. These fungi are even more diverse than the discomycetes, and are almost ubiquitous in their distribution. They include parasites as well as saprobes and symbionts, many of which are lichenised.

The flask fungi have tiny fruitbodies, some less than a tenth of a millimetre wide and none exceeding about two millimetres across. Most are dark-walled, appearing black to the eye, although some, such as coral spot, *Nectria cinnabarina*, are bright red or orange. The fruitbodies are usually gregarious but often developed inside plant tissue and largely hidden from view with only the ostioles breaking the surface. Others, however, develop conspicuous and sometimes massive areas of sterile tissue in which numerous perithecia are immersed. Since this tissue, known as a 'stroma', is typically black, many of these flask fungi appear burnt or carbonised, hence the term 'pyrenomycetes' (literally 'fire fungi'). Stromatic tissue varies greatly in structure and extent. At its simplest it merely comprises dark hyphae in the epidermal cells of the host, covering just a single perithecium, as in species of *Anthostomella* (*Xylariaceae*). In other cases, including most *Diatrypaceae*, it may blacken the host surface over extensive areas, or become crust-like or cushion-like with numerous embedded perithecia. Discrete, often massive, fruitbodies are formed in some pyrenomycetes, particularly in the *Xylariaceae* and *Hypocreaceae*. Amongst the largest of these are *Daldinia* species, called 'cramp balls' or 'King Alfred's cakes', common in Britain, and species of *Xylaria* (Fig. 11), a genus which includes the familiar black and white candlesnuff fungus, *Xylaria hypoxylon*, and dead man's fingers, *X. polymorpha*, on old stumps and logs. Cutting open one of these blackened 'fingers' reveals a core of whitish, sterile tissue with a multitude of tiny flask-shaped perithecia embedded in the surface layer.

Ascus characters are again fundamental to the classification of pyrenomycetes and on this basis two major groups can be distinguished. The first includes the true flask fungi, ascomycetes with flask-like fruitbodies and unitunicate asci. These are currently divided into at least 12 orders and over 40 families, although their taxonomy remains inadequately understood.

FIG 11. *Xylaria longipes*, recently dubbed 'dead moll's fingers', an ascomycete with large, stromatic fruitbodies. This species, distinguished by its slender, upright, unbranched fruitbodies, is quite common in Britain and occurs almost exclusively on dead roots and branches of sycamore (B. Spooner).

Most have a well-defined hymenium of asci and paraphyses, with spores released by extension of the asci though the ostiole. In some, however, the fruitbody is a completely closed structure (known as a 'cleistothecium'), and the asci break down so that forcible discharge of spores is lost. Most characteristic of such fungi are the *Eurotiales*, with asexual stages in the mould genera *Aspergillus* and *Penicillium*. Their fruitbodies are tiny, usually bright-coloured structures found on decaying plant matter. Other cleistothecial pyrenomycetes may be dark-coloured, such as species of *Thielavia*, often found on dung, and *Preussia*, sometimes found on old rope and rotting cloth. Also cleistothecial are the powdery mildews (*Erysiphales*; see Chapter Six), which are parasites of higher plants.

Lichenised pyrenomycetes are numerous and involve several families. They may exhibit a wide range of thallus types though most are encrusting. The large genus *Verrucaria*, worldwide in distribution and well represented in Britain, is a typical example.

Superficially similar to pyrenomycetes, though quite different in ascus structure, are the 'loculoascomycetes' or 'false flask fungi'. They again are hugely diverse and encompass a vast array of species. They have structurally complex asci termed 'bitunicate' which commonly have two wall layers, the outermost being a rigid structure which ruptures at maturity and allows the inner wall to extend through the ostiolar region and forcibly discharge the spores. Fruitbodies of the loculoascomycetes (known as 'pseudothecia') are stromatic, usually comprising dark, often carbonised tissue, within which unwalled cavities or 'locules' are developed which contain the asci. They exhibit a great diversity of form including minute, flattened shield-shaped structures, elongated or upright fruitbodies shaped like the shell of a bivalve mollusc, and flask-like forms resembling those of true flask fungi. Some are even discoid, mimicking discomycetes in form. *Patellaria*, for example, has blackish, saucer-shaped fruitbodies very like those of *Patellariopsis* in the *Helotiales*. As with other ascomycetes, loculoascomycetes exhibit a wide range of habitats and life styles. Saprobes abound on all kinds of decaying vegetation, parasites are common, and lichenised species are frequent.

Taphrina and Protomyces: gall-causing species

Amongst the most conspicuous of the plant parasitic fungi are those which gall their hosts. This is characteristic of the *Taphrinales* (*Taphrinomycetes*), which lack proper fruitbodies but instead form asci either internally in the host tissue or in a palisade on the host surface. Their asexual states are yeast-like, formed by budding of ascospores in a similar way to that in the basidiomycete order *Exobasidiales* and some of the smuts. The *Taphrinales*, comprising only about 115 species worldwide, is unique in this respect and now considered ancestral to the whole phylum *Ascomycota*.

Two families, *Taphrinaceae*, with a single genus *Taphrina*, and *Protomycetaceae*, with five small genera, are now referred to the *Taphrinales*. Some species of *Taphrina* induce conspicuous and often spectacular galls, including witches' brooms and severe deformation and enlargement of leaves and fruit (Fig. 12). They infect many woody hosts, though about 25 species occur on ferns, a few, such as *T. cornu-cervi* on *Arachniotes* in the eastern tropics, causing remarkable antler-like outgrowths of the host leaves.

FIG 12. *Taphrina deformans*, the cause of 'peach leaf curl', a common but disfiguring disease of almond and peach in which the leaves are characteristically swollen and distorted, the galls being bright red at maturity and lined with the asci of the fungus (B. Spooner).

Ascomycetous yeasts

Yeasts are microscopic, usually single-celled fungi which reproduce asexually, typically by budding. They occur as stages in the life cycle of many different fungi, both ascomycetes and basidiomycetes, though in some cases the sexual stages are rarely formed or even lost entirely. Due to their simple form, their classification has presented many problems and species identification is still a difficult and specialist task involving chemical, physiological and developmental as well as morphological characters. However, yeasts are of immense economic importance, both as agents of fermentation in the production of food and drink (Chapter 17), and as human and animal pathogens (Chapter 15), and have therefore received detailed study. Around 700 species have been recognised worldwide, the majority being ascomycetous yeasts. Most belong to the ubiquitous order *Saccharomycetales* in which no fruitbodies are formed, but asci are produced either singly or in chains from vegetative cells from which they are often scarcely morphologically distinct. Asci may contain just a single spore, and commonly are evanescent, the wall breaking down to release the spores.

The so-called 'fission yeasts', a tiny group including just two genera and five species, are also ascomycetes and comprise a distinct order *Schizosaccharomycetales*. In these, vegetative reproduction is by splitting or fission of the cells and there is no budding. The best known species, *Schizosaccharomyces pombe*, is an important fermentation yeast.

Hyphomycetes and coelomycetes

Hyphomycetes and coelomycetes are amongst the most commonly enountered microfungi. They are asexual, most of them being stages in the life cycles of ascomycetes, and are basically dispersive stages, usually able to reproduce themselves rapidly to colonise new hosts and take advantage of ephemeral substrates. In this, they are supremely successful, making their presence known even in the home by colonising everything from stale bread to damp wallpaper. Many produce vast quantities of conidia, which are easily dispersed and quick to colonise any suitable food source.

The terms 'hyphomycete' and 'coelomycete' refer merely to the form of the fruiting structure and have no taxonomic value. In the former, conidia are developed on specialised hyphae ('conidiophores'; Fig. 13) or sometimes

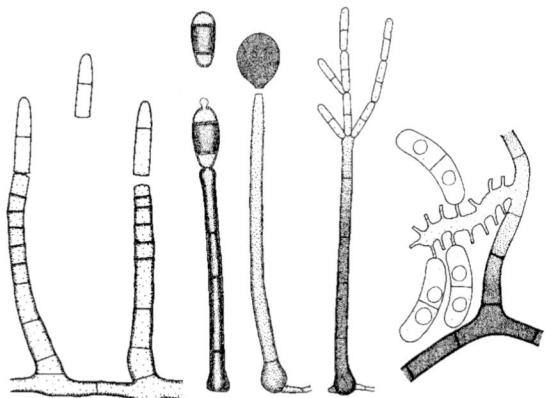

FIG 13. A range of conidiophores, the specialised hyphae on which conidia of asexual or anamorphic fungi are borne, showing some of the many different methods by which the conidia are developed (P.M. Kirk).

from unspecialised mycelium and there is no well-defined structure on which these are borne. The fungi popularly known as 'moulds', including many ubiquitous species in the genera *Penicillium, Aspergillus* and *Cladosporium*, mainly belong here.

Coelomycetes, in contrast, do produce a defined structure in which the conidia are formed. Commonly, these structures are flask shaped, resembling the fruitbodies of pyrenomycetes, and known as 'pycnidia'. The common genera *Phoma* and *Phomopsis*, found on many plants and sometimes parasitic, are examples. As might be imagined, there is a vast array of forms produced by asexual fungi and in some cases the distinction between 'hyphomycetes' and 'coelomycetes' becomes blurred. These fungi, sometimes referred to as the 'deuteromycetes', 'fungi imperfecti', or 'mitosporic fungi', are anamorphs or asexual stages of ascomycetes, though many have no known teleomorphs and are accordingly known as 'orphan anamorphs'. They may have lost the sexual stage in their life cycle or their appropriate teleomorph has not yet been discovered or recognised. This presents considerable difficulties in understanding numbers of fungal species. Although at least 16,000 species of hyphomycetes and coelomycetes have been described worldwide, the number of independent species which this represents is very uncertain.

The genera of hyphomycetes and coelomycetes can be regarded only as artificial 'form-genera', belonging variously in a system which is defined by their sexual stages, and with no taxonomic value. Their classification has been based largely on the method of production and characteristics of their conidia, pigmentation of the hyphae, and the development and structure of the fruitbody. Amongst the hyphomycetes, many species have dark pigmentation in some part, and are known as 'dematiaceous'. They are amongst the best known and most comprehensively studied of the hyphomycetes, in contrast to the numerous hyaline or unpigmented species many of which are still little known.

KINGDOM FUNGI: BASIDIOMYCOTA

The phylum *Basidiomycota* contains most of the familiar larger fungi, including mushrooms and toadstools, bracket fungi, and puffballs, as well as the rusts, the smuts, and much else besides. All produce their sexual spores externally on modified hyphae called 'basidia', the defining characteristic of the phylum (Fig. 14). The phylum itself is now divided into three classes –

FIG 14. Examples of different basidia: a) auricularioid (tubular with lateral septa), possibly the most ancient basidial form, found in many *Urediniomycetes*; b) tremelloid (ellipsoid with longitudinal or diagonal septa), typical of the *Tremellales*; c) tulasnelloid (with swollen sterigmata or epibasidia, septate at the base), characteristic of the *Tulasnellales*; d) holobasidioid (aseptate), typical of agarics and most basidiomycetes (P. Roberts).

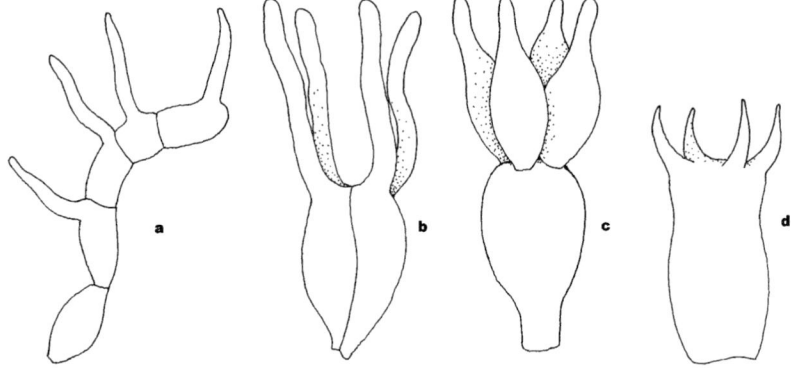

the *Basidiomycetes*, *Urediniomycetes*, and *Ustilaginomycetes* – based mainly on molecular and ultrastructure studies. The last two of these classes contain all the rusts and smuts (once lumped together as 'teliomycetes'), together with some related plant parasites and a few of the jelly fungi. The *Basidiomycetes* contain the rest, including all the larger and more conspicuous members of the phylum.

Approximately 30,000 basidiomycete species are known worldwide, with many more yet to be described. Some 3,600 have been recorded to date from the British Isles.

Mushrooms and toadstools

Mention the word 'fungi' to most people, and this is the group that first comes to mind. The old taxonomists placed all mushrooms and toadstools (including boletes) in the order *Agaricales* and referred to them as 'agarics'. This is still the preferred scientific term for fungi producing agaricoid (mushroom-shaped) fruitbodies, most of which are ephemeral structures seldom lasting more than a few days (Fig. 15). Typically, these fruitbodies have gills (lamellae) on which the spores are produced although in most *Boletales* there are tubes instead.

There is no real distinction between a 'mushroom' and a 'toadstool'. Historically, vernacular usage in England has considered edible species to be mushrooms (as in field mushrooms, horse mushrooms, parasol mushrooms, St George's mushrooms, etc.) and poisonous species (everything else, according to English belief) to be toadstools, though in a sense mushrooms are just edible toadstools. Amongst mycologists, the word 'mushroom' is often restricted to species of *Agaricus* (which includes the cultivated mushroom, *A. bisporus*, and the field mushroom, *A. campestris*).

The classification of agarics into orders and families is still unsettled. The classical division, between those with white spores and those with dark or coloured spores, is still a useful starting point for practical identification, but taxonomically far too simple. Three major orders are now recognised: the *Agaricales*, where most species belong, the *Boletales*, and the *Russulales*. The last, which includes the important ectomycorrhizal genera *Russula* and *Lactarius*, are quite distinct and have long been recognised as forming a separate evolutionary line. Their hyphal structure often produces large cells

FIG 15. *Phaeolepiota aurea*, a typical agaric. Fruitbody development shows cap, gills, and ringed stem. The ring is formed from the partial veil, a membrane which covers and protects the gills during development (B. Spooner).

which generally impart a fragile, often crumbly, consistency to the fruitbodies. However, it should be emphasised that many non-agaricoid forms are also now placed within these three orders. Furthermore, not all fungi with gills belong with the agarics! Some bracket fungi, such as *Lenzites betulina*, have gills, and typical agaricoid forms produced, for example, by *Panus* and *Lentinus* species, are more closely related to bracket fungi than to agarics.

Worth noting in the context of *Agaricales* are the so-called 'secotioid' fungi. In these, the caps remain closed and never expand. Gills are formed and produce spores, but the caps, instead of opening like a normal toadstool, fragment like distintegrating puffballs to release the spores. Although no secotioid fungi occur in Britain, several species are known from southern Europe, and many more in North America and Australia. Their unusual form conserves moisture and many, notably the Mediterranean *Montagnea arenaria* and the widespread *Podaxis pistillaris,* are fungi of deserts or arid areas. Further modifications of such forms also occur, so that one can find a series of species running from normal agarics, to secotioid agarics, to those that resemble puffballs or truffles. Indeed, it is now believed that most of the basidiomycetous false truffles are more closely related to their respective agaric ancestors than they are to each other. *Hydnangium carneum,* for example, a pinkish false truffle not uncommon in Britain with *Eucalyptus,* is closely related to the agaric genus *Laccaria* and has similar spiny spores. *Zelleromyces* species, with a single species (*Z. stephensii*) in Britain, have spores similar to *Lactarius* species and are related (they even exude a milky latex when broken). More recently and more surprisingly, DNA evidence is strongly suggesting that ordinary puffballs (*Lycoperdon* species) belong in the same family as mushrooms (*Agaricus* species), though morphologically they could hardly appear more different.

Ecologically, most agarics are either saprotrophs or ectomycorrhizal associates, though a few are parasites of plants or other fungi. The saprotrophs include many common grassland species (Chapter Eight), leaf and litter-rotting species (Chapters Three and Nine), and some specialist dung and firesite species (Chapter 13). Ectomycorrhizal toadstools associate with the roots of living plants, mainly forest trees, and include boletes, amanitas, russulas, and other familiar woodland fungi (Chapters Four and Nine). The plant parasites include such notorious species as honey fungus (the *Armillaria mellea* group), whilst among the parasites of other fungi are the piggy-back toadstools (*Asterophora* species) and the rare and peculiar *Squamanita* species (Chapter Six). Altogether, some 2,200 agaric species have been recorded from Britain.

'Gasteromycetes': puffballs, stinkhorns, and their allies

'Gasteromycetes' (literally 'stomach fungi') is the old collective name for a diverse range of fungi whose spores are typically produced and mature inside their fruitbodies. They are more appropriately referred to as the 'gasteroid fungi'. They include the puffballs, earthstars, earthballs, bird's-nest fungi, stinkhorns, and false truffles, and over 100 species occur in the British Isles.

Four main types of gasteroid fungi can be distinguished: 1) the phalloids, exemplified by our common stinkhorn (*Phallus impudicus*); 2) the puffballs and allied species; 3) the bird's-nest fungi; and 4) the false truffles. Phalloids produce gelatinous, egg-like fruitbodies which break and expand rapidly at maturity into upright, branched or cage-like structures on which spores are formed in a sticky and usually foul-smelling mass known as the 'gleba'. These spores are dispersed by insects attracted by the smell. The phalloids are almost all bizarre-looking fungi, and include some particularly unusual and brightly coloured species in genera such as *Aseroë* and *Clathrus* (Chapter Seven). The more commonplace puffball-like fungi produce fruitbodies in which the spores at maturity form a powdery mass dispersed on the wind. The bird's-nest fungi (*Nidulariales*) have spores which are formed in small, egg-like structures in cup- or goblet-shaped fruitbodies and are dispersed by rain-splash. The false truffles are subterranean basidiomycetes, superficially resembling the true truffles, some of which are quite common in the British Isles.

Unfortunately, these main forms have little taxonomic value and, based mainly on molecular evidence, the gasteroid fungi are now placed in a variety of different groups, some of which may be rather surprising. For example, puffballs, until recently referred to their own order, *Lycoperdales*, are now thought to be atypical members of the *Agaricales*. On the other hand, the superficially similar earthstars (*Geastrum* species) are now placed in the order *Phallales*, whilst *Astraeus hygrometricus*, which looks like an earthstar, is placed in the *Boletales*, along with the earthballs (*Scleroderma* species). The bird's-nest fungi have their own family within the *Agaricales*, as do the stilt-puffballs (*Battarraea* and *Tulostoma*). The false truffles are variously dispersed, mostly within the *Agaricales*, *Boletales*, *Phallales*, and *Russulales*.

Many of the false truffles are ectomycorrhizal, as are earthballs and the dyeball *Pisolithus arrhizus*. Most other gasteromycetes are saprotrophs in grass and woodlands, *Sphaerobolus stellatus* and *Cyathus stercoreus* being most frequent on dung. None appears to be parasitic.

Aphyllophoroid fungi: brackets, corals, and hedgehogs
Having divided off the agarics and the gasteromycetes, the old taxonomists were left with a large and confusing assortment of differently shaped basidiomycetes which they placed in a catch-all order 'aphyllophorales' (meaning 'non-gilled' fungi). Needless to say, this is an entirely artificial and

diverse assemblage, including all the bracket fungi, the corticioid or patch-forming fungi, the club and coral fungi, the hedgehog fungi, and more besides.

The bracket fungi, or polypores, are a diverse group of primarily wood-rotting species in which the hymenium is poroid or sponge-like, or gill-like in a few species. The fruitbodies are typically produced on dead trunks and stumps, on fallen wood, occasionally on living trees, or on dead, buried roots. Species growing on exposed wood are often highly adapted, having evolved specialist ways of resisting desiccation. Many produce tough, perennial fruitbodies such as the big, woody-hard *Ganoderma* brackets often seen on stumps or at the base of old but still living trees, which can last twenty years or more. The southern species, *Rigidoporus ulmarius*, typically found on old elms, produces some of the largest of all known fungal fruitbodies, with brackets up to two metres across. Altogether, around 100 species of polypores occur in Britain, divided into several different orders.

The corticioid fungi, typically forming patches on the underside of branches or fallen logs, play a similar role, though a few species are ectomycorrhizal. They lack gills or pores and generally have a simple, smooth hymenium, though in some species this is variously toothed, warted, or 'reticulate' (net-like). Over 300 species are known from Britain, often superficially similar but now divided into several different orders and families. The bright blue *Terana caerulea* is one of the few that can be readily identified in the field, without microscopic examination, but likes a damp, mild climate and is uncommon outside Wales and the Westcountry.

The club and coral fungi are far fewer in number (around 100 species in Britain), but equally mixed. All produce fruitbodies which are simple (cylindrical or club-shaped) or variously branched (coral-like), with spores developed on the surface of the clubs or branches. Some of the club fungi (*Clavaria* and *Clavulinopsis* species) grow in large clusters and can be quite conspicuous in old unimproved lawns and pastures in autumn, producing white, yellow, orange, brown, or even violet fruitbodies (Fig. 16). Smaller, less conspicuous species (mostly in the genus *Typhula*) occur commonly on decaying herbaceous stems and leaf petioles. Many of the coralloid fungi (mainly *Ramaria* species) are ectomycorrhizal and can produce large, yellow,

FIG 16. *Clavaria zollingeri* is an attractive example of a club or coral fungus, in which spore-bearing basidia are formed on the smooth surfaces of the branches. This particular species is widespread but uncommon in old, unimproved grassland (S. Evans).

ochre, or pinkish, compound fruitbodies in old woodlands, particularly of beech.

The ground-dwelling hedgehog fungi are also ectomycorrhizal. They resemble mushrooms and toadstools, but produce their spores on spines rather than gills. Only 20 or so species occur in Britain, *Hydnum repandum* being one that is common and edible (it is sometimes sold as 'pieds de mouton'). Other unrelated hedgehog fungi (in the genera *Bankera, Hydnellum, Phellodon,* and *Sarcodon*) may be indicative of ancient woodlands and are scarce outside the New Forest and Caledonian pinewoods. All these latter species seem to be getting rarer throughout Europe and are now collectively of conservation concern (Chapter 18).

'Heterobasidiomycetes': the jelly fungi

The heterobasidiomycetes are a very mixed bunch indeed, some now placed within the *Basidiomycetes*, others within the *Urediniomycetes*. The larger species are typically highly gelatinised, hence the common name 'jelly fungi', but this is not a character of the whole group. The name 'heterobasidiomycetes' comes from their unusual basidia, which are often strangely-shaped and segmented in contrast to those of the 'holobasidiomycetes' (the agarics, gasteromycetes, bracket-fungi, and the rest). Many of the heterobasidiomycetes have anamorphic yeast states, very similar to those found in ascomycetes. Such yeast states are unknown in the holobasidiomycetes.

Among the more conspicuous British heterobasidiomycetes are 'jew's ear' (*Auricularia auricula-judae*) and 'tripe fungus' (*A. mesenterica*), both wood-rotting species with large, gelatinous fruitbodies. These, as well as the equally gelatinous genera *Exidia*, *Guepinia*, and *Pseudohydnum* plus some other less conspicuous fungi are now, despite differences in the form of their basidia, placed in the order *Auriculariales* on the basis of ultrastructure and molecular evidence. In contrast, superficially similar species of *Tremella*, together with several less frequently encountered genera including *Filobasidiella* and *Syzygospora*, are placed in a separate order *Tremellales*. All *Tremellales* are now known to be parasites of other fungi, most producing yeast states. The bright yellow *Tremella mesenterica*, parasitic on corticioid fungi, is one of the commonest species, often seen on gorse. The yeast *Cryptococcus neoformans*, a stage of *Filobasidiella neoformans*, is a dangerous human pathogen (Chapter 15). Many other heterobasidiomycetes are also parasites of other fungi, often occurring inside the fruitbodies of their hosts. A few are plant parasites and a very few (principally *Sebacina* species) have recently been recognised as ectomycorrhizal. At least 200 different heterobasidiomycetes are known from Britain.

The *Auriculariales* and *Tremellales* belong in the class *Basidiomycetes*, but data on septal pore ultrastructure confirmed by molecular research has shown that a number of heterobasidiomycete genera belong in the class *Urediniomycetes*, together with the rusts. Orders in this group include the *Platygloeales*, an as yet uncertain assemblage of mainly inconspicuous genera, including several fungal parasites and the plant pathogen *Helicobasidium purpureum*; the *Atractiellales*, which includes *Phleogena faginea*, an odd wood-inhabiting species which superficially resembles a slime mould; and the *Septobasidiales*, which are symbionts of scale insects (Chapter Six), not yet known in Britain.

Rusts and smuts

The rusts and smuts are almost without exception parasites of higher plants. They are found anywhere that potential hosts occur, though are most abundant in temperate regions. Rusts have almost 7,000 known species and, because of their economic importance as crop pathogens, have been extensively studied. Their life cycles are complex, commonly involving more than one host plant and up to five different spore stages (Chapter Six). Though placed in the phylum *Basidiomycota*, rusts belong to the class *Urediniomycetes*, distinct from the *Basidiomycetes* to which most of the other fungi discussed above belong.

Smuts are less numerous than rusts but nevertheless comprise almost 1,500 species worldwide. Although a few occur on bryophytes, the great majority are parasites of vascular plants. Infection of the hosts may be localised, but many smuts are systemic, with their mycelium present throughout the host plant. Effects on the host therefore vary in severity, some species being of little significance, others inducing conspicuous galls and some being much more serious in destroying the inflorescence. Some, particularly species of *Ustilago*, cause important diseases of cereals. The classification of smuts, based largely on ultrastructure and developmental characters such as the presence or not of yeast-like stages in the life cycle, has recently been revised. They are now considered to represent a distinct class, the *Ustilaginomycetes*, developing their sexual spores within the host tissue. However, the few smuts known on dicotyledonous plants have recently been shown to be phylogenetically distinct and are now referred to the *Urediniomycetes*, along with the rusts.

KINGDOM FUNGI:
GLOMEROMYCOTA AND ZYGOMYCOTA

The *Glomeromycota*, only recently distinguished as a phylum distinct from the *Zygomycota*, includes just a single class *Glomeromycetes* and a single order *Glomerales*. Although no more than about 160 species are known worldwide, 11 of which occur in Britain, they are amongst the most widespread and biologically important of all fungi, formers of the ubiquitous vesicular-arbuscular (VA) endomycorrhizas (Chapter Four). This is the most widely distributed type of mycorrhiza, both geographically and with regard to plant partners, being found with many herbaceous species. Fruitbodies in the *Glomeromycota* may be totally lacking, their spores (which are comparatively large and thick-walled) being formed individually from hyphae in the soil, but many species produce small, underground fruitbodies known as 'pea truffles'. Some of these can reach 20 mm across, though most are smaller.

The *Zygomycota* are also comparatively few in number, with less than 1,000 species worldwide. They include saprobes as well as some important mycoparasites and pathogens of humans, insects and other invertebrates. The *Zygomycota* reproduce both sexually, by the formation of 'zygospores' (Fig. 17) which result from the fusion or 'yoking together' of specialised cells ('zygo' means yoke), and asexually, by non-motile spores produced in 'sporangia'. These sporangia are diverse in form but are often globose and multisporous and in some cases, such as the dung-inhabiting genus *Pilobolus* (Fig. 124), are adapted for violent discharge.

Perhaps the best-known of the *Zygomycetes* belong in the orders *Endogonales*, *Entomophthorales* and *Mucorales*. The first of these resemble the *Glomerales* in the general form of their fruitbodies (also known as 'pea truffles') but, although some develop ectomycorrhizal associations, they do not form endomycorrhizas. In Britain, just three species are known (Pegler *et al.*, 1993), forming fruitbodies in surface litter or upper layers of the soil.

The *Entomophthorales* are mostly pathogens of arthropods, especially insects, although some attack other invertebrates such as nematodes and tardigrades, as well as desmids or even fern prothalli, and a few are non-parasitic. Most belong to the family *Entomophthoraceae*, with 130 or so species

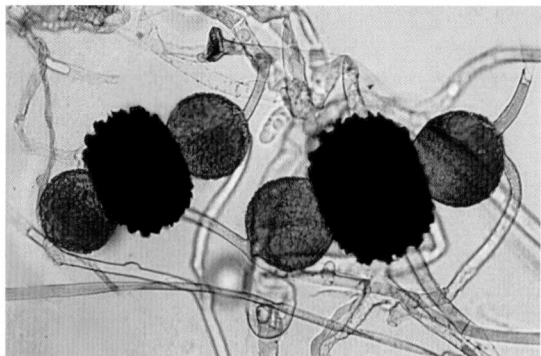

FIG 17. Zygospore of *Rhizopus sexualis* (Mucorales) formed during sexual reproduction. The dark, rough-walled zygospores with suspensor cells represent the isogamous gametes typical of most zygomycetes. (Kaminski's Digital Image Library).

known worldwide. They occur on various insect groups, though flies and aphids are especially important hosts. Dead insects in damp places are often seen to have a thick, whitish felt around the abdominal joints, sometimes covering the whole body. Hoverflies, especially of the genus *Melanostoma*, and sometimes other flies, may be killed in swarms by *Entomophthora muscae*, their bodies clinging to the leaves of trees, herbs and other vegetation. *Basidiobolus*, previously placed in the *Entomophthorales* but now referred to its own order, is notable in associating with vertebrates. There are just four species, two of which, *B. meristosporus* and *B. ranarum*, may be pathogenic to humans although the latter, a common and widespread species, is usually a saprobe typically found in the gut of frogs and often isolated from their dung.

Some of the most widely distributed *Zygomycetes* belong to the *Mucorales*, characterised by the production of non-motile, asexual spores. They are common in soil and are mainly saprobes, but include some obligate mycoparasites as well as parasites of plants, humans and other animals. Some of the 130 or so species are virtually cosmopolitan in distribution. Perhaps the most familiar belong to the *Mucoraceae* and *Pilobolaceae*. The latter are dung fungi, whose spores are forcibly discharged like miniature cannons (Chapter 13). The *Mucoraceae* includes 18 genera, the most important of which are *Mucor* and *Rhizopus* (Fig. 18), including the common species

Mucor hiemalis and *Rhizopus stolonifer,* which usually occur as saprobes but may also behave as parasites. They are mould-like and can be found on various kitchen substrates, including fruit and vegetables as well as bread and other food products. A number of *Mucorales* occur as parasites on other members of their own order (Chapter Six).

Finally, the *Zygomycota* also includes the *Trichomycetes.* These microscopic fungi are almost all found in the guts of arthropods, developing simple thalli attached to the host (or partner) by a holdfast. They are highly evolved fungi, apparently living as symbionts rather than as parasites (Chapter Five).

FIG 18. The common 'bread mould' *Rhizopus stolonifer* showing the typical creeping hyphae or 'stolons', with forked rhizoids and a clump of sporangiophores with apical dark-coloured sporangia (painting by E.Wakefield, RBG Kew).

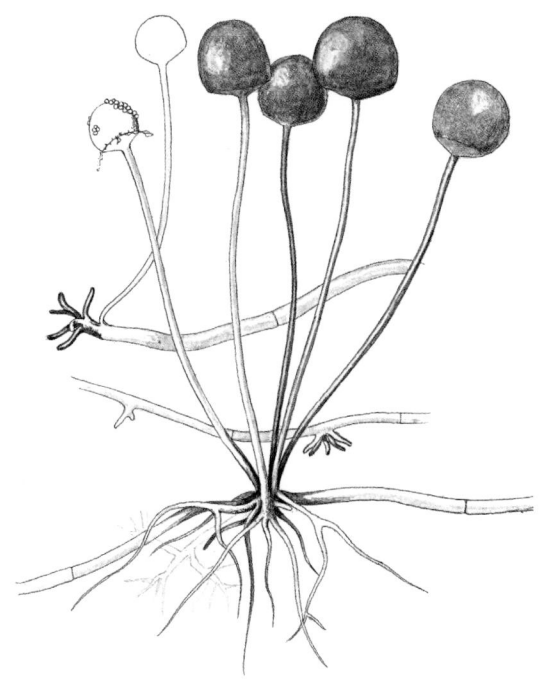

KINGDOM FUNGI: CHYTRIDIOMYCOTA

The *Chytridiomycota* or 'chytrids' are microfungi, widely distributed and abundant in appropriate habitats, but unlikely to be encountered except by specialists. Chytrids only rarely produce typical fungal mycelium and frequently resemble plankton-like cells. They all reproduce through 'zoospores' which can move around in liquid thanks to a posterior, whip-like 'flagellum' (Fig. 19). In many ways, particularly the possession of these motile zoospores, chytrids resemble the fungus-like species referred to

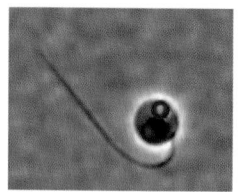

FIG 19. Zoospore of a chytrid showing the characteristic single flagellum. This zoospore also has a single oil globule, which is typical of many members of the *Chytridiales* (J.E. Longcore).

FIG 19A. Zoosporangium of a simple chytrid, formed on a system of branched rhizoids. Rhizoids with broad tips (> 0.5 μm) such as these are typical of the *Spizellomycetales*, found widely in soil and organic substrata. The zoosporangium is globose and contains numerous uniflagellate zoospores (J.E. Longcore).

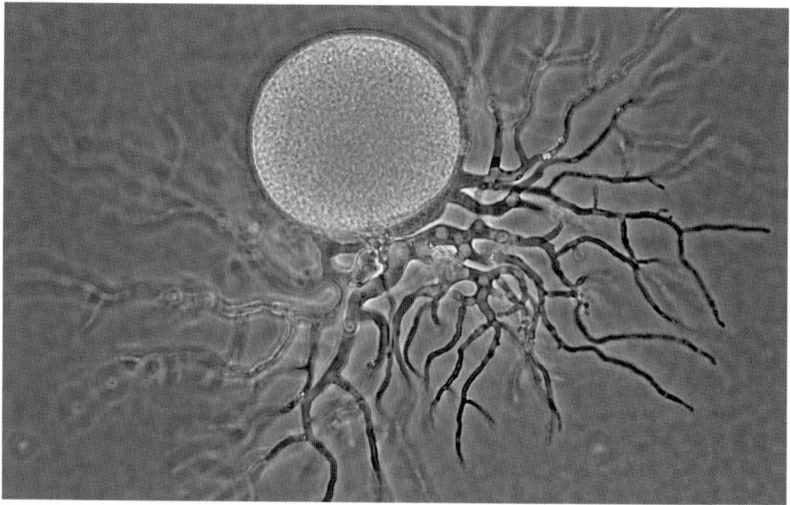

the kingdom *Chromista* (see below) and have often been placed with these organisms. However, chytrid cell walls are made of chitin and their mitochondrial ultrastructure is also characteristic of the kingdom *Fungi*, a conclusion now supported by molecular analysis.

Chytrids include around 1,000 species, many of them aquatic and occurring either as saprobes in decaying organic matter, or as parasites. They are found mainly in freshwater (Chapter 11) or in soil, although a few species are marine and some have recently been found in the guts of herbivorous mammals, where they help break down plant material (Chapter Five).

Six orders in two classes are currently recognised based on microanatomy, details of sexual reproduction and zoospore ultrastructure. The majority (at least 600 species) belong in the order *Chytridiales* in which four families are currently recognised. One of these, *Synchytriaceae*, comprises plant parasites which include some conspicuous gall-causing species. Amongst them is the plurivorous *Synchytrium aureum*, which produces small warts on the leaves of many herbaceous plants, and the well-known and host-limited *S. endobioticum*, the cause of the commercially important 'potato wart disease'. Eleven species of *Synchytrium* are now known in Britain.

KINGDOM CHROMISTA: OOMYCOTA AND OTHER PHYLA

The kingdom *Chromista* includes a wide range of both unicellular and filamentous organisms, many of which are photosynthetic (like plants), whilst others are fungus-like. Their classification remains unsettled, with even the most recent treatments varying in interpretation. Some ten phyla have been recognised, including brown seaweeds, yellow-green algae and diatoms, as well as the so-called 'lower fungi', all of which have characteristic zoospores (usually 'biflagellate' – with two whip-like appendages). The zoospore flagellum is distinctively ornamented with structurally complex, tripartite, tubular hairs for which the term 'straminipilous' has been proposed (Dick, 2001), and provides one of the main diagnostic characters of the kingdom. The fungus-like chromistans, once known as 'phycomycetes', closely resemble true fungi but differ notably in having hyphal walls typically made of cellulose, like the cells of plants. Molecular research has confirmed that the *Chromista* is a kingdom of eukaryotic organisms distinct from true fungi, animals, and plants. However, these fungus-like organisms are included here, since they have long been thought of as 'fungi' and have traditionally been studied by mycologists.

There are various suggested classifications of the fungus-like chromistans. Dick (2001) has placed them all in the phylum *Heterokonta*, but most authors have recognised three phyla: *Oomycota*, a large and widespread group of at least 1,500 species including some important plant and animal parasites, and the much smaller and less familiar *Hyphochytriomycota*, microscopic fungi found mostly on algae and fungi in soil and fresh water, and *Labyrinthulomycota*, mostly containing microscopic marine species.

Most of the chromistan fungi are microscopic, and include saprotrophs as well as parasites, in marine and freshwater habitats, including damp soil. Among the best-known are the *Saprolegniales*, or water moulds, some of which are parasites of fish, and plant parasites such as *Pythium* species, which cause 'damping-off' in seedlings, *Phytophthora* species responsible for serious timber and crop blights, including the Irish potato famine (Chapter Six), and the downy mildews and their relatives.

Pythium and Phytophthora

Pythium and *Phytophthora* belong to the family *Pythiaceae*, and together include almost 200 species worldwide. They are virtually cosmopolitan in distribution and include many important plant pathogens. As with other chromistans they reproduce asexually by 'sporangia' (packets of spores, released together). These are developed on 'sporangiophores' (microscopic sporangia-producing organs) which resume growth after the production of the sporangia. In *Pythium*, specialised sporangiophores are lacking and sporangia develop on hyphae which are little-differentiated. *Pythium* species occur commonly as saprotrophs in soil and water but can frequently turn parasitic, attacking seedlings of herbaceous plants and becoming a major cause of 'damping-off' diseases. In *Phytophthora*, saprotrophic stages are commonly lacking and most species are parasites, many of them destructive plant pathogens. Unlike *Pythium* species, they develop 'haustoria' (specialised parasitic hyphae) which penetrate the host cells. Their sporangia are developed on comparatively well-differentiated sporangiophores which usually emerge via the host stomata, so that leaves and stems of infected plants may be liberally covered with sporangia.

Downy mildews and blister rusts

The most frequently encountered fungus-like chromistans belong to the order *Peronosporales*. These are obligate plant parasites, commonly host specific and sometimes commercially important (Figs. 20 and 21). They include two families, *Peronosporaceae*, known as the 'downy mildews', and *Albuginaceae*, the 'blister-rusts' (Chapter Six). The mycelium of these fungi is intercellular, penetrating host cells by means of haustoria. Many species produce large, thick-walled 'oospores', which may be easy to see in the host tissue. In the downy mildews, sporangiophores emerge through host stomata

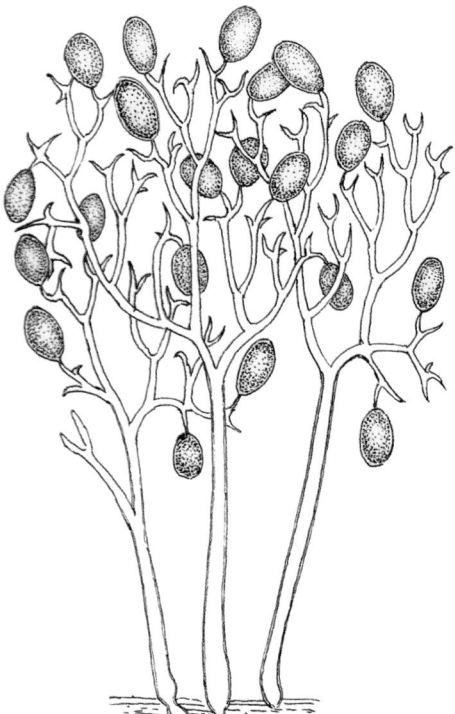

FIG 20. The downy mildew *Peronospora grisea*, a parasite of species of *Veronica*, showing the forked conidiophores and ellipsoid conidia characteristic of the genus (illustration by C. Crossland, RBG Kew).

FIG 21. *Peronospora farinosa* f.sp. *betae*, one of the downy mildews, fungus-like parasites now referred to the phylum *Chromista*. This species, found on sugar beet and other species of *Beta*, can damage plants and cause significant commercial loss (RBG Kew).

and form a white, cob-web like covering to the surface of leaves, often on yellowed or discoloured patches. The sporangiophores are characteristically forked near the tips, and produce oval sporangia which are dispersed by the wind. Species of *Albugo*, the only genus of the *Albuginaceae*, produce conspicuous white blisters on the host surface, in which sporangia are produced in chains on the short sporangiophores. Many of these fungi may cause considerable distortion of their host plants, especially in heavy infections.

KINGDOM PROTOZOA: MYXOMYCOTA AND OTHER PHYLA

The classification of the kingdom *Protozoa*, which includes many fungus-like species, is a complex and controversial system based largely on ultrastructure. The kingdom contains at least 14 different phyla but of these only the *Myxomycota*, the 'slime-moulds' and their allies, are fungus-like. In addition, however, the *Plasmodiophoromycota*, although placed by

Dick (2000) closer to the *Oomycota*, are commonly referred to the *Protozoa*.

Unlike true fungi, the *Myxomycota* lack hyphae and have a life-cycle that includes a free-living unicellular or plasmodial (amoeboid) stage. Commonly, they also produce distinct spore-bearing fruitbodies (sporangia) which may be very fungus-like in appearance. The phylum is not a large one, including less than 900 species worldwide. There are three classes, of which the true slime moulds (*Myxomycetes*) with almost 800 species is by far the largest. Some of these, including species of *Enteridium*, *Fuligo* and *Lycogala*, produce large fruitbodies reminiscent of puffballs, though unstalked and usually developed on rotten wood (Fig. 22). Most myxomycetes, however, produce far smaller fruitbodies, though these are often gregarious and easily visible after a period of wet weather (Fig. 23). The slimy plasmodial stage is sometimes also visible, particularly when it is brightly coloured, as in the striking, usually yellow species *Fuligo septica*.

The other two classes, *Dictyosteliomycetes* ('dictyostelids' or 'cellular slime

FIG 22. *Lycogala terrestre*, sometimes known as 'wolf's milk', one of the myxomycetes or slime moulds with large, compound sporangia that almost resemble puffballs when mature. This is a common species on rotten wood, the pink colour of the young sporangia being characteristic (B. Spooner).

moulds' with amoeboid stages) and *Protosteliomycetes* (or 'protostelids'), are comparatively small. The first of these is sometimes treated now as a separate phylum. The latter class, however, includes the common and widespread genus *Ceratiomyxa*, which produces soft, white fruitbodies which are almost ubiquitous on damp, rotten wood after rain. This small genus of just three or four species is easily distinguished from other slime moulds in having spores (which are dry and powdery at maturity) produced on the surface of its fruitbodies.

The phylum *Acrasiomycota*, to which the dictyostelids were previously referred, also belongs in the *Protozoa*. This phylum, the 'acrasid cellular slime moulds', has amoeboid stages with lobed pseudopodia and is now maintained as distinct based largely on molecular data. It is a tiny group

FIG 23. The myxomycete *Comatricha nigra*, a common species found on rotten wood throughout Britain. The globose sporangia and long, black stalks up to about 0.5 mm high are characteristic (painting by R. Baker, RBG Kew).

of only 12 known species, placed in a single order *Acrasiales*, which may be found on dung, on decaying plant matter, or in soil.

The final phylum, *Plasmodiophoromycota*, comprises obligate endoparasites of plants, algae and fungi. These organisms have been placed by some authors among the chromistans, by others (more recently) among the protozoans, but their true position has yet to be resolved. The phylum includes a single order *Plasmodiophorales* with just two families and 47 species. These fungus-like organisms occur within the cells of their hosts and produce multinucleate plasmodia and motile zoospores. They commonly induce conspicuous galls. Perhaps the best known species is the notorious and widespread *Plasmodiophora brassicae* which induces the disease known as 'club-root' in cabbages and other crucifers (Chapter Six).

CHAPTER 2

Evolution and Diversity

AN ANCIENT LINEAGE: PHYLOGENY AND THE FOSSIL RECORD

FUNGI are undoubtedly an extremely ancient group of organisms, but tracing their lineage and understanding their origin are far from easy. The fossil record, so helpful for many groups of organisms, provides very limited data for fungi. Their fruitbodies, the parts which provide the most useful information for systematic studies, are mostly ephemeral and readily decay, so that chances of successful fossilisation are remote. Even hard, woody brackets are rare as fossils. However, spores and hyphal remnants often do remain and these, together with a few comparatively recent bracket fungi, lichens, and other oddments, make up the known fossil record.

Altogether, around 950 fossil species ranged in 230 genera (Kalgutkar & Jansonius, 2000) have been described, a considerable increase over the 500 reported just a decade earlier (Stewart & Rothwell, 1993), but still not much compared to animals and plants. Nevertheless, a surprising amount of information can be gleaned from these fossils, not just about structure and systematics but also about biology and ecology as well as fungal diversity. The interactions between fungi and other organisms in ancient environments have been increasingly explored since the mid-1960's, following a study by Dilcher (1965) of leaf-inhabiting fungi from the Eocene of Tennessee. Examples of symbioses, parasitism and saprotrophism have all been demonstrated, as has the role of fungi in sedimentology and other geological processes, shown not least by trace fossils of fungi in the shells of marine molluscs.

How far back do these fungal fossils go? A remarkable paper by Hallbauer *et al.* (1977) described two lichen-like species, *Thuchomyces lichenoides* and *Witwateromyces conidiophorus*, from pre-Cambrian carbonaceous deposits some 2,500,000,000 years old. This would make fungi the oldest of all eukaryotic organisms by more than half a billion years, so it not surprising that the authors acknowledged that 'the observations described in this paper do not conform with current theories on the evolution of life'. Sadly, these hyphae-like, fossilised, pre-Cambrian pioneers are more likely to be filamentous bacteria than fungi. Equally remarkable is the hypothesis put forward by Retallack (1994) that the much later (ca. 670,000,000 years old) Ediacaran fossils, a peculiar group of organisms pre-dating the famous Burgess Shale fauna, were not animals, as conventionally thought, but lichenised fungi. If so, the origin of fungi and development of mutualisms may be much earlier than currently envisaged.

Such problems of interpretation continue with later fossils, many of which can only be termed 'fungus-like'. The oldest reliable records of fungi appear to be from the Ordovician, Silurian and Devonian periods, some 460–400,000,000 years ago, preserved among fossils of the first land plants. Many of these early fungi have been found in the exceptional and now famous Rhynie Chert formation in Scotland, which represents one of the most completely preserved ancient ecosystems in the world.

The earliest identifiable fossils are of *Glomus*-like fungi (*Glomeromycota*), from mid-Ordovician formations in Wisconsin around 460 million years old, which closely resemble modern plant-associated VA-mycorrhizal fungi in the *Glomerales* (Chapter Four). Though these pre-date the first vascular plants, it is known that some *Glomerales* can associate with hepatics and hornworts and may well have played a crucial role in allowing such early plants to colonise the land. The Lower Devonian *Aglaophyton major*, from the Rhynie Chert, is just such an early plant and has been shown to be VA-mycorrhizal (Fig. 24). It has even been suggested that some early land plants developed specialist organs (called 'roots'!) in order to interact with their associated fungi, a development which proved immensely important to the evolution of plants and fungi and provides a quite remarkable interpretation of the significance of mycorrhiza.

Members of the *Chytridiomycota* are first known from the Rhynie Chert, where they are well-preserved and quite common. Indeed, a species called *Milleromyces rhyniensis*, parasitic on algae and apparently very similar to the modern genus *Endophlyctis*, was so abundant that even the stages in its life cycle can be demonstrated from the fossil record (Taylor & Taylor, 1997).

The earliest well-documented *Ascomycota* are also from the Rhynie Chert and resemble modern pyrenomycetes (Taylor *et al.*, 1999) (Fig. 25). The *Basidiomycota*, many of which have characteristic clamped hyphae, are known from such hyphae preserved from the Upper Carboniferous, 300,000,000 years ago, and subsequently from a polypore, dubbed *Phellinites digiustoi*, from the Jurassic period almost 200,000,000 years ago. The earliest known toadstool is a *Marasmius*-like species found in fossil amber from New Jersey, believed to be over 90,000,000 years old.

Although fossil evidence is limited, it is clear that fungi were highly evolved by at least the end of the Carboniferous almost 300 million years ago and of major ecological importance in the terrestrial environment. Indeed, thanks to a unique event that occurred at the end of the Palaeozoic era, fungi were for a while the dominant organisms on earth. The Palaeozoic closed, at the end of the Permian period some 248,000,000 years ago, with a mass extinction probably as a result of geological upheaval and exceptional volcanic activity. This immense ecological catastrophe is estimated to have destroyed more than 90% of all species on Earth. But for fungi, as the prime agents of decay, it appears to have been a period of opportunity and plenty. The fossil record from this time contains 'unparalleled abundances of fungal remains' (Visscher *et al.*, 1996) and it seems that, following catastrophic dieback of terrestrial plants and ecosystem collapse, wood and litter-rotting fungi proliferated exceptionally. It was a time of extreme fungal dominance, known appropriately as the 'terminal Palaeozoic fungal event'.

Where direct evidence in the form of unequivocal fossil remains is lacking, the origin and evolution of fungi can be inferred from various indirect methods. These include comparative morphology, biochemistry, cytology and ultrastructure, but the most useful method stems from the advent of molecular techniques and analytical methods such as cladistics

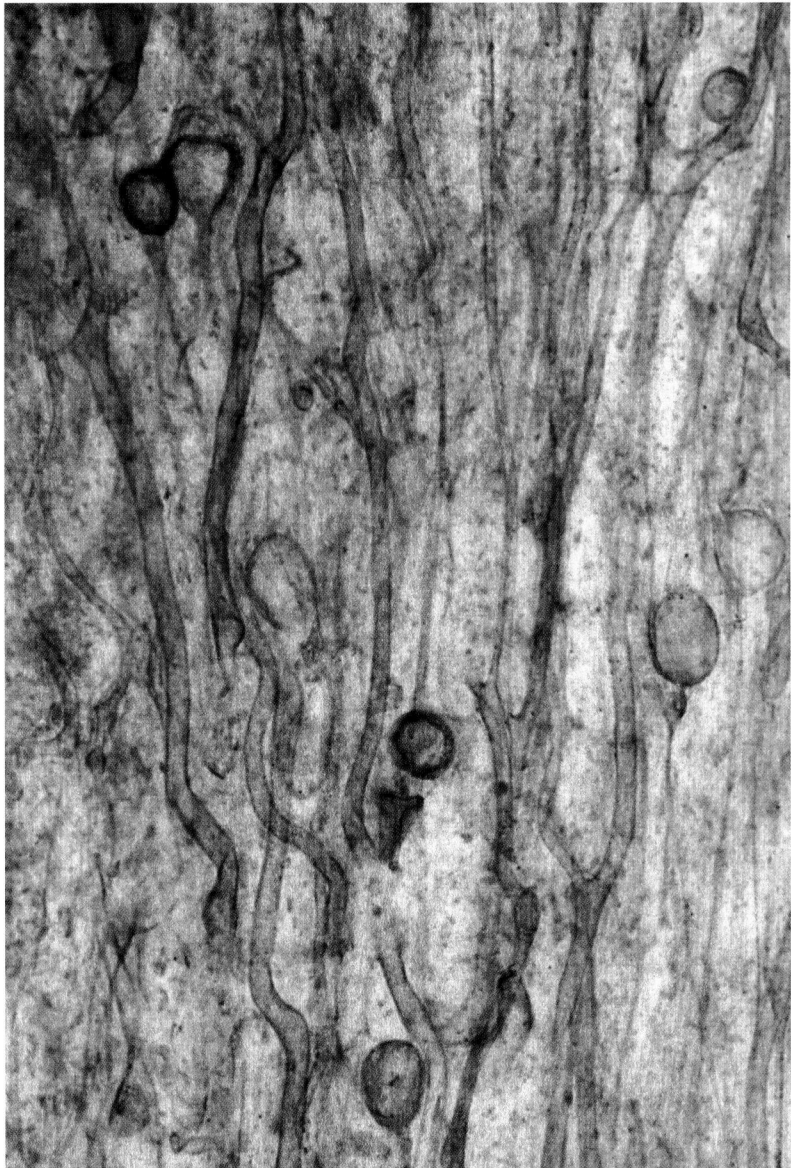

FIG 24. *Glomites rhyniensis* in *Aglaophyton major*, an early land plant, from the 400 million year-old Rhynie Chert. Longitudinal section of stem showing well-developed, branching hyphae and numerous spores (H. Kerp).

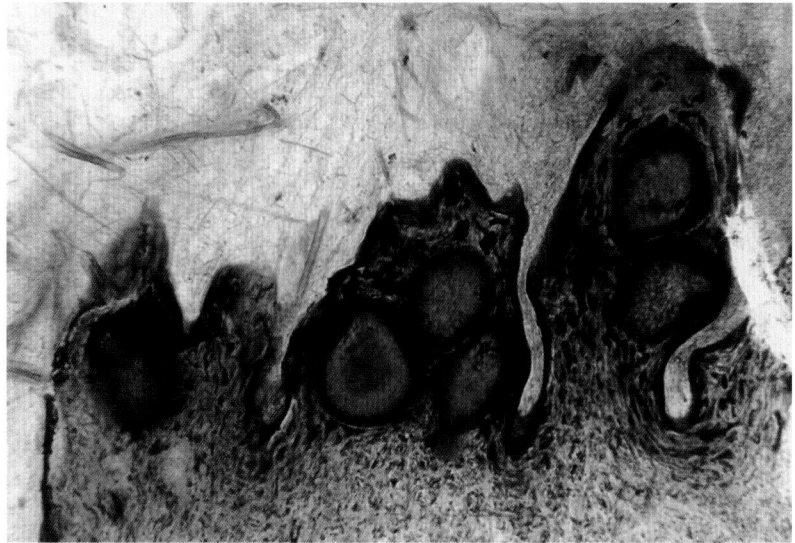

FIG 25. Fossilised fruitbodies of a pyrenomycete found in stems and rhizomes of *Asteroxylon*, a club-moss ancestor, from the Rhynie Chert. They resemble modern species but represent the earliest known fossil ascomycetes (H. Kerp).

which allow possible phylogenies to be constructed. This is the so-called 'molecular clock', a powerful tool based on the study of genetic sequences from existing species. The method relies on the fact that the genes selected for study, being essential for protein synthesis, are highly conserved and universally present amongst organisms, changing only slowly through time. This suggests it is possible to work backwards from sequences of existing species and postulate the gene sequence of an ancestor by calculating the simplest way in which differences in the sequence could have come about (assuming a single common ancestor). From this theoretical sequence the number of genetic changes by which such an ancestor differs from an existing organism can be studied. By applying frequencies to these changes the age of the lineage can also be established. The method is not without problems, however, since there is uncertainty as to whether the frequency of these changes is constant over time. There is also the problem that apparently small changes may have resulted from multiple events. However, by calibrating this method using fossils of known age it does seems to work quite well, at least for some organisms, if not for fungi. Berbee & Taylor (2001), for example, have estimated that the kingdom *Fungi* diverged from other eukaryotes around 1,000,000,000 years ago, whilst Heckman *et al.* (2001) have estimated the split as dating back more than 1.5 billion years. Berbee & Taylor estimated the divergence of the *Ascomycota* and *Basidiomycota* at around 500,000,000 years ago, Heckman *et al.* at around 1,200,000,000 years ago. Clearly, these differences indicate a more than considerable degree of uncertainty as to the date of origin of the *Fungi*, but at least these studies do confirm that these organisms are (by eukaryote standards) very ancient indeed.

Phylogeny and diversification

The *Chytridiomycota* are now considered to be the oldest true fungi, and directly ancestral to mushrooms, toadstools, and more familiar groups. Available evidence points to their origin from protozoan ancestors, specifically the choanoflagellates. However, there remains considerable uncertainty as to the details of ancestry and date of origin, not least because so few DNA sequences from appropriate modern species are yet available for analysis. Nevertheless, alternative theories of the origin of fungi, such as their derivation from algae by loss of chloroplasts, can now be safely abandoned. Furthermore, since the work of Wainright *et al.* (1993), it has been increasingly clear that not only are fungi not plants but that they are much more closely allied to animals, both *Animalia* and *Fungi* having arisen from choanozoan-like ancestors. The exact nature of the origin of chytrids, whether from a saprotrophic or a parasitic ancestor, is still unknown and alternative scenarios were discussed by Cavalier-Smith (2001). What is known is that the chytrids arose in marine environments probably around a billion years ago, and certainly long before the colonisation of the land and the origin of vascular plants.

The remaining fungal phyla diverged from the chytrids at least 600 million years ago (Berbee & Taylor, 2001). The *Zygomycota* and *Glomeromycota* appear to have had different chytrid ancestors, and the latter are considered ancestral to the ascomycete-basidiomycete lineage. The *Ascomycota* and *Basidiomycota* therefore had common ancestry and diverged after colonisation of the land by plants (though before the appearance of vascular plants) around 500 million years ago, early in the Palaeozoic era. The early basidiomycetes evolved rapidly to form the three classes (*Basidiomycetes*, *Urediniomycetes*, and *Ustilaginomycetes*) which are recognised today. However, many commonplace groups appear to be of comparatively recent origin. For example, the homobasidiomycetes, which include mushrooms and toad-stools, are known from fossil evidence no earlier than the mid-Cretaceous, about 100 million years ago, and may date back no more than about 200 million years (Hibbet *et al.*, 1997). The ascomycetes also evolved rapidly and again diverged into three major lineages (Berbee & Taylor, 2001). The earliest of these, the *Archiascomycetes*, includes some yeast-like species and the *Taphrinales*, known today as plant parasites. They arose around 450 million years ago, whilst the other groups, the *Hemiascomycetes*, comprising the yeast-like *Saccharomycetales* (which lack fruitbodies and have little or no development of mycelium) and the filamentous ascomycetes (*Euascomycetes*), which include all other species, diverged perhaps 50 million years or so later. The ascomycetes are now the largest and most diverse of all the fungal phyla.

The organisms called 'microsporidia' are all obligate intracellular parasites of insects and occasionally other animals, including fish. A few have achieved some notoriety as the cause of commercially important diseases such as 'pébrine', due to the microsporidian *Nosema bombycis*, which devastated the French silkworm industry in the 19th century. Another species, *Nosema apis*, is the cause of an important disease of honeybees, and there are many others. These organisms lack cell walls in their vegetative state and also lack mitochondria, so that until recently they were placed with the *Protozoa*. However, based largely on molecular data, their affinity with the true fungi now seems likely and a relationship was persuasively argued by Cavalier-Smith (2001). Microsporidia may have arisen from zygomycete ancestors (probably *Trichomycetes*) by loss of the cell wall and development of organelles for penetration of animal cells. This position within the *Fungi* requires confirmation from further study, but it may be that an additional phylum should be recognised.

The origin of fungus-like organisms in the *Chromista* and *Protozoa* appears to be comparatively recent. Although the fossil record is lacking, molecular evidence suggests they evolved independently from different ancestors during the late Cretaceous period and perhaps no more than 50 million years ago (Cavalier-Smith, 2001).

HOW MANY SPECIES?

It is now almost universally accepted that fungal diversity is high, but its true magnitude is still far from clear. It is a difficult question to tackle. Most regions are mycologically vastly understudied and, indeed, so little is known about the fungi of most areas, regardless of size, that even an approximate figure for how many species exist worldwide is almost impossible to establish. Even better-known areas, such as the British Isles, have few comprehensive checklists or inventories available, and for much of the world, especially the tropics, the cataloguing of fungi has hardly started.

Estimates of the numbers of fungal species have been put forward on various occasions, and have been continually amended upwards since a figure of 100,000 was suggested by Bisby & Ainsworth (1943). In 1991, a landmark paper by Prof. David Hawksworth sought to answer this question and place our knowledge of fungi in proper perspective in relation to other organisms (Hawksworth, 1991). Based on various independent sets of data, Hawksworth estimated that as many as 1.5 million species of fungi might exist, a figure since challenged by some authorities as being far too high or even far too low. Cannon (1997), for example, suggested the true number of fungal species might exceed nine million. However, revisiting the estimate a decade later Hawksworth (2001a) maintained the 1.5 million figure. The estimate was based upon the ratio of vascular plant to fungus species, extrapolated to the world as a whole using data from particular regions, well-studied sites, specific communities, and host specificity of fungi (including endophytes, symbionts and pathogens).

The vascular plant : fungus ratio

The plant to fungus ratio is of most interest when examined and compared for areas of different size. Although our limited knowledge of fungal distribution leads to a high degree of uncertainty, the ratio can still provide an initial guide to how many different fungi a particular area is likely to support. In the British Isles there are just over 2,000 species of vascular plants (excluding microspecies), compared to some 12,000 or so fungi, a ratio of 1: 6. On a smaller scale, given sufficient surveying, the ratio is usually somewhat higher. At Slapton Ley in Devon, for example, with 490 plants and 2,400 fungi, it is 1: 5, whereas at Esher Common in Surrey, with 420 plants and 3,200 fungi, it is already 1: 7.5 and rising. A survey of a much smaller area (just 4 ha and 170 plants) at Mickleham Down in Surrey, has produced an astonishing 1400 species of fungi to date, a ratio of 1: 8. In none of these sites, however, have fungi been fully recorded, and many additional species, especially in groups which need specialist attention, will undoubtedly occur in all of them. The true ratio for small woodland areas in England may, therefore, be 1: 10 or higher. In the British Isles overall, where unrecorded fungal species may be numerous but represent only a small percentage increase on the total already known, it seems unlikely that the ratio is higher than 1: 7 or 1: 8. For entire continents, and indeed for the world as a whole, this ratio will be smaller, but how much smaller is not yet clear. Extrapolating Hawksworth's estimated 1: 6 ratio to a world scale suggests that the 270,000 known vascular plant species might translate to over 1.5 million fungi, but there are various factors which might affect this total.

Firstly, could this be a conservative estimate? Studies on fungi from palm petioles and rachides in northern Queensland, for example, showed not only that 75% of the species were undescribed, but that the ratio of fungi to palm species was as high as 26: 1 (Hyde, 1996). Furthermore, this figure excluded lichens, fungi from palm flowers and seeds, and those on palm-associated arthropods. A study of banana pathogens (Wardlow, 1972) concluded that about half of the 50 species recorded were specific to this host genus. Shivas & Hyde (1997) considered this to be an average ratio for tropical host plants and concluded that perhaps 270,000 species of plant pathogenic fungi occur in the tropics alone. In another example, Aptroot (2001) reported 200 species of just ascomycetes from a single *Elaeocarpus* tree in Papua New Guinea. Half these species were undescribed and included at least two genera new to science.

However, there is a powerful counter-argument to these estimates. Many fungi are known to be extremely widespread (even cosmopolitan), and many are plurivorous – the pathogenic ascomycete *Colletotrichum gloeosporioides*, for example, has been recorded from over 470 different host genera. Furthermore, many host-linked fungi specialise not in a single host species but in a whole genus of plants. In other words, many of the same fungi can be found on African and Asian palms as well as Queensland species, and many generalist (non host-specific) species have a much wider geographical range than do plants. Available evidence from well-studied areas, in Britain and elsewhere, suggests that generalists account for a high percentage of the total, which might significantly reduce the number of species of fungi worldwide to closer to half a million.

Recently, Schmit *et al.* (2002) analysed and compared data from different geographical regions to try to obtain the most conservative estimate of diversity, i.e. the lowest possible number of fungal species which might exist worldwide. From this analysis they postulated a minimum figure of 500,000 species, in line with the reduced estimate above.

Ninety percent of fungi still undescribed?

How do these extrapolated estimates of diversity compare with the actual number of fungal species described to date? Unfortunately, this is another difficult question to answer. Figures ranging from 72,000 to 150,000 have been put forward for known fungal species, reflecting a surprising degree of uncertainty.

One of the problems concerns synonymy (several names for the same species). Well over 340,000 names have been introduced for fungi, but all too frequently the same species has been described over and over again and Hawksworth (1991) estimated that, on average, each species has been described no less than 2.5 times. Equally problematic is the linking of anamorph names with teleomorph names. Thousands of anamorphic states have been described and named, but how many are actually stages in the life cycle of already named teleomorphs, currently unlinked and erroneously counted as two separate species?

Whatever estimate is accepted, the difference between the number of species which exist and the number so far described is undoubtedly huge. It places our current lack of knowledge in perspective and highlights the enormity of the task ahead. It may be that only around 5–10% of the world's fungi have yet been described or, conversely, 90–95% of fungal species remain to be discovered. This vast, uncounted number presents an immensely daunting task because, at the current rate of description (around 1,500 new species per annum), it may take almost another millennium to describe them all.

FUNGAL DIVERSITY IN BRITAIN

The British Isles rank amongst the world's most thoroughly recorded areas for fungi. Yet even here our native mycota remains inadequately documented. New and additional species are reported regularly and, in fact, over just a ten year period, between 1980 and 1989, no less than 460 species of fungi new to science were described from Britain (Hawksworth, 2001).

Altogether, some 12,000 fungal species have been recorded to date from the British Isles. There is no complete checklist of these fungi, but this figure can be estimated with reasonable confidence from various data sets. These include the Fungus Records Database administered by the British Mycological Society which is an important source, though highly selective and uncritical in its compilation. The book *Fungi of the Hebrides* (Dennis, 1986) provided a complete analysis of all British genera (other than lichens) and is still a major source of information, and a comprehensive checklist of ascomycetes (including lichens) was published by Cannon *et al.* (1985), though is now in need of revision. A modern revised list of lichens (Coppins, 2002) is kept updated by the British Lichen Society, and a comprehensive checklist of the British *Basidiomycota*, currently being finalised at Kew, is scheduled for publication in 2005. There are also good sources for some other groups, though conidial fungi (hyphomycetes and coelomycetes) continue to present problems.

To produce a complete checklist of British fungi would be a daunting task, despite much progress since Cooke's Handbook of British Fungi (which included most species known at the time) was first published in 1871. Several regional mycotas, though mainly concerned with larger fungi, have appeared within the last thirty years or so including accounts for Dorset

(Bowen, 2000), Warwickshire (Clark, 1980), Yorkshire (Bramley, 1985), South East England (Dennis, 1995), the New Forest (Dickson & Leonard, 1996), Shetland (Watling, 1992a), Orkney (Watling *et al.*, 1999), and the Hebrides (Dennis, 1986), with more currently in preparation. These regional mycotas are supplemented by some all-taxa studies of specific sites. Most notable among these is the SSSI at Esher Common and Oxshott Heath in Surrey, comprising 380 ha of mainly acid, sandy, lowland heath with both planted and semi-natural secondary woodland on the outskirts of London. With records of almost 3,300 species to date, this is perhaps the most comprehensively inventoried site for fungi in the world. Other richly-recorded sites include Kew Gardens in Surrey (132 ha) with almost 2,600 species, and Slapton Ley in Devon (250 ha) with some 2,400 species. These studies are not just of local interest but are important on a global scale, providing the best available benchmarks to date for fungal diversity at any given site or area worldwide.

As far as can be ascertained, the British mycota is broadly similar to that of continental Europe, with a few predictable exceptions. Species associated with European trees not native in Britain, such as spruce and silver fir, are mostly absent, though a few have been introduced in parks and plantations (Chapter Nine). The same is true of fungi associated with other introduced continental plants. Also absent are thermophilic Mediterranean fungi (though some very southern species, such as the bracket fungi *Perenniporia ochroleuca* and *Flaviporus brownei* occur in coastal southwest Britain) and most Arctic and Alpine fungi (though a few are present in the Scottish Highlands). Eastern European species, typical of areas with a strongly continental climate, are also largely absent.

Few if any endemic species (those found nowhere else) are likely to occur in Britain, although over 300 species, mainly microfungi, originally described from Britain are as yet unknown elsewhere. Though they will almost certainly prove more widespread, this highlights how little is known of fungal distribution. However, among the more conspicuous and better recorded macrofungi, there are a few species where the British Isles hold a substantial proportion of the European and world population. For example, around 50% of known European sites for the pink waxcap *Hygrocybe calyptriformis* (Fig. 26), a distinctive toadstool of unimproved, grazed or mown

FIG 26. The pink waxcap *Hygrocybe calyptriformis*, a species of unimproved grassland rare in continental Europe but not uncommon in the British Isles. It is the subject of a Biodiversity Action Plan (Chapter 18) and has excited widespread conservation interest (S. Evans).

FIG 27. *Podoscypha multizonata* is a rare but conspicuous, rosette-forming basidiomycete usually found with old oaks. Most of the known localities for this species world wide are in southern England (P. Roberts).

grasslands, are in the British Isles. Indeed waxcap species as a whole are well-represented here. This almost certainly reflects the extent of our remaining species-rich grasslands, a habitat which is threatened throughout Europe. Two other examples are *Podoscypha multizonata* (Fig. 27), a large rosette-forming root parasite, for which some 80% of the known world sites are in England, and the oak polypore *Piptoporus quercinus* (Fig. 164) , which may equally be an English speciality. Both are typical of woodland pasture with veteran trees (exclusively oaks for the latter species). As such, the ancient deer parks and royal forests of England, with their pollarded oaks up to 800 years old, represent a further habitat which has become increasingly rare throughout Europe.

CHAPTER 3

Agents of Decay

THE DECAY of plant and animal debris is perhaps the most essential process in nature. Without decay, the nutrient cycle would grind to a halt, and life could no longer survive. Worldwide, vast quantities of such debris are continually produced and continually recycled. Temperate woodlands, for example, produce as much as five tonnes of plant and animal debris per hectare every year, and this figure increases to almost 60 tonnes in tropical rain forests, amongst the most productive of all the world's ecosystems.

It is fungi, along with bacteria and some invertebrate groups, that are the main agents of decay, especially in terrestrial ecosystems. Indeed, the contribution of fungi in the process of decomposition and nutrient recycling is almost certainly their most important environmental role. In all such habitats they are the major players, breaking down complex organic compounds into simple elements which are released into solution in the soil. Worldwide, it has been estimated that around 90% of all nutrient recycling in terrestrial ecosystems is due to fungal activity. Even in aquatic ecosystems fungal decay of littoral vegetation and submerged plant litter plays a significant role (Chapters 11 & 12). Fungal biomass in such habitats may exceed 10%, although this is small compared to some forest soils where the figure may be closer to 90%.

Almost any naturally occurring source of organic carbon can be broken down and used as food for fungi. Simple sugars (such as glucose and fructose) found in plant and animal tissues are readily assimilated by the majority of species, whilst more complex polymers (like cellulose and lignin of plant cell walls, chitin in insect exoskeletons, or keratin in hair and feathers) are degraded and utilised by specialists. Even petrochemicals, such as oil and bitumen, can be tackled by a number of fungal species (see Chapter 14, and Cooke & Rayner, 1984, for a comprehensive list).

A minority of fungi depend on living organisms for their food supply, as mycorrhizal partners (Chapter Four), parasites (Chapter Six), or other symbionts (Chapter Five). This chapter looks at the majority of fungi, the 'saprobes' or 'saprotrophs', which derive their sustenance from the discarded and the dead.

TURNING LEAVES TO HUMUS

Forest ecosystems are perhaps the most conspicuous example of nutrient recycling in which fungi play an essential role. Falling leaves typically form a litter layer which gradually breaks down into humus, becoming part of the soil structure. The main constituent of leaf litter is cellulose, the commonest organic substance on earth. This is not easily degraded, if at all, by animals, plants, or bacteria, but many fungi do have the requisite enzymes to break down cellulose into simpler compounds (principally glucose) and utilise it as a food resource. Worldwide this fungal breakdown has been calculated to release some 85,000,000,000 tonnes of carbon into the atmosphere as CO_2 each year, an essential part of the global recycling system.

The process starts whilst leaves are still on the tree. Phylloplane microfungi (those which live on the leaf surface; see Chapter Six), such as ascomycetous *Alternaria* and *Cladosporium* species and some basidiomycetous yeasts, are present on the surfaces of most living leaves where they subsist mainly on exudates without injury to their hosts. As leaves age, however, these phylloplane fungi tend to increase in numbers and may extract nutrients from senescent tissues. They continue to do so after leaf fall, but probably play a very minor role in leaf decay, since experimentation has shown that they have little ability to degrade cellulose.

Endophytic microfungi, occurring within the leaves, are capable of more active decay. These are typically present in living leaves as minute propagules, triggered to growth by senescence or leaf fall. Common examples include the discomycete *Mollisina acerina*, mostly found on sycamore, and the plurivorous coelomycete *Discosia artocreas*. These produce fruitbodies on fallen leaves in the spring following autumnal leaf fall. *Lophodermium* species, which often appear on senescent pine needles before they drop, represent another example, and there are many others.

In temperate forests, the next and most obvious stage is the decomposition of fallen leaves on the forest floor. But in some nutrient-poor tropical rainforests, specialised fungi have evolved which are capable of trapping leaves before they reach the ground. These fungi produce webs of rhizomorphs below the canopy, effectively catching leaves as they fall. Trapped leaves are quickly invaded by hyphae, becoming firmly attached to the rhizomorphs. Occasionally, whole tangles of these webs collapse under their own weight and fall to ground, typically revealing fruitbodies of *Marasmius* and *Crinipellis* species (toadstools with more conventional representatives in the British Isles) and xylariaceous ascomycetes. On reaching the ground, leaves may be rapidly comminuted by animals, principally earthworms, gradually decayed by fungi and bacteria, or (typically) a combination of both. Over time, layers build up over the underlying mineral soil, the uppermost 'L' layer consisting of intact leaves and other fallen matter, the middle 'F' layer of partly degraded leaves, and the lowest 'H' layer of wholly decayed and comminuted humus. The L-layer of discrete leaves tends to be dry and often disturbed, but within a few months of leaf fall may be colonised by smaller fungi. These need to be capable of forming fruitbodies from the nutrients available in a single leaf (not many, in the case of a conifer needle) and also need to tolerate comparatively low levels of moisture. In the F-layer, where the litter becomes more compacted and less dry, larger and more extensive fungal communities form which combine the nutrients from large numbers of leaves and other organic matter (twigs, insect frass, and so on) within the litter.

Not all leaves decay at the same rate, of course. Soft leaves from trees such as ash, sycamore, or alder may be turned to humus within a year, harder oak and beech leaves may take several years, and conifer needles as much as ten years. In addition, leaves with a high phenolic content, such as conifer needles, tend to be toxic to many organisms (including earthworms) and take longer to break down. This is particularly true on acid ground, typical of uplands, where litter and humus decomposition is slow. The result in such conditions is a 'mor' soil, often very productive for larger fungi, less so for invertebrates and plants. Where the pH is high, worms and other invertebrates are active, litter breakdown is rapid, and 'mull' soils form. In plant terms, these are often highly fertile, but tend to support fewer macrofungi.

The first colonisers of the L-layer are small and specialist, comprising a range of microfungi, ascomycetes (particularly discomycetes), and basidiomycetes, including clavarioid *Typhula* species and smaller agarics such as species of *Marasmius*. Some of these, for example *Marasmius hudsonii* on fallen holly leaves, and the discomycete *Lachnum capitatum* on fallen oak leaves, are host specific, though many other more plurivorous species occur. Fallen, decaying oak leaves, for example, may be host in Britain to at least forty different species of discomycetes. All are capable of growing and fruiting on individual leaves, sometimes on specific parts of the leaves such as the ribs or petioles.

As leaves begin to degrade, the tissues collapse and the water potential increases, so that the more compact, damper, and homogeneous F-layer forms through which fungal hyphae can spread. Colonisers at this stage tend to be larger fungi, particularly (but not exclusively) agarics, sometimes forming extensive fairy rings within the deeper litter. Common examples in British woodlands include *Collybia dryophila* and *C. maculata*, *Mycena galopus*, and the wood blewit *Lepista nuda*. Conspicuous wefts of their mycelia can be found below the topmost surface in autumn and winter, binding the litter together. Because of the homogeneity of this litter, the fungi growing within it are mostly generalists, though conifers attract a different set of fungi from broadleaf trees, and soils with high pH a different set from those with low pH.

The litter degraders in the F-layer are principally saprotrophic fungi, breaking down cellulose and lignin in a process similar to the 'white rots' produced by many wood-degrading fungi, and indeed compacted leaves in damp litter often appear bleached and friable. Some mycorrhizal fungi may also contribute to litter breakdown, though they obtain most of their carbon requirements from living plants.

In the H-layer, litter is so highly decomposed that it supports few if any larger fungi, partly because exploitable nutrients are exhausted and partly because fine particles increase competition from bacteria and other microorganisms. In mull soils, however, with hardly any litter accumulation some discomycetes, clavarioid fungi, and smaller agarics, particularly *Lepiota* species, appear on bare, humus-rich earth, though whether they are degrading the fine remnants of leaf litter or depend on some other niche resource is not clear.

WOOD ROTTERS

Wood-rotting is such a commonplace phenomenon that it tends to disguise the difficulties faced by any organism trying to break it down. In wood, the plant cell walls are hardened by lignin, a polymer that coats cellulose. The resulting lignocellulose is highly resistant to degradation. Furthermore, wood contains many oils, resins, gums, tannins, and other 'extractives' some of which are widely toxic. Wood is also deficient in nitrogen, can build up high levels of carbon dioxide, and often becomes excessively wet or excessively dry. It should be no surprise, therefore, that only a few specialised organisms can decay wood, and these are principally fungi and specifically the wood-rotting basidiomycetes together with the xylariaceous ascomycetes.

As with the litter-decomposers, wood-rotting fungi use cellulose as a food resource, but must release this from its lignin bonds to make it accessible. 'White rot' fungi break down both lignin and cellulose enzymatically, leaving the wood stringy, bleached, and soft, though the lignin itself may not be utilised as a resource. The less common 'brown rot' fungi manage to break down cellulose whilst leaving the lignin intact, probably by releasing a chemical solvent, hydrogen peroxide, using iron within the wood as a catalyst. Rotten wood is brown, often cubically cracked, and powdery rather than stringy. Though the white- and brown-rot fungi are the main degraders of wood, many less specialised fungi, mostly small ascomycetes, can produce superficial 'soft rots' by penetrating wood surfaces and exploiting the limited quantities of immediately accessible cellulose. They are particularly active in saturated wood and as such are the main agents of decay in marine drift-wood, but are of less importance as wood degraders in forest systems. Other ascomycetes utilise starches and sugars in wood, colonising the substratum without rotting it. An example is the discomycete *Chlorociboria aeruginascens*, the well-known green-staining fungus of oak.

The toxic extractives produced by trees are often concentrated in the heartwood and vary from species to species. Many are broadly effective against a range of organisms. Oak, for example, is said to produce acetic acid in sufficient concentration to corrode metal. Other extractives are specifically antifungal, and can only be tolerated by a few highly specialised fungi capable of breaking down and neutralising the chemicals involved or of growing in their presence. Variations in these extractives between tree species may be the reason why they attract different species of wood-rotting fungi. Heartwood of oak and chestnut is particularly resistant to degradation, as can be seen by their fallen, skeletal remains in old woodland, some of which may persist for more than a century. *Fistulina hepatica*, the beefsteak fungus, is one of the few specialist species capable of decaying oak and chestnut heartwood and is rarely found on other trees. Cedar produces particularly toxic extractives (called thujaplicins) which makes its wood naturally resistant to decay, and hence of commercial use in outdoor timber structures.

Low nitrogen content is another feature of heartwood which wood-rotting fungi have to deal with. Undecayed wood excluding bark contains between 0.03% and 0.3% nitrogen by weight compared to 0.6–6% for non-woody stems and foliage, so specialist wood-decay fungi have to be able to function at low nitrogen levels. They may achieve this by translocating nitrogen from old hyphae into new hyphae, effectively recycling themselves as they grow, or by scavenging nitrogen from bacteria, other fungi, or even nematode worms. Species of *Hohenbuehelia* and *Pleurotus* (oyster caps) are examples of wood-degrading specialists which produce remarkable nematode-trapping hyphae (Chapter Six), possibly to supplement their nitrogen intake. Bulky wood also contains high concentrations of carbon dioxide (around 10–20%) compared to leaf litter (under 1%). As a result, most wood-degrading fungi can tolerate high CO_2 levels, in some cases up to 70%, and concomitant low levels of oxygen. Indeed, many species are actively stimulated to growth by high levels of CO_2.

Water stress is a further major factor for wood-rotting fungi. Dead standing wood in particular can rapidly dry out and wood with a moisture content below 20% is effectively protected from decay (an important factor for timber used in construction; Chapter 14). Many wood-decayers, however, have evolved strategies for surviving seasonal and even longer-term droughts once they have become established within the wood. These include the production of sclerotia (hardened masses of thick-walled hyphae), chlamydospores (thick-walled resting spores), and long-lasting fruitbodies. Growth may halt when the wood becomes too dry, but can continue when the moisture content rises.

The process of wood-rotting starts in the living tree, which typically harbours a wide range of endophytic fungi comprising different species in the bark, the xylem, and the roots. A study of alders in Devon and Switzerland, for example, isolated 85 different species from wood and bark, almost all of them ascomycetes (Fisher & Petrini, 1990). Most of these are considered to be neutral symbionts, but several, specifically those in the *Xylariaceae*, are capable of extensive wood-rotting and may represent latent fungal infections which remain quiescent until senescence or death of the host tree or tree part.

Pioneer wood-rotting species can also enter through areas of insect and other damage. Dead attached twigs and branches are almost universally colonised in this way, mainly by corticioid basidiomycetes, such as *Peniophora* and *Vuilleminia* species, and by some resupinate polypores. These pioneer decay fungi are restricted to this habitat and quite rapidly disappear when branches eventually fall. Nonetheless they can cause substantial degradation of the wood (up to 13% weight loss per year, based on figures quoted in Rayner & Boddy, 1988) whilst it is still above ground.

A number of fungi, including bracket fungi like *Phaeolus schweinitzii* and *Heterobasidion annosum* or toadstools like *Armillaria mellea*, are parasites entering through roots and capable of infecting otherwise healthy trees. Their root infections produce 'butt rots' which invariably topple and destroy trees. Other specialists, already noted, are heart-rot species, mainly bracket fungi such as *Fistulina hepatica* on oak and chestnut, *Fomes fomentarius* on birch and sometimes beech, and *Ganoderma* species on various trees. By attacking heartwood, these fungi ultimately produce hollow trees which (if stable) may continue to grow for many years. Indeed, it has been suggested that this is an essential part of the natural development of 'veteran' trees and may even be beneficial to them and other organisms, establishing complex communities of invertebrates, fungi and other micro-organisms which may have no other niche.

Once timber has fallen, the fungal community changes, with only a few of the pioneer species persisting. New colonisers typically gain access either through newly exposed surfaces (sawn or fractured ends) or at points of contact with the ground. In the former case, the colonising fungi may enter as spores or via insect vectors. Siricid wood wasps are, for example, associated with wood-rotting *Amylostereum* and *Stereum* species with which they have a mutually beneficial association (Chapter Five). Fungi entering from the ground typically arise from hyphae already present in the litter or nearby woody debris. Such hyphae are frequently in the form of 'rhizomorphs', root-like strands composed of multiple agglutinated or interwoven hyphae, capable of foraging for new food sources sometimes at considerable distances (several metres or more) from their parent mycelium. Many of the larger rhizomorphs are easily visible in the F-layer of leaf litter or at the base of fruitbodies. The stinkhorn *Phallus impudicus*, the puffball *Lycoperdon pyriforme*, and the toadstool *Megacollybia platyphylla* are three very common examples of wood-rotting fungi forming conspicuous white rhizomorphs, though the black 'bootlace' rhizomorphs of *Armillaria* species, the honey fungus (Fig. 28), may be even more familiar.

Rotting of fallen wood typically involves a succession of fungal species, the earliest colonisers being quick to establish themselves, but later giving way to slower but more aggressive species. On deciduous logs, common and ubiquitous species such as *Trametes versicolor*, *Bjerkandera adusta*, and *Stereum hirsutum* will typically replace the original, specialist species rotting dead standing wood. They in turn may be replaced by species like the agarics *Hypholoma fasciculare* and *Megacollybia platyphylla*. This kind of replacement has been termed 'secondary resource capture' (Rayner & Boddy, 1988) and may involve a wide range of antagonistic interactions. These include better metabolisation of resources (out-competing the original colonisers),

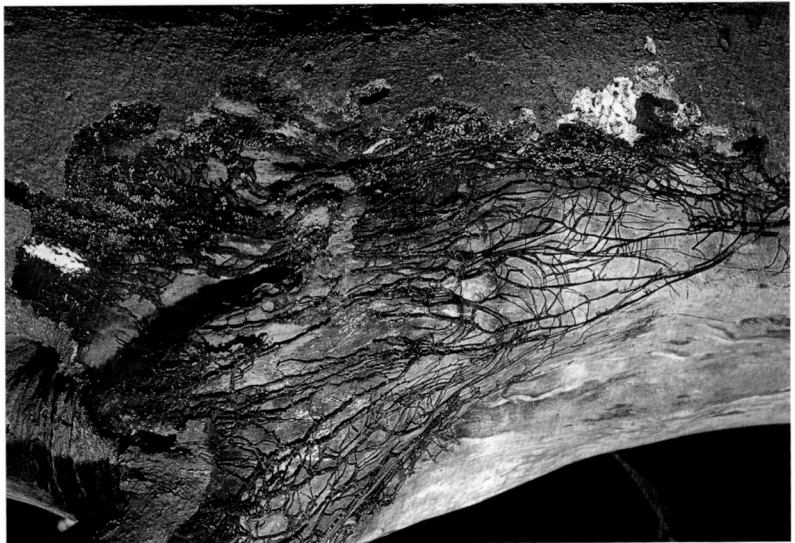

FIG 28. The black, bootlace-like rhizomorphs of honey fungus (*Armillaria*) by which the fungus is able to infect a wide range of trees and shrubs, characteristically developing under the bark. The fungus causes a root rot leading eventually to the death of the plant (P. Livermore).

production of specific antifungal enzymes or other combative chemicals, and mechanical attack by invading hyphae. Some strategies are effectively parasitic. *Trametes gibbosa*, for example, a common bracket fungus on beech logs and stumps, parasitises and eventually replaces the earlier colonist *Bjerkandera adusta*. *Lenzites betulina*, on birch and other hardwoods, parasitises and replaces *Trametes versicolor*. The conifer species *Skeletocutis carneogrisea* was unknown in Britain till 1994, when it was found growing on or close to the common *Trichaptum abietinum*. Once this niche was identified, it was reported with its presumed host from numerous sites country-wide.

Some of these secondary resource capture techniques can be seen by growing two different species together in the same Petri dish and observing what happens when the expanding hyphal fronts meet. Any given wood-rotting species may be successful against some competitors, but fall prey to others. Research in this area has led to the employment of one fungal species as a biological control agent for another. The best–known is the use of the corticioid fungus *Phlebiopsis gigantea* to control infection of cut stumps by the polypore *Heterobasidion annosum*, a potentially damaging parasite in conifer plantations. Cut stumps are painted with a conidial suspension of the *Phlebiopsis* immediately after felling. The species, once established, is antagonistic to most other potential invaders, particularly *Heterobasidion*, but is itself non-pathogenic and harmless to living trees.

Plantations and other managed woodlands often have unusual wood-rotting regimes, where certain species (including pathogens) may become dominant. This is partly the result of monocultures (trees of the same age and same species, often non-native and grown close together) and partly the result of artificial management. Brash, limbs, and eventually whole trunks are cut or felled when healthy and fresh, so that the colonisers of dead attached wood are rarely present and the wood-rotting succession may be highly atypical compared to that in natural forests. It is noticeable that certain wood-rotting species, for example the small brown toadstool *Melanotus horizontalis* or the jelly fungus *Calocera pallidospathulata*, have spread rapidly and epidemically through forestry plantations since the 1970s and 1980s. Both are probably non-European in origin.

ANIMAL SCAVENGERS

Unlike the rather tough and intractable remains of plants, most parts of dead animals are easily assimilated by carrion eaters and bacteria, leaving little scope for fungal saprotrophs under natural conditions. As a result, fungi are normally left with nothing much more than fur, feathers, and bones from vertebrates plus the chitinous exoskeletons of insects and their relatives.

One rather macabre exception is the Japanese corpse toadstool, *Hebeloma vinosophyllum*. Although not known in the British Isles, its close relative *Hebeloma radicosum* does occur in Britain where it is associated with underground mole latrines (Chapter 13). Both species are ammonophilic, but *H. vinosophyllum* has been found growing on soil above buried animal carcasses and, as such, may be of possible forensic value in locating the bodies of murder victims. A range of other species, both ascomycetes and basidiomycetes, also show selective fruiting on nitrogen or ammonia rich substrates (Sagara, 1992). They include the very common *Laccaria amethystina*, which was studied in Japan and found in urea-treated plots to fruit up to 300 times more densely than in untreated plots. Several other 'ammonia' fungi have also been associated with the later remains of corpses, notably *Hebeloma spoliatum* and *Laccaria bicolor*. The latter has been reported from forest soil over the decomposing body of a cat. However, these fungi are not solely associated with vertebrate remains, but also occur in other nitrogen-rich situations. Both *Hebeloma radicosum* and *H. spoliatum* have also, for example, been reported from the decomposing nests of wasps, utilising nitrogen compounds present in faecal pellets of the larvae. These two species have also been found to fruit after artificial application to forest soil of nitrogenous materials which decompose to form urea and ammonium compounds. It is of interest to note that these agarics form ectomycorrhizas with the roots of forest trees and therefore also require living tree roots to be present before they are able to develop.

Bones, horns, hooves, and hair are degraded by specialist keratinophilic fungi. Most are microscopic and are more or less ubiquitous in soil. They can even occur in the home. In a study of house dust in India at least 15 species were isolated, including nine species of the ascomycetous mould genus *Chrysosporium*.

Some of the larger and best-known keratinophiles belong to the ascomycete order *Onygenales*. Species of *Onygena* produce a profusion of whitish, drumstick-like fruitbodies a few millimetres high on substrates such as rotting horns or feathers. Two species are found in Britain: *Onygena equina*, which usually occurs on rotting horns of sheep (Fig. 29), or occasionally on shed horse hooves or owl pellets, and *O. corvina* which is found on rotting feathers, sometimes in nests, or on bird skulls. Other keratin specialists tend to be microfungi, some of which, such as *Microsporum gypseum*, are commonplace in soil where they live off skin flakes, hairs, and other detritus. They can be found by burying strands of hair as baits. Related species occur in bird nests (Chapter 13) or as saprotrophs in fur and feathers of living animals. Occasionally they can create problems by invading the outer layers of human and animal skin or finger and toenails, where they are effectively parasitic (Chapter 15).

FIG 29. The drumstick-like fruitbodies of *Onygena equina*, clustered on a rotting sheep's horn. The species can be quite common, and is one of the keratin specialists, producing special enzymes which enable it to degrade horn and similar substances (P. Livermore).

Keratinophilic species also occur amongst the chytrids and oomycetes. Some of the chytrids, such as *Rhizophydium apiculatum* and *R. keratinophilum*, can be obtained from damp soil by baiting techniques. Amongst the *Oomycota*, *Aphanodictyon papillatum* and *Lagenidium humanum* occur on keratin but their biology and ecology are little known. In addition, a range of non-keratinophilic fungi are sometimes capable of colonising keratinised substrata, utilising some part of the substrate as a sole source of nutrients. Various strategies are employed, notably intercellular sheets or 'fronds' of mycelium, and narrow, boring hyphae which penetrate layers of keratinised cells but which cannot directly digest the keratin. These were investigated by English (1965) and include species of ascomycetous genera such as *Chaetomium*, *Curvularia*, *Fusarium*, *Memnoniella*, and *Penicillium*.

Perhaps surprisingly, many common moulds, particularly species of *Penicillium* and *Trichoderma* are capable of breaking down chitin, the main component of insect exoskeletons, and are known to do so in the litter and humus layers in woodlands. Specialist ascomycetous chitinophiles are found in the genera *Cordyceps* and *Paecilomyces*, but these are generally parasitic species rather than saprotrophs (Chapter Six).

Decomposers of inorganic matter

Perhaps even more surprising is that some inorganic materials are also degraded by fungi. This capability can have significant and sometimes serious economic consequences, for example in the degradation of stonework, plastics, and even glass (Chapter 14). In nature, fungi play an important role in the breakdown of inorganic substances in animals, such as the calcareous shells and tests of *Foraminifera*, molluscs, and perhaps other groups, particularly in the marine environment (Chapter 12).

Luminescent fungi

Luminescence, a curious but well-known phenomenon in a wide range of organisms, also occurs in fungi where it appears to be a by-product of the decay process. Its biological value (if any) remains unclear, but certainly, many fruitbodies or mycelia of larger basidiomycetes emit light, usually of a pale blue-green hue, which is easily visible to the human eye in suitably dark conditions.

These luminescent fungi are mostly saprobes attacking wood and leaf litter. The phenomenon is quite commonplace, to the extent that, even in temperate forests in the United States and Europe, decomposing leaf litter may produce a faint but distinct glow at night. This glow is popularly known as 'foxfire' or 'faerie fire', and is most evident late in the year as the nights become cooler. It is said to fuel stories of ghosts and fairies and other folk myths. Most frequently, it is the mycelium of the fungus that is luminescent, though it may also be all or part of the fruitbody itself, such as the gills or stems of some agarics. In one case, *Mycena rorida* var. *lamprospora*, reported from southeast Asia and South America, only the freshly discharged spores emit light.

To date, over sixty species of fungi have been reported as luminescent (Table 1), including both tropical and temperate species. In British woodlands, honey fungus (*Armillaria mellea*) is the commonest such species. On dark nights, it is said that any freshly damaged wood containing honey fungus mycelium will be seen to glow faintly. Certainly, if such wood is gathered and taken to a dark room, the glow can be quite easily seen once the eyes have become fully accustomed to the darkness (Fig. 30).

Infected wood will continue to glow whilst the mycelium is fresh and damp, and sufficient oxygen is available. Indeed, as long ago as 1667, Boyle proved that oxygen was essential for the production of bioluminescence from wood. Later authors have gone further and noted that there is a distinct oscillation in the emission of light from mycelium, which may increase in response to injury. As a result freshly broken infected wood emits a brighter glow than older, exposed wood.

Fungal luminescence has been known in Europe for centuries, coming to the attention of Aristotle and later Pliny, who described a light-emitting species now considered to have been *Omphalotus olearius*, an orange, chanterelle-like, Mediterranean agaric which grows clustered at the base of olive trees. A related, more northerly species, *O. illudens*, occurs on chestnut in south-east England and is so well-known for its glow that it is called 'jack o'lantern' in the United States.

The earliest scientific study of luminescent wood can be attributed to Francis Bacon in the latter part of the 17th century. Bacon proved that such

FIG 30. Freshly broken dead wood containing the mycelium of honey fungus (*Armillaria*) is faintly luminous, but requires a long exposure to see clearly (G. Kibby).

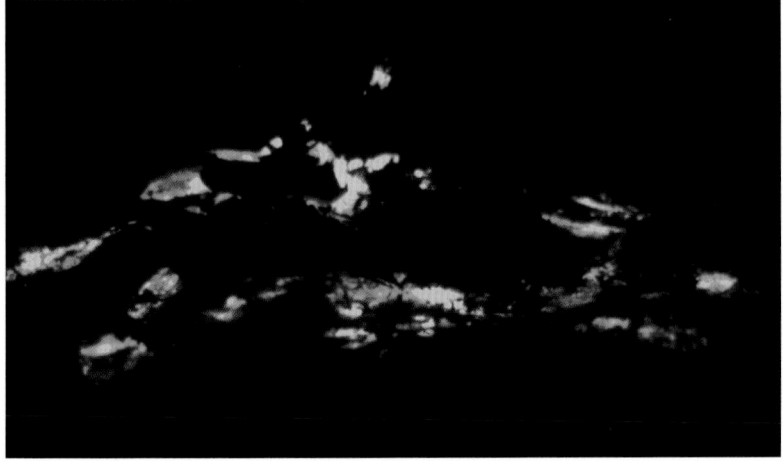

light is emitted only from decayed wood, and occurs only whilst the wood is damp. However, it was not until well over a century and a half later that J.F. Heller conclusively demonstrated that the luminescence was due to fungal mycelium. He called this mycelium *Rhizomorpha noctiluca* ('nightlights'), which was later shown to belong to *Armillaria mellea*.

Though the biochemistry of bioluminescence has been studied in many organisms, it is still not well understood for fungi. It is probable that a phosphate-rich chemical ('luciferin') is always involved. Luciferin combines with oxygen in the presence of the enzyme luciferase to generate light. However, non-enzyme precursors of luciferin are also known. The biological value of bioluminescence is also unclear. It has been considered that it may serve in some species to attract night-flying insects which have a role in spore dispersal. It has also been suggested, though, that bioluminescence may have a purely biochemical role, breaking down organic molecules using oxygen, emitting light and carbon dioxide as a result.

Perhaps surprisingly, at least 25 different luminescent fungi are known from the British Isles. However, it should be noted that not all populations of any given species are necessarily luminescent. This has been demonstrated, for example, in the shelf-like, wood-inhabiting toadstool *Panellus stipticus*. American specimens of this species are consistently luminescent, whilst British material is not.

A world list of fungi reported as luminescent is given in Table 1. Those species known from the British Isles are indicated, but it should be borne in mind that their luminescence in Britain has not necessarily been reported.

TABLE 1. Fungal species reported as luminescent

SPECIES	REGION	BRITISH
Agrocybe semiorbicularis	Europe	+
Armillaria mellea	N. & S. temperate	+
Armillaria tabescens	N. & S. temperate	+
Boletus impolitus	N. America	+
Collybia cirrhata	Europe	+
Collybia tuberosa	Europe	+
Dictyopanus foliicolus	Japan	
Dictyopanus gloeocystidiatus	Japan	

SPECIES	REGION	BRITISH
Dictyopanus luminescens	S.E. Asia	
Dictyopanus pusillus	Tropics, subtropics	
Favolaschia peziziformis	S. America	
Filoboletus manipularis	Africa, tropical Asia	
Flammulina velutipes	N. temperate	+
Heterobasidion annosum	N. temperate	+
Hypholoma fasciculare	Europe	+
Ileodictyon cibarium	New Zealand	(+; introduced)
Laetiporus sulphureus	cosmopolitan	+
Lampteromyces japonicus	E. Asia	
Locellina illuminans	Sulawesi	
Locellina noctilucens	Papua New Guinea	
Lysurus corallocephalus	Africa	
Marasmius phosphorus	E. Asia	
Mycena chlorophanos	S.E. Asia, Australia	
Mycena citricolor	S.America, Caribbean	
Mycena citrinella var. *illumina*	Japan	
Mycena cyanophos	Micronesia	
Mycena dasiyogunensis	Japan	
Mycena epipterygia	Europe	+
Mycena galericulata var. *calopus*	Europe	
Mycena galopus	Europe	+
Mycena inclinata	N. temperate	+
Mycena lux-coeli	Japan	
Mycena microillumina	Japan	
Mycena parabolica	Europe	
Mycena photogena	Japan	
Mycena polygramma	Europe	+
Mycena pruinoso-viscida var. rabaulensis	S.E. Asia	
Mycena pseudostylobates	Japan	
Mycena pura	Europe	+
Mycena rorida var. *lamprospora*	S.E. Asia, S. America	
Mycena sanguinolenta	Europe	+
Mycena stylobates	Europe	+
Mycena sublucens	S.E. Asia	
Mycena tintinnabulum	Europe	
Mycena yapensis	Japan	
Mycena zephira	Europe	

SPECIES	REGION	BRITISH
Omphalia martensii	S.E. Asia	
Omphalotus nidiformis	Australia	
Omphalotus illudens	N. temperate	+
Omphalotus olearius	Cosmopolitan	
Panellus stipticus	N. temperate	+
Phellinus igniarius	Europe	+
Phellinus pini	Europe	+
Pleurocybella illuminans	S.E. Asia, Australia	
Pleurocybella noctilucens	S.E. Asia	
Pleurotus canescens	Australia	
Pleurotus japonicus	E. Asia	
Pleurotus luminosus	Africa	
Pleurotus lux	Tahiti	
Pleurotus phosphoreus	Australia	
Pleurotus prometheus	China	
Polyporus noctilucens	Africa	
Polyporus rhipidium var. *pusillus*	Asia, Australasia, S. America	
Terana caerulea	widespread	+
Xerula longipes	Europe	+
Xylaria hypoxylon	temperate	+
Xylaria polymorpha	temperate	+

CHAPTER 4

Mycorrhizas – Promoters of Growth

T HOUGH saprotrophic fungi play a major and indeed essential role in the plant community by nutrient recycling through the breakdown of organic remains, some fungi play a more direct role by actively associating with living plant roots to form 'mycorrhizas'.

A 'mycorrhiza' ('fungus root') has been succinctly defined as 'a symbiosis in which an external mycelium of a fungus supplies soil-derived nutrients to a plant root' (Smith & Read, 1997). In other words, fungal hyphae and root cells interconnect, always to the benefit of the plant and often to the benefit of the fungus. These mycorrhizal relationships are ancient, and may have been instrumental in enabling early plants to colonise land, stimulating the evolution of the first root systems. Even today, it is mycorrhizas, not roots, which are the chief organs of nutrient uptake by plants, occurring in over 90% of plant species.

Mycorrhizas have evolved in several different and independent ways, and can be conveniently divided into four main groups. The most conspicuous of these are the 'ectomycorrhizal' fungi (principally toadstools) which mainly form associations with forest trees. Less conspicuous, but more universal, are the 'vesicular-arbuscular' (VA) mycorrhizal fungi (*Glomeromycetes*) which form associations with a wide range of plants, including grasses and food crops. 'Ericoid' mycorrhizal fungi (principally *Ascomycetes*) form associations with ericaceous plants, whilst 'orchid endomycorrhizal' fungi (principally *Basidiomycetes*) are hosts for terrestrial orchids. The few plant families which do not (or rarely) form mycorrhizas (i.e. the *Amaranthaceae, Brassicaceae, Chenopodiaceae, Cyperaceae, Juncaceae, Polygonaceae,* and *Portulacaceae*) tend to contain wetland or annual species, including many commonplace weeds. A checklist of British mycorrhizal plants was published by Harley & Harley (1987).

ECTOMYCORRHIZA

Only around 3% of the world's plants are believed to be ectomycorrhizal, but in temperate zones these include many dominant woodland trees. Such trees form the main ectomycorrhizal component in the British flora and include oaks, birches, beech, pine, alder, willows, and most plantation conifers (Table 2).

As well as trees, a small number of British shrubs and herbaceous plants also form ectomycorrhizas, notably mountain avens (*Dryas*), rock-rose (*Helianthemum*), and creeping willow (*Salix repens*). This means that in tree-less areas like dune slacks or limestone pavements, some familiar woodland macrofungi may appear, their fruitbodies often taller than the plants with which they associate.

TABLE 2. The main native and introduced ectomycorrhizal plant genera in Britain. Those which only occasionally form ectomycorrhizas are marked with an asterisk (*).

Abies	fir
Alnus	alder
Betula	birch
Carpinus	hornbeam
Castanea	chestnut
Corylus	hazel
*Crataegus**	hawthorn
Dryas	mountain avens
Eucalyptus	gum
Fagus	beech
Helianthemum	rockrose
Larix	larch

TABLE 2 – CONT.

Nothofagus	southern beech
Picea	spruce
Pinus	pine
Populus	poplar
Prunus*	cherry, sloe, etc.
Pseudotsuga	western hemlock
Quercus	oak
Salix	willow
Sorbus*	rowan, beam, service, etc.
Tilia	lime
Ulmus*	elm

In ectomycorrhizas, the fungal partner forms a mycelial sheath or mantle around the plant root from which hyphae grow outwards into the soil and inwards between the outer, cortical layer of roots cells, often forming a characteristic coralloid (coral-like) appearance (Fig. 31). This inward growth is mesh-like and forms a typical structure called the 'Hartig net'. It surrounds but does not penetrate the cells, hence the term 'ecto' (outer) mycorrhizal,

FIG 31. The ectomycorrhiza of a *Pisolithus* species and *Eucalyptus globulus*. The plant root hairs in ectomycorrhizal associations are characteristically swollen and coralloid in appearance (K. Ingleby).

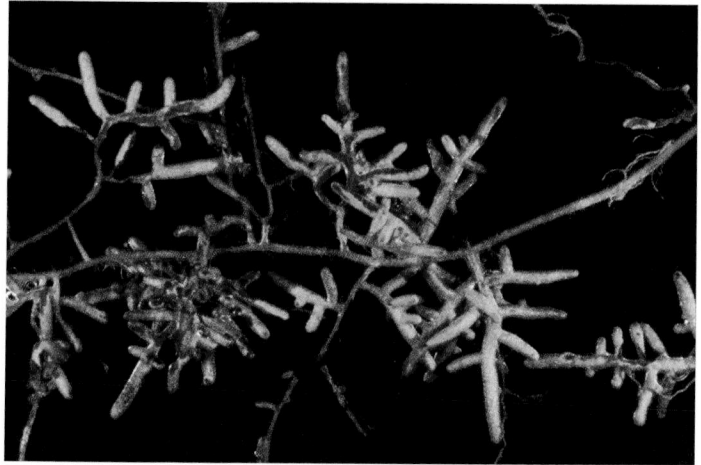

and provides an extensive plant-fungus interface across which nutrients can pass. Many ectomycorrhizal plants typically produce an abundance of short laterals from their primary roots specifically to maximise the fungal interface. In the absence of fungal colonisation, these lateral roots may abort.

In this mutually beneficial partnership, the fungus derives most of its organic nutrients, principally glucose and fructose, ultimately produced by photosynthesis, directly from the plant roots. Since the fungal biomass may be quite large, this places a considerable burden on the plant. Indeed, it has been estimated that as much as 15% of the plant's photosynthetic products goes towards maintaining its fungal partner (Finlay & Söderström, 1992).

In return, the ectomycorrhizal plant obtains nitrogen from its fungal partner, principally from soil ammonia (NH_4) and nitrates (NO_3), as well as phosphorus in both organic and inorganic forms. These nutrients are essential to healthy plant growth, but are often present in meagre quantities in poor soils. On their own, roots can only absorb a small proportion of the locally available nitrogen and phosphorous. The ramifying hyphal network of the fungal partner can, however, increase the absorption area by 40-fold or more, hugely extending the resources available to the plant.

In temperate forests, dominated by ectomycorrhizal trees, germinating seedlings rapidly contact their fungal partners, possibly by releasing chemical attractants, and can form initial mycorrhizas within as little as two to four days. Individual mycorrhizas may only last for a matter of months before becoming senescent, but new ones are constantly formed as roots and hyphae continue to grow. As root systems develop, plants may simultan-eously associate with several different fungal partners. Additionally, with age, the fungal partners may change, typically from 'early-stage' generalist to 'late-stage' specialist species.

These partner fungi, mainly basidiomycetes, include some of the most familiar forest toadstools, as well as many boletes, chanterelles, and tooth fungi, together with the earthballs, false truffles, and some corticioid and clavarioid species. Ascomycetous ectomycorrhizal fungi are fewer, but include the true truffles, hart's truffles (Fig. 32), and some of the cup-fungi. A very few zygomycetes (pea truffles) also form ectomycorrhiza. Additional

FIG 32. Hart's truffle *Elaphomyces granulatus*. The fruitbodies of this common species develop in ectomycorrhizal association with the roots of various deciduous and coniferous trees (P. Roberts).

genera have sometimes been reported as ectomycorrhizal, e.g. *Clavulina* (club fungi) and *Morchella* (morels), but further research is required to discover their true status.

TABLE 3. Known fungal genera containing ectomycorrhizal species in the British Isles (from Smith & Read, 1997; Agerer, 1987–1993).

ASCOMYCETES	
Balsamia	truffle-like fungi
Cenococcum	peppercorn truffles
Choiromyces	truffle-like fungi
Elaphomyces	hart's truffles
Genea	truffle-like fungi
Helvella	saddle-fungi
Humaria	cup fungi
Hydnotrya	truffle-like fungi
Pachyphloeus	truffle-like fungi
Sphaerosporella	cup-fungi

TABLE 3 — CONT.

Sphaerozone	truffle-like fungi
Tuber	truffles
BASIDIOMYCETES	
Amanita	toadstools
Amphinema	corticioid fungi
Astraeus	earthstar-like fungi
Bankera	tooth fungi
Boletinus	boletes
Boletopsis	bolete-like fungi
Boletus	boletes
Byssocorticium	corticioid fungi
Byssoporia	corticioid fungi
Cantharellus	chanterelles
Coltricia	poroid fungi
Cortinarius	toadstools
Craterellus	chanterelles
Entoloma	toadstools
Gautieria	false truffles
Geastrum	earthstars
Gomphus	chanterelle-like fungi
Gymnomyces	false truffles
Gyrodon	boletes
Gyroporus	boletes
Hebeloma	toadstools
Hydnangium	false truffles
Hydnellum	tooth fungi
Hydnum	tooth fungi
Hygrophorus	toadstools
Hymenangium	false truffles
Hymenogaster	false truffles
Hysterangium	false truffles
Inocybe	toadstools
Laccaria	toadstools
Lactarius	toadstools
Leccinum	boletes
Leucocortinarius	toadstools
Leucogaster	false truffles
Lyophyllum	toadstools
Naucoria	toadstools
Octavianina	false truffles

TABLE 3 – CONT.

Paxillus	toadstools
Phellodon	tooth fungi
Phylloporus	toadstools
Piloderma	corticioid fungi
Pisolithus	dye-balls
Porphyrellus	boletes
Pseudocraterellus	chanterelles
Pseudotomentella	corticioid fungi
Pulveroboletus	boletes
Ramaria	coral fungi
Rhizopogon	false truffles
Rozites	toadstools
Russula	toadstools
Sarcodon	tooth fungi
Scleroderma	earthballs
Sebacina	jelly fungi
Strobilomyces	boletes
Suillus	boletes
Thelephora	thelephoroid fungi
Tomentella	corticioid fungi
Tomentellopsis	corticioid fungi
Tricholoma	toadstools
Tylopilus	boletes
Tylospora	corticioid fungi
Xerocomus	boletes
Zelleromyces	false truffles
ZYGOMYCETES	
Endogone	pea truffles

It appears that nearly all of these fungi depend entirely on their specific plant associates in order to grow. This is why woodlands without ectomycorrhizal trees (e.g. some ash-sycamore coastal woodlands in Devon) lack many familiar species of macrofungi. It is also why some commercially important food species, including ceps and chanterelles, cannot be cultivated *ex situ* but are still gathered from the wild.

As field mycologists know, ascertaining which fungus fruitbody is associated with which tree species in a typical mixed woodland is an almost impossible task, especially since the fungal mycelium is capable of spreading as far as 100m from its partner. This problem extends to all *in situ* mycorrhizal studies. Uncovering and examining the mycorrhizas themselves can, however, help determine some of the partnerships. The gross morphology of a mycorrhiza differs from species to species in terms of precise shape and colour, and microscopic examination of the hyphal mantle can add further information. As a result, some mycorrhizal associations can be identified by using a guidebook, such as the *Colour Atlas of Ectomycorrhizae* (Agerer, 1987 – 1993). But increasingly the use of molecular methods is enabling fungal-plant partnerships to be identified with precision, both at the species and population level.

A somewhat surprising result of such studies is the frequent lack of correlation between the fungi found fruiting on the ground and those forming the ectomycorrhizas below. A four-year study by Gardes & Bruns (1996), for example, found that fruitbodies of *Amanita* and *Suillus* were most commonly collected in trial pine plots, but that *Russula* and *Tomentella* species were forming most of the ectomycorrhizas. A similar study in spruce plantations (Taylor & Alexander, 1989) showed that over 70% of ectomycorrhizas were formed with a species of *Tylospora*, though no *Tylospora* fruitbodies were ever collected. A possible explanation is that the dominant non-fruiting species are composed of many individuals, none of sufficient size to produce fruitbodies. Alternatively, the more successful associates may fruit rarely or lack the stimulus to fruit at all.

Ectendomycorrhizas: arbutoid and conifer variants

A variant form of ectomycorrhiza, in which hyphae penetrate the cortical cells of the plant roots as well as surround them in a sheath, is sometimes known as 'ectendomycorrhiza' (meaning that the fungus is both outside and inside the root). This is a purely descriptive term and does not imply that all ectendomycorrhizas are related or identical in function.

Ectendomycorrhizas (with well-developed sheaths) are typical of some members of the *Ericales*, principally *Arbutus* (the strawberry tree, native in south west Ireland) and *Arctostaphylos* (bearberry, a northern shrub commonest in the Scottish Highlands). Similar associations occur in *Pyrola* species (the wintergreens). The fungal components of these 'arbutoid mycorrhizas' are the same as those in ordinary ectomycorrhizal associations.

Zak (1976), for example, showed that a number of commonplace fungi (including *Hebeloma*, *Laccaria*, and *Lactarius* species) formed ectendomy-corrhizas with *Arctostaphylos uva-ursi*, but ordinary ectomycorrhizas with forest trees. Similar results were obtained for *Arbutus menziesii*. The determining partner in arbutoid mycorrhiza must therefore be the plants, rather than the fungi.

Rather different ectendomycorrhizas (with poorly developed sheaths) are sometimes found in conifers, particularly in seedling pine and larch. They are common in tree nurseries, and as a result have been quite closely investigated. The fungi responsible are mainly discomycetes (cup-fungi) in the genus *Wilcoxina*, and seem to have a beneficial effect on the health of the conifer seedlings. As the seedlings mature, more normal ectomycorrhizas replace the ectendomycorrhizas.

Plant parasites: the monotropoid cheats

A stranger variant is found in the 'monotropoid mycorrhiza' formed by a number of achlorophyllous (non-photosynthesising) plants, including the yellow birdsnest, *Monotropa hypopitys*, which is occasionally found in British woodlands, pine plantations, and dune systems. Since these plants lack green leaves they must obtain all their carbohydrates and nutrients from some other source, and they do this by tapping into existing ectomycorrhizal associations. Monotropoid mycorrhizas, though structurally related to arbutoid mycorrhizas, are entirely parasitic.

Recent research has shown that these monotropoid plants tend to be host specific, parasitising particular groups of fungi. In North America, for example, where such plants are quite common, Indian pipes *Monotropa uniflora* (Fig. 33) specialises in members of the *Russulaceae*, whilst *Pleuricospora fimbriolata* specialises in false truffles in the genus *Gautieria*. The British *Monotropa hypopitys* parasitises ectomycorrhiza formed by *Tricholoma* species, specifically *Tricholoma cingulatum/Salix* associations and *Tricholoma terreum/Pinus* associations (Bidartondo & Bruns, 2002).

The achlorophyllous orchids, a quite different group of plants, have evolved a similar method of mycorrhizal exploitation (see 'orchid mycorrhiza' below).

FIG 33. Indian pipes *Monotropa uniflora*, an achlorophyllous plant which parasitises mycorrhizal associations. This particular species is associated with members of the *Russulaceae* (P. Roberts).

Fungal interlopers

A number of larger fungi also appear to be parasites on existing ectomycorrhiza, notably species of the agaricoid genus *Gomphidius*. It has long been noticed, for example, that fruitbodies of *Gomphidius roseus* always occur in company with the bolete *Suillus bovinus* (Fig. 34) which is ectomycorrhizal with pine. Further investigation (Olsson *et al.*, 2000) has shown that the *Gomphidius* almost certainly parasitises both fungal and plant partners, using the bolete mycelium to locate mycorrhizas and then penetrating the pine root cells. A similar parasitism may occur with *Gomphidius glutinosus*, *Suillus* species (or their truffle-like relatives *Rhizopogon*), and spruce, and between *Chroogomphus rutilus*, *Suillus granulatus*, and pine.

Also known to many field mycologists is the relationship between the fly agaric *Amanita muscaria* and the bolete *Chalciporus piperatus*. The latter is almost always found fruiting in close proximity to the former, suggesting a mutualistic or parasitic relationship. However, this putative association does not appear to have been investigated to date.

FIG 34. The pink agaric *Gomphidius roseus* is always found in association with the brownish bolete *Suillus bovinus*. The *Gomphidius* has been shown to be parasitic on the mycorrhiza established between the bolete and the roots of pine (P. Roberts).

VESICULAR-ARBUSCULAR MYCORRHIZA

VA (vesicular-arbuscular) mycorrhizal associations are ancient and ubiquitous, uniting the plant and fungal kingdoms at least since the Triassic (240 million years B.P.) and probably since the Early Devonian (400 million years B.P.). Almost all plant families, from mosses and ferns to grasses and trees, are involved in this symbiosis and indeed it is thought that VA associations played an important role in the colonisation of land by vascular plants.

Unlike ectomycorrhizas, VA associations are 'endo' (inside) mycorrhizal, the fungal partner forming branching structures (arbuscles), and sometimes also bladder-like vesicles, within the cortical cells of plant roots. Thus the plant-fungus relationship is not always obvious, unless roots are dissected and examined microscopically. Indeed, though VA mycorrhizas were first noticed in the nineteenth century, their ubiquity and importance were largely overlooked until the 1970s, since when the VA plant-fungus relationship has become a major area of research.

The fungi involved in this cryptic relationship are themselves easily overlooked. Belonging to the order *Glomerales* (*Glomeromycota*), they represent one of the smaller groups of true fungi, distinguished in part from ascomycetes and basidiomycetes by having hyphae without septa (cross-walls) and by rarely producing macroscopically visible fruitbodies. Many produce no fruitbodies at all and can only be found outside plant roots in the form of hyphae or large spore-like bodies, some (in the family *Gigasporaceae*) up to 400 mm or so across. A further peculiarity of VA fungi is that they show little or no specificity in their choice of partners, so that almost any given species can associate with almost any VA mycorrhizal plant. Spores of VA fungi can be found (by fine sieving techniques) in almost all soils, including ploughed fields. They germinate readily in culture, but fail to develop into a mycelium unless and until they become established within the cells of a VA plant partner. The fungi are thus obligately symbiotic, incapable of living independently. It has even been suggested that they may lack some essential genetic material for growth and reproduction which can only be supplied by their plant partners.

The arbuscles typical of the VA plant-fungus association are formed by hyphal penetration of plant cell walls followed by subsequent hyphal growth. The plant cell membrane is not pierced, however, but surrounds the invading hyphae keeping them apart from the living plant cytoplasm. These arbuscles (together with the intercellular hyphae) provide an extensive and intimate interface between hyphae and cell across which are exchanged similar nutrients to those already noted for ectomycorrhizas.

Since VA mycorrhizas occur in food plants, including cereals, they are potentially of considerable economic importance, especially since their effects on plant health and yields are almost invariably beneficial. Their very ubiquity, however, means that these benefits are frequently discounted. VA mycorrhizal associations are part of normal, everyday existence for most of the world's plants.

ERICOID MYCORRHIZA

Most plants in the order *Ericales*, including heathers (*Calluna, Erica*), rhododendrons, and bilberries (*Vaccinium*), form distinct 'ericoid' mycorrhizas. The rather simple 'hair' roots typical of ericoid species are initially surrounded by a loose tangle of fungal hyphae which gradually penetrate the root cells, thus forming an endomycorrhizal association. The main fungal partner is an apparently ubiquitous discomycete, *Hymenoscyphus ericae*, with stalked, yellowish-orange cup-shaped fruitbodies about one mm across, originally isolated from *Calluna vulgaris* in Yorkshire (Read, 1974). This is now known to have an asexual state, *Scytalidium vaccinii*, first isolated from roots of *Vaccinium angustifolium* in Canada (Dalpe *et al.*, 1989). Recent molecular work has shown *H. ericae* to represent a complex of closely related species including *H. monotropae*, found on roots of *Monotropa uniflora* in North America. The biology and structure of these fungi are unlike those of typical *Hymenoscyphus* species and, as shown by recent Norwegian studies (Vrålstad, 2001), they probably require a new genus to accommodate them. Other ascomycetes, principally *Oidiodendron* species, more rarely form such associations. Evidence suggests that these fungi are particularly good at extracting nutrients from the impoverished, acidic, often toxic, organic soils typical of the heathland habitats in which most ericoid plants are found.

Indeed, they are so specialised that they can enable ericoid plants to out-compete any invasive ectomycorrhizal species whose fungal associates cannot break down and release organic nitrogen bound up in toxic (phenolic) ericoid residues in roots, twigs, and leaves. In this way, ericoid plants can dominate their communities by excluding competitors. Forestry spruce, for example, cannot be successfully established in heathland unless the *Ericales* are removed or a source of mineral nitrogen is supplied. Inadvertantly increasing nitrogen, through farming residues and other pollutants, is endangering many lowland heaths (an increasingly scarce habitat in Britain) by providing an opportunity for grasses and non-ericoid plants to invade.

ORCHID MYCORRHIZA

Orchid seeds are extremely small, contain very limited reserves of starch, and are incapable of growth beyond germination without an external supply of carbohydrates and additional nutrients. Though these nutrients can be artificially provided in the laboratory, they are entirely supplied by fungal associates in nature.

The association starts soon after germination. The young orchid protocorms develop epidermal hair cells which are extensively penetrated by fungal hyphae (Fig. 35). Individual orchid cells surround the invading hyphal tips with cytoplasm and remain active. Hyphal branching creates coils ('pelotons') within the cells (Fig. 36), so the association is endomycorrhizal. In most, though possibly not all, orchids the association continues throughout the life of the plant.

This is no partnership, however. The flow of resources is from fungus to plant, with little evidence that the fungus derives any benefit at all. In effect, orchids are parasitic on their fungal hosts.

In terrestrial orchids, including native British species, these hosts are free-living basidiomycetes and ascomycetes which form 'rhizoctonias' (anamorphic states characterised by their intermittently swollen, 'moniliform' hyphae and the occasional production of sclerotia). They include several plant pathogens, such as *Thanatephorus cucumeris* (and its

FIG 35. Developing orchid seedling showing a weft of fungal hyphae. These 'rhizoctonia' fungi form intimate associations with the orchid and are essential for seed germination and seedling development (G. Prendergast & A. McRobb, RBG Kew).

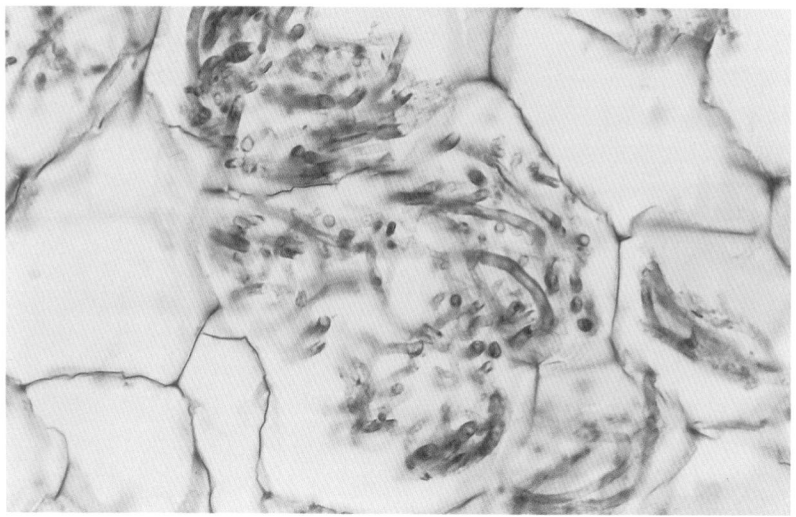

FIG 36. Fungal 'pelotons', coils of branching hyphae developed within orchid root cells; these are typical of orchid endomycorrhizas and are essential to the development of the plant (M. Ramsay, RBG Kew).

anamorph, *Rhizoctonia solani*). It appears that these soil-dwelling parasitic fungi attack terrestrial orchids in the same way as they attack other plants, but that orchids have evolved chemical and structural defence and control mechanisms which turn such attacks to their advantage. Non-parasitic rhizoctonia-forming soil and litter fungi (such as saprotrophic *Tulasnella* and *Ceratobasidium* species) may be chemically lured into orchid associations.

Some tropical epiphytic orchids are known to form associations with wood-rotting toadstools, including the honey fungus (*Armillaria mellea*), a particularly aggressive plant parasite. In this case, the orchid is doubly parasitic, using the mycelium of the honey fungus as a channel to derive nutrients from trees and other plants which the fungus has attacked.

The non-photosynthesising birdsnest orchid *Neottia nidus-avis*, not uncommon in British woodlands, appears to parasitise the ectomycorrhizal associations of nearby trees, specialising in those involving heterobasidiomycetous *Sebacina* species. This is quite surprising, since *Sebacina* species themselves have only recently been shown to be ectomycorrhizal. Their fruitbodies either form waxy gelatinous patches on damp soil and fallen wood, as in *Sebacina epigaea* and *S. dimitica*, or encrust the basal parts of plants, particularly woody seedlings, as in *Sebacina incrustans*.

The much less common British coralroot orchid *Corallorhiza trifida* is a similar parasite, said to invade ectomycorrhizas of *Thelephora* and *Tomentella* species, whilst in the United States *Corallorhiza* species parasitise ectomycorrhizas involving members of the *Russulaceae*. The rare British ghost orchid *Epipogium aphyllum* is presumably a further parasite, though its hosts are as yet unknown.

FERN MYCORRHIZOMES

Mycorrhizal associations ('mycorrhizomes') are widespread amongst ferns and fern allies and are found in virtually all pteridophyte groups, if not in all species. Only in some of the aquatic ferns (*Marsiliaceae, Salviniaceae*) are they apparently lacking. These fungus-fern associations were reviewed in detail for lycopods and *Psilotales* by Burgeff (1938), and for the whole of the pteridophytes by Boullard (1957, 1979), who found mycorrhizomes in no less than 420 species.

As might be expected, these associations are ancient, having been found in fossilised rhizomes of *Rhynia* and *Asteroxylon* as early as the Devonian period, 400 million years ago. These fossils are of VA mycorrhizas, and provide the earliest known examples of such associations. Almost all of the more ancient fern groups are now known to develop mycorrhizas of this kind. Indeed, they are virtually the only type to be found in pteridophytes, although some ectomycorrhizal associations have been reported in New Zealand species. It has been suggested that mycorrhizas may be less frequent in more advanced (leptosporangiate) ferns, perhaps indicating an evolutionary progression towards a non-mycorrhizal habit. However, this has not been supported by other studies.

Fungal associates are essential to the growth and development of mycorrhizal ferns as they are to all plants. In some species, fungi may even be essential for the germination of spores. This has been demonstrated for the leptosporangiate ferns as well as for eusporangiate ferns in the *Ophioglossaceae*. Species of *Ophioglossum* (adder's tongue), for example, have VA mycorrhizal associations with members of the genus *Glomus*. It has been shown that the spores of *Botrychium* cannot develop beyond the 3–4-cell stage in the absence of mycorrhizal fungi which supply appropriate organic materials. The gametophyte is unable to develop on sterile soil, and all older gametophytes have been shown to have mycorrhizas. The same is true for many of the fern allies.

MYCOTHALLIC ASSOCIATIONS AND AN UNDERGROUND LIVERWORT

Endomycorrhizal (or 'endomycothallic') associations occur commonly in liverworts and appear to be restricted to the gametophytes. These associations, reviewed by Boullard (1988) and Read *et al.* (2000), are surprisingly varied, although rather little is known about the fungi involved. However, research has shown that some are similar to VA mycorrhizal fungi, whilst others involve ascomycetes, including *Hymenoscyphus ericae*, the same discomycete that forms ericoid mycorrhizas. Basidiomycetes are also involved in mycothallic associations, particularly with liverworts in the orders *Jungermanniales* and *Metzgeriales*, and some appear similar to the haustoria-forming monotropoid mycorrhizas.

An interesting example is furnished by the peculiar underground liverwort *Cryptothallus mirabilis* (ghostwort), which lacks chlorophyll. This occurs in Britain and was initially believed to be associated with endomycorrhizal basidiomycetes, possibly involving the same group of rhizoctonia-forming species parasitised by terrestrial orchids, being entirely dependent on them for the provision of organic carbon. Subsequent investigation showed that the association was actually with ectomycorrhizal basidiomycetes linked to nearby birch trees, so that the ghostwort was effectively epiparasitic on the tree-fungus mycorrhiza. The latest research (Bidartondo *et al.*, 2003) suggests on molecular evidence that the associated fungi are related to rhizoctonia-forming *Tulasnella* species. These are normally associated with orchids, so finding them also present in the mycorrhizal roots of trees (birches and pines) is an unexpected new development.

These mycothallic associations are widespread and undoubtedly very ancient, although direct evidence from the fossil record is so far lacking. They do not occur in some more advanced liverworts, but are consistently present in primitive groups. It seems likely that coevolution with fungi has played a major role in the evolution of the *Hepaticae*, modifying their biology and facilitating their colonisation of otherwise unfavourable habitats.

PRACTICAL APPLICATIONS

In recent years, considerable research has been undertaken into the practical application of mycorrhizal fungi to promote plant growth. This research tends to suggest that inoculating plants with mycorrhizal fungi can be worthwhile where natural mycorrhiza are lacking, e.g. in nurseries or in disturbed or reclaimed ground. The inoculum typically consists of spores of various VA and ectomycorrhizal fungi in granular, gel, liquid, or pelleted form.

In forestry, young ectomycorrhiza-forming trees are now routinely inoculated with appropriate fungal associates when planting out in non-forest situations. These include former agricultural land, 'waste' land, and reclamation sites (Chapter 17). Ericoid mycorrhizas have also been used to inoculate commercial blueberries for planting on pasture soils and other non-ericoid sites.

CHAPTER 5

Partners and Providers

A ROUND two thirds of all fungi are believed to be involved in some form of association with other organisms. These may be mutualistic relationships, in which both partners benefit equally, or more one-sided forms of symbiosis in which one partner tends to benefit at the expense of the other. Lichens (involving fungi and algae) and mycorrhizas (involving fungi and plants) are two of the better-known examples of mutualistic partnerships. Using a partner for spore dispersal or for protection from predators (both typically involving fungi and insects) are examples of the latter. Parasitism and predation (Chapter Six) are particularly aggressive forms of symbiosis, though even these may not be entirely one-sided.

Many fungal associations have only recently been discovered and are far from being fully explored. Endophytic fungi (living inside plants) and phylloplane fungi (living on leaf surfaces), for example, are both now believed to be of fundamental importance to plant health, but the complex mutualistic relationships involved are still not wholly understood. Anaerobic gut fungi were unknown until 1975, but may be essential to the ruminant way of life. Many more associations are certainly waiting to be discovered; others may continue to elude us. We know, for example, that soil fungi are highly interactive with plant roots, bacteria, insects, nematodes, and a host of other organisms, not only in one-to-one partnerships, but in multiple and shifting symbioses the extent of which may never be fully appreciated.

Much of what we do know about the biology of mutualistic fungal associations was reviewed by Carroll (1992). This chapter provides a selective introduction to a wonderfully complex subject.

FUNGI AND ALGAE: THE LICHENISED LIFESTYLE

The development of lichenisation, the intimate and usually highly specific symbiosis of a fungus with an alga or cyanobacterium, is one of the best known partnerships between two different organisms. It is also by far the most successful and widespread of the fungal-algal symbioses, producing a stable, self-supporting association adapted to an extraordinarily wide range of environments, including many which could not be tolerated by either one of the partners living alone.

So successful is the association that at least 15,000 lichen species exist worldwide, amounting to almost 20% of all known fungi. Lichenisation is a way of life, and is found throughout a wide range of different fungal groups, so that the organisms commonly referred to as 'lichens' do not represent a single taxonomic assemblage, but are extremely diverse. Lichenisation, in other words, has evolved several times over.

The majority of lichens involve a single fungus (the dominant 'myco-biont', after which the partnership is named) and a single photosynthetic partner (an algal or cyanobacterial 'photobiont'). Almost all of the 15,000 mycobionts (98% or so) are ascomycetes, many producing cup-like fruiting bodies resembling those of their non-lichenised relatives. The photobionts are far less diverse. Only some 100 species have so far been described, most of which are capable of associating with a range of different fungal partners. Around 85% of lichenised fungi associate with algae, 10% with cyanobacteria (the 'blue-green algae'), and the remaining 5% with both simultaneously. The commonest algal associates belong to the genus *Trebouxia*, species of which are partners in at least 50% of all lichen associations. They can exist independently, but are rare and probably uncompetitive in a free-living state. The commonest cyanobacterial associates belong to the genus *Nostoc*, some species of which can be found free-living as gelatinous, seaweed-like blobs on the ground. Most of the fungal partners cannot exist independently.

Lichen-forming fungi are basically parasitic on their much smaller partners, which typically contribute no more than 5% or so to the combined biomass. The fungi obtain the nutrient products of their partners' photosynthesis through various interfaces, such as haustoria (specialised hyphal pegs which attach to the host). However, the photobionts not only survive this drain on their resources, but grow and prosper thanks to the protection against competitors and the outside environment afforded by their fungal associates. It is this mutualism that enables lichens to colonise some of the most inhospitable places on earth, not only distant polar wastes and sun-baked deserts, but suburban stone walls and asbestos roof tiles.

Lichens range from very loose and perhaps casual symbioses which lack a specialised 'thallus' (the visible body of a lichen), to much more organised unions which generate thalli of highly specific and distinctive shapes. These thalli are essentially the mycelium of the fungus, modified to contain algal cells and exposed to the light to promote photosynthesis. This contrasts, of course, with non-lichenised fungi in which the mycelium is normally hidden. As a result, a lichen is the whole fungus not just the fruitbody.

Typical ascomycetous lichens, of which almost 1800 species occur in Britain, comprise a wide range of thallus types. Many are crust-like (Fig. 37), such as the pollution-tolerant *Lecanora conizaeoides*, once common on tree trunks, whereas others are foliose (Fig. 38), with lobed, leaf-like thalli, for example the yellow *Xanthoria parietina*, another common and pollution-tolerant species on nutrient-rich substrata including trees, walls and roofs. Yet others have branching, often bushy 'fruticose' thalli (Fig. 39), such as the species of *Usnea* sometimes referred to as 'beard moss'.

In some lichens the fungal partner is able to form an association with different species of the same algal genus, although the resulting thalli may not look very distinct. An example is *Xanthoria parietina*, noted above, which may form a partnership with either *Trebouxia albulescens* or with *T. decolorans*. More remarkable are the fungi which can form associations with either an algal or a cyanobacterial partner, producing totally different thalli or 'morphotypes'. Indeed, so different are these thalli that they have sometimes been mistakenly described as separate lichen genera. The shrubby, cyanobacterial thallus of the New Zealand species *Sticta filix*, for example, was

FIG 37 & 38. The grey-green *Lecanora muralis* is an example of a crustose lichen, common on stone and wooden surfaces (here on a park bench). It is accompanied by the equally common, bright yellow *Xanthoria parietina*, an example of a foliose lichen (P. Roberts).

formerly placed in the genus *Dendriscocaulon*. Many such examples are now known, especially amongst the *Peltigerales*. Environmental factors, especially light and humidity, strongly influence the choice of photobiont and the different growth forms may be developed separately or in different parts of the same thallus, when they can look like two distinct lichens, one growing on the other. A good example is *Sticta canariensis*, frequent in the Canary Islands and the Azores, which forms large, leaf-like lobes in partnership with green algae but entirely different, greyish, shrub-like thalli with cyanobacteria.

In some cases, a lichen may have an obligate association with a particular alga (usually a marine seaweed – see Chapter 12) or moss. Indeed Poelt (1985) listed no less than 19 examples of lichen genera that occur exclusively on mosses and other bryophytes. One interesting case was described from the Austrian alps in which an anamorphic ascomycete, *Velutipila poeltii*, forms a specific, symbiotic association with an alga and with the moss *Ditrichum pusillum*. The fungus produces an irregular crust involving algal cells and fragments of the moss in a gelatinised matrix, appearing as greenish-black patches in the moss cushions. The exact nature of such a complex, partially parasitic association remains obscure.

Lichenicolous fungi (fungi which grow on lichens) provide a further level of complexity. Many appear to be simple parasites and are discussed in the next chapter. But some form mutualistic and commensalistic associations,

FIG 39. *Usnea ceratina*, an example of a fruticose lichen. *Usnea* species are sometimes called 'beard mosses', though they bear no relationship to the true mosses (P. Roberts).

sharing in the products of the lichen photobiont. Even more complex relationships are formed by lichenicolous lichens, effectively involving four partners.

Though almost all lichenised fungi are ascomycetes, a very few basidiomycetes also form mutualistic relationships with algae. These include agarics in the genus *Lichenomphalia* (previously referred to *Omphalina*) which are associated with algae in the genus *Coccomyxa*. The fruitbodies are ordinary toadstools, but the hyphae form associations with algal clusters, the resulting structures (sometimes seen like tiny green bobbles or scales around the toadstool base) being referred to the anamorphic genera *Botrydina* and *Coriscium*. Several such species occur in Britain, the commonest being the dull yellowish *Lichenomphalia ericetorum*, frequent in damp, peaty areas. In addition, a few simple, clavarioid basidiomycetes placed in the genus *Multiclavula* are associated with algal mats. *Multiclavula fossicola* is particularly common in parts of the tropics, producing troops of small, whitish fruitbodies on algae-covered rocks and mud. The similar *M. mucida* occasionally occurs in Europe on green, slimy wood. Though neither *Lichenomphalia* nor *Multiclavula* form typical lichen thalli, a few corticioid species (in the genus *Dictyonema*) produce true thalli looking like green brackets, occasionally found in Britain.

More on lichen and lichen-like relationships can be found in Hawksworth (1988) and Honegger (1992), but there is a vast literature on lichens in general. A separate New Naturalist volume (Gilbert, 2000) provides a useful and readable introduction to this extraordinarily diverse group of fungi.

FUNGI AND PLANTS: THE HIDDEN COMMUNITIES OF LEAVES AND STEMS

Perhaps the most important of the plant-fungal mutualisms is provided by mycorrhizas (Chapter Four), an association which is so intimate that in some form or another it is found in the great majority of all the world's plants. But there are other associations, the extent and significance of which are only now becoming clear. The most interesting of these concern fungi which live as endophytes, inside living plants, and the phylloplane fungi which live on leaf surfaces.

Endophytic fungi – secret plant symbionts

The term 'endophyte' is generally applied to fungi which colonise the tissues of healthy living plants and are symptomless, showing no external sign of their presence. Almost all plants investigated to date have yielded such endophytic fungi, often present in complex and diverse communities. In Britain, for example, no less than 58 different fungi were isolated from just five species of *Ericaceae* by Petrini (1984), and more than 60 fungi from bracken at just two localities (Petrini *et al.*, 1992). Endophytes in tropical areas may be even more diverse, as indicated from a study by Arnold *et al.* (2000) in which the extraordinary total of 418 species was isolated just from the leaves of two forest tree species in Panama.

Although some endophytic fungi are highly specific, as with *Epichloë* in grasses (see below), others seem to be much more plurivorous and include species which might be quite unexpected in such a habitat, such as discomycetes and even agarics. The *Xylariaceae*, for example, are normally encountered as large fruitbodies on rotting wood, but some are also known as endophytes. These include *Nemania serpens*, a common British species, now known as an endophyte in a wide range of plants, from temperate trees to tropical palms.

Endophytic fungi can be isolated from all tissue types, including roots and rhizomes, leaves and stems, seeds, bark, xylem, and even galls. Different assemblages of fungi are usually present in the different tissues, often influenced by season, and some species may dominate with others only occasionally present. In the bracken study noted above, only 22 out of the 60 species found were commonly present and only six of those were considered to be seasonally dominant.

Plant-endophyte associations typically benefit both partners in terms of nutrient and chemical cycling, the fungus in terms of enhanced survival, and the plant in terms of protection against disease organisms. In some cases the plant may also gain protection against plant-feeding invertebrates (and possibly even larger animals) thanks to the production of toxic compounds.

Many of the most extensively studied and highly evolved endophytes belong to the genus *Epichloë* (Fig. 40). These systemic, grass-infecting ascomycetes, with at least six species in Britain, cause 'choke' disease, in which flowering is prevented and no seeds are produced. The disease is spread by vegetative growth of the host plants, by seeds from infected plants in which the fungus does not fruit, and by spores developed on fertile stromata (a process which involves a specific fly, itself representing an interesting mutualism further discussed below). Though long thought of as simple parasites, it now seems that infection by *Epichloë* confers a range of benefits on the host grasses.

These benefits have been extensively studied in *E. festucae*, endophytic in various species of *Festuca*. As a result it is now clear that, though the fungus may 'choke' some tillers, the overall seed yield in endophyte-infected plants increases dramatically, up to 80% higher than in uninfected plants. Since the fungus can be disseminated with the seeds, this a major benefit to both parties.

Epichloë species also produce toxic alkaloids, such as ergovaline, similar

FIG 40. *Epichloë typhina*, one of several British species which occur as endophytes in grasses. They are the cause of choke disease that prevents flowering but also confers a range of benefits to the host plants (B. Spooner).

to those found in ergot (Chapter 15). These can have a serious effect on grazing animals such as cattle and sheep. Indeed, a debilitating condition known as 'ryegrass staggers' results from infection of *Lolium perenne*, one of the most important forage grasses, by the *Epichloë*-related endophyte *Neotyphodium lolii*. Similar alkaloids are produced by other *Epichloë* and *Neotyphodium* species, with the amount of toxin actually increasing in response to grazing pressure. This was demonstrated in an interesting study of Soay sheep in the Hebrides (Bazely *et al.*, 1997) in which alkaloid production in ungrazed grasses was shown to be considerably lower than that in grazed plants.

Additional alkaloids such as peramine and lolines are active against many invertebrate feeders, including locusts, beetles, caterpillars, bugs, and aphids. This has led to the investigation of endophytes as potential biocontrol agents, through the development of new host varieties with higher levels of endophyte infection (Clay, 1989). Unfortunately, there is evidence that in some plants pests may actually benefit from the presence of endophytes. The common sycamore endophyte *Rhytisma acerinum*, for example, apparently increases the tree's susceptibility to aphids, since it improves the nutritional quality of its leaves. Nonetheless, a number of endophytic ascomycetes in conifer needles, such as *Hormonema*, *Phyllosticta* and *Rhabdocline* species, produce enough toxins to be of practical use in controlling populations of the spruce budworm moth, a major pest of commercial forestry in the USA (Clark *et al.*, 1989).

More on fungal endophytes can be found in Bacon & White (2000) and Redlin & Carris (1996).

Phylloplane fungi – leaf-surface colonisers

The surfaces of living leaves, known as the 'phylloplane', offer extensive and valuable substrata for colonisation by microorganisms, including bacteria, algae, and fungi. Usually this goes unseen, but in certain places, such as tropical rain forests, the colonisation can be readily observed. The large, long-lived leaves of rainforest trees often become densely and visibly covered by a mosaic of epiphyllous lichens, sooty moulds (*Capnodiales*), mildews, and other fungi, as well as mosses and epiphytic plants. A few sooty moulds and dark hyphomycetes also occur on leaves in temperate regions, often feeding on the sugary honeydew secreted by aphids, and some pathogens such as powdery mildews, obligate parasites on their hosts, are equally conspicuous. However, even the surfaces of leaves which appear comparatively 'clean' will be covered in an abundance of yeasts and other microfungi, if examined with a microscope or plated out in culture.

Fungal spores are constantly impacting on leaf surfaces, some dispersed by air currents, some by rain drops and rain splash mechanisms. The number of spores and their species composition vary according to prevailing conditions of rainfall and temperature. They are also distinctly seasonal, greatest during late summer and autumn, and the resulting fungal communities change accordingly. Most spores are capable of germination on living leaf surfaces, but factors such as climate, competition, and antagonism influence their success and future development. Many remain dormant, only germinating and invading tissues when their host leaves die. Comparatively few species actually colonise the living phylloplane, but when they do they interact directly with their hosts, and may be important in protecting the plant from potential pathogens. This relationship is thus mutualistic, of benefit to both partners.

The plant's contribution to the partnership includes exudates and leachates from the leaf surface containing organic substances such as sugars, amino acids and vitamins as well as a variety of inorganic compounds. These stimulate the germination and growth of some fungi whilst inhibiting others. Exudates can vary between the upper and lower leaf surfaces, hence influencing the precise sites in which particular fungi may be found. Leaf surface characters and differences in humidity and temperature also have an influence.

In return, the resident phylloplane fungi and other microorganisms help keep pathogenic species at bay through a variety of means, including several different forms of antagonism and parasitism. A similar 'natural defence system' is found in the microbiota of our own skin, a population of normally harmless bacteria usually acquired in infancy whose antagonism towards newcomers helps protect us against invasive diseases.

A wide range of fungi, both resident and transient species, can contribute to the phylloplane community. In a study of leaf-surface fungi on three endemic trees in Hawaii, Baker *et al.* (1979) recorded more than 160 different species. The fungal communities varied according to host plant, site location and other factors, but mainly involved widely distributed and generalist fungi with just a few host-specific species. Other studies have been summarised by Dickinson (1976) who listed almost 80 fungal genera recorded in the phylloplane of 35 different plants. Amongst these the yeasts, especially basidiomycetous yeasts such as *Rhodotorula* and *Sporobolomyces*, are especially abundant. Together with bacteria they may be the major components of phylloplane communities, and are early colonisers of new leaves. Hyphomycetes are also commonly present, especially *Aureobasidium pullulans*, which is an abundant early coloniser of many angiosperm leaves, and species of ubiquitous genera such as *Alternaria, Aspergillus, Cladosporium, Epicoccum, Fusarium* and *Penicillium*. Many of these are rapid invaders of damaged tissue, and are commonly found as secondary colonisers of leaf spots caused by pathogenic fungi or bacteria. As with most phylloplane fungi, they are not usually host specific, their spores, abundantly present in the atmosphere, being deposited randomly on the leaves of many different plants.

It is now known that the balance between phylloplane populations depends not only on available conditions and nutrients, but also on parasitic and antagonistic interactions. Mycoparasitism may be unspecialised, as in some species of *Trichoderma*, or obligate as in *Ampelomyces quisqualis* and *Verticillium lecanii*, both common ascomycetes which attack powdery mildews. *Verticillium lecanii* also attacks rusts, and both have been used as biocontrol agents (Chapter 17). Many bacteria and yeasts as well as some filamentous fungi, notably *Aureobasidium pullulans*, produce antibiotics which are antifungal. These specifically inhibit the development of pathogens, and hence help protect the host plant from infection.

Other antagonistic interactions include competition for nutrients. It has been shown, for example, that infections of rye by the pathogens *Cochliobolus sativus* and *Septoria nodorum* are greatly reduced by spraying the crop with a nutrient solution to boost natural populations of the yeasts *Cryptococcus laurentii* and *Sporobolomyces roseus*. When the latter species is present, a similar reduction in infection of corn by *Colletotrichum graminum* has been demonstrated, seemingly because nutrient competition inhibits the pathogen's ability to produce the enzymes necessary for penetrating the leaf cuticle. Antifungal substances, including terpenoids and phenolic compounds, are also produced naturally by the leaves of many plants. These may be formed in glandular hairs, be present in leachates or be a component of cuticular waxes, and may themselves act to regulate or influence the phylloplane mycota. It is known, for example, that leaves of Norway maple (*Acer platanoides*) produce antifungal inhibitors which, compared to other plants, substantially reduce the number of fungal colonies they support. In some cases the production of antifungal substances (phytoalexins) is specifically stimulated by the presence of pathogenic fungi on the leaf surface.

Not surprisingly, pollution, particularly from lead and sulphur dioxide, has severe adverse effects on the phylloplane community, upsetting the balance of species and, as a result, increasing the susceptibility of plants to disease. The application of pesticides and fungicides to crop plants may have equally adverse effects, damaging or even eradicating populations of non-target species. Perversely, this may destroy the plant's ability to resist infection, leaving it defenceless against the very diseases the sprays were supposed to prevent.

Further details of the ecology and biology of phylloplane fungi, as well as the techniques employed in their study, can be found in Blakeman (1981), Dickinson & Preece (1976), Fokkema & Van den Heuvel (1986), and Preece & Dickinson (1971). The potential for biocontrol was explored in Dubos & Bulit (1981 – see also Chapter 17).

FUNGI AND BACTERIA: MICRO-MUTUALISMS & ANTAGONISMS

The lichenisation of fungi with relatively large, alga-like cyanobacteria (see above) is perhaps the best known of the associations between bacteria and fungi. However, although comparatively little understood, there are various other ways in which these organisms interact. A few of these appear to be mutualistic, but bacteriophagy (Chapter Six) and antagonism (due to competition for nutrients, parasitism and the production of antibiotics) may be much more common.

Communities of phylloplane and coprophilous fungi are known to be influenced by bacterial action, although the extent and significance of the interactions have not been fully explored. Antagonistic fruiting, well known between coprophilous fungi, may for example be mediated by the presence of certain bacteria, and this has been clearly demonstrated for some species of the ascomycetes *Ascobolus*, *Chaetomium*, and *Sordaria*. The last two may together severely suppress the fruiting of *Ascobolus* though, in the presence of certain bacteria, this situation is reversed: *Ascobolus* is then able to produce fruitbodies whilst the other fungi are inhibited.

Fungal-bacterial mutualisms may also be important in wood-rotting species. Blanchette & Shaw (1978) found that species of *Enterobacter* in combination with some yeasts and wood-rotting bracket fungi in the genera *Trametes*, *Trichaptum* and *Postia* substantially increased mycelial growth and enhanced decay rates by up to ten-fold according to species. This was observed experimentally as well as in nature and appears to be a mutualistic association since the bacteria and yeasts occur only in those cells which are occupied and modified by the basidiomycetes.

Another highly significant association between fungi and bacteria, probably mutualistic, involves mycorrhiza development. Certain bacteria (for example, *Pseudomonas* species) have been shown to consistently promote the establishment of mycorrhizal fungi on plant roots. These have been termed 'mycorrhization helper bacteria' by Garbaye (1994), who studied the process especially in the common toadstool *Laccaria laccata*. These bacteria may live in association with the fungus, and some at least appear to be species-specific to the fungus rather than the plant. For example, bacteria associated with *Laccaria laccata* were shown to stimulate mycorrhizal formation of this species as well as *L. bicolor* with a range of host trees. These bacteria had no effect with *L. proxima* and were inhibitory to mycorrhizal development in other fungi. Further examples of fungus-bacterial interactions can be found in Barron (1992) and Bennett & Feibelman (2001).

FUNGI AND ANIMALS – FROM APHIDS TO ELEPHANTS

Insects and other arthropods

At least 1000 species of invertebrates have been recorded in association with fungi in Britain (Paviour-Smith, 1960), with beetles (*Coleoptera*) and flies (*Diptera*) providing the majority of examples. Only some of the most interesting and important associations can be considered here, but the subject has been more fully explored by Wilding *et al.* (1989), Wheeler & Blackwell (1984), Howard & Miller (1996), and Pirozynski & Hawksworth (1988).

Ambrosia beetles

Several hundred species of small, wood-boring beetles in the families *Scolytidae* and *Platypodidae* (Beaver, 1989) have a remarkable mutualistic relationship with a variety of fungi. Although known for well over a century, the extent and ecological importance of this relationship has become clear only in recent years, and many aspects of the chemistry, physiology and evolutionary development of the relationship remain to be studied.

Some of these beetles, especially bark beetles of the genera *Dendroctonus* and *Ips*, attack living trees, but most feed in dead wood, either by tunnelling under the bark, where they make characteristic galleries, or by boring into the heartwood. Adults act as dispersal agents for the fungi involved, typically carrying spores or propagules in specialised fluid-filled organs called 'mycangia'. When boring into wood, the beetles release spores which then germinate in their tunnels. The fungi degrade the cellulose and lignin, otherwise indigestible to the beetles which lack the appropriate enzymes, converting it into 'ambrosial' fungal tissue which lines the beetle tunnels. This is grazed by the beetles and their larvae, which do not feed until it has been developed. The ambrosia fungi provide a rich source of protein and other nutrients, including ergosterol and perhaps other steroids which are essential for pupation and adult fertility, as well as vitamins. In turn, the beetles, physically or by various excretions, are able to promote growth of the ambrosia fungi, including sporulation, and inhibit growth of its competitors. When the beetles leave, their old galleries are quickly invaded by more combative wood-rotting fungi.

This mutualistic association, though highly specialised, has evolved repeatedly and independently in different beetle groups. The mycangia of different ambrosia beetles are not homologous and, depending on the genus of beetle concerned, occur on quite different parts of the body, from the mandibles to the elytra. The associated fungi are equally polyphyletic, and in most cases are not species-specific to the beetles. The fungi involved are mainly asexual stages of ascomycetes, including species of *Ambrosiella*, *Cephalosporium*, *Fusarium*, and *Monilia*. They also include many of the 'blue-stain' or 'ophiostomatoid' fungi, species of *Ceratocystis* and *Ophiostoma*, which are commonly spread by bark-beetles. Additionally, some ascomycetous yeasts, such as *Hansenula* and *Pichia* species, are known as ambrosia fungi and, in a few cases, basidiomycetous fungi have also been implicated.

Dutch elm disease

The life cycle of fungi associated with bark beetles is exempified by *Ophiostoma novo-ulmi*, the cause of the most recent Dutch elm disease epidemic. The devastating effects on the British countryside of this disease are all too well known. Infected elms, showing yellowing of foliage and die-back of branches (Fig. 41), became a common sight in the latter part of the 20th century. Although recovery is sometimes possible if reinfection is avoided during the following season, death is inevitable in severe infections. The loss of mature elm trees during the 1970s (Chapter Six) dramatically altered the appearance of large tracts of countryside, and took an inevitable toll of elm-associated wildlife. A similar disease, caused by the related species *O. ulmi*, was present in Britain much earlier last century, having been first recognised in south-east England in 1927. This also caused widespread destruction at the time but declined in severity after 1937.

Both these diseases result from cooperation between the fungus and an insect vector, mainly the common bark beetles *Scolytus scolytus* and *S. multistriatus*, which spread the spores. In infected trees, the presence of the fungus stimulates the water-conducting vessels to produce 'tyloses', bladder-like extensions which block the vessels and effectively prevent water conduction. These tyloses cause the dark marks characteristic of

FIG 41. The effects of Dutch elm disease, caused by the ascomycete *Ophiostoma novo-ulmi* the spores of which are carried by bark beetles. Leaves gradually yellow and die, followed almost inevitably by death of the tree (T. Cope).

infected timber. The fungus fruits in the galleries made by the bark beetles, which pupate in them. Emerging beetles are readily covered in spores, and the fungus is spread when the young beetles feed on healthy branches.

Gall midges

A similar association can be demonstrated in many plant galls induced by gall midges (*Cecidomyiidae*). The term 'ambrosia fungi' was, in fact, originally coined for such an association and galls induced by these midges are now usually referred to as 'ambrosia galls'. Essentially, species of *Asphondylia*, many species of *Lasioptera* and some other genera of tribe *Lasiopterini*, as well as most *Alycaulini*, induce galls in which fungi are always present. The midge larvae feed solely upon the mycelium which develops to form a thick layer sheathing the inside of the gall cavity. This replaces the nutritive tissue which is developed from the plant cells in response to larval activity in those galls which lack fungi. However, in some cases the fungus is apparently not utilised as food, and in others it may play a role in protecting the larva from attack by parasitoids. This latter situation is exemplified by *Asteromyia carbonifera*, an American species which galls species of golden rod. Here, the developing larva is enveloped by the mycelium which forms a black protective 'rind' around it when mature.

In true ambrosia galls, the fungus is introduced into the gall on oviposition, spores being carried by the adult female midges which therefore aid the dispersal of the fungus. These midges, at least in tribes *Asphondyliidi* and *Lasiopterini*, are now known to have special spore-carrying structures similar to the mycangia of ambrosia beetles, although these are not homologous and indicate independent evolution of the habit. The mycangia take the form of special pockets on the abdomen and may contain 40–150 fungal conidia according to species. However, the methods by which the female gall midge locates and collects the conidia are not yet known. After hatching, the larva appears to modify the behaviour of the fungus which usually does not develop further until after the gall is well established. At this stage it rapidly grows to line the gall chamber, serving as food for the developing insect. Further fungal development may not occur until after pupation and the fungi do not fruit on the host plant until some later stage. The species involved have not been easy to isolate in culture, making identification difficult. However, based largely on studies by Bisset & Borkent (1988), they are now known to be ascomycetes, mostly in the genera *Macrophoma* and *Dothiorella*. These are asexual stages of *Botryosphaeria*, a genus which is widely distributed on many host plants and includes both parasitic and saprotrophic species. The fungi may form pycnidia (asexual fruitbodies) on the surface of the gall after the emergence of the adult gall midge, but do not sporulate before then.

Woodwasps

Another highly evolved and obligate mutualistic relationship involves certain woodwasps (*Siriciidae*) and wood-rotting basidiomycetes in the genus *Amylostereum*, patch-forming, white-rot fungi which are pathogens of pine, spruce, larch and some other conifers. Woodwasps are *Hymenoptera* whose larvae feed by tunnelling in moribund or sometimes living trees. In this relationship, species of *Sirex* and *Uroceras* are instrumental in spreading the spores of at least three of the five known species of *Amylostereum*. A similar relationship between the woodwasp *Tremex columba* and the bracket fungus *Cerrena unicolor* infecting beech (*Fagus grandifolia*) is known in Canada.

Amylostereum species are able to seriously damage and even kill their host trees and may cause significant losses in plantations. They are potentially of considerable economic importance, particularly in New Zealand and more recently South Africa, where the introduced *A. areolatum*, native to Europe, has led to major loss of *Pinus radiata*. In Europe, the wasps are only minor pests and the fungus does little harm. A balance exists between the fungus, its normal host trees and natural parasites, absent where it has been introduced, that prevents serious damage to trees.

In Britain, the commonest species with such a relationship is *Amylostereum chailletii*, spread by the woodwasp *Urocerus gigas*. Elsewhere this fungus is spread additionally by species of *Sirex*. *Amylostereum areolatum*, comparatively rare in Britain, is spread by *Sirex noctilio*, a relationship more intensively studied in New Zealand because of the damage caused in commercial plantations. More recently, a third species *A. laevigatum* has been shown to have a symbiotic relationship with the woodwasp *Uroceras japonicus* in Japan and it seems likely that the two other known species of *Amylostereum* will prove to have a similar ecology.

The relationship here is mutualistic since the woodwasp larvae are only able to ingest wood which has been rotted by the fungus. This is again a highly evolved relationship, the wasps, like the ambrosia beetles and gall midges, having special mycangial pouches for carrying conidial spores, released through the ovipositor during egg-laying. After germination the mycelium rapidly develops and invades the sapwood around the oviposition site, later producing conidia in the tunnels created by the larvae. Since the woodwasps only spread asexual spores, *Amylostereum* populations tend to be clonal, comprising genetically identical populations, present over large areas and stable over time. The wasp-fungus relationship is yet more specialised, since mucoid secretions by the insects, introduced during oviposition, appear to be important in the development of the fungal mycelium. Furthermore, female larvae develop special organs in folds of the abdominal wall which carry the fungus, transferring it to the young adults after hatching. If the fungus is not present the larvae cannot develop successfully, and the relationship is therefore an essential and obligate one for both partners.

There is an additional inter-relationship with parasitoids of the woodwasps. Some species of ichneumon (*Hymenoptera*), for example, including *Rhyssa persuasoria* in Britain, are able to detect substances produced by the fungus and hence locate tunnels in which eggs or larvae are present. Some nematodes also exploit the wasp-fungus association, being not only parasitic in the larvae but also feeding, in a morphologically different form, on the fungus mycelium.

Termites

In the Old World tropics, termites (*Isoptera*) of several genera in the tribe *Macrotermitinae* maintain what are known as 'fungus gardens', highly specialised structures essential to the survival of the colony. These fungus gardens, or combs, are established deep in subterranean chambers, either centrally or sometimes in scattered pockets. They are protected by the surface mounds (or 'termitaries') whose often complex architecture helps regulate temperature and humidity, both of which are kept within narrow limits favouring the development of the fungus. The termites constantly tend the combs, which are sponge-like in appearance and made of faecal pellets added by workers. During the life of the colony, the fungus produces specialised conidial outgrowths called 'mycotêtes' which are fed to the queen and also eaten by workers. These mycotêtes are nitrogen-rich and appear to provide nutrients essential to egg-production in the queen.

The fungi cultivated by the termites are toadstools, distantly related to the common British genus, *Tricholoma*, but so specialised that they are placed within a separate genus, *Termitomyces*, sometimes even referred to its own family, *Termitomycetaceae*. Almost 40 species of *Termitomyces* are known to have a relationship with termites, their fruitbodies appearing on old abandoned termitaries after rain. They vary in size according to species, and can be small and appear in vast troops, as with *Termitomyces microcarpus*, scarcely more than 1 cm across, or variously larger up to the giant *Termitomyces titanicus*. The latter is a truly impressive species sometimes a metre wide across the cap and with a deeply rooting stem a metre or so in length. It is quite probably the largest toadstool on earth (Fig. 42). Strangely, despite its size and being widely eaten in Africa, it remained undescribed until 1980.

The termites involved in the partnership occur throughout tropical Africa and Asia, and are all members of the *Macrotermitinae*. They belong to the 'higher termites', the huge family *Termitidae*, with over 2000 species, almost three-quarters of all known termites. Many of the *Macrotermitinae* build massive mounds, sometimes as much as 9 m high, which are a striking and impressive feature of the landscape. Unlike most other termites, the *Termitidae* lack the symbiotic gut protozoa which produce cellulose- and

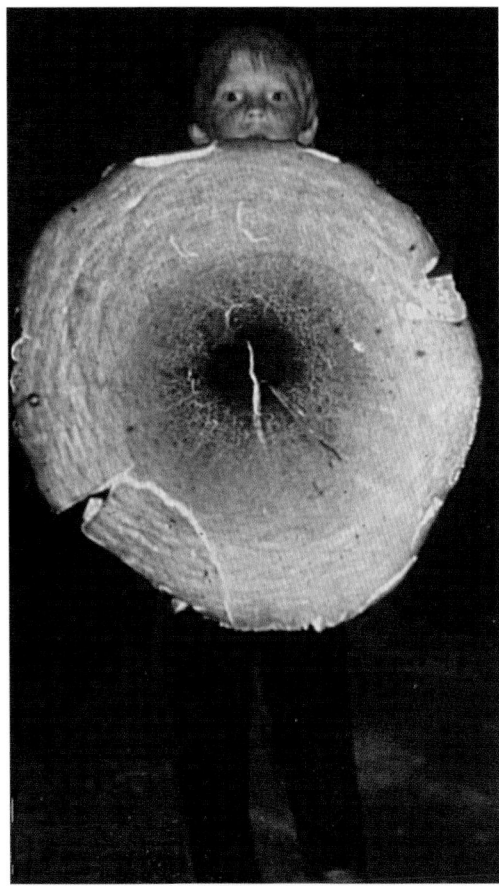

FIG 42. A fruitbody of the giant *Termitomyces titanicus*, found in association with termite mounds in Africa and probably the largest toadstool on earth (G. Piearce).

lignin-degrading enzymes and are essential in enabling the termites to digest plant tissue. Instead, they may utilise other symbiotic microorganisms or even produce their own enzymes but, in the *Macrotermitinae*, the enzymes obtained from the *Termitomyces* are of major importance for their digestion of plant matter. The comb is regularly reingested and recycled by the workers after development of the mycotêtes, supplying enzymes essential to digestion as well as fungal spores later passed out in faecal deposits. These may be the source of inoculum in new colonies, though these are also founded to coincide with the production of the *Termitomyces* fruitbodies. Workers ingest basidiospores which inoculate the new comb, hence ensuring sexual recombination and effective spread of the fungus.

Many other fungi are associated with termites, perhaps in excess of 100 species having been isolated from some part or another of termite mounds. Most are generalist saprotrophs, introduced by termite activity, but others are obligate associates. Some also appear to have symbiotic relationships, though in most cases the interrelationships between species are little understood. Some aspects of these fungal communities were considered and illustrated by Heim (1977). He described several species of macrofungi, including the toadstool *Lepiota termitophila*, the false truffle *Protubera termitum*, and the puffball *Bovista termitum*, as apparent specialists in this habitat, and discussed 15 others as common or occasional saprotrophs in the mounds.

Recently, *Termitomyces* fungi have also been reported from the New World, based on three species from Costa Rica. Unlike the Old World species, these fungi are associated with termites of the genus *Nasutitermes*. They belong to a quite different tribe, *Nasutitermitidae*, the species of which form nests above ground and in trees. The exact nature of their relationship remains as yet unknown.

Leaf-cutting ants

With this recently discovered exception, there are otherwise no fungus-gardening termites in the New World. Instead, there are some 190 species of ants in the tribe *Attini* that also cultivate fungi for food. The ants occur throughout the warm temperate and tropical Americas but are particularly important in Central and South America. The best known are the leaf-cutting ants, mainly species of *Acromyrmex* and *Atta*, many of which form large colonies of several million individuals. Different species are found in forests and in grasslands, but all cut living leaves from plants and carry them back to their nests where they are used as the substratum for extensive fungus gardens. The relationship is an obligate one, the ant larvae depending on the fungus as their sole source of food.

This ant-fungus association is ancient (at least 23 million years) and highly developed, to the extent that both partners have evolved special structures linked directly to it. The female ants have unique organs located near the oesophagus which are similar to mycangia and used for carrying fungal mycelium, the source of inoculum for new nests. The fungus partner produces special knob-like clusters of swollen hyphae termed 'gongylidia', which have no apparent function other than to feed ants. The ants harvest these regularly and feed them to the larvae which obtain essential growth proteins and nutrients from the fungus (adult workers obtain most of their food from plant juices). In return, the fungus is not only provided with a ready-made substratum, but is protected from competitors and transported from old to new nests. Together, the ant-fungus association enables both partners to exploit an almost unlimited range of food plants. Indeed, the association is so successful that leaf-cutting ants are the dominant herbivores in many ecosystems and hence may be hugely destructive of unprotected crops.

Successful nests develop substantially within a year or two, the fungus gardens being established within subterranean chambers which are sponge-like in appearance and composed of leaf material cut up by the workers. This leaf material is obtained from the vicinity of the nest by foraging workers, many species creating well marked trails radiating out from the nests in all directions. Leaves are initially cut into disc-like pieces about 1 cm in diameter, carried to the nest, and there further cut into much smaller fragments by other workers, before being eventually reduced to a pulp. Faecal deposits from the workers provide added nutrients for the fungus. These ants continually tend the gardens, maintaining conditions for optimum development of the fungus and apparently weeding out other invading fungi. They also secrete antibiotic substances, including myrmicacin and phenylacetic acid, which are inhibitory to the growth of opportunist saprotrophic fungi as well as bacteria. The main fungus associate appears rarely to fruit in nature and does not survive in abandoned nests, but has been successfully developed in culture from the gongylidia. It is now known to be *Leucoagaricus gonglyophorus*, a relative of the parasol mushroom (*Macrolepiota procera*) found in Britain. A few attine ant species cultivate a range of other fungi, but all are members of the *Lepiotaceae*. Further details of this remarkable ant-fungus association can be found in Weber (1979), Cherrett *et al.* (1989), and Fisher & Stradling (2002).

Other specialised associations between ants and fungi occur in Britain. Species of the ant genus *Acanthomyops*, for example, utilise fungi in their nests, though for structural purposes rather than solely for food. The nests of these ants, built in trees or in the ground, are constructed of material termed 'carton', consisting of digested food and soil, cemented by secretions from the ant, and intimately invaded by fungal hyphae. The nests are again sponge-like in appearance, the fungal hyphae binding the material and strengthening the structure. The ants also take fungi as food, though it does not make up their sole diet. The fungi involved, dark coloured hyphomycetes, appear to be specific to these nests, and are again cultivated by the ants to the exclusion of other species. In Britain, two fungal species, *Cladosporium myrmecophilum* and *Hormiscium pithyophilum* var. *myrmecophilum*, have been identified as ant associates and are apparently obligately present in the nests.

Epichloë, grasses and flies

The remarkable mutualistic relationships between endophytic fungi and vascular plants, noted above, include several grass endophytes in the order *Clavicipitales*. These are stromatic ascomycetes, of which the genus *Epichloë* is most interesting because of its intimate link with insects.

Like its relatives, it is a genus of heterothallic fungi, with two mating types. This means that individuals are self-incompatible and must be cross-fertilised to produce fruitbodies and continue the life cycle. This cross-fertilisation is now known to be achieved by a specific fly, *Botanophila* (= *Phorbia*) *phrenione*, which transfers fungal spermatia of one mating type to another during oviposition.

This highly evolved relationship has profound consequences for all three partners, the fungus, the insect, and the host plant. Bultman *et al.* (1995) found that the flies feed on the young *Epichloë* stromata, ingesting spermatia which pass intact through the gut before being deposited in faecal matter during egg laying. This initiates the development of the sexual stroma. In the absence of flies, some perithecia may develop anyway, and it seems that some wind-transfer may also occur. The *Epichloë* stroma is grazed by the developing fly larvae, with consume on average over 40% of the perithecial material, a significant loss to the fungus, but a cost it must pay for successful cross-fertilisation. However, the fly may also pay a price as the *Epichloë*, in common with other endophytic *Clavicipitaceae*, produces toxic alkaloids. These help to protect the grass host from herbivorous insects and may reduce the larval success rate. The grass host itself pays a price for protection as the fungus causes sterility and prevents flowering.

Aromatic plant pathogens
Many of the fungal plant pathogens which rely on insects for spore dispersal or cross-fertilisation have evolved distinctive methods for attracting their unwitting partners.

One of the most successful and surprising is the production of aromatic compounds, an evolutionary adaptation found most commonly in the rusts. As part of their complex life-cycle, many rusts produce pycnidia (see Chapter Three) which are cross-fertilised by insects attracted to their sweet-smelling exudates. This was first demonstrated in a study of the sunflower rust (*Puccinia helianthi*) but is now known to be a widespread phenomenon.

The thistle rust *Puccinia punctiformis* (previously known as *P. suaveolens,* the epithet 'suaveolens' meaning sweet-smelling) is a commonplace example in Britain. In late April and early May, heavily rusted thistles (*Cirsium arvense*) have a sweet, honey-like smell which even humans can appreciate from a few feet away. This comes from pycnidia which are dotted over the upper leaf surfaces, each producing masses of pycnidiospores (spermatia) which ooze out in a sugary droplet. Insects (flies, beetles, ants) feeding on these droplets intermix pycnidiospores from different plants, cross-fertilising the rust and thus instigating the formation of aecidia and aecidiospores on the undersurface of the leaves. The European mustard rust *Puccinia monoica* goes a stage further by galling its host (*Arabis* sp.) so that it produces bright yellow, sweet-smelling pseudo-flowers complete with a sugary fluid. Conversely, in some more primitive rusts such as *Chrysomyxa* and *Melampsorella* species, the pycnia, which are formed on conifer needles or cones, are not fragrantly scented but instead have a distinct, unpleasant odour of carrion. The function is the same however, since the noxious smell is equally successful at attracting flies.

Ergot (*Claviceps purpurea*), the toxic pathogen of rye and other cereals (see Chapters Six and 15), is an example of an ascomycete which has an aroma attractive to insects. Ergot produces overwintering sclerotia which, in late spring, release thread-like, wind-borne ascospores to infect the year's new cereal growth. Subsequently, the fungus produces conidiospores in the ovaries of its host which exude a sweet 'honey dew', comprising sugars and amino acids, which is attractive to various insects. The insect vectors help spread ergot from plant to plant, potentially turning an initial infection into an epidemic.

Trichomycetes: fungi that live in the gut

Fungi belonging to the *Trichomycetes* are a highly evolved group comprising well over 200 species in 55 genera, all adapted to living in the guts of freshwater, terrestrial, and marine arthropods, ranging from mosquito and fly larvae to beetles, millipedes, woodlice, and crabs. These are microscopic fungi, but sometimes grow in dense clusters which impart a hairy appearance to the gut lining to which the name 'trichomycetes' (hair fungi) refers. Although such fungi have been known since the middle of the 19th century, it is only recently that their true nature, diversity and ecology have become apparent (Moss, 1979; Lichtwardt, 1986). They are now known to be worldwide in distribution and to be obligately associated with their host, unable to develop outside of the host gut. As far as can be ascertained, the relationship between fungus and host is in most cases mutualistic, the fungi being commonest in healthy and successful host populations. A study by Horn & Lichtwardt (1981) involving the trichomycete *Smittium culisetae* and larvae of the yellow fever mosquito *Aedes aegypti* indicated that infected larvae faired better than uninfected larvae in conditions of nutritional stress, the fungus supplying some of the missing nutrients. However, one species, *Smittium morbosum*, appears to be pathogenic to mosquito larvae and may even have some potential as a biocontrol agent.

Trichomycetes form small, typically branched mycelial growths in various parts of the host gut, living off ingested food. They are attached to the gut wall by holdfasts and have evolved a lifecycle which takes account of periodic moults (the chitinous gut lining being shed along with the exoskeleton) to stimulate spore production. Spores are typically released from the gut and ingested by new hosts, in a cycle similar to the dunging-grazing cycle found in many coprophilic fungi. As a result, all the arthropod hosts of trichomycetes are detrivorous (feeding off decaying vegetation and detritus), not carnivorous.

Trichomycetes are true fungi, belonging to the phylum *Zygomycota*, and include three orders. These are distinguished largely on characters of the spores and thallus (Misra & Lichtwardt, 2000, have provided identifications and descriptions), though these tend to reflect their host ranges. Species in the *Harpellales* occur mostly in the freshwater larvae of midges, mosquitoes, and other flying insects, but not in the adults. However, in a study of British blackflies, Moss & Descals (1986) discovered that at least one species, *Harpella melusinae*, infects the ovaries of some adult flies so that females oviposit chlamydospores instead of eggs. These form asexual spores called 'trichospores' which are ingested by newly emerged larvae which graze the surface of the eggs, thus ensuring that each new larval generation is infected with the fungus. This may be more widespread than is currently known. Species in the *Asellariales* occur in freshwater and seashore isopods and in freshwater or marsh-living springtails. Species in the *Eccrinales* are more diverse, occurring in marine isopods, such as gribbles, in hermit crabs, freshwater crayfish, true crabs and lobsters, millipedes, woodlice, and beetles. Another order, *Amoebidiales*, also includes gut-inhabiting species found in freshwater arthropods and has traditionally been treated within the *Trichomycetes*. However, it now seems they are probably unrelated and better referred to the *Protozoa* rather than the *Fungi*. Species of the *Amoebidiales* produce amoeboid cysts and are atypical in sometimes being found externally, rather than internally, on a range of insects and crustaceans. *Amoebidium parasiticum* is a particularly common example, known worldwide (including the British Isles) on various freshwater hosts, especially in polluted pools and ditches.

Yeast endosymbionts

Microorganisms living as mutualistic associates within the cells of their hosts is a common and widespread phenomenon in insects. This association, known as 'endocytobiosis', frequently involves bacteria but, in some insects, notably *Homoptera* and *Coleoptera*, yeasts or yeast-like fungi are also important. The larvae of some wood-boring beetles, for example, particularly the longhorns (*Cerambycidae*) and woodworms (*Anobiidae*), have yeasts constantly present in their guts. These occur in special structures termed 'mycetomes', pockets of special cells (mycetocytes) which are filled with yeast. Mycetomes also occur in the reproductive tracts, enabling yeast cells to be attached to the eggs during oviposition, and subsequently ingested by the newly-hatched larva. The yeasts involved include species of *Candida* or related genera (*Saccharomycetales*) as well as, in anobiid beetles, species of *Symbiotaphrina*. The yeasts play an important, possibly essential, role in the nutrition of the host, facilitating the utilisation of woody substrates by supplying nutrients such as vitamins, sterols and amino acids, in which wood is severely deficient. Furthermore, *Symbiotaphrina* species produce hydrolytic enzymes and are uniquely capable of metabolising toxic compounds produced by plants, thus allowing the larvae to feed unharmed. The yeasts, in return, thrive in a protected, nutrient-rich environment.

Not only beetles, but some coccids (*Hemiptera*) also have such an association. In these, yeasts are found in the ovaries and are able to infect the eggs. Amazingly, this determines the sex of the individual coccid, infected eggs developing into females, uninfected eggs into males. The mechanism for this strange sex selection is currently unknown.

Fungi and bees

Although bees are subject to parasitism by fungi (Chapter Six), many saprotrophic fungi are also commonly found in their nests, and some bee-fungus associations appear to be mutually beneficial. These mostly involve yeasts, including species of *Candida* and *Saccharomyces*, which, sometimes in company with bacteria, play an important role in fermenting the foodstuffs eaten by the bee larvae. Bees in the genus *Ptiloglossa*, for example, regularly have healthy larvae with abundant yeasts in their cells, and the fermented provisions appear to be important for larval nutrition. Conversely, certain other saprotrophic fungi, notably *Bettsia alvei* (Fig. 65), which may occur in the larval cells, actually spoil the food, even producing toxins which can kill.

There are several other known bee-fungus associations. For example, bees have been implicated in the dispersal of spores of stinkhorns, including species of *Dictyophora*, *Phallus* and *Staheliomyces*, although flies are the commoner vector for these fungi. As long ago as 1833, Curtis mentioned bees attracted to the gleba of *Phallus hadriani* found in sand dunes near Lowestoft, though this observation was later queried. In South America stingless bees of the genus *Trigona* have certainly been reported to lick the gleba of stinkhorns and may have a role in spore dispersal. These bees have also been recorded as packing portions of stinkhorn gleba into their pollen baskets, the significance of which is unknown but is presumably for larval food. Similarly, honey bees are well known to collect the spores of some rust fungi and have also been reported to collect spores of species in the ascomycete genus *Neurospora*. In these cases, the pollen baskets of the bees were packed exclusively with the spores of the fungus. Bees may also serve as dispersal agents for the spores of anther smuts, though butterflies may be more important in this respect.

Septobasidium and scale insects

Septobasidium is a widespread genus of patch-forming fungi distantly related to the rusts. All species are intimately associated with scale insects, sap-sucking plant feeders which are related to aphids, and occur on the stems and leaves of living plants (mostly trees and shrubs).

Apart from free-flying males, scale insects lose their mobility at an early moulting stage and remain fixed on their plant host covered by an exuded waxy scale. *Septobasidium* species grow in extensive patches over colonies of scale insects, the fruitbodies forming chambers to accommodate their hosts with tunnels for males to enter and mobile young to emerge. The fungus thus helps protect the scale insects from predators and changes in the environment (principally desiccation), but at a price. A proportion of the insects is parasitised, fungal hyphae (typically in the form of coiled haustoria) entering through the body-wall and growing within the circulatory system or haemocoel. The parasitised insects remain alive, but are normally dwarfed and sterile, the fungus taking a high proportion of the sap they suck up for its own growth. The insect-fungus relationship is thus effectively symbiotic, if the scale insect colony is considered a single organism, since both more or less depend on the other (the scale species typically found with *Septobasidium* species rarely survive in the open).

Species of *Septobasidium* are quite common in the tropics and subtropics, extending well into warm temperate areas, particularly the southern United States. A few occur further north, *Septobasidium carestianum*, for example, being not uncommon on young willow branches in Europe as far north-east as Estonia. Rather surprisingly, none have yet been recorded in the British Isles, though their unusual habitat (typically on young living twigs) may mean they have been overlooked.

Sheep, cows, and anaerobic fungi

In 1975, to almost everyone's surprise, a whole new group of fungi was discovered growing anaerobically (in the absence of free oxygen) in the rumen of sheep in Britain. Subsequently, more have been discovered in other herbivores worldwide and it seems that these highly specialised fungi are part of the normal biota of the rumen along with anaerobic bacteria and protozoa. Though a number of more conventional fungi, including brewer's yeast, *Saccharomyces cerevisiae*, are facultative anaerobes capable of living in low oxygen environments, or even without oxygen if certain nutrients are available, these unusual rumen fungi are the only obligate anaerobic fungi discovered to date.

The species concerned are now known to be true fungi, belonging to the *Chytridiomycota*. At least 16 species have been recognised so far (Theodorou *et al.*, 1996). They include *Neocallimastix frontalis, N. patriciarum* and *Piromyces communis*, found in sheep, *N. variabilis* and *Anaeromyces elegans* found in cows, *Caecomyces equi* and *Piromyces mae* found in horses, and *Piromyces dumbonica*, which, as the epithet indicates, is found in elephants. Additional hosts include yaks, llamas, camels, musk ox, impala, reindeer, wapiti, kangaroos, zebras, and rhinoceroses. These fungi are not parasites, but have a mutually beneficial relationship with their hosts, helping break down cellulose and other plant material into simpler, more accessible nutrients, some of which are taken up by the herbivores themselves. This process is essential to the animals which are themselves unable to produce cellulases, the enzymes necessary for breakdown of plant matter. Indeed, the key to a successful herbivorous diet for all vertebrates (and many invertebrates) is a partnership with some other organism. This mostly involves bacteria and protozoa, widely present in animal guts and considered until 1975 to be the only microorganisms involved in the process. It was not until the discovery that the protozoan-like cells found in the rumen of sheep were actually fungal spores that the contribution of fungi was realised. This was effectively the discovery of an entire mode of life previously unknown amongst the fungi and led to the recognition of *Neocallimastigales*, a previously unknown order of fungi.

Though these fungi are obligate anaerobes which grow, sporulate, and complete their life-cycles within the rumen, they are also tolerant of oxygen in transferring to new hosts, forming thick-walled zoosporangia which can survive in aerobic conditions and remain viable in dried dung for many months. Their biology and ecology were fully reviewed by Mountfort & Orpin (1994) and by Trinci *et al.* (1994).

ANIMALS THAT FEED ON FUNGI

Eating fungi (mycophagy) as the main or sole item of diet is widespread, particularly among the invertebrates. It too is a form of association, since both the fungus and the fungus-eater may have evolved a range of specialist adaptations for their roles. The association can even be a mutualistic one, when being eaten helps spore or mycelial dispersal (see, for example, the sections on ambrosia fungi, termites, and ants above).

Fungus-eating invertebrates

Fungus-eating is surprisingly important to invertebrates and, indeed, in soil and litter, the majority of invertebrates primarily and selectively consume fungal mycelium. Their activities play a key role in the distribution and recycling of nutrients (Cooke & Whipps, 1993) as well as having a major impact on the composition of the fungal community. For example, larvae of the cranefly *Tipula flavolineata* feed in fallen oak twigs and, by eating mycelium along with the wood, they help change the fungal community of the twigs from an association of specialised primary wood-rotters to one which resembles a generalised soil community. Almost every group of invertebrates has at least some specialist fungus-feeders. The arthropods are by far the largest such group, but many pot-worms (*Enchytraeidae*) and eel-worms (*Nematoda*) also feed on hyphae, some of the last being specialist fungivores.

Fungus-invertebrate associations are typically specific, but a few are more wide-ranging. The common fly *Drosophila phalerata*, for example, has been recorded from many species of agarics, boletes, and some polypores, as well as other fleshy fungi and even slime moulds.

Conversely, many different invertebrates may utilise a particular fungus. A study of *Daldinia* species (*Xylariaceae*), which form large, blackish fruitbodies commonly known as 'cramp-balls', recorded over 100 species of invertebrates from sites mainly in south-east England (Hingley, 1970). The invertebrates included nematodes, annelids, molluscs, crustacea, chilopods, diplopods, and a wide range of insects and arachnids. Some occurred only in decaying fruitbodies, others entered at much earlier stages. However, only five out of the 100 or more species were specific to *Daldinia*: the moth *Apomyelois bistriatella* ssp. *neophanes*, the fly *Amiota alboguttata*, and three beetles.

Basidiomycete fruitbodies are also host to many invertebrates, again serving as a food source for developing larvae (and their attendant parasites and predators) and for more generalist feeders. The latter include springtails, mites and nematodes, all of which are common in soil, many feeding primarily on fungal mycelium. Also notable are slugs and snails, the raspings of which can often be seen on toadstools and other soft-fleshed fungi.

Lichens too are eaten. As well as flies, beetles, moths and mites, lichenophagous invertebrates include several rotifers (which feed on the ascospores), nematodes, tardigrades, some *Protozoa*, and pot-worms. Some of the lichen-feeding psocids or book-lice can have quite an impact. Laundon (1971), for example, noted almost total destruction of lichen communities dominated by *Evernia prunastri* and *Hypogymnia physodes* as a result of feeding activities by the psocid *Reuterella helvimacula*. The larvae of certain psocid species also cover themselves with detritus, mostly comprising fragments of lichen thalli, as a camouflage against predators. In this case, the association is a mutualistic one, since the fragments can serve as a means of dispersal for the lichens. Some lacewing larvae do the same thing.

Fungus flies

As every field mycologist knows, fleshy fruitbodies of agarics and boletes often contain maggots – fly larvae (*Diptera*) – which can be present even in young stages, and eventually may completely destroy the fruitbody. A study of insect mycophagy in the *Boletales* in North America (Bruns, 1984) recorded flies from no less than 16 different families and beetles from four families, all utilising fruitbodies. It seems that these insect species have found a way to overcome the many problems presented by unfavourable aspects of agaric and bolete fruiting, such as marked seasonality, irregular and sometimes unpredictable appearance and, frequently, very ephemeral fruitbodies. With the production of appropriate enzymes they have also overcome toxins, such as those produced for example in species of *Amanita* and *Cortinarius*.

A catalogue of dipteran associations with fungi in Britain, most involving basidiomycetes, was published by Chandler (1978). Altogether, some 375 species in 33 different families were listed, and more have been added since. Of these associations, the *Mycetophilidae*, commonly known as 'fungus-gnats', are the most numerous, involving at least 130 species in Britain. The families *Drosophilidae*, *Phoridae*, and *Sciaridae* also have many fungivorous representatives, some feeding and developing in living fruitbodies, others specialising in their decaying remains. The drosophilid *Steganina coleoptrata*, for example, develops in stromata of *Hypoxylon fuscum* and other examples can be found in Buxton (1960).

Fungus flies can be of economic importance when they attack crops of cultivated mushrooms. Several species of *Phoridae*, *Sciaridae*, and *Cecidomyiidae*, in particular, are well-known pests of mushroom beds, sometimes causing serious damage. Certain species feed on the mycelium, others directly in the fruitbodies. Commercially collected wild fungi may also be targets. Morels are particularly attacked by flies of the families *Drosophilidae* and *Phoridae* whilst truffles have their own associated group of 'truffle flies', species of *Suillia* (*Heleomyzidae*) which hover in swarms above the surface of the ground. These indicate the location of the underground fruitbodies and, in the absence of dogs or pigs, expert truffle-hunters claim to be able to locate their quarry using the flies as a guide. However, the flies breed in the fruitbodies, so their larvae may severely damage the truffles.

Most dipteran larvae feed directly in fungal tissue, but a few are gall-causers. Until recently, only two were known in Britain: *Brachyneurina peniophorae*, which galls the hymenium of the common corticioid fungus *Peniophora cinerea*, and *Mycocecis ovalis*, which induces blister-like swellings on the stroma of *Hypoxylon rubiginosum*. However, another midge, *Agathomyia wankowiczii*, has now been discovered in south-east England inducing conspicuous galls in the hymenium of the bracket fungus *Ganoderma applanatum* (Fig. 43). The midge is a good taxonomist, since it seems never to gall the closely related *Ganoderma australe*, a species which most mycologists find hard to distinguish. Another fly, *Megaselia Intescens* (*Phoridae*), galls the gills of some common *Panaeolus* species and *Panaeolina foenisecii* (Fig 44). The larva of the fly lives between two greatly inflated gills which envelop it like a tent.

FIG 43. Galls of the bracket fungus *Ganderma applanatum* caused by the midge *Agathomyia wankowiczii*. The distinctive galls, only recently discovered in Britain, are found only on this host species (B. Spooner).

FIG 44. Galls of the common brown toadstool *Panaeolina foenisecii* caused by the midge *Megaselia lutescens* whose larvae live between adjacent, greatly enlarged gills. It is one of very few insects which are able to gall ephemeral toadstool fruitbodies (RBG Kew).

Beetles

Beetles as well as flies make use of basidiomycete fruitbodies, including boletes, puffballs, and bracket fungi, particularly the larger, perennial species.

About 25 beetle families are strictly mycophagous, feeding directly on fungi, with many others feeding on wood or other plant matter which has been decayed and altered by fungal activity. These fungivorous beetles belong mainly to the *Ciidae, Elateridae, Nitidulidae,* and *Staphylinidae,* with species of *Atheta, Bolitobius, Bolitochara, Oxyporus,* and *Quedius* feeding primarily or exclusively in fungi. *Oxyporus* species (a confusing name applied both to beetles and bracket fungi) are, for example, specialists in agaric and bolete fruitbodies, and are associated with these both as adults and larvae. Particularly common is *Oxyporus rufus,* recorded from over 100 different species of agaric hosts. In addition, many species of *Phalacridae* also feed on fungi, including some smuts as well as the fruitbodies of *Daldinia.*

According to Paviour-Smith (1960), 346 species of beetles were recorded as fungal associates in Britain to that date, although many of these were considered accidental and non-specific. Of these, some 115 species are 'true fungicolous beetles', obligately and specifically associated with fungi. Commonly, these beetles exhibit adaptations to this habit, such as enlarged and strengthened mandibles characteristic of feeders in tough brackets.

Although some of these beetles may utilise fruitbodies of various different fungi, others are more specific. The tenebrionid *Eledona agaricola*, for example, occurs only in fruitbodies of the bracket fungus *Laetiporus sulphureus*, though at least 38 other non-specific species have been obtained from this host. Some beetle larvae occur in living fungi, others are associated only with dead fruitbodies and a few, such as *Necrophorus vespertilloides*, are found in rotten fruitbodies. In some cases, notably species of *Mycetophagus* and *Orchesia*, the beetle larvae are found under bark or in well-rotten wood, feeding on the fungal mycelium. Among the true fungus beetles, one of the most important families is the *Ciidae*, the entire life histories of which occur in fruitbodies of bracket fungi. About 26 species are known from Britain, their hosts including *Laetiporus sulphureus*, *Lenzites betulina*, *Piptoporus betulinus*, *Polyporus squamosus*, and species of *Trametes* and *Ganoderma*. The beetles have host preferences but are not strictly host limited, except in a few cases such as *Cis acritis* restricted to *Trichaptum abietinum* in North America. However, a study of the beetles' biology noted a clear succession in the colonising of brackets by different species, and also differences between the species colonising brackets at different heights on a single tree.

Beetles also feed on slime moulds, those having large fruitbodies, such as *Fuligo septica* and some species of *Lycogala* and *Enteridium*, being favourites. A few beetles, especially among the *Leiodidae*, are obligate slime mould feeders, but a number of others, as well as some diptera and mites, are frequent associates. Though direct feeding on plasmodia may damage the slime mould, the host probably benefits to some extent by dispersal of spores.

More details of fungus-beetle associations in Britain can be found in Walsh (1975).

Moths

Though beetles and flies are the most numerous of the insects which obligately breed in fungi, there is also a surprising number of moths with the same habit.

Megaselia lutescens has already been noted from *Daldinia* fruitbodies, but there are many others whose caterpillars feed either on lichens, on bracket fungi, or on various moulds. Most of these are 'micromoths', particularly of the families *Oecophoridae, Psychidae,* and *Tineidae.* About 50 such micromoth species may feed on fungi in Britain, some restricted to particular lichens, others being more generalist. Oddly, one of them, *Dryadaula pactolia* (*Tineidae*) appears to specialise in feeding on the wine-cellar fungus, *Rhinocladiella ellisii* (see Chapter 14).

Several larger moths are also lichen feeders, perhaps the best known in Britain being the footman moths and related species (*Arctiidae*) which specialise in lichens on trees. A few of the geometers (*Geometridae*), notably the 'Brussels lace' (*Cleorodes lichenaria*) and the 'speckled beauty' (*Fagivorina arenaria*), feed in a similar way, as does the 'beautiful hook-tip' (*Lespeyria flexula*), a member of the large family *Noctuidae.* The 'waved black' (*Parascotia fuliginaria*), another noctuid, is a well-known feeder on bracket fungi, and, at least in Britain, is perhaps the only larger moth to do so. Its larvae are found on various bracket fungi, particularly *Phaeolus schweinitzii, Piptoporus betulinus,* and *Trametes versicolor.*

In many cases the larvae of lichen-feeding moths exhibit cryptic coloration and markings which provide an effective lichen-like camouflage. This also applies to some adult moths which commonly rest on lichen-covered bark, species such as the 'frosted green' (*Polyploca ridens*) and 'mottled beauty' (*Alcis repandata*) being good examples. With the former disappearance of lichens from polluted areas, some of these species have shown signs of 'industrial melanism', whereby sooty individuals (dark and little-marked) have become commoner than lichen-coloured individuals. This has been noted most famously in the 'peppered moth' (*Biston betularia*), but has also been demonstrated in various other insects (Gilbert, 2000).

Mites

Mites (*Acarina*) occur abundantly in most habitats and many are associated either directly or indirectly with fungi. Some simply use fungal fruitbodies as a convenient habitat, others are associated with mycophagous invertebrates, and a few actually feed on fungal spores or mycelium. For generalist soil and litter mites, the fungal habit may be opportunistic, as in many of the oribatids. But for mites such as the *Astigmata*, living on fungi may be a specific and obligate way of life.

Mites are especially common on fruitbodies of agarics and bracket fungi, particularly among the gills or in the tubes, and these are the species which tend to feed on spores or mycelium. The genus *Boletoglyphus* (*Acaridae*) provides an interesting and highly evolved example, species being adapted to feed exclusively on spores of bracket fungi. The mites have become very elongated to inhabit the narrow tubes of their host fungi, and some, especially *B. ornatus*, have developed massive jaws to crush thick-walled spores (*Ganoderma* spores, in the case of *B. ornatus*). A similar situation occurs in some other mite groups. Species of *Hoploseius* (*Ascidae*), for example, also have elongated bodies to inhabit the tubes of bracket fungi, whilst feather mites (*Astigmata*), exclusively found amongst the feathers of birds, feed extensively on the spores of keratinophilic fungi.

One of the best known examples of a mycelium feeder is *Tyrophagus putrescentiae*, a common and destructive pest in laboratory cultures. Another pest of fungal cultures is *Tarsonemus fusarii*, widely distributed on fungal fruitbodies, whilst a related species, *T. myceliophagus*, causes problems in commercial mushroom beds.

Some mite-fungus associations appear to be mutualistic. This is especially highly evolved in species of *Siteroptes* (*Trombidiformes*) which are obligately and specifically associated with pathogenic fungi (*Nigrospora* and *Sporotrichum* species) in grass inflorescences. These fungivorous mites possess specialised 'sporothecae', internal spore-carrying structures, and are species-specific, the sporothecae carrying spores of only a single fungal species.

Slugs and snails

Slugs and snails are familiar feeders on soft-fleshed fungi, quite often destroying mushroom and toadstool fruitbodies before they are even mature. Surprisingly, however, they may have a role to play in the dispersal of fungi, since their gut enzymes have been reported to stimulate the germination of spores, even those of the mycorrhizal genera *Russula* and *Lactarius*.

Slugs and snails are also frequent feeders on lichens, 28 species being listed as lichen associates in Britain by Peake & James (1967), though whether they gain their nutritional benefit from the mycobiont or the photobiont is uncertain. Lichen acids, often considered as protective against predators, generally have no adverse effects on molluscs and pass unaltered through the gut, though the most toxic are avoided. These acids may similarly be ineffective against some lichen-feeding moth larvae. However, as the acids are not present in the larval frass, their fate and function in the lichen-moth relationship requires further study.

Mammals

Fungal fruitbodies form an important part of the diet for a wide range of small mammals, particularly rodents and lagomorphs (hares and rabbits). It is easy to find toothmarks on the caps of various agarics and boletes and it seems that fungi are a valuable and regular resource, particularly in early winter when other food is scarce. This applies especially to rabbits and squirrels, though some voles and mice are known to consume fungi at times. It seems likely that they are attracted to the fruitbodies mainly by smell, though it is possible that the bright colours of some species may also play a part.

The food value of fungi and their relative importance in small mammal diets require further study. Fruitbodies are clearly good sources of protein, carbohydrates, and minerals and may also supply vitamins and additional organic compounds. However, their overall percentage intake compared to other foods must vary greatly according to species. Also little known is the manner in which small mammals deal with poisonous species. Rabbits and squirrels seem to consume toadstools toxic to humans, including the death cap (*Amanita phalloides*), without any apparent harm.

Experiments and field observations on the consumption of fungi by rabbits and grey squirrels by Hastings & Mottram (1917) revealed a wide range of species being eaten. These included various boletes and fruitbodies of *Russula* and *Lactarius*, *Agaricus*, *Hypholoma*, *Cortinarius*, *Paxillus* and *Tricholoma*. Other species were taken when offered, particularly after starving the animals for 48 hours. However, some fungi were refused by rabbits even then, including, surprisingly, chanterelles. They also refused *Amanita muscaria* and *A. rubescens*, though the latter had been reported in field observations as eaten naturally by rabbits. Grey squirrels appeared to eat a similar range of species, though with differences in preference. For example, *Paxillus involutus* was readily eaten by rabbits but only rarely and in harsh conditions by squirrels. Stomach contents from red squirrels in Scotland have also shown that fungi are an important part of their diet, particularly truffles and boletes. It is worth noting that the Dutch name for the cep (*Boletus edulis*) is 'eekhoorntjesbrood', translated as 'squirrel's bread'.

Squirrels and their relatives are mycologically the most polyphagous of mammals, having been reported to take no less than 89 different species of fungi (Fogel & Trappe, 1978). Voles and other rodents also eat fungi, some specialising in truffles and hypogeous species (see below). Hares as well as rabbits eat fungi, as do various marsupials, and there are occasional reports of mycophagy from other mammal orders. These include baboons, armadillos and shrews, though fungal spores found in stomach contents of the last of these may originate from their insect prey. Even horses and sheep have been reported to eat field mushrooms (*Agaricus campestris*).

Lichens are also an important food source for some mammals. This is especially true of reindeer, for which lichens form a substantial part of their diet, particularly during the winter. Ground lichens, notably 'Iceland moss' (*Cetraria islandica*) and various species of *Cladonia* are the main species eaten by Scandinavian reindeer, but arboreal lichens, including species of *Alectoria*, *Hypogymnia* and *Usnea*, are utilised by North American caribou.

Various small mammals, especially voles, may also eat lichens, particularly when other food sources are scarce. This was well demonstrated by Hansson & Larsson (1978) who found that lichens, especially *Alectoria* species, formed up to 90% of the diet of voles in experimental reforestation areas in Sweden.

Small mammals and truffles

'Hypogeous' fungi (those with underground fruitbodies) are a highly diverse and heterogeneous assemblage of species which may look outwardly similar, but belong to quite different fungal groups. They are also surprisingly numerous, with almost 80 species in Britain alone. The species involved are almost always ectomycorrhizal and therefore of ecological importance to the habitats in which they occur. In fruiting underground, they have lost the ability to forcibly discharge their spores and instead must rely on some other means of dispersal. This is achieved primarily by mammals which utilise, and in some cases virtually rely on, the fruitbodies as a food source. Not only are the fungus spores passed safely through the animal's gut, to be liberated in the faeces and washed into the soil, they may actually be stimulated to germinate by the action of digestive enzymes. The fruitbodies of most hypogeous fungi have a strong smell by which they can be readily located by the mammals which feed on them. This is particularly true of commercial truffles, the smell of which not only accounts for their extraordinary popularity among humans, but also allows them to be hunted for by keener-nosed pigs and dogs (Chapter 17).

Dogs need to be trained to find truffles, but pigs find them as part of their natural diet. Many other large mammals, including elk, deer, and kangaroos, may play a role in spreading the spores of hypogeous fungi, but it is small mammals, particularly squirrels, mice, chipmunks, and voles, which are their main agents of dispersal. Truffles can often form the major part of their diet. In some voles and chipmunks, for example, truffles have been found to constitute over 70% of the stomach contents. These animals are, therefore, essential partners for the successful spread of the fungi involved. It is an obligate and specific mutualistic relationship which is also of immense benefit to the forest itself, ensuring the spread of mycorrhizal fungi and hence the health and survival of the trees themselves. Understanding the importance of these small mammals to the forest ecosystem has led to some changes in commercial forestry practice, whereby the habitat needs of the animals are fully considered and their perceived pest status re-evaluated.

In Britain, several native mammals, especially bank voles and squirrels, are known to feed on hypogeous fungi, though not as an exclusive part of the diet. Stomach contents of red squirrels examined in Scotland were found to contain spores of five different species: the asco-truffles *Elaphomyces muricatus* and *Hydnotrya tulasnei*, basidio-truffles *Melanogaster ambiguus* and *Rhizopogon roseolus*, and the tiny pea truffle *Endogone flammicorona* (Turnbull, 1995). The last is a member of the *Endogonales* (*Zygomycota*), many of which do not produce proper fruitbodies and it is considered that their dispersal may largely involve invertebrates rather than mammals.

CHAPTER 6

Parasites and Predators

WHEN we talk of 'parasites', we tend to think in human, pestilential terms – lice, fleas, tapeworms – unwelcome guests making a living at our expense. But parasitism as a way of life is a much broader and far more complex phenomenon. This is particularly true of the fungi, all of which, like animals but unlike plants, derive their nutrients from other organisms.

In the animal kingdom, parasitism often involves a high degree of specialisation, with the parasite being morphologically adapted and intimately linked with the life-history of the host. In the fungi, such specialisation is comparatively rare, although it is found in several ascomycete groups, as well as the rusts and smuts. More typically there is a continuum of relationships between fungi and their food sources. These range from the wholly saprotrophic to the wholly parasitic, with a large grey area of opportunistic and mutualistic interactions in between. The last is well exemplified by the complex interactions which commonly occur between plants, herbivorous insects and pathogenic fungi in which a wide range of direct and indirect mutualistic and antagonistic reactions can be demonstrated. For example, insect damage to plant hosts may greatly facilitate invasion by fungal pathogens. Conversely, some insects may feed on the spores or mycelium of parasitic fungi and render invasion more difficult, or the plant may secrete chemicals which protect it against fungi or insect attack. There are many other kinds of tripartite interactions, reviewed by Hatcher (1995).

In this chapter, we shall primarily consider those fungal pathogens which cause disease or even death of their host organisms. Additionally, we shall take a look at predatory fungi, a surprisingly diverse range of highly specialised species that trap and consume nematode worms and other microfauna.

PARASITES OF PLANTS

Even a casual look at our native trees, shrubs and herbs reveals the presence of parasitic fungi, most noticeably as leaf spots, stem lesions, swellings and distortions. These fungi are everywhere, with no plant species being entirely free from attack. They are hugely diverse, with representatives in all taxonomic groups, and have an equally huge impact on the natural environment, as well as on agriculture, horticulture, and forestry.

Some, including the rusts (*Uredinales*), smuts (*Ustilaginales*), and powdery mildews (*Erysiphales*), are obligate parasites, unable to grow except on the host plant and often markedly pathogenic, causing severe diseases. Others are less specialised, occurring on a wide range of hosts and also able to grow as saprotrophs on decaying plant parts. These are facultative parasites, and the majority of plant disease fungi are of this type. Parasites which cause the death of their hosts are termed 'necrotrophic', whereas those which keep their hosts alive are normally termed 'biotrophic', although these biotrophs may have various adverse effects on the hosts, ranging from sterility, to weak or impaired growth and development, chlorosis, deformations and galls.

The study of plant pathology, including the fungi themselves, the diseases they cause, their biology, ecological and economic importance, is a vast undertaking and is accompanied by an equally extensive literature. Many aspects can be found in the New Naturalist volume 'Plant Disease' (Ingram & Robertson, 1999) and there are plenty of popular guides available, such as Buczacki & Harris (1998) and Brooks & Halstead (1999). Arx (1987) provided a descriptive account of all major plant pathogenic fungi in an illustrated compendium which included keys for the identification of the most import-ant groups together with lists of species known from cultivated plants.

Rusts: specialists with a complex lifestyle

Rusts are plant parasite specialists, attacking a wide range of living plants, including many of our staple food crops. They belong to the *Basidiomycota*, and as such are very distant cousins of mushrooms and toadstools, but have become so radically adapted to their lifestyle that they are now placed in their own class, *Urediniomycetes*. Almost 7000 rust species exist worldwide, of which some 260 occur on native, crop, and garden plants in Britain.

The extent to which rusts have adapted to their parasitic habit is quite remarkable. They exhibit a range of strategies, often involving more than one host species and no fewer than five different spore-producing stages, four of them forming discrete spore-bearing structures or 'sori'. These complex life cycles have evolved to match the host cycles, enabling rusts to track their hosts through the seasons. The cycle is, of course, continuous, but traditionally the various spore stages are numbered O – IV, though not all stages are present in all species. The cycle (Fig. 45) starts with the 'spermogonium' or 'pycnium' stage (numbered 'O'), producing 'spermatia' or 'pycniospores'. The spermogonia are immersed in the host tissue and are commonly inconspicuous, but sometimes developed in leaf spots. They vary in form from tiny, flask-shaped bodies to more diffuse areas without well defined margins. Spermogonia exude haploid spermatia which need to be cross-fertilised with spermatia from a rust of a different mating type. As in many flowers, this is achieved by producing a sweet-smelling liquid (pycnial nectar) which is attractive to insects. Spermatia in the liquid are thus insect spread and, following cross-fertilisation, give rise to a diploid mycelium.

The next stage, the 'aecidium' (producing 'aecidiospores' and numbered 'I'), is usually conspicuous and often causes hypertrophy of host tissues. Aecidia vary in form, but are typically cup-like and densely gregarious, and are commonly referred to as 'cluster cups'. The aecidia of some *Gymnosporangium* species are particularly noticeable, producing elongated, horn-like structures up to 5 mm high on leaves and fruits of hawthorn and other rosaceous trees. Aecidiospores are actively discharged and wind-borne, allowing the rust to colonise new host plants. The spores germinate on reaching a suitable host to produce mycelium within the host tissue.

The following stage, the 'uredinium' (producing 'urediniospores' and

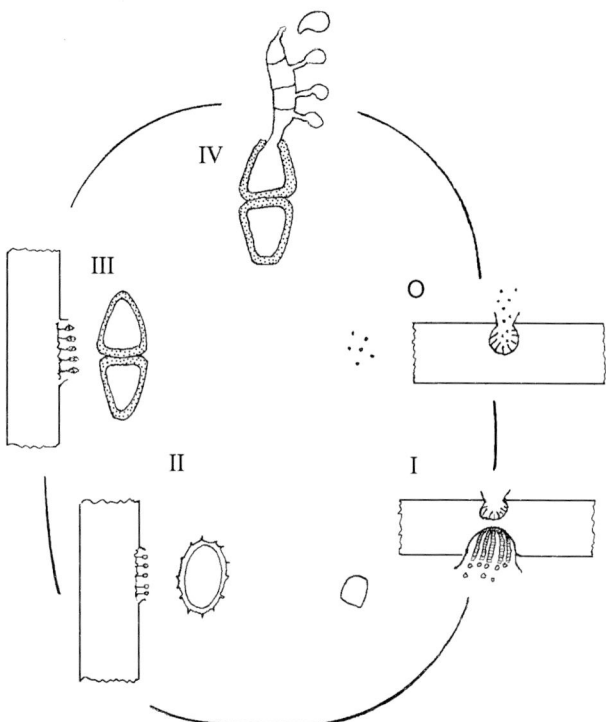

FIG 45. Simplified life cycle of the rust *Puccinia graminis*: O) germinating basidiospores on the upper surfaces of barberry leaves produce flask-like pycnia which in turn produce tiny pycniospores; I) if successfully cross-fertilised, aecidia are formed on the undersurfaces of the leaves and release aecidiospores; II) the aecidiospores infect cereal grasses, producing uredinia (rust-like patches) and releasing urediniospores which can infect more cereal hosts; III) towards the end of the year, teleutospores are produced which are thick-walled and capable of over-wintering on dead cereal stems; IV) the following spring, the teleutospores produce an auricularioid basidium on which basidiospores are formed; these disperse and germinate on barberry leaves to start the cycle over again (P. Roberts).

numbered 'II'), arises from this mycelium and serves to spread the rust to yet more host plants. It is effectively the epidemic stage, particularly in cereal rusts, allowing the fungus to spread from a few isolated plants to a whole crop. The uredinium typically develops below the surface of leaves and stems which split apart when the uredinium matures to reveal the wind-borne, thick-walled urediniospores. This is the stage when leaves and stems look 'rusty'.

The next stage, the 'telium', producing 'teliospores' or 'teleutospores' (numbered 'III'), is non-dispersive. The spores are thick-walled propagules, capable of overwintering in dead leaves or stems or in the soil. In most rusts teleutospores are developed in well differentiated sori, though these exhibit various different forms. In the genera *Melampsora* and *Melampsoridium*, common rusts on poplar, willow, and birch, the teleutospores form discrete subcuticular or subepidermal layers, appearing as conspicuous, dark, slightly raised areas on fallen leaves. In other genera the teleutosori may rupture at maturity to form powdery, dark brown spore masses. In *Gymnosporangium* the teleutosori often become exceptionally conspicuous. In the four British species they occur on swollen branches of juniper, the spores being closely cohesive and forming orange, gelatinous columns up to 10 mm or more high.

Teleutospores germinate, typically in the spring, to produce basidia which form basidiospores, the final stage (number 'IV') in the sequence. The basidiospores are forcibly discharged from the basidia, are wind-borne, and reinfect their hosts to initiate another cycle.

Puccinia graminis, the well-known 'black stem rust' of wheat and other cereals, is an example of a 'macrocyclic' species, one in which all five spore stages are present. It is also 'heteroecious', involving a second, separate host plant as part of its annual infection cycle. In the case of *P. graminis*, the alternate host is barberry (*Berberis vulgaris*) or *Mahonia*, on which the spermogonia and aecidia are produced. In Britain, *Puccinia graminis* is not a substantial problem to cereal growers since *Mahonia* is not native and barberry is a local and uncommon plant. But in North America, where barberry is more widespread, the disease can cause severe crop losses. Removing nearby barberry may be of little help, since the cereal-infecting airborne urediniospores are capable of travelling several hundred miles on favourable winds. In some warmer countries the rust, once established, can cause problems despite the absence of barberry. The lack of cold winters allows some aeciospores to survive till spring, reinfecting the crop without the intervening stages.

Comparatively few British rusts exhibit the full range of spore stages, only

38 species being capable of doing so. Among the commonest of these are the almost ubiquitous birch rust, *Melampsoridium betulinum*, and the equally abundant *Coleosporium tussilaginis* which occurs on many hosts in the Campanulaceae, Compositae, and Scrophulariaceae. Although these rusts can form the full range of spore stages, they do not necessarily develop them, some persisting as the uredinium stage on their primary hosts and not forming aecidia on their alternate hosts. Examples include *Puccinia caricina* and *P. urticata*, both common species which develop uredinia and telia on various sedges, but which may or may not form aecidia on their alternate hosts, currants and nettles respectively. In a few species, all five spore forms develop on a single host and there is no alternation. These include rose rusts in the genus *Phragmidium*, of which *P. mucronatum*, common on various wild and cultivated roses, is a good example.

Other rusts are less complex. They have fewer stages in their life cycles and are 'autoecious', completing their cycles on a single host. In some, the uredinial stage is lost from the cycle, although in Britain this applies to only a few species, such as the common *Puccinia smyrnii*, which forms conspicuous gall-like hypertrophy on stems and leaves of alexanders (*Smyrnium olusatrum*). Rarely, only uredinium and telium stages occur, as in the very scarce rust *Puccinia oxyriae* found on mountain sorrel (*Oxyria digyna*) in the highlands of Wales and Scotland. Simplest of all are the rusts which develop only telia and/or a spermogonial stage. An example is *Puccinia cnici-oleracei* on various species of *Achillea, Aster, Chrysanthemum*, and thistles (*Cirsium*).

Many of the British rusts are common and quite conspicuous. *Puccinia coronata*, for example, is often abundant on grasses, whilst *Puccinia punctiformis* is common on creeping thistle (*Cirsium arvense*) and is notable for developing sweet-smelling spermogonia in the spring which cover the entire leaf surface and cause distortion of the host, often preventing flowering. Common rusts in the garden include *Phragmidium mucronatum* on roses, *Puccinia malvacearum* on hollyhocks and wild mallows, *Puccinia menthae* on mints, and *Puccinia vincae* on periwinkle.

British rusts have been treated in detail by Wilson & Henderson (1966), with a revised checklist by Henderson (2000). As with other fungi, the British rust mycota is far from static. Fourteen species have been recorded as new to Britain since 1966, and it seems likely that others will turn up in future. Most (though not all) are considered to be new arrivals rather than overlooked native or long-established species. Amongst them is a rust on common daisy (*Bellis perennis*), first noticed in Britain in 1996 and now spread widely. It causes yellowed, rather distorted leaves (Fig. 46), easily visible in lawns because they tend to become erect instead of flattened. This rust seems to be the Australian species *Puccinia distincta* (Weber *et al.*, 1998a, b) although there is some doubt about this. The same daisy rust has also been found in the USA, where its identity with another Australian species, *P. lagenophorae*, has apparently been confirmed by cross-inoculation experiments. *Puccinia lagenophorae* has also been introduced to Britain, where it was first recorded in 1961 on groundsel at Dungeness in Kent. The species spread rapidly and is now common and widespread on this host as well as Oxford ragwort and pot marigold.

FIG 46. Daisy rust, *Puccinia distincta*, a recent introduction to Britain which causes marked yellowing of leaves and is readily visible in lawns (B. Spooner).

Smuts: the systemic specialists

The smuts are another major group of specialist, biotrophic plant parasites. Though once considered as a single related taxon, these are now split between the mainly monocot-hosted species, placed in their own class (*Ustilaginomycetes*), and the mainly dicot-hosted *Microbotryales* which appear to be more closely related to the rusts (*Urediniomycetes*). The smuts include far fewer species than the rusts, with some 1500 taxa known worldwide, only around a hundred of which are found in Britain. Many smuts attack grasses, including cereal crops, but others are found on a wide range of other native and garden flowering plants.

Smuts are typically systemic parasites, living within plant tissue and only conspicuous when sporulating. Sporulation tends to be restricted to particular parts of the host, and it is therefore possible to recognise stem smuts, leaf smuts, inflorescence smuts (Figs 47 & 48), and root smuts, although these categories are only used for identification purposes and do not reflect taxonomic groups.

In a typical inflorescence smut the fungus invades the flowering parts of plants, replacing the pollen with its own blackish, thick-walled 'ustilospores', the equivalent of teliospores in rusts. These are carried to other host plants by wind or insects, germinating to produce germ tubes or mycelia which function as basidia and produce basidiospores which infect the new host plant. The cycle is thus much simpler than in rusts, with fewer spore stages and no alternation of hosts.

Smuts are now of lesser economic significance than in the past, since they can be fairly easily controlled by the application of appropriate fungicides. Amongst crop plants, oats and other cereals were once the most affected, host to a range of damaging smuts which are now normally seen only in wild grasses. It is still easy to find smuts whilst walking through an overgrown meadow in early summer. The smutted inflorescences of tall grasses often cover hands and clothes with 'smutty' soot-like ustilospores. The commonest of these in Britain is *Ustilago avenae*, known as 'loose smut of oats'. Although still found on oats, it is much more frequent and often abundant on oat grass (*Arrhenatherum elatius*).

Leaf smuts include several British species of *Urocystis* which occur in leaves and petioles, sometimes also in stems and roots, and form blister-like

FIG 47. *Sphacelotheca hydropiperis*, a common smut fungus found in the ovaries of water pepper *Persicaria hydropiper*. It destroys the florets and develops a purple, powdery mass of spores at maturity but does not cause galls (B. Spooner).

swellings which rupture at maturity to expose a powdery, blackish spore mass. Some of the 15 leaf-inhabiting British species, such as *U. violae*, on various species of *Viola*, are quite common. There are also about 16 species of *Entyloma* in Britain, usually developed as leaf spots of various kinds. One of the commonest is *E. ficariae* on lesser celandine, most frequently seen in its conidial stage forming whitish spots or patches on leaves.

Root smuts are mostly gall-causers, and include species of *Entorrhiza* and *Melanotaenium* though, since they develop underground, they are rarely encountered. The three British species of *Entorrhiza* occur in rushes and sedges, whereas *Melanotaenium*, with two root-infecting species in Britain, occurs in dicotyledonous herbs: *M. hypogaeum* in the root stock of fluellen (*Kickxia spuria*) and *M. lamii* in roots of white deadnettle (*Lamium album*).

A few smuts, especially species of *Thecaphora*, occur in seeds. These may not be uncommon but are inconspicuous and difficult to find. Only three such smuts are known in Britain: *Thecaphora deformans* in seeds of dwarf furze (*Ulex minor*), *T. lathyri* in seeds of meadow vetchling (*Lathyrus pratensis*), and *T. seminis-convolvuli* in seeds of bindweed (*Calystegia* and *Convolvulus* species).

Although far fewer in number than rusts, there have been several additions to the list of British smuts since 1984, when a comprehensive treatment was published (Mordue & Ainsworth, 1984), and no doubt others will be discovered in the future. These additions include *Melanopsichium nepalense* and *Entyloma veronicae*. The former, reported in 1985 from Ham in Surrey, forms conspicuous galls on the stems of knotgrass (*Polygonum*

FIG 48. Galls in the ovaries of water pepper *Persicaria hydropiper* caused by the smut fungus *Ustilago utriculosa*. The smut, which also infects some related host species, is less common than *Sphacelotheca hydropiperis* but may be more conspicuous (B. Spooner).

aviculare). It has not been recollected and appears to have been a casual introduction which did not persist. The sori of *E. veronicae* are much less conspicuous, just tiny circular spots on leaves of thyme-leaved speedwell (*Veronica serpyllifolia*). Material of this smut was collected near Esher in Surrey in 1997.

Altogether, over 450 species of smuts are known from Europe, details of which can be found in the comprehensive monograph by Vánky (1994).

Mildews: a mixed bag of pathogens

The term 'mildew' is a well-known one but taxonomically imprecise, referring to a plant disease in which the pathogen appears as a superficial growth on the host. It covers a range of unrelated fungi, many of which are of economic importance. 'Powdery mildews' (*Erysiphales*) are ascomycetes, worldwide in distribution, and include some notable pathogens of crop plants. 'Downy mildews' (*Peronosporales*), though sometimes macroscopically similar, are not related to the powdery mildews, but belong to the *Oomycota* (kingdom *Chromista*). 'Dark mildews' are ascomycetes belonging to the *Meliolales* and *Capnodiaceae* (*Dothideales*), and are mostly tropical with just a few species known from Britain.

All these fungi are obligate plant parasites and mostly strictly host-limited. Powdery mildews, with over 90 species in Britain, cover plant leaves and stems with white superficial mycelium penetrating the host tissue by means of haustoria. It is the conidial or asexual states that are most frequently encountered. The sexual state, consisting of 'cleistothecia' (tiny closed spherical structures which are blackish at maturity and contain the asci and spores), is less frequently developed. Many of these mildews are common and are familiar to gardeners, particularly late in the season when fading plants are more susceptible to attack. One of the most conspicuous examples is the oak mildew, *Microsphaera alphitoides*, often seen smothering the leaves of saplings and young shoots of oaks (Fig. 49). This species, common throughout much of Britain, is found mainly in the asexual state although cleistothecia, found mostly on the leaf underside, are increasingly frequent, perhaps due to warmer summers.

Around 150 species of powdery mildews are known from European host plants, for which Braun (1995) has provided a comprehensive account.

FIG 49. Oak mildew, *Microsphaera alphitoides*, often forming a conspicuous white coating on leaves of young oaks and sucker growth. Due to the warmer climate of recent years production of cleistothecia is now frequent (P. Roberts).

In the downy mildews (*Peronosporales*), with around 120 British species, the mycelium is intercellular, with haustoria penetrating the host cells. These mildews are almost exclusively confined to dicotyledonous plants, with just a few species of *Bremia* and *Plasmopara* known from grasses. The downy mildews form greyish 'mould', usually on the leaf underside, and commonly cause leaf yellowing. They are important pathogens of a wide range of herbaceous plants, including crops and garden plants. The British species, documented by Francis & Waterhouse (1988) and Preece (2002), occur in five genera, the largest and most important of which is *Peronospora*. This includes potentially damaging species such as *P. destructor* on onions and *P. viciae* on peas, which may be particularly prevalent in wet or humid conditions. Another genus, *Bremia*, includes just a single species in Britain, *B. lactucae*, which occurs on many genera in *Compositae* and may be damaging to lettuce. Some species of *Plasmopara* and *Pseudoperonospora* are also of economic importance, particularly *Plasmopara viticola* on vines, an American species introduced to Europe in 1878. This is now present in all grape-growing areas worldwide and, despite the advent of Bordeaux Mixture and other fungicides, may sometimes do considerable damage to vine crops. Hop downy mildew (*Pseudoperonospora humuli*), common in Britain and now widespread throughout the northern hemisphere, is considered one of the most serious diseases of cultivated hops. More detailed information on the biology, ecology, distribution, and control of downy mildews can be found in Spencer (1981) and Bélanger *et al.* (2002).

Related to the downy mildews are the 'white blister-rusts' (*Albuginaceae*), although these include only about 30 species worldwide. Of these, just four are known from Britain. The most abundant and well-known is *Albugo candida*, the white blister of cabbages and other crucifers. This can cause significant crop damage and is an economically important pathogen as well as being common on many wild plants. Frequently, attacked plants are conspicuously distorted, with bent and often thickened stems (Fig. 50). Also frequent but with a more restricted host range are *Albugo tragopogonis*,

FIG 50. Bent and distorted stems of shepherd's purse *Capsella bursa-pastoris* infected with the white blister-rust *Albugo candida*, a common species on many cruciferous hosts (B. Spooner).

on groundsel and goatsbeard (*Tragopogon*), and *A. lepigoni* on spurrey (*Spergularia*), particularly S. *marina* and other coastal species. The fourth species, *Albugo amaranthi*, was only reported from Britain in 2001 on leaves of *Amaranthus retroflexus* from the Royal Botanic Gardens, Kew.

Of the mainly tropical dark mildews, only three species of *Meliolaceae* and about six of *Capnodiaceae* occur in Britain. The former include *Appendiculella calostroma*, which forms blackish patches on leaves and stems of bramble, and *Meliola ellisii* on leaves of bilberries. Most notable amongst the *Capnodiaceae* is *Trichomerium grandisporum*. This was first collected in Ireland but appears now to have become more widespread in England and Wales, forming conspicuous blackish mycelium on the leaves of evergreens such as holly, ivy, cherry laurel, and yew.

Leaf-spot fungi

Leaf spots, usually circular or irregular discoloured areas on living leaves, are a familiar sight on almost every kind of wild and cultivated plant. Although some are caused by bacteria and viruses, or even the activities of insects and other invertebrates, many are produced by plant pathogenic fungi. Rusts, smuts, and downy mildews are sometimes to blame, but the fungi most responsible are some of the smaller ascomycetes, particularly the anamorphic stages.

These leaf-spotting fungi include the hyphomycete genera *Ramularia* and *Cercospora*, as well as *Cercosporella*, *Mycovellosiella*, and *Pseudocercosporella*. Most of them develop conidiophores on the leaf underside, often in tufts emerging from the stomatal pores, and can be seen under a hand lens as tiny whitish or sometimes dark felty patches covering the leaf spot. Species of various coelomycete genera, particularly *Ascochyta*, *Phomopsis*, *Phyllosticta*, and *Septoria*, may also cause leaf spots. In these, the fungus usually develops fruitbodies on the leaf upperside, appearing as minute black dots under a hand lens.

Other leaf-spot fungi include certain ascomycete teleomorphs, a common example being *Venturia rumicis* which forms conspicuous spots with red or purple margins on various species of dock. Most of these fungi are strictly host-limited, but different kinds of leaf spot may occur on a single host, sometimes developing together, so microscopic examination is required for successful identification. Most of these fungi can be found in Ellis & Ellis (1997), but the early work by Grove (1935-37) is still important for identification.

Many of these leaf-spotters are extremely common in Britain. *Cercospora depazeoides*, for example, is frequent on elder leaves, forming darkish spots particularly later in the season. *Ramularia simplex* on buttercups and *R. rubella* on docks are equally common. However, a few species are unaccountably rare. *Septoria cymbalariae* on ivy-leaved toadflax (*Cymbalaria muralis*) is apparently known in Britain from just four collections, despite the abundance and wide distribution of the host.

Tar spot: a pollution-detecting pathogen

Among the most familiar of the leaf parasites are the 'tar-spot' fungi, belonging to the genus *Rhytisma* (*Ascomycota*). Their stromatic fruitbodies cause dark brown or blackish tar-like blotches which are unsightly in ornamental trees but usually cause little adverse effects on the host. There are three British species, of which *Rhytisma acerinum* on sycamore is by far the most common. Ascomata develop on leaves in summer, and mature the following spring on overwintered fallen leaves. Sycamore tar spot is widely distributed and generally common, though being sensitive to sulphur dioxide pollution, particularly during the infection stage in the spring, it may be rare or absent in urban areas. As with lichens, its distribution can be used as an indicator of air quality (Bevan & Greenhalgh, 1976), though other urban factors must be taken into account. According to Leith & Fowler (1988) it is the effective clearance of fallen leaves rather than air pollution that is the most important factor explaining its rarity in urban areas. The other British species, *R. salicinum* on willows and *R. andromedae* on marsh rosemary (*Andromeda*), are comparatively scarce, the latter only known from a few localities in northern England and Wales.

Rhizoctonia-forming fungi

Rhizoctonias are sterile fungi, the mycelial states of patch-forming basidiomycetes belonging to the genera *Ceratobasidium*, *Helicobasidium*, and *Thanatephorus* (the last meaning 'death bringer' in Greek). Of these, *Rhizoctonia solani* (the mycelial state of *Thanatephorus cucumeris*) is one of the most widespread and devastating plant pathogens having an "enormous capacity for destruction of man's crops" (Baker, 1970). The fungus can live saprotrophically in soil, persisting as 'sclerotia' (brownish hyphal propagules) when hosts are absent or weather conditions are poor. It will attack almost any plant, typically through roots, tubers, or stems, producing a variety of symptoms including blights, rots, and damping-off. In England, it causes widespread yield losses of potatoes through 'stem canker' and 'black scurf', but also attacks cabbages, sugar beet, tomatoes, lettuce, rape, cereals, bulbs, forestry seedlings, and turf grasses (where it causes 'brown patch' disease). It is even more of a problem in tropical areas, resulting (for example) in crop losses of up to 50% in rice-growing areas.

Curiously, however, known pathogenic strains of *Rhizoctonia solani* form endomycorrhizal associations with orchids (Chapter Four): a good example of the grey area between saprotrophic, mutualistic, and pathogenic fungal-plant relationships.

Vascular wilts and Dutch elm disease

Vascular wilts are confined, at least in early development, to the vascular system of their hosts, and are characterised by loss of turgidity and subsequent collapse of the plant. Most are due to highly specialised pathogens, including bacteria as well as fungi, and can result in severe losses in many crop plants, from potatoes to bananas. Comparatively few fungal species are involved, but some of these are exceptionally important.

In Britain the most notorious vascular wilt is 'Dutch elm disease' caused by species of *Ophiostoma* (*Ascomycota*). This has had a devastating effect on the British countryside since it first appeared during the early 1970s, resulting in the complete disappearance of mature elm trees through large tracts of England.

At first the disease was attributed to *Ophiostoma ulmi*, the cause of a milder epidemic in northwest Europe between 1910 and 1940. Although this resulted in a significant loss of elms in some countries, the disease declined markedly during the 1940s. The more recent and serious outbreak is now known to be caused by a different and previously undescribed species called *Ophiostoma novo-ulmi*. This species was first detected in the 1940s in two widely separated areas in North America and eastern Europe. These represented two distinct subspecies of the fungus, both of which are now present in northwest Europe, including Britain. *Ophiostoma novo-ulmi* is highly destructive (Fig. 41) and has resulted in the estimated loss of more than 25 million trees in the UK alone (Brasier, 2000). The fungus has rapidly replaced *O. ulmi* during its spread across Europe.

Both species are introductions in Europe and North America (the disease was named after its Dutch investigators, not because it came from there) and have no natural balance with their hosts. Their origin remains unknown although it has been suggested that they may occur naturally in the eastern Himalayas. A more detailed discussion of Dutch elm disease can be found in Dunn (2000) and Ingram & Robertson (1999). The fungus is spread by bark beetles, a mutualistic association treated further in Chapter Five.

The symptoms of Dutch elm and other wilt diseases include yellowing and shrivelling of leaves, drooping of leaf stalks, and wilting, sometimes suddenly so in hot weather. Dark discolouration in the vascular tissues is diagnostic of true wilts, if present in aerial stems well above ground level. The wilting itself is normally caused by the simple, physical presence of the pathogen, clogging up the xylem vessels with mycelium, rather than any specific disease effects on the host plant. Perversely, the development of counter-measures by infected plants, such as gums and tyloses which isolate and block off infected cells, often exacerbates the wilt. Most vascular wilt fungi belong to just a few ascomycetous genera, notably *Fusarium* and *Verticillium* in herbaceous plants, *Cephalosporium* and *Ophiostoma* in woody plants. With the exception of *Ophiostoma* species, which are spread by bark beetles, these are almost exclusively soil-borne pathogens. The fungi are able to survive for long periods in the soil as resting stages, either as chlamydospores, especially characteristic of *Fusarium* species, or as microsclerotia, aggregations of dark, thick-walled cells, characteristic of *Verticillium* species. These resting stages are induced to germinate only in the presence of the host roots. In crop plants the devastation caused by vascular wilts has been almost exclusively due to the activities of man, spreading the pathogens into soils worldwide in conjunction with the development of intensive crop monocultures. One of the most famous examples of this is 'Panama disease', a wilt of bananas caused by *Fusarium oxysporum* var. *cubense*. The fungus spread from eastern Asia throughout the tropics during the

18th and 19th centuries, devastating crops to such an extent that banana-growing in Central America and the Caribbean region was abandoned for many years.

Blights, rots, scabs, and diebacks

These are descriptive and rather imprecise terms for the effects that some parasites have on their host plants. They may be induced by a range of fungi, as well as bacteria and viruses, and vary in severity according to the disease concerned. 'Dieback' refers to the death of shoots and stems, usually from the tip downwards, and can have a variety of causes. It may result from girdling cankers lower on the stem, or from a specific pathogen attacking that particular stem. Dieback affecting entire plants is usually due to root parasites, including species of *Phytophthora*, though non-fungal causes (including frost or drought stress) can produce similar effects. One dieback familiar to many garden owners commonly occurs on hedges of box and is due to the wound-parasite *Volutella buxi*. This causes dieback of twigs and areas of brown foliage and produces minute, pinkish fruitbodies on the dead leaves.

'Scabs' are usually restricted to diseases of fruits or tubers characterised by roughened, often corky lesions. 'Powdery scab of potato' has already been mentioned, but perhaps the best known is 'apple scab' caused by the ascomycete *Venturia inaequalis*. This is very common, not only on apples but on many other rosaceous trees, and is commercially important for the damage it can do to crops. The scabby effects are rarely more than disfiguring surface features, but are more than enough to destroy a crop's retail value. A related fungus, *Spilocaea pyracanthae*, is common on *Pyracantha*.

'Rots' again cover a huge range of diseases having in common the breakdown of plant cells leading to a rotting mass of tissue. They are caused by a wide range of fungi, and occur in soft or woody plant tissue. Rots of bulbs, corms and flowers are sometimes due to basidiomycetous rhizoctonia-forming fungi, such as *Helicobasidium purpureum* and *Thanatephorus cucumeris*, but are mostly caused by ascomycetes, particularly species of *Fusarium* or *Penicillium*. Some species of *Sclerotinia* and related discomycetes are also involved, as in the very common 'brown rot' of apples and pears. This is produced by *Monilinia fructigena*, the characteristic pale brown felty pustules of the asexual state being frequent on soft, rotting brown areas of the fruit. Infected fruits ultimately shrivel and may long remain attached to the tree.

Perhaps the most ubiquitous of all the rots is 'grey mould', usually due to *Botrytis cinerea*, the asexual state of another *Sclerotinia* relative, *Botryotinia fuckeliana*. This may induce a wide range of symptoms, including flower and bud rots, as well as diebacks of woody plants. The fluffy, greyish mould is usually quite noticeable, and may also be seen on stored fruit and dead or moribund plant parts. A black, sclerotial state is also common on dead stems of many herbaceous plants.

'Blights' have no precise definition, the term usually referring to sudden death of twigs or stems resulting from the rapid invasion of a pathogen. Bacteria are often to blame, but some blights are caused by fungus-induced diseases, such as 'raspberry cane blight' due to the ascomycete *Leptosphaeria coniothyrium*, and 'early blight' of potatoes and tomatoes due to another ascomycete, *Alternaria solani*. Perhaps the most important of the blights are those produced by fungus-like *Phytophthora* species. Their range is large, and they attack both woody species, including some of ornamental or forestry importance, and herbaceous plants, including commercial crops. *Phytophthora ramorum*, the cause of 'sudden oak death', has received a lot of publicity because of the severity of its effects on oaks in North America and the quarantine procedures introduced to prevent its spread to Britain. Other important examples of blights are considered below, in Chapter Nine, and in a substantial review by Buczacki & Harris (1998).

Potato late blight and the Irish famine

The most notorious of the *Phytophthora* pathogens is the potato late blight, *P. infestans*, which can also attack tomatoes (Fig. 51). The blight typically starts as black infection spots on leaves, quickly rotting the haulms and subsequently the potato tubers themselves. Once established it will also rot stored potatoes in clamps. Nowadays potato late blight is a serious hazard for potato growers, but a treatable one. When it first arrived in Europe in the 1840s, however, it came with all the virulence and mystery of a mediaeval plague. In Britain, the first news came in August 1845, when The Gardener's Chronicle reported that "a fatal malady has broken out among the potato crop. On all sides we hear of the destruction ... There is hardly a sound sample in Covent Garden

FIG 51. The potato late blight *Phytophthora infestans* also affects tomatoes and can cause rapid and severe damage to crops. It can be quite common at times (G. Kibby).

market." By September, the "potato murrain" had spread to Ireland, causing the Chronicle to stop the presses and declare the issue "of the first national importance; for where will Ireland be, in the event of a universal potato rot?"

In the 1840s, the Irish poor relied on potatoes as their staple diet, the average labourer typically eating 3–6 kilos per day and little else. When they rotted in the fields and the clamps, as they did in 1845 and again in 1846, the people faced disaster. It has been estimated that *Phytophthora infestans* caused over 1,000,000 deaths from starvation in Ireland, as well as the mass emigration of much of the rural population, and the economic ruin of the country. It took well over 100 years for the population of Ireland to climb back to its pre-1845 level.

The discovery, by the Rev. Miles Berkeley in England and Dr Jean Pierre Montagne in France, of the cause of late blight was a landmark in the history of plant pathology. At the start of the outbreak, it was generally assumed that the murrain was directly caused by heavy rain or by the degeneration of plants grown without rotation. Stranger theories included unspecified problems due to static electricity (generated by the vapours of steam engines), mortiferous miasmas rising from blind volcanoes in the interior of the earth, or "by simple eremacousis or excolation in consequence of a deficiency of vital energy". Berkeley, however, demonstrated that a particular fungus (described by Montagne) was always present on affected potatoes and moreover that this fungus (*Phytophthora infestans*) was the cause of the blight, and not something that followed in its wake. This and other investigations into potato late blight helped found the new science of plant pathology and led, later in the century, to the development of fungicides as control agents (see Chapter 14).

Berkeley's original specimens from the Irish potato famine are still retained in the herbarium at Kew and have been used in molecular detective work to discover where the disease came from (probably Mexico) and how it is related to modern strains (Ristaino, 1998; Kleiner, 2001).

Damping-off diseases

'Damping-off' is one of the commonest diseases destructive to seedlings, affecting a wide range of herbaceous and woody plants. Symptoms vary according to plant species and the pathogens responsible, but seedlings commonly collapse due to rotting at the stem base, and become susceptible to attack by grey mould (*Botrytis cinerea*) and other parasites. Damping-off is mainly caused by species of *Pythium* and by *Rhizoctonia solani* which are commonly present in soil. The wide host range of these fungi and the ability of both species to live as saprotrophs in soil may severely hinder successful control of these diseases. Improved drainage of soil, avoidance of overcrowding of seedlings and use of sterilised soil in greenhouse situations are recommended.

Virus vectors

Many, possibly most, fungi carry viruses. In a few species these viruses (harmless in the fungi) can be passed on to crops and other plants, some causing significant diseases. The chytrid *Olpidium brassicae*, for example, carries *lettuce big vein virus* (viruses have English names, not Latin binomials), whilst the chromistan *Polymyxa graminis* carries *barley yellow mosaic virus*. Extensive research has been undertaken on these diseases and the role which fungi play in their transmission (Adams, 2002). Altogether, around 30 viruses are known to have such fungus vectors, and more may yet be discovered.

GALLS, CANKERS, AND WITCHES' BROOMS

The development of abnormal tissue, causing swellings of various kinds, occurs in response to a wide range of organisms, including bacteria, nematodes, insects, mites, and fungi. Such abnormal development, involving either 'hypertrophy' (cell enlargement) or 'hyperplasia' (cell proliferation), is generally called a 'gall'.

Galls caused by rusts

Among the *Basidiomycota*, perhaps the most significant 'cecidogenic' (gall-causing) species belong to the rust fungi. Many of these induce hypertrophy or hyperplasia of the host tissue at some stage in their life cycle. Indeed, almost 100 species of British rusts are considered to be gall-causers, the most important listed in Preece & Hick (1994). It is usually the aecidial stage of the rust which is cecidogenic, the characteristic 'cluster cups' often developing on abnormally swollen host tissue parasitised by species of *Puccinia* and *Uromyces*. Aecidial *Puccinia graminis*, for example, causes marked hypertrophy of the leaves of barberry, as does the same stage of *P. urticata*, commonly found on the leaves of nettles in spring. Other stages of these rusts, on grasses and sedges respectively, do not cause galls. It is rather less common for other stages of the rust life cycle to be cecidogenic, though telial stages may do so and there are some impressive examples of these amongst the British rusts. *Puccinia adoxae*, for example, a common rust on moschatel in spring, occurs only as telia, causing distinctly swollen stems and petioles and blistered leaves, and often abundantly present in local patches in a host population. The colourful and striking telial stages of *Gymnosporangium* species, which occur on conspicuously swollen branches of juniper, provide another example (Fig. 52).

FIG 52. The rust *Gymnosporangium clavariiforme* develops striking, yellow, cylindrical masses of teliospores on swollen branches of juniper. Its alternate host is hawthorn (B. Spooner).

Edible galls and other strange smuts

Many smut fungi are also cecidogenic (see Fig. 48). One of the most spectacular is *Ustilago maydis* on sweetcorn, inducing large swellings, often over 10 cm long, in the inflorescence and other aerial parts of the host plant. Surprisingly these galls are edible, being considered a delicacy in Mexico, where they are known as 'cuitlacoche'. Another smut gall used as food is *Ustilago esculenta* which galls wild rice (*Zizania aquatica*) in Taiwan, China and Japan. The smut affects the buds, and the young shoots are markedly hypertrophied as a result. Wild rice is cultivated in Taiwan especially for the galls, the smut being perennial in the rhizomes of the grass.

Other smut galls are less obvious. *Microbotryum violaceum*, the common anther smut of campions (Fig. 53) and other *Caryophyllaceae*, induces slight swelling of the anthers but is of interest for causing hermaphroditism in its hosts, a phenomenon known as 'parasitic castration'. The smut sporulates only in the anthers but causes stamens to be formed in female flowers of dioecious hosts. Linnaeus, unaware of the true cause of such stamens, described the resulting plants as if they were a new taxon, 'forma *hermaphroditis*'. It is not the only example of new taxa having been described based on smut-induced modifications.

Other secondary effects produced by smuts on their host plants are equally surprising. These were ably summarised by Fischer & Holton (1957) and include 'phyllody' (transformation of flower parts into leaves), dwarfing or, more rarely, gigantism, reduced root development, induced 'tillering' (proliferation of side shoots), and seedling deformation. Also of interest is modification of host resistance to other fungal parasites. The smut *Tilletia caries*, for example, causes wheat to become more susceptible to stripe rust, but less susceptible to powdery mildew infection.

FIG 53. Anther smut *Microbotryum violaceum*, common in the anthers of red campion *Silene dioica* (P. Roberts).

Leaf apples and antler galls

Another group with important gall-inducing representatives is the *Exobasidiales*, simple heterobasidiomycetous fungi in which the mycelium is endophytic (growing within the host tissue). Fruiting bodies are not produced, but instead basidia are developed directly on the surface of host plants, often emerging through the stomata on the underside of leaves. Most of the host plants are members of the *Ericaceae*, especially species of *Rhododendron* and *Vaccinium*. Parasitised leaves or shoots frequently turn bright red and are sometimes variously thickened or swollen, making infected plants easy to spot. *Exobasidium vaccinii* is the most frequent such species in Britain, locally common in stands of bilberry. A few of the *Exobasidiales* produce much more conspicuous galls. Amongst the largest and most familiar in Britain are *Exobasidium japonicum*, causing fleshy white leaf galls on garden species of *Rhododendron*, and *E. camelliae* which swells leaves of *Camellia* to such a spectacular degree that they resemble apples (Fig. 54). In the Mediterranean and (especially) in the Canary Islands, a further species, *Laurobasidium lauri*, produces massive, antler-like stem galls on branches of laurel trees (*Laurus azorica*) (Fig. 55). The European *Exobasidiales*, reviewed by Ing (1994a), include at least 23 gall-causing species, 11 of which occur in the British Isles.

Pocket plums and witches' brooms

The lack of a fruiting body is equally characteristic of members of the ascomycetous order *Taphrinales*. These are obligate parasites of ferns and dicotyledons, often causing leaf or fruit galls, or a proliferation of twiggy growth (popularly called 'witches' brooms'). Some species are highly conspicuous, for example *T. deformans* which forms bright red, thickened and blistered leaves on almond and peach, a condition known as 'peach leaf curl'. Another species, *T. pruni*, is the cause of 'pocket plum' disease of sloes and plums, in which the asci develop over the surface of swollen young fruits. These galled fruits can be locally frequent in the late spring and summer. *Taphrina padi* causes similar fruit galls on bird-cherry (*Prunus padus*), but is much less common. *Taphrina alni* produces colourful tongue-like galls on alder catkins (Fig. 80), and was once thought to be rare in Britain, but is now more widespread and appears to be spreading. In woody hosts some *Taphrina*

FIG 54. *Exobasidium camelliae* infects the leaves of *Camellia* species causing highly conspicuous galls which often resemble apples. In Britain the fungus is found mostly in south-west England (B. Spooner).

FIG 55. The distinctive antler-like galls caused by *Laurobasidium lauri* on the trunk of *Lauris azorica*. The fungus is found only on this host and is quite common in the Canary Islands (B. Spooner).

species induce witches' brooms, that on birches, caused by *T. betulina*, being particularly conspicuous on leafless trees during the winter. *Taphrina* species are also associated with ferns, some of which also induce broom-like growths (Chapter 13).

Club-root and other galls

Some members of the *Chromista* and *Protozoa* also cause galls. Most of the former are also parasites of algae (see Chapter 11), but amongst the *Protozoa* is the economically important genus *Plasmodiophora*, as well as the related genera *Sorosphaera*, *Spongospora*, and *Tetramyxa* (all *Plasmodiophorales*). These are parasites of vascular plants, infecting roots and stems and often causing marked swellings. *Plasmodiophora brassicae*, responsible for 'club-root disease' of cabbage and other *Cruciferae*, is common and causes substantial problems to gardeners and commercial growers. The roots of infected plants are distorted, with large, irregular swellings, and the plants themselves are often stunted, readily wilt during the day, and may eventually die. The fungus is difficult to eradicate and may persist in the soil as resting spores for many years. *Spongospora subterranea* is also of economic importance, attacking roots and tubers of potatoes and tomatoes, causing 'powdery scab' disease. It too has long-lasting resting spores and may be difficult to eradicate.

Cankers and conks

True cankers occur only on woody plants, and are lesions resulting from the death of the cambium where no new bark is formed. They may be caused by bacteria or by various fungi which induce abnormally developed, hypertrophied tissue. Commonly, the canker enlarges each year as the fungus continues to spread around the infected branch or twig. This may sometimes be entirely girdled by the canker, resulting in die-back. Many fungi from unrelated groups are canker-forming but amongst the better-known species are two ascomycetes, *Nectria galligena* and *Lachnellula willkommii*. The former causes a serious canker of apple and pear trees, and is also responsible for the large cankers frequently seen on ash trunks and branches. *Lachnellula willkommii* causes larch canker which may be commercially damaging in plantation trees.

A specific canker-like development not uncommon on the trunks of birch trees in parts of Scotland and northern England is caused by the poroid fungus *Inonotus obliquus*. The fungus produces conspicuous 'conks', swellings on the surface of living trunks having dark, rough bark, although the fruitbody itself is not developed until after the death of the tree. The species is the source of a possible anti-cancer agent (see Chapter 16).

FUNGI PARASITIC ON OTHER FUNGI

It is perhaps no surprise to discover that fungi parasitise each other as readily as they parasitise plants and animals, but the extent and variety of these interfungal relationships is quite remarkable. Almost every group of fungi, from the larger toadstools to inconspicuous moulds, contains its wolves in sheeps' clothing: predators ready and able to attack and assimilate their own kind.

Much of this predation goes unseen and its true extent is yet to be discovered. In some cases, too, the nature of the relationship is unclear. Take, for example, the bolete *Boletus parasiticus* and its 'host', the common earthball, *Scleroderma citrinum*. Here the parasitism seems so obvious that it is celebrated in the very name of the fungus. Yet Rayner *et al.* (1985) have asserted that *B. parasiticus* is non-parasitic and merely requires the presence of the *Scleroderma* to stimulate fruiting, so that the relationship may be neutral or mutually beneficial rather than antagonistic. This has, however, been questioned by Redhead *et al.* (1994).

Another visible association of fruitbodies involves the polypore *Phaeolus schweinitzii*, frequent at the base of old conifers, and the rare bolete *Pulveroboletus lignicola*. The latter, known from less than a dozen records in the British Isles, seems only to occur with the former suggesting some sort of relationship between the two.

Similar field observations suggest additional relationships among macrofungi, possibly of a parasitic nature. The poroid fungus *Skeletocutis carneogrisea*, for example, commonly grows on or close to fruitbodies of *Trichaptum abietinum*, a very common violaceous polypore found in swarms on fallen conifer trunks and logs. The *Skeletocutis* species was unknown in

Britain until the apparent relationship was pointed out in a standard text (Ryvarden & Gilbertson, 1994). Since then, over twenty records of *Skeletocutis carneogrisea* have been sent to Kew from around the country, suggesting that the association previously went unnoticed but is in fact a common one.

Other hidden relationships may occur when fungi compete for the same resources. In most cases this involves antagonistic responses, rather than parasitism, such as the release of chemicals which restrict or curtail the growth of competitors. On occasion, however, there is direct evidence of hyphal interference involving a form of specialised parasitism. This has been demonstrated (Rayner *et al.*, 1987) in the bracket fungus *Lenzites betulinus*. *Lenzites* is typically a secondary coloniser of dead birch wood, gaining access by attacking and destroying the hyphae of a primary coloniser, the very common, non-specialist bracket fungus *Trametes versicolor* (the 'many-zoned polypore'). The interesting thing here is that the *Lenzites* is primarily a wood-rotting saprotroph. It attacks the *Trametes* purely to remove competition and gain access to its food resource. This has been termed 'secondary resource capture' and may be much more commonplace than presently known.

Piggy-back toadstools

A few toadstools are much less secretive about their parasitism and actually grow directly on the fruitbodies of their hosts. The 'piggy-back toadstools', *Asterophora lycoperdoides* and *A. parasitica*, are prime examples, obligate parasites commonly found on the old fruitbodies of *Russula* species, most commonly on *Russula nigricans* and related blackening *Russula* species. Both *Asterophora* species produce abundant powdery masses of asexual chlamydospores. These are larger and more thick-walled than normal basidiospores and appear to persist long enough to reinfect new host fruitbodies as and when they arise.

The rare *Volvariella surrecta* (Fig. 56) is another conspicuous toadstool which grows on the caps of its host, in this case the clouded agaric *Clitocybe nebularis*, a large and common late season woodland toadstool. However, whether it is an obligate parasite, or may sometimes develop as a host specific saprotroph is unclear, since the *Clitocybe* is frequently decomposing when the *Volvariella* produces its fruitbodies. The same is true for a group of small *Collybia* species, including *C. cookei* and *C. tuberosa*, which arise from

FIG 56. The rare parasitic toadstool *Volvariella surrecta*, showing its conspicuous basal volva, growing on the caps of the much commoner woodland species *Clitocybe nebularis* (P. Livermore).

the remains of rotting toadstools. Some of these *Collybia* species produce small tuber-like sclerotia, densely agglutinated, thick-walled hyphae, which appear to serve the same function as chlamydospores in *Asterophora*, persisting in the soil and leaf litter to reinfect host fruitbodies when they appear.

Squamanita: the toadstool chimaera

Perhaps the strangest and certainly the rarest of the toadstool parasites are species of the genus *Squamanita*. When first described these were thought to be ordinary toadstools, though with a number of puzzling, sometimes contradictory features which made their systematic placement difficult. It has now been shown (Redhead *et al.*, 1994) that they are in fact parasitic toadstools, unique amongst agarics in systemically infecting and galling the host, and replacing the cap and gills of the host fruitbody with their own cap and gills. In effect, the fruitbodies are chimaeras, most of the stem belonging to the host, the rest to the parasite. In *Squamanita paradoxa*, an occasional species in the British Isles, this is quite obvious, once pointed out, since the host species, *Cystoderma amianthinum*, has a distinctive, densely scaly stem, also seen in specimens of the *Squamanita*. Indeed, the 'join' between host stem and parasite cap can sometimes be conspicuous.

Heterobasidiomycetes: the secret fungal parasites

Parasitism is particularly common amongst the heterobasidiomycetes, the largest of which are sometimes called 'jelly fungi'. The bright yellow *Tremella mesenterica*, for example, is common on dead twigs and branches, particularly of gorse. It is now known to be parasitic on species of *Peniophora*, which form reddish to grey or violaceous patches on the undersides of the same twigs and branches. The *Tremella* parasitises the mycelium of the host, hidden within the wood. Turn over a branch with the *Tremella* on, and a *Peniophora* will often be found fruiting on the underside. A second large, bright yellow species, *Tremella aurantia*, not uncommon in Britain but only discovered here in the 1990s, parasitises the abundant, bracket-like *Stereum hirsutum* which grows in large tiers on old deciduous trunks and logs (Fig. 57). A related species, *Tremella encephala*, attacks *Stereum sanguinolentum* on conifers. Both these *Tremella* species parasitise the fruitbodies of their host, rather than the underlying mycelium. Indeed, if a specimen of *Tremella encephala* is cut, a hard whitish 'kernel' will be found in the centre, surrounded by an outer gelatinous layer. This 'kernel' is all that is left of the parasitised *Stereum* fruitbody, completely enveloped by the *Tremella*.

An obscure group of fungi related to *Tremella* and belonging to the genus *Syzygospora*, are also parasites but, unlike *Tremella*, mostly specialise in agarics. A favourite host in Britain is the common woodland toadstool, *Collybia dryophila*. When attacked by the parasite *Syzygospora tumefaciens*, large semi-gelatinous galls are formed on the cap and sometimes the gills and stem of the host, the galls containing the basidia and basidospores of the parasite. When first noticed in Britain, these peculiar fruitbodies were dismissed as monstrosities, their true nature being discovered only later.

FIG 57. The gelatinous, orange-yellow fruitbodies of *Tremella aurantia* resemble those of *T. mesenterica* but are firmer in texture and parasitise the bracket-like fruitbodies of *Stereum hirsutum* (P. Roberts).

Ascomycetes and parasitic moulds

Parasitism as a way of life is even more prevalent among the ascomycetes, though the majority are inconspicuous and only recognisable with a microscope. An exception is the genus *Cordyceps*, several species of which parasitise the underground fruitbodies of hart's truffles (*Elaphomyces muricatus* and *E. granulatus*). The mycelium of the *Cordyceps* penetrates and takes over the truffle, later producing large drumstick or club-like fruitbodies which rise above the soil surface to release their spores. Interestingly, most other *Cordyceps* species are insect parasites (see below), some attacking underground moth pupae in a very similar manner. It is worth remembering that both insects and fungi contain the structural material chitin, and from a parasite's point of view may not be too dissimilar. Three species occur on *Elaphomyces* in Britain. Perhaps the commonest is *C. ophioglossoides* recognised by its greenish-yellow stromatic fruitbodies with cylindrical fertile head (ophioglossoides means 'like a serpent's tongue').

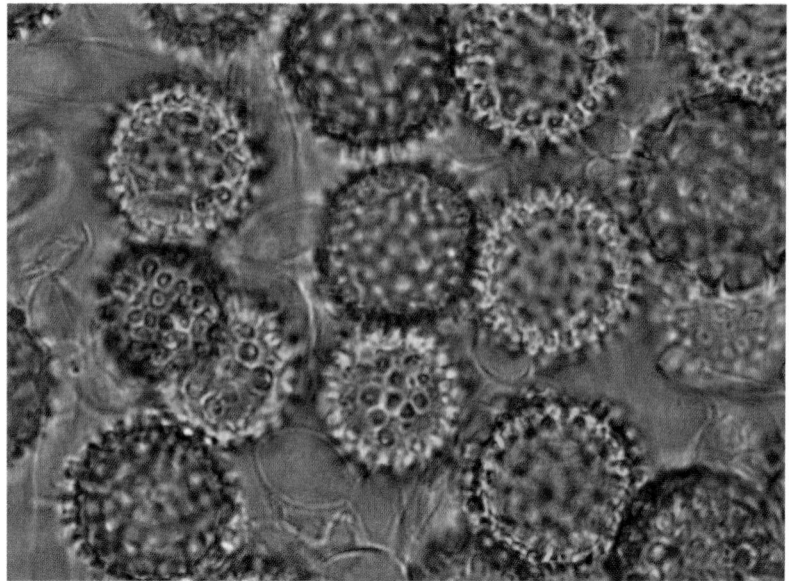

FIG 58. The distinctive chlamydospores formed by *Hypomyces chrysospermus*, a common parasite of boletes, rotting the flesh of the host and developing a powdery mass of spores at maturity (RBG Kew).

Cordyceps capitata and *C. longisegmentis* both differ in having drumstick-like fruitbodies.

Boletes are often attacked by ascomycetes of the genus *Hypomyces*. Both the perfect, ascospore-producing state and the mould-like asexual state may be involved. *Hypomyces chrysospermus* is a particularly conspicuous species, turning boletes into bright yellow powdery masses which collapse on touch. The powdery mass consists of globose, warted chlamydospores (Fig. 58), the sexual state of the fungus being rarely if ever developed in Britain. This fungus provides a good example of necrotrophic parasitism, in which the parasite wholly destroys its host. Several other *Hypomyces* species are found in Britain, parasites on various agarics and bracket fungi. Amongst these, *H. aurantius* is quite common, particularly on the bracket *Trametes versicolor*, producing an orange growth over the host surface. *Hypomyces rosellus* is similar but is deep pink or violaceous. It can be found on various agarics and bracket fungi and is also the cause of 'cobweb disease' in cultivated mushrooms, so called for the coarse mycelium which rapidly spreads over infected crops, rotting the fruitbodies.

Also notable are three other *Hypomyces* species which are found exclusively on fruitbodies of *Russula* and *Lactarius*. The parasites distort the host fruitbody, abort the gill tissue, and form a usually brightly-coloured layer over the underside of the cap, completely replacing the gills. Infected toadstools have firm, solid flesh which does not readily decay. The most frequent species in Britain are *H. lateritius*, mainly on *Lactarius deliciosus*, and *H. lithuanicus* on *Lactarius torminosus* and *L. pubescens*. *Hypomyces luteovirens* (Fig. 59) is similarly destructive to some species of *Russula*. In North America, a closely related species, *H. lactifluorum*, turns infected fruitbodies entirely bright reddish-orange. These are popularly known as 'lobster mushrooms' and are surprisingly edible, so much so that they are now commercially imported into Britain (see Chapter 17).

FIG 59. *Hypomyces luteovirens*, parasitic on species of *Russula*, forming greenish-yellow mycelium and fruitbodies. Host fruitbodies are distorted and gill development is suppressed (B. Spooner).

Several other fungal diseases are all too well known to mushroom growers. *Mycogone perniciosa*, the cause of 'wet bubble disease', is particularly destructive. It can turn young button mushrooms into large, cauliflower-like distortions, oozing brownish droplets. Some species of *Verticillium* may be equally bad, notably *V. fungicola*, responsible for 'dry bubble disease'. This is one of the most serious fungal infections of mushroom crops, causing distortion and discoloration of fruitbodies which remain dry and do not rot. It is capable of destroying an entire crop within 2–3 weeks. Unlike these fruitbody parasites, the false truffle *Diehliomyces microsporus* parasitises the mushroom mycelium. It has small, irregular fruitbodies no more than a centimetre or so across and has only been found as a pest in mushroom beds, never in the wild. It can seriously reduce crop yield, but is now rare in Britain.

Zygomycetes as fungal parasites

The zygomycetes are perhaps best known as parasites of invertebrates (see below). However, they also include a surprising number of specialised fungal parasites. These exhibit a range of strategies, and include both necrotrophs and biotrophs, many of them being parasites of other zygomycetes. Most belong to two orders, the *Dimargaritales* and *Zoopagales*. The *Dimargaritales* are composed solely of species parasitic on other fungi, with three genera, *Dimargaris*, *Dispira* and *Tieghemiomyces*, whereas within the *Zoopagales* only *Piptocephalis* and *Syncephalis* are fungal parasites. Species of these five genera mainly attack members of the *Mucorales*, usually those found on dung, though some have ascomycete hosts.

Other zygomycetes, notably species of *Spinellus*, are found on agarics, usually species of *Collybia* and *Mycena*. Although they occur on moribund fruitbodies, they are probably necrotrophic parasites, killing their hosts and fruiting on the decaying remains.

Fungi on rusts

The sori of rust fungi are prone to attack by parasitic microfungi, the majority of which are specific to rusts and not found elsewhere. In Britain they include at least two species of *Cladosporium*, *C. aecidiicola* and *C. uredinicola*, and three species of another hyphomycete genus, *Tuberculina*.

The *Cladosporium* species occur, as their names suggest, on the aecidia or uredinia of various rusts and are not otherwise host-specific. *Tuberculina persicina* is common on many rust aecidia, but *T. maxima* appears to be restricted to aecidia of *Cronartium* species, and *T. sbrozzii* occurs only on sori of *Puccinia vincae*. The last causes a pale, pinkish coating to the sori and seems to be constantly present on this rust which is quite common on greater periwinkle, its only host.

Perhaps the most abundant and ubiquitous of the rust parasites is the ascomycete *Eudarluca caricis*. In Britain, this is almost always found in its conidial state known as *Sphaerellopsis filum*, which produces tiny, blackish fruitbodies often densely clustered in the rust sorus. Another rust associate is the tiny discomycete *Mollisina oedema*. This seems to be strictly host-limited and occurs only on the telial sori of *Phragmidium violaceum* on bramble leaves. The tiny, clustered fruitbodies are developed in spring or early summer on dead or fallen leaves and it may be that the species is more of a saprotroph rather than a true parasite. Overseas, one of the odder examples is the hyphomycete *Verticillium lecanii*, perhaps better known as a parasite of scale insects and aphids. Rather surprisingly, it is also a parasite of the economically important coffee rust, *Hemileia vastatrix*, and is capable of attacking many other rust species. It directly infects uredospores of the rust and may completely prevent development of the sori, making it of potential use as a biocontrol agent.

Parasites of slime moulds

Despite the mostly small size of their fruitbodies, myxomycetes are an important substratum for a range of parasitic fungi, some generalist, some specialist. Worldwide, about thirty such parasites have been recorded, and well over half of these are now known in Britain. All are ascomycetes, most of them belonging to the family *Hypocreaceae*. They include several species of *Nectriopsis* and anamorphic stages in the genera *Acremonium*, *Gliocladium*, and *Verticillium*. Most parasitise a wide range of myxomycetes. For example, *Verticillium rexianum*, the anamorph of *Nectriopsis exigua*, is quite common on at least 19 genera of myxomycetes, and *Polycephalomyces tomentosus*, the anamorph of *Byssostilbe stilbigera*, is equally plurivorous. In contrast, a few species seem to be much more restricted. The rare *Nectriopsis violacea*, for example, only parasitises *Fuligo septica*, coating its host with its distinctive violaceous mycelium.

'Mouldy' myxomycetes can be found quite commonly and are not too difficult to identify, thanks to useful keys by Ing (1974) and Rogerson & Stephenson (1993).

Fungicolous slime moulds

Several myxomycete species are obligate fungivores, attacking the fruit-bodies of a range of larger basidiomycetes and some lichens. Chief amongst these are some *Badhamia* species, especially *B. utricularis*, a widespread and common species found on various corticioid and bracket fungi as well as agarics. It has a rather conspicuous, bright yellow plasmodium and later develops grey, lime-rich clusters of stalked, pendant sporangia. *Badhamia capsulifera* and the much rarer *B. nitens* are also fungivorous, as are a few species of the related genus *Physarum*, though these are mainly tropical (Ing, 1994b).

Lichenicolous parasites

Lichens, with their long-lived, exposed thalli, are prey to an exceptionally large number of fungal parasites, though until comparatively recently many of these were unstudied and unknown. For example, almost all of the forty or so known heterobasidiomycetous parasites of lichens were first described in the 1990s by a single researcher (Diederich, 1996) who effectively discovered a whole new and previously unsuspected ecosystem. Twelve of these new species have now been found in the British Isles, all belonging to *Syzygospora* and *Tremella* in the *Tremellales*. Altogether, well over 1500 species of lichenicolous fungi have now been described worldwide (Lawrey & Diederich, 2003).

Initial investigations into the lifestyles of lichenicolous fungi actually suggest a wide variety of biotrophic and necrotrophic relationships, with some parasites causing galls, others altering the whole appearance of the host lichen. Some species actually steal the algal partner of their hosts for their own use, gradually taking over the lichen. This happens, for example, with *Arthrorhaphis citrinella* which parasitises *Baeomyces rufus*, eventually capturing the photobiont and forming its own thallus. Others, however,

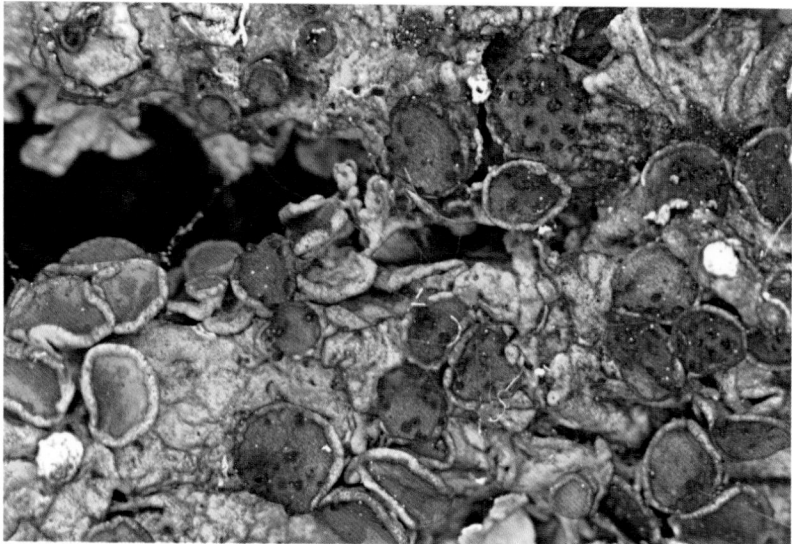

FIG 60. *Lichenoconium xanthoriae*, a parasite in the yellowish fruitbodies of the common lichen *Xanthoria parietina*, forming numerous tiny, blackish pycnidia (B. Spooner).

appear to enter a stable relationship with their hosts which they may use merely to gain some living space, like permanent half-tolerated guests. A few of these commensal parasites are lichenised themselves.

Most lichenicolous fungi are ascomycetes (including conidial stages), with over 380 British species recorded to date (Hawksworth, 2003). A few of these are common and widespread, such as *Lichenoconium xanthoriae* which forms tiny, black pycnidia in fruitbodies of *Xanthoria* and some other lichen species (Fig. 60), though they are not always conspicuous and even with a hand lens are rarely easy to find. Some gall-causing species induce only slight hypertrophy of the host thallus. The fruitbodies of *Polycoccum peltigerae* on *Peltigera*, for example, are sunken in the slightly thickened and discoloured host thallus and are consequently rather inconspicuous. In contrast, species such as *Abrothallus parmeliarum* and *Refractohilum galligenum* cause much more noticeable, convex or convoluted galls.

Other than those noted above, basidiomycetous lichen parasites are few, with less than twenty species in Britain. Amongst the commonest and most conspicuous is *Marchandiomyces corallinum*. This forms tiny, pinkish cushions on various lichens, most frequently on *Lecanora conizaeoides* found on the trunks of many trees. *Marchandiomyces* was long considered to be a genus of ascomycetous affinity, but recent molecular studies have suggested a relationship to the rhizoctonia-forming basidiomycetes. *Biatoropsis usnearum* which galls various *Usnea* species, was also originally misidentified as an ascomycete, but has now been shown to be a heterobasidiomycete with auricularioid basidia. The corticioid fungus *Athelia arachnoidea* is also quite commonly seen overgrowing *Lecanora* on tree trunks, appearing as whitish, cobweb-like patches.

TOADSTOOL TERATOLOGY AND MONSTER MUSHROOMS

The abnormal development of fruitbodies of larger fungi, especially agarics, has long been the subject of curiosity. A strange specimen of the cultivated mushroom (*Agaricus bisporus*) which bore another perfectly formed but inverted specimen on its cap was described in the Gardener's Chronicle as long ago as the 1850s , though an even earlier illustration of abnormal toadstools was published by Sowerby in 1799. Sowerby's plate depicted specimens of the meadow waxcap *Hygrocybe pratensis* with fused fruitbodies and proliferate gills which he referred to as 'somewhat sportive'.

Such teratological developments have a variety of causes involving physical, physiological, and perhaps genetic factors. These are little understood, though van der Aa (1997) discussed some aspects in relation to development of the fruitbody primordium. Abnormalities due to chemical pollution and radiation, notably following the Chernobyl disaster in the Ukraine, have also been documented. Growth in the absence of light, a frequent occurrence in mines and caves (Chapter 13), is also known to cause strange forms quite unlike typical fruitbodies. Other abnormalities are akin to galls and may be induced by viruses and mycoplasmas or even bacteria. Potentially, it would seem that any fungus may at times exhibit teratological fruitbodies.

A catalogue published by Penzig (1922) included well over 200 different species for which abnormalities had been reported at that time. Perhaps the most comprehensive work on abnormal toadstools was, however, compiled by Worsdall (1915), as part of his classic two-volume treatment of plant teratology. Worsdall recognised different teratological forms under seven main headings broadly including abnormal branching, hymenium inversion, fusion and abbreviation. Abnormal branching occurs especially in fruitbodies which have developed in the dark, including the strange stagshorn-like structures frequently reported for *Lentinus* and *Polyporus*. Some may be so proliferate as to form dense, coralloid masses. Fusion of developing fruitbodies is much more common. This may occur when fruitbodies develop in intimate contact, and is seen most frequently in species which normally produce tufted fruitbodies. It may be due to fusion in the primordial stage and can lead to a range of structures. Worsdall (1915) for example figured specimens of the field mushroom, *Agaricus campestris*, which were fused at their stipe bases and again at their cap centres. Linked with such development is the proliferation of fruitbodies, seen particularly in agarics, in which a second, and rarely even a third fruitbody, develops from the cap of the main one, producing structures known as 'twins' or 'triples'. In many such cases, the secondary cap is inverted and sessile, or sometimes even stalked, though still producing gills which bear normal spores. A good example of a twin development of *Lepista nuda*, the common wood blewit, was illustrated by Ramel & Webster (1995). In this case, a small but well-formed fruitbody about 3 cm high occurred on the cap of a specimen about twice that size. Another type of inversion of the hymenium may also occur in which a distinctly morchelloid (honeycomb-like) form is produced. Such development has been entirely misinterpreted at times and species erroneously described on the basis of abnormal specimens. *Laccaria laccata* and more especially *L. amethystina* are prone to production of such grossly distorted fruitbodies in a variety of irregular shapes. It seems likely that such distortion is due to infection by virus or mycoplasma though this has apparently not yet been demonstrated. However, microcephalous fruitbodies, with long stem and tiny cap, are well known in this genus, and these as well as irregularly warted caps of chanterelle (*Cantharellus cibarius*) have been shown to be due to a virus infection.

PARASITES OF ANIMALS

Parasites of insects and other invertebrates

Fungal parasites of insects ('entomopathogenic' fungi) have been known for centuries, indeed since at least the ninth century judging from accounts of the silk-worm industry in Japan. Silkworms, larvae of the moth *Bombyx mori*, are susceptible to several fungal diseases, most importantly those referred to as 'muscardine', often common in rearing houses. Muscardine is due to *Beauveria bassiana* and perhaps also to other fungi, such as species of *Metarhizium* and *Paecilomyces*, which produce a superficial, white 'coat' of mycelium and spores on infected larvae. The dead larvae, known as 'Bombyx Batrycatus' are believed to have a wide range of medicinal properties and are even traded commercially.

The main groups of entomopathogenic fungi were outlined in Samson *et al.* (1988), who listed 52 genera ranged in *Chytridiomycota*, *Oomycota*, *Zygomycota*, and *Ascomycota*, including anamorphic fungi. Only the *Basidiomycota* among the major phyla are poorly represented, although the genus *Septobasidium* (see Chapter Five) is a notable exception.

Amongst the known genera of fungi on insects, the great majority are comprised exclusively of obligate entomopathogenic species. Only *Nectria*, with its anamorphs *Acremonium*, *Fusarium*, and *Verticillium*, has fewer insect parasites than plant parasites and saprotrophs.

The chytrids and *Oomycota* are mainly aquatic (see Chapter 11). They include many saprotrophic species as well as parasites of a wide range of organisms, with entomopathogenic species occurring mostly on dipteran larvae.

Pathogenesis

All entomopathogenic microorganisms other than fungi infect their hosts via the mid-gut. Fungi are different, infecting instead though the host cuticle. The way in which they do this has three phases. The first is attachment and germination of the spore on the insect cuticle, the second is penetration of the host body wall, and the third is the development of the fungus within the host body. Contact with the host may be by chance for most fungi with airborne spores, but for oomycetes such as *Aphanomyces* with motile zoospores there is a chemical attractant which utilises metabolites produced by the host. Commonly, fungal spores appear to be passively attached to the host cuticle but in many cases they have a mucilaginous coat which assists in the adhesion process. Others have a lipoprotein surface layer which facilitates attachment, and in some there appear be specific processes which involve mutual host-fungus recognition. Spore germination requires appropriate conditions of humidity and temperature, which vary according to the fungus involved, but may also involve the availability of appropriate nutrients on the host cuticle, and be influenced by the presence of various lipids, phenols and other compounds. After germination, the fungus must successfully penetrate the host cuticle and body wall, a difficult and uncertain process given the thickness and chemistry of these structures, and one which usually requires the production of a complex range of enzymes. Once inside the host body the fungus must be able to overcome the natural defence mechanisms of the host, another uncertain process for which success is not guaranteed. If successful, the fungus continues to develop, eventually leading to death of the host due to various causes such as toxin production or starvation by gut paralysis or metabolic failure. After death of the host, the fungus grows as a saprobe, producing fruitbodies or some form of resting spores according to environmental conditions.

In some cases, notably *Cordyceps* and *Entomophthora*, the fungus affects the behaviour of the host, and the development of entomogenous species frequently occurs in time cycles directly linked to host numbers. The potential for biological control of insect pests using entomopathogenic fungi is therefore great, and is likely to become of increasing commercial significance (see Chapter 16).

Ecological importance

Entomogenous fungi can be found in all primary ecosystems as well as in agricultural environments, and may be abundant at times. They play an important role in regulating host populations and may also be significant in supplying a natural control of agricultural pest organisms. The latter has been well documented, particularly in the Americas and Africa. For example, in citrus orchards in Florida entomopathogenic fungi, including species of

Aschersonia and *Podonectria*, have been referred to as the 'friendly fungi' for their role in controlling scale insects and whitefly.

In aquatic environments, entomogenous fungi are mostly chytrids, such as *Coelomomyces* and other parasites of mosquito and midge larvae, or fungus-like *Oomycota*. Some species of *Entomophthorales* are also specialist pathogens of aquatic insects, particularly diptera, stoneflies and caddis flies, the bodies of their victims often to be seen on the water surface or in damp marginal litter. Their life cycles are highly adapted to the habitat with, for example, the production of stellate secondary conidia developed from branched primary conidia and adapted to impaction on their aquatic hosts.

In terrestrial ecosystems, it is perhaps the tropical rain forests that support the greatest diversity of insect pathogens. The genus *Cordyceps* reaches it evolutionary peak in such forests, and related genera such as *Hypocrella* and *Torrubiella* also occur commonly. Conversely, the common entomogenous genera of agricultural and secondary habitats, *Beauveria* and *Metarhizium*, are poorly represented in tropical forests. In temperate forests and non-forest habitats, *Cordyceps* species also occur, but species of *Entomophthorales* and other entomopathogens are usually more frequent.

Entomogenous fungi in the British isles

In the British Isles, entomogenous fungi, particularly those of commercial importance and the more common or conspicuous species, have been studied for well over a century. Petch (1932) published the first catalogue of British species, later enlarged and extended to include a total of 86 species, with the exclusion of the *Laboulbeniales* which were not regarded as pathogens. Slightly more recent are the host catalogues compiled by Leatherdale (1958, 1962, 1965), later updated with a fungus list (Leatherdale, 1970), which, whilst still useful for some groups, are now considerably out of date and also did not include *Laboulbeniales*. Many more have been reported since then and the total of entomogenous fungi currently known from Britain is probably in excess of 250 species.

Entomophthoraceae: insect controllers

Entomophthoraceous fungi (*Entomophthorales*) are obligate parasites found mainly on insects. They attack the living host, germ tubes from conidia penetrating the cuticle and forming hyphal structures which fill the haemocoel and invade other tissues, ultimately leading to death. The fungi may affect the host's behaviour, indicating a highly evolved and very specific association. An example is the remarkable influence *Entomophthora muscae* (Fig. 61) has on its host flies, affecting them in two ways according to whether conidia or resting spores are produced. Infected flies producing conidia die above ground in the late afternoon, conidial production being rapid and discharge being at night when conditions are ideal for germination. Infected flies producing resting spores move downwards into the soil, where conditions are suitable for the spores to overwinter and affect a new generation of flies emerging from pupae in the ground.

Aphids are susceptible to the greatest number of entomophthoraceous pathogens and infections may at times reach epidemic status, influenced by factors such as weather conditions and population density. Such infections may have significant effects, and these fungi have therefore been involved in

FIG 61. *Entomophthora muscae*, a parasite of muscid flies, showing the typical swollen abdomen of the host and thick, whitish layer of conidia. The fungus alters the behaviour of the host, causing it to die in a position favourable to the dispersal of the spores (B. Spooner).

developing biological controls, and in the preparation of mycopesticides.

Almost 200 species of *Entomophthorales* are known world-wide, with at least 70 recorded from Britain. The great majority are insect pathogens, but some attack other invertebrates including nematodes and tardigrades, and a few even occur on algae or ferns (see Tucker, 1991). Amongst the commonest are *E. muscae* which parasitises hoverflies and various other diptera, and *E. dipterigena* which attacks mosquitoes and small aquatic diptera. These may be conspicuous at times, particularly on hoverflies which sometimes die in swarms, and the bloated bodies of small gnats can often be found on the surface of ponds. Others are usually more difficult to find, and should be searched for amongst damp litter. However, identification often presents problems. No comprehensive account is available, though keys to *Entomophthora* by Waterhouse & Brady (1982) are still useful, and many species were dealt with in the revisionary work based on Swiss species by Keller (1988, 1991).

Cordyceps: the 'plant worms'

Species of *Cordyceps* (*Ascomycota*) have long been a source of strange fascination. In the British Isles, just eight entomogenous species have been recorded, some of which are rare and seldom collected, but worldwide over 100 species are known, mostly from the tropics. Many are striking, forming brightly coloured, upright, club-shaped structures. Fine illustrations by Kobayasi & Shimizu (1983) provide an insight into their diversity of form and structure. Most species develop on insects or spiders, although a few are parasitic on the truffle-like fruitbodies of species of *Elaphomyces* (see above). Their development on insects has led to common names such as 'caterpillar fungi', 'vegetable wasps', or 'plant worms', giving the appearance of strange composite organisms whose true nature was long a mystery.

Bizarrely, in China the species *Cordyceps sinensis* has been used as a tonic since ancient times, recently hitting the headlines as a result of the record-breaking achievements of Chinese athletes, whose diet was said to have included caterpillar fungi. It has also been used to alleviate a variety of ailments, including tuberculosis and anaemia. This fungus was first brought to England in 1842, where it was scientifically described by the Rev. M.J. Berkeley. *Cordyceps sinensis* is parasitic on larvae of the moth *Hepialus armoricanus*, killing the host after the larva has buried itself in readiness for pupation in the autumn. It develops in the stromatised larval body and fruits the following summer.

In Britain, the commonest of the entomogenous species is *C. militaris*. This develops attractive, bright orange, club-shaped fruitbodies on the buried larvae of lepidoptera in autumn. Also on lepidoptera are *C. gracilis*, a less common and less brightly coloured, spring-fruiting species which produces pale yellowish, club-shaped fruitbodies (Fig. 62), and *C. tuberculata*. Other British species occur on beetles, flies, and wasps and are generally rare. Indeed, *C. memorabilis*, on beetle larvae, appears to be known from only a single locality in Norfolk.

FIG 62. The upright, pale yellow fruitbodies of *Cordyceps gracilis* can be found in the spring and are parasitic on larvae of moths of the family *Hepialidae* (B. Spooner).

Hypocrella: colourful parasites of scale insects

Although almost exclusively tropical or sub-tropical, the abundance of *Hypocrella* species in appropriate habitats, their bright orange or yellow colours, and their close relationship to *Cordyceps*, makes them worth mentioning briefly. Unlike *Cordyceps* they have sessile, cushion-shaped fruitbodies and are specialised parasites of scale insects or whiteflies. Around 30 species have been described but, despite their conspicuous appearance, there is little recent work on the genus. In fact, an early monographic study by Petch (1921) is still important. It is the asexual states of *Hypocrella*, referred to the genus *Aschersonia*, which are most commonly found, though both states may occur together. The fungi develop their fruitbodies on the surfaces of living leaves and superficially appear to be plant parasites, though in fact they attack larval or pupal stages of their insect hosts. These are sometimes so totally obliterated that *Hypocrella* species were not even recognised as insect parasites by early collectors.

Laboulbeniales: little-known ectoparasites

The *Laboulbeniales* (*Ascomycota*) (Figs 63 & 64) comprise a large group of inconspicuous fungi which occur as obligate parasites on a wide range of arthropods, particularly insects. Beetles (*Coleoptera*) and flies (*Diptera*) are the most important host groups, but mites and millipedes are also host to a number of species. Over 2000 species of *Laboulbeniales* are now known, although they have been largely neglected by mycologists and many more species may await discovery. This seems especially true in the light of recent work on British species by Alex Weir which more than doubled the number of species from 45 known in 1985 to around 110 today.

Laboulbeniales are ectoparasites, lacking normal hyphae and comprising an organised cellular thallus on which the reproductive organs are borne. This thallus is attached to the exoskeleton of the host by means of a basal foot cell, but scarcely penetrates the host cuticle. Specially modified hyphal branches, designed to absorb nutrients from the host, have been observed in some genera, and it seems likely that all obtain their nutrition through such 'feeding cells'. The fungi appear to have no significant effects on their hosts, although damage to muscle and abdominal tissues has been reported for a few species, and some, including *Hesperomyces virescens*, have been linked

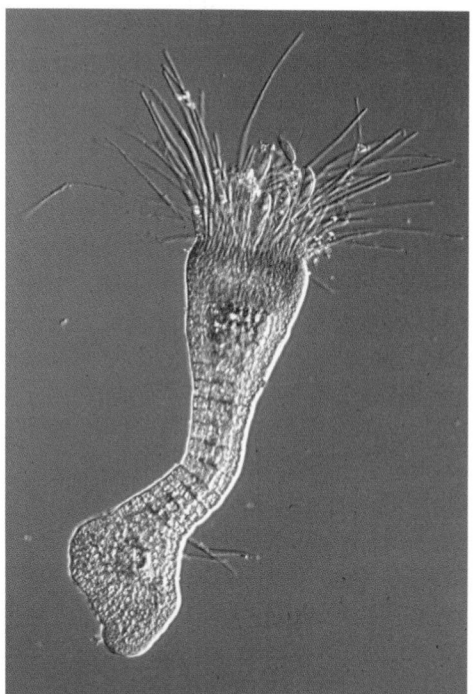

FIG 63. *Zodiomyces vorticellarius,* a distinctive species of *Laboulbeniales* with many-celled thallus and multiple 'tentacles'. It occurs widely through parts of Europe (though not Britain), Africa and the Americas on water beetles (*Hydrophilidae*) (A. Weir).

FIG 64. A species of *Laboulbenia* showing the distribution of the dark-coloured fruitbodies, scarcely more than 0.5 mm high, on the dorsal surface of a ground beetle in England. (A. Weir).

with premature mortality of their ladybird hosts. Most species are strictly host limited, and some occur only on a particular part of the host (position specific). Distribution is evidently by direct contact between individuals, although details of the process are lacking for most species.

The *Laboulbeniales* were unknown until the mid-19th century, the first of them, in the type genus *Laboulbenia*, not being described until 1853. Little interest was shown in these fungi until the pioneering studies carried out by Roland Thaxter at Harvard. The first of his papers appeared in 1890 and in 1896 he published a comprehensive monograph of the 152 species known at the time. Four further major additions to this monograph were published between then and 1931, the total work including over 1300 species and running to more than 1200 pages.

The first report of these fungi from Britain was not until 1909, when two species, *Laboulbenia vulgaris* and *Stigmatomyces purpureus*, were reported. As noted, at least 110 British species are now known. Knowledge of them elsewhere, especially in tropical regions, is even less than it was in Britain, and there can be little doubt that many species still remain to be documented.

Bee parasites

Batra *et al.* (1973) listed no less than 124 species of fungi known to occur in association with the nests of bees (*Apoidea*), including parasites as well as saprotrophic and mutualistic species. Some of the parasites are of economic importance since they attack honey bees (*Apis mellifera*) and pollinating species, such as the leaf-cutting bees (*Megachilidae*) and bumble-bees (*Bombidae*), but almost every kind of bee can be affected. Mould species in the genera *Aspergillus* and *Rhizopus* as well as the ascomycete *Bettsia alvei* (Fig. 65), a common hive fungus, have even been blamed for the decline of some bee species by infecting and destroying the provisions stored in the hive cells, hence killing the larvae that feed on them. Other parasites, including *Saccharomyces* and *Torulopsis* yeasts, *Trichothecium roseum*, and some species of *Aspergillus*, *Penicillium* and *Mucor*, directly and sometimes obligately infect and kill both larvae and adults. The yeast-like *Melanosella mors-apis* also infects honey bee queens, apparently causing 'melanosis', melanised patches of tissue around egg cells in the ovaries.

FIG 65. Conspicuous white mycelium of the ascomycete *Bettsia alvei* developed on the surface of honeycomb. The fungus utilises the larval food stores and produces toxins which may kill the larvae (J. Rickwood).

One of the best-known parasites is *Ascosphaera apis*, an ascomycete which attacks honey bee larvae causing a lethal disease known as 'chalk brood', characterised by the chalky-white appearance of the dead, mummified larvae. Although widespread and quite common especially in parts of Europe (including Britain) and in North America, the disease usually only infects part of a colony and can be kept under control by appropriate ventilation of the hive and avoidance of damp conditions. The bees are apparently capable of doing this themselves, deliberately increasing the temperature of infected hives to a level too high for fungal growth. Chalk brood nevertheless weakens the colony and may significantly reduce honey production. Three other species, *Ascosphaera aggregata*, *A. major*, and *A. proliperda* cause similar diseases in leaf-cutting bees (*Megachile* spp) and mason bees (*Osmia* spp). Another fungal disease, 'stone brood', is caused by species of *Aspergillus*, especially *A. flavus* and *A. fumigatus*. The fungus kills the larvae before pupation, transforming them into hard, stone-like objects, and is also able to attack the adults. Fortunately, although widespread, this disease is less common and of less commercial importance than chalk brood.

FUNGI THAT PREY ON ANIMALS

The nematode-trappers

Nematodes (eelworms) are probably the most abundant and ubiquitous animals on earth. Soil and leaf litter can contain up to 20,000,000 individuals per square metre whilst decayed standing wood can contain around 1000 individuals per 100 ml. Other favoured substrata include dung, bryophytes, coastal vegetation, brackish water, and sewage works where they mostly feed on bacteria and on fungi. Most species are microscopic, but a few can reach a millimetre or more in length.

With such a limitless food resource, it is no surprise that over 150 fungal species parasitise nematodes. What is surprising is that some fungi actively trap the eelworms, crossing the line between parasite and predator. Calling them 'carnivorous mushrooms' (Thorn & Barron, 1984) may be an over-statement, but, like the sundew and the Venus fly-trap in the plant kingdom, these fungi are certainly capable of actively trapping animals to supplement their diet.

There are many ways to catch a nematode, and an intricate variety of mechanisms has evolved independently in different fungal groups (Fig. 66).

FIG 66. A selection of nematode traps; a) an hour-glass trap of an oyster fungus, secreting an immobilising glue; b) an adhesive stephanocyst of a *Hyphoderma* species; c) the strange shoe-shaped spores of *Harposporium dicerarum* which lodge and germinate in the gut; d) a constricting ring of a *Drechslerella* species (P. Roberts).

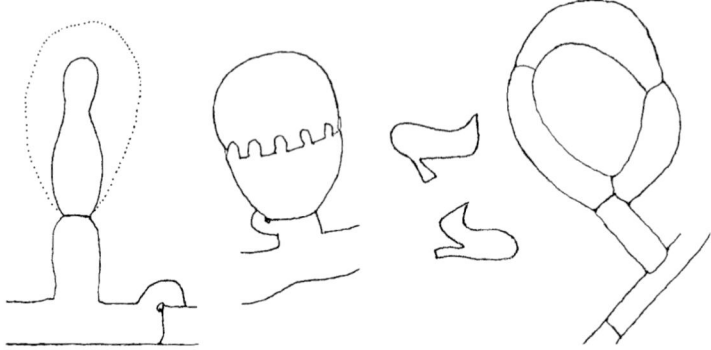

One is the 'super-glue' method, utilized by many ascomycetes and basidio-mycetes. This typically involves the production of specialised hyphae by the predator fungus which secrete a polymeric adhesin that specifically bonds to nematodes. Various adhesive trapping devices exist, having evolved separately within some of the pleurotoid and corticioid fungi (*Basidiomycetes*) and the *Orbiliaceae* (*Ascomycetes*).

The most familiar nematode-trappers are the edible, toadstool-like oyster caps (*Pleurotus* species). These are wood-rotters, but wood, especially heartwood, is frequently nitrogen-deficient. The addition of nematodes to the diet may compensate for the lack of nitrogen, though most other wood-rotters manage without any such supplement. *Pleurotus* species may nonetheless have gained some competitive advantage through evolving a means of trapping nematodes. They do this by producing hourglass-like projections on some of their hyphae. These projections not only exude a viscous substance which adheres to nematodes on contact, but also release an immobilising toxin which paralyses the prey within a minute. From this point of attachment, hyphae grow out into the nematode. *Hohenbuehelia* species, belonging to a related group of oyster-cap-like fungi, produce similar traps. It was some time before their nematode-trapping hyphal stage, discovered independently and dubbed *Nematoctonus*, was linked with the fruitbody stage, *Hohenbuehelia*, but the connexion is now well-established. Thorn & Barron (1986) have provided an illustrated key to *Nematoctonus* species and their fruitbody stages.

Some wood-rotting corticioid fungi in the genus *Hyphoderma* also capture nematodes, using specialised adhesive projections called 'stephanocysts', long noted as occurring as peculiar, toothed cells on the basal hyphae of fruitbodies, particularly in the common *Hyphoderma praetermissum*. Their adhesive, nematode-trapping capabilities were only discovered much later, but have subsequently been observed in seven *Hyphoderma* species. A further twelve species were found to be lethally poisonous to mycophagous nematodes, producing assimilative hyphae to coil round and consume their would-be predators (Tzean & Liou, 1993).

Nematode-trapping in the ascomycetes has evolved within the *Orbiliaceae*, a family producing small, often brightly coloured, disc-shaped fruitbodies on dead standing branches and rotting woody material. Their anamorphic forms can be grouped into four genera depending on the manner in which they trap nematodes, a morphological character which accurately reflects their phylogeny. Species of *Dactylellina* and *Gamsylella* produce adhesive projections on their hyphae superficially similar to those found in the pleurotoid fungi. In at least some species, however, these projections are detachable but still viable. This allows the nematode to make a temporary escape, carrying the detached hyphal propagule with it.

Even more sophisticated are the noose and net-like traps produced by *Arthrobotrys*, *Drechslerella* and some *Dactylellina* species (*Orbiliaceae*). Noose-like traps are formed by a straight piece of hypha curving back on itself and anastomising to create a ring, which may be simple (*Dactylellina*) or actively constricting (*Drechslerella*). In species with non-constricting rings, nematodes enter the rings by hazard, typically breaking them free. The detached ring is a self-sufficient propagule and will produce new hyphal growth that penetrates the host nematode. The common *Dactylellina haptotyla*, first reported in Britain from leaf debris in the pond of the Chelsea Physic Garden, produces both non-constricting rings and adhesive nodules to capture nematodes. Several species of *Arthrobotrys* trap nematodes by producing complex, three-dimensional, web-like structures similar to multiple rings. These are non-constricting, but adhesive. In species with constricting rings, such as *Drechslerella brochopaga*, the presence of a nematode causes the hyphae of the ring to swell inwards, a trigger mechanism that operates in less than one tenth of a second.

Many, possibly all, of these predatory fungi actively entice nematodes into their traps, using chemical exudates. A study by Field & Webster (1977) showed that species of *Arthrobotrys* growing in culture without traps were only visited randomly by nematodes, whereas cultures with traps attracted five to six times the random number. Other studies have shown similar levels of attraction to traps.

As well as predatory nematode-trapping fungi, there are a number of obligate fungal parasites for which nematodes are the primary food source and not just a supplementary additive. These include ascomycetes (*Hirsutella* and *Drechmeria* species), chytridiomycetes (*Catenaria* species), and some of the fungus-like oomycetes. Most produce adhesive or motile spores, chemically attracted to nematodes, which germinate and destroy the host.

The commonest of these is the chytrid *Catenaria anguillae* which produces zoospores with a whiplash flagellum capable of swimming after nematodes, tracking them down through their exudates. On contact, the zoospores encyst and produce germ tubes which penetrate their host.

Species of *Harposporium* (*Ascomycota*) produce unusual spores which are typically sickle-shaped or (in *H. dicerarum*) high-heeled-shoe-shaped. These spores are ingested by nematodes, but lodge in the digestive tract where they produce hyphae and infect their host.

Cooke (1977) and Gray (1987) have written useful and detailed reviews of the ecology of nematode-trapping fungi. An illustrated key to almost 100 different species was published by Cooke & Godfrey (1964) and a more recent key to genera was provided by Rubner (1996). A note on fossil nematode-trapping fungi, preserved in 25 million year-old amber, was published by Jansson & Poinar (1986).

Hunting rotifers, springtails, and other microfauna

As well as nematodes, fungi are known to hunt for other small animals, including amoebas, rotifers, arthropods, crustaceans, and tardigrades. The techniques deployed are, in most cases, similar to those used to catch nematodes. The ascomycetous *Cephaliophora navicularis*, for example, uses adhesive knob-like traps to catch bdelloid rotifers (*Adineta* species) in soil. Interestingly, these traps have no affect on nematodes, so appear to be prey-specific. Two additional species, *Cephaliophora muscicola* and *C. longispora*, prey on rotifers in damp moss and leaf litter but are also capable, at least in culture, of trapping tardigrades. Observations indicate that the prey species are actively attracted to the adhesive knobs, most frequently becoming attached by the mouth-parts. *Sommerstorffia spinosa*, an oomycete only known in Britain from Kew, captures loricate (hard-bodied) rotifers on adhesive pegs, as do the zygomycetes *Zoophagus insidians* and *Z. tentaculum*. *Dactylellina copepodii* uses adhesive projections to catch copepods (tiny shrimp-like crustacea) found in damp compost, whilst at least two *Arthrobotrys* species have developed 'multiple-ring' techniques to capture springtails (*Sminthuroides* and *Gressittacantha* species), which are comparatively large and very active prey. A much more surprising predator of springtails is the mycorrhizal agaric *Laccaria bicolor*, a close relative of the abundant *L. laccata*.

It has been found recently (Klironomos & Hart, 2001) that *L. bicolor* is able to capture, kill and infect the springtail *Folsoma candida* and then to supply nitrogen from its prey to its mycorrhizal tree partner in exchange for plant carbon. Capture of the springtail is by a toxin which paralyses the insect prior to its infection by mycelium. Only 5% of springtails were found to have survived after two weeks' exposure to *L. bicolor*, whereas almost all survived in the presence of other fungi or in the absence of fungi. 25% of the nitrogen used by the tree was found to have been derived from the springtails, a remarkable discovery which if more widespread amongst mycorrhizal fungi paints an even more complex picture of fungal ecology and the nitrogen cycle than hitherto realised.

Dactylella passalopaga is one of several species which prey on amoebas. Its prey species, a testaceous amoeba (rhizopod) called *Geococcus vulgaris*, normally feeds on fungal hyphae and spores by fastening to the wall and sucking out the contents. Instead of providing a meal, however, *Dactylella passalopaga* responds by producing a bulbous outgrowth which first traps the amoeba and then gives rise to assimilative hyphae. A number of zygomycetes in the order *Zoopagales* also prey on amoebas, mainly by adhering to them when brushed against. Dayal (1975) provided a key to 92 species of *Zoopagales* in ten genera which are associated either with amoebas or with nematodes.

Bacterivory

Although many flagellate *Protozoa* are known to feed on bacteria, both in soil and aquatic habitats, bacterivory by fungi is a comparatively little-known phenomenon. However, it now seems that various fungi can utilise bacteria as a food source. This has been shown, for example, for the cultivated mushroom *Agaricus bisporus* which is grown on a composted substrate rich in microbes and utilises bacteria as a major source of nitrogen. Other basidiomycetes may also attack and degrade bacterial colonies, including the oyster cap *Pleurotus ostreatus* and the wood blewit *Lepista nuda*, although such abilities have not been found in mycorrhizal species, nor in other groups of fungi. Some ascomycetes and zygomycetes, however, are able to degrade dead bacterial colonies. Recently, it has been discovered that some marine thraustochytrids (*Chromista*) are also able to ingest bacteria.

This has so far been shown for two species, *Thraustochytrium striatum* and *Schizochytrium mangrovei*, both of which produce amoeboid stages in the presence of bacteria, engulfing and destroying the bacterial cells (Raghukumar, 1992).

CHAPTER 7

Dispersal

F OR ALL organisms, dispersal is one of the most important of all
biological goals. It is essential for extending range when local
sources of nutrients are exhausted and also for successfully
colonising and exploiting suitable ecological niches. It also provides an
opportunity to maintain genetic variation within populations and perhaps
to exploit this variation in adaptation to new habitats. Successful dispersal,
however, presents a wide range of problems, and fungi have tackled these
by adopting an equally wide range of strategies, the most important and
interesting of which are considered in this chapter.

Most fungi are dispersed by specialised units, the 'spores', which may be
produced asexually or following sexual recombination. Though all spores are
microscopic, they show an extraordinary degree of variation in size, shape,
colour, and structure, all of which are linked in some way to different
dispersal strategies. Thus, for example, large, brown, thick-walled spores
withstand harsh conditions better than small, colourless, thin-walled spores,
but may take longer to produce and be slower to germinate. Which kind of
spore a species produces will depend on its dispersal strategy.

In addition to sexual and asexual spores, other units such as fragments
of hyphae, particles of lichen thallus, thick-walled sclerotia, and similar
structures may function as dispersal agents, or 'diaspores'. Some fungi
produce a range of different diaspores at different stages in their life cycle.
For example, asexual conidia may be formed by anamorphic stages, sexual

spores by the teleomorph, and other units, such as chlamydospores or hyphal fragments, as the opportunity arises or conditions dictate. This can be nicely demonstrated in the ascomycete *Hypomyces chrysospermus*, a common parasite of boletes, in which three types of diaspores are produced. These include large, ornamented chlamydospores as well as small, smooth-walled conidia, both of which lack forcible discharge, plus rough-walled ascospores which are forcibly discharged. Another ascomycete, *Dipodascus aggregatus*, has at least four methods of conidiogenesis.

In general, there are four main agents of dispersal for fungal diaspores:

- wind or air currents, utilised by the majority of species;
- water, utilised mainly by aquatic fungi (Chapters 11 & 12), though it can play a role in the liberation of spores of terrestrial fungi that are otherwise air-dispersed);
- animals, involving vertebrates as well as invertebrates, and both internal and external transmission;
- dispersal with plant hosts, particularly with seeds.

Most methods of active spore-discharge in terrestrial fungi rely on turgid cells – either the basidium or ascus – for which water is an essential component. It is no accident that most active periods of spore release in many ascomycetes, for example, correspond to periods of rainfall. Water is also used in other ways. In the ascomycete genus *Daldinia* water retained in the gelatinised parts of the stroma is used to achieve continuous spore release even during prolonged periods of drought. The gelatinous fruitbodies of some discomycetes, such as the rubbery, black *Bulgaria inquinans* which occurs in swarms on oak and beech, can similarly discharge spores for some time in dry conditions. Gelatinous basidiomycetes, such as *Auricularia* and *Tremella* species, are able to resume spore release by rapid rehydration whenever wet conditions return. This is not an option generally available to fleshy, short-lived fruitbodies such as toadstools which stop sporulating permanently when the weather turns dry. But even here, a few species, notably the fairy-ring toadstool *Marasmius oreades*, are capable of rehydrating. Longer-lasting fruitbodies, especially those of perennial bracket fungi, are resistant to drying and can resume spore liberation even after extended periods of drought. This is also a feature of *Schizophyllum commune*, the split-gill fungus. Fruitbodies dried for 50 years were found by Ainsworth (1962) to be still capable of spore release after wetting.

Before being dispersed, all spores must be successfully liberated from the parent fungus. This again involves a diversity of strategies and mechanisms, and provides the starting point for this chapter.

SPORE LIBERATION AND DISCHARGE

Active liberation

In the majority of fungi, including most of the larger terrestrial species, spores are actively and often violently discharged from the 'hymenium' (spore-producing surface) of a fruitbody, using a number of specialist adaptations based around a few long-evolved themes.

In the ascomycetes, sometimes referred to as the 'spore-shooting fungi', ascospores are typically shot out of the ascus under pressure. The distance to which they can be shot varies greatly according to species, but generally ranges from two to 400 mm. In some cases, notably species of *Saccobolus* which occur mostly on dung, the spores are not released singly but adhere in packets. The resulting projectile is then more massive and can be shot to greater distances. *Saccobolus*, in common with many other dung-inhabiting genera, also has asci which are positively phototropic, bending towards the light and therefore maximising the chances of spores being discharged into air currents above the dung.

Commonly, asci mature successively so that spores are released continually throughout the life of the fruitbody, though in a few cases, such as the large cup-fungi in the pantropical genus *Cookeina*, asci mature simultaneously and all the spores are released at once. The phenomenon known as 'puffing', in which many thousands of asci in a single fruitbody simultaneously discharge their spores to produce a visible cloud, can often be seen in larger cup-fungi, particularly *Peziza* species. Puffing is typically triggered by small changes in air pressure, and can usually be demonstrated clearly and impressively by enclosing a fruitbody in a container for some time, and then removing the lid. It has been claimed that, in some cases, puffing can actually be heard as well as seen. Smaller cup-fungi, including members of the *Helotiales*, also puff, but with less dramatic results.

The *Basidiomycota* have evolved a quite different method of spore release, producing spores externally on club-shaped cells called 'basidia', each spore developing on a small stalk called a 'sterigma'. Typically, four basidiospores are produced per basidium and, when mature, are forcibly discharged by a rather complex mechanism. Each spore is attached to the sterigma asymmetrically by a small projection termed the 'apiculus'. Discharge occurs following the production of a drop of fluid at and apparently from this projection (Fig. 67). This is known as 'Buller's drop', studied in detail by Reginald Buller and published in his 'Researches on Fungi' between 1922–1934, and is essential to the effective discharge of the spore. A similar drop is formed on the adaxial surface of the spore itself. More recent work (Webster *et al.*, 1995) has shown that these drops contain concentrated sugars, mannitol and hexoses, which allow their rapid expansion by adsorption of water vapour from the atmosphere. As they make

FIG 67. Active spore release in basidiomycetes. Each basidiospore develops from the sterigma asymmetrically; at maturity, a drop of fluid (Buller's drop) forms on the apiculus and fluid also builds up on the adjacent spore surface; when the expanding drop touches the surface fluid, the two instantly coalesce and the momentum discharges the spore (P. Roberts).

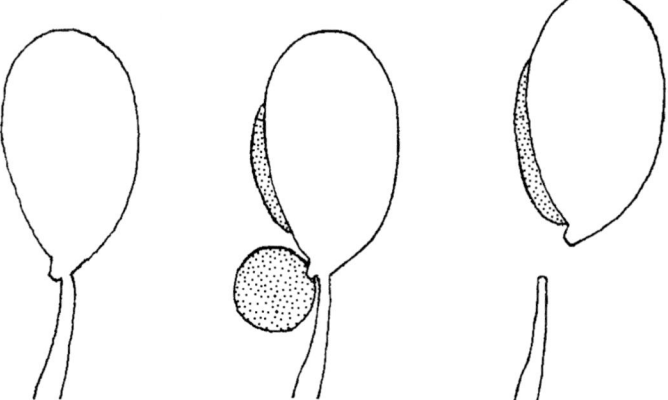

contact, it seems that the liquid in Buller's drop is rapidly displaced from the sterigma causing a momentum which effects discharge of the spore. The speed at which this takes place is so great that it cannot be successfully filmed and so, although there is now good evidence for this mechanism, precise details of its action still remain unclear.

This ingenious mechanism is much less powerful than that employed by the ascomycetous spore-shooters, discharging basidiospores no further than about 0.2 mm. However, this is just enough to clear the spore-producing surface and then drop by gravity into the air-stream, without impacting on a neighbouring surface. As a result, basidiomycetes can turn their hymenia into a complex of folds, gills, spines, or tubes to make maximum use of their surface areas. In doing so, they can also maintain a damp microclimate within the hymenia, extending their periods of spore production.

For basidiospores to drop into the air-stream it is essential that the hymenial surfaces remain absolutely vertical, otherwise spores from one surface – an agaric gill for example – would fall onto the next, whilst spores produced in the narrow tubes of bracket fungi would never reach the exit pore. This of course requires the cap itself to remain horizontal and, other than in teratological specimens, it is rare to find fresh, undisturbed fruitbodies in which the cap is otherwise. In many agarics, even after specimens have been picked or knocked sideways, it is common for their stems to curve, exhibiting a marked negative geotropism, so as to regain and maintain the horizontal position of the cap. This phenomenon, quite easy to demonstrate, was investigated by Buller in 1909. He showed that after placing the fruitbody of the ink-cap *Coprinus plicatilis* in a horizontal position, gradual curvature of the stem began after about two hours and the cap (kept in a moist atmosphere) regained its horizontal position after three hours. A similar phenomenon can be seen in bracket fungi. Where an old standing trunk bearing actively developing brackets has fallen, new brackets will form at right angles to the old ones, each perfectly aligned to the earth's gravitational field.

Basidia typically form in succession, releasing spores continuously over a period of time. In large, long-lived fruitbodies, such as the perennial brackets produced by some species of *Ganoderma*, spore production can be

FIG 68. Spores of a bracket fungus (*Ganoderma* species) released in such vast quantities that, in appropriate light, they are visible as a cloud (P. Bridge).

extraordinarily high. In moist but sunny conditions, particularly in the tropics, clouds of spores can be seen emanating from such brackets (Fig. 68). The spores are dispersed by air currents over considerable distances, though many will be blown back onto and around the brackets which produce them, covering everything in a layer of brownish dust. Such visible dissemination of spores has also been reported for various other bracket fungi. Buller observed spore clouds produced continuously over 13 days by the common bracket *Polyporus squamosus* and an interesting account by Stone (1920a) reported the same phenomenon in *Fomitopsis pinicola*, another species with large, perennial fruitbodies. The number of spores produced is vast. Buller (1909) estimated that a single bracket of *Polyporus squamosus* may produce 50,000,000,000–100,000,000,000 spores during a year. Even ephemeral toadstools produce spores in billions. The field mushroom *Agaricus campestris* has been estimated to release around 40,000,000 spores per hour, and the ink cap *Coprinus comatus* more than double that, at 100,000,000 spores per hour. With an average fruitbody sporulating for 48 hours, this produces a total of well over 5,000,000,000 spores. The jelly fungus *Exidia glandulosa* (the common 'witches' butter') is rather less prolific, estimated to produce no more than 200,000,000 spores during a 24 hour period.

Active spore release is also found in some conidial fungi, either resulting from movements of the spore-producing 'conidiophores' in response to changes in relative humidity or, in a few cases, relying on turgid cells. The former mechanism is utilised, for example, by the common grey mould *Botrytis cinerea* in which the conidiophores twist as humidity changes thereby releasing spores. In some species, such as the tropical *Deightoniella torulosa*, differential thickening of the wall of the conidiophore has a similar effect.

Liberation based on turgid cells seems to be much rarer, but has been demonstrated for *Pyricularia oryzae*, the cause of rice blast disease, as well as the cosmopolitan *Nigrospora sphaerica*. In both these species the rupture of a turgid cell at maturity discharges the conidia. The abundant litter saprotroph *Epicoccum purpurascens* may also rely on turgid cell discharge but in this case by sudden inflation rather than rupture.

In some fungi, active discharge not just of spores but of whole 'sporangia' (packets of spores) or other spore-containing bodies occurs. Species in the dung-loving zygomycete genus *Pilobolus* can shoot their spore packets, developed like black caps atop a colourless, transparent 'stem', to a height of up to one metre. If grown in a Petri dish, these sporangia can clearly be heard impacting on the lid. The basidiomycete *Sphaerobolus stellatus*, the shooting star or cannon-ball fungus, is even more impressive and is capable of shooting its spore mass a distance of well over five metres.

Passive spore liberation

Passive liberation of spores, effected by external agencies such as wind, rain or animals, occurs in many fungi, but amongst the larger species most notably in the so-called 'gasteroid' fungi such as puffballs, earthstars, and stinkhorns.

Spores of puffballs and their allies are usually liberated either by wind or by rain-splash. In the stilt-puffball *Battarraea phalloides*, as well as in myxomycetes and a few genera of smut fungi, passive liberation is aided by sterile threads called 'elaters' which occur freely within the spore mass. These often have spiral or ring-like thickenings and react to water by moving and twisting around, presumably helping separate and free the spores.

Another unusual form of spore liberation is found in the common grassland puffballs *Bovista nigrescens* and *B. plumbea* (Fig. 73). These produce their spore mass in a ball-shaped structure which, when mature, flakes off its white outer surface to reveal a smooth, grey or blackish inner wall (peridium). With the outer surface gone, the inner peridium becomes detached and blows around in the wind, releasing spores as it tumbles about. These fungi are rather restricted in habitat, usually occurring in short, often rabbit-grazed turf, over which fruitbodies can travel for considerable distances. In the giant puffball *Calvatia gigantea* the peridium simply breaks apart to expose the spore mass inside, spore liberation relying partly on wind though mechanical abrasion of the ripe fruitbodies – including their common use as footballs – is a useful contributing factor.

Surprisingly, many kinds of fungi rely on rain drops or rain splash mechanisms for liberation of their spores. Equally surprising is the diversity and often the complexity of the mechanisms they have evolved to take advantage of this. Perhaps the most familiar 'rainfall fungi' are puffballs of the genus *Lycoperdon*. Like *Bovista* and *Calvatia* species, these produce spores inside a sack-like peridium, where they remain until maturity. As with other puffballs, the internal hymenium and basidia quickly disintegrate, leaving only a dusty spore mass interspersed with a specialised, rather elastic network of hyphae called a 'capillitium'. When mature, the peridium ruptures at the apex leaving a hole rather like a salt-shaker. Water drops falling onto the puffball sharply depress the peridium shooting a puff of spores into the air, after which (thanks to the elastic capillitium) the peridium springs back into shape, ready for the next drop of water.

A more or less identical mechanism has evolved in the earthstars (*Geastrum* species), though curiously these are not closely related to the puffballs. In *Geastrum*, the outer peridium is tough and at maturity splits into four or more arm-like segments (or 'rays') which peel back to reveal the puffball-like inner peridium, complete with apical hole and powdery internal spore mass. The rays, still attached to the base of the inner peridium, curve under the earthstar effectively raising it from the ground. In some species the rays split in two, so that the whole fruitbody is cantilevered into the air. The basidiome of *Geastrum fornicatum*, the largest of the two British cantilevering species, is a truly astonishing object considered by some to represent the height of fungal fruitbody evolution

In a few earthstars (Fig. 69) and also in the remarkably similar but unrelated species *Astraeus hygrometricus* (the barometer earthstar), the rays are hygroscopic, opening up in rain to reveal the inner peridium, but closing back over it in dry weather. *Astraeus* and the hygroscopic earthstars are uncommon in Britain, but much more frequent in southern and eastern Europe where they can be found in arid scrub and grasslands. Their highly evolved spore release strategies allow them to grow in near desert conditions, sporulating only during periods of rain, whilst closed up and protected

FIG 69. *Geastrum floriforme*, a scarce earthstar probably introduced to Britain, has fruitbodies which are hygroscopic, opening when damp but closing up in dry weather (T. Læssøe).

from wind and sunlight during dry periods. A detached fruitbody of *Astraeus* in a Devon garden was seen to keep up this cycle for several years, before eventually weathering away.

An entirely different strategy for spore release has evolved in the bird's-nest fungi, a group of basidiomycetes represented in Britain by five species, *Crucibulum laeve* (Fig. 70), *Cyathus olla*, *C. striatus*, the rare *C. stercoreus*, and *Nidularia deformis*. These employ 'splash cups' or other special mechanisms for the purpose. Young fruitbodies are more or less drum-shaped, but at maturity the drum-skin surface ruptures to reveal a flask or cup-shaped receptacle at the bottom of which are several discrete, lentil-shaped structures termed 'peridioles'. The immediate impression is of a miniature bird's nest complete with a clutch of tiny eggs. The peridioles each contain a mass of basidiospores and, except in *Nidularia*, are loosely attached to the receptacle by a coiled hyphal cord termed a 'funiculus'. Sufficiently heavy raindrops falling into the receptacle splash out the peridioles and also uncoil and release the sticky funiculus. This serves to liberate and disperse spore

packets, ejecting them up to a metre away, where the funiculus glues them
to leaves, sticks, and other vegetation.

Commoner, but less complex, methods of splash liberation and dispersal
are found in many conidial ascomycetes, both saprobes and parasites. In
Fusarium and related genera, for example, the conidia are agglutinated and
cannot be liberated by air currents. For these, rain splash is an important
release mechanism, though dispersal distances may be short and spores
are not generally transferred to the air stream but remain in water droplets.
Similar rain-splash mechanisms play a part in the dispersal of spores of
many phylloplane microfungi (those growing on living leaf surfaces).

Passive spore liberation by wind action is the commonest dispersal
mechanism in most microfungi, particularly among the hyphomycetes.
In many species, the spores (conidia) are dry, powdery in mass, and readily
liberated either directly or indirectly by air movement. Direct liberation
appears to rely on turbulence rather than wind speed, involving such things
as the surface characteristics of the leaves and stems on which the fungi

FIG 70. *Crucibulum laeve,* one of the bird's-nest fungi. The fruitbodies act as
splash-cups for dispersal of the spore-containing 'eggs' or peridioles which nestle
within them (P. Roberts).

grow. Spores are also shed indirectly by wind action due to the shaking and knocking together of host leaves and stems.

A detailed exploration of spore liberation in all its many forms can be found in Ingold (1971).

DISPERSAL BY AIR

Airborne dispersal is the method of choice for most fungi, whether or not there is forcible discharge of spores. The great majority of our familiar larger species have evolved to take advantage of wind and air currents, as also have many microfungi. Because of the importance of airborne spore dispersal in understanding the epidemiology of crop diseases, it has received detailed study and is probably the best documented of all the various dispersal methods (Malloch & Blackwell, 1992).

Fungal spores are a very significant component of the so-called 'air spora' which comprises all kinds of microbial diaspores, including those of bacteria, plants and animals. The existence of an air spora has long been known, but the abundance of spores present was more firmly established during the 1940s when specially designed suction traps were introduced by Hirst (1952). These provide accurate and continuous sampling, allowing detailed analysis of the numbers and types of spores present at different times. The constituents of the air spora vary considerably according to time of day, weather conditions, season and a range of other factors, reflecting the way in which the spores of different species are liberated. However, spores are always abundantly present in the air, and may reach concentrations of up to two million per cubic metre. Concentrations are obviously greatest near the ground, closest to the source of freshly liberated spores, but spores may also be present in surprising quantities at high altitudes, as shown by sampling undertaken from balloons or aircraft. In general, there is a logarithmic decrease in spore concentrations with altitude and, although complexities in air movements and temperature inversions may affect this pattern, above about 3000m the number of fungal spores decreases to around three per cubic metre. However, even at much higher altitudes of up to 20km some fungal spores have been found.

Air is an efficient medium, potentially able to carry spores over very great distances. However, in order to be dispersed effectively by air, it is essential that spores are successfully discharged into moving air currents. These currents occur only above the so-called 'laminar air', a thin layer adjacent to the ground surface, in which the air is virtually still and in which no effective spore dissemination is possible. For those fungi which fruit on trees or other above-ground substrata, spore discharge into turbulent air is no problem, but it may be less easy for ground-fruiting fungi to achieve. Most agarics overcome the problem by having fruitbodies with stems which raise the cap to a sufficient height, but stalkless cup fungi have a different solution, relying on violent spore discharge to shoot the spores through the laminar zone and into the turbulent air.

The way that spores and other propagules move in the air is complex. Because they are denser than air, spores fall under gravity until eventually impacting on a surface. But there are numerous interacting factors which affect their movement up to that point. Successful dispersal depends very much on the characters of the spores themselves, especially their size, surface ornamentation, and viability, as well as on conditions of the atmosphere, such as turbulence and wind speed. Size and surface characters significantly affect the distance spores can travel before being deposited, particularly their rate of fall through the air, which is directly linked to the spore radius, and the efficiency with which they can impact on appropriate surfaces. In addition, electrostatic charges carried by individual spores may affect their dispersal due to interaction with other particles. Of course, many spores may fail to escape at all from their parent fruitbody, and of those which do escape most normally travel no more than a few metres. Conidia of the common mould *Botrytis cinerea*, for example, have been found up to three metres from their source and no further, although some rust and smut fungi have been shown to infect neighbouring host plants at distances up to 150 metres away.

The potential for long-distance dispersal does not, therefore, seem to be realised in most cases, although some considerable distances have been reported, such as the conidia of *Fusarium moniliforme* trapped up to 500 km from their source. Rishbeth (1959) noted that spores of the wood-rotting species *Heterobasidion annosum* and *Phlebiopsis gigantea*, were detected in air spora in Shetland, over 300 km from their source. Other cases of long-distance dispersal over hundreds of kilometres, effecting international spread, were given by Zadoks (1967), although these may attest to the fecundity of the pathogens involved and relentless rapid spread from successive infections rather than long-distance dispersal and viability of individual spores. He cites, for example, the case of grape vine mildew (*Uncinula necator*) which was first discovered in England in 1845 in Kent. In 1847 it was present in Paris, and within six years the whole of the vine-growing areas of the Mediterranean and into North Africa were affected by the disease. It is not always clear that these long-distance travellers retain their viability on arrival, although the spread of certain rust fungi from Australia to New Zealand, a distance of around 2000 km, suggests that it may be possible. Many myxomycetes have spores that are thick-walled and can remain viable for decades, presumably an important factor in the unusually wide distribution of species, some of which appear to be cosmopolitan in appropriate habitats. In contrast, fungi which are geographically restricted may be unable to spread over long distances partly or wholly because of poor spore viability. Climatic and ecological requirements are, of course, just as important, and it may well be lack of suitable conditions that restricts the geographic distribution of most fungi.

Fungi with bipolar distribution represent the extreme for long distance dispersal. This is known for a surprising number of lichens, including species from at least 20 families, reviewed by Galloway & Aptroot (1995). Dispersal by air may explain such extreme disjunct distributions, though it is also possible that other reasons – such as relict populations persisting over geological time – are the cause. It has been suggested that the mechanism for such long-distance dispersal involves characters of the lichen diaspores, usually ascospores, which in species with disjunct distributions are small and highly tolerant of long-range air transport. Nevertheless, the problems of traversing equatorial regions, where air movements are slight, are great, and may partly explain why the majority of lichenised fungi are not so widely distributed.

Deposition of spores from the air and successful impaction on substrata are also essential to the dispersal process, although only in comparatively few cases will the substratum be an appropriate one for the full growth and development of the spore; natural wastage is high. Spore deposition depends on a range of characters and, though essentially random, may occur in one of several ways. Commonly, impaction occurs on surfaces which protrude into the air stream. Leaves of living plants are a good example of this, and the spores which impact here are part of the phylloplane community (Chapter Five). This community represents potentially a great diversity of fungi, varying according to the size and surface characters of the leaves, differences in which markedly affect the rate and success of spore deposition. In general, leaves of broad-leaved trees, with greater surface area, tend to capture more spores. This was clearly demonstrated by Rishbeth (1959) in studies of the pathogen *Heterobasidion annosum* where the spore count on Scot's pine leaves was 700 as opposed to 6000 on birch.

Electrostatic deposition may also be a factor in spore deposition if the minute electric charge carried by the spore is opposite to that of the substratum it encounters. Spores may also be deposited directly by sedimentation under gravity if they enter the laminar air near ground level, and be washed out of the air by rain or snow. Rishbeth found, for example, that heavy deposition of spores of both *Heterobasidion annosum* and *Phlebiopsis gigantea* occurred after periods of prolonged rain. Characters of the spore, particularly size and surface ornamentation, as well as wind speed and rain all interact to affect the rate of deposition. Larger spores fall more readily and impact more efficiently, but conversely will travel less far.

Rhythms of dispersal

Annual cycles in the development of fungal fruitbodies and spore production for particular species are rhythms which are well known to field mycologists as well as to aerobiologists. However, the use of spore traps to sample the air spora has revealed unexpected diurnal rhythms of spore dispersal and remarkable differences in the way in which different fungi operate. Time of spore discharge varies according to ecology, and almost all species show distinct patterns of discharge according to temperature, relative humidity, light, season, and other factors. Fungi dependent on water availability are, for example, most active after rain, or at night when humidity levels are higher. In contrast, fungi which liberate spores through mechanical means, which often involve temperature increase or turbulence, show midday maxima. In some fungi, notably *Daldinia concentrica*, spore discharge is inhibited by light and almost entirely nocturnal. In contrast, sporulation in some powdery mildews, notably the common *Erysiphe cichoracearum*, is stimulated by light, again resulting in marked diurnal patterns. Rhythms of spore discharge that are directly light-related are evidently frequent amongst the ascomycetes though much less common in basidiomycetes and other fungi. In temperate regions, air spora is at its lowest during winter, a seasonal rhythm which is obviously absent in the tropics. Crop cycles will additionally influence the abundance of spores of pathogenic fungi. Whilst most fungi release their spores late in the day or at night, plant pathogens seem do so in the morning. Because of the potential devastation caused by crop diseases, it is no surprise that the aerobiology of plant pathogens has received extensive study. An understanding of both long-distance dispersal of pathogens into new crop-growing areas and local spread amongst their crop hosts is essential to the forecasting and control of plant diseases. Aspects such as the timing of spore liberation in crop diseases and conditions affecting spore dispersal and viability have been extensively studied and used to create mathematical models which can successfully simulate epidemics (Scott & Bainbridge, 1978).

ANIMAL DISPERSAL

The use by fungi of animals as agents of spore liberation and dispersal is a surprisingly widespread phenomenon, involving mammals and birds as well as numerous insects and other invertebrates. Such usage ranges from passive liberation through incidental animal activity to highly-evolved symbiotic relationships dispersing diaspores externally (on the surface of an animal) or internally (through ingestion of fruitbodies and propagules).

Spore-bearing voles and other mammals

Truffles and other underground fungi do not actively liberate their spores. Instead, most species produce strong-smelling fruitbodies attractive to voles and other small mammals which eat them and disperse spores in their droppings. This apparently simple mechanism actually has much more wide-ranging implications and may form an essential component of highly evolved and complex partnerships (Chapter Five). Other fungi which actively rely on mammals include many of the dung fungi dispersed by grazing animals (Chapter 13), the anaerobic rumen fungi (Chapter Five) also dispersed through dung, and, not surprisingly, animal pathogens such as ringworm (*Microsporum* and *Trichophyton* species; Chapter 15). Many keratinolytic fungi which degrade hair also occur in the fur of living mammals, providing opportunities to colonise new hosts, new nest sites and moulting areas. A wide range of additional fungi may also be isolated from the fur and skin of mammals (Malloch & Blackwell, 1992), allowing the possibility of opportunistic spore dispersal.

Humans, of course, are by far the greatest dispersers of fungi worldwide, though apart from ringworm, athlete's foot, and a few other host-specific pathogens, this form of dispersal is just a bonus for the fungi concerned, and not yet an evolutionary adaptation.

Woodpeckers, swallows, and truffle-eating birds

Birds have also been implicated in the spread of fungi, particularly pathogenic species (Malloch & Blackwell, 1992). Woodpeckers and treecreepers, for example, are known to carry large numbers of spores, some of which belong to tree pathogens. Indeed, they are believed to have been vectors for the long-distance spread of the devastating chestnut disease caused by *Cryphonectria parasitica*, whose wind-borne spores are only effective for local dispersal. Whether this is an example of mutualism (dead wood being beneficial to the birds) or merely opportunistic, is unclear. Other fungi isolated from woodpeckers include species of the ubiquitous moulds *Cladosporium*, *Penicillium* and *Trichoderma*, as well as keratinolytic fungi in their feathers (the last certainly being mutualistic). Migratory swallows are known to carry spores of rust fungi and it seems probable that water fowl may play a role in the dispersal of aquatic fungi which lack air-borne diaspores. As noted by Ingold (1953), the distribution of such fungi, even to isolated systems, is efficient and likely to be effected by birds. A few birds even appear to play a role in the dispersal of certain truffle-like fungi. The desert truffle *Phaeangium lefebvrei*, for example, is said to be specially sought out and eaten by birds.

Wasps, worms, and other invertebrates

There are many ways, ranging from incidental activity to highly evolved mechanisms, in which fungi are dispersed by invertebrates. Some involve complex, often symbiotic partnerships. Others are simpler, but often surprising.

In some habitats, dispersal of spores occurs freely and commonly amongst invertebrates, which often become covered with spores of both saprotrophic and parasitic fungi. Wasps, for example, have been shown to transport spores of *Monilia fructigena*, an ascomycete causing soft rot of fruit such as apples and plums. The fungus forms conspicuous pustule-like fruitbodies with powdery spore masses which are normally wind-dispersed. However, wasps feeding on the rotting fruit also pick the spores up and transport them to any healthy fruit they sample. Similarly, studies on woodlice have shown they are capable of distributing spores simply by walking over surfaces and picking them up on their legs or body parts. They are equally capable of eating and defecating viable spores, and it is evident that passage through invertebrate guts is an important method of dispersal for many fungi. In some cases, it may actually stimulate spore germination. This has been suggested for species of the mycorrhizal toadstools *Lactarius* and *Russula*, fruitbodies of which are often eaten by slugs. The slug *Malacolimax tenellus*, a rare woodland species, appears to be a specialist feeder on fungi, including *Russula* fruitbodies, and may be a significant agent of spore dispersal.

Most of the VA-mycorrhizal *Glomerales* produce tiny fruitbodies (pea truffles) or just loose, unprotected spores whose dispersal may well rely on the activities of invertebrates. McIlveen & Cole (1976) found earthworms to be especially important as vectors of these fungi. Worms are well known to be of major significance in the movement and mixing of soil, and intestinal contents of all specimens examined contained spores of *Glomerales*. These are voided in worm casts and have been shown to be viable and capable of developing new VA-mycorrhizas. Many ant species also move soil, particularly when nest building, and again these have been shown to have a role in the dispersal of *Glomerales*, bringing spores to the surface and directly transporting them over small distances. Spores of these fungi have also been found in wasp nests and in the mud-built nests of swallows. Erosion and wind dispersal from old nests, and indeed from worm casts, may help long-distance dispersal of the otherwise subterranean spores.

Many of the yeasts which occur on flowers are also known to be vectored by invertebrates, this time by pollinating bees as well as various non-pollinating beetles and flies. These are evidently specific associations between the yeast, the insect and the flower host, and often represent highly evolved symbiotic relationships in which the yeast cells are used as food by the larvae of the insects involved. Although this has apparently not yet been researched in Britain, some interesting results have been obtained from studies carried out in various parts of the New World and Australia. For example, Lachance *et al.* (2001) found four groups of flower yeasts, including many previously undescribed species of *Candida* and *Metschnikowia*, to be intimately associated with insect vectors. Individual scarab and sap beetles (*Nitidulidae*) were shown to each carry around 10,000 yeast cells, voided in their faecal pellets, and fruit flies also to carry significant numbers of yeasts. These yeasts readily formed new colonies on flowers visited by the insects.

Myxomycete spores are also found in invertebrate dung, and some species appear to be dispersed by passage though the gut of certain beetles and earthworms.

Flies and phalloids

The stinkhorn, *Phallus impudicus*, is the commonest British example of a group of largely tropical basidiomycetes – the phalloids – whose spores are spread mainly by flies (Fig. 71). Fruitbodies of these fungi develop in leaf litter as smooth, white, leathery, egg-like receptacles inside which the slimy spores, passively released by basidia, mature. The 'egg' then ruptures and the slimy spore mass, or gleba, is exposed at the apex of a hollow stipe. As the common name suggests, the gleba stinks and does so mainly of rotting flesh, though with a hint of violets according to some. It also contains sugars. This immediately attracts bluebottles and similar carrion-loving flies, which swarm over and feed on the sticky spore mass. The ingested spores pass through the flies' gut unaltered, to be defecated and spread elsewhere. The

FIG 71. The common stinkhorn *Phallus impudicus*, swarming with flies which are attracted by the foul-smelling gleba and act as agents of spore dispersal (P. Roberts).

flies involved in this process in Britain mainly belong to the genera *Calliphora* and *Sarcophaga*, but Smith (1956) recorded no less than fourteen species visiting stinkhorns in England. Two rare and bizarre 'clathroid' fungi, both naturalised in England from their native Australasia, are related to stinkhorns and have a similar form of spore dispersal. *Clathrus archeri*, the commoner of the two, opens its egg to reveal four or more pink to reddish tentacle-like arms which open up like some strange flower, the foul-smelling slimy spore mass being spread along each arm. It has been suggested it arrived in Europe with fodder for the ANZAC cavalry during the Great War, but the British introductions, in Cornwall and south-east England, appear to be have been with exotic garden plants. The second species, *Aseroe rubra*, is only known in Britain from Oxshott Heath near London, where it was first found in 1993. Like *Clathrus archeri*, it produces paired, tentacle-like arms surrounding a centralised spore mass but the resemblance to some strange fungal flower is even greater. This may be a strategy for attracting insects by sight as well as by smell.

A native European clathroid, *Clathrus ruber*, has been known in Britain since the 1840s and has either been imported or has extended its range naturally (it is common in the Channel Islands and now widespread on the south coast). Sometimes called 'the cage fungus', it produces a lattice-like structure of interlinked pink arms, with the slimy spore mass spread along the inner sides of the arms. The structure is similar to some flowers (such as those of *Ceropegia* species) which temporarily trap insects, though whether this strategy is employed by *Clathrus ruber* is unknown.

Lichens hitching a ride

Some lichenised fungi benefit from external transport on invertebrates. One unusual method involves larvae of certain booklice (*Psocidae*) and lacewings (*Chrysopidae*) which cover themselves with fragments of lichens and algae to provide camouflage against the bark lichens on which they feed. Nymphs of the British psocid *Trichadenotecnum fasciatum*, for example, are covered with sticky hairs that attract bits of lichen and other fragments, whilst larvae of one lacewing species, *Nodita pavida*, selectively use lichens for this purpose. These fragments include spores and other propagules, thus helping disperse the lichens. Springtails (*Collembola*), ants, mites and molluscs have also been reported to disperse lichens.

On a different scale, an elegant, if slow method of dispersal has been discovered for the lichen *Physcia picta*. This typically grows on rock and bark, but has also been found in the Galapagos on the shells of living giant tortoises.

Smuts and moulds disguised as pollen

Many of the systemic smuts rely largely or entirely on insects for dispersal to new, healthy hosts. A common and easily observed example of this is provided by species of *Microbotryum*, the 'anther smuts', on campions and other host genera in the *Caryophyllaceae*. In infected plants, the smut modifies the flowers so that they release spores, not pollen. Superficially the flowers look the same and to insects they smell the same, but the anthers are commonly dark purple-brown not white. Smut spores are distributed to new hosts mainly by the agency of night-flying moths, but some butterflies and bees are also carriers. Other British smuts dispersed this way are *Ustilago succisae* on scabious, *Urocystis primulae* on primroses, and *Thecaphora seminis-convolvuli* on convolvulus.

A similar life history is found in a quite unrelated fungus, the hyphomycete *Botrytis anthophila*, the cause of 'anther mould' of red clover. This is a systemic disease in which ash-grey conidia are developed in the anthers of the clover, partly replacing the pollen. The fungus relies on bees, the normal pollinating agents of the clover, to disperse its conidia to healthy flowers, thereby infecting the resulting seeds.

Cryptoporus: an insect-dispersed bracket fungus

Some parasitic, wood-rotting fungi are actively dispersed by wood-boring insects in highly evolved, mutualistic relationships (Chapter Five), but insects can also act as vectors for dispersal simply by carrying spores on their outer surfaces. The insects gain nothing from this, but it enables the fungus to colonise new and suitable substrata very effectively. One interesting example involves *Cryptoporus volvatus*, a bracket fungus which develops small, hoof-like fruitbodies on recently killed conifers, often those which have been severely attacked by bark beetles. This species, known from North America and parts of East Asia, has a pore-layer which is covered by a membranous veil or volva. The veil has a small, basal pore through which many of the spores shed at maturity are released to be dispersed by air currents. However, many more are deposited on the inner surface of the veil and trapped inside. These are dispersed on the surface of beetles which forage inside the veil and then go on to forage in the bark and wood of other trees.

Mites

Surprisingly, mites (*Acarina* species) have proved to be important agents of dispersal for many fungi. Some are partners in mutualistic relationships but others may accidentally pick up fungal spores during their normal activities and these can be dispersed over a wide range, particularly by phoretic mites (those which hitch a ride on insects) and mites dispersed by wind. Moser *et al.* (1989) found no less than 85% of the 20 mite species they studied carried spores, and these represented at least ten different ascomycetes. Many mites also feed on fungi, and their faecal pellets are known to contain fungal spores which remain viable, helping disperse the fungi involved.

SEED-BORNE FUNGI

A surprisingly wide variety of organisms, including bacteria, viruses, and insects, are adapted for dispersal either on or in the seeds of plants. Predominant among them are the seed-borne fungi, most of them pathogens, often of considerable economic importance, but also including saprobes and symbionts beneficial to the plants involved.

As long ago as 1755, Tillet demonstrated that 'bunt of wheat', a devastating smut disease caused by the fungus now named *Tilletia tritici*, was seed-borne. However, it was more than a century later that fungal pathogens other than smuts were also recognised as being spread in this way. In 1883 Frank showed that 'anthracnose of beans', caused by the ascomycete *Colletotrichum lindemuthianum*, was seed-borne and since then, more than 600 fungal species have been found to use seeds to spread their spores (listed in Noble *et al.*, 1958, and Richardson, 1979). Indeed, almost all crop plants are subject to disease from at least one seed-borne fungus. Some are particularly prone. Rice, for example, has at least 13 species of associated seed-borne fungal pathogens, as well as several bacteria.

Seed-borne fungi are frequently endophytes, causing systemic infections of their hosts. They may occur in roots, stems or other parts and infect the ovaries after flowers are produced. The important genus of grass endophytes, *Epichloë* is a prime example, utilising seeds for dispersal but employing other mechanisms as well. It is the cause of 'choke' disease, which prevents flowering of the host, but it also occurs as an endophyte in choke-free hosts and is then transmitted via the seeds. Some grass smuts, including the potentially serious cereal smuts such as *Tilletia tritici* already mentioned, and *Ustilago hordei*, are also seed-borne, ensuring immediate infection of germinating seedlings. These are amongst the most commercially important seed-borne plant pathogens. Their strategy is unlike that of *Epichloë*, however, since they destroy the inflorescences of infected plants, releasing spores from a powdery mass to infect the ovaries of healthy plants, and thus infecting the seeds. 'Blind seed disease', caused by the ascomycete *Gloeotinia temulenta*, is also commercially important. Although infected seeds do not germinate, they are easily distributed with viable seeds, the fungus soon forming cup-shaped fruitbodies which sporulate and infect the seedlings.

It is not just grasses that are infected. Many other plants, including herbs and woody plants, wild and crop species, are equally susceptible. A recent study of tropical dipterocarp forest, for example, found no fewer than 31 species of seed-borne fungi infecting a single tree species, *Dipterocarpus alatus*. There are many other examples, particularly amongst the smuts and ascomycetes, and it is clear that seed-borne dispersal is an important and efficient mechanism for the transmission of plant pathogenic fungi to new hosts.

In the modern world, seed-borne pathogens are mainly transported and spread by man, often with devastating results. The most obvious is the introduction of crop-destroying diseases to new areas. But seed-borne pathogens also damage seed viability resulting in poor harvests, and, in some cases, they can lead to serious poisoning of people and livestock, by contaminating grains, pulses, and other seeds used for food (Chapter 15).

To combat the spread of pathogens, seed is now regularly tested before sale. This began as far back as 1869, when the first official seed-testing station was established in Saxony by Friedrich Nobbe. The need for international guidelines for seed testing was soon recognised and these were developed as early as 1875. Since then, seed-testing stations have been established throughout Europe and methods have been refined and standardised for speed and accuracy. They are now regulated, revised and updated by the International Seed Testing Association (ISTA), founded in 1924. It publishes the internationally binding 'International Rules for Seed Testing' and also produces the Manual for the Determination of Seed-borne Diseases.

CHAPTER 8

Grass and Grassland

T HE GRASSLAND areas which today occur extensively throughout Britain and much of Northern Europe represent valuable habitats, supporting diverse and complex communities of species, not just grasses but many herbs, insects and other invertebrates, and of course fungi. With few exceptions, these communities have been traditionally considered to result from human activity, created in historic times as the ancient, post-glacial forests were relentlessly cleared for agriculture. Today, these grasslands are maintained and stabilised by continued human activity, by mowing, either for hay or amenity use, by providing pasture for horses, sheep or cattle, and by the grazing of deer and rabbits, all of which effectively remove trees, shrubs, and other potential climax vegetation. This clearance of ancient forests was thought to have began during the Neolithic period about 4000 BC or even earlier, following recolonisation of the British Isles after the last Ice Age, and continuing into Anglo-Saxon times. Early Neolithic settlers, using only flint axes, cleared just the less densely wooded slopes, and so created the first hill pastures for the grazing of cattle and sheep. Such forest clearance spread gradually into more lowland areas, so that the chalk downlands were established by the late Neolithic. Even though some of these grasslands have been established for hundreds or even thousands of years, they have been regarded, at best, as semi-natural habitats, with all but a few upland areas susceptible to rapid colonisation by scrub and woodland when stabilising activities are removed.

The traditional view of a once-continuous primeval wildwood, in which trees regenerate in naturally-formed gaps in the canopy, is based largely on the study of ancient pollen and of sub-fossil trees which has shown that oaks, hazel, and other trees such as lime, elm and hornbeam, were present over large areas. Nowadays, derelict fields rapidly revert to scrub and woodland which appear therefore to be a natural climax vegetation. Recently, however, this interpretation has been challenged by the Dutch ecologist F.W.M. Vera (Vera, 2000), who suggests that these trees cannot, in fact, regenerate in closed forests but do so only in mosaic landscapes in which open grassland, areas of scrub, woodland and solitary trees occur. The existence of large grazing herbivores (their role today replaced by domestic livestock) may support this view. This difference of interpretation has yet to be proven but has important implications for our understanding of the ecology and conservation of grassland communities.

More intensive clearance and the development of arable fields and hay meadows undoubtedly took place during Anglo-Saxon times from about 450 AD. From the mediaeval era to the present, improvements in agriculture have further altered many of the early grasslands, so that today typical farmland fields are highly modified – 'improved' from a commercial point of view. They may be recently sown with hybrid seed mixes and further dressed with fertilisers, weedkillers, and pesticides. As a consequence of this long history, a wide range of ancient and modern British grassland types can be distinguished, many of them increasingly being recognised as rich and valuable habitats for fungi.

Grasslands are extremely diverse, largely due to edaphic factors (those linked directly to soil type) and climate and, regardless of their origin, are now constantly moulded by human activities. Although floristically dominated by various different grasses, they characteristically also include a wide range of herbaceous plants, mostly native species many of which are now becoming rare due to loss of unimproved grassland. The traditional species-rich 'wild flower' meadows are an increasingly scarce resource. Grazed unfertilised pastures are similarly scarce and, although these may be less diverse from a floristic viewpoint, they are especially important for larger fungi, supporting a range of waxcap toadstools (*Hygrocybe*) and other species rarely found elsewhere. The threat to these pastures and their equally threatened fungi deserves greater recognition, though a start has now been made on recording and conserving some of the best remaining sites (Chapter 18). Wild flower meadows are not so interesting for macrofungi, perhaps because the moss layer is less developed, and perhaps also because tall sward inhibits the production of fruitbodies (it certainly makes them more difficult to find). It may be that some macrofungi are present as mycelium but seldom fruit, a possibility which merits further investigation. Wild flower meadows are, however, rich in microfungi, particularly plant parasites, soil and litter saprotrophs, and insect associates.

Mosses are also components of many grasslands, and their ecological importance, particularly with regard to fungi and invertebrates, is perhaps greater than is generally realised. They directly support a large number of species, offer shelter and provide indirect support to many others, and help retain moisture. A well-developed moss layer has been found to be positively correlated with the number of macrofungi present in a grassland (Arnolds, 1981) and these moss layers are best formed in short sward, promoted by regimes of grazing or mowing. It has been suggested that *Hygrocybe* species may have a specific relationship with mosses. Although this relationship is little-studied and remains unproven, it might explain why waxcaps are sometimes found in mossy areas of woodlands. It may even be that waxcaps are actually woodland fungi which have expanded their habitat range into man-made short-sward grassland along with their associated mosses. Certainly in North America the majority of waxcaps, including important grassland indicators in Europe such as *Hygrocybe pratensis* and *H. calyptriformis*, are known as fungi of forests or copses.

Lichens may also be found in grasslands, though few are specific to such habitats. Their presence varies according to conditions, with closely-grazed grasslands on calcareous soils usually being richest in lichens, to the extent that some authors have termed them 'lichen grasslands' (Rodwell, 1992). More than 200 species have been recorded from this habitat (Gilbert 1993, 1995), although many of these were on chalk pebbles and flints rather than on the ground or turf itself. Also, the 70 or so genuinely terricolous lichens recorded, mainly species of *Cladonia*, *Leptogium*, and *Peltigera*, mostly have a wider ecology. Upland, acidic grasslands can also support lichens, especially *Cladonia* species, but such areas tend to be heath-like in composition. It seems that disturbance by man is a factor in encouraging the development of grassland lichens, one of several further aspects of the subject considered in Lambley (2001).

The development of grassland habitats in Britain has been described in the classic work by Tansley (1939) and, more recently, by Rackham (1986). These habitats include fine downland grassland overlying chalk or limestone, impoverished rough upland grassland, lowland acid grassland, and lowland meadows and pastures. Most are defined by soil pH and by their associated grasses and herbs, for which detailed community descriptions were given in Rodwell (1992). In terms of the fungi, it is convenient to talk broadly about semi-natural acid grasslands and calcareous grasslands, both of which have some typical species, particularly amongst the microfungi, and also to include more visibly artificial habitats such as old, unimproved lawns and recent or ephemeral grasslands.

Ecology of grassland fungi

In general, the fungi of grassland are as characteristic as the flora, and an integral part of the biotype. Fungal communities may vary markedly, however, according to the different types of grassland. Only a few non-specialist fungi are able to colonise widely and may also occur in non-grassland habitats. It should also be noted that many species which are not characteristic or typical of grassland habitats may be of incidental occurrence in them (perhaps occurring with a single old tree or a piece of buried wood). These different categories were carefully distinguished by Arnolds (1982) in an extensive and detailed ecological study of grassland macrofungi in the Netherlands.

There are many factors which influence the species composition of fungi in grassland, as well as their growth, development and fruitbody production. Soil type, pH, mineral content, carbon and nitrogen availability, water relations and other climatic factors all play a part, although the interaction between these factors is highly complex. Because of the comparatively exposed nature of grassland habitats, microclimatic factors can also vary greatly. Considerable fluctuations in species composition and fruitbody production may occur as a result, summarised by Arnolds (1992) for fungi of grasslands as well as other non-forest habitats. In Britain, pioneering studies on the ecology of grassland fungi were undertaken by Wilkins & Patrick (1939, 1940), who recorded a total of 172 species at 20 sites in southern England chosen to represent different soil types. They also investigated the presence and frequency of fungi on each soil type and their seasonal frequency in relation to environmental factors such as temperature, rainfall, soil water content and pH. Although it is difficult to generalise from these studies, there were some interesting conclusions. For example, they found the highest number of species to occur on chalk soils, fewer on sandy soils and the lowest on clay. The density of fruitbodies, however, was greatest on sandy soils, four times greater than on chalk and no less than eight times greater than on clay.

True grassland fungi are present as members of a range of ecological niches, either as saprotrophs, as parasites, or as mycorrhizal partners with plants. Eleven ecological groups of fungi obligately associated in some way with grassland habitats were recognised by Arnolds (1982), including saprotrophs on humus and on plant remains, parasites on herbs and on bryophytes, and coprophilous and nitrophilous species. The last group colonises the dung of herbivorous mammals, not only cattle, sheep and horses but rabbits and deer. These grazing animals are essential to the maintenance of short sward and the dung-loving fungi associated with them are a characteristic part of the pasture community. Fungi parasitic on invertebrates represent a further ecological group (Chapter Six), of which the scarlet caterpillar fungus *Cordyceps militaris* is a striking example.

Characteristic macrofungi of semi-natural grasslands

The most characteristic grassland macrofungi, including those associated with dung, are referable to three main groups of basidiomycetes and two of ascomycetes. Prominent among the former are the mushrooms and toadstools, which include such well-known species as the field mushroom *Agaricus campestris*. Genera with most or all of their species in grassland include *Agaricus* (the true mushrooms), *Hygrocybe* (waxcaps), *Dermoloma*, *Entoloma*, and *Porpoloma*. Other frequent grassland agarics include representatives of the genera *Conocybe*, *Galerina*, *Mycena*, *Panaeolina*, *Stropharia* and *Agrocybe*, although the majority of species in these genera typically occur in other habitats.

Another major group of grassland basidiomycetes is the clavarioid (club and coral) fungi. These include a range of simple or branching, white, yellow, pink or violaceous species in the genera *Clavaria, Clavulinopsis* and *Ramariopsis* (Fig. 72).

Puffballs also have several grassland representatives. These include the meadow puffball *Vascellum pratense*, several species of *Lycoperdon* and *Bovista*, the larger and more spectacular mosaic puffball *Handkea utriformis*, and the giant puffball *Calvatia gigantea*. The last of these produces one of the largest fruitbodies of all fungi, reaching 70 cm or more across. The grassland *Bovista nigrescens* and *B. plumbea* (Fig. 73) have a tumbling, wind-borne method of spore dispersal specifically adapted to short turf conditions and are consequently found nowhere else.

The larger ascomycetes are represented by the earth-tongues

FIG 72. The club fungus *Clavulinopsis fusiformis*, a common species of unimproved grassland recognised by the clustered, spindle-shaped, yellow fruitbodies (P. Livermore).

FIG 73. The grassland puffball *Bovista plumbea* showing the outer layer breaking away. The greyish inner spore sac is then freed to tumble about in the wind gradually releasing the spores (P. Livermore).

(*Geoglossaceae*), especially species of *Geoglossum*, most of which are grassland fungi, and *Microglossum*. These have upright, club-shaped fruitbodies not unlike some clavarioid fungi in form, but mostly blackish. Although a few of them, particularly *Geoglossum umbratile* and *G. fallax*, remain fairly common and widely distributed, sometimes even appearing in garden lawns, the majority of the dozen or so British species are becoming increasingly scarce. The greenish *Microglossum olivaceum* (Fig. 74) is of conservation concern in the UK and is a priority Biodiversity Action Plan species (Chapter 18).

Extensive lists of the principal larger fungi associated with grassland habitats were published by Watling (1973) and Ramsbottom (1953).

FIG 74. The greenish earthtongue *Microglossum olivaceum*, a scarce grassland species which is of conservation concern in the UK (S. Evans).

Increasing loss of habitat and the threat of commercial 'improvement'

The widespread and continual loss of old-established grasslands has had a major impact on the abundance and distribution of many characteristic grassland species. Commercial improvement of pasture by drainage, ploughing and reseeding, plus the application of inorganic fertilisers and herbicides, has been extensive, recent, and rapid. The extent of this loss in Britain was highlighted in a survey by Fuller (1987) of lowland grasslands in England and Wales. This found total grassland area to have declined by an alarming 3 million hectares between 1930 and 1984, to a total of just 4.8 million ha. Of these, only 0.2 million ha were categorised as unimproved pasture, a mere 3% of the area which existed in 1930. The complex communities of native herbs, grasses and bryophytes which once existed have been replaced with virtual monocultures of highly productive crop species such as perennial rye-grass (*Lolium perenne*).

This kind of commercial improvement is detrimental not only to the native grassland flora, but also to the saprotrophic soil fungi which are part of the same community. The effects have been well documented and were ably demonstrated, for example, by Arnolds (1989) in a study over a seven-year period of a sheep meadow in the Netherlands. Within five years the application of artificial fertilisers and liquid manure to a previously low-productive, moss-rich grassland community resulted in the almost complete loss of the dominant grasses and species-rich moss layer. There was a marked decrease in the terrestrial macrofungi previously known from the site and a total loss of fungi associated with bryophytes. Seven species of macrofungi, including the waxcap *Hygrocybe ceracea*, the club fungus *Clavulinopsis helvola* and the earth-tongue *Geoglossum glutinosum*, disappeared within a year, whilst nitrophilous species such as the common brown toadstools *Panaeolina foenisecii* and *Panaeolus* species, the puffball *Vascellum pratense*, and the fairy-ring toadstool *Marasmius oreades* (Fig. 78) increased. In general, the fungi were affected more rapidly and more drastically than the flora. Once fertilised and improved for agriculture, sites take at least 30 years to recover their characteristic grassland fungi.

FIG 75. A species of *Panaeolus*, slender toadstools with dark spores, several of which can be found commonly in semi-improved grassland, sometimes forming fairy rings (P. Roberts).

Waxcaps and other 'old grassland' indicator species

The importance of fungi as indicators of the conservation value of semi-natural grasslands is now widely accepted, and is based in particular on the numbers and diversity of waxcap species. These are mostly attractive, brightly-coloured toadstools which are readily seen and, as noted by Arnolds (1989), are 'pre-eminently appropriate indicator fungi of old, not or very weakly fertilised meadows'. They are entirely absent from temporary and recent grasslands, though a handful of common species such as *Hygrocybe conica* and *H. virginea* may start to appear after ten to twenty years if no further 'improvement' or other inappropriate management has been carried out. Old, unimproved grasslands may, in contrast, contain well over 20 waxcap species, with a few sites in the British Isles having 30 or more. Many of the waxcap species involved are now increasingly endangered throughout Europe, and it appears that the ever-decreasing British grasslands are paradoxically among their last European strongholds. For example, over 50% of the sites known in Europe for the pink waxcap (*H. calyptriformis*) are to be found in the British Isles.

Here, as throughout northern Europe, waxcaps are mostly found in dry, unimproved grasslands on well-drained soil, in dune grassland and in upland meadows, although some are characteristic of wetter habitats, including bogs. Over 50 species of *Hygrocybe* are known in the British Isles, of which only a few such as *H. conica*, *H. virginea*, and the edible *H. pratensis* are common in a wide range of grassland sites. These three are distinctive and readily identifiable, and a few others such as *H. psittacina*, often known as the 'parrot waxcap' on account of its multicoloured fruitbodies (Fig. 76), and the uniquely pink *H. calyptriformis* are also easy to recognise. The majority require more specialist attention. Boertman (1995) has provided excellent photographs, with keys and descriptions, for identifying European species, and keys to British species (and other grassland agarics) were given by Henrici (1996).

As well as the waxcaps, a range of other genera with similar ecological needs can also be used as indicators of these habitats, notably species of club and coral fungi, toadstools in the genera *Entoloma* and *Dermoloma*, and the earth-tongues. Various rating systems to reflect the value of any given site have been developed based on the presence of such fungi. The survey of

FIG 76. The parrot waxcap *Hygrocybe psittacina*, a common grassland species readily recognised by its green and yellow colours to which the common name refers (P. Roberts).

waxcap grasslands, which has been carried out by voluntary recorders from the British Mycological Society since 1996, has identified important grassland sites throughout the British Isles employing the 'CHEG' rating system to indicate the value of a site. This was developed from a Danish system, first proposed by Rald (1985), in which four categories of sites ranging from 'unimportant' to 'nationally important' were recognised, based solely on the number of *Hygrocybe* species present. Additional grassland fungi were added to form the CHEG system (*Clavariaceae-Hygrocybe-Entoloma-Geoglossaceae*) developed by Nitare (1988) in Sweden. CHEG brings together more information than the Rald system and is considered more flexible. However, it gives each species, common or rare, the same 'weighting' or value, so a more complex methodology with species weighted according to their perceived rarity was proposed by Jordal & Gaarder (1993). Although the result from this system may be more accurate, it presents greater difficulties in identification and, in practice, a similar rating is achieved regardless of the method used. The practical difficulty with all these systems is that they rely, inevitably, on the presence of fruitbodies at the time of investigation. For this reason, it is important that rating scores achieved after a single visit be compared and modified by scores achieved after several visits over more than one season.

Using a modified version of the original Rald system, Vesterholt *et al.* (1999) have suggested that the presence of 22 waxcap species constitutes a grassland site of international importance. England had 12 such sites in 2003, whilst Wales had 14 and Scotland at least 11. The top-scoring English site, Longshaw Estate in Derbyshire, has 33 *Hygrocybe* species, almost two-thirds (65%) of the total British waxcaps, whilst the best Welsh site was Garn Ddyrys on the Blorenge near Abergavenny, Monmouthshire, with 32 species. In Scotland, the grasslands at Abernethy in Inverness-shire rank amongst the best sites, with 28 *Hygrocybe* and 24 *Entoloma* species recorded. Some of the Hebridean islands are equally important. Even remote St. Kilda supports at least 23 different waxcaps. The most highly rated site in Ireland, The Curragh in Co. Kildare, largely comprises acidic grasslands in which no fewer than 33 *Hygrocybe* species have been recorded.

These threatened waxcap grasslands vary considerably in size, ranging from small garden lawns and churchyards to large estates and upland ranges. Although the relative importance for fungi of such disparate areas cannot be directly compared, all are valuable from a conservation point of view and it is essential that they are identified, recorded, properly protected and managed.

Calcareous grassland sites in the British Isles

Perhaps the most widespread semi-natural grasslands in the British Isles are those on calcareous soils, chalk and limestone. These tend to be dry grasslands because of the free-draining nature of the soil, and are rich in calcium but poor in available nitrogen and phosphate. They have been considered as the most species-diverse of all grasslands and are herb-rich with plants such as rock-rose (*Helianthemum* species), stemless thistle (*Cirsium acaule*), salad burnet (*Sanguisorba minor*), various sedges and orchids. Characteristic grass genera include *Bromus, Brachypodium, Briza, Helictotrichon, Phleum,* and *Sesleria.*

Dry calcareous grasslands are the most thoroughly studied from a mycological perspective, with intensive work carried out in the Netherlands by Arnolds (1981, 1982, 1989). They are potentially rich in waxcaps and *Entoloma* species, as well as other fungi (Fig. 77). However, many of the species are also found in acidic grasslands, their ecology seeming to depend more on the moss species present than on the pH of the soil. This may reflect the still undefined relationship between waxcaps and mosses, particularly *Rhytidiadelphus squarrosus*. This is a common and widespread moss which, as noted by Watson (1955), is 'indifferent as regards soil reaction, and grows equally in chalk grassland, among grass on lawns, in neutral pastures and on acid heaths. Grassy rides in woods are also a favourite habitat . . .'. Nevertheless, a recent report for English Nature (Evans, 2003) suggests that at least some waxcap species are restricted to alkaline sites,

FIG 77. The inkcap *Coprinus stanglianus*, a rare species of calcareous grassland usually found fruiting after rain in late spring and summer (T. Læssøe).

notably *Hygrocybe spadicea*, *H. calciphila*, and *H. persistens* var. *konradii*. Others, noted below, occur mostly in acidic grasslands, and some species prefer dry sites (*H. spadicea*), boggy meadows (*H. helobia*, *H. coccineocrenata* and *H. substrangulata*), or dune grassland (*H. conicoides*, *H. constrictospora*).

Amongst the most important examples of unimproved calcareous grassland in England are Greenham Common, Berkshire, which has at least 20 species of *Entoloma*, and Dancer's End, Buckinghamshire, where over 500 fungi have been recorded to date. The chalk downs around Box Hill and Norbury Park in Surrey also include extensive areas of unimproved calcareous grasslands which are rich in fungi. One site in Wales, Cwm Clydach in Breconshire, with 22 *Hygrocybe* and 17 *Entoloma* species recorded, has been designated a Site of Special Scientific Interest on the basis of its fungi.

Acid grassland sites in the British Isles

On sandy, acid soils, grasslands have a different suite of plant species. Grasses such as *Agrostis*, *Aira*, *Festuca*, *Nardus* and *Vulpia* species occur, and *Molinia* is abundant in wetter areas. Herbs include species of *Campanula* (harebell and its relatives), *Hieracium* (hawkweeds), *Polygala* (milkworts), *Thymus*, and *Viola*, and mosses may be abundant, notably species of *Dicranum*, *Hypnum*, and *Polytrichum*. Unimproved, well-drained acidic grassland can be rich in macrofungi, including many species of waxcap as well as *Entoloma* and *Dermoloma*. *Hygrocybe laeta*, *H. miniata* and *H. turunda* seem to have a special preference for acidic grasslands.

One of the most interesting acid grasslands, at The Patches (Little Moseley) in the Forest of Dean, is around 500 years old. This has been carefully managed, including a grazing regime and, with 29 species of *Hygrocybe* recorded, is amongst the richest sites for these fungi in Britain. It is also rich in species of *Entoloma*, including *E. infula* var. *chlorinosum*, for which it is currently the only known locality in Britain. Another acid grassland at Clitheroe, Lancashire, has 29 different waxcaps including the rare *H. aurantiosplendens*, a European Red List species. Well over 500 fungi have been recorded at this privately owned site, including the scarce earth-tongue *Trichoglossum walteri*.

Old lawns and cemeteries

Old lawns, churchyards and cemeteries represent artificial but often long-established grassland habitats. They are usually closely mown at regular intervals, and are of considerable wildlife importance. Where nitrogenous fertilisers have not been applied they may be herb- and moss-rich and, in addition, play host to a wide range of interesting fungi. Cemeteries, for example, are commonly amongst the best waxcap sites, especially in built-up areas and in parts of the country where unimproved pasture has virtually disappeared.

A good example is Darlington West Cemetery in County Durham, the fungi of which have been studied since 1971 (Legg, 1991). Around 400 species, including some significant rarities, have now been recorded from this site, although many microfungi are included in this total. Another well-studied site is Brookwood Cemetery in Surrey, the largest cemetery in the UK and once the largest in the world, covering almost 150 ha. Over 200 species of macrofungi have been recorded from Brookwood, including 23 *Hygrocybe* species, qualifying the site as an Important Fungus Area in the UK. Smaller sites may also be rich, as for example Danehill and Slaugham Churches in Sussex, each with 22 species of *Hygrocybe*, and St. Nicolas' Churchyard at Rotherfield Greys in Oxfordshire, where 17 species of *Hygrocybe* have been recorded.

Old lawns are of equal potential. One of the best known examples is at Down House in Kent, the former home of Charles Darwin now owned by English Heritage. Twenty species of waxcap have been recorded here, as well as eleven species of *Entoloma* and nine clavarioid fungi. In Wales, the lawns of Llanerchaeron Manor in Pembrokeshire have been proposed for SSSI (Site of Special Scientific Interest) status based on their macrofungi which include 20 waxcaps and various rare clavarioid fungi. In Leicestershire, the lawns of Roecliffe Manor at Charnwood are one of the best sites for grassland fungi so far known anywhere in the British Isles. No fewer than 27 species of waxcap and 28 species of *Entoloma* have been recorded there. Smaller garden lawns where fertilisers have long been avoided may also be of considerable interest. This is evident from an extensive study by Bond (1981) of lawns near Bristol, just 380 square metres in area, where 86 species of macrofungi were recorded during an eight-year period.

Ordinary garden lawns like these, which cover a vast area nationwide, are of immense potential value to wildlife. Avoiding fertilisers and other chemicals is a positive way to enhance their value and something every home-owning naturalist should take to heart. An unwarranted obsession with moss-free lawns not only represents a threat to waxcaps and other harmless fungi, but to insects and other invertebrates, the birds on which they feed, and the whole miniature ecosystem which is the traditional British garden.

Macrofungi in ephemeral and improved grasslands

Roadside verges, urban lawns and parks, and fallow farm fields represent less established, usually nitrogen-enriched and sometimes ephemeral grassland types. These may be of comparatively little mycological interest, although a surprising range of larger fungi can occur, mainly of commonplace nitrogen-tolerant species. Waterhouse (1957) recognised ten macrofungi which were more common on ordinary garden lawns than in other habitats, including the fairy-ring toadstool *Marasmius oreades* and, perhaps the most abundant of all, the ubiquitous *Panaeolina foenisecii*. This is the typical little brown toadstool of suburban lawns, the fruiting of which is apparently stimulated by mowing. The delicate parasol ink-cap *Coprinus plicatilis* is another of the common lawn fungi. Other species from 'improved' or fertilised lawns include the mildly hallucinogenic toadstool *Psilocybe semilanceata* (commonly known as 'liberty caps'), mushroom-like *Agrocybe* species, especially *A. praecox* and *A. dura*, the poisonous ring-forming toadstool *Clitocybe rivulosa*, the shaggy ink-cap *Coprinus comatus*, and the horse mushroom *Agaricus arvensis*. As commonplace nitrophiles, most of these can also be found in dung-rich areas of unimproved grasslands.

Several small, brown *Galerina* toadstools are frequently present on lawns, growing in association with mosses, and the equally small *Mycena olivaceomarginata*, which has a yellow tinge to the cap and a distinctly coloured gill edge, often occurs in troops. Some species of the brown-spored toadstool genus *Conocybe* may also be present, as may the larger fruitbodies of the whitish mushroom-like *Leucoagaricus leucothites*. A longer list of species recorded from lawns was given by Waterhouse (1957).

Fairy Rings

Though not restricted to grasslands, 'fairy rings' can be one of the most noticeable year-round indicators of the presence of macrofungi in lawns and pastures (Fig. 78). The term owes its origin to superstitious beliefs which developed in the Middle Ages to explain the existence of ring-like patterns and circles in grass. The existence of such rings has been recorded for centuries, and they may well have been the earliest disease of cultivated turf to be described.

Because of their apparently mysterious nature, a range of folk beliefs, myths and superstitions concerning fairy rings has arisen in Britain and throughout much of Europe. References occur abundantly in early literature and poetry, and detailed accounts of their history and associated superstitions were given in Ramsbottom (1953) and Rutter (2002). In early writings they were attributed to supernatural beings, particularly dancing fairies, and popular names such as 'fairy dances', 'hag tracks', 'hexen rings' and 'ronds de sorcières' occur throughout Europe. However, even as early

FIG 78. A circle of the common fairy ring champignon *Marasmius oreades*. This species forms conspicuous rings with a characteristic marked zonation with lush grass on either side of a rather dead zone in which the toadstools are formed (F. Hora).

as the sixteenth century, some authors attempted a more scientific explanation and attributed their formation to natural events, notably the effects of lightning. This remained a popular explanation even into the late eighteenth century, though other natural explanations such as the mating trails of slugs and the activities of insects were also put forward. It was not until the end of the eighteenth century that the true nature of fairy rings was understood, their formation finally being correctly attributed to *Marasmius oreades* (the commonest ring-forming toadstool) by the English botanist William Withering in 1792. The scientific study of their nature and biology has progressed apace since then, though even now they can still excite superstitions appropriate to the times. A fine photograph of a well-formed ring was published in the letter column of *Fortean Times* (Feb. 1999) as a 'mysterious circle' possibly formed by 'Earth energies' or alien crop-circle makers.

The prosaic truth is that fairy rings result from the growth of various fungi, particularly agarics and puffballs. Around 100 fungal species have been reported to form rings, mainly in grasslands, but also in other habitats such as woodlands. However, in the woodland environment the ring structure is only seen when fruitbodies appear, is frequently disrupted, and hence not so readily appreciated. A fundamental difference between grassland and woodland rings was identified by Gregory (1982). Grassland fungi, not tied to the roots of trees, form 'free' rings, potentially able to expand indefinitely, whereas those dependent on trees, usually in ectomycorrhizal associations, form 'tethered' rings. The latter, involving toadstool and bolete genera such as *Amanita, Lactarius, Boletus* and *Suillus*, exhibit only limited increase in diameter according to the growth of the tree.

Most ring-forming fungi develop in the soil, and as such are recognised as creators of 'edaphic' fairy rings. In contrast, a few basidiomycete species develop in the grass litter and form 'lectophilic' or 'superficial' fairy rings. They include some species of *Coprinus*, but the fungi involved are often sterile and their identity uncertain. Although most have no effect on the grass, some lectophilic fungi may be pathogenic on the grass roots, and cause severe injury to turf.

In grassland, three types of edaphic rings may be recognised. Type I, in which the grass is severely damaged or killed, is exemplified by the fairy-ring toadstool *Marasmius oreades*. This species is especially common in parks, lawns, and amenity turf, and the fruitbodies (buff-coloured, edible toadstools 2–5 cm across) may occur in large numbers in summer and autumn. It is the most important fairy-ring former in grassland because of the persistent disfiguring effects it causes in turf. In Type I rings, three different zones are clearly visible: two of lush, stimulated grass, separated by one of dead or stunted grass. The fungal fruitbodies develop in the outer edge of the dead zone, in which the fungal mycelium is most dense. In this dead zone permeation of surface water into the soil is much reduced, stunting the development of the grass. The inner lush zone is due to the presence of old, decaying fungus mycelium releasing accumulated nitrogen into the soil which stimulates grass growth. A similar though less marked effect occurs in the outermost zone of the ring where actively growing mycelium also produces excess nitrogen. *Marasmius oreades* is also pathogenic and may produce hydrogen cyanide, which is toxic to grass roots. Type I fairy rings produced by this species are perennial, increasing in diameter annually at a variable rate of between 0.2 m and 0.7 m according to environmental conditions. In undisturbed areas, rings up to 800 m across and estimated to be over 1000 years old have been reported. Although potentially able to expand indefinitely, rings typically reach their limits by physical disruption or mutual inhibition by competing and overlapping ring-forming fungi.

Fairy rings of Type II, in which the grass is stimulated but not killed, are caused by a range of fungi, notably species of *Agaricus*, the true mushrooms, the common blewits *Lepista nuda* and *L. saeva*, and puffballs such as *Vascellum pratense*. These are not parasites and do no damage but nutrients made available from their decomposition of organic matter in the soil stimulate grass growth. Although these fungi are generally common, perennial and often long-lived, the rings they form tend to be obvious only during their main fruiting season in the autumn, and are much less conspicuous (and less damaging) than those of *Marasmius oreades*.

Type III rings are produced by fungi which have no apparent effects on the growth of the grass. By their nature, these rings can only be appreciated when the fungal fruitbodies are formed, being otherwise completely inconspicuous. Waxcaps are perhaps the best-known formers of this type of ring, though species of *Calocybe* and *Panaeolus* (Fig. 75) are also involved. These fungi are saprotrophs, usually confined to the uppermost layers of the soil and decaying the root hairs of grass and dead mosses.

Grassland microfungi

As well as the larger fungi which are characteristic of grassland habitats, vast numbers of microfungi are present, particularly ascomycetes, and play an essential role in maintaining these habitats.

Many of these microfungi are soil saprobes, fruiting on and decaying dead parts of grasses, herbs and mosses and thereby recycling grassland nutrients. The majority occur on a wide range of grasses, although some, including various species of *Ascochyta* or *Phaeosphaeria* (*Ascomycota*), appear to be much more host-restricted. Other fungi occur as symbiotic partners in a range of associations with grasses and grassland herbs. Most grasses are now known to develop VA-mycorrhizal associations (Chapter Three) and fungal endophytes within living grasses may also play a significant role in maintaining the health of the community. The genus *Epichloë*, the cause of grass 'choke' (Chapter Five), is especially significant in this respect. Many further species are associated with grassland invertebrates and other animals, as parasites, saprobes or mutualists, or are associated with the dung of herbivores. All are an integral and important part of the grassland mycota.

Parasitic fungi of grassland plants are also characteristic, and some, notably diseases of crop and pasture grasses, are economically important. These include the rust fungi (*Uredinales*), some smuts (*Ustilaginales*), downy mildews (*Peronosporales*), powdery mildews (*Erysiphales*) and other ascomycetes such as ergot (*Claviceps purpurea*) and choke. These are all obligate parasites of grasses and are considered to have evolved in intimate association with their hosts, including the development of mutualistic relationships. *Neotyphodium lolii*, an *Epichloë* anamorph has, for example, been isolated as a symptomless endophyte of ryegrass, *Lolium perenne*. Ryegrass is a widespread and common species, much planted in improvement schemes. Its fungal endophyte plays a defensive and protective role within the plant, providing competitive benefits such as increased drought tolerance, increased tillering, and resistance to herbivory. The last is due to the secretion of chemicals such as alkaloids and neurotoxins which may be toxic to mammals and a deterrent or poison to invertebrate feeders. Perhaps the best-known of these toxic alkaloids is 'ergotamine', produced by the sclerotium of *Claviceps purpurea* which parasitises the ovary of many grasses. Once commonly present in cereal crops such as wheat and barley, ergotamine poisoning was responsible for many deaths in the Middle Ages and is today strictly monitored and controlled.

Smut fungi are not numerous in grassland but some, such as 'loose smut' (*Ustilago avenae*) and 'covered smut' (*Tilletia* species), may be abundant on certain wild grasses. The former infects and replaces the ovaries of oat grass (*Arrhenatherum elatius*) and has a blackish, powdery spore mass, yielding copious spores which can make hands and clothes 'smutty' when walking through infected plants. Species of *Tilletia* infect various grasses, the commonest being *T. holci* on species of *Holcus*, and *T. sphaerococca* on *Agrostis*. They again destroy the ovaries and may also cause stunting of infected plants, but the spore mass is largely concealed by the glumes and is not exposed and powdery. Another common grassland smut, *Ustilago striiformis*, infects the leaves of a wide range of grasses and forms conspicuous, longitudinal raised streaks beneath the epidermis, later rupturing and splitting the leaf into ribbons. Rust fungi may be abundant, and many grasses are potential hosts. Crown rust (*Puccinia coronata*) is one of the commonest species, alternating with buckthorn (*Rhamnus*), and infecting many kinds of grasses. Wheat rust (*P. graminis*), once an important disease of wheat, remains common but is controlled by removal of its alternate host, barberry (*Berberis* species). Over 20 different grass rusts occur in Britain, some of them very common. They include several which are strictly host limited, such as *Puccinia festucae* on some *Festuca* species, but others may infect a wide range of host genera and, since these are frequently found in their closely similar uredial stages, they can often prove difficult to identify.

Many other microfungi are also common as parasites of grasses. The most important British species were effectively dealt with in an early account by Sampson & Western (1941), but there are several more recent and detailed surveys, such as those provided by Smith *et al.* (1989), Smiley *et al.* (1992), and Couch (1995). All wild grasses are host to a range of such fungi, which in natural grasslands present no special problems. However, in ornamental and amenity grasslands, which are often artificial monocultures, they can attack and damage seedlings of fine grasses and established turf. This makes them a perpetual worry (and expense) to groundkeepers responsible for lawns and sports fields, especially since they involve a surprising number of fungi which may variously attack seeds, roots, leaves or inflorescences. One of the commonest in Britain is snow mould, a severe and disfiguring disease of fine turf found mainly during the winter months. It is caused by the ascomycete *Microdochium nivale* which initially produces small brownish spots in turf which gradually coalesce into larger patches, often killing the grass. Annual meadow-grass (*Poa annua*), as well as species of *Agrostis* and *Festuca*, are particularly susceptible. During the summer months, red thread disease caused by the corticioid basidiomycete *Laetisaria fuciformis* may occur. This tends to produce bleached areas of grass, often containing visible pink mycelial threads. Other important diseases due to ascomycetes include dollar spot caused by *Sclerotinia homoeocarpa* and take-all patch caused by *Gaeumannomyces graminis*. Dollar spot is fairly common and widespread but in the British Isles seems to be virtually confined to *Festuca rubra*. It causes small, yellow-green and then bleached areas in turf, these gradually enlarging and sometimes coalescing into more diffuse, disfigured areas. Take-all patch may affect a range of grasses and is often encouraged by over-liming. It typically produces bleached or brown rings in fine turf, most noticeable from late summer, eventually killing the grass. Baldwin (1990) has provided a brief overview of the commonest British turf diseases, with colour photographs of the symptoms.

CHAPTER 9

Trees and Woodland

I T IS NO surprise and certainly no accident that fungi attain their greatest diversity in woodlands. As decomposers of plant litter and wood, as ectomycorrhizal associates of trees, and as leaf and plant parasites, fungi can find innumerable niches in woodland ecosystems within which they play an essential, nutrient-recycling role.

British woodlands

In Britain, both woodlands and their associated fungi date back no further than the end of the last Ice Age, some 12,000 years ago. When the glaciers retreated, trees returned from the south in a series of recolonisations which have been dated by examining ancient pollen trapped in peat bogs and lake sediments. From this we know that the earliest colonisers included birch, aspen, and willow, followed by hazel and pine, then alder, oak, and lime, and finally beech, ash, and hornbeam. From these arose, around 7000 years ago, the original 'wildwood' of Britain and Ireland, covering most of the land except for the highest moors, mountains, and the northenmost parts of Scotland.

The pattern of natural vegetation has changed surprisingly little since then. Our main native beech woods, for example, are still confined to southeastern England, the Midlands, and south Wales. Our native pine woods are still confined to Scotland. What has changed, of course, is the arrival of people. Between the Bronze Age and the Roman period, most of the original wildwood was cleared for agriculture and settlement. By the time of the Domesday Book, only 15% of England was still wooded (Rackham, 1986), and even this was managed, exploited, and entirely tamed. By the beginning of the twentieth century, the figure had dropped to around 5% and today has sunk to below 1%, representing around 10% of total 'tree cover'. Extensive replanting in the last 200 years has maintained or even increased tree cover in Britain, but these replantings, often of exotic trees, are highly artificial. England today has around 7.5% tree cover, with Sussex, Surrey, Hampshire, and Northumberland the most wooded counties; Wales has around 12% tree cover, with West and Mid Glamorgan the most wooded counties; Scotland has around 19% tree cover.

Traditional woodland management involved 'coppicing' trees (cutting them at ground level) to promote the growth of poles which were harvested every few years and principally used as fuel. In wood-pastures or other areas subject to grazing, trees were 'pollarded' (cut above the reach of animals) rather than coppiced. In many woodlands, a minority of trees were left uncut to produce timber for construction. Coppice 'stools' (the tree base itself) can be exceptionally old and large, as can some pollarded trees. In both cases, the coppicing and pollarding appear to prolong the life of the tree almost indefinitely. This ancient woodland regime fell into disuse in the twentieth century, but has recently been revived in many nature reserves. Coppicing clearly eliminates fungi growing on dead standing wood (though some non-lichenised species may survive if woods are coppiced in rotation) and also curtails the production of fruitbodies, since newly coppiced woodland becomes open, drier, and choked with new herbaceous growth. From a purely mycological point of view, old abandoned woodlands tend to be richest in species, though epiphytic lichens prefer old wood pasture where trees are less shaded.

Veteran trees, those 'of interest biologically, culturally, or aesthetically because of their age, size, or condition' (Read, 2000), are a particular feature of the British landscape. They are often 'working trees' which were once pollarded and may be (as in some wood pasture oaks) up to 800 years old. Such trees are of exceptional interest to nature conservation because of the habitats they offer to otherwise rare organisms, many of which are the last survivors of the ancient pre-mediaeval wildwood. In terms of fungi, veteran trees are of particular significance for their epiphytic lichens, and indeed medieval wood-pasture with its ancient trees is considered the richest of all woodland types for lichens. They support many rare and relict species which are indicators of age and ecological continuity. A list of 30 such lichens was provided by Rose (1976), including the crustose species *Pachyphiale carneola, Lecanactis premnea, Thelotrema lepadinum* and *Opegrapha lyncea* which still occur in southern England but are now found only on ancient trees. The foliose *Lobaria, Nephroma* and *Sticta* species are similarly restricted. A few non-lichenised fungi (notably the oak polypore *Piptoporus quercinus*) also seem to be restricted to this habitat. In 1993, the Ancient Tree Forum (ATF) was formed which led in turn to the Veteran Trees Initiative, a partnership between ATF, landowners and conservation agencies set up in 1996. This has already led to a substantial guidebook on managing veteran trees (Read, 2000), with particular reference to their wood-rotting and epiphytic fungi.

Plantations, even exotic and fairly recent conifer plantations, can often contain a rich assortment of fungi (Humphrey *et al.*, 2002), sometimes including uncommon native species which have managed to exploit a niche in the ecosystem. If the number of fungal species is lower in plantations, then it is almost certainly because plantations tend to be monocultures lacking diversity. There is no proof for this, however, as no comparative work on numbers of fungal species in different woodlands has been undertaken. In Britain (and indeed the world), the most comprehensively recorded site for fungi is Esher Common in Surrey, where over 3200 different species have been found to date. This site has extensive pine plantations and secondary woodland on residual heath but also offers many other habitats. Whether even more species could be found in a similar area of ancient, native woodland is as yet unknown.

In summary, what we have now in Britain is a mix of ancient managed woodland, secondary woodland, plantation, and open parkland or wood-pasture. Despite all the depredations and reductions in the last 2000 years, this man-made mix still provides us with a rich and varied woodland mycota.

Woodland fungi

Fungal communities in woodlands vary considerably depending on a number of factors which are clearly influential, though difficult to assess and compare. The following are some of the more important:

- *composition of the woodland*, particularly in terms of tree species (or more properly, genera). Most trees have their own fungal associates, so that a mixed woodland with many different trees will inevitably contain a greater variety of fungi than woodland dominated by a single species. By the same token, a beech wood will contain a very different set of species from a pine wood.
- *soil composition*, whether it is acid or alkaline, mull (with little or no litter layer) or mor (with a substantial litter layer). Acidic ground with mor soil is typical for the majority of British woodlands simply because it is not good for agriculture. It is, however, good for both ectomycorrhizal and litter-degrading macrofungi, so often appears rich in species. Woodlands on alkaline ground with mull soil have a quite different and often less immediately visible mycota.
- *climate and location.* Though fungi tend to be widely distributed, there are many northern species in Scotland which do not occur in the south of England, and vice-versa. Some also show an east-west preference, and a few are unaccountably localised (e.g. the bolete *Strobilomyces strobilaceus*). Whether this is entirely due to differences in climate is not clear.
- *moisture.* Not surprisingly, different fungi grow in woodlands on wet ground from those on dry ground, but humidity and rainfall are also important and one of the reasons for the east-west divide noted above. The extent to which woodlands are sheltered from the wind certainly influences fruitbody production.
- *past and current management.* Dense, old coppice woodland will have many more species than heavily managed new coppice or open woodland pasture (though the latter, if old, may be ideal for epiphytic lichens). Similarly, woodland with plenty of dead standing and fallen wood supports more species than 'tidy' commercial or amenity woodland. Heavily grazed woodlands are poor for fungi, mainly

because of soil disturbance and nitrification through dunging. Farm residues, particularly from fertilisers, also degrade the fungal composition of adjacent woodland.

- *age*. The age of the woodland is clearly important for fungi though difficult to gauge. Ancient, continuously wooded sites support far more species than recent plantations, but that is partly a matter of variety and tidiness. Some macrofungi, notably ectomycorrhizal Cortinarius species, may be associated with ancient woodland, but potential indicator species (other than lichens – see Chapter 18) have yet to be found.
- *size*. The larger the wood, the more fungal species it will contain. This is partly a factor of habitat diversity, always likely to be equated with size, but is also a factor of integrated plant-fungal-animal communities, whose diverse interactions may be destroyed when woodlands become too small to support certain key species.

From the list above, the tree composition of a woodland is probably the single greatest influence on the mycota, and it therefore seems best to consider the fungi of British woodlands in terms of their tree species.

Before doing so, however, it may be useful to recall the three main ecological niches for woodland fungi. The most obvious group is the wood-rotters (Chapter Three), many of which are specialised in terms of the species of tree they rot, whether they rot standing or fallen wood, and whether they rot heartwood, sapwood, bark, or twigs and branches. Also important are the leaf- and litter-rotters, some of which specialise in particular kinds of litter which may be influenced by soil acidity and the availability of nutrients. The third group is the ectomycorrhizal fungi (Chapter Four), most of which are associated with living trees and are frequently specific to particular tree genera.

In addition to these, of course, there are numerous parasitic fungi attacking woodland plants and invertebrates (Chapter Six), as well as lichenised epiphytes and insect associates (Chapter Five), and fungi of specialist niches within woodlands (Chapter 15).

For each of the major genera of trees a table is given listing important fungal associates in Britain, including mycorrhizal species, pathogens and saprobes. Lichenised species are not included, as epiphytic lichens tend to grow on barks of different pH values and different textures, rather than on specific tree genera. Thus, of over 300 species of lichen recorded from oak bark in Britain (Rose, 1974), none are specific to oak.

Extended lists of fungal associates of British trees were published by Watling (1973) and Dennis (1986), and many microfungi were treated in Ellis & Ellis (1997).

General woodland macrofungi

Table 4 lists widespread, generalist basidiomycetes found in deciduous and mixed woodland in the British Isles, based on the top 50 species recorded during British Mycological Society spring and autumn forays (Rayner, 1979). The list includes many familiar agarics, such as *Amanita rubescens* (the blusher), which may form ectomycorrhizal associations with a wide range of tree species. In Britain, such fungi may be found in almost every mixed woodland. The same applies to many generalist wood and litter saprotrophs, like *Armillaria* species (the honey fungus group), *Collybia peronata* (Fig. 79) *Hypholoma fasciculare, Mycena galopus,* or *Trametes versicolor.* Being based on

FIG 79. *Collybia peronata* is a common woodland toadstool growing in leaf litter. The species is sometimes called 'wood woolly-foot' due to its shaggy stem base (B. Spooner).

foray records, the list is biased towards conspicuous and easily recognised species, and may also miss out some late-season generalists like *Lepista inversa* and *Clitocybe nebularis,* both extremely common in late autumn and early winter. More extensive lists of general woodland agarics were provided by Orton (1986).

Among the commoner larger ascomycetes, not covered in the survey, are *Xylaria hypoxylon* (the candlesnuff fungus), ubiquitous on stumps and decaying wood, the false morels *Helvella crispa* and *H. lacunosa,* and the brownish cup-fungi *Peziza badia* and *P. succosa. Elaphomyces granulatus,* the hart's truffle, is also worth noting since it is almost universally present in mixed woodlands, even though it has to be searched for under the litter layer.

TABLE 4. Some typical basidiomycetous macrofungi of deciduous woodland, based on Rayner (1979). Species marked with an asterisk were found on more than 20% of the foray excursions; the remainder on 10 – 20%.

SPECIES	ECOLOGY	SUBSTRATA
*Amanita fulva**	mycorrhizal	on soil, litter
*Amanita rubescens**	mycorrhizal	on soil, litter
*Boletus chrysenteron**	mycorrhizal	on soil, litter
Boletus edulis	mycorrhizal	on soil, litter
*Boletus subtomentosus**	mycorrhizal	on soil, litter
*Cantharellus cibarius**	mycorrhizal	on soil, litter
Clavulina cinerea	mycorrhizal	on soil, litter
Clavulina cristata	mycorrhizal	on soil, litter
Hebeloma crustuliniforme	mycorrhizal	on soil, litter
Hydnum repandum	mycorrhizal	on soil, litter
*Inocybe geophila**	mycorrhizal	on soil, litter
*Laccaria amethystina**	mycorrhizal	on soil, litter
*Laccaria laccata**	mycorrhizal	on soil, litter
*Russula cyanoxantha**	mycorrhizal	on soil, litter
*Russula fragilis**	mycorrhizal	on soil, litter
*Russula ochroleuca**	mycorrhizal	on soil, litter
*Scleroderma citrinum**	mycorrhizal	on soil, litter
*Armillaria mellea s.l.**	parasitic	clustered on logs, stumps, buried wood
*Auricularia auricula-judae**	saprotrophic	on fallen or dead standing wood

SPECIES	ECOLOGY	SUBSTRATA
Bjerkandera adusta*	saprotrophic	on stumps, fallen or dead standing wood
Calocera cornea	saprotrophic	on fallen or dead standing wood
Clitocybe infundibuliformis	saprotrophic	on soil, litter
Clitopilus prunulus	saprotrophic	on soil, litter
Collybia confluens*	saprotrophic	on soil, litter
Collybia dryophila*	saprotrophic	on soil, litter
Collybia maculata*	saprotrophic	on soil, litter
Collybia peronata*	saprotrophic	on soil, litter
Coprinus micaceus*	saprotrophic	on rotten stumps and logs
Dacrymyces stillatus*	saprotrophic	on fallen or dead standing wood
Entoloma conferendum*	saprotrophic	on soil, litter
Galerina mutabilis*	saprotrophic	on dead trunks and branches
Ganoderma adspersum*	saprotrophic	on heartwood
Hypholoma fasciculare*	saprotrophic	on rotten stumps and logs
Laetiporus sulphureus	saprotrophic	on heartwood
Lepiota cristata	saprotrophic	on soil, litter
Lycoperdon perlatum	saprotrophic	on soil, litter
Lycoperdon pyriforme*	saprotrophic	on rotten stumps and logs
Megacollybia platyphylla	saprotrophic	near rotten stumps and logs
Mycena galericulata*	saprotrophic	on rotten stumps and logs
Mycena galopus*	saprotrophic	on soil, litter
Mycena pura	saprotrophic	on soil, litter
Mycena sanguinolenta*	saprotrophic	on soil, litter
Mutinus caninus	saprotrophic	in woodland litter
Oudemansiella radicata*	saprotrophic	on buried wood
Phallus impudicus*	saprotrophic	near rotten stumps and logs
Pluteus cervinus*	saprotrophic	on rotten stumps and logs
Polyporus squamosus	saprotrophic	on rotten stumps and logs
Schizopora paradoxa*	saprotrophic	on fallen or dead standing wood
Stereum hirsutum*	saprotrophic	on fallen or dead standing wood
Trametes versicolor*	saprotrophic	on rotten stumps and logs

BROADLEAVED TREES

The following A-Z entries provide some details of the fungi associated with all the major native and naturalised trees in the British Isles. A few additional fungi associated with exotic garden or parkland trees are considered briefly in Chapter 14.

Alder

Alder (*Alnus glutinosus*), widespread throughout the country, is predominantly a tree of wet and flooded woodland, most frequent along water-courses but often forming more substantial carrs. It also occurs in some upland areas, less obviously associated with water. It was frequently coppiced, particularly for charcoal, but little used for timber. Alder is ectomycorrhizal and has a distinctive set of associated fungi. Amongst the commonest are the milk caps *Lactarius omphaliformis* and *L. obscuratus*, comparatively small and similar tawny-orange species, the latter being distinguished by its olivaceous tints. *Naucoria escharioides* is the commonest of about nine or ten species of *Naucoria* associated with alder in Britain, all of which are delicate toadstools with yellowish-brown or date-brown caps and are reliably distinguished only on microscopic characters. Less common ectomycorrhizal species include *Amanita friabilis*, *Paxillus rubicundulus*, *Russula alnetorum*, and the rare but distinctive bolete *Gyrodon lividus*.

Dead branches and logs often bear fruitbodies of *Daedaleopsis confragosa*, the 'blushing bracket', so named for its red-staining pore layer. It is equally common on birch and willow. The yellow-brown, tiered brackets of *Inonotus radiatus* are also frequent on dead alder trunks, as well as on birch. An ascomycetous saprotroph, *Camarops polysperma*, has dark stromatic fruitbodies which develop under the bark, eventually causing the top of the tree to collapse (a rather obvious clue to its presence). Amongst the parasites are three species of *Taphrina*, all of which induce galls. *Taphrina tosquinetii*, quite common on young trees and sucker growth, causes conspicuously wrinkled and blistered leaves which are much paler than uninfected foliage. *Taphrina sadebeckii* also occurs on leaves, but forms isolated, yellowish blisters. Much more spectacular are the galls of *T. alni* which transform the

FIG 80. Once thought rare, *Taphrina alni* appears to be extending its range in Britain. The fungus induces conspicuous pinkish, tongue-like galls on female alder cones (B. Spooner).

scales of female cones into long, conspicuous tongue-like structures (Fig. 80). This species, once rare and restricted to parts of western England, Wales and Ireland, appears to be spreading and has been found recently in several localities in northern and central England. More serious parasites are species of *Phytophthora*, especially *P. cambivora*, a root pathogen which may cause die-back and pale leaves which are greatly reduced in size.

TABLE 5. Some typical fungi found with alder (*Alnus glutinosus*).

SPECIES	ECOLOGY	SUBSTRATA
Amanita friabilis	mycorrhizal	in litter and soil
Cortinarius alnetorum	mycorrhizal	in litter and soil
Gyrodon lividus	mycorrhizal	in litter and soil
Lactarius omphaliformis	mycorrhizal	in litter and soil
Lactarius lilacinus	mycorrhizal	in litter and soil
Lactarius obscuratus	mycorrhizal	in litter and soil
Naucoria escharioides	mycorrhizal	in litter and soil

SPECIES	ECOLOGY	SUBSTRATA
Naucoria striatula	mycorrhizal	in litter and soil
Paxillus rubicundulus	mycorrhizal	in litter and soil
Russula alnetorum	mycorrhizal	in litter and soil
Taphrina alni	gall-forming	on attached female catkins
Taphrina sadebeckii	gall-forming	on leaves
Taphrina tosquinetii	gall-forming	on leaves
Microsphaera penicillata	parasitic	on leaves
Phytophthora cambivora	parasitic	on roots
Camarops microsperma	saprotrophic	on trunks
Camarops polysperma	saprotrophic	on trunks
Ciboria amentacea	saprotrophic	on fallen male catkins
Ciboria viridifusca	saprotrophic	on fallen female catkins
Daedaleopsis confragosa	saprotrophic	on logs, trunks, branches
Encoelia furfuracea	saprotrophic	on dead branches
Inonotus radiatus	saprotrophic	on trunks
Peniophora erikssonii	saprotrophic	on dead attached branches
Rutstroemia conformata	saprotrophic	on dead leaves
Uncinia foliicola	saprotrophic	on dead leaves
Vuilleminia alni	saprotrophic	on dead attached branches

Ash

Ash (*Fraxinus excelsior*) was widespread but rather uncommon in the original wildwood but is an effective coloniser which appears to have increased its presence in surviving woodland as a result of clearance and management. Trees are rather short-lived, typically lasting less than 200 years, but the oldest living coppice stools may be 1000 years old. Ash was widely utilised for timber (it was the second favourite, after oak), but more frequently coppiced or pollarded, the wood used for poles, hoops, and handles. The foliage was also sometimes used as fodder, for which it was the second favourite tree after elm.

Ash is not ectomycorrhizal and consequently has few agaric associates, though the late-fruiting *Phaeogalera oedipus* occurs typically in decomposing ash litter. It does, however, have several conspicuous non-agaric associates, notably *Daldinia concentrica*, commonly called 'King Alfred's cakes' (on account of its black, burnt-looking fruitbodies) or 'cramp balls'. The fruitbodies, on dead trunks and fallen wood, have a conspicuous concentric zonation easily seen when specimens are cut across. At least six other *Daldinia* species occur in Britain on a variety of hosts. Another large fungus is the bracket *Inonotus hispidus*, often growing quite high up on mature trees and distinguished by its hirsute ('hispid') cap. It is most frequent on ash, but occasionally fruits on apple and other deciduous trees.

Other species are much less conspicuous. The tiny, blackish, flask-shaped fruitbodies of the ascomycete *Cryptosphaeria eunomia* are common and occur in swarms, but are sunken in dead branches and visible on the surface only as minute dots. The ascomycete *Nectria galligena* is equally small, but is the cause of a very conspicuous and fairly common canker of trunks and branches.

TABLE 6. Some typical fungi found with ash (*Fraxinus excelsior*).

SPECIES	ECOLOGY	SUBSTRATA
Inonotus hispidus	parasitic	on standing trunks
Nectria galligena	parasitic	on cankered wood
Phyllactinia fraxini	parasitic	on leaves
Hymenoscyphus albidus	saprotrophic	on fallen leaves, petioles
Cryptosphaeria eunomia	saprotrophic	on dead branches
Cryptosphaeria fraxini	saprotrophic	on dead branches
Daldinia concentrica	saprotrophic	on dead wood
Hypoxylon fraxinophilum	saprotrophic	on dead branches
Hypoxylon rubiginosum	saprotrophic	on dead wood
Hysterographium fraxini	saprotrophic	on bark of dead branches
Phaeogalera oedipus	saprotrophic	on leaf litter
Phomopsis pterophila	saprotrophic	on fallen samaras

Beech

Beech (*Fagus sylvatica*) was one of the last native trees to arrive in Britain and largely colonised the country south-east of a line from Weymouth to Swansea to King's Lynn with some outliers further north. Since then, it has been widely planted and become naturalised throughout the country. Veteran trees, such as those in Epping Forest, Essex, are at least 400 years old. Trees were mostly coppiced or pollarded to provide fuel wood (particularly billets and logs) and only rarely grown as timber. In the West Country, beech was frequently used in hedging, resulting (through neglect) in some old beech avenues in areas where beech was never native. More recently it has been used as a shelter-belt tree for conifer plantations.

Beech has numerous associated fungi, including many ectomycorrhizal species, some common parasites and a host of obligate saprotrophs. Perhaps the most familiar of its mycorrhizal partners are the red-capped *Russula mairei*, the yellowish *R. fellea*, which has a distinct fruity odour, and the milk-cap *Lactarius blennius*. Beech is also an important host for the best of our edible truffles, *Tuber aestivum*, found particularly on chalky soil in southern England.

Several large bracket fungi occur on standing trunks. These include at least two species of *Ganoderma*, *G. australe* and *G. pfeifferi*, both plurivorous but particularly frequent on this host. *Fomes fomentarius* is of interest, since it normally grows on birch in the north of Britain, where it is common, but tends to switch host further south where, until recently, it was much more rare and occurred mainly on beech. *Trametes gibbosa* is also common on beech, forming tough, sometimes tiered brackets on dead trunks and logs. Whitish when young, they are soon colonised by algae giving a characteristic green colour to the upper surface. Other plurivorous bracket fungi such as *Bjerkandera adusta* and *Trametes versicolor* are also common on beech logs.

Beech leaf litter provides an equally rich substratum. The tiny white agaric *Mycena capillaris* is restricted to beech litter, as is the larger and more attractive *M. crocata*. The latter has a distinctive orange-brown cap and copious orange-red latex which exudes from damaged flesh. *Xylaria carpophila*, a close relative of the candle-snuff fungus *X. hypoxylon*, develops wiry blackish or white-tipped stromata on decaying beech cupules in fallen litter (Fig. 81).

Trunks and branches of beech are commonly seen to bear patches of a blackish, encrusting fungus on the bark. This is *Ascodichaena rugosa*, an ascomycete which, although abundantly producing asexual spores, rarely if ever develops asci. It also occurs on oak. One of the most distinctive agarics on dead trunks and branches is *Oudemansiella mucida*, an attractive toadstool with whitish, translucent, slimy caps which have given it the common name 'porcelain fungus'. It grows in tufts, often high up in old trees (Fig. 82). Two large ascomycetes should also be noted: *Hypoxylon fragiforme* produces hemispherical stromata up to 1 cm across which are brick-red at first,

FIG 81. *Xylaria carpophila*, a relative of the candlesnuff fungus, grows only on decayed and fallen beech cupules. It can be quite common in litter under beech trees in the autumn (B. Spooner).

FIG 82. The porcelain fungus, *Oudemansiella mucida*, typically grows in tufts on dead attached branches of beech, often quite high up in the tree. The English name refers to its white, translucent fruitbodies, the Latin epithet to their sliminess (P. Roberts).

becoming blackish with age, and often occur in swarms on decaying branches and logs; *Neobulgaria pura* is a cup-fungus with pale violaceous, gelatinous, top-shaped fruitbodies 1 – 3 cm across, often found growing in dense clusters on fallen trunks.

TABLE 7. Some typical fungi found with beech (*Fagus sylvatica*).

SPECIES	ECOLOGY	SUBSTRATA
Boletus satanas	mycorrhizal	on soil and litter
Cortinarius cinnabarinus	mycorrhizal	on soil and litter
Cortinarius elatior	mycorrhizal	on soil and litter
Cortinarius splendens	mycorrhizal	on soil and litter
Cortinarius stillatitius	mycorrhizal	on soil and litter
Cortinarius torvus	mycorrhizal	on soil and litter
Elaphomyces muricatus	mycorrhizal	on soil and litter
Hygrophorus cossus	mycorrhizal	on soil and litter
Lactarius blennius	mycorrhizal	on soil and litter
Lactarius subdulcis	mycorrhizal	on soil and litter
Russula fellea	mycorrhizal	on soil and litter
Russula mairei	mycorrhizal	on soil and litter
Tuber aestivum	mycorrhizal	on soil and litter
Nectria ditissima	parasitic	on trunks, branches
Ascodichaena rugosa	parasitic	on trunks and branches
Collybia fagiphila	saprotrophic	on fallen leaves
Coprinus picaceus	saprotrophic	in leaf litter
Fomes fomentarius	saprotrophic	on trunks
Ganoderma australe	saprotrophic	on trunks
Ganoderma pfeifferi	saprotrophic	on trunks
Hericium erinaceus	saprotrophic	on living trunks
Hypoxylon fragiforme	saprotrophic	on dead trunks and branches
Marasmius alliaceus	saprotrophic	amongst leaf litter
Melanconis chrysosperma	saprotrophic	on dead branches
Mycena capillaris	saprotrophic	on leaf litter
Mycena crocata	saprotrophic	in leaf litter
Mycena pelianthina	saprotrophic	on or amongst leaf litter
Neobulgaria pura	saprotrophic	on fallen trunks and logs
Oudemansiella mucida	saprotrophic	on dead attached branches
Pezicula carpinea	saprotrophic	on dead twigs and branches
Trametes gibbosa	saprotrophic	on stumps
Xylaria carpophila	saprotrophic	on beechmast cupules

Birches

Our two common birches (*Betula pendula* and *B. pubescens*) are rapid colonisers and were among the earliest trees to appear in the British Isles after the last Ice Age. They are, however, comparatively short-lived, rarely reaching 100 years, and are also intolerant of shade. In the original wildwood they were abundant only in northern Scotland though surviving further south in fens and other marginal areas. Birches have no heartwood and fallen trees rot so rapidly that logs often consist of a more or less hollow tube of bark. In Scandinavia, this tough but pliable bark was valued, particularly for roofing, but there are few if any records of such uses in Britain. Here, the tree was coppiced for underwood, the twigs used for birch-brooms, and the bark occasionally employed in tanning. With the decline of traditional woodmanship, together with the decline in maintenance of heathlands, birch has invaded previously cleared ground and has become increasingly common throughout Britain, to the extent that it is often now regarded as a weed species. Dwarf birch, *Betula nana*, a much scarcer species restricted to moors mostly at altitudes over 250m, is found only in northern England and Scotland. It is a shrub rarely over a metre in height, yet supports many of the typical birch fungi.

Birches are ectomycorrhizal and have a distinctive and substantial mycota of associated agarics. One of the most conspicuous is *Amanita muscaria*, the fly agaric, almost ubiquitous with birch, less commonly also with pine, spruce, or beech. *Amanita fulva*, the tawny grisette, is also common with birch, whilst the attractive, but uncommon orange species, *A. crocea*, occurs with birch and beech. Several of the *Russulales* are only found with birch, notably the coconut-scented *Lactarius glyciosmus* and, in *Sphagnum* bogs and on wet ground, the bright yellow *Russula claroflava*. Numerous *Cortinarius* species are birch associates, often hard to distinguish but including some attractive species such as *C. armillatus* and *C. hemitrichus*, and the larger *C. triumphans*. Various boletes including *Leccinum versipelle*, the orange birch bolete, *L. holopus*, a whitish species, and several brown species formerly referred to *L. scabrum*, also specialise in birch.

Birch has few specialist litter-rotting species, but does have a number of distinctive wood-rotters. Chief among these is the well known birch polypore or 'razor-strop fungus', *Piptoporus betulinus*, which is restricted to this host and can be found almost everywhere birch grows, particularly on dead standing trees. In Scotland and northern England, *Fomes fomentarius*, the 'hoof fungus', is equally common and has a similar habit (Fig. 83). In recent years it has spread on this host to southern England, where it was first found on birch at West End Common, Esher, Surrey in 1990. Orton (1986) provided lists of agarics he considered typical of Highland birch woods and of more general birch woods throughout Great Britain. Watling (1984) also provided lists and notes on British macrofungi in birch woods.

FIG 83. The hoof-like fruitbodies of *Fomes fomentarius* were once almost restricted to old birch trees in Scotland and the north of England, but are now occasionally found on birch and other hosts in the south (B. Spooner).

TABLE 8. Some typical fungi found with birches (*Betula* species).

SPECIES	ECOLOGY	SUBSTRATA
Amanita crocea	mycorrhizal	in soil and litter
Amanita muscaria	mycorrhizal	in soil and litter
Cortinarius armillatus	mycorrhizal	in soil and litter
Cortinarius betuletorum	mycorrhizal	in soil and litter
Cortinarius hemitrichus	mycorrhizal	in soil and litter
Cortinarius triumphans	mycorrhizal	in soil and litter
Lactarius glyciosmus	mycorrhizal	in soil and litter
Lactarius torminosus	mycorrhizal	in soil and litter
Lactarius turpis	mycorrhizal	in soil and litter
Lactarius vietus	mycorrhizal	in soil and litter
Leccinum holopus	mycorrhizal	in soil and litter
Leccinum scabrum	mycorrhizal	in soil and litter
Leccinum versipelle	mycorrhizal	in soil and litter
Russula betularum	mycorrhizal	in soil and litter
Russula claroflava	mycorrhizal	in soil and litter
Russula gracillima	mycorrhizal	in soil and litter
Tricholoma fulvum	mycorrhizal	in soil and litter
Melampsoridium betulinum	parasitic	on leaves
Melanconis stilbostoma	parasitic	on branches
Taphrina betulina	parasitic	causing witches' brooms
Fomes fomentarius	saprotrophic	on trunks
Hypoxylon multiforme	saprotrophic	on dead stumps, branches
Inonotus radiatus	saprotrophic	on trunks
Lenzites betulina	saprotrophic	on trunks, branches
Piptoporus betulinus	saprotrophic	on trunks

Chestnut

Sweet chestnut (*Castanea sativa*) is believed to have been brought into Britain in the Roman period, but has long become naturalised and part of the woodland landscape. It was valued not only for its edible chestnuts, but as coppice wood and to a lesser extent as timber. Ancient trees, such as the Tortworth chestnut in Gloucestershire, are probably over 500 years old and some large coppice stools may be even older.

Chestnut is an ectomycorrhizal tree, but has no specific associates, at least in Britain, and mycorrhizal fungi in chestnut woods are typically common and promiscuous species, such as chanterelles (*Cantharellus cibarius*), but also include some less common associates of the *Fagaceae*, such as the stipitate hydnums, *Hydnellum concrescens* and *Phellodon melaleucus*, both typical of old woodland.

Chestnut wood is hard, enduring, and as such very similar to oak. Indeed, chestnut shares many species with oak, including the heartwood-rotting beefsteak fungus (*Fistulina hepatica*), *Daedalea quercina*, and *Hymenochaete rubiginosa*. Again, it appears to have no specific wood-rotting associates.

From a fungal point of view, the most notable aspect of chestnut woodlands is the old discarded nut cupules which have a distinctive mycota of microfungi. These include a characteristic range of hyphomycetes such as *Anavirga laxa, Phialocephala truncata, Pleurotheciopsis pusilla*, and *Tricladium castaneicola*, and others which were catalogued by Sutton (1974). Several discomycetes are also typical of rotting cupules, notably *Lanzia echinophila* (Fig. 84) and *Ciboria americana*, both fairly common in autumn when they form brown, stalked, disc- or cup-shaped fruitbodies which arise from the blackened, stromatised surfaces.

A serious disease of chestnut caused by the ascomycete *Cryphonectria*

FIG 84. The brown, stalked, cup-shaped fruitbodies of the discomycete *Lanzia echinophila* are quite common on decaying cupules of sweet chestnut (B. Spooner).

parasitica has resulted in severe losses of trees in the USA and some parts of Europe. Fortunately, it has not yet appeared in the British Isles, but may well prove a problem in the future.

TABLE 9. Some typical fungi found with sweet chestnut (*Castanea sativa*).

SPECIES	ECOLOGY	SUBSTRATA
Cantharellus cibarius	ectomycorrhizal	in soil and litter
Cryptodiaporthe castanea	parasitic	on branches
Septoria castaneicola	parasitic	on leaves
Ciboria americana	saprotrophic	on decaying cupules
Lanzia echinophila	saprotrophic	on decaying cupules
Lachnum castaneicolum	saprotrophic	on spines of decaying cupules
Fistulina hepatica	saprotrophic	on heartwood
Hymenochaete rubiginosa	saprotrophic	on stumps and logs

Elms

Elms (*Ulmus glabra* and *U. minor*) are often thought of as non-woodland trees, but can occur extensively within woods or occasionally form distinct woodlands in their own right. Their tendency to spread by suckering often leads to substantial scrub-formation, nowadays (at least in the south of England) the predominant phenotype of elm, following the devastation caused by Dutch Elm Disease. Elm was widely distributed in the original wildwood and later became the commonest hedgerow tree. It was quite frequently used as timber (the third most important tree after oak and ash), and coppiced or pollarded for underwood and for fodder (ancient elms pollarded for fodder are also found in western Norway).

The advent of Dutch Elm Disease in the 1970s inevitably produced large quantities of dead wood and as a result a number of usually scarce fungi became temporarily common. These wood-rotting species, on stumps and fallen trunks, are not restricted to elm, but seem to have a marked preference for its wood. They include the large and distinctive agaric *Volvariella bombycina*, with silky whitish fibrils on the cap surface, and the attractive *Rhodotus palmatus* whose pinkish fruitbodies have a thickly gelatinous and wrinkled cap cuticle. The uncommon but eyecatching vermilion-capped *Pluteus aurantiorugosus* is perhaps most frequently found on elm. The funnel-shaped oyster fungus *Pleurotus cornucopiae* is another associate, often covering fallen trunks and logs in vast numbers in the early 1980s. It is an edible species, as is the common and well-known *Flammulina velutipes*, also most abundant on elm. This species, easily recognised by its orange-brown cap and dark brown, velvety stem, is a very late season toadstool, found mostly after the first frosts and fruiting throughout the winter. The bracket *Rigidoporus ulmarius* is typically found on elm stumps and can form huge, record-breaking fruiting bodies, the largest in the world, according to the Guinness Book of Records, growing (entirely by coincidence) outside the Mycology Building at the Royal Botanic Gardens, Kew (Fig. 85).

Elm is typically VA-mycorrhizal, but can occasionally form ectomycorrhizas probably with a limited number of species. One of the few such associates is the spring agaric, *Entoloma aprile*. This has greyish-brown fruitbodies, with pinkish gills and a distinct mealy taste and odour.

Apart from the *Ophiostoma* species, elm has comparatively few parasites,

FIG 85. The bracket fungus *Rigidoporus ulmarius* is common on elms, but also grows on other deciduous trees. This record-breaking, perennial fruitbody grew to a circumference of 490 cm (16 ft) before finally decaying. (RBG Kew).

although the powdery mildew *Uncinula clandestina* occurs on its leaves, and the ascomycete *Mycosphaerella ulmi* is not uncommon in leaf spots, usually in its asexual state (*Phloeospora ulmi*). More conspicuous on leaves are the dark grey stromata of another common ascomycete *Platychora ulmi*, initially developed in its asexual state (*Septogloeum ulmi*) on living leaves and forming the ascus state on those which have fallen and overwintered.

TABLE 10. Some typical fungi found with elms (*Ulmus* species).

SPECIES	ECOLOGY	SUBSTRATA
Entoloma aprile	mycorrhizal	on soil
Mycosphaerella ulmi	parasitic	on leaves
Ophiostoma novo-ulmi	parasitic	on wood
Platychora ulmi	parasitic	on leaves
Taphrina ulmi	parasitic	on leaves
Uncinula clandestina	parasitic	on leaves
Auricularia mesenterica	saprotrophic	on stumps and logs
Eutypella stellulata	saprotrophic	on dead branches
Flammulina velutipes	saprotrophic	on dead stumps and logs
Hypochnicium vellereum	saprotrophic	on dead wood
Peniophora lilacea	saprotrophic	on dead attached branches
Pleurotus cornucopiae	saprotrophic	on stumps and logs
Pluteus aurantiorugosus	saprotrophic	on stumps and logs
Rhodotus palmatus	saprotrophic	on stumps and logs
Rigidoporus ulmarius	saprotrophic	on stumps and at base of trees
Quaternaria dissepta	saprotrophic	on dead branches
Volvariella bombycina	saprotrophic	on stumps and logs

Hawthorns, cherries and other rosaceous trees

Hawthorns (*Crataegus laevigata* and *C. monogyna*) are widespread native trees, with *Crataegus laevigata* more typical of hedgerows and *C. monogyna* more typical of woodlands, though many hawthorns are natural hybrids. Alive or dead, they were important for stock-proof hedging or fencing and were also coppiced for fuel. The English word 'spinney' is derived from the Latin 'spinetum', a place of thorns. Trees are quite long-lived and some are certainly over 300 years old.

Hawthorn has several obligate associates, notably the little brown agaric

Tubaria dispersa, recognised by its yellowish gills, and the ascomycete *Xylaria oxyacanthae*. Both grow on old fallen haws which have become buried and may be found in swarms in appropriate conditions. More frequent and sometimes readily attracting attention is the sweet-smelling conidial state of the ascomycete *Monilinia johnsoni* which covers greying, wilting leaves at shoot tips in spring. This fungus is quite common, although the ascus state, a stalked cup-fungus which develops early in spring on overwintered fruit, is rarely found. It is the ascospores which infect the developing leaves in the spring.

Cherries (*Prunus avium* and *P. padus*) together with blackthorn or sloe (*Prunus spinosa*) are also native, though the bird cherry (*P. padus*) is mostly northern and localised. Wild cherry, *Prunus avium*, had limited use as timber for furniture making, whilst blackthorn (like hawthorn) was used for hedging. Both (unlike *P. padus*) have edible fruits, as do non-native species like plum or damson (*P. domestica*) and almond (*P. dulcis*). The non-native cherry laurel (*P. laurocerasus*) was at one time widely planted and has become invasive in many woodlands.

Common fungi associated with *Prunus* species are listed in table 12. Perhaps the most conspicuous is *Taphrina deformans*, which causes bright red, convoluted leaf galls on almond. Two other *Taphrina* species parasitise fruits: *T. pruni* causes elongated and enlarged sloes, known as 'pocket plums', whilst *T. padi* does the same with bird cherries. These fungi may be of commercial importance when present in abundance. Other *Prunus* parasites, notably *Apiognomonia erythrostoma* and *Blumeriella jaapii* which cause leaf wilt and 'shot hole' respectively, may also cause problems to growers, as occasionally do the *Tranzschelia* rusts.

Crab apple (*Malus sylvestris*) and pear (*Pyrus pyraster*) are widespread but infrequent native trees, often occurring singly in old woodlands. Their timber was occasionally used for specialist purposes and the fruit possibly once used for cider and perry, though quickly supplanted by cultivars.

Wild and cultivated trees are subject to a range of parasitic fungi, including powdery mildew (*Podosphaera leucotricha*), and the ubiquitous fruit-rotting ascomycete *Monilinia fructigena*. This is commonly seen in its asexual state, forming pale brown felty cushions often in concentric rings on the surface of rotting fruit. Scab, caused by the ascomycete *Venturia inaequalis*, is

FIG 86. *Sarcodontia crocea* on the trunk of an old apple tree. This rare but distinctive species forms yellowish, sweet-smelling fruitbodies with characteristic spines or teeth on which the spores develop (B. Spooner).

another common disease of these trees, and no less than three species of *Pezicula*, another of the ascomycetes, cause rot or canker of fruit and branches. Pear rust *Gymnosporangium sabinae*, which alternates with *Juniperus sabina*, occurs occasionally, and apparently became more frequent in the 1990s. The aecidial sori form conspicuous swollen, orange patches on leaves. On old, dead apple wood the distinctive, yellow fruitbodies of the now rare basidiomycete *Sarcodontia crocea* may occasionally be found (Fig. 86). This has a hymenium of well-developed teeth or spines. The species was once frequent in orchards, but has declined greatly with the advent of modern fungicidal treatments.

Rowan (*Sorbus aucuparia*) is a widely distributed native, occurring frequently in lowland woods as well as in more upland regions, to an altitude of around 900m. Whitebeam (*S. aria*) is a less common and more southern tree, found on chalk and limestone. Other native *Sorbus* species, such as service (*S. torminalis*), are occasional in old woodlands, mostly in southern England. Two rusts occur on the leaves: *Gymnosporangium cornutum*, most frequent in parts of Scotland, and *Ochropsora ariae*, a rare species confined to Scotland. Leaf spots due to the asexual *Septoria sorbi*, and perhaps also to other species, are sometimes conspicuous and disfiguring.

Rosaceous trees and shrubs are typically VA-mycorrhizal, but some can form ectomycorrhizas, probably with a limited number of species. Among the few such associates is the spring agaric, *Entoloma clypeatum*, typically found with blackthorn. Another spring species, the ascomycete *Verpa conica*, typically occurs with hawthorn, but is able to produce fruitbodies only following hot summers (Fig. 87). This became particularly evident in 1977 when, following the hot, dry summers of the preceding two years, it occurred in exceptional abundance throughout central and southern England and Wales, with some fruitings numbering over 1200 specimens.

FIG 87. *Verpa conica*, a relative of the morels, is a spring-fruiting fungus found in grass and litter near hawthorn. It is rare most years, but can fruit abundantly after a hot summer (P. Roberts).

TABLE 11. Some typical fungi found with hawthorn (*Crataegus* species).

SPECIES	ECOLOGY	SUBSTRATA
Verpa conica	mycorrhizal	on soil
Tubaria authochthona	saprotrophic	on fallen haws
Vuilleminia cystidiata	saprotrophic	on dead attached branches
Xylaria oxyacanthae	saprotrophic	on fallen haws
Diplocarpon mespili	parasitic	on leaves
Gymnosporangium clavariiforme	parasitic	on leaves, stems & haws
Gymnosporangium confusum	parasitic	on leaves, stems & haws
Monilinia johnsonii	parasitic	on leaves, later on haws

TABLE 12. Some typical fungi found with *Prunus* species.

SPECIES	ECOLOGY	SUBSTRATA
Entoloma clypeatum	mycorrhizal	with blackthorn
Dermea cerasi	saprotrophic	on branches of cherry
Dermea padi	saprotrophic	on branches of cherry
Dermea prunastri	saprotrophic	on branches of sloe and damson
Pezicula houghtonii	saprotrophic	on branches of cherry laurel
Phellinus pomaceus	saprotrophic	on dead trunks and branches of blackthorn
Trochila laurocerasi	saprotrophic	on fallen leaves of cherry laurel
Vuilleminia cystidiata	saprotrophic	on dead attached branches
Apiognomonia erythrostoma	parasitic	on shoots, leaves
Blumeriella jaapii	parasitic	on leaves of cherry
Diaporthe perniciosa	parasitic	on branches of sloe and damson
Monilinia laxa	parasitic	on flowers and fruit
Taphrina deformans	parasitic	on leaves of almond and peach
Taphrina padi	parasitic	on fruit of bird cherry
Taphrina pruni	parasitic	forming galls on sloes and plums
Tranzschelia discolor	parasitic	on leaves
Tranzschelia pruni-spinosae	parasitic	on leaves
Venturia carpophila	parasitic	on shoots, leaves and fruit

TABLE 13. Some typical fungi found with *Malus*, *Pyrus* and *Sorbus* species.

SPECIES	ECOLOGY	SUBSTRATA
Dermea ariae	saprotrophic	on dead branches of *Sorbus*
Rutstroemia rhenana	saprotrophic	on dead branches of apple
Sarcodontia crocea	saprotrophic	on dead standing apple wood
Tympanis conspersa	saprotrophic	on dead branches of apple and *Sorbus*
Eutypella sorbi	saprotrophic	on dead branches of *Sorbus*
Gymnosporangium sabinae	parasitic	on leaves of pear
Gymnosporangium juniperi-virginianae	parasitic	on leaves of apple
Gymnosporangium cornutum	parasitic	on leaves of *Sorbus*
Ochropsora ariae	parasitic	on leaves of *Sorbus*
Podosphaera clandestina var. *aucupariae*	parasitic	on leaves of *Sorbus*
Podosphaera leucotricha	parasitic	on leaves of apple and pear
Monilinia fructigena	parasitic	on apples
Pezicula alba	parasitic	on apples, causing rot
Pezicula corticola	parasitic	on branches of apple, causing canker
Pezicula malicorticis	parasitic	on apple, causing cankers and fruit rot
Septoria sorbi	parasitic	on leaf spots of *Sorbus*
Taphrina bullata	parasitic	on leaves of pear
Venturia inequalis	parasitic	on leaves, fruit of apple, causing scab
Venturia pirina	parasitic	on leaves, flowers, fruit of pear

Hazel

Hazel (*Corylus avellana*) was one of the earliest post-glacial colonisers in the British Isles and remains extremely widespread. It can form substantial trees, but is typically found as understorey and was principally managed by coppicing (though it is often self-coppicing). The largest stools may be around 300 years old. As well as the edible nuts, hazel was widely used for its pliable wood, which can be twisted to form wattles (used to make wattle and daub buildings), fences, thatching broaches, and faggot bands (Rackham, 1980).

Hazel is ectomycorrhizal, but has few specialist associates. By far the

FIG 88. The milkcap *Lactarius pyrogalus* is a typical ectomycorrhizal associate of hazel. Its latex tastes as fiery as a chilli pepper (P. Roberts).

commonest of these is *Lactarius pyrogalus* (Fig. 88), which has a greyish-fawn cap, pale orange gills, and white, acrid latex ('pyrogalus' means fire-milk). The bolete *Leccinum carpini* occurs locally with hazel, as well as with hornbeam.

A wide range of microfungi occurs on hazel, including some specialist parasites such as *Asteroma coryli* and *Piggotia coryli*, both coelomycetes found in leaf spots. The plurivorous powdery mildew *Phyllactinia guttata* is also quite common on leaves. Several ascomycetes are well-known saprotrophs of dead branches, including three species of the discomycete genus *Pezicula*, and the common and conspicuous *Encoelia furfuracea* which produces clusters of leathery, furfuraceous, pale brown fruitbodies bursting through the bark of trunks and branches. Also very common on dead branches are the stromatic ascomycetes *Hypoxylon fuscum*, which has blackish, cushion-like fruitbodies 2–4 mm across developed in swarms, and *Diatrypella favacea*. The latter, also common on birch, has blackish stromata erumpent through the bark.

Basidiomycete specialists on hazel wood are few, but include the common resupinate species *Vuilleminia coryli* and *Hymenochaete corrugata*, both on dead attached branches. In dense growth, where branches from different trees touch each other, *H. corrugata* can rapidly produce mycelium which binds the branches together, allowing the fungus to move from one host tree to another, a survival tactic quite common in tropical rain forests but rare in temperate woodlands. The red-listed ascomycete *Hypocreopsis rhododendri*, found in Britain only in parts of western Scotland, Ireland, Devon and Cornwall, occurs on hazel branches in association with *Hymenochaete corrugata*. The large, yellow- or red-brown stromatic fruit-bodies form irregular, often radially arranged, lichen-like lobes (Fig. 89) and are quite distinctive.

FIG 89. The rare ascomycete *Hypocreopsis rhododendri* is associated with the patch-forming fungus *Hymenochaete corrugata* and, despite its name, typically grows on hazel (B. Spooner).

TABLE 14. Some typical fungi found with hazel (*Corylus avellana*).

SPECIES	ECOLOGY	SUBSTRATA
Lactarius pyrogalus	mycorrhizal	on soil and litter
Leccinum carpini	mycorrhizal	on soil
Mamiania coryli	parasitic	on living (and fallen) leaves
Phyllactinia guttata	parasitic	on living leaves
Encoelia furfuracea	saprotrophic	on dead attached branches
Encoelia glauca	saprotrophic	on dead branches
Hymenochaete corrugata	saprotrophic	on dead attached branches
Hymenoscyphus fructigenus	saprotrophic	on fallen nuts
Hypocreopsis rhododendri	parasitic	on or with *Hymenochaete corrugata*
Hypoxylon fuscum	saprotrophic	on dead branches
Hypoxylon howeianum	saprotrophic	on dead branches
Ophiovalsa corylina	saprotrophic	on dead branches
Pezicula coryli	saprotrophic	on branches
Sillia ferruginea	saprotrophic	on base of standing branches
Vuilleminia coryli	saprotrophic	on dead attached branches

Hornbeam

Hornbeam (*Carpinus betulus*) is native in roughly the same parts of Britain as beech, forming a major component of woodland in parts of south-east England. It was traditionally managed in much the same way as beech, its wood being used for fuel. Old hornbeam pollards can be 300 years old or more. The species belongs to the *Corylaceae* but shares most of its associated fungi with beech and oak, as well as hazel.

Hornbeam has comparatively few specialist fungi of its own. Among the ectomycorrhizal associates are *Lactarius circellatus* and the bolete *Leccinum carpini*, the latter also occurring with hazel. A notable ascomycetous parasite is *Taphrina carpini* which causes conspicuous witches' brooms on trunks and branches throughout the year. The fruitbody of the fungus, a simple layer of asci, develops on the surface of developing leaves in spring.

Several saprotrophic fungi occur exclusively with hornbeam, though they are generally inconspicuous and need to be searched for carefully in fallen litter or sometimes on dead, attached branches. The coelomycete

Melanconium stromaticum is sometimes conspicuous on dead twigs and branches, exuding masses of black spores resembling lava flows from tiny volcanoes. A related species, M. *bicolor*, the conidial state of the ascomycete *Melanconis stilbostoma*, occurs on birch.

Two notable fungi which occur as obligate associates of *Carpinus* in continental Europe, the rust *Melampsoridium carpineum* and the discomycete *Ciboria bolaris*, have not yet been recorded from Britain.

TABLE 15. Some typical fungi found with hornbeam (*Carpinus betulus*).

SPECIES	ECOLOGY	SUBSTRATA
Lactarius circellatus	mycorrhizal	in soil and litter
Leccinum carpini	mycorrhizal	in soil and litter
Taphrina carpini	parasitic	causing witches' brooms
Peniophora laeta	saprotrophic	on dead attached branches
Sphaerognomonia carpinea	saprotrophic	on rotting, overwintered leaves
Diaporthe carpini	saprotrophic	on dead branches
Encoelia glaberrima	saprotrophic	on dead branches
Pezicula carpinea	saprotrophic	on dead branches
Melanconium stromaticum	saprotrophic	on dead branches

Limes

Limes (*Tilia cordata* and the rare *T. platyphyllos*) were once amongst the commonest trees of the lowland (southern and eastern) wildwood, but have gradually been displaced by other species so that now they are either local (as a dominant tree) or infrequent. Small-leaved lime (*T. cordata*) was grown occasionally for timber, more frequently as coppice for fuel and for fibre ('bast') used for rope-making. Some English trees are over 300 years old, with coppice stools much older still.

Despite its long history, *Tilia* has a surprisingly meagre mycota. Perhaps no more than 40 or so associated species have been recorded in Britain. Although an ectomycorrhizal tree, only one agaric, *Russula praetervisa*, is considered a typical associate, and amongst other basidiomycetes only the corticioid *Peniophora rufomarginata* on dead attached branches, is a lime specialist. Although various plurivorous microfungi occur on limes, obligate associates are few. Amongst the most conspicuous of these are the hyphomycetes *Corynespora olivacea* and *Exosporium tiliae*, both of which form thick, dark brown or blackish, felty colonies on dead branches, reliably distinguished only by microscopic examination. *Tilia* also seems to have few pathogens, although trees are occasionally susceptible to attack by species of *Phytophthora*.

TABLE 16. Some typical fungi found with limes (*Tilia* species).

SPECIES	ECOLOGY	SUBSTRATA
Russula praetervisa	mycorrhizal	on soil and litter
Corynespora olivacea	saprotrophic	on dead branches
Cryptodiaporthe hranicensis	saprotrophic	on dead branches
Diaporthe velata	saprotrophic	on dead branches
Encoelia tiliacea	saprotrophic	on dead branches
Exosporium tiliae	saprotrophic	on dead branches
Hercospora tiliae	saprotrophic	on dead branches
Peniophora rufomarginata	saprotrophic	on dead attached branches
Splanchnonema ampullaceum	saprotrophic	on dead branches
Stegonosporium cellulosum	saprotrophic	on dead branches

Maples and sycamore

Field Maple (*Acer campestre*) is a native tree, believed to have been uncommon in the original wildwood and possibly restricted to the south-east of England. It was occasionally grown as timber and sometimes coppiced, its wood used for furniture and other small items. Some trees and coppice stools are at least 300 years old. Sycamore (*Acer pseudoplatanus*), introduced from central Europe in the Middle Ages, was widely planted in the eighteenth and nineteenth centuries, and has since become extensively naturalised. It is a rapid coloniser of clearings and abandoned land, so that it is now commonly regarded as a weed species.

Neither tree is ectomycorrhizal and there are no specific agaric associates. However, they support several plurivorous and some specific fungi, including parasites as well as saprotrophs. The corticioid basidiomycete *Dendrothele acerina* is almost ubiquitous with *Acer campestre*, forming conspicuous white patches on mossy living trunks, but is strangely rare on sycamore. The latter tree is famous for its highly visible 'tar spot', *Rhytisma acerinum*, on living leaves in summer and early autumn. Fallen branches often support the upright black stromata of *Xylaria longipes*, recently dubbed 'dead moll's fingers' (Fig. 11).

Norway maple (*A. platanoides*), a native of continental Europe, was introduced to Britain in the 17th century. It is widely planted in suburban parks and gardens and, being vigorously self-seeding, is also now naturalised in many areas. It has few specific associated fungi, although the powdery mildew *Sawadaea tulasnei* may sometimes develop a conspicuous white coating to the leaves. Its branches, as with sycamore, are a common substratum for coral spot (*Nectria cinnabarina*).

TABLE 17. Some typical fungi found with maple* (*Acer campestre*) and sycamore** (*Acer pseudoplatanus*).

SPECIES	ECOLOGY	SUBSTRATA
Cristulariella depraedens	parasitic	on leaves**
Cryptostroma corticale	parasitic	on trunks**
Dendrothele acerina	parasitic	on living trunks * (rarely **)
Rhytisma acerinum	parasitic	on leaves**
Sawadaea bicornis	parasitic	on leaves*, **
Lanzia luteovirescens	saprotrophic	on rotting petioles**
Mollisina acerina	saprotrophic	on fallen leaves**
Pyrenopeziza petiolaris	saprotrophic	on rotting petioles**
Xylaria longipes	saprotrophic	on roots and fallen branches **
Stegonosporium pyriforme	saprotrophic	on dead, often attached branches **

Oaks

Oaks (*Quercus robur* and *Q. petraea*) are celebrated as the quintessential English trees, native and common throughout the country (in Wales and lowland Scotland too), particularly in the west. Their usefulness to man, their ability to grow on poor, often acidic soils, and their readiness to colonise new ground have increased their representation in surviving woodland and in broadleaf plantations. Oaks were valued as timber trees, accounting for most early timberwork in buildings and ships. But they were also commonly coppiced or pollarded to provide wood for fuel, fencing, wattle, and charcoal. Stripping oak bark for leather tanning was at one time a major industry, particularly in the north. Pannage, the feeding of acorns to pigs, was a minor side-benefit.

Oak trees are enduring, maturing in 100–200 years and continuing for several hundred more. The oldest living oaks in Britain, such as some of those in Windsor Great Park in Berkshire, are around 800–1000 years old, and trees 400 years old are not uncommon. In the old deer park at Staverton in Suffolk, there are some 4000 oaks of this age, and the Birklands area of Sherwood Forest in Nottinghamshire has around 1000 such trees. Around 2000 ancient pollarded oaks occur in the National Nature Reserve at Ashtead in Surrey. Many of the veteran oaks at these sites are now 'stag-headed', forming new crowns below the dead limbs of old crowns, a natural feature typical of older oaks and in no way detrimental to their long-term survival.

Oaks are ectomycorrhizal, forming partnerships with a wide range of agarics and boletes (no less than 57 species, according to Watling, 1974). Indeed, ectomycorrhizal fungi in Britain are predominantly associated with oaks, as the commonest native trees. Oakwoods on acidic soils in autumn can therefore be rich in species of *Amanita, Cortinarius, Hebeloma, Inocybe, Laccaria, Lactarius, Russula,* and *Tricholoma* among the agarics, *Boletus* and *Gyroporus* among the boletes, *Cantharellus* and other chanterelle-like fungi, and more rarely stipitate hydnoid species in the genera *Hydnellum* and *Phellodon*. Many of these species, such as *Amanita rubescens* (the blusher), *Laccaria amethystina,* or *Cantharellus cibarius* (the chanterelle), are promiscuously ectomycorrhizal, associating with a wide range of trees. Others, such as *Gyroporus castaneus* and *Hydnellum concrescens,* may be restricted to the *Fagaceae,* including not only oak, but beech, chestnut, and hornbeam. Commonest of the exclusive oak associates is *Lactarius quietus,* the oak milk cap, with its distinctive oily smell, said to be of bed bugs. Also common are *Lactarius subumbonatus,* with a similar but even stronger smell (Fig. 90) and *L. chrysorrheus,* with bright yellow latex.

Fallen oak leaves are comparatively tough and full of unsavoury chemicals. On acidic ground they tend to build up, forming mor soils with fairly deep litter. These are mainly degraded by agarics in the genera *Clitocybe, Collybia, Marasmius,* and *Mycena*. Of these, the tiny *Marasmius quercophilus* is restricted to oak leaves. Old acorns and acorn cupules are also rotted by various specific as well as plurivorous fungi such as the

FIG 90. The milkcap *Lactarius subumbonatus* is an ectomycorrhizal associate of oak. It is better-known as *L. cimicarius*, the epithet referring to its oily smell, said to be of bed bugs (*Cimex* species) (P. Roberts).

discomycetes *Hymenoscyphus fructigenus*, a small but common yellowish species, and *Ciboria batschiana*, which forms larger, brownish, long-stalked fruitbodies up to 1.5 cm across on buried, mummified acorns.

Freshly fallen or cut oak wood frequently bears masses of the black, gelatinous, button-shaped fruitbodies of *Bulgaria inquinans*, an ascomycete whose rapid appearance strongly suggests it lives endophytically in living oak awaiting its opportunity to claim a fallen branch as soon as it is detached. Rotten fallen oak wood is often stained turquoise by the ascomycete *Chlorociboria aeruginascens* which produces small, similarly coloured, cup-shaped fruitbodies. Almost 100 additional species of fungi have been recorded from rotting oak wood.

Old oak heartwood is extremely difficult to degrade (Chapter Three) and can take decades to rot down. A specialist species on such wood is *Hymenochaete rubiginosa*, forming thin, hard, brown brackets with a smooth undersurface.

Occasionally found arising from buried or exposed roots of living oak are the large and peculiar fruitbodies of *Podoscypha multizonata*, composed of leathery fronds in dense rosettes (Fig. 27). This conspicuous species, whose nearest relatives are mostly tropical, was originally described from England in the nineteenth century and is scarcely known elsewhere. It is quite frequent in the Midlands and southern England, particularly in old parkland and forests. Even larger, but more widespread, is *Grifola frondosa*, an annual root-rotting polypore which produces massive clumps of soft, leathery fruitbodies at the base of trees and around old stumps. In similar situations is the wood-rotting agaric, *Collybia fusipes*, dark reddish-brown and always in dense clusters. The most familiar polypore on old trees (though not confined to oak) is *Fistulina hepatica*, sometimes called the 'beefsteak fungus' because of its raw-meat colour and texture and its habit of oozing blood-red liquid in damp weather. It is a heartwood specialist, helping hollow out old oaks and thus prolonging their lives. *Piptoporus quercinus*, the oak polypore (Fig. 164), has a similar habit, but is exclusive to oak and found only on veteran trees (over 250 years old). It is a rare species on the European mainland and England appears to be its world stronghold. It is one of the few fungi protected under the Wildlife & Countryside Act 1981, making it illegal to damage sites where it grows (Chapter 18). Other large polypores on oak include *Phellinus robustus*, a perennial species, not recorded in Britain till the 1980s and still known only from ancient woodlands in the New Forest, Windsor, and Shropshire; *Daedalea quercina*, a common species with maze-like pores; and *Inonotus dryadeus*, which weeps distinctive droplets.

A specialist assemblage of species occurs as wood-rotters on dead attached oak branches, including the corticioid fungi *Peniophora quercina*, *Stereum gausapatum*, and *Vuilleminia comedens*, and the common, black, gelatinous *Exidia glandulosa*. All of these are adapted to fluctuating weather conditions, and have waxy, gelatinous, or leathery fruitbodies capable of surviving dry periods and reviving rapidly in rain to produce spores.

Among the many microfungi on oak, perhaps the most conspicuous is *Microsphaera alphitoides*, the oak mildew (Fig. 49). This parasite first appeared in Britain at the beginning of the twentieth century, probably introduced from America, and is now ubiquitous, especially on the leaves of sapling oaks in early summer turning them a conspicuous grey-white. It causes no serious harm to established trees, but has been blamed for the failure of seedlings to regenerate in shaded woodland. Another leaf parasite is *Microstroma album*, a member of the *Ustilaginomycetes* and related to the smuts, which develops tiny, white flecks on the undersides of leaves, but causes little damage. It is probably common and widespread in Britain, though inconspicuous and easily overlooked. Oaks also have a rust, *Cronartium quercuum*, but this is surprisingly uncommon in Britain.

Various other pathogens occur on oak, reviewed by Murray (1974), including *Phytophthora quercina*, a recently described cause of epidemic oak dieback in Europe. This is now known in Britain and must be considered a potential threat to oaks here although it is apparently less destructive than the plurivorous *P. cinnamomi*. An even more recent threat is *P. ramorum*, the cause of 'sudden oak death' in America and the subject of strict quarantine regulations in Britain. This species has a broader host range and has been found in several English nurseries on other host genera including *Camellia*, *Rhododendron* and *Viburnum* but in all cases successfully eradicated. Fortunately, English oaks appear to be resistant to this pathogen.

Additional species of oak occur as introductions in Britain. Their attendant fungi have not been much investigated, though the evergreen holm oak (*Quercus ilex*), extensively naturalised particularly in coastal woodlands, has proved rich in leaf litter microfungi with at least 70 species having been recorded from this substratum in Britain.

TABLE 18. A selection of typical fungi found with oak (*Quercus* species).

SPECIES	ECOLOGY	SUBSTRATA
Amanita phalloides	mycorrhizal	on soil and litter
Boletus pulverulentus	mycorrhizal	on soil and litter
Boletus radicans	mycorrhizal	on soil and litter
Boletus rubellus	mycorrhizal	on soil and litter
Cortinarius nemorensis	mycorrhizal	on soil and litter
Cortinarius alboviolaceus	mycorrhizal	on soil and litter
Gyroporus castaneus	mycorrhizal	on soil and litter
Hebeloma crustuliniforme	mycorrhizal	on soil and litter
Hydnellum concrescens	mycorrhizal	on soil and litter
Lactarius chrysorrheus	mycorrhizal	on soil and litter
Lactarius quietus	mycorrhizal	on soil and litter
Lactarius sumbumbonatus	mycorrhizal	on soil and litter
Leccinum quercinum	mycorrhizal	on soil and litter

SPECIES	ECOLOGY	SUBSTRATA
Russula sororia	mycorrhizal	on soil and litter
Russula vesca	mycorrhizal	on soil and litter
Tricholoma acerbum	mycorrhizal	on soil and litter
Ciborinia candolleana	parasitic	at first on living leaves
Colpoma quercina	parasitic	on dead attached branches
Cronartium quercuum	parasitic	on living leaves
Microsphaera alphitoides	parasitic	on living leaves
Microstroma album	parasitic	on living leaves
Phytophthora cinnamomi	parasitic	on roots
Phytophthora quercina	parasitic	on roots
Podoscypha multizonata	parasitic	on roots
Taphrina caerulescens	parasitic	on living leaves
Aleurodiscus wakefieldiae	saprotrophic	on dead attached branches
Amphiporthe leiphaemia	saprotrophic	on dead branches
Bulgaria inquinans	saprotrophic	on fallen branches
Ciboria batschiana	saprotrophic	on mummified acorns
Coccomyces dentatus	saprotrophic	on fallen leaves
Chlorociboria aeruginascens	saprotrophic	on fallen branches
Collybia fusipes	saprotrophic	on roots and stumps
Daedalea quercina	saprotrophic	on stumps and fallen trunks
Diatrypella quercina	saprotrophic	on dead branches
Exidia glandulosa	saprotrophic	on dead attached branches
Fistulina hepatica	saprotrophic	on trunks, heart-rotting
Ganoderma lucidum	saprotrophic	on trunks, heart-rotting
Ganoderma resinaceum	saprotrophic	on trunks, heart-rotting
Grifola frondosa	saprotrophic	on dead roots
Hymenochaete rubiginosa	saprotrophic	on fallen heartwood
Inonotus dryadeus	saprotrophic	on trunks, heart-rotting
Lachnum soppittii	saprotrophic	on fallen leaves
Marasmius quercophilus	saprotrophic	on fallen leaves
Mycena inclinata	saprotrophic	on stumps and dead wood
Peniophora quercina	saprotrophic	on dead attached branches
Phellinus robustus	saprotrophic	on trunks, heart-rotting
Piptoporus quercinus	saprotrophic	on trunks and limbs, heart-rotting
Plagiostoma pustula	saprotrophic	on fallen leaves
Poculum sydowianum	saprotrophic	on decaying petioles
Rutstroemia firma	saprotrophic	on fallen branches
Stereum gausapatum	saprotrophic	on dead attached branches
Vuilleminia comedens	saprotrophic	on dead attached branches

Poplars

Aspen (*Populus tremula*) is a predominantly northern, woodland tree and was one of the first post-glacial colonisers in Britain. It prefers wet ground and is short-lived (around 50 years), but was nonetheless occasionally used for timber. Other native poplars (*Populus nigra*, *P. alba*, and hybrids) originally grew along watercourses rather than in woodlands, and still do so, although *P. nigra*, the black poplar, is now an extremely rare species much replaced by various hybrids.

Populus species are all ectomycorrhizal, although associated fungi, including two boletes in the genus *Leccinum*, are generally uncommon in Britain. Poplars are host to various parasitic fungi, including three rust species, of which *Melampsora larici-populina* is common on black poplar and its hybrids, and *M. populnea* is common on aspen and white poplar. Both produce their uredial and telial stages on *Populus* leaves and their spermogonia and aecidia on other hosts – *M. larici-populina* on larch, *M. populnea* on larch, pine, and mercury. *Melampsora allii-populina*, also on black poplars, is less common, and alternates with *Allium* and *Arum*. Other poplar parasites include *Taphrina populina*, which forms bright yellow, gall-like blisters on leaves, mostly of black poplars, and *T. johansonii*, a much rarer species which galls catkins. Another leaf parasite, *Sphaceloma populi*, forms conspicuous leaf spots and lesions. Though widely distributed in Europe, it has been reported from Britain only recently. Equally interesting is *Phellinus tremulae*, a bracket fungus found on dead trunks and branches of aspen and, although forming sizeable fruitbodies and apparently widespread in parts of the Scottish Highlands, was discovered there only in 2000.

TABLE 19. Some typical fungi found with poplars (*Populus* species).

SPECIES	ECOLOGY	SUBSTRATA
Lactarius controversus	mycorrhizal	on soil and litter
Leccinum aurantiacum	mycorrhizal	on soil and litter
Leccinum duriusculum	mycorrhizal	on soil and litter
Tricholoma populinum	mycorrhizal	on soil and litter
Cryptodiaporthe populea	parasitic	on branches
Drepanopeziza populi-albae	parasitic	on leaves
Drepanopeziza populorum	parasitic	on leaves

SPECIES	ECOLOGY	SUBSTRATA
Melampsora allii-populina	parasitic	on leaves
Melampsora larici-populina	parasitic	on leaves
Melampsora populnea	parasitic	on leaves
Sphaceloma populi	parasitic	on leaves
Taphrina johansonii	parasitic	on catkins
Taphrina populina	parasitic	on leaves
Uncinula adunca	parasitic	on leaves
Auriculariopsis ampla	saprotrophic	on dead attached branches
Encoelia fascicularis	saprotrophic	on dead branches
Leucostoma nivea	saprotrophic	on twigs
Peniophora polygonia	saprotrophic	on dead attached branches
Phellinus tremulae	saprotrophic	on dead trunks and branches
Pholiota populnea	saprotrophic	on dead logs

Willows and sallows

Willows and sallows, all species of *Salix*, occur widely and commonly in many habitats throughout Britain. They hybridise readily and their identification and nomenclature is far from straightforward. They have also long been planted for timber and whips for basket-making, so their natural distribution is difficult to ascertain. Of the larger species, often abundant in damp woodland habitats, perhaps eleven are indigenous to Britain, although the status of the long-leaved willows *Salix alba* and *S. fragilis* and of the osier *S. viminalis* is uncertain. There are also seven native species of dwarf willow, creeping willow (*S. repens*) being the commonest and most widely distributed, often found in woodland. The other dwarf species almost exclusively grow in upland or mountainous regions, especially in Scotland and Ireland.

Willows are ectomycorrhizal and are associated with several common agarics, including *Hebeloma leucosarx*, *Tricholoma cingulatum* (one of the few *Tricholoma* species to have a ring), and the attractive, copper-coloured *Dermocybe uliginosa*. Less common are *Lactarius aspideus*, with violaceous latex (Fig. 91), the miniature *Laccaria tortilis*, the bolete *Leccinum salicicola* (mainly with *S. repens* in Scotland), and *Amanita nivalis* (with *S. herbacea* in Scotland). Watling (1992b) provided a list of ectomycorrhizal and other macrofungi associated with British willows.

Willows are subject to a range of fungal diseases, though these rarely cause severe damage. Perhaps most frequent are species of the ascomycete

FIG 91. *Lactarius aspideus*, an uncommon ectomycorrhizal associate of willow, is an attractive, pale yellow milkcap, exuding a latex which slowly turns violaceous (P. Roberts).

genus *Drepanopeziza*, the cause of anthracnose. Three are associated with *Salix* in Britain, causing leaf lesions in their asexual stage but developing the sexual stage only in spring on overwintered leaves. Equally common are rust fungi, species of *Melampsora*, of which six occur on willow leaves in Britain. Some of these alternate with other hosts and may be difficult to identify to species. Another parasite, the plurivorous ascomycete *Glomerella cingulata*, often attacks willows and is the cause of die-back, canker, and blackening of leaves.

Several larger fungi are found commonly on *Salix* wood, including the bracket fungi *Daedaleopsis confragosa* and *Phellinus igniarius*. The latter forms large, perennial hoof-shaped, woody brackets, mostly on old trees, and causes a white rot of the heart wood. Agarics include *Agrocybe cylindracea*, a distinctive pale buff species which has large, tufted fruitbodies with a ring on the stem, and the small but attractive *Phaeomarasmius erinaceus*, occasionally found on dead twigs. Equally attractive, but rather rare, is *Lentinus tigrinus*, with speckled, funnel-shaped fruitbodies. The orange-brown jelly fungus *Exidia recisa* is locally common on dead attached twigs (Fig. 92), as is the

FIG 92. The jelly fungus *Exidia recisa* is typically found on dead attached twigs of willow in late autumn and winter (P. Roberts).

corticioid species *Hymenochaete tabacina*. The latter is very probably the host to an extremely rare but conspicuous ascomycete, *Hypocreopsis lichenoides*, only known from a handful of collections in Britain.

There are many microfungi associated with *Salix*, some of them parasitic, but many of them saprotrophs on leaves, wood and bark. No specific inventory of these fungi has been made, but they probably include over 200 species in Britain.

TABLE 20. Some typical fungi found with willows (*Salix* spp.).

SPECIES	ECOLOGY	SUBSTRATA
Amanita nivalis	mycorrhizal	on soil and litter
Dermocybe uliginosa	mycorrhizal	on soil and litter
Hebeloma leucosarx	mycorrhizal	on soil and litter
Inocybe salicis	mycorrhizal	on soil and litter
Laccaria tortilis	mycorrhizal	on soil and litter
Lactarius aspideus	mycorrhizal	on soil and litter

(Fig. 95), and the handsome dark red and yellow agaric *Tricholomopsis rutilans*, found clustered on old stumps and commonly known as 'plums and custard'.

Ascomycetes on pine are many, though most are microscopic. They include some important pathogens, notably *Rhizina undulata* which causes a highly destructive root disease particularly of seedlings. This species is interesting for its dependence on fire (Chapter 13). Another pathogen is *Lophodermium seditiosum*, the cause of needle cast of saplings. Several further *Lophodermium* species occur on dead and decaying needles, by far the commonest being *L. pinastri*, which forms characteristic dark, transverse zone lines. Other saprotrophic ascomycetes include the attractive discomycete *Lachnellula subtilissima*. This forms gregarious fruitbodies with bright yellow-orange discs surrounded by white hairs, often abundant on fallen branches in autumn. Other species such as *Lachnellula pseudofarinacea* are much less common. Another discomycete, *Pezicula livida*, with orange-brown, gregarious fruitbodies, is common on pine, but also found on other conifers. Several other tiny discomycetes are frequent on decaying needles, including

FIG 94. The yellow, globose fruitbodies of *Rhizopogon luteolus*, commonest of the British 'beard truffles'. It forms an ectomycorrhizal association with pine and can often be found in groups, half-buried at the soil surface (B. Spooner).

FIG 95. The cauliflower fungus, *Sparassis crispa*, is a common and edible species typically found at the base of old pine trees. (P. Roberts).

Cenangium acuum, various species of *Lachnum*, particularly the pure white *L. acuum*, and *Cyclaneusma minus* which has tiny, immersed fruitbodies exposed by a tiny flap of host tissue. *Desmazierella acicola* is also found on decaying needles, forming brownish, hairy fruitbodies in spring, but this fungus is much more frequent in its asexual state (*Verticicladium trifidum*) which occurs throughout the year.

TABLE 22. A selection of fungi found with Scots pine (*Pinus sylvestris*).

SPECIES	ECOLOGY	SUBSTRATA
Amphinema byssoides	mycorrhizal	in soil and litter
Bankera fuligineoalba	mycorrhizal	in soil and litter
Boletus badius	mycorrhizal	in soil and litter
Boletus pinicola	mycorrhizal	in soil and litter
Cortinarius cinnamomeus	mycorrhizal	in soil and litter
Cortinarius paleaceus	mycorrhizal	in soil and litter
Cortinarius sanguineus	mycorrhizal	in soil and litter
Cortinarius semisanguineus	mycorrhizal	in soil and litter
Cortinarius speciosissimus	mycorrhizal	in soil and litter
Hebeloma mesophaeum	mycorrhizal	in soil and litter
Hydnellum ferrugineum	mycorrhizal	in soil and litter
Hygrophorus hypothejus	mycorrhizal	in soil and litter
Lactarius deliciosus	mycorrhizal	in soil and litter
Lactarius hepaticus	mycorrhizal	in soil and litter
Lactarius rufus	mycorrhizal	in soil and litter
Phellodon tomentosus	mycorrhizal	in soil and litter
Rhizopogon luteolus	mycorrhizal	in soil and litter
Russula amara (R. caerulea)	mycorrhizal	in soil and litter
Russula sanguinea	mycorrhizal	in soil and litter
Russula sardonia	mycorrhizal	in soil and litter
Sarcodon imbricatum	mycorrhizal	in soil and litter
Suillus bovinus	mycorrhizal	in soil and litter
Suillus granulatus	mycorrhizal	in soil and litter
Suillus luteus	mycorrhizal	in soil and litter
Suillus variegatus	mycorrhizal	in soil and litter
Tricholoma pessundatum	mycorrhizal	in soil and litter
Chroogomphus rutilus	parasite of mycorrhiza	in soil and litter
Gomphidius roseus	parasite of mycorrhiza	in soil and litter
Coleosporium tussilaginis	parasite	on needles
Cronartium flaccidum	parasitic	on branches

SPECIES	ECOLOGY	SUBSTRATA
Cronartium ribicola	parasitic	on branches
Heterobasidion annosum	parasitic	on roots
Phaeolus schweinitzii	parasitic	on roots and trunks
Rhizina undulata	parasitic	on seedlings
Sydowia polyspora	parasitic	on needles and twigs
Antrodia xantha	saprotrophic	on fallen branches and logs
Auriscalpium vulgare	saprotrophic	on fallen cones
Baeospora myosura	saprotrophic	on fallen cones
Calocera viscosa	saprotrophic	on rotten stumps
Cenangium acuum	saprotrophic	on decaying needles
Cyclaneusma minus	saprotrophic	on fallen needles
Desmazierella acicola	saprotrophic	on fallen needles
Exidia saccharina	saprotrophic	on dead attached branches
Gloeophyllum sepiarium	saprotrophic	on rotten logs
Gymnopilus penetrans	saprotrophic	on fallen branches
Hyaloscypha aureliella	saprotrophic	on rotten trunks and branches
Hypholoma capnoides	saprotrophic	on rotten stumps
Ischnoderma benzoinum	saprotrophic	on rotten logs
Lachnellula subtilissima	saprotrophic	on fallen branches
Lophodermium pinastri	saprotrophic	on fallen needles
Marasmius androsaceus	saprotrophic	on decaying needles
Mycena capillaripes	saprotrophic	in needle litter
Mycena vulgaris	saprotrophic	in needle litter
Nectria cucurbitula	saprotrophic	on twigs and needles
Paxillus atrotomentosus	saprotrophic	on stumps, roots
Pezicula livida	saprotrophic	on fallen branches and cones
Phacidium lacerum	saprotrophic	on needles
Phellinus pini	saprotrophic	on rotten logs
Postia stiptica	saprotrophic	on dead wood
Pseudohydnum gelatinosum	saprotrophic	on rotten logs
Sparassis crispa	saprotrophic-parasitic	on roots
Stereum sanguinolentum	saprotrophic	on rotten logs
Strobilurus tenacellus	saprotrophic	on rotten, buried cones
Tapinella panuoides	saprotrophic	on rotten wood
Trichaptum abietinum	saprotrophic	on rotten logs
Tricholomopsis rutilans	saprotrophic	on dead wood

Silver fir

Silver fir (*Abies alba*) was once planted for forestry and still has some extensive plantations in Britain. It is also used as an ornamental. Firs are ectomycorrhizal but few of their associated fungi are present in Britain, the milk-cap *Lactarius salmonicolor* being a rather uncommon exception. It is related to *L. deliciosus* (with pine) and *L. deterrimus* (with spruce), having a bright orange latex which, however, does not turn green on exposure to air. Firs provide an alternate or potential alternate host for some of the fern rusts. Two species of *Milesina, M. blechni* and *M. kriegeriana*, may develop spermatia and aecidia on the needles, and three other *Milesina* species have been shown to do so in inoculation experiments. The same stages of the common willow-herb rust *Pucciniastrum epilobii* and *Melampsorella caryophyllacearum*, otherwise on *Cerastium* and *Stellaria*, also occur on *Abies*. Firs are host to various microfungi, though only a few, such as the ascomycetes *Delphinella abietis*, and *Herpotrichia parasitica*, both parasitic on the leaves, and the stromatic *Camarops tubulina* on rotten wood, are restricted to this host genus.

Spruces

After pine, the commonest plantation trees in Britain are Norway spruce (*Picea abies*) and Sitka spruce (*P. sitchensis*). Norway spruce, native in pre-glacial times, was reintroduced to Britain as early as the 16th century and is now extensively planted for commercial use.

Spruce is ectomycorrhizal and on the continent has a wide range of host-specific associates, though few are found in Britain. The most familiar is probably *Lactarius deterrimus*, similar to *L. deliciosus*, but often brighter-coloured with a tendency for the whole fruitbody to change from orange to jade-green. The rare stipitate hydnoid fungus, *Bankera violascens*, was found in a spruce plantation in Scotland in 1996, but ironically appears to have been rendered extinct in the UK as part of a Habitat Action Plan which recommended the removal of non-native trees. *Melanotus horizontalis*, a small, brown, bracket-shaped agaric with dark gills and spores, often occurs in swarms on fallen trunks and brash. It appears to be a comparatively recent introduction, now frequent in spruce plantations, though it also found on other woody substrata. *Strobilurus esculentus* is a slender agaric growing exclusively on old, fallen and often buried spruce cones.

Parasites of spruce are rather few, but include three scarce rust fungi in Britain. Two of these occur on the needles, *Chrysomyxa abietis* which forms telia only and is restricted to *Picea*, and *C. ledi* var. *rhododendri* which forms aecidia on *Picea* and alternates with *Rhododendron. Pucciniastrum areolatum* is also scarce, forming aecidia on cone scales and alternating with *Prunus padus.* Another parasite is the ascomycete *Gemmamyces piceae*, of interest because, although scarce, it is a gall inducer, causing swollen, distorted buds. Various microfungi occur commonly on decaying needles and branches, but only a few, such as *Lophodermium piceae* on needles, and the scarce *Pseudophacidium piceae*, a small, blackish cup-fungus on logs and branches, are restricted to *Picea*.

TABLE 23. A selection of fungi found frequently or exclusively with spruce (*Picea* species).

SPECIES	ECOLOGY	SUBSTRATA
Bankera violascens	mycorrhizal	in soil and litter
Lactarius deterrimus	mycorrhizal	in soil and litter
Ramaria abietina	mycorrhizal	in soil and litter
Russula queletii	mycorrhizal	in soil and litter
Tylospora fibrillosa	mycorrhizal	in soil and litter
Chrysomyxa abietis	parasitic	on needles
Chrysomyxa rhododendri	parasitic	on needles
Gemmamyces piceae	parasitic	on buds
Aleurodiscus amorphus	saprotrophic	on attached branches
Heyderia abietis	saprotrophic	on fallen needles
Lophodermium piceae	saprotrophic	on needles
Melanotus horizontalis	saprotrophic	on brash and fallen wood
Micromphale perforans	saprotrophic	on fallen needles
Merulicium fusisporum	saprotrophic	on brash
Panellus mitis	saprotrophic	on brash and fallen wood
Pseudophacidium piceae	saprotrophic	on dead branches and logs
Strobilurus esculentus	saprotrophic	on buried cones

Yew

Yew (*Taxus baccata*) is one of only three coniferous species native to the British Isles. It is a characteristic tree of the southern chalk downlands, the yew forest at Kingley Vale in Sussex, for example, being one of the finest such forests remaining in Europe. Yew is also widespread in limestone areas throughout most of Britain. Furthermore, it is abundantly planted as an ornamental and is well known as a churchyard tree, where ancient specimens in excess of 1000 years old can often be encountered.

Yew is not ectomycorrhizal and has few parasites, though is subject to species of *Phytophthora*, especially *P. cinnamomi*, which may cause die-back of branches and serious root disease. The large, shiny, reddish-brown brackets of *Ganoderma carnosum* occur occasionally on trunks and the patch-like fruitbodies of *Amylostereum laevigatum* are common on living trunks and branches of mature trees. The sooty mould *Capnobotrys dingleyae* forms thick, spongy, reddish-brown colonies on living leaves and branches but causes no great problem to the tree. Various saprotrophic microfungi are specific to *Taxus*, and occur mainly on dead leaves and twigs. These include the ascomycetes *Botryosphaeria foliorum* and *Dothiora taxicola*, and the coelomycetes *Cytospora taxi* and *Diplodia taxi*, all of which occur on dead, attached leaves or twigs. However, one of the commonest and most conspicuous fungi on yew is *Laetiporus sulphureus*, with its unmistakeable bright yellow to orange, soft-fleshy brackets. This species, popularly known as 'chicken-of-the-woods', is also common on non-coniferous hosts.

TABLE 24. A selection of fungi found frequently or exclusively on yew (*Taxus baccata*).

SPECIES	ECOLOGY	EUBSTRA
Amylostereum laevigatum	saprotrophic	on trunks and branches
Botryosphaeria foliorum	saprotrophic	on dead leaves
Cytospora taxi	saprotrophic	on dead leaves and twigs
Diplodia taxi	saprotrophic	on dead leaves and twigs
Dothiora taxicola	saprotrophic	on dead leaves
Ganoderma carnosum	saprotrophic	on living trunks
Laetiporus sulphureus	saprotrophic	on living trunks
Capnobotrys dingleyae	parasitic	on living leaves and branches
Phytophthora cinnamomi	parasitic	on roots

CHAPTER 10

Dunes and Heathland

ALTHOUGH dunes and heathlands represent independent and quite distinct habitats, they nevertheless share a range of characteristics and may occur next to each other in some coastal regions, as part of a natural shoreward succession. It seems useful, therefore, to consider these habitats together. Both are highly specialised ecosystems with a unique mycota and are fragile, vulnerable, and often threatened.

DUNE SYSTEMS

Zones and habitats

Dunes in the British Isles are invariably coastal systems, formed by the wind moving and shaping the sand over long periods of time. They exhibit a marked zonation, from the strand line, inland across mobile sand to inner fixed systems (with grass or heaths), and eventually to woodland. Nearest the coast the sand remains free and is readily blown by wind currents, creating continually moving and unstable dunes. Further inland, the sands are colonised by characteristic vegetation and become stable, fixed, and mature dunes which support a greater range of fungi as well as other organisms. It is important to distinguish these zones in the succession of dune development as they reflect differences which are highly significant in defining habitats.

In general, different zones support an equally different range of plants and fungi.

Rotheroe (1993) has provided a guide to zones that can be recognised in any mature dune system in the British Isles. Dunes vary greatly in their development and characteristics depending on geological, topographical, and climatic factors. Some occur only as narrow coastal strips where geological factors limit sand availability, but others may extend inland by several kilometres. These are the hindshore dunes, exemplified in Britain by well-known systems such as Braunton Burrows in north Devon and Culbin Sands in Scotland. These big dune systems can be split into a series of zones which begin at the strandline (where higher plants and mycorrhizal fungi are absent), followed by embryo dunes (comprising unfixed sand with little or no higher vegetation or macrofungi), 'yellow' dunes (unstable and constantly shifting, but colonised by marram grass, *Ammophila arenaria*, and lyme-grass, *Leymus arenarius*), semi-fixed dunes (or 'grey dunes'), and finally fixed dunes where vegetation varies depending on calcium carbonate (pH) content. Acid conditions give rise to a typical heathland flora; alkaline conditions to a species-rich grassland which, with appropriate grazing, may be similar to that found on chalk or limestone. Dune slacks, hollows or depressions where the water table is close to the surface and where seasonal flooding often occurs, are frequently found among the fixed dunes. Such slacks are characterised by the ground-hugging, ectomycorrhizal creeping willow, *Salix repens*, and are the most important areas of the dunes for fungal diversity. Beyond the fixed dunes, the system may develop into scrub and eventually climax woodland, the final successional stage, which, unfortunately, is virtually absent from the British Isles.

Sand dunes occupy around 10% of our total coast length. Although some are degraded and of comparatively little mycological interest, there are still some major systems remaining, including those at Ynyslas and Newborough Warren in Wales, Whiteford Burrows, Ainsdale, and Braunton Burrows in England, Culbin Sands (the largest system in Britain) and Bettyhill in Scotland, and Les Quennevais in Jersey. In general these dune systems represent a comparatively unspoiled and in many ways unique ecosystem which, as well as being of special mycological interest, supports a wide range of other organisms.

Dune mycorrhizas

The presence and influence of mycorrhizas in sand dunes were studied by Read (1989). These change markedly, both in type and function, through the dune zonation. Vegetation near to the high tide line comprises non-mycorrhizal species, and the sand supports few if any macrofungi. In the embryo dunes the only mycorrhizal fungi present are those which form facultative VA-mycorrhizas (Chapter Four) associated with pioneer grasses, particularly sand couch, *Elymus farctus*, which is the earliest coloniser of the open sand. The fungi concerned are mainly species of *Glomus* (*Glomeromycota*) and appear to be of critical importance to the vegetation, particularly in the early stages of colonisation, enabling the grasses to capture growth-limiting elements such as phosphorus which are essential to their development. The fungi are also important in binding the sand grains and further facilitating the colonisation of other grasses (especially marram grass), as well as sea holly (*Eryngium maritimum*) and species of ragwort (*Senecio*), restharrow (*Ononis*), and spurge (*Euphorbia*).

Similar VA-mycorrhizal fungi are present throughout the semi-fixed dunes, but further into the succession (notably in the dune slacks where there is abundant accumulation of organic matter and a lower pH) nitrogen rather than phosphorus becomes the most important growth-limiting element. It is here that the ectomycorrhizal species predominate. Creeping willow is the main ectomycorrhizal plant typical of dune slacks and a surprisingly wide range of fungi can occur with it. Low-level colonisation of the willow by VA-mycorrhizal species also occurs, sufficient at least to cover its phosphorus requirements. Indeed, the relative abundance and interaction between VA- and ectomycorrhizal species apparently contribute to the broad habitat range of *Salix repens*. Further into the succession the soil pH is reduced still further with a greater accumulation of organic matter and more extensive leaching out of the calcium carbonate. Here, the plants of the earlier succession cannot survive and instead there is the development of ericoid mycorrhizas which are characteristic of acidic heathlands. These mycorrhizas function both to liberate phosphorus and nitrogen and also to assimilate toxic organic acids and metal ions. This allows the development of ericaceous species such as ling (*Calluna vulgaris*), and in some areas species of heathers (*Erica*) and crowberry (*Empetrum*) as well as unwelcome alien invaders notably species of *Rhododendron* and *Gaultheria*.

Larger dune fungi

It is the stable dunes, particularly the dune slacks, which are most important for larger fungi. They support a surprising diversity of species including obligate dune fungi (Table 25) as well as many facultative taxa. Based mainly on studies at Ynyslas in Wales and Bettyhill in Scotland, Watling & Rotheroe (1989) compiled a list of dune macrofungi that contained over 150 species. The majority were widespread non-mycorrhizal species such as the agarics *Agrocybe praecox*, *Agaricus arvensis*, *Panaeolina foenisecii*, *Hygrocybe psittacina*, *H. virginea* and *Lepista nuda*, all commonly found in grassy places even away from the coast, together with equally widespread ectomycorrhizal species like *Dermocybe cinnamomea*, *Hebeloma leucosarx* and *Inocybe lacera*. About 40 of the listed species, such as *Cortinarius ammophilus* and *C. fulvosquamosus*, were only known from dune slacks. Studies in the Netherlands (van der Heijden *et al.*, 1999) recorded 78 ectomycorrhizal species in association with *Salix repens* in dune systems. These belonged to no less than twelve different genera although the majority were in *Cortinarius*, *Hebeloma* and *Inocybe*.

Mobile dunes also support a range of larger fungi, including species which are specifically associated with marram and other dune grasses. They include widespread generalists such as the agarics *Bolbitius vitellinus*, *Crinipellis scabellus*, and *Volvariella speciosa*, as well as several obligate species, notably *Peziza ammophila* and *Phallus hadriani*, both of which occur in most well-developed dunes. The last is similar to the common stinkhorn, *Phallus impudicus* (also frequent in dunes), but can be distinguished in the field by its pinkish 'egg' (Fig. 96). Also found in the mobile, yellow dunes is the much less frequent though widespread agaric *Hohenbuehelia culmicola*, which produces small greyish-brown, kidney-shaped fruitbodies on dead culms of *Ammophila* and *Leymus*. Another obligate dune agaric, *Stropharia halophila*, is so far known in Britain only in Norfolk. It has a yellow cap and is reminiscent of the much commoner grassland species *S. coronilla*, though more robust and with a thicker, well-developed ring. A few species,

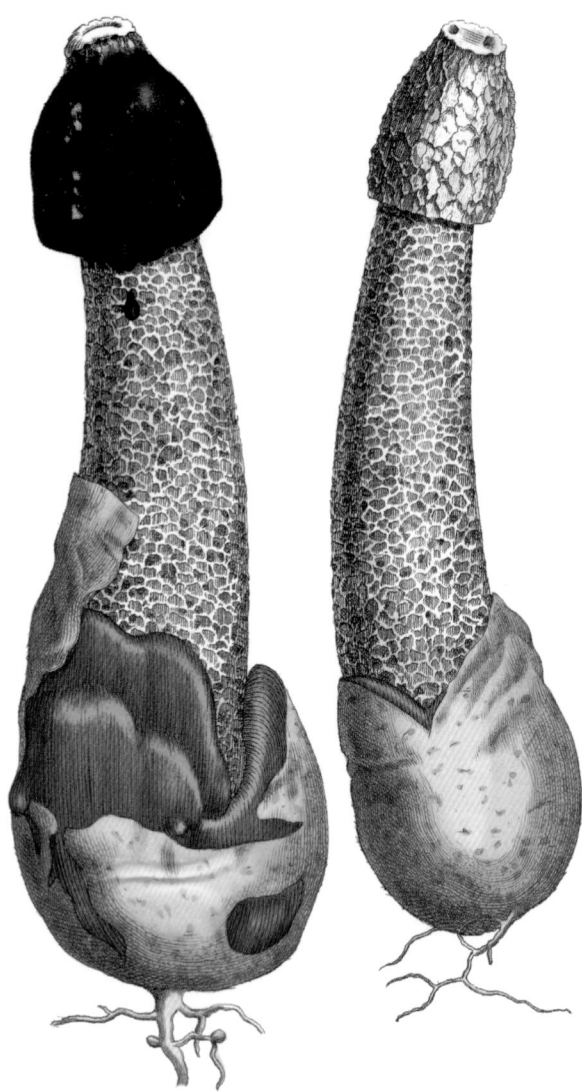

FIG 96. The dune stinkhorn, *Phallus hadriani*, is found in Britain only in sand dunes. It closely resembles the common *P. impudicus* but differs especially in having a pink egg (RBG Kew).

particularly the dune wax-cap (*Hygrocybe conicoides*), can occur throughout much of the dune succession.

Dung associates provide further examples of facultative dune fungi, one of the most notable being *Cyathus stercoreus*, the 'dung bird's-nest'. This occurs on rabbit droppings in dunes, though its other requirements are uncertain. So far the only British collections are from dunes in Wales. Other coprophilous dune species on rabbit dung include the agarics *Panaeolus sphinctrinus* and *Psilocybe coprophila*.

There are also many arenicolous fungi (sandy soil specialists), of which the agarics *Agaricus devoniensis* (Fig. 97), *Lepiota alba* and *Rhodocybe popinalis*, the earth-tongue *Geoglossum arenarium*, the puffball *Bovista limosa*, the stilt-puffball *Tulostoma melanocyclum*, and the earth-star *Geastrum schmidelii* (Fig, 98) are good examples. The last, known as the 'dwarf earthstar', is particularly frequent amongst grass and moss in dune slacks, but is

FIG 97. The dune mushroom *Agaricus devoniensis* develops under the surface of the sand and emerges only when it expands (P. Roberts).

occasionally found inland in sandy places. Bryophytes offer another niche, the conspicuous orange discomycete *Octospora rutilans*, for example, being frequent with *Polytrichum*.

Curiously, the lichens often include normally epiphytic species, such as *Evernia prunastri* and *Usnea hirta*, growing on the sand of fixed dunes. Otherwise they tend to be dominated by *Cladonia* species, the species changing from zone to zone. Many other generalist macrofungi will be found in any dune system. Further lists were published by Ramsbottom (1953), Rotheroe (1993), and Watling (1973).

FIG 98. The dwarf earthstar *Geastrum schmidelii* (once called *G. nanum*) is a small species typically found in dune slacks and sandy places (B. Spooner).

TABLE 25. Macrofungi known in Britain only from sand dunes

SPECIES	DESCRIPTION
Agaricus devoniensis	saprotrophic agaric
Agrocybe subpediades	saprotrophic agaric
Bovista limosa	puffball
Conocybe dunensis	saprotrophic agaric
Coprinus ammophilae	saprotrophic agaric
Cortinarius ammophilus	mycorrhizal agaric
Cortinarius fulvosquamosus	mycorrhizal agaric
Entoloma nigrella	mycorrhizal agaric
Hohenbuehelia culmicola	saprotrophic agaric
Hygrocybe conicoides	saprotrophic agaric
Hygrocybe phaeococcinea	saprotrophic agaric
Inocybe dunensis	mycorrhizal agaric
Inocybe fastigiata f. arenicola	mycorrhizal agaric
Inocybe halophila	mycorrhizal agaric
Inocybe heimii	mycorrhizal agaric
Inocybe impexa	mycorrhizal agaric
Inocybe inodora	mycorrhizal agaric
Inocybe serotina	mycorrhizal agaric
Inocybe vulpinella	mycorrhizal agaric
Laccaria maritima	mycorrhizal agaric
Melanoleuca cinereifolia	saprotrophic agaric
Melanoleuca schumacheri	saprotrophic agaric
Mycena chlorantha	saprotrophic agaric
Oudemansiella xeruloides	saprotrophic agaric
Peziza ammophila	ascomycete
Phallus hadriani	stinkhorn
Pluteus lepiotoides	saprotrophic agaric
Psathyrella ammophila	saprotrophic agaric
Psathyrella dunensis	saprotrophic agaric
Pyrenocollema arenisedum	lichenised ascomycete
Pyrenocollema subarenisedum	lichenised ascomycete
Stropharia halophila	saprotrophic agaric
Tulostoma melanocyclum	stilt-puffball

Dune microfungi

Whilst larger fungi have received considerable attention, especially in recent years, microfungi of dune systems remain less well known. However, several important studies, in Britain and elsewhere, have shown many species to be common in dune soils.

Brown (1958) researched dune microfungi at eight localities in England, Scotland, and Wales, including both alkaline and acid systems. She examined the different successional zones, at soil depths between 1 and 30 cm, and isolated over 160 species. These included 21 species of *Mucorales*, mainly belonging to the genera *Absidia*, *Mortierella* and *Mucor*, and many hyphomycetes, particularly *Penicillium* species. All parts of the succession yielded microfungi and, although the semi-fixed and fixed dunes were in general the most productive zones, a significant number were obtained from open sand and embryo dunes. At Sandwich in Kent, for example, 32 species were isolated from the embryo dunes. Some, notably several penicillia and the ubiquitous *Cladosporium herbarum*, were found to occur throughout the system, even in acid and alkaline dunes. *Penicillium nigricans* was the commonest species isolated and considered to be the most widespread microfungus in British dune soils. Rather few ascomycetes were found in this study, mostly widespread and plurivorous species of *Chaetomium*, *Gelasinospora* and *Sporormiella* which normally occur on vegetable debris and dung. Other than *Peziza ammophila*, listed in the table as a macrofungus, few obligate sand-dune ascomycetes are known. However, *Sordaria arenicola*, a tiny pyrenomycete described from amongst sand and algae in dunes in Lincolnshire, is apparently not known from other habitats, and the hyphomycete *Asteromyces cruciatus*, only found in open sand between high and low tide marks, is considered a pioneer species in young dunes.

There are also many fungi associated, both as saprotrophs and parasites, with the dune grasses *Ammophila arenaria* and *Leymus arenarius*. Dennis (1983) listed around 100 species on marram grass in Europe, most of which are known from Britain. However, few if any appear to be specific to *Ammophila*, many also occurring on *Leymus* and other grasses, or on other herbaceous substrata. Obligate marram associates include some larger fungi, such as *Psathyrella ammophila*, as well as a number of microfungi. The variety *ammophilina* of the rust *Puccinia pygmaea*, the typical form of which occurs on *Calamgrostis*, occurs only on *Ammophila*, and the coelomycetes *Septoria ammophilae*, a leaf-spot parasite, and *Rhodesia subtecta*, on dead leaves, may also be host-specific. The rust *Puccinia elymi* occurs only on dune grasses, infecting both *Ammophila* and *Leymus*, as well as the hybrid x *Ammocalamagrostis baltica. Leymus* is host to a number of plurivorous, saprotrophic microfungi, often shared with *Ammophila*, but again appears to have few obligate associates.

Myxomycetes are not common in dunes, and those which do occur are generally characteristic of particular substratum types rather than dunes themselves. However, a few slime moulds can be found in this habitat, and an interesting paper by Howard (1948) listed 20 such species from Norfolk dune systems. These mostly occurred on *Ammophila* and stems of *Senecio*, and included rarities such as *Diderma asteroides* which is supposedly typical of evergreen forests in the Mediterranean. Among the more frequent dune species are *Diderma spumarioides* growing in moss and *Mucilago crustacea* colonising living grass stems. Other species are associated with dune lichens, notably the rare *Listerella paradoxa* and *Diachaeopsis mitchellii*, both of which have been recorded from *Cladonia* species in dry dune slacks.

HEATHLAND

Heathland represents a distinct and well-defined habitat which is characteristic of poor, acid soils and may be developed either inland or in coastal areas as a late successional stage of dune systems. It is dominated by ericaceous dwarf shrubs, especially ling, the most characteristic of the defining species, and, on wetter heaths, species of *Erica*, the true heathers.

Ling is also characteristic of moorland, which differs in being developed on peat and is mainly found in upland areas at altitudes above 300m. Heathlands, in contrast, occur in lowland areas and are found almost exclusively in northern Europe, particularly in southern and south-eastern England. Indeed, Britain's 58,000 ha of remaining heathland includes a significant proportion of the world's total heathland habitat.

Although characteristically developed on sandy soil, like dunes, heaths are never calcareous, but have a low pH, calcium carbonate and most of the nutrients having been leached out since the land was deforested. However, despite being acidic, heathland may develop over chalk or limestone bedrock if a thin layer of sandy drift is present.

History and conservation

Heathlands are now regarded as man-made habitats, created following extensive clearance of the forest which continued from late neolithic times to the eighth century AD and, indeed, earlier than 6000 BC heathland scarcely existed at all. Grazing on poor soils where agriculture was unsustainable prevented the return of climax vegetation which, in parts of the continent, is pine forest, but in England is usually oak. The introduction of rabbits in the Middle Ages and the development of heathland warrens were further factors in sustaining the habitat. Heathlands have therefore become established over at least 1500 years, sometimes much longer, and are now unique habitats with a community of organisms, particularly insects and fungi, that occur nowhere else. Their flora, however, is comparatively poor, although various herbaceous species such as tormentil (*Potentilla erecta*), heath milkwort (*Polygala serpyllifolia*), heath bedstraw (*Galium saxatile*) and sheep's sorrel (*Rumex acetosella*) are characteristic and regularly present even in dry heaths. Gorse and bracken are also typical heathland plants, as are grasses such as sheep's fescue (*Festuca ovina*) and wavy hair grass (*Deschampsia flexuosa*), together with various mosses, especially *Polytrichum juniperinum*. The ecology of heathlands was further discussed by Gimingham (1972) and the whole habitat explored by Webb (1986).

Unfortunately, heathlands are fragile systems and are declining or being degraded throughout most of their range. In southern England the remaining heaths are often invaded by birch and pine which transform the habitat, destroying the heather and associated species which cannot thrive in shade. Commercial encroachment also takes its toll, such 'worthless' land being ideal for forestry, holiday camps, and industrial estates. In Surrey, still one of the most important counties for heathland, a survey undertaken in 1985 for the Nature Conservancy Council and Surrey County Council found that only about 15% of the original heathland cover as recorded in 1762 now remains. The decline of heathland in Dorset shows a similar pattern, with rapid destruction during the past century. The heaths of the Bovey Basin in

Devon have almost all been destroyed by ball clay quarrying, industrial development, conifer plantation, and housing estates. Overall it is estimated that during the past 50 years no less than 75% of British heathlands have been lost.

Currently, among the most notable inland heaths that remain are those of the New Forest (amongst the most extensive anywhere), Wangford Warren in the Suffolk Breckland, Hartland Moor and Arne Heath in Dorset, Ambersham-Heyshott Common in Sussex, Chobham Common in Surrey, Cawton-Marsham Heaths in Norfolk, and Risby Warren in Lincolnshire. Coastal heaths include the Lizard in Cornwall, Studland Heath in Dorset, Bardsey Island, and Culbin Sands in Scotland.

Ericoid mycorrhizas

One of the most important aspects of the mycology of heathlands is the existence of the unique ericoid mycorrhizas found with *Calluna*, *Erica* and other ericaceous plants typical of the habitat (Chapter Four).

The *Ericaceae* are the dominant members of the heathland community, and are obligate mycorrhizal plants. They form a variety of mycorrhizas, but most important is the ericoid type, a characteristic association which enables ericaceous plants to grow and thrive in soils where nitrogen and phosphorus are limiting, conditions in which other plants cannot survive. Ericoid mycorrhizas infer a range of benefits to the plant partners, not just allowing colonisation of acid, heathland soils but also providing resistance to toxic pollutants including heavy metals such as copper, zinc, and arsenate. Furthermore, ericoid mycorrhizas prevent invasion of spruce by suppressing the development of ectomycorrhizal fungi and preventing the growth of young trees although they seem to actually stimulate the growth of some ectomycorrhizal species, notably the agaric *Paxillus involutus* and the bolete *Suillus grevillei* (Mitchell *et al.*, 1992). This is perhaps reflected in the ease with which pine and birch are able to colonise heathlands. The basidiomycete *Clavaria argillacea* also has an intimate association with *Calluna* involving an exchange of nutrients, although the exact nature of this association is unclear.

Larger heathland fungi

The larger fungi of heathlands have been studied in detail in the Nether-lands, especially by Arnolds (1982, 1988), and also in Germany and Poland. The number of species present is not high in comparison to habitats such as woodland and grassland but, as noted by Arnolds (1992), they often fruit in high densities.

Perhaps the most important heathland macrofungi belong to the agaric genera *Mycena* (Fig. 99) and *Galerina*, although few are obligate species, many also being found in other habitats. Moss associates include the discomycetes *Octospora rutilans* (Fig. 100) associated with *Polytrichum*, and *Cheilymenia fibrillosa* (Fig. 101), both with orange-yellow apothecia, and the small, orange species *Lamprospora carbonicola* and *Octospora roxheimii* which occur on burnt heath with the moss *Funaria hygrometrica*. Burnt areas of heathland frequently

FIG 99. *Mycena epipterygia*, a fairly common though quite variable heathland toadstool. The yellow stem is character-istic and the species has a gelatinous pellicle or 'skin' which covers the cap and can be pulled away (P. Livermore).

FIG 100. The discomycete *Octospora rutilans* is associated with mosses of the genus *Polytrichum* and is found on sandy soils in both dunes and heathlands (B. Spooner).

FIG 101. The discomycete *Cheilymenia fibrillosa*, with cup-shaped fruitbodies, a rather scarce species found mostly on sandy, heathland soils (B. Spooner).

also support the discomycetes *Peziza pseudoviolacea* and *Plicaria endocarpoides*, and the orange-brown toadstool *Pholiota highlandensis*.

Marasmius androsaceus is of particular interest in being a parasite of *Calluna* and *Erica*, continuing to develop on dead stems, and spreading by means of characteristic black, wiry, horsehair-like rhizomorphs. It is common on *Erica* though occurs in various other habitats, being frequent for example on decaying pine needles, as well as in oak woodland. It is the cause of branch dieback of heather, rhizomorphs penetrating the living stems through wounds and killing the stem by causing separation of the bark. In some areas, particularly in Scotland, the death of extensive stands of heather has been of significant economic importance. The periodic burning of heathland, so removing dead stems which harbour the fungus, was a recommended management procedure, doubly useful in also controlling the damaging heather beetle (*Lochmaea suturalis*).

Lichens are well represented in heathland communities, various attractive and distinctive species occurring on soil and plant litter, or as epiphytes on heathland plants. Soil-dwelling lichens are dominated by *Cladonia* species such as *C. arbuscula*, a robust, much-branched species that often occurs in the bare areas which develop in the centre of old *Calluna* plants as their branches expand. Other lichens typical of this habitat include *Cladonia coccifera* and *C. floerkeana* (Fig. 102), both with attractive red fruiting bodies. Foliose lichens such as *Peltigera didactyla*, crustose species such as *Placynthiella icmalea* and *P. uliginosa*, and the dark-brown, mat-forming *Cornicularia aculeata* are also common on heathland soil. The widespread and plurivorous *Hypogymnia physodes* is a common epiphyte on stems of *Calluna* and *Erica*, often colonising dead branches. After fires, common on heaths, lichen communities follow a well-marked succession. Pioneer species such as *Placynthiella icmalea* appear rapidly, followed within 2–3 years by *Cladonia* species, though the succession back to the fully developed lichen community may take 10–15 years.

The myxomycetes of lowland heaths are generally similar to those of acid woodland, though a number of interesting species can be found among *Calluna* and bracken on damper heaths. The uncommon *Hemitrichia leiotricha* is an example of the former and, where litter is sufficiently developed, *Diderma simplex* and *Lepidoderma chailletii* can also occur. The common

FIG 102. The lichen *Cladonia floerkeana*, a typical heathland species, with attractive red fruitbodies (RBG Kew).

Leocarpus fragilis, characterised by large, shiny, chestnut-coloured fruitbodies which form grape-like bunches, is often found in gorse litter, together with *Didymium melanospermum*. Various other common slime moulds may also be frequent in heathland, but none are specialists in this habitat.

TABLE 26. Some typical heathland macrofungi in the British Isles (including moss associates)

SPECIES	DESCRIPTION
Aleurodiscus norvegicus	corticioid fungus on heathers
Cheilymenia fibrillosa	discomycete
Cladonia arbuscula	lichenised ascomycete
Cladonia coccifera	lichenised ascomycete
Cladonia floerkeana	lichenised ascomycete
Clavaria argillacea	club fungus
Collybia dryophila	saprotrophic agaric

SPECIES	DESCRIPTION
Collybia impudica	saprotrophic agaric
Cornicularia aculeata	lichenised ascomycete
Cystoderma amianthinum	saprotrophic agaric
Entoloma bloxami	saprotrophic agaric
Entoloma cetratum	saprotrophic agaric
Entoloma helodes	saprotrophic agaric
Entoloma turbidum	saprotrophic agaric
Galerina atkinsoniana	saprotrophic agaric
Galerina calyptrata	saprotrophic agaric
Galerina hypnorum	saprotrophic agaric
Hygrocybe laeta	saprotrophic agaric
Hygrocybe miniata	saprotrophic agaric
Hygrocybe turunda	saprotrophic agaric
Lycoperdon ericaeum	puffball
Marasmius androsaceus	parasitic/saprotrophic agaric
Mycena cinerella	saprotrophic agaric
Mycena epipterygia	saprotrophic agaric
Mycena sanguinolenta	saprotrophic agaric
Octospora rutilans	discomycete
Omphalina grisella	saprotrophic agaric
Omphalina griseopallida	saprotrophic agaric
Omphalina rustica	saprotrophic agaric
Peltigera didactyla	lichenised ascomycete
Placynthiella icmalea	lichenised ascomycete

Heathland microfungi

Calluna and *Erica* have few if any fungal parasites other than *Marasmius
androsaceus*, though root death due to *Phytophthora* has been recorded.
However, on dead stems various microfungi characteristically occur. On
Calluna these include most notably the discomycetes *Godronia callunigera* with
leathery, blackish, urn-shaped fruitbodies, and *Pseudophacidium callunae* with
part-sunken fruitbodies which burst through the bark at maturity to expose a
yellowish disc. Both of these are apparently restricted to this host, though
scarce. Various plurivorous discomycetes also occur commonly. Most
notable are species of *Mollisia*, with gregarious, greyish fruitbodies often
seated on a dark brown mat of hyphae, several species of which are frequent
on damp, dead stems.

Other microfungi occur as parasites on invertebrates, such as the white hyphomycete *Beauveria bassiana*, a common heathland species, sometimes found on the heather beetle *Lochmaea suturalis*. These again are mostly plurivorous fungi, not restricted to heathland hosts. Other species occur in the soil, and the presence, distribution and ecology of heathland soil fungi were investigated by Thornton (1956) and Sewell (1959a, b, c), based mainly on sites in southern England and Wales. In total, over 80 microfungi were isolated in these studies, including 17 species of *Mucorales*, mostly in the genera *Mortierella* and *Mucor*, and a wide range of hyphomycetes of which *Penicillium* was the dominant genus. Most species were found to occur in the immediate subsurface layer, with the presence and abundance of fungi decreasing with depth. Although the microfungi isolated were mostly widespread and found in various habitats, some, particularly *Beauveria bassiana*, *Mucor ramannianus*, *Trichoderma viride* and some *Penicillium* species, were constantly obtained and considered to be characteristic species of heathland soils.

CHAPTER 11

Freshwater

A LL FUNGI, even xerotolerant species, are linked in some way with water. It is an essential requirement for fungal growth and development, just as it is for other organisms. But a number of fungi are specifically adapted to freshwater habitats, rivers, lakes, bogs, marshes, fens and other wetlands, or are directly associated with plants that are found in these habitats. They include the so-called 'indwellers', species which complete their entire life cycle in aquatic habitats and which often show specific adaptations to an aquatic existence, as well as 'immigrants', which are only partially aquatic.

Most groups of fungi have some freshwater representatives, although the majority are microfungi. Goh & Hyde (1996) noted more than 600 species of *Fungi*, the ascomycetes being particularly well represented, with almost 500 species (excluding lichens and anamorphic forms) reported to date (Shearer, 2001). Including lichens and various fungus-like groups, around 900 fungal species are now known from freshwater habitats.

As in other habitats, freshwater fungi play important roles in the environment, particularly in the degradation of organic matter and recycling of nutrients, and interact in various ways with other aquatic organisms, involving not only saprotrophic, but parasitic and mutualistic associations.

Specialist adaptations to life in water

Many unique adaptations to an aquatic existence are exhibited by freshwater fungi. These adaptations reflect the wide range of environments they inhabit, from rivers and streams, to lakes and ponds, puddles and even raindrops and include mechanisms for drought resistance, substrate location and colonisation, reproduction and dispersal.

The periodic drying up of habitats is a common occurrence, and fungi may endure such times either as endophytes in living plants or as mycelium in rotting wood or other substrata. Some, particularly amongst the chytrids, form resting spores or cysts which can lie dormant in the mud. Immigrant species may continue in their terrestrial stages until conditions improve.

Spore dispersal is equally specialised. Many of the fungi with motile spores respond to chemical compounds released from their hosts or to substances leached from decaying plant material. Fungi with non-motile spores often display special adaptations for efficient spore dispersal. This is most clearly demonstrated by the remarkable water-borne spores and propagules of the Ingoldian and aero-aquatic hyphomycetes.

The spores of Ingoldian hyphomycetes are commonly branched, allowing them to float freely until the branches catch upon suitable substrata. These and many other aquatic spores are invested in mucilage or have mucilaginous appendages which provide effective adhesion after contact.

In the aero-aquatics, the spores are commonly globose or helicoid and are non-wettable and buoyant. As a result they readily rise to the surface when their terrestrial substrata are flooded and are then appropriately situated to colonise fallen leaves and other floating debris.

Stream foam and leaves: the Ingoldian hyphomycetes

Amongst the best known of the aquatic fungi are the hyphomycetes, of which over 300 species (in around 100 genera) have been described to date. They exhibit a variety of ecological strategies and are fundamental to the ecology of most freshwater ecosystems, particularly in the breakdown of organic matter and the recycling of nutrients.

The foremost pioneer of the study of these fungi has been Prof. C.T. Ingold who has made extensive contributions to their ecology and biology since he first discovered abundant conidia in stream foam in

Leicestershire in 1938. Indeed, hyphomycetes of this ecological type, which
develop and sporulate on submerged substrata, are now commonly referred
to as 'Ingoldian fungi', a term introduced by Webster & Descals (1981). Over
200 species have been recognised, many of them worldwide in distribution.
They are particularly characteristic of fast-flowing woodland streams and
well-aerated lakes, though these are not their sole habitats. Some are clearly
pollution-tolerant, a surprising range of species being isolated in Germany
from sites with high levels of heavy metal contamination. Two species,
Heliscus lugdunensis and *Tetracladium marchalianum*, were present in all
sites sampled.

Ingoldian fungi grow on submerged, decaying leaves and other
vegetation, and their conidia, liberated and dispersed below water, are often
abundantly present in stream foam. They may be readily examined if
decaying, part-skeletonised, submerged tree leaves are washed and placed
under water in a Petri dish. Within a day the crop of developing
hyphomycetes can usually be observed. They occur on many kinds of leaves,
although those of beech and conifers are generally unproductive. Ingoldian
fungi are most abundant in late autumn after the main leaf fall, and play a
major role in the decay of dicotyledonous leaves in streams. This has
important consequences for the nutrition of aquatic invertebrates which
utilise the decaying leaves as a food source. The fungi degrade the cellulose
and lignin in the leaves, making them available to invertebrates which lack
the appropriate enzymes to digest these compounds. Fungal activity also
increases the protein content of decaying leaf litter. The invertebrates
(including insects, crustaceans, and worms) in turn provide food for fish,
waterbirds, and other larger animals.

Ingoldian fungi can also be obtained in their conidial form by direct
examination of stream foam. Foam is an effective trap for such spores,
particularly tetraradiate types (those with four appendages or arms) and
other branching conidia, and a few species are as yet only known from foam.
However, foam samples should immediately be placed in a fixative, since the
conidia start to germinate as soon as the foam collapses.

Ingoldian hyphomycetes exhibit distinctive, curved and usually branched,
frequently tetratradiate conidia developed as an adaptation to aquatic
dispersal (Fig. 103). They provide an interesting example of convergence in

conidium morphology, as they are now known to be stages in the life histories of widely separated fungi, not only within the ascomycetes and the basidiomycetes, but also in some zygomycetes. The tetraradiate form is the commonest, the most effective shape for lodging on underwater surfaces and thus a significant adaptation to an aquatic existence. A sigmoid form is also common and has again been independently evolved in a wide range of fungi. The advantage of such a form is less clearly understood but was investigated by Webster & Davy (1984). They found that, although impaction efficiency on substrata is less than for branched conidia, adhesion still occurs at two points of contact – at one end and at an intermediate position – and orientation on contact parallel to the water flow minimises the chances of being washed off.

Although such general patterns are common, the conidia of many individual species are highly distinctive in their precise form and size. Some are extremely large; for example, the conidia of *Actinospora megalospora*, described from Britain, may reach over 350 µm across (50 to 100 times larger than most terrestrial conidia). Others, such as

FIG 103. Examples of spores formed by aquatic hyphomycetes. The coiled spores belong to aero-aquatic species, evolved to be buoyant. The complex, branched spores belong to the so-called Ingoldian hyphomycetes, evolved for dispersal in water (H. Voglmayr).

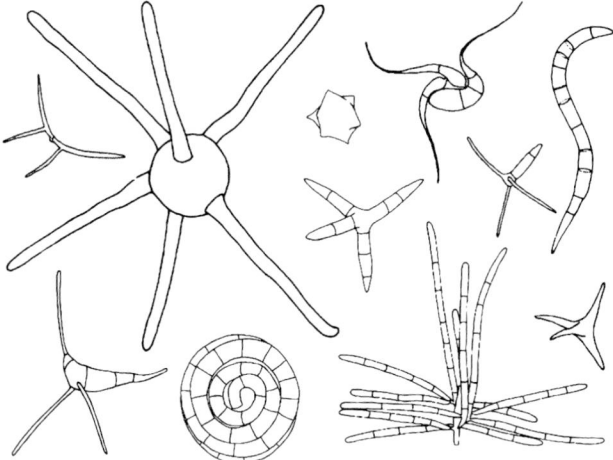

species of *Gyoerffyella*, are readily recognised by their radially curved, catherine-wheel-like form. Keys for the identification of these conidia were provided by Ingold (1975).

As yet, the sexual stages of Ingoldian fungi have been established only for a minority of species, but several are now known to be cup-fungi. The common *Tricladium splendens*, for example, is the anamorph of a *Hymenoscyphus* species (described as *H. splendens*). Two additional new species with aquatic anamorphs, *H. tetracladius* and *H. foliicola*, were described in the same account. Another discomycete, *Mollisia uda*, forms small, usually gregarious, greyish fruitbodies on submerged or water-soaked wood. Its anamorph is the well-known Ingoldian, *Anguillospora crassa*. Other Ingoldians with ascomycetous teleomorphs were discussed by Webster (1992).

An example of an Ingoldian hyphomycete with a basidiomycetous anamorph is *Ingoldiella hamata*, a widely distributed tropical species first described in 1972. This has conidia of typical Ingoldian form but with clamp-connections (found only in *Basidiomycota*), and was shown a decade later to be a stage in the life-cycle of a corticioid fungus described as *Sistotrema hamatum*. Other species of *Ingoldiella*, as well as species referred to *Fibulotaeniella*, *Taeniospora*, *Dendrosporomyces* and *Tricladiomyces*, are also conidial basidiomycetes, some of which occur in the British Isles.

Stagnant pools and ditches: the aero-aquatic hyphomycetes

A quite different ecology to the Ingoldians is exhibited by many other hyphomycetes which are characteristic of aquatic habitats. These are known as aero-aquatics, though two further ecological groups, the submerged-aquatic and terrestrial-aquatic hyphomycetes, have been recognised recently.

Aero-aquatics are indwellers, adapted to a fully aquatic existence. Unlike the Ingoldians they develop in stagnant conditions, such as pools and ditches, which are seasonally dry. They grow underwater in the decaying leaves and other plant debris and, when conditions are dry, produce buoyant conidia which readily float to the surface when the substratum is reflooded. Even small, temporary pools in forests are known to be productive of many species of aquatic hyphomycetes, sporulating as the pools dry out, their spores released by any new influx of water. Plant debris from suitable habitats which has been rinsed in clean water and incubated for a few days in a moist chamber will usually yield abundant aero-aquatic species. The conidia of these fungi tend to differ in form from the Ingoldians, and are commonly spirally coiled in either watch-spring or barrel-like forms. Other conidial types include cage-like structures and bulbils comprised of clusters of cell-like hyphae, often surrounded with incurved arms. All these aero-aquatic conidia are adapted to trap air and to float.

An aero-aquatic ecology is found worldwide and has again been evolved by fungi from many unrelated groups, including both basidiomycetes and ascomycetes. In Britain, two common basidiomycete examples are the corticioid species *Bulbillomyces farinosus* and *Subulicystidium longisporum*, both of which produce white, bulbil-like propagules (known as *Aegerita candida* and *Aegeritina tortuosa* respectively) which are often abundant and easily visible under a lens on wet, rotting wood on stream banks or ditches (Fig. 104). However, most aero-aquatics are ascomycetous, the helical conidia

FIG 104. The tiny, white propagules of *Aegeritina tortuosa* develop in swarms on rotting wood in damp places. The perfect, spore-bearing state is the corticioid (patch-forming) species *Subulicystidium longisporum* (RBG Kew).

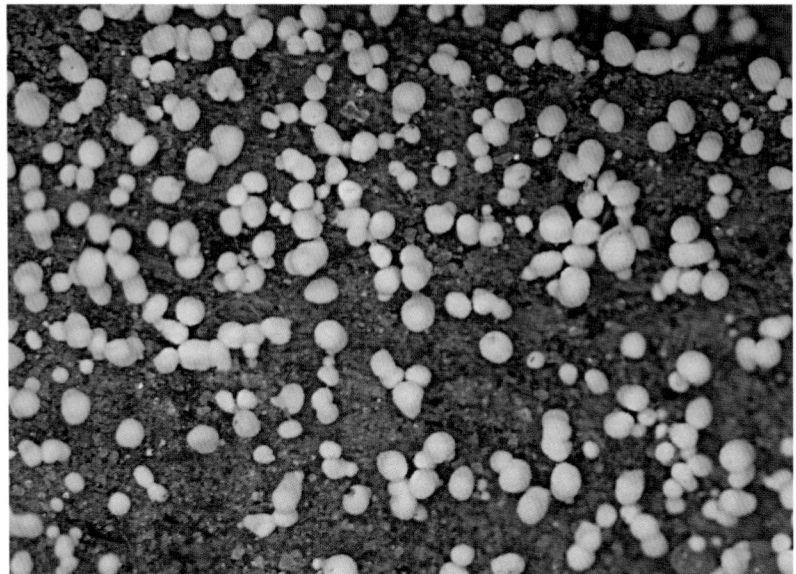

of genera such as *Helicomyces* and *Helicodendron*, for example, being stages of pyrenomycetes (*Tubeufia*) and discomycetes (*Lambertella*) respectively.

Air and water: the submerged-aquatic hyphomycetes

The submerged-aquatic (or sometimes 'facultative-aquatic') hyphomycetes grow on submerged, decaying plant debris, but are mainly lignicolous and found in fast-flowing streams. They represent a rather heterogeneous assemblage of species with an ecology which is in some ways similar to that of both the Ingoldians and the aero-aquatics. They are mainly dark-coloured (dematiaceous) fungi, unlike most of the previous groups, and develop conidia on distinct conidiophores. They may sporulate either underwater or, more commonly, on exposed substrata, when their conidia may be air-dispersed. Conidia dispersed underwater are often branched and reminiscent of those of the Ingoldian fungi; airborne conidia are comparatively simple, cylindric, ellipsoid or clavate.

A British example of a submerged-aquatic hyphomycete is *Casaresia sphagnorum*, which has characteristic, dark, branched conidia. It is now known that the sexual state is a discomycete, *Mollisia casaresiae*, fruitbodies of which were discovered on submerged wooden dowels in a Devon stream.

Raindrops and morning dew: the terrestrial-aquatic hyphomycetes

The so-called terrestrial-aquatic hyphomycetes occur in the smallest of water bodies in terrestrial ecosystems, in raindrops on the leaf surface or in rainwater trickling down the surface of living trees. They produce branched, often tetraradiate conidia, similar to those of the Ingoldian fungi, but formed on simple cells rather than conidiophores. Even the most ephemeral of water bodies, those formed by morning dew, which evaporate during the day and are replaced the next day in a continuing cycle, are exploited by terrestrial-aquatic hyphomycetes.

Specialist wood-rotters in freshwater systems

As in the marine environment, most of the fungi that break down wood in freshwater habitats are ascomycetes, typically causing superficial but increasingly invasive soft rots. These soft-rot pockets, produced by freshwater lignicolous genera such as *Pseudohalonectria*, are especially important for aquatic invertebrates many of which need fungus-softened wood for boring or grazing.

Many of the aquatic wood-rotters are pyrenomycetes or members of the *Dothideales*, with representatives worldwide. Although most belong to genera more commonly represented in terrestrial habitats, such as *Leptosphaeria*, *Phaeosphaeria*, *Ophiobolus*, *Pleospora*, *Massarina* and *Nectria*, some genera are entirely comprised of aquatic species. These include *Aniptodera* and *Pseudohalonectria*, the former including both marine and freshwater species, as well as several more recently described genera now referred to the *Annulatascaceae*. These fungi, all saprotrophs on submerged wood, include many tropical aquatic species belonging to the genera *Annulatascus*, *Aquasphaeria*, *Aquaticola*, *Diluviicola*, *Submersisphaeria*, *Torrentispora*, and *Vertexicola*. Two species of *Aniptodera* are also known from Britain, the most recently discovered being *A. fusiformis*, the tiny, flask-shaped fruitbodies of which were found on rotten wood in a stream at Perivale in Middlesex. The species had previously been known only from Illinois, USA.

Pseudoproboscispora caudaesuis, a pyrenomycete described from submerged, decorticated twigs in the English Lake District, is a good example of convergent adaptation since its water-borne ascospores have evolved in a similar way to many of the conidia produced by aquatic hyphomycetes. The large, ellipsoid, two-celled spores are packed with small oil drops and furnished at each end with a remarkable mucilaginous appendage. This appendage, sometimes over 100 μm long and more than three times the length of the spore itself, is finely tapered and tightly coiled towards the tip. Similar appendages occur in some species of *Aniptodera*, as well as marine and brackish water species of *Halosarphaea*, *Cucullospora* and other genera, and actually unfurl as the spores are released. They may at first appear as solid, hook-like structures but in water rapidly unwind into characteristic long, fine threads.

Discomycetes are also represented in freshwater habitats, though few genera are entirely adapted to an aquatic mode of life. One of the few is *Vibrissea*, a small but virtually cosmopolitan genus which, together with two other small genera *Chlorovibrissea* and *Leucovibrissea*, constitutes the family *Vibrisseaceae*. All members of this family are aquatic or semi-aquatic, producing fruitbodies on submerged wood which release long, filiform ascospores adapted for dispersal in moving water. Five species are known from Britain including *Vibrissea truncorum*, the largest and most impressive of them. This occurs on branches and roots which are lodged in severely water-splashed areas in small waterfalls in streams and ditches. It can readily be identified by its long-stalked, capitate fruitbodies with yellowish-orange, strongly convex caps. The species is widespread throughout north temperate regions, but in Britain is uncommon and mostly northern. Other *Vibrissea* species are sessile and not so easy to distinguish at species level.

Larger cup-fungi, members of the *Pezizales*, also have a few representatives typical of freshwater habitats. In Britain they include *Miladina lechithina* and *Pachyella babingtonii*, characteristic species of water-soaked, often submerged wood. *Miladina lechithina* is now known to have an aquatic hyphomycete stage (*Actinospora megalospora*) the conidia of which can be found in stream foam. It is also found elsewhere in Europe and in North America, and has broadly attached, yellowish, disc-shaped fruitbodies about 5 mm across. *Pachyella babingtonii*, an uncommon but also widespread species in Britain has larger, sessile, brownish, cushion-shaped fruitbodies about

FIG 105. *Pachyella violaceonigra* is a large but uncommon cup fungus associated with wet rotten wood in marshes and fens (P. Roberts).

10 mm across, mostly developed in spring, either on water-soaked wood or on submerged wood in moving water. A related species, *P. violaceonigra*, is even larger and more rarely encountered (Fig. 105).

Wood-rotting aquatic basidiomycetes are comparatively few, but in Britain include the aero-aquatic species *Bulbillomyces farinosus* and *Subulicystidium longisporum*, noted above. In America, a tiny puffball-like basidiomycete, *Limnoperdon incarnatum*, was unexpectedly found floating on the surface of water-filled Petri dishes containing submerged twigs from marshes. It appears that fruitbodies develop on rotten wood and are released when the substratum is flooded.

Freshwater lichens

As in marine and terrestrial environments, lichens are found in most freshwater habitats, either as obligate aquatic species, often fully submerged, as species tolerant of inundation, or as species on damp waterside rocks. The lichens of British rivers, streams, tarns and lakes were thoroughly reviewed in the New Naturalist volume by Gilbert (2000) and are surprisingly many, with around 160 species in all. They are typically found in zones similar to those of the shoreline lichens on seacoasts (Chapter 12), from fully submerged to occasionally flooded. Among the fully aquatic lichens of the submerged zone is the 'river jelly lichen' *Collema dichotomum*, resembling a small brown seaweed, which can occur half a metre below the water surface. Although still locally frequent in some Scottish rivers, it is sensitive to pollution and has disappeared from many places. It is included on Schedule 8 of the Wildlife and Countryside Act 1981 (Chapter 18) and listed as 'vulnerable' in the lichens Red Data Book. Around 15 aquatic lichen species can be found in acid streams, far fewer in alkaline waters. The self-explanatory amphibious zone is richer in species, with some 25 acid and 20 alkaline lichens. The two higher zones contain damp-loving species, including many found elsewhere and not restricted to rivers and streams. These lichens are almost entirely restricted to Grade A waters and are highly intolerant of pollution. The acidity or alkalinity of their rock and stone substrata seems to be more of an influence on species than the pH of the water itself.

Lake margins have a similar set of lichen zonations to rivers, with at least some species in common. Their widespread exploration was apparently neglected until the 1980s when a supposedly extinct species, *Lecanora achariana*, was rediscovered in the Lake District (it is now known from three additional sites in Ireland, Scotland, and Wales), encouraging a hunt for other rarities. A peculiarity of some western lakes is the presence on damp rock outcrops of large, foliose, epiphytic lichens, such as *Parmeliella triptophylla* and *Pseudocyphellaria intricata*, normally regarded as ancient woodland indicator species.

Mycorrhiza and aquatic plants

Mycorrhizal associations between living aquatic plants and fungi are limited because many muds and waterlogged soils are anaerobic. In partly or seasonally oxygenated soils, however, such associations do occur, principally involving VA-mycorrhiza fungi (*Glomerales*) together with a surprisingly wide range of aquatic plants, including submerged and free-floating species (Khan & Belik, 1995, provided an extensive list and references). In addition, ectomycorrhizal species habitually form associations with willows, alders, and other wetland trees, often in conditions of seasonal flooding.

Saprotrophs on aquatic plants and plant debris

Mitrula paludosa, a spring-fruiting discomycete, is one of the most striking British fungi on decaying leaf litter and water plants, occurring in swarms in ditches and boggy pools, usually in May (Fig. 106). It is popularly known as 'bog beacon' on account of its bright orange-yellow, mitre-shaped, upright fruitbodies which break the water surface and make an eye-catching display against the background of a dark ditch.

Other aquatic discomycetes are much less evident though often common in appropriate places. They include representatives of the large, cosmopolitan genera *Hymenoscyphus* and *Mollisia*, a few of which, as noted, have an aquatic hyphomycete as an asexual state. Freshwater species of *Mollisia* can be found on sedges, reeds, and rushes, developing fruitbodies on rotting, sometimes submerged culms. Two closely related genera, *Belonopsis* and *Niptera*, have a similar host range and are mostly found in freshwater habitats. One of the commonest is *Niptera pulla* on submerged parts of various monocotyledonous plants, but the greyish, discoid fruitbodies of all

FIG 106. The bog beacon, *Mitrula paludosa*, an attractive species which often occurs in swarms in ditches and bogs in late spring. The bright yellowish head is conspicuous amongst the dark substrata, hence the common name (B. Spooner).

species are rather similar in appearance and can only be distinguished microscopically.

Notable among freshwater pyrenomycetes is the unique genus *Loramyces*, now known to have an *Anguillospora*-like aquatic hyphomycete stage. There are two species, both found in Britain, which occur on dead, submerged stems of marsh plants such as *Juncus*, spike-rush (*Eleocharis*), and horsetails (*Equisetum*). They were studied by Ingold & Chapman (1952) who described *Loramyces macrospora* as a new species from submerged stems of *Equisetum fluviatile* in the Lake District. *Loramyces* species have tiny, dark-coloured fruitbodies and distinctive sperm-shaped spores which are adapted to aquatic dispersal. These are full of oily droplets and are two-celled, with a long 'tail' and the head enveloped in a broad, mucilaginous sheath. Other British aquatic pyrenomycetes include several species of *Leptosphaeria* and *Phaeosphaeria*, closely related genera more commonly found in terrestrial habitats, often as saprotrophs on herbaceous stems. Some species, however, such as *Phaeosphaeria juncicola* and *P. typhae*, occur only on leaves and culms of marsh plants.

Another specialist aquatic genus is *Coleosperma*, with a single species *C. lacustre*. This was described from Britain but known so far only from the Lake District and Hebrides. It has tiny, colourless fruitbodies no more than about 0.5 mm across found on dead, submerged stems of club-rush. The large spores, packed with tiny oil drops, are surrounded by a delicate mucilaginous sheath.

Basidiomycetes on submerged water plants are mostly known only from their status as Ingoldian hyphomycetes, as noted above. However, some larger basidiomycetes occur on decaying marsh plants above the water surface, one example being *Epithele typhae*, a corticioid species which forms whitish, effused fruitbodies on old leaves and culms, sometimes of reedmace but more commonly of sedges. Several other corticioid fungi occasionally occur in similar situations. These include *Phlebiella paludicola* (the epithet means 'marsh-dwelling'), described from Slapton Ley in Devon and otherwise known only from Wheatfen Broad in Norfolk, Petworth in Sussex, and Aveyron in France. Another species of this genus, the enigmatic *Phlebiella aurora*, was described from a collection on sedges at Batheaston, Somerset, in 1851, and has been found nowhere else since.

Several small but distinctive agarics also grow on marsh plants. The little pinkish-brown *Mycena belliae* grows on dead reeds whilst *Mycena bulbosa*, with its distinctive swollen base, occurs on *Carex*, *Juncus*, and other decaying stems. *Psathyrella typhae*, *Coprinus martinii*, *Marasmius limosus*, and *M. menieri* are further examples of British species associated with marsh plants, and several more were listed in Watling (1973). The last of these species, *Marasmius menieri*, can apparently trap air bubbles in its cap and continue to sporulate when periodically submerged. *Gloiocephala aquatica*, a South American species on bulrush, apparently always produces submerged fruitbodies and is, as yet, the only known underwater toadstool.

The genus *Mycocalia* is also notable, its several species being characteristic of bogs and wetland habitats. These are closely related to bird's-nest fungi, but have tiny, globose or lenticular fruitbodies no more than about 2 mm across looking very like plant seeds and easy to miss amongst wet vegetation. Four *Mycocalia* species are now known in Britain, at least one of them, *M. denudata*, being common and widespread, usually on wet culms of marsh plants or on wet, rotting wood in acid bogs. The other three species, *M. duriaeana*, *M. sphagneti*, and *M. minutissima* – the last only a quarter of a millimetre across – seem to be less common but may just be overlooked.

Equally easy to overlook is a strange little heterobasidiomycete which parasitises sclerotia of *Rhizoctonia* species lying among marsh plants. Called *Tetragoniomyces uliginosus*, it has four-celled basidia resembling those of *Tremella* species, but the basidia produce no sterigmata or spores. Instead, each basidium becomes detached and functions as a spore-like propagule. These may well be water dispersed, together with their host sclerotia (themselves functioning as propagules). This unique species, the only member of its genus, has been found at Slapton Ley in Devon and Wheatfen Broad in Norfolk, but may well prove to be more widespread.

Although few myxomycete species can be considered as truly aquatic, several of them occur regularly in wetland habitats or are able to fruit on submerged substrata. The common *Didymium difforme* is a good example, first recognised as an aquatic species over a century ago and frequently found in freshwater habitats. Thirteen further species are known from swamps in Illinois, USA, occurring regularly on submerged plant remains, though these include such common species as *Arcyria denudata*, equally well known in the terrestrial environment. *Didymium aquatile*, a Brazilian species, appears to be exclusively aquatic. Ing (1994b) has reviewed wetland myxomycetes and notes that *Didymium applanatum*, in Britain and elsewhere, is a species typical of lake margins, fruiting on decaying aquatic plants. Similarly, species such as *Physarum pusillum* and *Diderma globosum* are frequent on decaying remains of *Phragmites*, *Glyceria*, *Cladium* and other wetland plants.

Fungi on diatoms and other freshwater algae

The fungal associations of freshwater algae are extremely diverse, although the fungi involved are mostly chytrids and fungus-like oomycetes. Indeed, algae are amongst the most important hosts for these organisms, especially amongst the families *Chytridiaceae* and *Synchytriaceae* (*Chytridiomycota*) and *Hyphochytriaceae* (*Oomycota*). Diatoms, desmids, and other unicellular or colonial species are the main algae affected, although some chytrids specialise in filamentous algae and stoneworts (*Characeae*).

Many planktonic diatoms and desmids are unwilling hosts to chytrids which attach themselves by haustorium-like structures or develop within the algal cells. Some of these cause galling, notably *Endodesmidium formosum* which produces swollen cells in desmids of the genera *Cylindrocystis* and *Netrium* in Britain. Other gall-causers parasitise filamentous algae, including *Canteriomyces stigeoclonii* (*Hyphochytriaceae*) in species of *Draparnaldia* and *Stigeoclonium*, causing marked hypertrophy of host cells, and *Micromyces zygogonii* and *M. petersenii* (*Synchytriaceae*), which commonly cause conspicuous swelling and elongation of host cells in *Mougeotia*, *Spirogyra*, and other genera. Other associations are more complex, involving hyperparasitic chytrids on algicolous parasites. A British example is *Rozella polyphagi*, a parasite of another chytrid, *Polyphagus laevis*, itself parasitic on species of *Chlamydomonas* and *Euglena*. A few chytrids are saprotrophs; *Diplophlyctis intestina*, for example, is a widespread species in decaying thalli of *Nitella* and other charophytes.

Controlling algal blooms

Research in the Lake District has revealed that the tiny planktonic algae which cause 'algal blooms', familiar to pond owners and often a serious problem for fish, are largely controlled by epidemics of parasitic chytrids. This is specifically true of desmid populations, whilst planktonic diatoms, dinoflagellates, and other algal groups suffer similar epidemics involving both chytrids and oomycetes (*Lagenidiales*). *Rhizophydium planktonicum*, a common parasite of the diatom *Asterionella formosa*, is one of the chytrids responsible. The effects of these epidemics are complex, allowing non-parasitised species to become dominant at times.

Some chytrids have a range of hosts which they affect in different ways. Thus *Rhizophydium couchii*, first described as a weak parasite of species of *Spirogyra* and *Mougeotia*, was later identified as a parasite of desmids in the Lake District, and the following year as a saprotroph in cells of *Pediastrum duplex* in Lake Manitoba, Canada. It seems that the conditions under which algal populations are parasitised by fungi are important, and may vary

FIG 106A. Zoospores of the chytrid *Rhizophydium planktonicum*, a common parasite of the diatom *Asterionella formosa*. The large image, taken with the transmission electron microscope, shows the various organelles (H.M. Canter & G. Beakes).

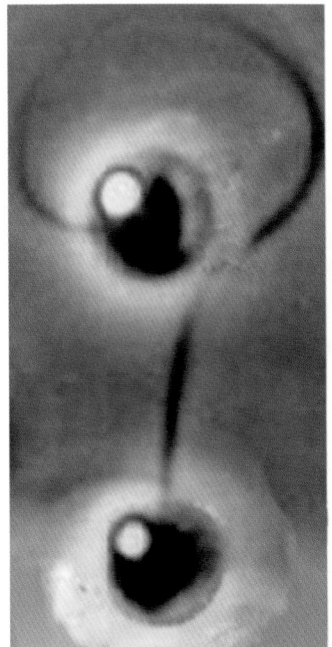
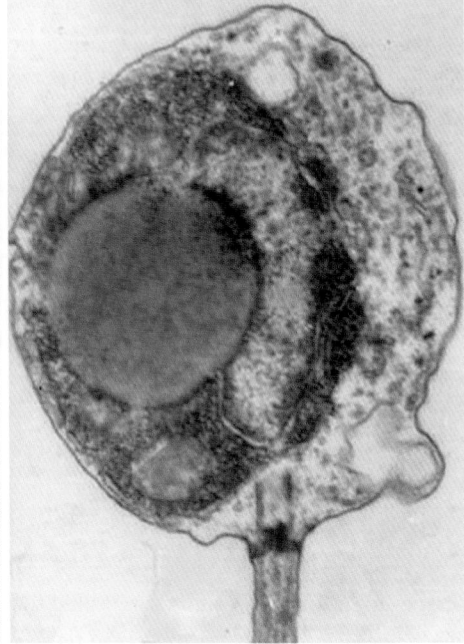

according to temperature and light. Some fungal zoospores may become inactive in low light regimes and unable to infect potential host cells. Similarly, either above or below threshold temperatures, which vary according to species, infection may again be limited.

Reviews of the biology and ecology of chytridiaceous fungi on freshwater algae have been published by Canter & Lund (1969), Lund (1957), Masters (1976), and Van Donk & Bruning (1992). Sparrow (1960) produced a comprehensive account of all species described to that date.

Other algal associates

A number of oomycetes (water moulds) are also associated with algae, either as parasites, some again causing galls, or as saprotrophs. *Aphanomycopsis bacillariacearum* and species of *Ectrogella*, for example, are parasites of diatoms in Britain, especially species of *Synedra* and *Pinnularia*. Another parasite, *Canteriomyces stigeoclonii*, may cause galling of the filamentous green algae *Draparnaldia plumosa* and *Stigeoclonium subuligerum*.

Among the ascomycetes associated with algae is the little-known *Phaeospora lemaneae*, notable as occurring, possibly in a mutualistic association, in the thallus of *Lemanea fluviatilis*. This is a species of fast-flowing streams, growing in tufts attached to submerged rocks. The fungus forms tiny, black, subglobose fruitbodies less than one tenth of a millimetre in diameter inside the host cells and occurs abundantly along the length of the algal filament. The alga is apparently unharmed by the fungus, and a symbiotic relationship between them has been suggested, although the fungus is not invariably present with the alga. The species occurs in Europe, and in England is known from Shropshire where it was first collected in 1865. It has rarely been recorded since then, though is undoubtedly overlooked.

Water moulds and freshwater fish

Though a few oomycetes are associates of algae, they are better known as parasites of freshwater animals, especially fish, crustacea, and molluscs. The group as a whole is sometimes called 'water moulds', since they are well-adapted to an aquatic existence and often give rise to mould-like underwater growths. These pseudofungi reproduce by releasing motile zoospores with hair-like appendages enabling the spores to swim to suitable sites for germination.

Many of the well-known skin diseases of ornamental fish are caused by water moulds in the genus *Saprolegnia*. The common and widespread *S. ferax* is the chief culprit, at least in Britain, where it produces skin lesions in a range of species, including goldfish. *Saprolegnia* can be a primary pathogen, but develops mainly as a secondary infection, entering a cut or graze on the fins, tail or head and growing out as a visible whitish mould. In bad infestations, this can lead to the flesh rotting away, and ultimately to death. A related species, *Saprolegnia parasitica*, is important elsewhere and others are occasionally involved.

Ulcerative dermal necrosis (UDN) is an epidemic skin disease principally of salmon and sea trout in the British Isles, rarely occurring elsewhere. It was first recorded as early as 1748 when a 'fatal distemper of roach in captivity' was reported to the Royal Society. The problem became worse in the 1870s, when an epidemic of 'salmon disease', spreading from the Conway and the Tweed, "threatened to deprive the wealthy of a favourite pastime" and caused "serious consternation among gentlemen, fish-wardens and gillies" (Large, 1940). *Saprolegnia* was certainly involved, since infected fish were conspicuously mouldy. However, why the disease had become an epidemic was a mystery. Some of the theories advanced to explain this seem surprisingly modern. Pollution by industrial effluents was, for example, suggested as a factor, as was the decrease in natural predators such as otters (a view put forward by Mordecai Cubitt Cooke, the first mycologist at Kew). Thomas Huxley, one of the foremost scientists of his day, noted that dead bluebottles, when rubbed against infected fish and placed in water, developed the same mould. He suggested the disease might be spread by flies, in which case there was no practical remedy except to let nature take its course. This is effectively what happened, since UDN disappeared again until the 1960s when there were further outbreaks in Britain and Ireland. The disease produces head lesions in infected fish, but the cause remains unknown. Secondary pathogens, notably the oomycete *Saprolegnia diclina*, extend the necrosis with fatal results.

Altogether, at least 14 *Saprolegnia* species occur in Britain, most of them saprotrophs or occasional parasites of plant and animal matter. They occur in various freshwater habitats, commonly in bogs and swamps but sometimes in damp soil. Most are dealt with in the works of Sparrow (1960) and Dick (2001).

The spread of crayfish plague

An oomycete called *Aphanomyces astaci* is responsible for 'crayfish plague', a lethal disease of freshwater crayfish which first appeared in Europe in Italy in 1860 and has spread inexorably ever since, wiping out wild populations. The disease is endemic in North America, but the native species there are relatively immune to its effects. When these American crayfish were imported into Europe, however, (as happened in Lombardy in 1860 and repeatedly elsewhere since) the disease spread into non-resistant European crayfish species.

Crayfish plague was first found in Britain (River Lea, Hertfordshire) in 1981 and since then has substantially destroyed populations of our native species, the white-clawed crayfish *Austropotamobius pallipes*. The cause of the destruction has been the importation by commercial interests of alien species of crayfish infected with *Aphanomyces astaci*. These include particularly the original carrier, *Pacifastacus leniusculus* (the signal crayfish), as well as a secondary carrier, *Astacus leptodactylus* (the long- or narrow-clawed or Turkish crayfish), feral populations of which are now widely established in the British Isles. By 1990, native crayfish populations from 88.6% of sites recorded since 1970 had either been eliminated, or were directly threatened, by crayfish plague, competition with introduced species, or pollution. As a result the native *Austropotamobius pallipes* belatedly received protection in 1986 under the Wildlife and Countryside Act whilst the further importation and keeping of alien crayfish was and is (partly) banned under the Prohibition of Keeping of Live Fish (Crayfish) Order, 1996.

Fungi on other freshwater animals

A few *Saprolegnia* species occur as mollusc parasites, as do many other members of the *Oomycota*. Indeed, laboratory studies of freshwater molluscs in Poland found no less than 57 of the 60 'fungal' species recorded to be oomycetes, many of these also known to be fish parasites (Czeczuga, 2000). Other oomycetes are insect parasites, amongst the most interesting being

Lagenidium giganteum, a widespread obligate endoparasite of dipteran larvae including mosquitoes. It has been the subject of considerable study for its potential as a biocontrol agent of mosquitoes including those which spread malaria. Oomycetes also parasitise protozoa and even *Cladocera* (water fleas). *Aphanomyces daphniae*, first described from Perthshire, attacks *Daphnia hyalina*, individuals often being so heavily infected as to appear covered in fur.

Some of the *Entomophthorales* produce conidia which resemble Ingoldian fungi in form, though they are insect parasites rather than leaf-litter rotters. *Entomophthora conica*, for example, is a parasite of aquatic diptera and caddis flies. Its primary conidia germinate underwater to produce tetraradiate secondary conidia. Some zygomycetes (*Entomophthorales* and especially *Trichomycetes*) may also be parasites of aquatic insects.

A few chytridiaceous species are parasites of protozoa, most attacking amoebas. They include *Nucleophaga amoebae*, a European species which develops sporangia in the hypertrophied nucleus of *Amoeba verrucosa*. There are also many chytrid parasites of rotifers, some of them further discussed in Chapter Five. Perhaps the most important are species of *Olpidium* and *Rhizophydium* which frequently parasitise rotifer eggs, some species also attacking adults.

Some zygomycetes, species of *Zoophagus*, also attack rotifers (Chapter Five). These fungi may themselves be prey to chytrids such as *Rozellopsis inflata*, which also parasitises species of *Pythium* – an example which illustrates the complex web of interactions between fungi and other organisms that is as intricate in the aquatic environment as in any terrestrial ecosystem.

Sewage filter beds and other polluted waters

A rather specialised and unpleasant aquatic habitat is to be found in sewage treatment plants. These represent an entirely man-made ecosystem which employs a trickling filter system designed solely for the treatment of sewage by microbial action. The microbiology of sewage sludge degradation is complex, and involves not just bacteria but a wide range of fungi and fungus-like organisms, as well as algae and protozoa. However, the role that fungi play in the process is a particularly important one which continues through all its stages, even including significant activity in anaerobic conditions. Any anaerobic activity was long considered impossible for fungi – they were once even defined as solely aerobic organisms – but such activity is now known to occur also in the gut-dwelling *Trichomycetes* and rumen fungi (Chapter Five).

Well over 200 species of microfungi have been recorded from sewage plants, many of them being widely distributed. They include species of the ubiquitous mould genera *Aspergillus*, *Fusarium* and *Penicillium*, as well as yeasts such as *Candida* and *Rhodotorula*, and species of *Pythium* and *Mucor*. One of the best known is *Leptomitus lacteus*, an oomycete, described as early as 1800 and one of the first 'water moulds' to be studied. It is characteristic of polluted waters and is often known as the 'sewage fungus' due to its prevalence and tendency to form extensive masses which commonly block sewage filters. Another notable and highly distinctive species is the tiny, long-necked ascomycete *Subbaromyces splendens*, known only from slurry and from slime in trickling filter beds. It can be recognised by the unique structure of the neck, which is narrowed in the upper part above a conspicuous, collar-like zone (Fig 107). This species, originally described from sewage filter beds in New York, has only recently been reported from the UK and is so far known only from Northern Ireland where material from simulated slurry tanks in Belfast was collected in 1992.

Polluted streams and other waters enriched with organic nutrients may offer similar conditions. Many fungi occur in such conditions, though fewer species are to be found in the most heavily polluted regions. They may again play important roles in nutrient transformation and consequent remediation of such pollution.

Some aquatic fungi are tolerant of toxic residues and as such can be a problem for other organisms. *Tetracladium marchalianum*, for example, is tolerant of pesticide residues and heavy metals, accumulating these pollutants in its mycelia, thereby building up potentially significant consequences for invertebrate feeders and organisms higher up the food chain. This build-up of toxins by fungi has already been recognised as a problem in salt marshes fed by polluted rivers (Chapter 12).

Conversely, some other aquatic fungi have the capacity to degrade and metabolise toxins, hence playing potentially valuable remediation roles. As an example, even the effects of DDT, a chlorinated hydrocarbon compound

FIG 107. The ascomycete *Subbaromyces splendens*, only recently recorded from Britain, showing the unique collared neck arising from the perithecium buried in sewage sludge. The species occurs only on sewage in trickling filter beds (RBG Kew).

which is highly toxic and a serious pollutant, may be ameliorated by a number of fungi. DDT has serious and long-lasting effects because most microorganisms cannot degrade it. As a result it can rapidly accumulate through the food chain, having catastrophic effects on species at the top. However, the aquatic hyphomycetes *Clavariopsis aquatica* and particularly *Heliscus submersus* can metabolise DDT, an ability that may prove extremely useful.

CHAPTER 12

Marine and Salt Marsh

I T MAY COME as a surprise to discover that fungi can and do live in the sea, but in fact they are well-represented and even abundant in marine environments. Indeed, it is becoming increasingly apparent just how important a role fungi play, not only in coastal regions but in all marine and littoral ecosystems, including the deep sea.

To date, well over 800 fungi and fungus-like species have been described as obligately or facultatively marine, with more being discovered regularly. Kohlmeyer & Volkmann-Kohlmeyer (1991) and Hyde & Venkateswara Sarma (2000) have published illustrated keys to most of the filamentous species, whilst Johnson & Sparrow (1961) dealt with many of the non-filamentous and fungus-like species. The number is tiny compared with the huge diversity of terrestrial species, and the sea is evidently very much a secondary habitat adaptation for fungi, even if the primordial fungal ancestor (possibly in the *Chytridiomycota*) originally evolved from a marine species. Only a single order of filamentous fungi, the *Lulworthiales*, are believed to be exclusively marine, although the *Halosphaeriales* are substantially so. Both are ascomycetous. The fungus-like thraustochytrids and labyrinthulids (the latter sometimes called 'marine slime moulds') are entirely marine. All other orders with marine species also have freshwater or terrestrial representatives, suggesting that the evolutionary return to the sea was comparatively recent. DNA sequence analyses appear to confirm this hypothesis (Spatafora *et al.*, 1998).

Specialist adaptations: salt-tolerance and water-borne spores

Like all marine organisms, fungi living in sea water need to be salt-tolerant.
For some groups this is no problem. Most cellular yeasts, for example, can
grow in high salt concentrations, making it difficult to determine whether
yeasts isolated from sea water are genuine marine species or terrestrial
vagrants. Certainly the majority of yeasts recorded from sea water are also
known on land. For other groups, however, particularly the fungus-like
water-moulds (*Saprolegniales*), even low concentrations of salt water may
lead to plasmolysis (disintegration) of hyphae and death. These moulds,
common as plant and fish parasites in fresh water, are almost entirely
absent from marine habitats. Ingoldian hyphomycetes, also common in
fresh water, can often survive in saline conditions, but appear unable
to sporulate.

Many specialist marine fungi have evolved distinctive spores adapted
for water dispersal. Such spores typically produce an extraordinary variety
of appendages. These may take the form of ribbons, spines, mucilaginous
sheaths, or filaments, and may cover the whole spore surface or form
equatorial or polar appendages. They help keep the spores buoyant, aiding
dispersal, and also facilitate attachment to host substrata, such as driftwood
or seaweed. Tests on how well such spores attach themselves to substrata
have shown some considerable variation in performance, suggesting that
the different types of appendage may be related to host preferences.

Like Ingoldian hyphomycetes in fresh water, appendaged fungal
spores can often be found in foam, the air bubbles efficiently trapping the
spores. Jones (1973) found an average of five to eight spores per litre of
filtered sea water, but far greater numbers in foam collected from beaches.
Some spores collected this way may have drifted in on oceanic currents,
but the majority appear to belong to species of *Corollospora* (Fig. 108) and
Carbosphaerella, tiny ascomycetes adapted to living on detritus in the upper
layers of sandy beaches, producing miniature fruitbodies attached to grains
of sand.

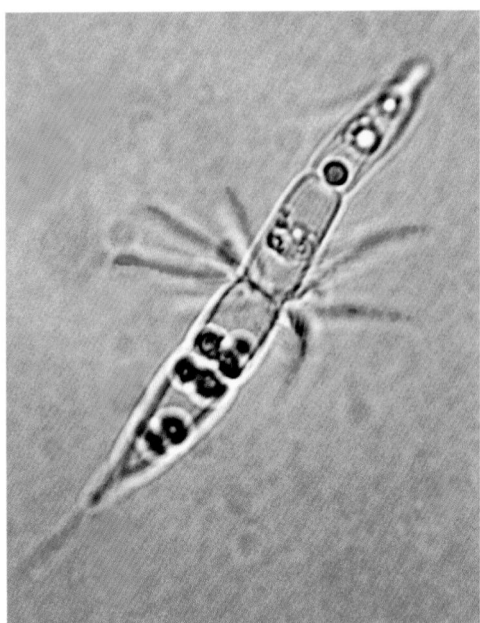

FIG 108. Ascospore of *Corollospora angusta* associated with the seaweed *Fucus serratus*. The filaments are part of the spore and an adaptation to dispersal by water (A. Zuccaro).

Fungi on driftwood

The majority of filamentous marine fungi described to date are wood-degraders, found on driftwood and man-made structures, as well as mangroves in the tropics. Wood is present in both inshore and oceanic waters, even 'common' in the deep sea, and is quickly and invariably attacked by marine fungi unless levels of dissolved oxygen are low.

Most of the ascomycetous marine fungi cause 'soft rot' of surface wood, whilst basidiomycetous species cause systemic 'white rot' similar to that seen in terrestrial wood-rotting species. Though these rots can cause significant degradation of wood, including treated timber used in jetties, pilings, and harbour walls, it is crustacean and molluscan wood-borers such as gribbles and shipworms which cause most commercial damage in the marine environment. There is some evidence, however, that these invertebrate wood-borers have a mutualistic relationship with marine fungi. The gribble (*Limnoria tripunctata*) is usually found on rotten wood and may distribute fungal spores (e.g. of the anamorphic ascomycete *Cirrenalia macrocephala*) by passing them unharmed through its gut. Though it can survive on undegraded wood, it may depend on fungal nutrients for reproduction.

The commonest wood-rotting fungal genera in British waters are *Zalerion* and *Lulworthia*, the latter named after Lulworth Cove in Dorset. *Zalerion* is a marine genus of anamorphic ascomycetes producing coiled conidiospores; *Lulworthia* has small, immersed fruitbodies and filamentous ascospores. Both genera are fairly typical of the ascomycetous wood-degraders. Like *Lulworthia*, the perfect states of almost all marine ascomycetes are pyrenomycetes, producing small, superficial or immersed fruitbodies. The cup-fungi, so abundant in terrestrial habitats, appear to have no fully marine representatives.

Marine basidiomycetes are comparatively rare and only two wood-degrading species occur in British waters. The tiny gastroid species *Nia vibrissa* (Fig. 109) has been found on timbers brought up from the wreck of the warship *Mary Rose*, which sank in the Solent in 1545. Oak barrel staves kept wet whilst awaiting conservation developed numerous globose fruitbodies, 0.5–5 mm across, many producing basidiospores with five tentacle-like appendages up to 20 µm long (Fig. 109A). It was not thought

FIG 109. Fruitbody of the tiny gastroid basidiomycete *Nia vibrissa*, a marine wood-rotting species, taken with a scanning electron microscope (R. Eaton).

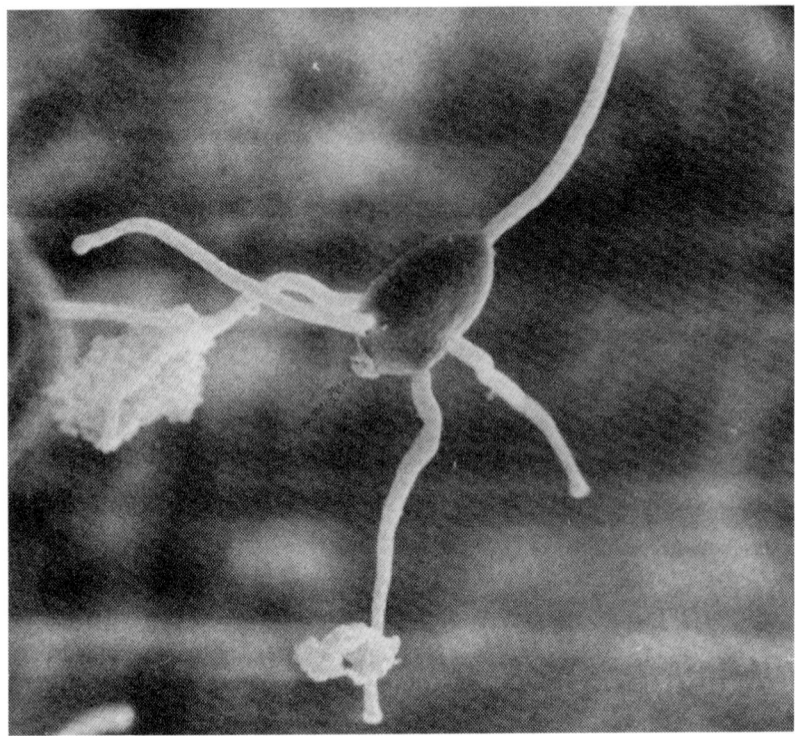

FIG 109A. The peculiar, long-armed basidiospore of *Nia vibrissa*, adapted for water dispersal, taken with a scanning electron microscope (R. Eaton).

that *Nia* had lain dormant for more than 400 years, but that the wood was recolonised by the fungus as it was brought up from the seabed (Jones & Jones, 1993). *Nia* is more normally found on driftwood and tolerates both temperate and tropical waters. The second species, *Digitatispora marina*, produces effused (corticioid) fruitbodies and elegant basidiospores with three radiating arms. It appears to be confined to temperate waters.

As might be expected, many of these marine wood-degraders are cosmopolitan, but for those with a restricted geographical range the main determining factor is sea temperature. Studies on growth and sporulation in culture have shown that certain species are exclusively tropical or temperate. *Digitatispora marina*, for example, has an optimum growth temperature of 15°C and will not grow at all above 25°C, which is why it is not found in the tropics.

Cosmopolitan species can tolerate a much broader temperature range.

A specialised mycota exists in tropical mangrove swamps. These attract both generalist marine species and a number of taxa found nowhere else. Mangrove roots, exposed to tidal waters, have a notably toxic bark containing large amounts of tannin, extracts of which have been tested as antifouling agents. Nevertheless, several saprotrophic ascomycetes are able to live on mangrove bark, whilst others can penetrate and rot damaged and dead mangrove wood.

In Britain and elsewhere, marine wood-degraders have largely been studied by suspending wood-block 'baits' in coastal waters and checking them for fungal colonisation and succession over a period of weeks and months. Natural driftwood is more difficult to study but may support a greater variety of species, especially if bark is still present and if it has been exposed to sea water for sufficient time. Techniques for studying marine wood-degrading fungi together with keys to genera and species can be found in Hyde & Pointing (2000).

Decay of shells and other inorganic matter

Fungi may play an important role in the breakdown of inorganic substances produced by animals. In the marine environment this is evident in the degradation of calcareous shells and tests produced by *Foraminifera* and various molluscs. Kohlmeyer (1985) has reported that fruitbodies on and within *Foraminifera* tests are widespread on tropical beaches in various parts of the Pacific and Atlantic Oceans. The fungi involved are ascomycetes, mostly species of the genera *Arenariomyces* and *Corollospora* (*Halosphaeriaceae*) and *Lindra* (*Lulworthiaceae*) (Fig. 110). These are capable of damaging the tests and contributing to their eventual disintegration. The hyphae of some species in these and other related genera such as *Remispora* are also able to penetrate calcareous substances secreted by other marine organisms, including barnacles and the tubes of wood-boring shipworms (*Teredinidae*). They cause degradation and decomposition of the calcium carbonate, probably by both chemical and physical means, although details of the process are not fully understood.

An important shell disease of oysters is caused by *Ostracoblabe implexa*, a filamentous fungus of uncertain disposition found in southern English and

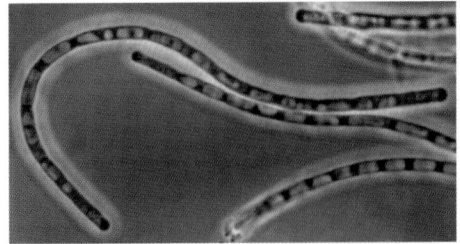

FIG 110. Serpentine ascospores of *Lindra* cf *obtusa*, one of a number of marine species that can degrade calcareous shells (A. Zuccaro).

Irish coastal waters. The fungus penetrates and degrades the shell matrix and, in severe infections, can be fatal. At one time, it caused substantial losses among young oysters in commercial beds, but removal of old shells appears to have helped prevent serious outbreaks.

Marine and maritime lichens

Lichens are a major component of the coastal (littoral and supralittoral) biota. A large number of specialist species occur on rocks and other substrata within the splash zone or just above the tide-line, where they may be regularly covered by sea water. Those which are able to tolerate regular inundation are generally considered to be true 'marine' lichens. Some are extremely common, but there are not many of them (just 16 species according to Gilbert, 2000) compared to the lichens which occur further up the shore. *Pyrenocollema halodytes*, for example, is frequently found forming subgelatinous brownish patches on tide-line rocks, barnacles, mussels, and limpets, and the frondose *Lichina pygmaea* forms large patches on intertidal rocks, typically infested with the tiny mollusc *Lasaea rubra*.

There are many factors which influence the distribution of lichens from the littoral zone (where they are regularly submerged) to the 'xeric-supralittoral zone' (which is most remote from the sea). However, in general, it seems that lichenised fungi occur in distinct, if overlapping, bands influenced by topography, available substrata, wave action, length of inundation, and insolation. However, this banding is well developed only on rocky shores and, furthermore, it is found only in temperate regions on coasts subject to marked tidal action. On non-rocky shores, salt-tolerant species of genera such as *Xanthoria*, *Caloplaca* and *Physcia* may occur but there is no clear zonation, and in the tropics such communities are generally absent.

Thanks to the conspicuous colour differences between the zones (Figs 111 and 112), this lichen banding is often readily visible, even to the non-specialist. Three distinct bands can be recognised. The marine lichens form the 'black zone', which is composed mainly of crustose species in the family *Verrucariaceae*. They include several species of *Verrucaria*, notably *V. maura*, the black 'tar-spot lichen' (Fig. 113) which is often considered to mark the upper limit of the marine lichen zone. Also characteristic are species of *Lichina*, in which the photobiont is a cyanobacterium, and *Pyrenocollema*.

Lichens which occur higher up the shore but remain within the splash zone are regarded as 'maritime' rather than fully marine. Many such maritime lichens are known in the British Isles, and keys for their determination were provided by Fletcher (1975 a,b). Two main colour bands can be recognised. The 'yellow or orange zone,' lying immediately above the black zone, is also known as the 'mesic-supralittoral' zone and is largely

FIG 111. Lichen zonation on rocky shores. The black strip towards the base forms a narrow but distinct band, typically composed of *Verrucaria* species; above is the less well-defined yellow or orange zone, often containing *Caloplaca* species; above that and partly intermixed is the white or grey zone of pale-coloured lichens (A. Fletcher).

FIG 112. Lichen zonation on rocky shores. The lower, black strip forms a conspicuous band in this photograph, with a patchier yellow strip above, merging into the white or grey zone (A. Fletcher).

FIG 113. The tar-spot lichen, *Verrucaria maura*, one of the commonest components of the coastal black zone (A. Fletcher).

comprised of members of the *Teloschistaceae*, and includes crustose species of *Caloplaca* (Fig. 114) as well as foliose species of *Xanthoria*. Immediately above this is the 'xeric-supralittoral' zone which dries out rapidly and where moisture is at a premium. This is the 'white or grey zone' and is composed mainly of members of the *Parmeliaceae* and *Lecanoraceae*, including conspicuous foliose and shrubby species of *Ramalina* and *Parmelia*, together with crustose species of *Buellia*, *Lecanora*, *Lecidella*, *Ochrolechia*, *Pertusaria* and *Tephromela* (Fig. 115).

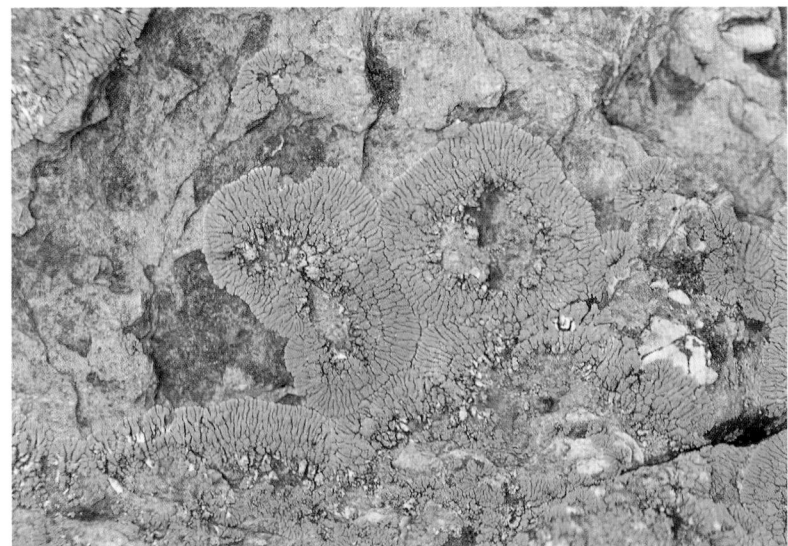

FIG 114. *Caloplaca verruculifera*, a typical crustose lichen of the yellow or orange zone (A. Fletcher).

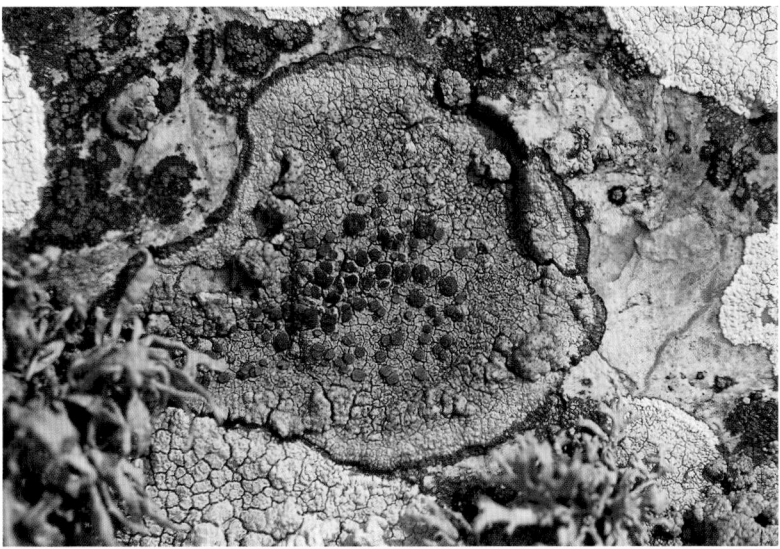

FIG 115. *Buellia subdisciformis*, one of several crustose lichens typical of the white or grey zone (A. Fletcher).

Saline lagoons also exhibit a range of lichens, including a mixture of marine, maritime, and terrestrial species. These were studied at twenty such lagoons in various parts of England by Gilbert (2001) who recorded 25 different lichens, including the new species *Caloplaca suaedae* growing on twigs of seablite (*Suaeda vera*) in lagoons in Dorset and Norfolk.

Submarine lichens and fungi on seaweeds

Only one true lichen is known to grow below the low tideline, namely *Verrucaria serpuloides*, which has been found at depths of 30 m in Antarctic waters. However, what can also happen below the tideline is that the normal fungal-algal roles are reversed and lichen-like associations occur in which the algal partner (now a full-size seaweed) determines the habit, leaving the fungus to take a secondary and often cryptic role.

Such a relationship exists between the ascomycete *Mycophycias ascophylli* (Fig. 116) and brown shoreline seaweeds (wracks) in the genera *Ascophyllum* and *Pelvetia*. The fungal hyphae are regularly present, growing between the cells of the host algae, and neither partner appears able to grow independently. The life cycles of *Ascophyllum nodosum* and *M. ascophylli* even appear to be synchronised, with fungal sporulation occurring on the algal receptacles; in some cases, a three-way symbiosis occurs between the brown alga, the fungus and a red algal epiphyte (*Polysiphonia lanosa*). *A. nodosum* is the host for the red alga, which buries its rhizoids into the brown algal thallus. The hyphae of *M. ascophylli* interact with both the rhizoids and the thallus filaments forming a link between the two seaweeds. It is thought that the fungus might be transferring nutrients between the two. *Pharcidia laminariicola* is another example of an ascomycete forming a partnership with a brown seaweed, *Ectocarpus fasciculatus* which grows epiphytically on the fronds of kelp.

Non-lichenised, parasitic relationships are far more common in the marine environment, with at least 30 ascomycete species found on living seaweeds worldwide. All appear to be specific to different classes of seaweeds (red, brown, or green – *Rhodophyta*, *Phaeophyta*, or *Chlorophyta*) but, within these classes, some are widespread generalists. The British species *Lulworthia fucicola*, for example, parasitises bladderwrack but can also occur saprotrophically on dead seaweeds and even on driftwood. Another British

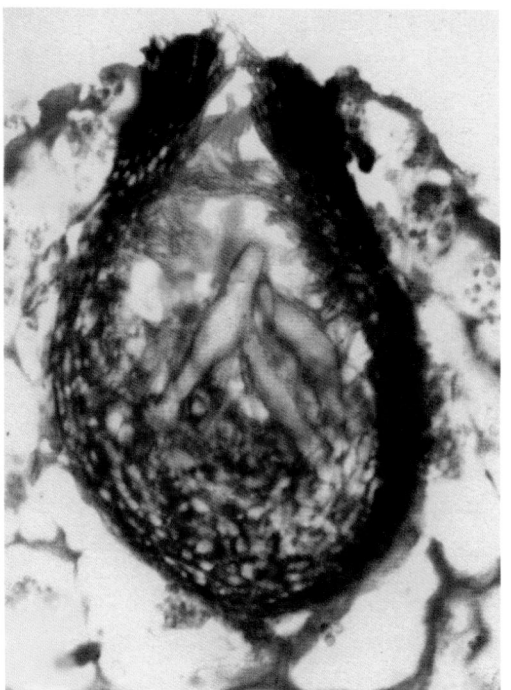

FIG 116. Cross-section of the fruitbody (perithecium) of the ascomycete *Mycophycias ascophylli* growing on the shoreline seaweed *Ascophyllum nodosum* (S. Stanley & S. Moss).

species, *Phycomelaina laminariae*, is much more specific, causing an infection known as 'stipe blotch of kelp'. Some ascomycetes even cause seaweed galls. The South Pacific *Spathulospora calva*, for example, induces proliferating hair-like growth in its host, similar to 'witches' brooms' on trees. Various chytrids are also parasitic on seaweeds. *Chytridium polysiphoniae* is one of the most widespread, known from the Atlantic coasts of North America and Europe though not yet recorded as British. Most of these fungal seaweed parasites are ascomycetes or chytrids. An exception is *Mycaureola dilseae*, a basidiomycetous spot-causing parasite of the edible red seaweed, *Dilsea carnosa* (dulse), known from coastal waters around Britain.

Among the fungus-like *Oomycota* are several species which parasitise seaweeds, notably *Pythium porphyrae* which does substantial damage to *Porphyra yezoensis* (laver) in Japan and Korea. This seaweed, popularly known as 'nori', has long been cultivated, with over 250,000 tons produced each year. 'Red rot' disease caused by the *Pythium* can be severe and commercially devastating. Another oomycete, *Petersenia pollagaster*, damages the economically important seaweed Irish Moss or Carrageen (*Chondrus crispus*), used to produce gelling agents in the food industry. Some oomycetes are also gall-causers. In British waters, they include *Eurychasmidium tumefaciens* on *Ceramium* species and *Eurychasma dicksonii* on species of *Ectocarpus*, *Pilayella* and *Striaria*.

Eelgrass (*Zostera marina*) is also subject to devastating epidemics. This is a vascular plant rather than a seaweed, but grows submerged in shallow estuarine and coastal waters, providing an important habitat and resource for young fish, wildfowl, and invertebrates. In the 1930s and 1940s, this habitat was substantially destroyed almost throughout its range on the Atlantic coasts of America and Europe by 'eelgrass wasting disease'. This was originally believed to be caused by an ascomycete, *Lulworthia halima*, which occurs in the leaves and rhizomes of the eelgrass, but it is now known that the real culprit is the fungus-like *Labyrinthula zosterae*. Additional pathogens of seaweeds and other marine algae were listed by Andrews (1976).

Another group of seaweed-associated fungi are the shoreline saprotrophs, which help rot down dead and dislodged weed. These include a single discomycete, *Laetinaevia marina*, described from bladderwrack in Scotland and now known on various species of *Ascophyllum* and *Fucus*. Other shoreline saprotrophs are a mixture of marine ascomycetes, adventitious terrestrial species, and yeasts. Most of the filamentous fungi occur on the larger and tougher brown seaweeds, the thinner red and green weeds generally rotting down too quickly, though some red algae (e.g. *Ceramium* species and *Chondrus crispus*) can be attacked.

Saltmarsh fungi

Salt marshes provide a specialised habitat, linked to the marine environment, in which fungi play an important though often cryptic role. Typical salt marshes are vegetated estuarine and coastal areas of high salinity, periodically inundated by the tide, often exposed to high daytime temperatures, and with poorly aerated soil turning into saturated mudflats on their seaward sides. Salt-loving plants such as glasswort or marsh samphire, thrift, sea poa, sea purslane, and cord grass (*Spartina anglica*) are usually dominant, and other grasses such as *Festuca rubra* may also occur, often providing grazeable pasture for sheep.

As might be expected, many microfungi are associated with these plants, well over 100 species having been recorded from *Spartina* alone. Others occur with animal dung, as well as in the saltmarsh soil. A few, such as *Ascochyta obiones* and *Scolecobasidium salinum*, are characteristic, and may be found in various situations. They have been recorded, for example, as dominant initial root surface colonists of sea purslane. However, the fungi in salt marshes tend to be generalists rather than specialist halophiles, though they are obviously salt-tolerant. This has been demonstrated in various studies. An extensive survey of ascomycetes in a Lincolnshire salt marsh, for example, recorded a total of 141 species (Apinis & Chesters, 1964). The majority were generalists, although a minority (17 species) were marine taxa mostly found associated with the grasses *Agropyron pungens* and *Spartina anglica*. The marine taxa typically occur on submerged parts of the plants, whilst the generalists grow above the water mark. One interesting exception to this is the ergot disease of *Spartina* species, recently recognised as a distinct taxon specially adapted to marine conditions. This fungus, *Claviceps purpurea* var. *spartinae* (Fig. 117), occurs widely with its host genus and differs from typical *C. purpurea* in the anatomy of its sclerotia ('ergots'). These are larger, less dense and specially adapted to float in sea water as an aid to dispersal of the fungus (Pazoutová *et al.*, 2002).

A list of marine fungi known from salt marshes was published by Kohlmeyer & Kohlmeyer (1979). They included 57 species, although others have been described since then.

Despite anoxic conditions produced by waterlogging in saline muds and sands, vesicular-arbuscular (VA) mycorrhiza are also present. These occur in a range of plants including *Agrostis* (bent-grass), *Armeria*, scurvy-grass, sea milkwort, *Glyceria*, and plantains. In a survey of salt marshes along the North and Baltic Seas, the main fungal associate was found to be *Glomus geosporum* (Hildebrandt *et al.*, 2001). This forms mycorrhiza with a range of plants, including genera such as *Salicornia* (samphire) in families which otherwise are not or rarely mycorrhizal.

There appear to be no larger fungi which are saltmarsh specialists, most of the agarics and other species being generalists. A few salt-tolerant species,

FIG 117. Ergots of *Claviceps purpurea* var. *spartinae* in the salt marsh grass *Spartina* x *townsendii*. The ergots are specially adapted for dispersal in the sea and are larger and less dense than those found in other grasses (RBG Kew).

such as *Agaricus bernardii*, may be particularly common in salt marshes, but are also found in dunes and coastal grassland. Some rare lichenised fungi, such as the yellow-green *Cyphelium notarisii* (Fig. 117A), are known from salt marshes and mud flats in East Anglia, principally on old jetties and worked timbers which carry communities of algae and lichens zoned by the tides. A few other marine lichen species typically occur on stones and debris on sheltered muddy shores.

Fungi on fish and marine animals

Though the fungi and fungus-like organisms associated with marine animals may be obscure from a mycological perspective, their impact on the marine environment can be devastating. Together with viruses and bacteria, fungi are increasingly responsible for mass mortalities in fish, corals, crustacea,

disease. An additional disease-causing fungus, *Trichomaris invadens* (*Ascomycota*), attacks crabs.

Certain yeasts (*Metschnikowia* and *Rhodotorula* species) are known pathogens of sea urchins and studies on holothurians (sea cucumbers) in the Sea of Japan have revealed some 27 associated species of fungi, a number of which may be pathogenic. Isolates from marine sponges have also revealed the presence of over 50 different genera of filamentous fungi, mostly in the *Ascomycota*.

Marine mammals and reptiles have been less studied, except for those in captivity. However, species of *Fusarium* (*Ascomycota*) and *Malassezia* yeasts (*Basidiomycota*) causing mycotic dermatitis have been isolated from dolphins, seals, and sperm whales and the dermatotroph *Epidermophyton floccosum* (*Ascomycota*) has been isolated from a manatee. Captive seals, dolphins, and whales are prone to candidiasis (caused by *Candida albicans*, the fungal agent of thrush in humans), possibly because of water treatments. A lethal epidemic among farmed saltwater crocodiles in Australia has been reported, caused by the ubiquitous *Fusarium solani*.

A general review of fungal diseases of marine animals was provided by Alderman (1976), with a more recent review (emphasising methodology) by Rand (2000).

Yeasts, North Sea oil, and commercial bioprospecting

Ascomycetous and heterobasidiomycetous yeasts are ubiquitous in the marine environment, present, for example, in 99% of stations sampled in the North Sea and averaging 5–500 cells per litre in oceanic waters, with higher counts in estuaries (Fell, 1986). Yeasts are capable of exploiting many nutrient sources (including hydrocarbons associated with petroleum products), and can be shown to do so under laboratory conditions. However, it is difficult to ascertain which of the available nutrients they might be using in sea water, or indeed whether they are utilising any at all and are simply present as seablown propagules.

Research, however, has shown that at least some yeasts may be associated with algal (*Noctiluca*) blooms at sea (producing substantially higher than normal counts, up to 3000 yeast cells per litre, in the North Sea), as well as with offshore pollution, and with oil spills. Changes in species populations were noted in yeast samples from the North Sea before and after the start of oil drilling and in yeast samples obtained after the 'Amoco Cadiz' tanker disaster. Studies have been made on fungi (both yeasts and ascomycetous moulds) as potential biodegradation agents for oil spills in open water and on coastlines (Chapter 17).

Fungi of the abyss

Very little research has yet been undertaken on deepwater fungi, but a few unusual species are known to occur in the bathyal and abyssal zones (down to 6000 m). *Periconia abyssa*, *Bathyascus vermisporus*, and *Allescheriella bathygena* have been found on submerged wood, whilst *Abyssomyces hydrozoicus* (*Ascomycetes*) was recovered from the exoskeletons of a deepwater hydrozoan colony. An undescribed ascomycete has even been found associated with the gastropod *Bathynerita naticoidea* in hydrothermal vents and it has been suggested that filamentous fungi may be involved in the precipitation of minerals making up the sulphide 'smokers' which surround the vents. The deepest known fungi have been isolated from the hadal zone, in muds of the Mariana Trench over 10,000 m below sea level. Some barotolerance tests have been undertaken on deep sea yeasts and deep sea isolates of filamentous fungi (*Aspergillus* and *Graphium* species). However, much remains unknown about the biology of these abyssal fungi or how they cope with low temperatures, perpetual darkness, and crushingly high pressure.

CHAPTER 13

Specialised Natural Habitats

W ITHIN THE wider habitats of woodland, grassland, and coastal dunes are many smaller, sometimes temporary but often highly specialised communities of fungi adapted to specific niches. Such communities include the phoenicoid or firesite fungi, the dung fungi, the fungi of bird nests, and those adapted to dry (xerophilic), cold (psychrophilic), and other extreme conditions. Specialised communities of fungi are also associated with specific plant groups, notably mosses, liverworts, and ferns. The present chapter looks at all of these, together with the fungi found in caves and other underground chambers.

PHOENICOID OR FIRESITE FUNGI

Firesite or 'phoenicoid' fungi (the term means 'phoenix-like', arising from ashes) are specialised species which typically appear after forest fires, controlled burns and bonfires, and on other heat–treated substrata. The term 'phoenicoid' was introduced by Carpenter & Trappe (1985) in recognition of the remarkable response of these fungi to severe heat. Following the eruption in May 1980 of Mount St. Helens in Washington State, USA, phoenicoid fungi (including species such as the cup-fungus *Peziza violacea* and the morel *Morchella elata*) were the first visible life-forms to appear amongst the devastation, producing fruitbodies in the tephra within two months of the eruption.

It was assumed initially that phoenicoid fungi were 'carbonicolous' (able to colonise charcoal and other burnt vegetable matter), but a series of investigations has revealed a more complex and less obvious ecology. Basically, many of these fungi respond either to severe heat or to secondary changes brought about by burning, but rarely if ever to charcoal itself. Nevertheless, it is still common to see fungi of burnt ground referred to as 'carbonicolous'.

Many phoenicoid species produce spores which are stimulated to germinate by heat. A short period of heat treatment at 50°C, for example, can enhance sporulation in a number of typical firesite cup-fungi, including *Peziza praetervisa*, *Ascobolus carbonarius*, and *Pyronema domesticum*. The last of these sometimes appears on steam-treated greenhouse soils in the absence of fire.

Fires, whether natural or manmade, not only burn and sterilise sites, but also cause substantial changes in the chemistry and structure of the soil. Chief amongst these is a marked increase in surface alkalinity, with initial pH values in the uppermost ash layers rising to 10 or so. This alkaline ash gradually diffuses into the subsurface soil layers through leaching, raising pH values throughout. Areas with high ash cover, such as woodland bonfire sites, are clearly more affected than areas with low ash cover, such as those found after stubble burns or natural, quick-burning, forest fires.

It appears that many phoenicoid fungi are alkaline specialists, able to tolerate or even thrive at pH levels inimical to more generalist species. This explains why typical firesite species such as the cup-fungi *Peziza praetervisa* and *Geopyxis carbonaria* can occasionally be found growing on old mortar and damp plaster.

Moser (1949) split macrofungi into four ecological groups, according to their dependence on burning. 'Anthracobionts' are obligate phoenicoid fungi and include, amongst others, species of the cup-fungi *Plicaria* and *Anthracobia*, as well as some agarics such as *Tephrocybe ambusta*. 'Anthracophiles' prefer burnt sites but may occur elsewhere; they include the chanterelle-like *Faerberia carbonaria*, the morel *Morchella elata*, and the discomycete *Trichophaea gregaria*. 'Anthracoxenous' species are of accidental occurrence on burnt ground but can tolerate such sites, and the remainder, including most (but not all) mycorrhizal species, cannot tolerate burning at all.

The firesite succession

Obligate anthracobiont species tend to appear in well-defined succession following burning, and may continue to develop for several years. This succession mirrors that exhibited by fungi on dung (see below), and has been studied or reviewed by Petersen (1970), Turnau (1984), and Lisiewska (1992). In some of the phoenicoid ascomycetes, it has been shown to reflect direct antagonism by later-fruiting species towards earlier colonisers.

The first macrofungi to appear after burning tend to be discomycetes, particularly *Pyronema* species which form pinkish-orange crusts of confluent fruitbodies over freshly burnt or sterilised soil. These are followed by species of *Anthracobia* which commonly continue to fruit for up to seven or eight months after burning. *Geopyxis carbonaria*, *Plicaria trachycarpa*, and some species of *Peziza* are next in succession. The toadstools *Pholiota highlandensis* and *Psathyrella pennata* also appear at this stage and may persist for many months. The discomycete *Octospora hetieri* and the toadstool *Myxomphalia maura* are examples of species which do not make an appearance for more than a year, but may then persist for up to four years. Other more generalist species finally supersede the true firesite fungi, but how and in what form the latter persist in the absence of fires remains largely unknown.

Larger phoenicoid fungi in the British Isles

In Britain there are around 30 species of phoenicoid discomycetes, all of which belong in *Pezizales*. Species of *Peziza*, *Plicaria*, and *Rhizina* are amongst the largest, the most spectacular being *Peziza proteana*. In its normal form this produces typical cup-shaped or discoid fruitbodies, but in the variety *sparassoides* fruitbodies are cauliflower-like forming large, whitish, compound structures up to 25 cm high and 15 cm wide. This strange-looking fungus is not common, but is unmistakeable when encountered. The other five or so British phoenicoid *Peziza* species (see Table 27) are more conventional, though often quite large and variously coloured in dull violet, brown, or black (Fig. 118).

Plicaria is closely related to *Peziza* but distinguished microscopically by its globose rather than ellipsoid ascospores. Three *Plicaria* species occur in Britain, all of which are restricted to fire sites and have dark brown,

FIG 118. The cup fungus *Peziza petersii* is one of the larger discomycetes found on firesites (P. Livermore).

cup-shaped or discoid fruitbodies. The commonest and also the largest of these is *Plicaria endocarpoides*, with fruitbodies to 6 cm or so across. *Rhizina undulata* is another conspicuous species, and one which appears to require heat-shock for germination of its spores. The species is fairly common on burnt ground in conifer woods from late summer to autumn and in such situations can be a serious parasite of newly emerging pine seedlings.

Much smaller, but far more abundant, are species of *Anthracobia* which can cover fire sites with hundreds of usually orange or reddish-orange, discoid fruitbodies. Three species, *Anthracobia macrocystis*, *A. maurilabra*, and *A. melaloma*, are particularly common (Fig. 119), whilst two others, *A. uncinata* and the blackish *A. subatra*, are distinctly rare. Indeed the last species was only recorded from Britain in 1996 based on a collection from Surrey. Phoenicoid species of *Tricharina* and *Trichophaea* have pale, yellowish-orange or whitish fruitbodies and occur singly or in clusters on burnt ground which has been colonised by mosses (Fig. 120). *Lamprospora carbonicola*, with tiny, orange fruitbodies only 1–2 mm across, shares the same habitat. Although always on burnt ground, its true association is with the moss *Funaria hygrometrica*, a common and early coloniser of fire sites. Dougoud (2001) has

FIG 119. *Anthracobia melaloma*, one of several small discomycetes which typically occur in swarms on firesites, sometimes developing within a few months of burning (P. Livermore).

FIG 120. *Tricharina praecox*, a discomycete associated with mosses on burnt ground. The fruitbodies are gregarious and are usually found in spring (P. Livermore).

provided a key for the identification of discomycetes on burnt ground, including obligate phoenicoid species as well as those only occasionally found in this habitat.

Several pyrenomycetous ascomycetes are also characteristic of fire sites ('pyrenomycetous' refers to their carbonised appearance, not their habitat preferences). In Britain, these include species of *Cercophora*, *Jugulospora* and *Strattonia*, some of which are fairly common although, being small and black, are almost impossible to see in the field. They are best located by collecting other, more conspicuous fungi and scanning the soil around them under a dissecting microscope. A general key to British phoenicoid ascomycetes was published by Ellis & Ellis (1988).

A number of British basidiomycetes are also burnt ground specialists. Most of these are agarics, such as *Pholiota highlandensis*, one of the commonest phoenicoid species recognised by its viscid, orange-brown cap (Fig. 121). The misleading epithet '*highlandensis*' comes from America, not Scotland, and the toadstool is perfectly at home in the lowlands. At least

FIG 121. The brown toadstool *Pholiota highlandensis* growing with the grey inkcap *Coprinus jonesii* in a typical firesite association (P. Roberts).

FIG 122. The inkcap *Coprinus jonesii,* a delicate species with characteristic shaggy veil and clustered fruitbodies, grows almost exclusively on burnt ground (B. Spooner).

three of the ink-caps are typical of burnt sites: *Coprinus jonesii,* a common agaric with large, tufted, greyish fruitbodies (Fig. 122), *C. gonophyllus,* and the tiny *C. angulatus,* a much less frequent species. Other phoenicoid agarics include *Myxomphalia maura,* a grey-brown species with striate cap and mealy smell, *Hebeloma anthracophilum, Psathyrella pennata,* and several rather dull, greyish species of the genus *Tephrocybe.* The stalked polypore *Coltricia perennis* (Fig. 123) is also not uncommon on firesites.

Obligate or typical British phoenicoid macrofungi are listed in Table 27. However, it should be remembered that many other species are occasionally found on burnt ground, especially amongst the discomycetes. *Byssonectria fusispora,* for example, together with *Geopora arenicola* and several species of *Peziza,* including *P. repanda,* are not infrequent, but are excluded from the table since they are more commonly found elsewhere. Monti *et al.* (1992) have published a useful selection of colour photographs of burnt ground fungi.

FIG 123. *Coltricia perennis* is an attractive stalked polypore with a zoned cap often found on old firesites (P. Livermore).

TABLE 27. Obligate or typical British phoenicoid macrofungi.

SPECIES	ORDER
ASCOMYCETES	
Anthracobia macrocystis	Pezizales
Anthracobia maurilabra	Pezizales
Anthracobia melaloma	Pezizales
Anthracobia subatra	Pezizales
Anthracobia uncinata	Pezizales
Ascobolus carbonarius	Pezizales
Geopyxis carbonaria	Pezizales
Lamprospora carbonicola	Pezizales
Octospora hetieri	Pezizales
Peziza echinospora	Pezizales
Peziza petersii	Pezizales
Peziza pseudoviolacea	Pezizales

SPECIES	ORDER
Peziza proteana	*Pezizales*
Peziza proteana v. *sparassoides*	*Pezizales*
Peziza vacinii	*Pezizales*
Peziza violacea	*Pezizales*
Plicaria carbonaria	*Pezizales*
Plicaria endocarpoides	*Pezizales*
Plicaria trachycarpa	*Pezizales*
Pulvinula carbonaria	*Pezizales*
Pyronema domesticum	*Pezizales*
Pyronema omphalodes	*Pezizales*
Rhizina undulata	*Pezizales*
Rhodotarzetta rosea	*Pezizales*
Sphaerosporella brunnea	*Pezizales*
Tricharina gilva	*Pezizales*
Tricharina praecox	*Pezizales*
Trichophaea abundans	*Pezizales*
Trichophaea woolhopeia	*Pezizales*
Cercophora arenicola	*Sordariales*
Jugulospora rotula	*Sordariales*
Strattonia carbonaria	*Sordariales*
Strattonia minor	*Sordariales*

BASIDIOMYCETES

Coprinus angulatus	*Agaricales*
Coprinus gonophyllus	*Agaricales*
Coprinus jonesii (= *C. lagopides*)	*Agaricales*
Hebeloma anthracophilum	*Agaricales*
Myxomphalia maura	*Agaricales*
Pholiota highlandensis (= *P. carbonaria*)	*Agaricales*
Psathyrella pennata	*Agaricales*
Tephrocybe ambusta	*Agaricales*
Tephrocybe anthracophila	*Agaricales*
Tephrocybe atrata	*Agaricales*
Tephrocybe impexa	*Agaricales*
Clavaria tenuipes	*Cantharellales*
Coltricia perennis	*Hymenochaetales*
Faerberia carbonaria	*Poriales*

DUNG FUNGI

Dung, particularly of herbivorous mammals, provides a nutrient-rich substratum for a large variety of specialist fungi. It typically contains easily accessible cellulose and hemicellulose, is high in nitrogen, ammonia, and organic compounds, has a high pH, and is water-retentitive. Moreover, herbivores eating and dunging in the same area provide an efficient re-cycling system for fungal spores and propagules. However, dung is clearly a complex substratum, varying greatly in its chemistry according to species, age and local conditions which affect the rate of decomposition. It has an equally complex ecology, being home to many kinds of organisms in addition to fungi, all of which interact in ways which are not yet fully studied.

The succession of fungi on dung

Dung fungi are highly successional, as can easily be demonstrated by keeping rabbit pellets or similar material in a moist chamber and noting which species appear and when. Simple methods for doing this, as well as keys to British species, can be found in Richardson & Watling (1997). The succession typically moves through three phyla of higher fungi, the *Zygomycota* appearing first, followed by the *Ascomycota* and finally the *Basidiomycota*. Although this is essentially a factor of the time it takes to produce fruit-bodies, competitive antagonism can also be demonstrated. Species of *Mucor*, for example, are more prolific on sterilised rather than unsterilised dung, their growth being restricted by the presence of other fungi. Further aspects of the dung succession, such as the effects of ecological factors on fungal growth and sporulation, have been investigated by Harper & Webster (1964), Ikediugwu & Webster (1970a,b), and Larsen (1971).

Fruitbodies of the *Zygomycota* can appear on dung within 2–3 days. Typically, they include examples of the genus *Pilobolus*, highly adapted fungi having glistening, colourless, pin-like fruitbodies about 2–5 mm high, each with a swollen tip surmounted by a shiny black, discoid structure ('sporangium') which contains the spores (Fig. 124). Despite their small size, *Pilobolus* species are capable of projecting these sticky packets of spores for distances of one metre or more from the dung surface. The sporangia adhere to grass leaves and other vegetation, where they can be grazed, ingested, and re-released with fresh dung. Species of another common genus, *Phycomyces*, have evolved an equally remarkable strategy by producing hair-like, attenuated fruitbodies up to a third of a metre long. Each is tipped with sticky sporangia which adhere to whatever they touch. Instead of projecting its spores onto grazeable grass, *Phycomyces* effectively reaches out and places them there. Many other zygomycetes are associated with dung, with around 20 genera recorded from the Britain. As well as *Phycomyces* and *Pilobolus*, these include species of *Mortierella*, *Mucor*, *Pilaira*, *Piptocephalis*, and *Rhizopus*, several of which are common, if rarely noticed. Of particular interest are species of *Syncephalis*. Though these always occur on dung, they are actually parasitic on their fellow zygomycetes. Two species, *Syncephalis depressa* and *S. nodosa* occur in Britain, parasites on various species of *Mucoraceae*.

After 6–12 days ascomycetous fruitbodies start to appear. These are the

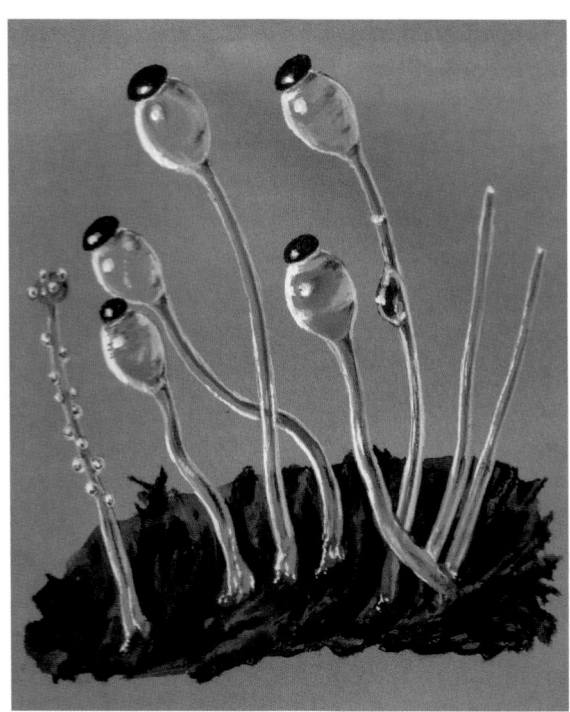

FIG 124. *Pilobolus crystallinus*, one of the Mucorales, is common on the dung of herbivores. The sporangiophores, swollen near the top and bearing a black sporangium which is forcibly discharged, are characteristic of the genus. From a painting by R. Baker (RBG Kew).

most numerous of the dung associates, and are a highly diverse assemblage. Most of the major orders of the *Ascomycota* include some coprophilous species, but the most significant on dung are the operculate discomycetes (*Pezizales*) together with pyrenomycetous groups such as the *Sordariales*, some *Xylariales*, *Dothideales*, and *Gymnoascales*. Curiously, members of the inoperculate discomycetes (*Helotiales*, *Orbiliales*) are scarcely represented. This is remarkable, given their ubiquitous presence elsewhere, on rotting plant remains. Only a few species, mostly in the genera *Lanzia*, *Martininia*, *Orbilia* and *Pezizella*, have been found on dung, although some *Orbilia* species are of particular interest in having anamorphic states which trap dung-dwelling nematode worms (Chapter Five).

Altogether, at least 150 species of coprophilous ascomycetes have been recorded from Britain to date. They occur on all types of droppings and present an astonishing diversity of form and structure, best appreciated by taking dung samples, keeping them in a damp container, and examining the succession of fruitbodies under a microscope. Many of these ascomycetes are rare, or apparently so, and are seldom seen. As with so many groups of fungi, species new to the British Isles are still being discovered. For example, the small, black, flask-shaped species *Podospora granulostriata* was first reported in 1995 based on collections on deer dung from Surrey and Cambridgeshire, whilst the remarkable *Subbaromyces splendens* was discovered in Belfast slurry tanks in 1992 (Fig. 107).

Much more frequent and far better known are species of *Ascobolus* and *Saccobolus* (*Pezizales*), the majority of which are strict dung-associates although a few occur on rotting vegetation or burnt ground. These can be readily recognised by their characteristic ascospores which at maturity are purple, and usually have a striate or sometimes warted surface. *Saccobolus* species are distinctive in having ascospores that are formed, mostly in consistent and regular patterns, into cohesive clusters which are ejected as a unit from the ascus. In *Ascobolus* species, spores are individually discharged and dispersed on air currents, but the clustered spores of *Saccobolus* form a large projectile which is shot over comparatively long distances into surrounding vegetation. A mucilaginous sheath surrounds the spore package in all dung-inhabiting species of *Saccobolus*, gluing the spores to nearby vegetation where, as with *Pilobolus*, they can be grazed, ingested, and re-released with fresh dung. Species of *Cheilymenia* and *Lasiobolus* are also characteristic of dung, most having small, disc-shaped, orange fruitbodies frequently ornamented with hairs. *Cheilymenia stercorea* is a typical example, often occurring in swarms on cow pats. Other discomycete genera such as *Thelebolus, Ryparobius, Trichobolus* and *Ascozonus* produce microscopic fruitbodies and, although some are very common, their taxonomy is not yet fully elaborated and species identification is no easy task. It is notable that many species of these last mentioned genera have multisporous asci, in some cases over 1000 spores being formed in each ascus. Similar asci also occur in some coprophilous pyrenomycetes, such as *Arnium leporinum* and *Podospora granulostriata*. In many such cases the spores may be discharged as a single unit, possibly indicating the development of polyspory as an adaptation to a coprophilous habit.

Most of the remaining ascomycetes on dung are pyrenomycetes belonging to the order *Sordariales*. These are characterised by having dark brown ascospores which have germ pores, are frequently 2-celled, and have either a gelatinous sheath or gelatinous appendages. These gelatinised elements almost certainly play a role in spore discharge and dispersal, helping them stick to surrounding vegetation. *Podospora* and *Schizothecium* are the commonest of the genera involved, with over 120 species between them, around 30 of which are known in the British Isles.

Most of the coprophilous pyrenomycetes are small to microscopic, though some species of *Podosordaria* and *Poronia* (*Xylariaceae*), are much larger and easily visible. The latter genus is well-known thanks to the status of *Poronia punctata* as a European priority species for conservation. The species is sometimes called the 'nail fungus' because of its distinctive nail- or golf-tee-shaped fruitbody. This roots deeply into the dung and has a flat or slightly concave disc about 10–15 mm across, dotted with the black mouths of the perithecia in which the asci and spores are formed (Fig. 125). It is associated with horse dung and was comparatively commonplace in Britain (as was its host) until the beginning of the twentieth century. It has now become so rare that it is virtually restricted to pony dung in the New Forest, with only occasional records from elsewhere. It is considered endangered throughout Europe, since it seems to be found only in areas of unimproved pasture, a threatened habitat which is being increasingly lost. The

FIG 125. The rare *Poronia punctata* on pony dung from the New Forest, one of its few remaining sites in Britain. The characteristic fruitbodies are golf tee- or nail-shaped, rooting into the dung (S. Evans).

widespread use of artificial fertilisers, as well as additives to feedstuffs and better veterinary care, have altered the nature of horse manure, possibly making it a less suitable substratum for the fungus. Another possible reason for the decline of *Poronia punctata* is that the natural, year-round, eating-dunging cycle has been broken for most British horses. The New Forest ponies, which still roam in a comparatively natural and unimproved environment, are an exception. A second British species, *Poronia erici*, is something of a curiosity. Although similar to *P. punctata*, it has larger spores and smaller, less deeply rooting stromata, and is typically found on rabbit pellets particularly near the coast. It is so far known in Britain only from Scolt Head Island in Norfolk, where it was first collected in 1933 but remained unidentified and unrecognised until 1988. It has now been recorded from various parts of northern Europe, mostly on rabbit pellets, but has a curiously disjunct distribution, occurring also much further afield in Australia where it grows on kangaroo and wallaby dung, as well as that of rabbits, sheep and horses. It is thought to have been introduced into Europe after successfully colonising rabbit dung following the introduction of rabbits into Australia during the 19th century. Anamorphic ascomycetes (hyphomycetes) are also common on dung, especially late in the succession, and include strict dung-associates as well as secondary invaders. Over 260 coprophilous species were noted by Seifert *et al.* (1983), although not all of these have yet been recorded from Britain. Most hyphomycetes are visible only as mouldy growths in the field, though some are distinctive under the microscope. A few 'synnematous' genera (forming drumstick-like fruitbodies) such as *Doratomyces* and *Stilbella* are more conspicuous and somewhat easier to identify. *Stilbella erythrocephala*, for example, is common, especially on rabbit pellets, and produces club-shaped fruitbodies, sometimes up to two millimetres high, which occur in swarms and have pinkish-orange heads. The species is known to inhibit the development of many other coprophilous fungi, providing an example of antagonistic competition in the fungal succession.

Basidiomycetes begin to appear on dung after nine days or more and include a number of toadstools, particularly ink caps of the genus *Coprinus* (derived from the Greek 'kopros', meaning dung). Some of these are extremely small and ephemeral, rarely if ever seen in the field, but commonly observed when dung is cultured. Other coprophilous agarics include species of *Conocybe, Panaeolus* and *Psilocybe*. Some of these grow directly on dung, others (including 'magic mushrooms') are more typically found on manured grassy ground and soil. Non-agaric basidiomycetes are comparatively few on dung, but two gasteroid species are particularly notable. *Sphaerobolus stellatus*, the 'shooting star' or 'cannon-ball fungus', is fairly common on dung though not restricted to this substratum. It is a highly distinctive fungus with densely gregarious, small, pale yellow fruitbodies which at maturity split to eject a globose spore-ball. This is a surprisingly powerful and efficient mechanism. It was investigated in detail by Buller (1933) who measured the horizontal range of the spore-ball to reach as far as 18 feet 7 inches (c. 5.7 m) and the vertical range to be as high as 14 feet 5 inches (c. 4.4 m). Also of note is the bird's-nest fungus *Cyathus stercoreus*, a rather rare or localised species associated with rabbit droppings in sand dune systems.

Dung, especially that of herbivores, also provides a suitable habitat for slime-moulds, particularly those otherwise associated with plant litter. Few of the species involved are thought to be obligately coprophilous, although some are as yet only known from dung, notably *Trichia fimicola* and *Perichaena luteola*. The former is very rare on hare and rabbit droppings in coastal dunes, and is only known from Britain and Belgium. The latter has been recorded from the Hebrides on cow and sheep dung, but is known elsewhere in Europe and in North America. Over 30 species of myxomycetes recorded on dung were noted by Eliasson & Lundquist (1979), and many additional species have since been found (Ing, 1994b).

In all, around 400 species of fungi have been recorded as dung associates in the British Isles, and no doubt others await discovery. Table 28 lists a selection of the commonest or most distinctive of these species, and a more comprehensive coverage, with illustrations and keys for their identification, was provided by Ellis & Ellis (1988) and Richardson & Watling (1997).

TABLE 28. A selection of typical British dung fungi.

SPECIES	ORDER
ASCOMYCETES	
Ascobolus furfuraceus	Pezizales
Ascobolus immersus	Pezizales
Ascophanus microsporus	Pezizales
Cheilymenia fimicola	Pezizales
Cheilymenia granulata	Pezizales
Coniochaeta scatigena	Sordariales
Coprotus granuliformis	Pezizales
Iodophanus carneus	Pezizales
Lasiobolus ciliatus	Pezizales
Orbilia fimicoloides	Orbiliales
Peziza bovina	Pezizales
Podosordaria tulasnei	Xylariales
Podospora intestinacea	Sordariales
Poronia erici	Xylariales
Poronia punctata	Xylariales
Pseudombrophila equina	Pezizales
Sporormia bipartis	Pleosporales
Stilbella erythrocephala	Ascomycota (anamorphic)
Thelebolus stercoreus	Thelebolales

SPECIES	ORDER
BASIDIOMYCETES	
Conocybe fimitaria	*Agaricales*
Coprinus stercoreus	*Agaricales*
Cyathus stercoreus	*Nidulariales*
Panaeolus semiovatus	*Agaricales*
Panaeolus sphinctrinus	*Agaricales*
Psilocybe coprophila	*Agaricales*
Stropharia semiglobata	*Agaricales*
ZYGOMYCETES	
Phycomyces nitens	*Mucorales*
Pilobolus crystallinus	*Mucorales*
Pilobolus kleinii	*Mucorales*

Specialist adaptations

An essential part of the biology of dung fungi is their ability to persist in an ephemeral environment and most species have adapted in some way to the eating-dunging cycle, particularly by producing spores capable of surviving passage through the gut. Larsen (1971) split dung fungi into three groups: obligate 'endocoprophilous' fungi (e.g. *Saccobolus* and *Ascobolus* species) whose spores germinate only after passage through the gut; facultative endocoprophilous fungi (e.g. *Coprinus* species) whose spores can survive passage through the gut; and 'ectocoprophilous' fungi (e.g. *Ascozonus* species) whose spores do not survive passage through the gut, but persist in dunged soil.

Given that most dung fungi are so highly adapted, it is perhaps surprising that very few of them appear to be strictly selective in their animal associates. Many are known to occur on a wide range of dung types, although most show definite preferences and are regularly more abundant on some types than others. Richardson (1972) examined the occurrence of ascomycetes on different herbivore dung, but found only a tendency for certain species to be associated with ruminant (cattle and sheep) dung or non-ruminant (rabbit and hare) dung. Many more species were common to both. Such differences as were observed could be due more to the composition of the dung (texture, nutrients, water content, and so on) than to its source.

Lundquist (1972), however, analysed host preferences for Nordic

Sordariaceae and showed that, whilst some common species may occur on dung of a wide range of animals, all species show definite preferences for one or two kinds of dung. For example, *Schizothecium conicum*, one of the commonest and most ubiquitous of the dung fungi, strongly favours that of cows and horses but occasionally occurs on dung of 14 other animal species. He recognised three ecological groups: species with a broad ecological tolerance and low preference for a particular substratum, those with a broad tolerance and high preference for a particular substratum, and specialised species restricted to one or a few kinds of substrata. He also found several surprising and unexpected relationships. The dung of deer, for example, has more species in common with that of rabbits than that of sheep and goats. Quite why is unclear.

Carnivore dung is obviously not part of the eating-dunging cycle, but can harbour a range of opportunistic fungi. Dog dung, for example, offers the enquiring mycologist a number of interesting species of which the cup-fungi *Ascobolus* and *Thelebolus* are particularly frequent. This area of research is surprisingly understudied, although Dennis (1960) noted encouragingly that 'a rich harvest may well await the man who cares to devote his leisure hours or his declining years to the study of stale dog dung.'

Even human faeces are known to yield various fungi, though the non-pathogenic species appear to be little studied. Fairman (1920) provided a brief synopsis of the fungi colonising this readily available substratum. These include the almost ubiquitous *Ascobolus furfuraceus* as well as the specifically named *Sordaria humana*, though the latter is equally common on dog dung.

Dung of small mammals, such as mice, voles, and bats, is not always easy to find, but can also be rewarding mycologically. Some of the zygomycetes, for example, are particularly frequent on these substrata, including species of *Coemansia, Kickxella, Mortierella, Mucor, Piptocephalis,* and *Rhopalomyces*. Among the discomycetes, *Ascobolus rhytidisporus* has been described from mouse dung in Britain, and the ascomycete genus *Guanomyces* was described from bat dung in Mexico.

Bird droppings, especially those of grouse and geese, also have associated fungi, Lundquist (1972), for example, recording 19 species of *Sordariaceae* and *Lasiosphaeriaceae* (*Ascomycetes*) on this substratum in the Nordic countries. Most of these, including various species of *Podospora* and *Sporormia*, are plurivorous, but a few, such as *Strattonia borealis*, seem strongly to favour grouse dung. Richardson (2001) found *Sporormiella minima* to be most frequent on grouse dung, and the discomycete *Ascobolus carletonii* to occur only on this substratum. Some other ascomycetes frequently encountered on bird droppings include *Saccobolus quadrisporus* and *Thelebolus cesatii*. A common zygomycete is *Coemansia scorpiodea*. Pigeon droppings (not hard to find) are notoriously a source of the yeast *Cryptococcus neoformans*, a serious and often fatal pathogen of humans (Chapter 15).

Though comparatively little investigated, the dung of amphibians such as frogs and toads hosts a range of species which, because of the ephemeral nature and small size of the dung, require specialist study to appreciate. However, working in such an obscure field can clearly prove rewarding. For example, the zygomycete *Dimargaris verticillata* was reported as new to Britain from toad dung by Kirk & Kirk (1984). This was previously known only from amphibian dung on the California-Mexico border. The same toad dung also produced the first British record of *Coemansia erecta*, and the uncommon species *Mortierella polycephala*.

FUNGI OF BIRD NESTS

Bird nests may seem a peculiar and unexpected place to look for fungi, but in fact they provide ideal habitats for a range of specialist saprotrophs and parasites.

Most of these fungi belong in a group of ascomycetes known as the *Onygenales*. This order, with around 90 species world-wide, contains keratinolytic specialists capable of decomposing hair, horns, bones, and feathers. Some are parasites, including the dermatotrophs which occur on the skin, hair and nails of humans (Chapter 15). Others are non-parasitic saprotrophs which are widely present in keratin-containing substrata such as dung, soil, and bird nests.

Species of *Onygena*, the type genus, are large and comparatively easy to name. Perhaps the commonest of these is *O. equina*, its club-shaped fruitbodies often occurring in swarms on rotting horn and hooves. Another, *Onygena corvina*, is found on bird skulls or on rotting feathers and its whitish,

2–3 mm high, club-shaped fruitbodies are also sometimes encountered in old nests. More typical, however, are genera with small to microscopic fruitbodies, particularly species of *Arthroderma* (Fig. 125A) and *Chrysosporium*, which may be present in high concentrations in occupied bird nests. Over 90% of nests sampled by Pugh (1966) from sites in England and Wales were found to contain these fungi, though their presence and abundance depended on the type of nest material, as well as its water content and pH. Of the twelve bird species sampled, the nests of blackbirds, song thrushes, sand martins, and hedge sparrows were most productive, but all nests except those of wrens and starlings yielded some fungi. Twelve different fungi were isolated, of which *Chrysosporium* species, especially *C. keratinophilum*, were the most frequent.

Keratinophilic fungi may also occur on the birds themselves and were investigated, again from British sites, by Pugh (1965) and Pugh & Evans (1970). Both studies, using feathers removed from ringed birds, found only about 37% of birds sampled had fungi on their feathers, and few individuals

FIG 125A. *Arthroderma curreyi*, a keratinophilic species, developing on damp, rotting feathers (RBG Kew).

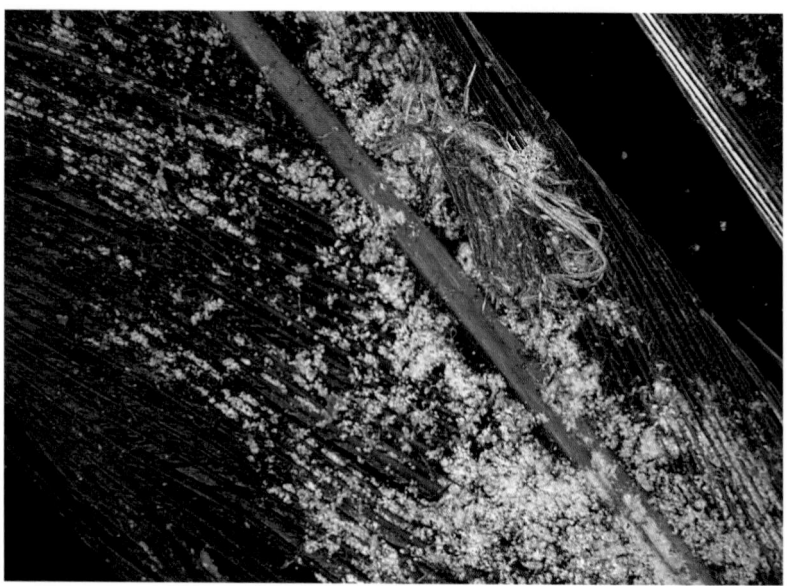

harboured more than two or three species. Fungi were most prevalent on blackbirds, pheasants, and grouse, whilst pigeons and starlings were largely uninfected. Some of these fungi appear to be host specific, or at least have a marked preference for certain birds. *Ctenomyces serratus*, for example, is almost exclusively found on partridges and pheasants, whilst *Arthroderma curreyi* occurs most frequently on blackbirds and song thrushes. It seems that the occurrence and distribution of keratinophilic fungi on birds is largely determined by the presence and quantity of feather fats.

In general, the fungi isolated from feathers of living birds were different to those found in nests, but a few were common to both, though in different ratios. For example, *Arthroderma curreyi*, the most common species on feathers and present in 67% of blackbirds sampled, was found in only 13.7% of blackbird nests. Conversely, *A. quadrifidum* was found only on 3.5% of birds studied, but occurred in almost half the nests. *Arthroderma* and *Chrysosporium* were again the most frequent genera obtained from feathers in these studies, and a similar study from 92 bird species in Yugoslavia and the Czech Republic also found these to be the most frequently isolated keratinophiles.

FUNGI OF MOSSES AND LIVERWORTS

Although the association between fungi and bryophytes (mosses and liverworts) has long been known, the ubiquity and diversity of this biologically remarkable phenomenon was slow to be recognised. Many hundreds of bryophilous fungi have now been described, reviewed by Felix (1988), but few have received detailed study. Indeed, Döbbeler (1978) noted that, given the abundance of bryophilous fungi, "their neglect is inexplicable". He provided an account of just the pyrenomycetes and *Dothideales* (*Ascomycota*) known to occur on the gametophyte stage of bryophytes and included no fewer than 123 species in 33 genera, 62 of which were described as new to science. They included some particularly notable species, such as *Bryochiton monascus* and *B. perpusillus* which have the smallest known fungal fruitbodies, less than 50 μm diameter and sometimes as small as 18 μm across. Many ascomycetes have individual spores which are bigger than this. Moreover, these miniature *Bryochiton* species are able to develop their tiny fruitbodies directly from a single spore without forming a mycelium. *Bryochiton perpusillus* has been recorded from Britain on *Polytrichum piliferum*. Another species, *Epibryon intracellulare*, is also notable, being the first known higher fungus in which the fruitbody develops to maturity inside a host cell. It was described from Sri Lanka in (rather than on) *Schistochila aligera*.

Bryophilous ascomycetes

Many bryophilous ascomycetes are saprotrophs, and play an important role in the decomposition of the thalli. Others are biotrophic parasites, developing mutualistic associations with their hosts without causing any appreciable damage. They include endophytic VA mycorrhiza-like associations, termed 'mycothalli', as well as the development of appressoria and intracellular haustoria, which in some species may induce conspicuous galls in moss rhizoids. These galls are caused by species of *Octospora* (*Pezizales*), obligate moss-associates which produce conspicuous orange fruitbodies, and a few others such as species of *Lamprospora* (Fig. 126). These are well-known and sometimes common fungi, with at least 15 species in Britain. As the host associations and ecology of these bryoparasitic *Pezizales* have gradually been brought to light, further new taxa have been recognised and it is significant that over half of the known species have been described since 1975.

Other discomycetes which are specific to bryophytes include species of *Bryoscyphus*, all of which are parasites, some being associated with liverworts. In Britain, five are known so far, including *Bryoscyphus atromarginatus* which frequently grows with *Marchantia* in plant pots in garden centres, turning the infected thalli brown. *Nectria muscivora* is necrotrophic on species of *Barbula* and other small mosses, developing its orange-yellow fruitbodies in the leaf axils. *Bryostroma trichostomi*, only discovered in Britain in 1999, forms tiny black fruitbodies, no more than 300 μm across, in the leaf axils of its host. It is now known from Suffolk on *Ceratodon purpureus* and from Somerset on *Barbula*. *Mniaecia jungermanniae*, an attractive species associated with leafy liverworts, has deep blue-green fruitbodies that develop in early spring and are well worth looking for (Fig. 127). They are not easy to spot in the field but the species is known to be widespread, especially in southern England and Wales.

FIG 126. *Lamprospora dictydiola* is one of several discomycetes associated strictly with mosses. Many of these species have small, orange fruitbodies and can be distinguished only under the microscope (J. Palmer).

FIG 127. The turquoise discomycete *Mniaecia jungermanniae* is a spring-fruiting species, found only in association with liverworts (RBG Kew).

Toadstools and bryophilous basidiomycetes

Many basidiomycetes are also intimately associated with bryophytes, mostly as biotrophic parasites, although their biology requires further study. Species of the agaric genera *Arrhenia*, *Rimbachia*, and *Rickenella* are typical moss associates, as are many species of *Galerina*, a large genus of small brown toadstools. A study by Redhead (1981) showed that *Galerina paludosa*, grown in culture with *Sphagnum*, produces peg-like hyphal haustoria which penetrate the moss cells, though plants appear to remain healthy. *Rickenella fibula*, an attractive little orange agaric common in patches of moss in damp turf, and *R. pseudogrisella*, a constant associate of the liverwort *Blasia pusilla*, produce similar haustoria. Both occur in Britain, though the latter has only recently been discovered here. Further study may show such haustoria to be typical of most bryophilous agarics. *Rimbachia* has three British species which are obligate moss associates, all of them rare. They are similar to species of *Arrhenia* in having small, often stemless fruitbodies with gills either lacking or reduced to shallow veins. *Arrhenia* has seven British species, of which *A. retiruga* is the most common, forming pale grey fruitbodies on various living mosses. Another gill-less moss associate, widespread but uncommon in Britain, is *Cyphellostereum laeve*, a small, whitish species found on various mosses, particularly *Polytrichum* and *Dicranella*.

Unlike these biotrophs, the greyish toadstool *Tephrocybe palustris* is a necrotrophic parasite. It has long been known to kill off patches of *Sphagnum*, its fruitbodies appearing among the bleached and decaying remains of the moss. It does precisely the same in culture, its hyphae overrunning the host, penetrating and destroying the host cells.

An unusual basidiomycete, *Eocronartium muscicola*, occurs on various mosses, including in Britain species of *Eurynchium*, *Fissidens*, *Hylocomium* and *Leskea*. It forms upright, club-shaped fruitbodies 0.5–2 cm high, but is readily distinguished from the true club-fungi (*Clavariaceae*) by its septate, tubular basidia (which places it in its own genus among the heterobasidiomycetes). It is extremely rare in the British Isles, known from England and Ireland but with only two collections since 1900. It is a phylogenetically interesting species, considered to be ancient and possibly ancestral to the rusts.

Although bryophilous fungi are so numerous and diverse, it is curious that none of the pathogenic rusts, smuts, and powdery mildews have yet been discovered on mosses. These obligate plant parasites have an ancient lineage going back at least 300 million years during which they have evolved in intimate association with their plant hosts, but not, apparently, with bryophytes. At one time, some smuts were believed to occur on *Sphagnum*, but it is now known that these are not true smuts, although their affinities remain unclear. The best known, *Bryophytomyces sphagni* (formerly in the smut genus *Tilletia*), is a widespread species recorded from Britain. It may be the anamorph of a discomycete, *Discinella schimperi* (*Helotiales*), but this connection has not been confirmed.

Basidiomycetes are also involved in 'mycothallic' (mycorrhiza-like) associations with liverworts, particularly in the *Jungermanniales* and *Metzgeriales* (Chapter Four).

Slime-moulds and other moss associates

Several myxomycete species can be found in association with bryophytes. Indeed some, such as *Fuligo muscorum*, *Physarum citrinum*, *P. confertum*, *P. virescens*, *Licea albonigra* and *L. lucens*, appear to be confined to mosses. A highly specialised assemblage occurs on wet rocks by waterfalls and in deep ravines (see Ing, 1983) and includes, amongst others, *Craterium muscorum*, *Lamproderma columbinum*, and several species of *Diderma*. Several myxomycetes occur with *Sphagnum*, including *Badhamia lilacina*, which appears to be confined to this host. This has small, gregarious, greyish-lilac fruitbodies, but its yellow plasmodial stage is much more conspicuous. *Amaurochaete trechispora* and *Symphytocarpus trechisporus* are also regular *Sphagnum* associates, and occasionally more general moss-associates such as *Lamproderma columbinum* will also be found on *Sphagnum*.

Curiously, only a few species of the fungus-like Oomycota infect bryophytes. Most notable amongst these is *Pleotrachelus wildemanii*, described from Denmark and also known in Britain, which galls the rhizoids of *Funaria hygrometrica* and *Tetraplodon mnioides*. Other bryophilous oomycetes include *Olpidiopsis ricciae*, a weak parasite in the rhizoids of liverworts such as *Marchantia* and *Riccia*, and *Lagenidium ellipticum* in moss rhizoids. Neither has been recorded from Britain, but may well occur here. Similarly, very few chytrids are bryophilous. Two species of *Synchytrium*, *S. musicola* which parasitises the leaves of various mosses and *S. pyriforme* in *Anomodon*, appear to be the only examples. Neither is known from Britain.

FUNGI AND FERNS

As with bryophytes, fungi play a highly significant and indeed vital role in the ecology and biology of pteridophytes (ferns and their allies). Some of these associations are ancient, having developed early in the long history of pteridophyte evolution, probably over 350 million years ago, but others may be more recent in origin. However, as noted by Bennell & Henderson (1985), who briefly reviewed the parasitic species, the study of fungi on pteridophytes has been largely neglected, to the extent that most potential host species have never been investigated.

British fern fungi

The most frequent British fern fungi are ascomycetes some of which are common and abundant. They include the tiny discomycetes *Microscypha grisella* on decaying fern fronds, *Micropodia pteridina* on blackened stem bases of bracken, and *Pezizella chrysostigma* on decaying *Dryopteris* petioles. Pteridicolous species amongst the pyrenomycetes are mostly associated with bracken, the almost ubiquitous *Rhopographus filicinus* appearing as black streaks on dead stems. Several hyphomycetes are also common, such as *Chalara pteridina* on bracken petioles, as are coelomycetes such as *Ascochyta pteridis*, an obligate fern associate and important pathogen of bracken. Many of these pteridicolous ascomycetes can be identified using Ellis & Ellis (1997) who dealt with over 50 British species.

Basidiomycetes are also well represented. Rarely recorded, but well worth looking for, is the tiny toadstool *Mycena pterigena* on old fern rhizomes and rotting stems; fruitbodies are a delicate whitish-pink, with the gill edges outlined in deeper coral-pink. Less immediately attractive, but equally uncommon, is another agaric, *Marasmius undatus*, which grows on old bracken stems on alkaline soils. The white club-shaped fungus, *Typhula quisquiliaris*, is commoner and appears in groups on decaying bracken stems. Effused, corticioid (patch-forming) fungi include *Aphanobasidium filicinum*, ubiquitous on dead, damp bracken stems where it forms thin, waxy, greyish patches, and *Parvobasidium cretatum*, not noticed in Britain till the 1990s, but evidently extremely common in early spring at the base of *Dryopteris* clumps, at least in the Westcountry. A parasitic species forming whitish patches on the sori of living *Dryopteris* leaves is the heterobasidiomycete *Herpobasidium filicinum*, possibly widespread in Britain but rarely reported. A survey of obligate and other non-agaricoid basidiomycetes on ferns, with a key for their identification, was published by Boidin (1993). This covered over 80 European species, most of which are known in the British Isles. Decomposers of bracken litter were investigated by Frankland (1966, 1969, 1976) who recorded a total of 390 species, including ascomycetes, basidiomycetes and zygomycetes, although many of these were sterile and remained unidentified. These fungi, isolated in damp chamber cultures from decomposing petioles over a six year period, mostly consisted of common and plurivorous saprotrophs with very few bracken-specific species. They showed a marked succession during the process of decomposition similar to that on rotting wood. Lignin and cellulose decomposers predominated at first, followed by those which utilise simple sugars and carbohydrates, and finally by members of the zygomycetous *Mucorales*. The common woodland toadstool *Mycena galopus* was found to be the most active decomposer of bracken, just as it is for mosses.

Mycorrhizal associations of ferns and fern allies are treated in Chapter Four.

Fern parasites

Pathogenic fungi on pteridophytes involve representatives of most major groups including rusts. Amongst the obligate host-specific fungi are species of *Taphrina* (*Ascomycota*), which lack proper fruitbodies and simply produce a layer of asci over the infected plant parts. The genus was monographed by Mix (1949), who included 24 species on fern hosts, with more described since. Most are tropical and several induce distinctive and conspicuous galls. The Asian species *Taphrina cornu-cervi*, for example, causes branched antler-like galls on leaves of *Arachniodes aristatum*, whilst *Taphrina laurencia* produces remarkable, bushy galls on fronds of *Pteris quadriaurita*. A few British *Taphrina* species are pteridicolous, mostly on species of *Dryopteris*. They cause galls but these are inconspicuous, amounting to little more than thickened spots on leaves. Few other significant ascomycetous fern parasites occur, though *Ascochyta pteridis*, the cause of curl-tip disease of bracken and a common endophyte of the pinnules, has been investigated as a potential biocontrol agent (Chapter 17).

The strange and unique genus *Mixia* is also worth noting here as an obligate fern parasite. It includes a single species, *M. osmundae*, known from Japan and USA, which forms yellowish spots on the pinnules of species of *Osmunda*. It was once referred to the genus *Taphrina* as it produces spore-sacs which are reminiscent of the asci of that genus. However, they actually produce their spores exogenously and are therefore not asci. The genus is now considered akin to the basidiomycetes, a position supported by molecular data, and placed in its own family *Mixiaceae*.

Other obligate parasites on ferns are rust fungi, of which thirteen species have been recorded from the British Isles. Eight of these belong in the genus *Milesina*, many of which have alternate stages on conifers, especially firs (*Abies* species). In Britain the genus includes some fairly common species, such as *Milesina blechni* on *Blechnum spicant*, *M. kriegeriana* on *Dryopteris* species, and *M. scolopendrii* on *Phyllitis scolopendrium*. There are also some rarities. *Milesina carpatorum* on *Dryopteris filix-mas*, for example, is currently known in Britain from just six collections, whilst *M. vogesiacum* and *M. whitei* are almost as rare on *Polystichum setiferum*. Other British fern rusts include the equally rare *Uredinopsis filicina* on *Thelypteris phegopteris*, *Milesia magnusiana* on *Asplenium adiantum-nigrum*, and three rare or localised species of *Hyalopsora*. Of the 120 species of fern rusts known worldwide, almost all belong in these three genera, considered to be the most primitive of all living rusts. Another rust, *Uredo vetus*, recently discovered in China on the fern-ally *Selaginella*, is also of special interest as this is the most primitive group of vascular plants on which a rust has ever been found.

In contrast to rusts, virtually no smut fungi have been found on ferns or fern-allies. Just two Asian species, *Melaniella oreophilum* and *M. selaginellae*, both on *Selaginella*, are known. These species were until recently referred to the genus *Melanotaenium*, but were shown by Bauer *et al.* (1999) to be better placed in a distinct genus in the order *Doassansiales*. They consider the presence of these smuts on *Selaginella*, the most primitive host group known for such fungi, to be due to a host jump. However, it is also possible that they represent extant examples of an ancestral smut group.

A few chytrids also infect ferns and fern allies, mostly occurring as parasites on the spores. These include *Rhizophlyctis rosea* on germinating spores of *Equisetum*, and some species of *Rhizophydium*. These fungi are not restricted to ferns, occurring also on soil or on pollen. However, *Ligniera isoetes* is apparently a specific parasite in *Isoetes*, and *Physoderma marsiliae* is parasitic on species of *Marsilia* in the United States. There are also two species of *Synchytrium* recorded from ferns, though both appear to be very rare. Various fungus-like *Pythium* species (*Oomycota*) are known to attack prothalli of ferns and horsetails. Prothalli of *Gymnogramme*, *Ceratopteris* and *Polystichum* are parasitised by *Completoria complens*, a unique member of the *Entomophthorales* most other species of which are parasites of invertebrates.

XEROPHILIC FUNGI

A remarkable demonstration of the adaptability of fungi and their ability to take advantage of varied and often extreme environments is provided by the xerophilic (dry-loving) and xerotolerant fungi, which have evolved to cope with conditions in which water is not or is scarcely available.

It is a common observation that most fungi, particularly the fleshy macrofungi, produce fruitbodies in damp conditions. The flush of fungi in wet autumn weather is a well-known phenomenon, as too is the scarcity of fruitbodies when the weather turns dry. Yet surprisingly, a wide range of macrofungi can also be found in extremely dry habitats, where they make the most of what little water is available.

Desert truffles

Some of these xerotolerant species escape the worst effects of desiccation by growing underground where they form ectomycorrhizal associations with desert shrubs. *Terfezia* and *Tirmania*, for example, are truffle-like ascomycetes of which 14 species are known, mostly occurring in association with *Helianthemum* and *Cistus* (rock-roses and their allies) in parts of southern

Europe and north Africa. Their fruitbodies are large, up to about 8 or 9 cm across, and have long been important as edible fungi, the Romans being especially fond of them. They are still much sought after and regularly sold in local markets (Chapter 17).

Earthstars and the gasteroid fungi

Quite a few gasteroid basidiomycetes are specially adapted to dry environments, notably species of *Battarraea*, *Montagnea*, *Podaxis*, *Pisolithus*, *Tulostoma*, *Myriostoma*, *Astraeus* and *Geastrum*. These occur in sandy soils and arid habitats, and may be common in semi-desert regions which are subject to occasional rains or floods. In the seasonally hot, dry parts of north-western Australia, for example, *Pisolithus arrhizus* and *Podaxis pistillaris* are both common species. The stilt-puffball *Battarraea phalloides* can be common in dried-out watercourses in Namibia, and in arid regions of Europe, Central America and south-east Australia. Given some moisture, all of these species produce fruitbodies which are woody or leathery and well-protected against drying out. As in puffballs, the spores develop inside the fruitbodies and are only released when mature, sometimes by a distinct hole as in *Astraeus*, *Geastrum*, and *Tulostoma* species, but more frequently by the whole outer surface breaking away.

Battarraea phalloides is a good example. Like a stinkhorn, the fruitbody grows from a gelatinised 'egg' (the matrix helping store water), but the 'egg' is underground and gives rise to a dry, puffball-like peridium (containing the spores) on an equally dry, shaggy, woody stem. The whole fruitbody can be as much as 40 cm tall. On maturity, the thin papery peridium breaks into pieces and releases a huge mass of rusty-brown spores (Fig. 128). Curiously this strange species was first described, not from a tropical desert, but from Bungay, Suffolk, in 1782. It has since been found elsewhere in Britain, in dry hedgerows and sandy ground, once even in the dry interior of a hollow tree, but is obviously on the edge of its range here and is extremely rare (see Chapter 18 for an interesting attempt to conserve it). Large forms of this species up to 50 cm high and with a thick, dry volva, occur commonly in the Mediterranean area and are also widespread in subtropical regions. These have been considered as a separate species, *Battarraea stevenii*, but this conclusion has not been upheld in recent studies based on molecular as

FIG 128. *Battarraea phalloides*, the 'sandy stilt puffball' has a dry, fibrous stem and is especially adapted to arid conditions. It is usually found on dry, sandy soil but is very rare in Britain and is a Biodiversity Action Plan species (RBG Kew).

well as morphological data. In Cyprus, where this dry form is quite common, it is known as the 'donkey fungus' and is even eaten in its 'egg' stage.

Montagnea arenaria, also found in the Mediterranean, resembles a woody, dried-up ink-cap (*Coprinus* species) and is indeed related to this group of toadstools. However, instead of the cap expanding to reveal the spore-bearing gills, in *Montagnea* it remains firmly closed and the spores develop inside, protected from drying out, before eventually being released as the cap breaks apart and flakes away. However, if cut open, *Montagnea* can still be seen to have toadstool-like gills. In evolutionary terms, it appears to have evolved from ordinary toadstools and is half-way to becoming a puffball.

Only three *Tulostoma* species are found in Britain, though there are many more in the Mediterranean area and in the steppes and drylands of eastern Europe. They resemble miniature puffballs on woody stalks and in Britain are most frequent in sand dunes and in dry, sandy grasslands. *Tulostoma brumale*, the commonest species, has also been found growing in the mortar of old walls, a suitably arid habitat. The rare *Tulostoma niveum*, considered to be threatened throughout its range, is a species of the arid subarctic. It was first found in Britain in 1989, in thin soil and moss on limestone boulders at Inchnadamph in Scotland.

Earthstars (*Geastrum* species) have a woody outer peridium which splits into rays and opens up to reveal a puffball-like inner peridium inside. There are 16 British species, most of them uncommon and some of them very rare. Though not so obviously xerophilic in their habitat, many still show a preference for growing in sand dunes, dry hedgebanks, and arid, often stony ground. Three species, together with the macroscopically similar but unrelated barometer earthstar (*Astraeus hygrometricus*), have hygroscopic rays. These only open up to reveal the spore-containing inner peridium when soaked with water. In dry conditions, the rays close up again for protection. The epithet '*hygrometricus*' means 'water-measuring'.

Fungi on bare, exposed wood

Other xerotolerant species develop and fruit on bare, exposed, often decorticated wood. Such wood, including trunks, branches and twigs, presents an extreme environment for fungi due to low nutrient availability, high temperature range, and aridity. Although crustose lichens are well known from such conditions, various non-lichenised fungi also occur. Many of the species involved are ascomycetes, adapted morphologically in having thick, gelatinised tissues which help to retain moisture. In this respect they also exhibit a remarkable degree of evolutionary convergence, with species from a range of unrelated genera presenting similar morphological features which have arisen in response to their environment. Sherwood (1981) reviewed the non-lichenised discomycete groups, and examined their biology, ecology and morphology. She found that taxonomically diverse species in such habitats often exhibit a range of characters not seen elsewhere. For example, all species with multiseptate, muriform, small-celled spores and a high proportion of those with filiform spores, occur in dry, weathered wood. Most also have a dark pigmented outer structure to the fruitbody or a dark layer which covers the hymenium when dry, all characteristics which help to minimise water loss.

Basidiomycetes on exposed wood show some of the same characteristics. Species of *Auricularia*, including the common jew's ear (*A. auricula-judae*), often grow on dead, exposed branches and are both highly gelatinised and capable of reviving after dry periods, to the extent that a single fruitbody can last a year or more, sporulating only when rehydrated after rain. The small agaric *Resupinatus applicatus* often grows on dead attached twigs and is also highly gelatinised. Another small toadstool, *Mycena rorida*, most frequently seen on old brambles and briars, has an unusual stem which (in wet weather) is almost hidden inside a thick, gelatinised coating. The porcelain fungus (*Oudemansiella mucida*, Fig. 82), a much larger, translucently white agaric, typically grows in clusters high up in the dead branches of old beech trees and is covered in a semi-gelatinised slime, the better to resist desiccation.

Many of the patch-forming heterobasidiomycetes and corticioid basidiomycetes growing on dead attached branches are equally gelatinised, or leathery (another way of resisting drying), or waxy, or filled with a protective layer of mineral matter. Though fruitbodies may persist all year, spores are only produced following rain. Bracket fungi too are adapted to drying out, many of them producing tough leathery fruitbodies, sometimes with a varnish-like or waxy coating (as in *Ganoderma lucidum* and *G. resinaceum*). They also protect their hymenia by producing spores in narrow pores, creating a damp microclimate away from drying winds. Many of these bracket fungi are so specialised at resisting drought that they are actually commoner on exposed trees in (for example) parks and woodland pastures, than on sheltered forest trees. Some, like the oak polypore, *Piptoporus quercinus*, are virtually restricted to this habitat in Britain.

Fungi on rocks and stones

Microfungi can colonise bare rock and stone surfaces, in natural pores and irregularities, as subsurface 'endoliths', or as components of surface biofilms. More surprisingly, they can actually cause considerable degradation of rocks, either by mechanical means (splitting apart rock particles by growth) or by chemical attack through the release of various organic and inorganic acids.

The acid-producing microfungi are mostly familiar ascomycetous moulds belonging to such genera as *Alternaria*, *Aspergillus*, *Botrytis*, and *Penicillium*. Some of these are now used commercially to produce acids (Chapter 17), so it is no surprise to find them doing the same thing when they colonise damp rock surfaces. The mechanically degrading fungi appear to be much more specialist and much more xerotolerant. They are mostly dematiaceous hyphomycetes (with dark hyphae) in genera such as *Exophiala*, *Sarcinomyces*, and *Lichenothelia*, and may be adapted to their niche. Many are slow-growing, but able to survive considerable changes in temperature and humidity. They can colonise rock surfaces in arid, semi-desert areas as well as in damper and more temperate regions, gradually causing 'biopitting' as a result of their growth (see Chapter 14 for their effects on buildings and other artefacts). Sterflinger (2000) has reviewed these rock-dwelling microfungi, providing species and reference lists.

It is claimed that these microfungi are responsible for changing the colour of the Acropolis over the last 150 years, but the most immediately visible fungi on rocks, as well as on cement and concrete structures, are the lichens. The coloured banding due to salt-tolerant marine and maritime lichens on coastal rocks (Chapter 12) provides a familiar example. The distinctive, often mottled effect of lichen thalli on gravestones is also well known, adding character to many cemeteries and, in older examples, often harbouring scarce and vanishing species. However, lichen growth may be rapid and, even on new concrete, colonisation of lichens may be well established within 4–5 years if the initial alkalinity is sufficiently neutralised by acid pollution.

Xerophilic and osmotolerant microfungi

The fungi just mentioned are not true xerophiles in the strict sense of the word, since they have merely evolved xerotolerant fruitbodies capable of resisting periods of drought. The true xerophilic fungi, mostly moulds and yeasts, are those which are capable of growing and sporulating in unusually dry situations. This includes the osmotolerant fungi which can grow on substrata with high salt or high sugar content, where the osmotic pressure is high.

Drying, salting, and sugaring are among the most ancient methods of preserving food against fungal and bacterial decay. However, all such preserved foodstuffs are susceptible to invasion by xerophilic fungi, notably species of *Eurotium* (*Ascomycota*), commonly seen in its mould-like *Aspergillus* state, species of *Penicillium*, and many ascomycetous and basidiomycetous yeasts. They include *Xeromyces bisporus* (*Ascomycota*), the most xerophilic fungus known, which can occur on sugar-saturated confectionery. Studies of the physiological adaptations of these fungi to dry conditions have been made, with particular attention paid to commercially important yeasts in the food industry, such as species of *Hansenula, Pichia*, and *Torulopsis*. Tolerance of dry conditions depends upon the ability of the fungus to modify the osmoregulatory pressure within its cells. Substances such as glycerol and polyols are accumulated or secreted, hence lowering the internal osmotic pressure below that of the external environment and preventing water loss. A general overview of these specialist fungi was provided by Dix & Webster (1995), with major aspects covered by Hocking (1993).

PSYCHROPHILIC & SNOW-MELT FUNGI

Psychrophilic fungi are species of cold environments, specially adapted not just to survive but even to thrive in low temperatures. Specifically, these fungi are able to make active growth and to produce fruitbodies below 5°C.

They are able to survive, however, at the much lower temperatures, sometimes below −40°C, which can occur in polar winters. Conversely, such cold-adapted fungi are, in general, unable to develop at temperatures above 20°C, and are usually unable to survive at all, either as mycelium or spores, after exposure for a few days to temperatures above 25°C or so. Most other fungi, in contrast, have growth optima above 15°C. A few are adapted to still higher temperature regimes, with optimal growth above 20°C and even as high as 50°C or more. These latter species are the thermophiles, found in places like compost heaps (Chapter 14).

Several psychrophilic moulds and yeasts can grow on food in cold storage, and many more find the coolness of domestic refrigerators an excellent climate for growth. Others find a more natural home in arctic and antarctic soils.

Polar fungi

Psychrophilic species have evolved in several different groups of fungi and include most of the species native to the coldest parts of the Arctic and Antarctica. The majority are yeasts and other microfungi, and are, for example, the dominant fungi in antarctic soils during spring and autumn. They include *Candida* and *Cryptococcus* yeasts and various zygomycetes, particularly in the genera *Mortierella* and *Mucor*. *Cryptococcus vishniacii* has been found in the dry valleys of Antarctica, possibly the most inhospitable place on the planet. Lichenised ascomycetes, including *Buellia*, *Lecidea*, and *Acarospora* species, are also able to survive in these dry valleys as 'cryptoendoliths', inhabiting the subsurface cavities of porous rocks. Ocean depths are more or less continually cold, typically just above freezing, and provide another habitat for psychrophiles.

Psychrotolerant fungi are able to survive extreme cold but cannot actively grow until temperatures rise above 10°C. Many of these are macrofungi, such as the bryophilous toadstool genera *Galerina* and *Omphalina* which are characteristic of subpolar vegetation dominated by grass tussocks and moss cushions. Several hundred agaric species and other macrofungi have been recorded from such cold environments, which include huge areas of the Canadian, Alaskan, and Russian tundra as well as much of Antarctica and the subantarctic islands, together with alpine and other montane regions. The maximum temperature in some of these areas rarely exceeds 10°C, even during the short summer season.

In the British Isles, a number of macrofungi typical of the arctic-alpine mycota have been found in Scotland, either in the Highlands or at lower altitude further north. An example is *Amanita nivalis*, originally described from the Cairngorms and there associated with the least willow *Salix herbacea*. Various *Omphalina, Russula, Laccaria, Inocybe,* and *Cortinarius* species may also form part of the Scottish subarctic mycota. A few species also occur in the English Lake District, including *Amanita nivalis*, the waxcap *Hygrocybe salicis-herbaceae*, and several *Omphalina* species.

Snow-melt fungi

Nivicolous or snow-melt fungi occur at the edge of snow banks and fruit when the melt is underway. They are surprisingly diverse and probably include representatives from most groups of fungi. Many alpine and arctic species develop under snow banks and much of the decomposition of plant litter and nutrient recycling in such places takes place under snow cover.

Snow-melt myxomycetes were not thought to occur in Britain, but Ing (1998), searching for them in the Scottish Highlands, duly found several specialist species otherwise known only from the Alps and other areas of more permanent snow. In late spring and early summer, especially where patches of snow remain which have been present for at least three months, a characteristic association occurs of myxomycetes which are rare or absent from other habitats. These are able to develop on plant litter from the previous year, protected from freezing by an insulating blanket of snow. The fruitbodies can be found within a metre or so of the edge of the melting snow, mostly from late March to early June. Several species are involved, around 16 being recorded from Britain to date. Most records are from Scotland, but a few have also been found in the English Lake District. Of the species involved, the commonest is *Diderma niveum*, frequent on a range of rotting vegetation between 700 and 1200 m, but others such as *Physarum vernum*, a widespread and conspicuous species, and *Diderma alpinum*, may be locally common.

Several of the larger discomycetes are also associated with snow-melt. These include species of *Peziza*, notably *P. ninguis* and *P. flos-nivium*, which were described from the French Alps. The former was recorded from the Isle of Skye in 1989, and has since been found in Cambridgeshire, though in both cases without specific association with melting snow. These alpine fungi, as well as further discomycetes, myxomycetes, and some agarics, were studied by Heim (1947). He attempted to distinguish between obligate and facultative nivicoles, the latter being able to develop under snow but having a much wider ecological range.

Amongst other cold-tolerant ascomycetes are species of *Thelebolus*. This is a genus of coprophilous fungi with tiny fruitbodies which appear in early winter or spring, and are known from the Antarctic. Their development was studied by Wicklow & Malloch (1971) who found that, although optimal growth was between 15–20°C for those investigated, all possessed the ability to develop fruitbodies at low temperatures. In addition, they had the ability to do so in the absence of light, suggesting their possible development under snow. The psychrophilic genus *Antarctomyces*, based on a single species, *A. psychrotrophicus*, has been isolated from Antarctic soil where the average annual temperature is –1.5°C. This species has rudimentary fruitbodies that merely comprise a cluster of asci and has been shown by molecular study to be closely related to *Thelebolus*.

In America, Cooke (1955) reported a range of fungi associated with snow banks in montane localities in the western USA. These included many agarics, such as species of *Lyophyllum*, *Tricholoma*, *Mycena*, and *Hygrophorus*, as well as species of the discomycete genus *Plectania*, all of which were found consistently in close proximity to the melting snow bank, either fruiting through the snow or developing beneath it. In the Swiss alps, Senn-Irlet (1988) found 88 species of larger fungi in snow-bed communities, including *Psilocybe chionophila* and *Galerina chionophila*, known only from such habitats. They also included 36 species mycorrhizal with dwarf shrubs, mainly *Salix* and *Dryas* species, a surprising diversity given that the vegetation period in such conditions lasts no longer than three months, even in favourable years.

Several plant pathogens are also adapted to these conditions, particularly those affecting cereals and turf grasses. Perhaps the best known is the disease commonly called 'pink snow mould' or 'Fusarium patch'. This is caused by the mould *Microdochium nivale*, or other cold-tolerant species such as *Fusarium avenaceum* and *F. equiseti*. These can grow under snow and form discoloured patches in turf which may be covered with white or pinkish mycelium and fruitbodies of the fungus. The disease can also occur in water-soaked areas in cool, wet weather. Other 'snow mould' diseases are caused by the clavarioid fungus *Typhula incarnata* and the discomycete *Myriosclerotinia borealis*, both psychrotolerant species which can develop under snow. The former occurs in Britain and can cause problems on crops such as winter barley. These and other such diseases have been treated in detail by Couch (1995).

ACIDOPHILIC AND ALKALOPHILIC FUNGI

Organisms able to grow above pH 8.5 are alkalophilic, whilst those able to grow at less than pH 4 are acidophilic. A number of fungi, particularly among the moulds and yeasts, are able to tolerate or even thrive in such extreme environments (Magan, 1997).

Highly alkaline conditions occur in volcanic areas (such as soda lakes), as well as some desert areas, and (more oddly) bird nests. Some of the *Chrysosporium* species found in nests can tolerate levels up to pH 11, whilst a range of moulds including *Botrytis*, *Cladosporium*, *Fusarium*, *Penicillium*, and *Paecilomyces* species, can grow at around pH 9.

Highly acidic conditions can also occur in volcanic areas (such as sulphur springs), as well as coal and copper mine spoil heaps, where specialised fungi may have a role to play in bioremediation (Chapter 17). Several moulds, including species of *Aspergillus*, *Eurotium*, *Fusarium*, and *Penicillium*, can grow at pH 2, and some yeasts can grow at even lower levels. These include brewer's yeast, *Saccharomyces cerevisiae*, and others which may have uses in industrial chemical processes.

FUNGI IN MINES AND CAVES

Fungi in mines and caves caused some puzzlement to early mycologists. Firstly, there were a few genuinely exotic species, presumably imported with foreign pit props, which were able to flourish in the comparatively mild, unchanging climate underground. As long ago as 1793, Baron von Humboldt described just such a subtropical species, the polypore *Flaviporus brownei*, from mines in Silesia (it has since been recorded in mines and tunnels in Britain). Secondly, many of the fungi found below ground were of bizarre appearance, elongated like stalactites or branched like stags' horns. Examination subsequently showed that these were abnormal fruitings of ordinary wood-rotting fungi growing in total darkness. One of the earliest reports of abnormal fruitbodies was by Martyn in 1744 who described a stag's horn growth of *Polyporus squamosus* found in a cellar in the Haymarket in London. Many other strange and abnormal forms were included amongst the no less than 75 species described from caves in Italy by Scopoli in 1772. Some of the unusual growth forms exhibited by agarics and bracket fungi, such as *Lentinus lepideus* or the polypore *Heterobasidion annosum*, include elongation of stipes, undersized caps, and loss of certain pigment (Fig. 129). In mines, the familiar many-zoned polypore, *Trametes versicolor*, produces fruitbodies which are normally shaped, but white and entirely unzoned.

Though most fungi have no need of light for growth, many are

FIG 129. The strange, stagshorn-like growth of *Lentinus lepideus* developed in the dark on timber in a mine (RBG Kew).

stimulated to produce fruiting bodies by light, even if artificial and of brief duration. Dry rot, *Serpula lacrymans*, is one such example. In the absence of light, some fungi will not produce fruitbodies at all or will produce fruitbodies of varying abnormality. Occasionally, for example, the common polypore *Laetiporus sulphureus* may develop sterile, stag's horn growths in dark conditions in woodlands. However, not all fungi develop abnormally in such conditions; fruitbodies of *Melanotus hartii*, described from spruce timbers in a gold-mine in Ontario, growing in darkness at depths of over 1600m, were not dissimilar to those obtained in culture.

Pilát (1927) provided an account of several species of larger fungi from mines in Příbram in the Czech Republic, most of which are now well-documented and known to be widespread. One of the commonest in Britain, to the extent that it was popularly known as 'the mine fungus', is the polypore *Antrodia vaillantii*, a pit-prop rotter occasionally also found in houses. Nowadays, the few remaining working mines in Britain use steel or other non-wooden props.

Many microfungi have also been recorded from mines, some developing on wood or debris, others obtained by isolation from soil or air. Fassatiova (1970) isolated 90 species of microfungi from the mines in Příbram. These involved 25 genera, although species of *Aspergillus* and *Penicillium* were most frequent. Many were ubiquitous airborne fungi, present in the mines only as spores. Elsewhere, however, some microfungi have been responsible for serious health problems in mine workers. Sporotrichosis, a lesion-forming disease caused by the anamorphic ascomycete *Sporothrix schenckii*, is a notable example. Back in the 1940s it reached epidemic proportions among workers in South African gold mines, probably as a result of growth on untreated timber in conditions of heat and high humidity.

Fungi in natural caverns

Caves are similar to mines in many respects, but with no wooden pit props or other obvious substrata for fungal development. Mycologically, they are best known as suitable locations for growing mushrooms (Chapter 17), but in fact fungi are surprisingly numerous in this environment. Although cave fungi have received little extensive research, some important studies were published last century by Lagarde (1913, 1917, 1922) on fungi from cave systems in France, Spain and Algeria. Lagarde reported around 120 species, and although some were well-known fungi such as *Stereum hirsutum* and *Peziza micropus*, presumably from debris in the caves, nine were described as new to science, and 25 other potentially unknown species were referred to genus only. Fungi in general are considered an important component of typical cave biota, functioning as decomposers of organic substances (including dung), and supplying nutrients to other cave organisms where there is no primary production from photosynthesis. They also play a significant role as parasites on cave-dwelling invertebrates.

Most fungi recorded from caves are known elsewhere and are only incidentally present. The agaric *Psathyrella corrugis*, for example, was reported fruiting in complete darkness in a cave in Italy. However, there are a few fungal species that have so far been recorded exclusively from caves. These include the specialist ascomycete *Laboulbenia lecoareri*, a microscopic species on the integument of the cave beetle *Trechus micros*, widely distributed in northern Europe and known in Britain from Oxfordshire. The trichomycete *Parataeniella scotonisci* is known only from the hindgut of cave-dwelling isopods in the Pyrenees. More peculiarly, a microscopic ascomycete, *Microascus caviariformis*, has been described from rotting flesh in a cave in Belgium. This species is so far known only from a single location, the Cave of Ramioul near Liège, where it is evidently common on proteinaceous substrates. It was first discovered covering a discarded piece of cooked chicken, its tiny, densely crowded fruitbodies resembling caviar. It has since been found to be common in the cave system, developing regularly on such substrates within 3–4 weeks. It has also been shown to grow well at temperatures as low as 10°C. Although there is no indication that the species is especially adapted to caves (it also develops well, for example, at temperatures up to 25°C), it has been suggested that it may be associated with cave animals. Another ascomycete, 'Lachnea spelaea', was described (albeit invalidly) from cave systems near Trento in Italy. This fungus, a discomycete with tiny, whitish, hairy fruitbodies c. 0.75 mm across, grew in complete darkness on the cave floor apparently in association with bat droppings. It appears to have had no modern revision, but from the published description it seems likely to be a species of *Trichophaea* (*Pezizales*), not obviously matching any currently known.

Microfungi are also present in cave systems, as clearly evident from the work of Lagarde noted above, although little recent research has been published. However, in the Carlsbad Caverns in New Mexico a surprising total of 92 species of microfungi representing 13 genera has been recorded. These fungi were found within the caves at depths of up to 466 m, where darkness is total and there is an extremely low organic input into the system. It was suggested that they might be associated with organic matter produced from chemolithotrophic bacteria which utilise iron, manganese and sulphur in the limestone baserock of the cave. Entomogenous fungi were investigated by Samson *et al.* (1984) from cave systems in the Netherlands. These included the ubiquitous species *Beauveria bassiana* and *Paecilomyces farinosus*, but also two species, *Hirsutella guignardii* and *Stilbella kervillei*, known only from cave insects. The last occurs only in association with the *Hirsutella* and is parasitic upon it. Both fungi have adapted to development in cool, humid conditions and the complete absence of light.

Fungi and stalactites

A remarkable group of cave fungi occur in drops of water at the growing tips of stalactites, possibly influencing their growth form. One species, the anamorphic ascomycete *Cephalosporium lamellaecola*, has been regularly isolated from terminal drops of stalactites in Nevada, the hyphae also occurring sparingly in the surface layer of the stalactite. These hyphae are considered to act as crystallisation nuclei helping to bind crystals and effectively control the orderly growth of the stalactite. The fungus was found to be present in all actively growing stalactites in the cave system under study, to the exclusion of all other microorganisms. Nevertheless, it is not universally present in cave systems, although some other fungi may be. The anamorphic ascomycete *Scolecobasidium anellii*, for example, has been isolated from stalactites in Italy.

Deep subsurface fungi

Since the 1980s, considerable research has been undertaken into organisms living deep below ground, in rocks, subsurface sediments, and groundwater. These unpromising depths team with life, but mostly of a simple, single-celled, bacterial kind. Some few fungi, nonetheless, have made their chthonic homes in the earth's dark places, over 100 (unspecified) taxa having been isolated from core samples up to 2.8 km below ground (Fredrickson & Onstott, 1996).

FUNGI IN ANIMAL BURROWS

Animal burrows are a further example of specialised underground habitats, and again have some interesting fungal associates. For example, no less than five taxa of *Penicillium* have been described from underground seed caches and cheek pouches of the banner-tailed kangaroo rat (*Dipodomys spectabilis*) in desert regions of North America (Frisvad *et al.*, 1987). Four of these are known only from the rodent burrows, and are now recognised as distinct species. In Britain, the corticioid basidiomycete *Trechispora clanculare* was described as new to science from puffin burrows on the Welsh island of Skokholm, but has since proved to be more widespread and less particular about its habitat.

The large agaric *Hebeloma radicosum* is also associated with animal tunnels, in this case the underground nests of moles and mice. The species is widely distributed throughout the northern hemisphere, and its association with moles and shrew-moles in Japan was studied by Sagara (1978) and Sagara *et al.* (1981, 1989). The fungus has been shown to be directly associated with deserted latrines of these animals, and provides a reliable method for detecting their nests. In Japan it is accordingly known as 'the mole nest finder'. *Hebeloma radicosum* has a long, rooting base which, if followed down to its origin, will be found to arise from a mass of soil and fungal mycelium. This mass unfailingly proves rich in animal excreta. The fungus has been found in Britain in association with the mole, and its association with the nests of wood mice has been subsequently reported from Switzerland. This fondness for the ammonium- and nitrate-rich soil of latrines provides an example of a specialised habitat which is shared by a number of other fungi, some of which commonly occur in the vicinity of corpses (Chapter Three).

CHAPTER 14

Man-made Habitats

AS FAR AS we know, no fungus is so recently evolved that it has become specifically adapted to man-made habitats. Even *Saccharomyces cerevisiae*, the yeast that ferments beer, finds its natural home in rotten, sugary fruits. We merely provide an additional convenient habitat where it can continue to grow naturally, albeit in the slightly alien surroundings of a brewery.

Brewers' yeast and a few other fungi are very welcome in our human world as are the microfungi that help break down compost and enrich our garden soils. Most other fungi in man-made habitats, however, are not there by invitation, but by accident, bad management, or neglect. Together with bacteria, they are the most frequent cause of biodeterioration and biodegradation in man-made products. This chapter looks at these uninvited guests in our homes and gardens, in our workplaces, transport, and artefacts, and at the way in which they survive and even prosper in novel and often unnatural surroundings.

To understand how these colonists adapt to man-made habitats, it is useful to refer back to Chapter Three and the three major ecological strategies employed by saprotrophic fungi (following Cooke & Rayner, 1984).

- 'Generalists': these include many of the household timber-rotters, though species tolerant of lower water levels and warmer indoor temperatures may out-compete our native outdoor fungi.

- Specialised 'stress-tolerant' species: adapted to very specific conditions are clearly at an advantage in habitats where these conditions are artificially maintained. An ability to withstand high levels of creosote, for example, is a winning adaptation for fungi in the human environment.
- Opportunistic 'ruderal' fungi: often capable of rapid reproduction and sporulation, are adapted to colonise temporary nutrient resources, like rotten food or damp plaster.

In man-made habitats, it is chiefly these last two classes of 'stress-tolerant' and 'ruderal' fungi which meet with the most success.

FUNGI IN THE HOME

Dry and wet rots

Fungi are the main agents of wood decay and this applies just as much in the home as in the forest. Structural timber, roof beams, floorboards, doors, wooden windowsills, skirting boards, and furniture are all food for fungi, given a chance, and it has been estimated that in the 1990s fungi caused around £400 million of damage to UK buildings every year.

Good quality, durable timber, properly treated and kept in dry condition will last almost indefinitely. But not surprisingly these ideal conditions are not always met.

To start with, different trees produce timber of differing durability under natural conditions, ranging from balsa at one extreme to teak at the other. Timber classed as 'perishable' or 'non-durable', such as ash, beech, birch, spruce, and scots pine, may be suitable for furniture or indoor use, but not for outdoor use unless specially treated. Timber classed as 'durable', such as chestnut, oak, yew, and cypress, can last for years outdoors even if untreated. Inevitably, the most durable timbers are also the most expensive, so most modern buildings compromise to keep down costs.

This is no problem as long as buildings remain dry and well-ventilated, with internal timber then having a typical moisture content of around 10–20%. But when buildings become damp, through floods, leaks, seepage, or condensation, and moisture content rises above 20%, then non-durable timbers rapidly become susceptible to fungal decay. The most notorious of these decay fungi is 'dry rot', *Serpula lacrymans*, which can rapidly turn solid timber into a cake of soft brown powder. Like most wood-rotters, the fungus belongs to the *Basidiomycetes*, specifically the *Boletales*, which includes the edible boletes or ceps. When mature, it produces large, pancake-like, brown fruitbodies with a wrinkled surface (Fig. 130A), capable of producing 3000 spores per cm^2 per day. Once established in damp timber, it may spread at a rate of around one metre per year, the fine hyphal threads often passing through masonry and other obstacles to infect any damp timber within reach. Spores, which may be so plentiful that they can be seen as a fine brown dust, can establish new colonies wherever conditions are suitable.

    Serpula lacrymans will normally only infect conifer wood (pine, spruce, and other softwoods), producing a brown (or cubic) rot (Fig. 130) which is typified by the wood losing its strength, cracking into cubes, and finally becoming soft and easily crumbled by hand (hence the name 'dry rot'). The fungus, though long known in Britain, is not native here and has not established itself in the wild. Its natural home appears to be in montane forests on the west coast of America, Central Europe, and the Himalayas in areas of low or

FIG 130. Dry rot *Serpula lacrymans* turns tough structural timber into a soft cake of cracked and easily crumbled, brown powder (RBG Kew).

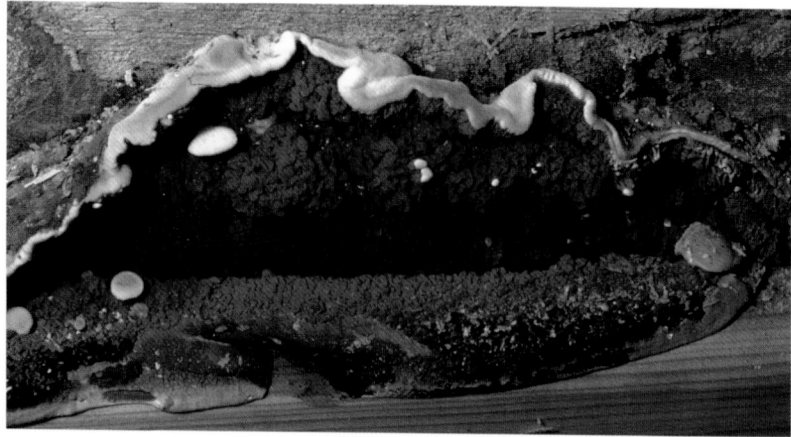

FIG 130A. The effused fruitbody of dry rot *Serpula lacrymans* can cover extensive areas. Its brown, spore-bearing surface is wrinkled and net-like (P. Livermore).

variable rainfall. Our forests may simply be too wet for *Serpula lacrymans* to grow successfully or compete against better-adapted native species. It is nonetheless prevalent in British buildings, accounting for some 15% of all reported timber decay. This figure peaked immediately after the Second World War, as a result of bomb damage and dereliction, and may gradually be decreasing. A useful collection of papers on *Serpula lacrymans*, its biology and control, has been published by Jennings & Bravery (1991).

The commonest of the so-called 'wet rots' is *Coniophora puteana*, sometimes known as the 'cellar fungus'. This is a relative of *Serpula lacrymans*, producing smooth to warty, yellowish to olive-brown, patch-like fruitbodies, and is a native British species commonly found on rotting logs in woodland. It is also a brown rot fungus, but favours wetter conditions (hence the name), typically infecting wood with moisture content above 50%. Together with other wet rots, it has accounted for some 35% of reported timber decay in UK buildings, tending to infect newer houses where structural timber has not been properly dried. It will readily attack wood of any kind.

A number of other wood-rotting fungi may occur in buildings, some causing fibrous white rots rather than cubic brown rots. Most are bracket fungi, many of which can be found in native woodlands, but they also include wood-rotting toadstools and even a false truffle, *Melanogaster ambiguus*. This species has often been found under floorboards or attached to damp timber, but causes more problems through its smell than its limited wood-rotting abilities. Aptly called the 'stinking slime truffle', one Victorian mycologist noted that the smell of "a single specimen in a room is so strong as to make it scarcely habitable" (Berkeley, 1844).

Thatched roofs, made from reeds (*Phragmites australis*) or wheat straw, are subject to decay by much the same white-rot fungi that attack structural timber, together with soft-rot ascomycetes and moulds. A study of thatched roofs in a Devon village (Kirby & Rayner, 1988) isolated 37 different fungal species from just four visible decay patches.

Some of the commonest wood-rotting fungi found in buildings are listed in Table 29 and illustrated in a useful pocket guide by Bravery *et al.* (1987). Of these, *Donkiopora expansa* and *Serpula lacrymans* do not occur outdoors in Britain, and *Asterostroma cervicolor* is known outdoors from just a few recent records. All three are presumably introductions from elsewhere.

TABLE 29. A selection of wood-rotting fungi found in buildings in Britain

Species	Fruitbody	Type of rot	Substrata (Kew specimens)
Antrodia serialis	poroid	brown	window sill
Antrodia vaillantii (mine fungus)	poroid	brown	dance floor
Asterostroma cervicolor	corticioid	white	door
Coniophora puteana (cellar fungus)	corticioid	brown	structural timber
Diplomitoporus lindbladii	poroid	white	structural timber
Donkiopora expansa	poroid	white	roof timber, floorboards
Ganoderma lucidum	poroid	white	floorboards
Gloeophyllum sepiarium	poroid	brown	house timber
Gloeophyllum trabeum	poroid	brown	window sill, door
Lentinus lepideus	agaricoid	brown	roof timber
Melanogaster ambiguus	gasteroid	white	floorboards
Phellinus contiguus	poroid	white	window sills, thatch
Pleurotus ostreatus	agaricoid	white	floorboards
Postia floriformis	poroid	brown	structural timber
Postia rennyi	poroid	brown	ceiling timber
Serpula lacrymans (dry rot)	merulioid	brown	structural timber

Moulds and mildews

Often the first sign of damp in any household is a musty smell and the discovery of mottled greenish or black patches on wallpaper or plaster. These are due to the ubiquitous moulds and 'mildews' whose minute airborne spores can settle and develop anywhere there is moisture and a minimum of sustenance. They are typical opportunistic 'ruderal' fungi, fast-growing, ephemeral, and able to metabolise any immediately available nutrient resources.

All the common moulds are imperfect (asexual) states of *Ascomycetes*, each producing millions of clone-like conidiospores capable of rapidly colonising any damp surface. Sampling estimates of airborne spores have found up to 450,000 spores per cubic metre in homes showing visible damp, far fewer (< 200) in drier buildings. It is possible that these spores can contribute to 'sick building syndrome' (the symptoms of which were listed in Gravesen *et al.*, 1994) and they can certainly trigger attacks of asthma and rhinitis in susceptible individuals (Chapter 15). Some, notably species of *Stachybotrys*, can produce toxic trichothecines particularly in conditions of high humidity and high temperature, and these may cause health problems. It has also been suggested (Van Asselt, 1999) that there may be mutualistic interactions between moulds and house-dust mites (a major cause of asthmatic attacks), each helping the other spread through an infected household.

Common moulds in the home include species of *Cladosporium*, *Stachybotrys*, *Penicillium*, *Aspergillus*, and *Alternaria* (Gravesen *et al.*, 1994, provided a list of species isolated from house dust). Their spores will germinate on any damp surface, including areas liable to condensation such as kitchen and bathroom walls. As long as there is sufficient moisture, i.e. a relative humidity above 70%, they will rapidly spread, living off dust and other surface detritus. As well as being found on damp plaster and wallpaper, moulds can also grow on manufactured organic products, not only natural ones like leather and cotton, but also man-made materials like nylon and cellophane. On plastics (shower curtains, for example) they can easily be wiped off, but on more porous materials like wallpaper or plasterwork, they can cause permanent disfigurement. Moulds and mildews cause no deep-seated or structural damage, but their presence always indicates some local area of dampness.

Even where dampness is generally absent in the home, moulds are familiar on spoiled food. Some are ubiquitous airborne species, others such as *Penicillium italicum* (blue rot) and *P. digitatum* (green rot) on citrus fruits or *P. expansum* (blue rot) on apples, are likely to have entered the home with the produce. Most of these moulds are harmless; we even deliberately eat some specialist moulds, such as *Penicillium camembertii* and *P. roquefortii* in cheese. But a few produce mycotoxins which can cause problems, though more usually in large scale food storage than in the home (see Chapter 15 and 'Fungi in Food' below).

The characteristic mouldy smells are produced by a number of 'microbial volatiles' (alcohols, ketones, esters, and hydrocarbons) released during growth. *Penicillium commune*, for example, gives off 2-methyl-isoborneol, an unpleasant musty odour, and other species also have their characteristic smells.

Foxing old books

Moulds are not always obvious. Old books are often disfigured by rust-coloured spots known as 'foxing'. These are mostly seen on machine-made paper from the 18th and 19th centuries and their cause has long been unclear. It is now known, however, that ordinary moulds are responsible for most if not all foxing. The presence of fungal hyphae in foxed areas was established by electron microscopy in the late 1970s, and molecular analysis of DNA obtained from such areas in early American books subsequently identified the hyphae as belonging to species of *Aspergillus*. No equivalent DNA was obtained from clean areas. It seems probable that metabolites produced by the fungi slowly interact with the paper to cause the rusty or fox-brown colour of the spots, although the detailed chemistry for this reaction is not fully elucidated (Florian, 1997, provided a detailed discussion of the problem).

Ruining the paintwork

Disfiguration of indoor and outdoor painted surfaces by darkening and spotting is another well known phenomenon caused mainly by moulds. Two common plurivorous fungi, *Cladosporium herbarum* and *Aureobasidium pullulans*, are the usual culprits on outside paintwork. Diffusion of pigment from the mycelium into the paint can additionally cause dark, reddish-violet marks several centimetres across, particularly on white lead paintwork formerly used in glasshouses. These marks are mainly made by *Phoma violacea*, although other, related species such as *Phoma glomerata* have also been implicated. Allsopp & Seal (1986) listed over a dozen fungal species isolated from paintwork.

Artistic paintwork, particularly frescoes, is also subject to attack and degradation whenever conditions become sufficiently damp. Once again the culprits are principally moulds, including species of *Alternaria, Aspergillus, Chaetomium, Cladosporium*, and *Penicillium*. Investigation of a single Italian fresco (in St Damian's monastery, Assisi) yielded 33 different fungal species, whilst investigation of a Florence church suggested a nice fungal differentiation between frescoes painted by Botticelli (primarily colonised by *Penicillium* species) and frescoes painted by Ghirlandaio (primarily colonised by *Aspergillus versicolor*). Ciferri (1999) has reviewed the subject of artwork degradation and provided a substantial bibliography.

Eating away the stonework

Most weathering of exterior surfaces takes place through physical and chemical damage, but there is also an important biological factor which can lead to the erosion and fragmentation of exposed surfaces. This degradation is caused by mechanical breakdown resulting from the actions of algae, bacteria, fungi, and their metabolic products. Given sufficient moisture, algae and blue-green bacteria may establish an organic 'biofilm' on surfaces which can then be colonised by microfungi.

Weathered stone surfaces that have become porous are able to support a wide range of moulds and other microfungi, including species of *Trichoderma, Acremonium, Aspergillus, Cephalosporium, Penicillium*, and *Mucor*, some of which produce organic acids, especially citric and oxalic acid, that decompose natural silicates. Non-porous surfaces can also suffer mechanical breakdown or 'biopitting' through the growth of microcolonies of dematiaceous fungi (ascomycete anamorphs with dark hyphae). A study of marble monuments from the Sanctuary of Delos in Greece (Sterflinger & Krumbein, 1997) showed considerable damage, with pits up to 20 mm wide and 15 mm deep caused by species of *Monodictys*,

Lichenothelia, *Sarcinomyces*, and others. Gaylarde & Morton (1999) have published a list of genera and research references for microfungi found on concrete and stone.

Crustose lichenised fungi are also common on buildings and may similarly cause etching and breakdown of surfaces by chemical decomposition and also by mechanical action (resulting from shrinkage and expansion in dry and wet weather). However, their ability to break down surfaces varies and, as shown in a study of sandstone weathering by Williams & Rudolph (1974), lichens may be less significant in degrading stone than non-lichenised fungi. Indeed, there is evidence that a number of lichens can actually help protect some types of stone by providing a shield against rainwater erosion (Mottershead & Lucas, 2000; Hawksworth, 2001b).

Etching glass

Perhaps surprisingly, fungi can even cause problems with glass when conditions are suitably humid. A number of xerophilic moulds, particularly *Aspergillus* species, can colonise such unpromising surfaces if there is sufficient moisture available, living off organic residues in superficial dust, fingerprints, and other contaminants. . If not cleaned away swiftly, the organic acids produced by the fungi can etch the glass surface. This is quite a common and expensive problem in camera lenses and field glasses, especially if packed away whilst still damp. In the humid tropics, it is a more or less constant problem.

Lichenised species can be a problem on old stained-glass windows, which are often difficult to access and therefore left uncleaned. Richardson (1975) listed over 15 species growing on this substratum, causing pitting and other damage

Opportunists and unexpected visitors

In addition to moulds, other much larger fungi may occasionally be found in the home. One of the most frequent is *Peziza cerea*, a cup fungus in the order *Pezizales*. It produces brittle, fleshy, cream or pale yellowish, cup-shaped or irregular fruitbodies which grow to several centimetres across and tend to occur gregariously (Fig. 131). One of its favourite habitats seems to be toilets, where a leaking cistern can cause extensive, sometimes spectacular, growths

FIG 131. The cup fungus *Peziza cerea* is a pale species common on old brickwork, plaster, and even damp carpets (B. Spooner).

FIG 132. The tropical canary-yellow toadstool *Leucocoprinus birnbaumii* has become quite frequent in Europe in greenhouses and plant pots (M. Love).

on sodden carpet, wood, or plaster. Apart from indicating extreme damp, they do little active harm.

Toadstools, especially *Coprinus* species ('ink-caps'), can sometimes occur in the same habitats or on sodden woodwork, but in most homes toadstools are more likely to be seen in potted plants. One species in particular has become widespread in this habitat: *Leucocoprinus birnbaumii*, a delicate and attractive canary yellow toadstool, which is an exotic from the tropics and subtropics (Fig. 132). It is presumably spreading into private houses from the suppliers of plants or potting compost, since it is not found in the wild in Britain.

FUNGI IN THE GARDEN

Perhaps the most noticeable fungi found in gardens are the plant parasites, against which is waged a constant battle. They include the rusts, smuts, and powdery mildews (Chapter Six) as well as many others for which Buczacki & Harris (1998) gave a thorough, illustrated coverage aimed at gardeners, and the New Naturalist volume by Ingram & Robertson (1999) provided a general review.

Other garden fungi include those typical of lawns, those found in woodchip mulch (an increasingly common substratum), greenhouse and garden exotics, and the beneficial microfungi which maintain healthy working soils and compost heaps. In addition, there are some specialist fungi associated with exotic trees and garden shrubs.

Honey fungus: the gardener's curse

Armillaria mellea and related toadstools, commonly called 'honey fungus', are highly evolved and often virulent parasites able to infect an almost limitless range of garden plants and timber trees. At least five species occur in Britain (Pegler, 1999, provided a key), two of which, *A. mellea* itself and *A. ostoyae*, are strongly pathogenic.

Honey fungus is able to spread through the soil by means of 'rhizomorphs', bootlace-like structures which are black at maturity and have a white core. These may grow to a length of 3 m or more, and are able to penetrate the roots of trees and other plants. The fruitbodies are large, conspicuous toadstools, recognised by their scaly, yellow-brown caps 5–12 cm across, slightly decurrent gills, woolly ring on the stems (absent in one species), and their tufted habit (Fig. 133). All honey fungus species can also grow as saprotrophs on decaying logs and stumps, and may be found in large numbers in woodlands.

Once established in gardens, honey fungus can ravage ornamental trees and shrubs, even attacking iris, potato, and other tuberous plants. Though some cultivars are more resistant to attack than others, there is at present no fully effective fungicidal control. The advice suggested in Fox (1999) is to move house.

FIG 133. Honey fungus *Armillaria mellea* is a common problem in gardens being a root parasite able to attack a wide variety of woody and some herbaceous plants (B. Spooner).

Compost heaps

Far less noticeable than pests and diseases, but far more beneficial, are the many garden fungi which form part of the natural cycle of decay and renewal. This cycle is most conspicuously at work in the compost heap where plant and other organic waste is gradually broken down into a nutrient-rich soil.

The fungi active in this process are capable of decomposing cellulose, hemicellulose, lignin, and other plant materials. In compost heaps, where internal temperatures can reach 50–60°C, they are also capable of growing at temperatures which ordinary soil fungi cannot survive. These compost thermophiles and heat-tolerant microfungi include species such as *Chaetomium thermophile*, *Talaromyces thermophilus*, *Humicola insolens*, *Thermomyces lanuginosa*, and *Aspergillus fumigatus*, which grow optimally at temperatures between 40 to 52°C. Ordinary (mesophilic) soil fungi grow optimally at temperatures between 20–23°C. Thermophilic and thermotolerant fungi are thus good examples of species utilising 'stress-tolerant' strategies enabling them to colonise substrata where more generalist fungi cannot grow. When conditions return to normal, the specialist colonisers give way to the generalists which will recolonise the remains of the compost heap. Under natural conditions, thermophilic fungi have been isolated from such substrata as leaf mold and peat, herbivore dung, and bird nests. A few may be agents of disease in warm-blooded vertebrates, including man, and a range of obligate thermophilic fungi occurs in heated soil and hot springs in regions of active vulcanism (Emerson, 1968).

More conspicuous heat-loving fungi include a number of toadstools typical of compost heaps. One of the ink-caps, *Coprinus cinereus*, frequently produces clumps of fruitbodies at the surface of large heaps, as do several other *Coprinus* and *Psathyrella* species. Less common are *Leucocoprinus cepistipes* and other white-spored *Lepiota*-like species, some of which may be exotics introduced into Britain and only surviving in greenhouses or outdoor sites where composting is both regular and extensive.

Fungi and soil health

Equally beneficial are the microfungi of soils, individually inconspicuous but accounting for as much as 70–80% by weight of the soil microbial biomass. Though often taken for granted, they are an essential component of the health and fertility of garden and agricultural soils.

Typical components of the soil mycota are saprotrophic microfungi living on decaying vegetable matter and vesicular-arbuscular (VA) mycorrhizal fungi associated with the living roots of various flowers, crops, and weeds. Both these groups contribute substantially to the aggregate structure of soil and to the distribution of accessible nutrients within the soil. In effect, without fungi, soils would be little more than dust, sand, or solid clay.

Fungi in lawns

The fungi in lawns are essentially grassland species (Chapter Eight) and, as such, reflect the age and quality of the lawns in which they occur. Lawns that have been re-seeded, doused in fungicides, moss-killers, and 'improving' chemicals are almost as dull and lifeless as artificial turf, whereas traditional British lawns that are simply mown and cared for become richer and more interesting as the years go by. Unfortunately, such traditional lawns are becoming an increasingly endangered habitat.

As with unimproved grasslands, the indicator species for fine old lawns are waxcaps (*Hygrocybe* species), mostly brightly coloured toadstools which occur in late autumn when mowing has finished. Some of them, such as the pink waxcap, *Hygrocybe calyptriformis*, are rare and endangered throughout Europe, but have a stronghold in Britain, particularly in old lawns since they prefer short, mown or grazed turf. Waxcaps colonise new (untreated) lawns slowly, the commonest species, like the white *Hygrocybe nivea*, appearing after 10–20 years, the rarer species taking perhaps 40 years or more to colonise, if they do so at all. Other old-lawn species include the 'earth tongues' (*Geoglossaceae*) and the often brightly coloured 'fairy clubs' (*Clavariaceae*).

New and nitrogen-rich lawns will, however, support some macrofungi, including those which are normally associated with dunged grass. Commonest by far is the ubiquitous little brown toadstool, *Panaeolina foenisecii*, the main culprit in poisoning enquiries in Britain. It seems to be a favourite target of toddlers exploring back gardens and local parks in summer time, but is normally harmless in small quantities.

Greenkeepers and others seeking billiard-table lawns are plagued with many fungal problems. Fairy rings are a particular bugbear, caused by a variety of macrofungi, notably the fairy ring champignon *Marasmius oreades*, but there are plenty of other species causing spots, patches, blotches, and blights in turf (Chapter Eight).

Mulched flowerbeds

Bark or woodchip mulch provides a further distinct habitat for fungi, most notably for a range of agaric species not or rarely found elsewhere. The mulch may be imported or made on site and typically contains wood-chippings and other left-overs from forestry and similar work. It protects the soil from drying out by providing a barrier between soil and air, whilst at the same time blocking out weeds and rotting down to provide a gradual source of compost and fibre.

Old woodchip mulch is an ideal substratum for a number of late-stage wood-rotting and compost fungi, such as bird's-nest fungi (*Cyathus* and *Crucibulum* species), and various toadstools including *Tubaria*, *Psathyrella*, *Coprinus*, and *Psilocybe* species. In addition, it has attracted a number of exotic fungi, some of which have now become common in municipal flower beds and urban roadside plantings. The orange-capped toadstool, *Stropharia aurantiaca*, is a conspicuous example (Fig. 134). Possibly a native of Australia and almost certainly misnamed, it has spread extensively in Britain through mulch beds. *Psilocybe cyanescens*, a brownish toadstool with bluish-green tints, is a fellow-traveller. It was described from Kew Gardens in 1946, but has become much more widespread in recent years and has now been reported from woodlands as well as flower beds. *Stropharia percevalii* and *Agrocybe putaminum* are more recent examples, both possibly American, and both apparently spreading in mulch from the south-east since the 1980s. *Panaeolus atrobalteatus*, described as new to science from mulched flowerbeds in Buckingham Palace, is another recent exotic arrival, its original habitat and home as yet entirely unknown. Even more recently, *Melanoleuca verrucipes* has become established in parts of the south-east as has the exotic maroon and

FIG 134. The orange-capped toadstool *Stropharia aurantiaca* is a recent introduction to the British Isles, but has spread rapidly and is now commonplace in mulched flowerbeds (P. Roberts).

FIG 135. The purple, scaly, clustered fruitbodies of *Gymnopilus dilepis*, only recently recorded in Britain, occur on rotting piles of wood-chips and are becoming increasingly frequent (M. Adler).

yellow *Gymnopilus dilepis* (Fig. 135). In all, over 150 species of larger fungi have now been recorded from woodchip mulch in Britain.

Garden and greenhouse exotics

Some other interesting and unusual exotics have also established themselves in British gardens and parks, possibly arriving with plants brought in from overseas.

Chief amongst these, in terms of visual impact, are some of the strange clathroid and phalloid species from Australia, New Zealand, and the southern temperate zone. One of the commonest is *Clathrus archeri*, sometimes called 'devil's fingers' or 'octopus fungus'. Originally described from Tasmania, the fruitbodies of this bizarre fungus have 4–8 pinkish-red, tentacle-like 'arms' covered in a greenish-brown, foul-smelling slime. The slime contains the spores which are distributed by flies attracted by the carrion smell, as happens in our native British stinkhorns. *Clathrus archeri* was first reported from Britain in a Cornish garden in the 1940s, and has since spread into gardens and parks throughout southern England. At the Royal Botanic Gardens, Kew, it regularly produces hundreds of fruitbodies in beds of bamboo. A second, rarer, clathroid species is *Ileodictyon cibarium*, sometimes known as the 'basket fungus' because of its cage-like structure. This is common in New Zealand, but is only known in Europe from a very few gardens in the south-east of England where it has been established since the 1950s. Even rarer is *Aseroë rubra*, a spectacular Australasian fungus looking like *Clathrus archeri* but larger and stalked (Fig. 136). This species was seen once in a greenhouse in Kew in the nineteenth century, but was not found again till a colony appeared in a Surrey woodland in the 1990s. Why and how remains a puzzle.

The origin of *Amanita inopinata* (the epithet means 'unexpected') is even more of a mystery. First discovered in south-east England and described as new to science from these collections, it has now fruited in gardens, churchyards, and parkland in several counties from Kent to Berkshire. With dark brown cap and stem, it is an unusual and distinctive species which has clearly been introduced from somewhere outside of Europe (Fig. 137). But to date, no one has discovered its true home.

Ectomycorrhizal species forming host-specific partnerships with

FIG 136. The extraordinary, tentacled fruitbody of *Aseroë rubra*, a distant Australasian relative of the stinkhorns, naturalised in an English woodland, its only known site in the northern hemisphere (B. Spooner).

non-European exotic trees are easier to trace, though fewer in number. This is partly because only a minority of introduced garden trees are ectomycorrhizal, and partly because many native fungi are non-host-specific and capable of forming ectomycorrhiza with new partners. *Nothofagus* (southern beech) has been widely planted in Britain. It has its own ectomycorrhizal associates in South America and New Zealand, but none have yet been reported from British trees, either in gardens or plantations. However, a rust *Mikronegeria fagi* has been found on *Nothofagus* in Britain, being first discovered at Westonbirt Arboretum in 1976. *Eucalyptus*, also extensively planted in gardens, has a wide range of associated ectomycorrhizal fungi in its native Australia, but only three of these have so far been found in the UK. *Laccaria fraterna*, a small reddish-brown agaric similar to our native *Laccaria laccata*, has been reported in several places from Devon to Scotland. A close relative, the false truffle, *Hydnangium*

FIG 137. *Amanita inopinata* is a large and distinctive toadstool, described from England in 1987 but probably originating elsewhere (RBG Kew).

carneum, has been known in Britain since 1875 and is perhaps the most frequent eucalypt associate over here. Another false truffle, *Hymenangium album*, first found in Glasgow Botanic Garden in 1830, and subsequently described as new from a collection in Edinburgh in 1880, has now reappeared under a *Eucalyptus* in Kew Gardens, its first English sighting. Fungi with long-established exotic trees (including chestnut, sycamore, larch, and spruce) are covered in more detail in Chapter Nine.

Other fungi of exotic trees and shrubs

A wide range of exotic trees, including conifers as well as broad-leaved species, can be found in gardens, public parks, and churchyards. These are mostly ornamental plantings, but some, such as *Laurus nobilis*, the bay tree, are grown for their culinary value. In general, they have few specific fungal associates in Britain, either amongst the mycorrhizals as noted above, or amongst the parasites and saprotrophs. Nevertheless, there is still considerable mycological interest in some of these trees, as can be shown by a couple of examples.

Cedars are native to parts of Mediterranean, eastern Europe, and Asia where a surprising number of associated fungi have been recorded, albeit few of them obligate. A few of these fungi occur in Britain, the most well-known being the cup-fungus *Geopora sumneriana*. The fruitbodies develop below ground as closed, hollow spheres, breaking the surface at maturity, splitting at the top and expanding to reveal the cream-coloured, deeply concave fertile surface. It is a spring fungus, not uncommon under mature cedars in March and April. Some species well known from native conifers may also occur with *Cedrus*, and over 40 species of cedar-associated fungi have been received at the Royal Botanic Gardens, Kew since 1995.

The bay tree, *Laurus nobilis*, is commonly grown in gardens, mainly for its aromatic leaves. Although bay is not ectomycorrhizal and has comparatively few fungal parasites or lignicolous saprotrophs, the decaying leaf litter is a surprisingly good substratum for microfungi. Studies by Kirk (1981, 1982, 1983, 1984) have shown bay litter to be richer in microfungi than any other known tree in Britain, despite its non-native status. To date, no less than 173 species have been recorded from its leaf litter, including 13 species new to science.

FUNGI IN STORED FOOD

Worldwide, it has been estimated that 5–10% of all food production is lost to fungal spoilage after harvest, a phenomenal waste of resources.

In grain and other food plants, natural rots and decay fungi are active as soon as the crop is harvested. Human intervention is likely to exacerbate such rots by bruising and rough handling, and by intensive storage where temperature, humidity, and proximity can rapidly spread a rot from damaged crops to sound crops.

Many different fungi (involving at least 50 different genera) are involved in such post-harvest rots. The blue to greenish moulds of *Penicillium* species are ubiquitous on rotten foodstuffs, but others are more specific. Tomatoes, for example, are prey to black rots caused by *Alternaria alternata* (blackish depression in skin together with internal blackening) and to watery rots caused by *Rhizopus* species (swelling, followed by collapse and a greyish mould). Leaf vegetables are most susceptible to *Botrytis cinerea*, the same grey mould that occurs in gardens, which will rapidly destroy cabbage, lettuce, broccoli, celery, and other commonplace foodstuffs. Bananas tend to get stem and crown rots which then spread into the fruits. *Colletotrichum musae* ('musa' means 'banana'), *Gleosporium musarum*, and *Fusarium semitectum* are among the commonest and most damaging of these host-specific banana fungi. Peaches, plums, and cherries are prey to *Rhizopus stolonifer* and *R. oryzae*, both of which are so typical of bruising and handling that they are known as 'transit rots'. Apples can develop 'white bloom' after picking caused by development of yeasts (*Tilletiopsis* spp) on the surface, whilst other yeasts (*Cryptococcus*, *Metschnikowia*, *Rhodotorula*, and *Sporobolomyces* spp) can cause 'russetting'.

All these rots of fresh produce result from high water content, which is why drying is the ancient and traditional method of storing and preserving food. Some stress-tolerant fungi, however, are xerophilic (capable of growing in dry conditions – Chapter 13) and can cause problems in foodstuffs where the relative humidity is far too low to support ordinary rots and moulds. In stored grain, the most common causes of spoilage are *Eurotium* species, ascomycetous fungi capable of growing in extremely dry conditions.

Beans, nuts, and other dried produce may also be spoiled by these fungi.

Foods preserved with sugars are susceptible to a number of xerophilic yeasts capable of growing in conditions of low water activity. *Xeromyces bisporus* and *Zygosaccharomyces rouxii* are two such yeasts which can cause problems in jams, fruit juices, cakes, and confectionery, usually entering somewhere in the processing stage. Infection of filled chocolates, for example, can produce enough growth and gas to split the chocolate casings. Salt preservation and acid preservation (e.g. pickles in brine or vinegar) similarly attract a range of specialised spoilage fungi, capable of surviving and replicating under abnormal conditions.

Psychrotolerant microfungi (those that can cope with low temperatures – Chapter 13) are important as contaminants of frozen foods. It has been known for well over a century that certain opportunistic moulds, including species of *Aspergillus*, *Penicillium*, *Rhizopus*, and *Mucor*, can survive long periods of storage at –10°C in packed fruit and vegetables, causing rapid deterioration on thawing. Other fungi can be similarly isolated from frozen meat. Surprisingly, these include the ubiquitous mould *Cladosporium herbarum*, which is able to grow on and damage meat at temperatures as low as –6°C. Many other moulds, notably species of *Penicillium* and *Fusarium*, as well as yeasts, develop optimally at temperatures of around 5°C. This is the temperature typically found in domestic refrigerators, home to many moulds on long-forgotten foods. Such cold-tolerant fungi are therefore a potential health hazard, as well as being of considerable commercial importance as the cause of biodeterioration in stored products.

A full review of food spoilage fungi was provided by Pitt & Hocking (1997), whilst a comprehensive, well-illustrated guide to post-harvest diseases of fruits and vegetables can be found in Snowdon (1991).

HONEYDEW, DISTILLERIES, AND WINE CELLARS

The dense, dark growth of fungi on the leaves of many street trees, and often on the surfaces of surrounding objects, is a well known phenomenon, and sometimes the cause of concern and exasperation when present, for example, on parked cars. It is due to mycelial growth of a mixture of fungi that are able to develop on 'honeydew', a carbohydrate-rich secretion from aphids which feed on sap from the trees. Some trees, especially the commonly planted urban lime, *Tilia x platyphyllos*, are particularly susceptible to aphid infestation and a major source of honeydew. This fungal growth was previously blamed on a single 'species', referred to as '*Fumago vagans*', but is now known to be composed of various fungi, commonly including *Aureobasidium pullulans* and *Cladosporium herbarum*. The latter is an abundant and ubiquitous saprobe on a huge range of decaying plant parts.

Similar dark growths of fungi, again encouraged by a carbohydrate source, are found around distilleries and in wine cellars, where they develop on walls and casks impregnated with carbohydrates from evaporating alcohol. Dark growths found outdoors around bonded warehouses in Aberdeen were examined by Watson *et al.* (1984), who identified eleven different fungal species. These fungi occurred abundantly on the walls of the warehouses, and were also present on surrounding buildings, fences, and other structures within 100m of the warehouses, especially in the direction of the prevailing wind. They also developed on street trees, sometimes causing severe disfigurement and damage. These fungi again included *Aureobasidium pullulans*, as well as common, plurivorous saprobes such as *Epicoccum nigrum* and *Cladosporium tenuissimum*.

Wine vaults, where casks are stored to mature, are also well known to be subject to infestation by fungi, although in this case only a single species, *Rhinocladiella ellisii*, is normally involved. This is sometimes called the 'cellar fungus', but should not be confused with the quite different, wood-rotting 'cellar fungus', *Coniophora puteana*. *Rhinocladiella ellisii* is again encouraged by the presence of evaporating alcohol, which provides a rich source of carbohydrates by soaking into the wood of the casks and permeating the air in the cellar. The fungus coats the casks with a thick, felty growth of mycelium which is at first yellow or pinkish, becoming olive or blackish-brown as it matures. The mycelium is often sterile, and is then frequently called *Zasmidium cellare* or *Racodium cellare*. It is capable of developing at low temperatures, around 10°C, and is also known from hillside caves used for storing wine casks in France and Spain. Another dark mould-like fungus occurs in cellars where casks of Cognac are aged. This fungus, known as

Torula compniacensis, blackens the stone walls of the cellars, again using the evaporating alcohol, the so-called 'Angel's Share', as a source of carbohydrate. *Torula compniacensis* was described well over a century ago, in 1881, but still requires taxonomic study. It seems to be a 'good' species but does not truly belong in the genus *Torula*.

FUEL-EATING FUNGI – PLANES, TRAINS, & PARAFFIN STOVES

Perhaps surprisingly, oil-based fuels like the kerosene used in jet engines provide easily assimilated hydrocarbons for a range of fungi, particularly moulds and other ascomycetous anamorphs. As many as 20 different species have been isolated from jet engine fuel (Allsopp & Seal, 1986, provided a list), the commonest being *Amorphotheca resinae*, sometimes known as the 'creosote fungus'. This species is able to metabolise kerosene as long as some water is present (as little as ten parts per million of fuel is sufficient), can survive in pure kerosene, and can withstand temperatures as low as –25°C. As such, it is a classic example of a stress-tolerant species. Once present in fuel tanks, it can form mycelial mats which can cause pitting and corrosion if attached to surfaces, or clogging and potential blockages if unattached and floating freely. Clearly this is a potentially lethal fungus in aircraft and rigorous checks are made to ensure fuel tanks are clear, especially where aircraft are grounded for long periods in humid conditions.

Dieso, the marine equivalent of kerosene used by gas-turbine naval vessels, is equally liable to degradation by fungi. Once again, the commonest species is *Amorphotheca resinae*. Large marine diesel engines circulating oil as a coolant can also have problems, since the oil never reaches the high temperatures which prevent fungus growth in the coolant systems of land vehicles. The thermophilic *Aspergillus fumigatus* is the main contaminating agent.

On land, *Amorphotheca resinae* can attack and degrade diesel stored in refineries and in the fuel tanks of trains, lorries, and cars if a little water is present. The average mechanic is unlikely to specify a fungus as the cause of a fuel blockage, so in the words of Allsopp & Seal (1986) "the results of infections are often reported as equipment malfunctions". Ordinary petrol is a poor source of easily assimilated hydrocarbons and non-diesel cars are seldom affected by fungal growth in fuel tanks.

Domestic paraffin and central heating oils are, however, subject to degradation by fungi, as are industrial oils and emulsions used as lubricants in metal-working (Allsopp & Seal, 1986, provided a list of isolated species).

SHIP-ROTTING FUNGI

Wooden ships have a long history of rotting at sea, sometimes even before they have left the docks.

In 1684 Samuel Pepys, as Secretary to the Admiralty Board, was called upon to inspect the fleet which was considered 'in danger of sinking at their very Moorings'. He blamed 'the plain Omission of the necessary and ordinary Cautions us'd for the preserving of New-built ships', noting that 'I have with my own Hands gather'd Toadstools growing in . . . them, as big as my Fists'. Rotting ships continued to plague the navy well into the nineteenth century. In 1812, the botanist and mycologist James Sowerby was called in to inspect a particularly notorious ship, the *Queen Charlotte*, which decayed before it was even commissioned. His list of over twenty fungi from the ship contained several of the wood-rotting species listed in Table 29, including dry rot. The cause throughout, as noted by Sowerby, was the use of timber which was not properly seasoned, exacerbated by poor ventilation and exposure to rainwater. Rots in sea-going wooden ships rarely if ever affect those parts of the wood below the waterline, since few damaging, wood-rot fungi are capable of growth in saturated saline conditions. Instead, the areas at risk are those above the waterline wherever there is high humidity and poor ventilation (e.g. cargo holds).

The *Queen Charlotte* affair encouraged a series of mostly unsuccessful but ambitious experiments in wood preservation, the most dramatic being the deliberate (if temporary) sinking of ships to kill off fungi. By order of the Admiralty, a 'fungus pit' was dug at Woolwich to test various methods. Initially the most successful was 'kyanisation', the soaking of wood in 'corrosive sublimate' (mercuric chloride), a process patented in 1832 by the

Irishman John H. Kyan and championed in a paper on dry rot by Faraday. For a time, kyanised timber was widely used in everything from the building of the British Museum to American railroad ties. However, the preservative which eventually proved of lasting value was an oil tar called 'creosote', introduced in the 1830s. Thanks to creosote, the last wooden warships in the British navy were protected, but within a few decades all were replaced by ironclads. Historic survivors of the wooden fleet, such as HMS Victory, have either had to be extensively repaired or scrapped. Findlay (1982) inspected HMS Implacable, a Trafalgar veteran, in 1949 and concluded it was beyond saving. The ship was ceremonially sunk off Spithead.

The same problems that afflicted naval ships continue on a smaller scale in yachts and small boats constructed of timber or plywood. Sowerby's strictures on using well-seasoned timber, avoiding dead air spaces where humidity can rise, and keeping out rain when not in use, apply equally well today.

DECAYING TELEGRAPH POLES AND RAILWAY SLEEPERS

Creosote was also put to use protecting railway sleepers, which, being exposed and in contact with the ground, were subject to severe decay. In Britain, most wooden sleepers were made from creosoted pine giving them a useful life of 25 years or more (now they are mostly made of concrete). Decay, when it happened, was frequently by the fungus *Lentinus lepideus*, a tough, toadstool-like relative of the polypores. This occurs as a comparatively uncommon conifer rot in the wild, but can tolerate levels of creosote lethal to most other wood-rotting fungi. By the exclusion of competitors, *Lentinus lepideus* effectively made railway sleepers and other outdoor, creosoted softwoods (such as telegraph poles) its major habitat in the British Isles. In the United States, decay of telegraph poles is such a problem that a manual has been issued detailing 132 decay fungi isolated from such poles (Wang & Zabel, 1990).

RADIOACTIVE FUNGI AND CHERNOBYL

A report by Zhdanova *et al.* (2000) listed 37 species of microfungi from Unit Four of the Chernobyl Nuclear Power Plant in Ukraine, destroyed by an explosion in 1986. Surfaces of walls, ceilings, and passages were sampled between 1997 and 1998 and the samples tested for fungal growth. Most of the samples produced ubiquitous moulds, such as *Alternaria alternata*, *Aspergillus niger*, *Aureobasidium pullulans*, *Botrytis cinerea*, *Cladosporium herbarum*, and *Penicillium* species, even though these fungi were subjected to constant radiation levels 100,000 times that of the natural background radiation and 10-100 times the dose which would cause severe radiation sickness in human beings.

Many of the fungi isolated at Chernobyl had dark, pigmented hyphae and spores, a fact already noted in fungi isolated from Bikini atoll after nuclear tests. This may be a factor in their survival under such hostile conditions.

MIR AND MUTANT SPACE FUNGI

As well as its many other problems, the Russian space station Mir was infested with fungi. According to a report by Novikova (2001), 126 species of microfungi from 25 genera were isolated in Mir between 1986 and 2000, including such ubiquitous moulds as *Aspergillus niger*, *A. flavus*, *A. fumigatus*, *Cladosporium herbarum*, and *Penicillium crustosum*. Some of these were growing so well that they were producing visible growth obscuring windows and damaging communications and other equipment. A number of human pathogenic microfungi were also isolated. Reports suggested that some of the Mir isolates had become more 'aggressive' than terrestrial isolates, giving the press a 'mutant space fungi' field-day when Mir was scheduled to crash-land back on earth. Clearly, these micro-organisms posed a genuine threat to the space station and its crew, and contamination remains a potential threat to any future long-term space missions.

An additional long-term threat concerns the possible survival of fungi and other micro-organisms on the external surfaces of spacecraft, posing quarantine problems on interplanetary voyages. Koike *et al.* (1992) have shown that fungi are capable of surviving such extreme conditions. They subjected the yeasts *Saccharomyces cerevisiae* and *Candida albicans*, together with spores of the mould *Aspergillus niger*, to a low-temperature (–195°C), high-vacuum environment and bombarded them with protons to simulate cosmic ray irradiation. The *Saccharomyces* did not survive such treatment, but 28% of the *Aspergillus* spores remained viable after the test equivalent of 250 years in space, whilst 7% of *Candida albicans* cells survived for the equivalent of 60 years.

FIGHTING BACK WITH FUNGICIDES

In 1882 the French botanist P.M.A. Millardet, working at the University of Bordeaux, discovered that a mixture of copper sulphate and lime prevented the growth of *Plasmopara viticola*, the grape vine mildew, and of *Phytophthora infestans*, the notorious potato blight. Called 'Bordeaux Mixture', Millardet's fungicide for the first time enabled farmers to combat many of the diseases that ravaged their crops. Although copper sulphate, as well as sulphur, had been previously used against fungi, particularly in seed treatment and for control of powdery mildew of fruit trees, this was a major discovery that helped make possible the advent of modern commercial agriculture.

Bordeaux Mixture is still in general use today as a control for a range of plant diseases, but a wide variety of additional chemicals have been developed in the intervening years. Indeed, hundreds of different fungicides are now available, often formulated for specific purposes. Some are preventatives, to protect against infection either by specific pathogens or against a broad array of fungi, others control diseases after infection. Many are applied externally, but the systemic fungicides are toxic to fungi after being taken up by plants. The most important of these fungicides are quite straightforward, involving sulphur or compounds of mercury and copper. Burgundy Mixture, for example, is a variation on the Bordeaux formula, using copper sulphate and sodium carbonate. Cheshunt Compound, familiar to gardeners as a preventative for damping-off in seedlings, is a mixture of copper sulphate and ammonium carbonate, and other copper-based fungicides are used for seed treatment.

Organic fungicides came into general use in the 1930s with the development of Thiram (tetramethylthiuram disulphide) which was successfully used for seed treatment. Related fungicides as well as quinones, imidazolines and others soon followed and they now include formalin for soil and seed disinfection, propionic acid for food preservation, and salicylinide for plant protection. Development of systemic fungicides, often useful against a range of fungal pathogens, has been of major commercial importance. Although the concept of systemic treatment has long been known, it was the introduction of organic fungicides in the mid-1960s that proved especially significant in this respect. Perhaps the most effective of these fungicides is benomyl which can be used successfully against a wide range of diseases. An interesting and more detailed account of the development of fungicides and their application was provided by Ainsworth (1981).

CHAPTER 15

Fungi and Health

T HIS CHAPTER looks at both the good and the bad in the fungal world in terms of human and (briefly) animal health. Fungal diseases, such as thrush and ringworm, are examined together with the more serious infections that have become prevalent in people whose immune systems are compromised. Fungal allergies and fungal toxins are also covered, including those produced by traditional 'poisonous toadstools'. The beneficial fungi include those used in traditional medicine and those which provide antibiotics and other modern pharmaceuticals.

FUNGAL DISEASES

It should be no surprise that under certain circumstances our own bodies can play host to a wide and unpleasant range of fungal pathogens and parasites, some of which we share with domestic and wild animals. Even healthy humans may be hosts to a variety of commensal fungi. No fewer than 63 genetically distinct yeasts, for example, were isolated just from the mouths and nails of 24 volunteers (Kam & Xu, 2002), suggesting that all of us are hosts to fungi right now. Most of these fungi are harmless, but at least 200 species are known to be capable of causing human and animal diseases, termed 'mycoses'. Illustrated descriptions of many of these fungi were published by de Hoog *et al.* (2000).

Athlete's foot and ringworm

Among the most widespread and familiar fungal pathogens are the dermatotrophs which causes 'athlete's foot' and 'ringworm'. The skin between the toes is the usual infection point for athlete's foot (tinea pedis), particularly when suitable damp, unventilated conditions arise. As might be expected, infection is highest in shoe-wearing cultures and reaches a seasonal peak in winter. Microscopic examination of infected skin will show hyphae and spores belonging to the mould-like *Trichophyton rubrum*, the conidial state of an ascomycetous *Arthroderma* species. This fungus belongs to the order *Onygenales*, the same group that degrades bones, horns, fur, and feathers in soil and leaf litter (Chapter Three). The fungus passes from person to person on shed skin flakes and attacks the outer layers of skin, decaying and breaking down the epidermis and spreading to new skin underneath. Left untreated, it can spread even more widely, causing severe lesions of the feet and hands.

The same organism (as well as various ascomycetous *Microsporum* species) can cause ringworm of the skin (tinea corporis), so called because the fungus develops a ring-like lesion as it grows outwards from the initial infection point (Fig. 138). Though rather macabre, the principle is the same as that seen

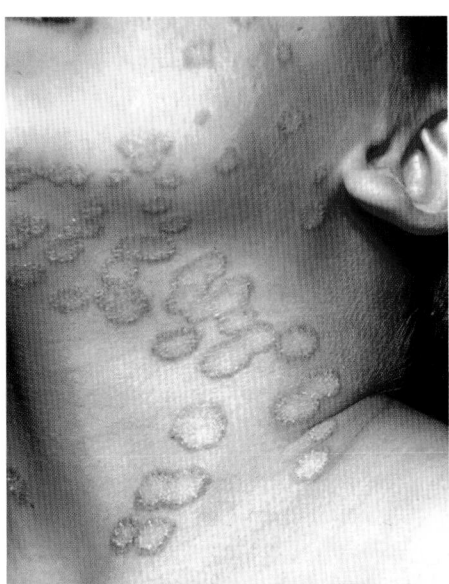

FIG 138. Symptoms of ringworm (tinea corporis). Young boy showing numerous characteristic circular lesions following infection by the ascomycete *Microsporum canis* contracted while playing with kittens (Kaminski's Digital Image Library).

in fairy rings in grassland. Ringworm of the scalp (tinea capitis) is caused by a number of *Trichophyton* and *Microsporum* species which degrade hair and cause inflammation of the hair follicles. The species responsible can be classed as anthropophilic (true human parasites), zoophilic (animal parasites), or, very rarely, geophilic (soil fungi). Until the 1980s, the zoophilic species *Microsporum canis* (teleomorph *Arthroderma otae*), was the commonest cause of scalp ringworm in the UK. As the epithet suggests, this is a parasite of dogs (and also cats) typically transferred to humans, especially children, by fondling pets. In the 1990s, *M. canis* gave ground to the anthropophilic *Trichophyton tonsurans*, at least in urban centres. The latter species is spread by hair and skin flakes on shared combs, clothes and towels, seat backs, and suchlike. In a south London primary school, up to 12% of the children were found to be carrying the disease, though not all showed symptoms (Hay *et al.*, 1996). The history, epidemiology, and treatment of tinea capitis were reviewed by Gupta & Summerbell (2000).

Thrush or candidiasis

A different group of *Ascomycetes* is responsible for another familiar but equally unpleasant fungal disease called 'thrush' or 'candidiasis'. *Candida albicans*, an ascomycetous yeast, is the organism responsible for most infections, typically causing superficial but unpleasant whitish lesions of the mouth (particularly in infants), the vagina (particularly during pregnancy), nails (Fig. 139), and more rarely the lungs.

The yeast itself is omnipresent and has been isolated from almost everything, from fruit to faeces, soil to sea water. We all constantly play host to *Candida albicans*, but it is only under certain conditions that the yeast, which is tolerant of high bodily temperatures, can overcome our natural defences and proliferate to become a problem (Fig. 139A). Sufferers from diabetes, patients undergoing prolonged antibiotic treatments, and HIV-positive patients are among the groups particularly at risk. A new species, *C. dubliniensis*, described from HIV patients in Ireland in the 1990s, also appears to be a significant human pathogen. In the wild, *Candida* species are probably opportunist saprotrophs of dung, rotting fruit, and other rich sources of nutriment. It is our misfortune that they may occasionally regard the human body as an equally rich source.

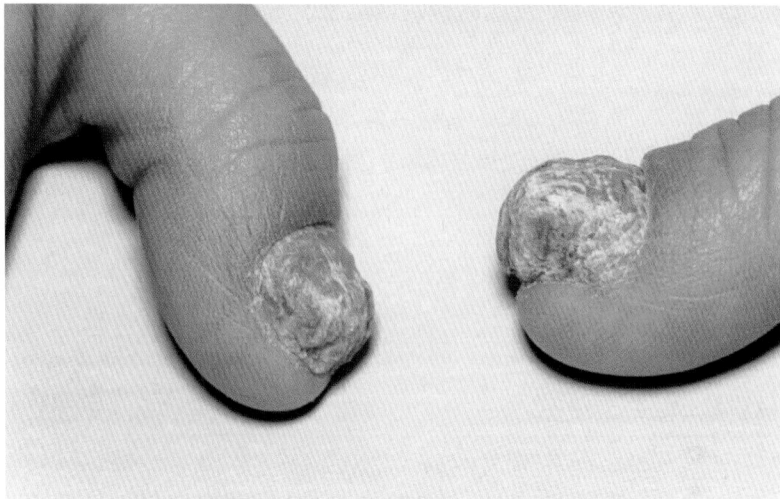

FIG 139. Chronic candidiasis of thumb nails showing destruction of tissue following infection by the ascomycetous yeast *Candida albicans* (Kaminski's Digital Image Library).

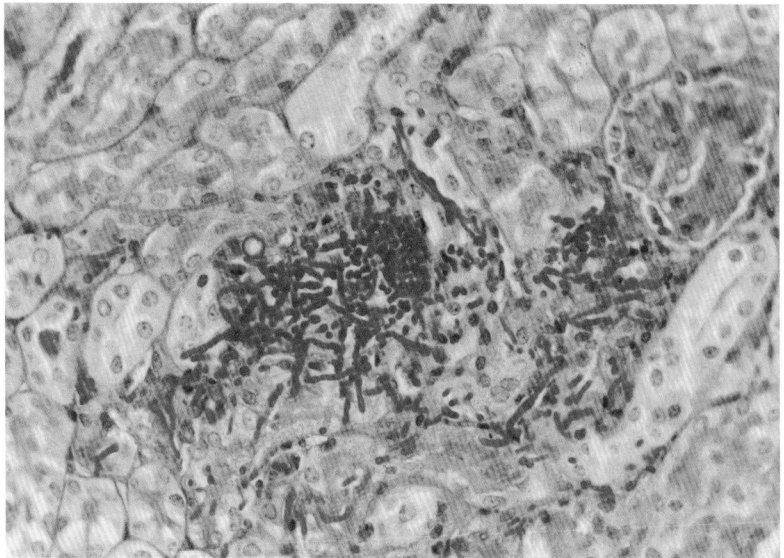

FIG 139A. Yeast cells of *Candida albicans* growing in mouse liver. The fungus is tolerant of high bodily temperatures and can proliferate in tissues if the normal immune system is compromised (N. Gow).

PCP and Sudden Infant Death Syndrome

One of the commonest infectious agents in human beings is the fungus *Pneumocystis carinii*, an atypical ascomycetous yeast adapted to human and animal tissues, and spread from person to person by inhalation. By the age of four, an estimated 94% of us have been infected by this fungus, usually without any apparent symptoms. However, it has long been known to produce *Pneumocystis carinii* pneumonia (PCP) in premature babies and malnourished infants and has more recently become one of the most serious secondary infections in AIDS patients, 60–80% suffering from PCP before new therapies were introduced in 1989, with more than 20% continuing to suffer thereafter. It is similarly common in other immunocompromised patients, and frequently fatal. Vargas *et al.* (1999) have shown that *Pneumocystis carinii* is often linked to cases of Sudden Infant Death Syndrome ('cot deaths'). It is quite possible that PCP and SIDS may be 'the tip of the iceberg' in *Pneumocystis* infections, as suggested by Dei-Cas (2000), and that further studies may implicate this fungus in a wide range of human pathogenic syndromes.

AIDS and the increase in opportunistic mycoses

The advent of AIDS, which disables the body's immune system, plus transplant surgery and other immuno-suppressant treatments, have led to a substantial increase in serious and previously little-known mycoses occurring as secondary infections, as noted above for candidiasis and PCP. Given the right conditions, almost any opportunistic, thermophilic fungus capable of growth at 37°C can invade the body. There are even cases of infection by toadstool mycelium involving species of *Coprinus* (ink caps), which more normally inhabit heat-producing compost heaps, and the bracket-like fungus, *Schizophyllum commune*, which is commonplace on insolated (sun-exposed) fallen wood, especially in the tropics. Both have been isolated from human tissue, the latter being the subject of a widespread scare story in England ("Nightmare threat of the terror toadstools", Hughes, 2002; "Danger mushrooms will eat your brains", Nicks, 2002). A brief mycological review of AIDS infections in the UK was published by Campbell & White (1989).

In the USA, fatalities from fungal diseases tripled between 1980 and 1992, whilst hospital admissions rose by 10% per annum to reach 30,000 in 1994. De Hoog & Garro (1995) noted that 'during the last few decades ... we are beginning to detect a logical spectrum of opportunistic fungi. A surprisingly large number of saprophytic species are able to survive in human tissue and cause chronic mycoses.' Fortunately, when the immune system functions normally, serious fungal infection is still rare.

Cryptococcosis and other basidiomycetous yeast infections

Cryptococcosis is a serious disease of the lungs and central nervous system caused by the fungus *Cryptococcus neoformans*. This is the asexual yeast stage of *Filobasidiella neoformans*, a basidiomycete related, rather surprisingly, to familiar woodland 'jelly fungi' (*Tremella* species). Like *Candida albicans* (the cause of thrush), this yeast has been isolated from a range of sources (it was originally discovered in peach juice), but occurs most commonly and abundantly in pigeon droppings, thought to be the main source of human infection. Curiously, the pigeons themselves are immune to the disease, having too high a body temperature for the fungus to grow.

Cryptococcus neoformans is not normally a hazard, but can proliferate in living tissue if the body's natural defences are compromised, causing cryptococcal meningitis and also, occasionally, pulmonary infections and fungaemia. In such circumstances it is frequently fatal. AIDS patients in developing countries are particularly at risk, because of the high cost of medication. By the 1990s, over 20% of AIDS patients in Central Africa were developing cryptococcosis, with close to 30% in Thailand (Hamilton, 2002).

Basidiomycetous yeasts in the genus *Malassezia* are part of the normal skin mycota, but can occasionally cause dermatitis and other skin complaints. In its mildest form, this may amount to little more than dandruff, but *Malassezia furfur* and *M. pachydermatis* have been known to cause deep-seated systemic infections, particularly in premature babies. *Malassezia pachydermatis*, originally described from a rhinoceros, is normally associated with animals and may be introduced into hospitals from healthcare workers' pets. The taxonomy and epidemiology of the genus was reviewed by Guého *et al.* (1998).

Trichosporon is another genus of basidiomycetous yeasts which form part of the normal skin mycota. Again, some species are associated with skin complaints, notably *Trichosporon cutaneum*, the cause of 'white piedra', a comparatively uncommon condition in which whitish fungal nodules are formed on hair shafts. In immunocompromised patients, however, *T. cutaneum* and other *Trichosporon* species can cause dangerous systemic mycoses.

Valley Fever and other mould infections

As well as yeasts, a number of moulds can cause infections in humans, particularly when the immune system is suppressed. Some of these infections are geographically localised, notably 'coccidioidomycosis' caused by *Coccidioides immitis* (Fig. 139B) another member of the *Onygenales*. This is a soil fungus which is particularly prevalent in American deserts and can cause various problems, from pulmonary infections to rheumatism, when inhaled during dust storms and the like. Its ubiquity in California's San Joaquin Valley, where 50–70% of the population may be infected, has led to coccidioidomycosis being dubbed 'valley fever' in the USA. Infection is often mild and symptomless, but up to 100,000 people may be infected each year in the US alone, with serious infections leading to an average 58 deaths annually (Weitzman, 1991).

'Blastomycosis' was also thought to be American and was originally dubbed 'Chicago disease', but is now known to occur in pockets worldwide, including Europe. The causative agent is another soil fungus, *Blastomyces dermatitidis*, also a member of the *Onygenales*. Infection is associated with disturbed soil near water. It is known, for example, to have attacked raccoon hunters (and their dogs) in swamps. 'Histoplasmosis' is caused by another anamorphic member of the *Onygenales*, *Histoplasma capsulatum*, and is associated with disturbed soil containing bird droppings (e.g. in chicken runs or below bird roosts). It is worldwide, but particularly common in the Mississippi and Ohio River valleys, where up to 80% of the population may be infected. In both blastomycosis and histoplasmosis, initial infection is typically by inhalation of conidiospores and the symptoms (which do not always occur) include a diverse range of pulmonary and other problems. The causative fungi are closely related, both having teleomorphs in the genus *Ajellomyces*. A series of papers on blastomycosis was published by Al-Doory & DiSalvo (1992).

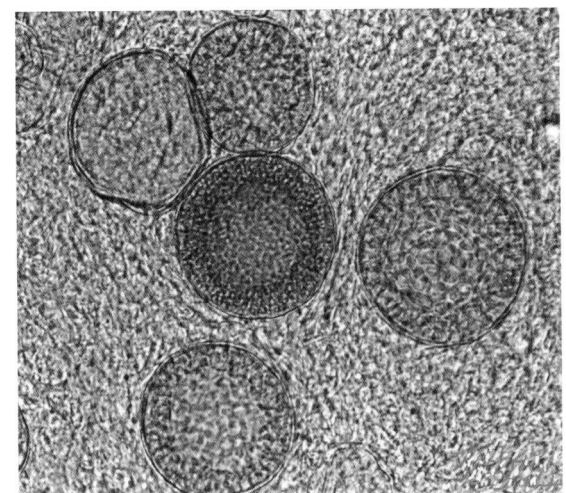

FIG 139B. Sporangia of *Coccidioides immitis* in human cells from skin lesions. The fungus is the cause of coccidio-idomycosis, initially a respiratory infection which may progress to systemic disease includ-ing infection of skin tissues (Kaminski's Digital Image Library).

'Sporotrichosis' caused by the anamorphic ascomycete *Sporothrix schenckii* is rather different in that it normally infects people through scratches and other skin damage, causing skin lesions and sometimes more deep-seated infections. It was at one time a serious problem in South African gold mines. The fungus typically grows on wood and decaying vegetation and may be picked up on thorns, splinters, or animal scratches. Bizarrely, armadillo hunters in Uruguay seem to be particularly at risk, the animals being covered in spores from the dried grass in their nesting burrows. They also have sharp claws. At least 75 cases of hunters infected by spore-bearing armadillos are on record (MacKinnon, 1969). Brazilian armadillo-hunters, on the other hand, are subject to coccidioidomycosis, the dust-borne disease noted above, whilst the armadillos themselves suffer from paracoccidioidomycosis caused by the ascomycetous *Paracoccidioides brasiliensis*, which also affects humans in Latin America, and indeed penguins.

'Aspergillosis' is caused by ubiquitous airborne *Aspergillus* moulds, most of which are thermophilic. *Aspergillus fumigatus*, is the commonest pathogen, but Pitt (1994) listed over 20 potentially pathogenic species, including *A. flavus*, *A. terreus*, and *A. niger*, all of which can grow at body temperature. All of us inhale *Aspergillus* spores with almost every breath we take, but in immunocompromised individuals the spores can germinate in the lungs allowing the fungus to spread through the body. Such invasive pulmonary aspergillosis is frequently fatal.

Zygomycetous moulds can also cause severe infections in susceptible people, particularly those with poorly controlled diabetes mellitus. 'Mucormycosis' is caused by a several species of *Mucorales*, including *Rhizopus oryzae*, *Cunninghamella bertholletiae*, and *Saksenaea vasiformis*, all common on decaying vegetation and spoiled food. Growth of these fungi in the body can rapidly lead to necrosis and death. Curiously, some of the zygomycetous *Entomophthorales* can also infect humans, notably *Basidiobolus ranarum* (more normally associated with frogs) and *Conidiobolus coronatus*. Both cause subcutaneous infections, possibly from cuts, and are largely confined to the tropics.

Various other moulds, including *Fusarium* and *Penicillium* species, can also cause problems. Matsumoto *et al.* (1994) listed no less than 57 genera of brownish anamorphic ascomycetes (dematiaceous fungi) containing 101 additional pathogenic species (not covered in the paragraphs above), causing a range of human diseases under the collective name 'phaeohyphomycosis'. Even baker's yeast, *Saccharomyces cerevisiae*, has recently been implicated in human infections (Pontón *et al.*, 2000).

FUNGAL ALLERGIES

Allergic reactions to fungal spores, both indoors and outdoors, are commonplace and possibly increasing. In many situations, the number of airborne spores substantially exceeds the number of pollen grains, frequently by 100 to 1000 times. The average number of fungal spores outdoors is around 10,000–20,000 per cubic metre, with highs up to 2,000,000; indoors, in excessively dusty situations, the spore count can reach 1,000,000,000 per cubic metre. In susceptible people, around 3 to 10% of the population, these spores can produce asthmatic attacks and rhinitis.

The fungi responsible are mainly ubiquitous moulds (including *Aspergillus*, *Alternaria*, *Cladosporium*, and *Penicillium* species) particularly in the home, in factories and processing plants, in offices (where they may play a part in 'sick building syndrome'), even in 'problem' buses. However, yeasts, rusts and smuts, plus some mushrooms and toadstools (notably *Pleurotus* and *Coprinus* species), puffballs and earthstars, and bracket fungi (notably *Ganoderma* species) have also been shown to provoke allergenic reactions. The problem is widespread, and Gumowski *et al.* (1991) listed almost 100 fungal genera associated with allergies. Kurup *et al.* (2000) have reviewed the respiratory allergies caused by moulds and yeasts, whilst Horner *et al.* (1995) have provided a detailed review of the subject.

Farmer's Lung and Organic Toxic Dust Syndrome

Straw and hay-making has traditionally been blamed for 'farmer's lung', a debilitating bronchial condition arising from the clouds of dust raised during pitching and turning, often in closed and poorly ventilated barns. Though fungi have long been held responsible for farmer's lung, the actual cause is believed to be an allergic response to bacterial spores (*Actinomycetes*), since they can contribute up to 98% of the airborne spores produced in disturbed hay in Britain.

Fungi are, however, believed to be responsible for the very similar 'Organic Toxic Dust Syndrome' (OTDS) which also causes an inflammatory, flu-like illness in farm workers, grain handlers, sawmill operators, and others likely to inhale large amounts of organic dust. OTDS is thought to require higher levels of exposure to dust than farmer's lung disease, but may affect a greater percentage of people. Brinton *et al.* (1987), for example, reported an outbreak at a college barn dance in which 82% of attendees became ill with OTDS. The organisms responsible are believed to be various ascomycetous moulds, including once again ubiquitous *Aspergillus*, *Penicillium*, and *Cladosporium* species, and related xerophilic fungi which are frequent contaminants of stored grain, hay, and animal feeds. The same moulds can cause allergic reactions in domestic animals stabled in damp conditions. The disease called 'heaves' is an example, causing particular problems in racehorses.

MYCOTOXINS

Fungi are probably best known not for the diseases they cause or the allergies they may provoke, but for the poisons that some of them produce. These mycotoxins occur in a many species, not just the infamous toadstools of fairy tales. Many less obvious fungi, including moulds, are toxic, some dangerously so, and one of the best-known of these is the cause of a mediaeval plague.

Ergot: St Anthony's Fire and Dancing Manias

Claviceps purpurea, sometimes called 'ergot of rye', is one of several related ascomycetous parasites of the ovaries of grasses and other mono-cotyledonous plants. The species forms sclerotia (ergots), small, blackish, banana-shaped storage organs (Fig. 139C), which fall to the ground in autumn, rest over winter, and develop fruit bodies in spring. Although rye is the commonest cereal host, the fungus also occurs on wheat and barley, and more rarely on oats.

The sclerotia contain alkaloids which are highly toxic to humans and animals. Bread made with parasitised grain can cause 'ergotism', a serious form of poisoning which takes two main forms: gangrenous ergotism and spasmodic (or convulsive) ergotism. The former, known as 'St Anthony's Fire', was common in the Middle Ages when the link with ergot was completely unknown. It results from constriction of the small blood vessels which restricts the blood supply to the extremities, causing gangrene. Spasmodic ergotism, common in parts of Europe, is said to have led to medieval dancing manias, with sufferers unable to control their movements. Both forms are severe and may result in death.

Matossian (1989) has suggested that ergotism was much more prevalent in rye-eating communities than has generally been recognised and may have been a significant factor in the poor health of mediaeval and later Europeans well into the eighteenth century. She has also suggested that spasmodic ergotism, with its fits and convulsions, hysteria and burning sensations, occasioned various outbreaks of religious revivalism, such as those seen at early quaker meetings, as well as outbreaks of

FIG 139C. Ergots, the sclerotial resting-stages of the ascomycete *Claviceps purpurea*, developing in inflorescences of *Phleum*. When the grasses die back, the ergots will fall to the ground and overwinter, infecting a new crop in the spring (RBG Kew).

witch-hunting in East Anglia and Salem, New England (both rye-growing areas).

The fungus is common in Britain on wild grasses, but is strictly controlled on commercial cereal crops. The last British outbreak of ergotism is believed to have been in Manchester in 1927, among Jewish immigrants eating bread made from rye grown in Yorkshire. Problems have occurred at a later date elsewhere, however, with severe outbreaks in France in the 1950s, in India in 1975, and in Ethiopia in 1978. The alkaloids involved include lysergic acid derivatives, particularly ergotamine, ergometrine, and ergotoxine. In small quantities, however, these can have therapeutic properties and are used in standard pharmaceutical preparations.

Poisonous toadstools

In Britain at least, 'poisonous' and 'toadstools' tend to go together in the public mind, but whilst it is true that many common British agarics are variously toxic, only a minority are dangerously so.

Amatoxins and the death cap

The most notorious of the poisonous toadstools is the aptly named 'death cap', *Amanita phalloides*, common at least in southern Britain with oak and beech trees, with which it forms an ectomycorrhizal association. The toadstool contains a number of toxins, most importantly cyclic octapeptides called 'amatoxins'. These are cytolytic (cell-destroying) poisons, inhibiting protein synthesis. They are resistant to heat, so are not destroyed by cooking. Within 8–15 hours of ingestion there are initial symptoms of nausea, vomiting, and acute diarrhoea, followed by a remission; two to three days later potentially fatal liver, kidney, and other damage occurs. Cooper & Johnson (1998) noted 11 poisonings by *A. phalloides* in the British Isles between 1973 and 1981, one of which proved fatal. The white gills, olive cap, and basal sack-like volva of mature *A. phalloides* should insure that it is not mistaken for anything edible, but only a small section of a single cap is a potentially lethal dose. The fact that modern treatments have reduced fatalities to around 20% is no great comfort.

The wholly white *Amanita virosa*, sometimes luridly called the 'destroying angel', is equally poisonous, but comparatively rare in Britain.

Commoner, and hence potentially more dangerous, are *Lepiota* species, relatives of the much larger parasol mushroom, *Macrolepiota procera*, which is edible and quite frequently collected for food. *Lepiota* species are small toadstools, typically with zoned, scaly caps, white gills, and coloured veil remnants on the stem. Many species have a distinctly southern distribution in Britain, preferring rich, calcareous soils, but can also grow in gardens, greenhouses, and flower pots. In 1997, a specimen of *Lepiota brunneoincarnata* was sent to Kew for identification, having caused serious poisoning in a child who had picked it from a plant container in London. Several other *Lepiota* species are equally dangerous (the toxin concentration varies from species to species), but all are best avoided.

Several *Galerina* species also contain amatoxins. These are mostly small, rusty-brown toadstools, often associated with mosses, but *G. unicolor* grows in troops on logs, and could be mistaken for the edible *Kuehneromyces mutabilis* (though the latter is rarely eaten in Britain). The rather similar *Conocybe filaris* also contains potentially dangerous amounts of amatoxins.

Orellanine poisoning and the mistaken chanterelles

'Orellanine' toxins are also cytolytic, eventually causing kidney failure. They are typified by the late onset of initial symptoms (nausea, etc.), which may not happen for several days or even several weeks after ingestion (2–21 days according to Benjamin, 1995). The toxins are found in toadstools of the very large genus, *Cortinarius*, which are ectomycorrhizal and typified by their rust-brown spores and thin, web-like ring (cortina). *Cortinarius orellanus*, after which the toxin is named, is a rare, mainly southern species in Britain, but commoner on the continent. However, several other species are equally toxic, including *C. orellanoides*, also known from southern England, and *C. speciosissimus* found mainly in conifer woods in Scotland.

Orellanine poisoning was unknown till the 1950s when a mass outbreak occurred in Poland involving over 100 toadstool-eating villagers, 19 of whom died. In Britain in 1979, three holidaymakers at a Scottish campsite ate a meal of *Cortinarius speciosissimus* under the impression that they were chanterelles and suffered severe poisoning some ten days later. Two required kidney transplants.

Gyromitrin poisoning: true and false morels

The ascomycete *Gyromitra esculenta* is a large, morel-like fungus, typically occurring in northern conifer woods in the spring (Fig. 140). As the epithet suggests, is has traditionally been considered esculent (edible), to the extent that it was once grown commercially in Poland. However, it contains a compound called 'gyromitrin' which is broken down in the stomach to form monomethylhydrazine (MMH), a chemical better known as a rocket fuel.

Gyromitrin poisoning can cause substantial, often fatal, damage to the liver and kidneys, but is curiously unpredictable. People have traditionally eaten *Gyromitra esculenta* and related species without any ill-effect, but occasionally, for no clear reason, the fungus can be lethal. There are cases of families sharing a meal in which some members showed no symptoms at all, others became slightly ill, and an unfortunate few died. There are also cases where regular eaters of the fungus were suddenly, and inexplicably, poisoned. Similar toxins may exist in the more common and widespread false morels (*Helvella* species), which are generally regarded as poisonous, and even the highly esteemed true morels (*Morchella* species). These latter,

FIG 140. The false morel *Gyromitra esculenta*, a potentially poisonous species despite is name (B. Spooner).

though sold in supermarkets and restaurants, have been known to cause gastric upsets if eaten raw or undercooked. There are stories of *nouvelle cuisine* chefs, keen to break with tradition, ruining receptions with elegant but poisonous new morel dishes.

Clitocybe, Inocybe, and muscarine poisoning

Species having dangerous amounts of the toxin muscarine are primarily toadstools in the genera *Clitocybe* and *Inocybe*. The former genus contains saprotrophic species, mostly found in woodland litter or grassland. The two most likely to cause poisoning are *Clitocybe dealbata* and *C. rivulosa*, both pale to whitish species typically forming rings in grass, where they could be mistaken for *Marasmius oreades*, the edible fairy-ring champignon. *Inocybe* species are ectomycorrhizal woodland fungi, some very common, and many very poisonous, the large *I. patouillardii* being notably so. *Omphalotus* species may also contain muscarine, but the only British species, *O. illudens*, is extremely rare and possibly confined to the south-east.

Muscarine poisoning rapidly produces a range of unpleasant symptoms (often within 15–30 minutes of ingestion) including profuse perspiration, salivation, and lacrimation, known as the PSL syndrome. Severe poisoning can lead to cardio-respiratory failure and death, but this is thankfully rare.

Haemolytic toxins and the Paxillus syndrome

Haemolytic toxins destroy red blood cells and can lead to anaemia. Three *Amanita* species, the blusher *A. rubescens* and the grisettes *A. fulva* and *A. vaginata*, contain haemolytic toxins, but are only poisonous if eaten raw or undercooked.

Paxillus involutus, the brown roll rim, is far more dangerous, however it is served. It is one of the commonest of all ectomycorrhizal toadstools, often occurring in quantity in birch and other woods, and has a long history of being eaten in eastern Europe, despite the frequency with which it causes stomach upsets. However, it can also provoke a peculiar, accumulative allergic reaction (the *Paxillus* syndrome) in a few people leading in time to severe and sometimes fatal haemolytic anaemia.

Alcohol and ink caps

The common ink cap, *Coprinus atramentarius*, has been given the name 'tippler's bane' because of the unpleasant consequences of drinking alcohol after eating it. The effect is similar to that produced by 'Antabuse' (the commercial name for disulfiram), sometimes used in the treatment of alcoholics. Any alcohol taken within three days of eating the *Coprinus* provokes flushing, nausea, and other unpleasant symptoms within a few minutes. Though a few other ink caps contain sufficient amounts of the active agent (coprine) to provoke the same reaction, none of them are common or likely to be eaten. Similar reactions are, however, said to occur in a number of unrelated toadstools, notably *Pholiota squarrosa* and *Clitocybe clavipes*, as well as the bolete, *Boletus luridus*.

Magic mushrooms and psilocybin

Two groups of toadstools have toxins which are psychotropic (affecting the brain), making hallucinations part of the poisoning syndrome. These hallucinations have been traditionally valued for religious and recreational purposes (Chapter 16).

The best known of these psychotropic fungi is the fly agaric, *Amanita muscaria*, a common ectomycorrhizal associate of birch and other trees. It contains a substance called ibotenic acid which the body breaks down into muscimol, thought to be the main toxic agent. Ibotenic acid was first isolated in Japan from *Amanita strobiliformis*, called 'ibo-tengu-take' ('the warty, long-nosed goblin toadstool') in Japanese. Onset of symptoms is quite rapid, within half an hour to two hours of ingestion, and can include intoxication, nausea, delirium, and alternating periods of hyperactivity and lethargy. Some deaths have been recorded, but these are comparatively rare. The much less common panther cap, *Amanita pantherina*, also contains ibotenic acid and produces similar symptoms.

The second group contains the toxin psilocybin and its associate psilocin, alkaloids appropriately related to bufotenine, the toad-skin toxin. Most toadstools in the genus *Psilocybe* contain varying amounts of the toxins, the best-known being the liberty cap, *Psilocybe semilanceata*, which is common in Britain in dunged grassland, and *Psilocybe cyanescens*, probably an introduced alien in Britain but now locally common on wood-chip mulch. Some other species with a similar habitat also contain psilocybin. By far the commonest is *Panaeolina foenisecii*, ubiquitous in suburban lawns and parks, though the species (frequently eaten by grazing toddlers) contains very small amounts of the toxin and is unlikely to cause problems.

Effects occur soon after ingestion, usually within half an hour, and may include euphoria (or dysphoria), hallucinations, anxiety attacks, palpitations, nausea and vomiting, often depending on the individual and the circumstances of ingestion. Poisoning is rarely serious, though can be sufficiently unpleasant for people to seek hospital treatment. For example, over a period of a single month in 1981, no less than 44 people (mainly teenagers) were seen in the admissions and emergency department of Ninewells Hospital in Dundee after ingesting *Psilocybe semilanceata*, of which there was a 'bumper harvest' locally that autumn (Peden & Pringle, 1982). A similar epidemic was reported from Glasgow. Bennell & Watling (1983) reported some unpleasant symptoms (numbness and lack of co-ordination) lasting several days in two adults who breakfasted on *Panaeolus subbalteatus*.

Other fungi not to eat

As well as the recognised and often serious toxic syndromes outlined above, there is a general gastro-intestinal syndrome (nausea, stomach ache, vomiting, diarrhoea) common to a range of additional fungi. The causes may be many and various, sometimes involving toxins, sometimes allergens, and are often not well-researched or understood.

Many only seem to affect a limited number of people, for no immediately apparent reason. The yellow-staining mushrooms, *Agaricus xanthoderma* and *A. placomyces*, are two of the commonest examples. Both resemble edible mushrooms, but can be distinguished by their bulbous bases which bruise bright chrome yellow when scratched. Although many people consume them without ill-effects, others receive an unpleasant bout of food poisoning, possibly caused by the phenol which these mushrooms are known to contain. Other examples include honey fungus, *Armillaria mellea* and its allies, which causes problems for some, but is eaten by others, and the sulphur-yellow bracket fungus, *Laetiporus sulphureus*.

Hebeloma and *Entoloma* species are generally poisonous. Indeed *Hebeloma crustuliniforme* has the common name 'poison pie'. Badham (1863) gave a dramatic account of eating *Entoloma sinuatum* by which he was 'so continually and fearfully purged, and suffered so much from headache and swimming of the brain, that I really thought that every moment would be my last.' Several *Russula* and *Lactarius* species are so acrid that, if they can be stomached at all, they can cause severe gastric irritation. Examples are the aptly named, bright red *Russula emetica*, ectomycorrhizal with pines, and the hazel associate, *Lactarius pyrogalus* (the epithet means 'fire-milk'). Others are equally bitter, notably the ubiquitous sulphur-tuft, *Hypholoma fasciculare*. This would seem to be wholly inedible, but was still served up as a substantial part of a 'wild mushroom' dish in an English restaurant, the remains of which were sent to Kew for identification. Those who managed to eat this unpleasant meal were hospitalised, but subsequently recovered.

The devil's bolete, *Boletus satanas*, causes gastric upsets, but is too uncommon in Britain to present any real problems. Other inedible boletes are either bitter, as in *Boletus calopus* and *Tylopilus felleus*, or acrid, as in *Chalciporus piperatus*. Less well-known is that *Suillus luteus*, a common ectomycorrhizal species with pine, can cause problems if the slimy cuticle is not removed.

Details of other poisonous species, plus a comprehensive account of toadstool poisoning in general, were published by Benjamin (1995). Cooper and Johnson (1998) provided an account of poisonous species in the British Isles, and Oldridge *et al.* (1989) a brief but useful British guide to toxins. Watling (1995) produced a short guide specifically on fungal poisoning in children (who account for more than half the suspected poisoning cases dealt with in British hospitals).

Aflatoxins and poisonous moulds

Far more of a problem than poisonous toadstools are the unseen and insidious toxins produced by poisonous moulds. Though mouldy foods are normally discarded, if only because they taste bad, some may still be consumed through poverty, through bulk processing, or because they are difficult to detect.

'Aflatoxins' are by far the worst of these poisons. They are mainly produced by *Aspergillus flavus* (hence the name 'a-fla-toxin'), a common and widespread fungus infecting many kinds of stored food, but particularly maize, peanuts, and oilseeds. The fungus grows optimally at around 33°C, so is not an endemic problem in temperate countries, though it still occurs as a contaminant in imported foodstuffs. The dangers of aflatoxins were first recognised in 1960 following the mysterious death of over 100,000 turkeys in Britain. Subsequent research discovered aflatoxins in mouldy grain fed to the birds. Aflatoxins may be acutely poisonous, even lethal, in trace amounts, and are serious liver carcinogens, indeed 'the most potent known' (Pitt & Hocking, 1997). They may also increase susceptibility to viruses, and in the tropics may be linked to kwashiorkor (protein malnutrition) in children. They are also persistent and heat-stable, resisting sterilisation and cooking. In the west at least, toxin levels are now monitored in susceptible foodstuffs, the maximum permitted level in the EU being around 2–5 μg/kg, depending on product. However, in many tropical and subtropical countries, foodstuffs have been found containing up to 1,000 times the maximum permitted level, causing lethal outbreaks in local populations. Pitt (2000) has estimated that in Indonesia alone 20,000 deaths per year may be caused by liver cancer resulting from alflatoxin consumption, and has further claimed that it is 'very likely that mycotoxins play a significant role in the perceived poor health of many tropical people'.

'Ochratoxin A' (OTA) is a temperate toxin, commonest in northern Europe. It was first described from *Aspergillus ochraceus*, but is mainly produced by *Penicillium verrucosum* which typically contaminates barley and wheat. The toxin is known to cause kidney failure, and has been held responsible for outbreaks of nephritis in Scandinavian pigs. Although quite high levels of the toxin have been found in people, it has not yet been linked to any human health problems. It is nonetheless classed as a carcinogen and in 2002 the EU set limits of 3–10 μg/kg for various cereal and dried grape products, including sultanas, currants, and raisins. Research is also being undertaken to assess the risk posed by its presence in European wine, and it may also occur in coffee, cocoa, and beer.

A standard, illustrated guide to food spoilage fungi, including those producing mycotoxins, has been published by Samson *et al.* (2000).

FUNGI AND FOLK MEDICINES

It seems that almost every culture from the Arctic to Australia has or once had its own folk traditions involving the use of fungi as medicines, tonics, and dressings. Even the mycophobic English and Inuit seem prepared to use a few fungi for medical purposes, whilst Chinese and Japanese traditional practices have elevated some species to the highest and most expensive class of sought-after panaceas.

European folk medicine

Comparatively few fungi have been used in European folk medicine or appear in classic herbals. Dioscorides and other classical writers championed the benefits of 'agaricum', believed to be the bracket fungus *Fomitopsis officinalis*, which typically grows on larch. Agaricum was considered to be a universal panacea, capable of curing everything from snake bites to hysteria. It was one of only three fungi featured in Gerard's Herbal published in 1633. Gerard recommended it as 'a sure remedy for cold shakings ... good for those that are bit by venomous beasts ... cureth agues and wandering feavers ... purges away grosse, cold and flegmaticke humours ... [and] is good against the paines and swimming in the head, or the falling Evill'. Agaricum was retained in the British Pharmacopoeia till 1788 and was still being imported (from Archangel) in the early nineteenth century.

Gerard's other two useful fungi were the jew's ear, *Auricularia auricula-judae*, boiled in milk or steeped in beer as a palliative for sore throats, and puffballs, the spores of which were used to dry out 'kibes'. Bacon in 1627 noted that jew's ear was 'used for squinancies and inflamations in the throat' whilst Berkeley, writing in 1860, reported that it was still sold at Covent Garden market 'in consequence of some supposed healing properties' together with *Elaphomyces*, the hart's truffle (the latter under the name 'Lycoperdon nuts' and considered an aphrodisiac). Puffballs, particularly the giant puffball (*Calvatia gigantea*), were also frequently used as styptics (to staunch bleeding), a practice which lingered into the twentieth century. Berkeley also noted the burning of puffballs as anaesthetics with properties 'similar to those of chloroform'.

The use of ergot in midwifery, a centuries-old practice, is a good example of a folk medicine that is based on fact rather than superstition. A possible companion is 'chaga', a traditional Russian folk cure for cancer made from the conks of the polypore *Inonotus obliquus*. The cure presumably originated in the resemblance of the gall-like conks to masses of cankerous tissue, a god-given signal to the mediaeval mind. But surprisingly, chaga was researched and medically approved as an anti-cancer agent during the soviet era when it was available under the name 'Befungin'. Pharmacological investigation and clinical trials still continue today.

Other polypores were also used. Fruitbodies of *Phellinus pomaceus* (found mainly on blackthorn in Britain) were ground on a nutmeg grater and used in Sussex as a poultice for a swollen face. In the same county *Piptoporus betulinus* was charcoaled and used as an antiseptic and disinfectant. Linnaeus noted that *Fomes fomentarius* was used in Lappland for moxa (a healing cauterisation of the skin), more normally undertaken by burning wormwood and other herbs. The polypores *Fomes fomentarius* and *Phellinus igniarius* were the source of amadou, mainly used as tinder (Chapter 16), but also for moxa. Léveillé in 1854 additionally recorded the use of amadou as a styptic and surgical dressing, for compresses and pessaries, and (when burnt with potassium nitrate) as an inhalant for asthmatics. Baker (1989) has published an interesting account of the use of polypores and puffballs as styptics and surgical dressings.

Cakes of brewer's yeast (*Saccharomyces cerevisae*) were used in poultices as an antiseptic and internally as a cure for various ailments, from acne to rheumatoid arthritis. Various moulds were also used in poultices, long before penicillin was isolated and recognised as an antibiotic. In Cornwall and Devon, for example, a Good Friday bun was suspended from farmhouse beams, allowed to go mouldy, and used as a cure-all.

A popular feature of mediaeval medicine was the 'doctrine of signatures', the belief that God had provided cryptic clues for medical usage in the shapes and colours of plants and other organisms. Several lichens were used on this basis, notably the hair-like *Usnea barbata* (used for strengthening hair), the lung-shaped *Lobaria pulmonaria* (used for lung problems), and the yellow *Xanthoria parietina* (used for treating jaundice). Lichens found growing on human skulls were highly valued as a cure for epilepsy. Other lichens were used, according to Lindsay in 1856, "as nutrients, demulcents, febrifuges, astringents, tonics, purgatives, and anthelmintics", though Lindsay also noted that "the virtues of Lichens in medicine are certainly more imaginary than real". Despite this, *Cetraria islandica* (once ground up for food) was still being employed in the 1970s by a Swiss company to make throat pastils and herbal teas.

In the realm of pure superstition, Swanton (1917) reported the carrying of 'cramp balls' (*Daldinia concentrica*) in Surrey and Sussex as a preventitive for cramp, specimens having been given to him 'by old villagers' in Haslemere.

Chinese traditional medicine

Fungi are mentioned in Chinese pharmacopiae dating back to the third century. Four species in particular were and are still considered to belong to the highest class of medicines (along with ginseng), promoting all-round good health. These are the wood-rotting polypores *Ganoderma lucidum* (ling zhi), *Polyporus umbellatus* (zhu ling), and *Wolfiporia cocos* (fu ling), together with the insect pathogen *Cordyceps sinensis*.

Ganoderma lucidum (also used in Japanese traditional medicine where it is known as 'reishi') is favoured as a general tonic and panacea. Once rare and expensive, it is now widely cultivated and available as whole fruitbodies (often attractively boxed), in tablet form, as '*Ganoderma* tea', as '*Ganoderma* wine' (a potent spirit having a flavour reminiscent of silage), and as concentrated spore preparations (Fig. 141).

Cordyceps sinensis, the 'Chinese caterpillar fungus' is a parasite of moth larvae. It is also used as a general tonic and panacea, but one which continues to be rare and expensive (Fig. 142). *Cordyceps sinensis* is reputed to have been the secret tonic which led to the success of Chinese athletes in the Olympic Games during the 1990s. Rolfe & Rolfe (1925) noted that 'it holds, together with 'toad-spittle cakes' and 'powdered tiger's bones', a worthy place in the ranks of that heterogeneous and mysterious medley which comprises Chinese materia medica.'

Many of these traditional medicines are considered to have spiritual or mystic qualities and as such are a frequent component of 'alternative' medical practice in the West, particularly in the United States. Thus

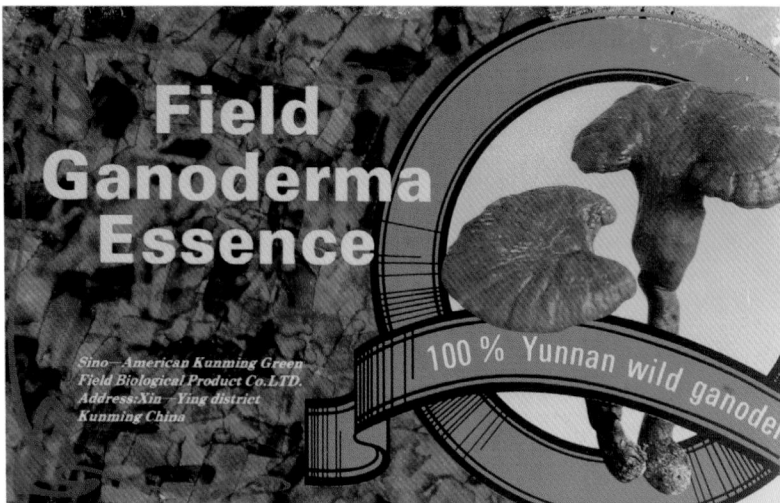

FIG 141. The polypore *Ganoderma lucidum* (ling zhi or reishi) is widely sold as a tonic in China and Japan (RBG Kew).

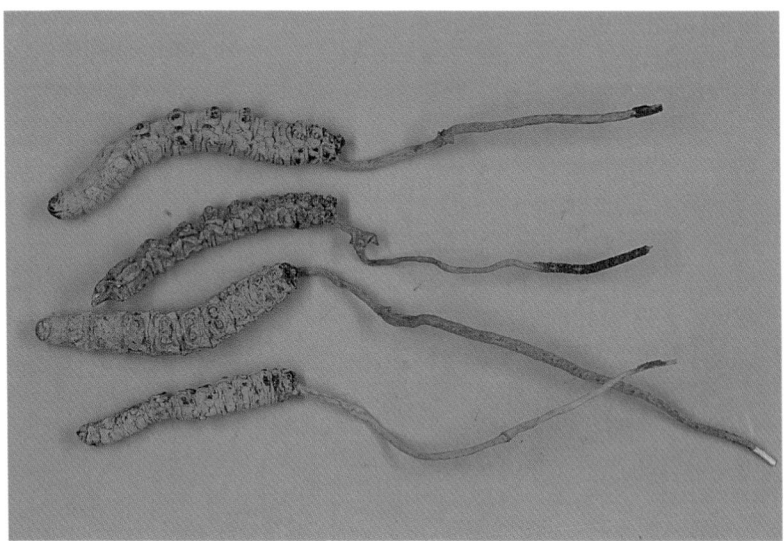

FIG 142. The 'Chinese caterpillar fungus', *Cordyceps sinensis*, which parasitises moth larvae and is sought-after as a tonic. The species is rare but collected from the wild for commercial sale and is of conservation concern (RBG Kew).

Beinfeld's introduction to Hobbs (1995) extolled the virtues of *Ganoderma lucidum* (reishi) by suggesting that 'just as young mushrooms feed on decomposing forest debris, so it seems that in the human body they assist in the neutralization of psychic waste and recycle such negativity into mental clarity and optimist' (sic). Despite this egregiously dippy introduction, Hobbs' book provides a useful and comprehensive guide to macrofungi in traditional and alternative medicine, with particular reference to Chinese practice.

Other folk remedies

In India, traditional ayurvedic medicine makes use of a bracket fungus called 'phansomba' for treating diarrhoea and dysentery, and for healing wounds. It is believed the name may be applied to several different species of *Phellinus*. Another bracket, *Daedaleopsis flavida,* is ground and used as a snuff for treating jaundice, whilst brackets of 'umbarache kan' (*Phellinus gilvus*) are simply threaded and worn for eight days to 'cure' kidney disorders. A survey of fungal folk remedies employed by the Baiga and Bharia peoples of Madhya Pradesh, revealed some ten macrofungi used to effect cures (Rai *et al.*, 1993; Harsh *et al.*, 1999).Traditional fungal remedies in Malaya were said to include 'tahi angin' (the lichen *Usnea barbata*) as a remedy for colds, 'chendawan merah' (the scarlet bracket *Pycnoporus sanguineus*) to cure dysentery, and 'susu rimau' (the polypore *Lignosus sacer*) to treat consumption. A large polypore sclerotium known as 'susu rimau' was also used to cure asthma. Tradition held that the sclerotium was the congealed milk of tigers.

Walleyn & Rammeloo (1994) noted that fungi were less frequently used in African traditional medicine than in Asian, but nonetheless compiled a substantial list of fungal treatments. In America, the Inuits, who traditionally shun most fungi as 'the excrement of shooting stars', nonetheless used and still use puffballs as styptics, a practice also reported among the Kwakiutl, the Pawnees, the Cherokees, the Mohegans, and the Navaho. The Mayans were said to collect various *Geastrum* species for the same purpose.

FUNGI AND MODERN MEDICINES

Back in 1925, Rolfe & Rolfe noted that 'the uses of fungi in medicine have now been largely abandoned . . . [and are] in danger of being forgotten in this more scientific age.' This was just three years before the discovery of penicillin. Since that date, fungi have not only made a resurgence in modern pharmacy, they have dominated the industry as a source for antibiotics, immuno-suppressive drugs, and cholesterol-lowering agents. In 1995, six of the top twenty best-selling prescription medicines were of fungal origin (Langley, 1997).

Ergot, obstetrics, and migraine

Ergot contains a large number of alkaloids, including acid amide derivatives of lysergic acid, many of which are highly toxic. However, in small quantities ergot can be beneficial in stimulating muscle contractions and restricting bleeding. As such, it was used in European midwifery at least as long ago as the sixteenth century, before its properties were officially recognised and incorporated into modern medical practice some 300 years later. The main active ingredients, principally ergotamine, are concentrated in the sclerotia ('ergots') which were formerly grown and harvested for medical use. The two main producers were Russia with an average annual crop of 100 tons, and Spain, with a crop of 70 tons. Nowadays, extracts are made from laboratory-grown cultures. The two main preparations in current use are ergotamine tartrate and ergometrine maleate, used in obstetrics and in the treatment of a number of conditions (e.g. migraine) involving dilation of blood vessels. A detailed review of ergot alkaloids was published by Křen & Cvak (1999).

Penicillin and cephalosporin

The discovery of penicillin was a breakthrough for modern medicine, introducing a whole new range of effective, fungus-derived antibiotics which are still of major importance today. By 1997, world sales of these 'β-lactam' antibiotics, which include the penicillins, cephalosporins, and their derivatives, were worth some £6,000,000,000 p.a. Penicillin itself is produced by a number of ascomycetous moulds, principally *Penicillium chrysogenum*. The related cephalosporins are also produced by ascomycetous moulds, notably *Acremonium chrysogenum* (formerly called *Cephalosporium chrysogenum*, hence 'cephalosporin'), as well as some actinomycetes and bacteria. Penicillin and 'first generation' cephalosporins are effective against Gram-positive bacteria such as *Staphylococcus* and *Streptococcus*, and modified 'second generation' cephalosporins are effective against Gram-negative bacteria such as the infamous 'E. coli' (*Escherichia coli*) and *Salmonella*. Many of these modified β-lactams are 'biosynthetics', in which the original products of fungal fermentation are altered or added to by chemical means.

Griseofulvin, fusidic acid, and pleuromutilin

Three less familiar antiobiotics are also derived from fungi and are used to treat specific conditions. 'Griseofulvin', originally derived from *Penicillium griseofulvum*, is used to treat infections caused by *Trichophyton* species and other dermatrophic fungi which are not susceptible to other antibiotics. 'Fusidic acid', first derived from an ascomycetous *Cylindrocarpon* species (formerly called *Fusidium coccineum*), is used against infections by Gram-positive bacteria which have become resistant to other antibiotics. 'Pleuromutilin' is unusual in being the only basidiomycetous antibiotic so far produced commercially. It was originally derived from the agarics '*Pleurotus mutilus*' (the name has been variously applied) and *Clitopilus passeckerianus*. Pleuromutilin is particularly effective against mycoplasma infections in animals and is used in veterinary medicine under the name Tiamutin®.

Other important pharmaceuticals from fungi

'Cyclosporins' are fungal metabolites (cyclopeptides) derived from *Tolypocladium inflatum* and other ascomycetous soil fungi. Their importance lies in their potent immunosuppressive effects and they are widely used (under the names Sandimmune® and Neoral®) to prevent organ rejection in transplant patients. Cyclosporins have also been approved as a treatment for psoriasis, rheumatoid arthritis and as an alternative to colectomy for patients with severe inflammatory bowel disease. Further research is being undertaken into the possible use of cyclosporins for HIV treatment.

'Mevinic acids', including mevastatin, lovastatin, simvastatin and pravastatin, are produced or partly synthesised from strains of ascomycetous yeasts and moulds such as *Monascus ruber, Aspergillus terreus,* and *Penicillium citrinum.* All are cholesterol-lowering drugs marketed under various names, including Zocor® and Mevacor®. These are currently among the biggest-selling prescription drugs in the United States, though now challenged by more recent synthetics, such as atorvastatin (Lipitor®).

VETERINARY MYCOLOGY

Animal mycoses, at least among birds and mammals, tend to be similar to those affecting humans. Indeed many fungal species do not discriminate between hosts and are capable of switching between species, if the overall environment is similar. Thus aspergillosis, candidiasis, cryptococcosis, and other human diseases are also known in a range of pets, farm animals, and (less widely investigated) wild animals. A somewhat dated, but still useful review of animal mycoses was published by Ainsworth & Austwick (1973), whilst opportunistic mycoses were reviewed by Smith (1989).

Among the mycoses we share with animals, blastomycosis is notable in affecting dogs, especially hunting dogs, often at the same time as their owners. The causative agent is a soil fungus with a preference for growing near water, and the shared mycosis is probably a result of being in the same place at the same time. Other wild animals which may suffer from habitat-specific diseases include burrowing mammals infected by soil fungi. Armadillos, as already noted, are prone to paracoccidioidomycosis caused by *Paracoccidioides brasiliensis,* whilst both armadillos and burrowing rodents may suffer from a lung disease, adiaspiromycosis, caused by the ascomycetes *Emmonsia crescens* and *E. parva* (*Onygenales*). In Britain, this has been linked to periodic fluctuations in the mole population. Marsupials, such as the hairy-nosed wombat, can also be infected. In desert areas in America, soil-disturbing animals are thought to play a role in maintaining populations of *Coccidioides immitis,* the cause of valley fever.

Host-specific animal dermatotrophs

Though most fungal infections of mammals can also be found in humans, some of the dermatotrophic fungi appear to be obligate parasites and have evolved host-specific associations. In the ringworm-causing genera *Microsporum* and *Trichophyton*, for example, there are species associated with horses (*T. equinum*), with pigs (*M. nanum*), with poultry (*T. gallinae*), with voles (*M. persicolor*), and even hedgehogs (*T. erinacei*). Many of these can switch hosts and cause problems in humans, *M. canis* on dogs and cats being the commonest such species, but (like fleas) do not seem able to persist in the absence of their preferred hosts. *Malassezia* species may have also evolved host preferences in animals (it has even been suggested that okapis harbour a distinct species, though this is less clear-cut).

Mycotoxins and farm animals

Farm animals are particularly susceptible to mycotoxins, either through non-selective grazing or more commonly through being fed contaminated foodstuffs. There are occasional cases of grazing animals eating poisonous toadstools, sometimes with fatal results. More common is gangrenous ergotism from silage, hay, or pasture grasses infected with *Claviceps purpurea*. It particularly affects cattle and in severe cases can lead to the loss of limbs, as happened to the poor beast Graceless in *Cold Comfort Farm*. This is no mere fiction. Ergotism is still a very real problem in Britain, where the incidence of *Claviceps* infection in pasture crops increased significantly in the 1980s. Other problems can be caused by unseen fungal endophytes, notably *Neotyphodium lolii* which is a symbiont of ryegrass. This produces a neurotoxin, 'lolitrem B', the cause of 'ryegrass staggers', a condition that principally affects sheep, but also cattle and horses. Animals become uncoordinated, stagger, and may collapse. In America, *Neotyphodium coenophialum*, symbiotic in tall fescue grass, produces a far more dangerous mycotoxin called 'ergovaline' which causes symptoms similar to ergotism. Tall fescue poisoning can be severe and in the United States has been credited with causing annual losses of over £400,000,000 among cattle and horses. Lupins, sometimes grown for forage, can produce a liver-damaging disease called 'lupinosis' when infected by the fungus *Phomopsis leptostromiformis,* which produces a toxin called 'phomopsin A'. Lucerne, a more common leguminous forage crop in Britain, may also be host to similar mycotoxins.

CHAPTER 16

Folklore and Traditional Use

T RADITIONAL uses of fungi are legion. As well as food and alcohol (Chapter 17), fungi have been used as fly-killers, bee-tranquillisers, night-lights, and dyes, and have been crafted into tinder, paper, ink, clothing, decorative woodwork, razor-strops, and cosmetics. In addition, they have been employed as intoxicants and hallucinogenic agents, in rituals and folk medicines, and have gathered around them a diverse and distinctive folklore, ranging from fairy tales and superstitions to cult and religious beliefs. It is an area of study known as 'ethnomycology', with a very substantial worldwide literature only part of which can be covered here.

PREHISTORIC USAGE

Mankind's use of fungi goes back at least 8000 years, and probably extends still further into the deep pre-human past. Their employment in prehistoric times is well established, having been documented from archaeological digs and artefacts. Although the soft fruitbodies of agarics are rarely preserved, tougher fruitbodies may persist and provide evidence of past uses.

One of the most famous and tangible examples of the prehistoric use of fungi involved the neolithic 'ice-man', discovered frozen in a Tyrolean glacier on the Austrian/Italian border in 1990. The man died over 5000 years ago attempting a journey through an alpine pass. Among the many strange devices he was carrying were three pieces of fungi whose usage has been the subject of considerable study and debate. Two of them, walnut-sized objects mounted separately on a leather thong, are parts of a fruitbody of *Piptoporus betulinus*, the common birch polypore, whilst the third, contained in a leather pouch, has been identified as tissue from the hoof-shaped polypore, *Fomes fomentarius*. The *Fomes* tissue had been mechanically treated so as to loosen the hyphae for use as tinder and possibly also for use as a styptic. Such usage is well documented elsewhere and has continued up to modern times. But why the ice-man should have taken *Piptoporus betulinus* with him is much more of a puzzle. The tissue of the birch polypore has been used as tinder (see below) and it is not impossible that it could have been carried for this purpose. However, the mounting of the objects on a leather thong separate from the *Fomes* tissue suggests some other use, possibly of a medical-spiritual nature.

A further ancient use of fungi has been inferred from excavations at Skara Brae in Orkney, where the remains of fruitbodies of the puffball *Bovista nigrescens* were discovered in 1972 and 1973. These finds, reported by Watling (1975), are around 2000 years old and, although the puffballs may have been used for tinder or medically (as styptics), their quantity and presence in buildings suggested that they may have had a secondary usage, providing effective insulation against draughts. Puffballs (*B. nigrescens* and *Calvatia utriformis*) have also been found at the Roman site of Vindolanda in Northumberland.

TRADITIONAL USES & FUNGAL CRAFTS

Tinder and amadou

The dried tissue of some bracket fungi, in particular *Fomes fomentarius* and *Phellinus igniarius* which have a hard, corky context, smoulders for a long time once alight, and can be applied to dried twigs or leaves to create flames (the epithet '*igniarius*' relates to fire). This was particularly important in primitive societies as a method of creating fire. Indeed, it remained of importance in not-so-primitive societies up to the invention of lucifer matches.

The tinder was produced by cutting the fruitbodies into strips, which were then beaten, rubbed and stretched until they became soft and pliable, at which stage it was often known as 'amadou' or 'German tinder' (Fig. 143). In Europe, up to the nineteenth century, amadou was sold as sheets or more commonly twisted into regular lengths or *'fusées'*. They could be used directly as tinder, but were much more effective when saltpetre (NaNO3) or gunpowder was added. This was known as 'black amadou', the untreated material as 'red amadou'.

The production of amadou was noted by Cooke in 1862, when it was still of commercial importance throughout northern Europe. Britten in 1877 claimed that it was 'formerly prepared . . . by the Highlanders' from *Fomes fomentarius* and that 'its value was from a shilling to eighteenpence an ounce' (£1.75–£2.65 per kilo). Other brackets such as *Piptoporus betulinus* and *Laetiporus sulphureus* also had some lesser use for the same purpose. Swanton (1917) observed that the fruitbodies of the birch polypore smoulder persistently when enclosed in a tin and were used in Surrey to transport fire. Britten noted that the sulphur polypore was powdered and used as tinder by some continentals and 'the Indians of Rupert's Land'.

Amadou was at one time also used extensively in medicine, principally as

FIG 143. Amadou, the dried suede-like tissue of polypore fruitbodies, was extensively used for tinder well into the nineteenth century (RBG Kew).

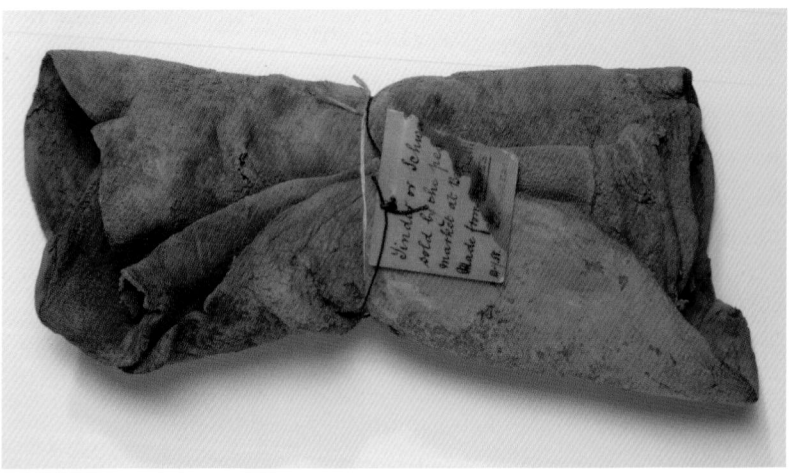

a styptic, although puffballs (species of *Bovista*, *Calvatia*, and related genera) were more valued for this purpose. Amadou derived from *Fomes fomentarius* is apparently still used in dry fly-fishing, being ideal for keeping the fly afloat. Small pieces can be bought in tackle shops at a cost of £5 or more per piece.

Bees and tranquillisers

Another use for puffballs was to tranquillise bees in order to gain access to the hive and its honey. The species most frequently used for this purpose seems to have been the giant puffball, *Calvatia gigantea*, which was set alight and allowed to smoulder giving off copious clouds of bee-befuddling fumes. According to Swanton (1917), fruitbodies of the bracket fungi *Piptoporus betulinus* and *Daedalea quercina* were also employed in this way, and at that time were still in such use by beekeepers in the Godalming district of Surrey. Placed beneath the hive, the fumes from the smouldering fruitbodies have the required effect on the bees, although it seems likely that their anaesthetic properties may simply be due to a high production of carbon dioxide on burning.

Nevertheless, use of puffballs as anaesthetics in hospital operations was recorded in the 19th century. The alarming effects of such use was colourfully described by MacMillan in 1861 who stated that they deprived 'the patient of speech, motion and sensibility to pain, while he is still conscious of everything that happens around him; thus realising that nightmare of our dreams in which we lie stretched upon the funeral bier, sensible to the weeping of friends, aware of the last screw being fixed in the coffin, and the last clod clapped down upon us in the churchyard, and are yet unable to move a hand or a lip for our own deliverance'!

Puffballs have been put to a surprising variety of other practical folk uses, including as tinder, and as pin-cushions in parts of Europe. North American Indians have used them as necklaces, as rattles wielded by medicine men, and even as dusting powder for baby talc. Additional uses, culinary, medical and practical, of puffballs and other gasteromycetes were given by Læssøe & Spooner (1994).

Razor strops

In the early part of 19th century, fruitbodies of *Piptoporus betulinus* were
sometimes used instead of leather to make razor strops. Swanton (1917) described how a piece of the fungus measuring about 6′ × 2′ × 1′ (15 × 5 × 2.5 cm)
was nailed to a length of wood, the stropping area being the pore surface
dusted with siliceous earth. Examples of such strops can be found in
the collections at Kew and at Haslemere Museum. Even today, *P. betulinus* is
sometimes known as the 'razor-strop fungus'. Another common species,
Polyporus squamosus, was also used for making razor strops in England, but
was apparently much less popular.

Dyeing

The use of fungi for dyeing wool and other fibres was for centuries
a traditional practice in northern Europe and North America and has
resurfaced today as an interesting craft pastime.

Lichens were originally the fungi most widely used, different species
producing a wide range of dyes in shades of red, violet, or brown. Amongst
the best known was 'orchil', produced from species of *Roccella*, mainly
R. canariensis, *R. fuciformis*, and the tropical *R. montagnei*, and 'cudbear' from
the crustose lichens *Ochrolechia tartarea* and *O. androgyna*. Both give a strong
reddish-purple colour, though this is fugitive to light. The lichens from
which orchil was obtained were known as 'Canary weed' because of their
economic importance in the Canary Islands where they grew in quantity on
sea cliffs. They were also found on other Atlantic islands such as Madeira
and the Azores, and supported an important export trade. This began in the
15th century and reached its peak in the 18th century when up to 120 tons
of lichens were collected annually for shipment to England and Spain. Such
gross over-exploitation of the lichen populations inevitably meant that by
1778 only half a ton could be gathered, and by the early 19th century the
trade had all but ceased.

Cudbear was a commercial enterprise started in 1758 in Edinburgh by
one George Gordon, who originally called his new dye 'cuthbert' after his
mother's maiden name. The manufactory moved to Glasgow where up to 250
tons of *Ochrolechia tartarea* were processed annually, originally collected from
the Highlands and islands, but later imported from Scandinavia, the Canary

Islands, and Malta. The ammonia used in processing the dye was distilled from Glaswegian urine, of which no less than 2000–3000 gallons were required each day. The Glasgow manufactory closed in 1852, much to the dismay of Lindsay (1856) who hoped that a 'revival and extension of this traffic would probably prove a great boon to that remnant of the Celtic race, which is fast disappearing from our shores'. Cudbear continued to be manufactured in small quantities in England up to the 1950s, most of it exported to the USA for use as a purple food colouring and for dyeing leather.

Other lichen dyes, such as 'crottle', from species of *Parmelia*, particularly *P. omphalodes* and *P. saxatilis*, are light-fast and reactive, giving a buff or brown colour. They were once extensively used for dyeing homespun yarn, particularly in Scotland where 'almost every farm and cotter-house had its tank or barrel of 'graith', or putrid urine, and its 'lit-pig', wherein the mistress of the household macerated some familiar crottle' (Lindsay, 1856). This home-dyeing industry (of which lichens were only a part) continued in some small way at least till the 1970s, the dyes being used for Harris tweed and other handmade fabrics.

Numerous non-lichenised fungi can also be used for dyeing, and indeed seem to be of increasing importance for the production of colour-fast and environmentally friendly dyes. Traditionally, perhaps the most important of these was the large, puffball-like *Pisolithus arhizus*, also known as *P. tinctorius* (the epithet referring to its dyeing qualities) or simply 'dye-ball'. It was formerly used in the Canaries, Italy, and the south of France to give 'an excellent brown' to silks. Another puffball-like species, the tropical *Podaxis pistillaris*, was used in Sudan to produce a yellowish dye for carpets.

Similar colours can be obtained from the bracket fungus *Inonotus hispidus* and were once also employed in silk dyeing. The same species was used by glovers and leather-dressers for colouring skins, and by cabinet-makers for colouring wood. Three further brackets, *Phellinus igniarius*, *Laetiporus sulphureus*, and *Polyporus alveolaris* give brownish-black, yellow, and yellowish-green dyes respectively, whilst the scarlet bracket fungus *Pycnoporus sanguineus* has been used to produce orange-grey or brownish dyes in West Africa. The dye potential for various other bracket fungi was investigated by Cedano *et al.* (2001). Of the fourteen species examined they found *Phaeolus schweinitzii* to have the greatest value of all, yielding, depending on the mordant used, five colours of excellent intensity. Other good dye sources amongst the bracket fungi are *Fomes fomentarius* and *Hapalopilus nidulans*.

In recent years in Europe and North America, there has been an upsurge of interest in craft-dyeing using natural products. As a result, modern craft dyers have discovered that fruitbodies of certain toadstools yield excellent dyes (Fig. 144). It has long been known that 'a very fine red' could be obtained from various *Russula* species, but species of *Gymnopilus*, *Hygrocybe*, and particularly *Dermocybe* also produce intense dyes. When combined with an appropriate mordant such as alum, tin, or iron, these produce attractive shades of orange, red, pink, brown, and yellow. The only elusive dye colour from fungi is said to be a good blue.

Methods for extracting the dyes and some of the fungi involved have been detailed in handbooks by Rice & Beebee (1980) and Bessette & Bessette (2001), with colour photographs of the results.

FIG 144. Dyed wool samples, showing a wide range of colours derived from modern and traditional fungal pigments (P. Livermore).

Litmus from lichens

Litmus, well known to chemists for its use in indicating pH, is another important dye produced from fungi (Fig. 145). It can be prepared from various lichens, including *Lecanora tartarea* and some species of *Roccella*, especially *R. tinctoria*, using ammonia in conjunction with potassium carbonate to produce the blue alkali azolitmin. This is turned red by acids and blue by alkalis. From the sixteenth century onwards, litmus was mainly produced in Holland, though in the 1940s it also began to be manufactured in Hendon, Middlesex. By the 1970s, this manufactory was importing 25 tons of lichens, mainly using *Roccella montagnei* from Madagascar for litmus production.

FIG 145. Litmus blocks prepared from lichens. Acids turn the blue lichen-dye pink (RBG Kew).

Paper making

The craft manufacture of paper from fungi is a comparatively recent innovation developed largely by Miriam Rice in the 1990s (Rice, 1991, 1992). She proposed using different species of bracket fungi to obtain fine, high quality papers using simple and straightforward methods. The species involved include *Bjerkandera adusta, Daedaleopsis confragosa, Datronia mollis, Trametes gibbosa, T. versicolor, Heterabasidion annosum, Fomes fomentarius, Inonotus radiatus, Lenzites betulina* and *Ganoderma applanatum*. These are all common bracket fungi, widespread throughout Britain. Those with a tough structure of thick-walled and binding hyphae give the best results. The process is fairly simple, the fruitbodies being cut into pieces, soaked and blended, the resulting puree then pressed between sheets of blotting paper until dry. Colour and fine texture of the finished paper vary according to the fungus used.

Toadstool ink

Not only can fungi be used to make paper, they can also serve as the basis for making ink. Traditional ink manufacture used bark and other plant materials rich in tannins, especially certain oak galls which were once of commercial significance for this purpose. However, an alternative tradition involved the production of ink from *Coprinus comatus*, the shaggy ink cap or lawyer's wig, and other fleshy species of *Coprinus*. Bulliard in 1791 noted that his new species, *Coprinus atramentarius* (the epithet means 'inky'), could be used to make ink suitable for drawing.

Fungal ink is simple to produce. The fruitbodies are placed in a suitable container, such as a glazed pot, and then left to deliquesce into a black liquid. This liquid is then poured off and can be used directly as ink or boiled down to darken the colour. Phenol can be added to preserve the ink, but it is generally agreed that fungal ink was and is less effective and less permanent than its vegetable counterparts.

Perfumes and pot-pourri

The use of fungi in the development of perfumes is a long-established though rather little known practice. It is centred on a few lichenised species, notably *Evernia prunastri*, commonly known as 'oak moss', and *Pseudevernia furfuracea* (Fig. 145A) or 'tree moss'. These produce chemicals that can be used in perfumes to reduce the rate of evaporation of other ingredients, hence making the fragrance last longer. 'Cyprus powder', once used to powder wigs, contained a mix of lichens scented with flowers. Surprisingly, these lichens

FIG 145A. Tree moss *Pseudevernia furfuracea* is a lichen still widely used in the perfume industry to 'fix' fragrances (RBG Kew).

are still used by the perfume industry today, an estimated 8000–9000 tons being collected per year in the 1970s, mainly from France, Italy, Morocco, and the Balkans. As a result, the lichens have been so commercially exploited in some parts of Europe that they have become of conservation concern due to overcollecting and damage to the environment.

Of ethnomycological interest is the former use of the polypore *Haploporus odorus* as a natural perfume. The species, which occurs on willow in high northern areas, has a strong aniseed smell which persists even in dried fruitbodies. Linnaeus noted that it was carried by young men out wooing in Lappland, whilst Blanchette (1997) illustrated its widespread use in necklaces, scalp trophies, and robe ornaments by the Blackfoot and Cree peoples. The latter were also said to use it as a form of incense.

The fruitbodies of several bracket-like fungi are commonly used for decorative purposes in pot-pourri mixtures in Britain. These include *Lentinus polychrous, Daedalea quercina, Microporus xanthopus* and *Lenzites acuta*, wood-rotting species with tough, inedible fruitbodies which do not lose their shape once dried. *Daedalea quercina* occurs throughout Europe on trunks and stumps of oak and chestnut, whereas the other species occur in the eastern tropics and in parts of Australasia. Most of the material imported into Britain originates in India, and is generally traded under common names such as 'golden mushroom' (*Microporus xanthopus*) and 'sponge mushroom' (*Lenzites acuta*). The fruitbodies of *Daedalea* and *Lenzites* are often dyed red, yellow, green, or blue for the pot-pourri mixture, using non-toxic textile dyes. Some lichens are also used in pot-pourri, mostly species of *Cladonia* and *Pseudevernia* obtained from Norway and Morocco; as noted above, these are mainly used to fix and extend the fragrance.

Though hardly an essential item, pot-pourri is of considerable commercial importance, with over 600 tons of dried ingredients, including fruit, flowers, leaves and fungi, being imported into Britain annually. The trade is now estimated to exceed £50,000,000 per annum in the UK alone.

A few oils derived from fungi, particularly lichens, are used in the modern art of 'psycho-aromatherapy'. The lichen *Parmelia nepalensis*, one of the main sources of such oils, which is currently marketed (in small quantities) at around £450 per litre. Oil of *Evernia prunastri* is said to have the emotional attribute of 'creating a sense of home, attachment, and belonging' and costs around £750 per litre. Oil of *Usnea barbata* is somewhat cheaper.

Well-dressings, wreaths and models

Lichens are also a constituent of 'well-dressings', a traditional pagan custom still observed in the Peak District of Derbyshire, whereby wells are annually dressed with intricate floral and mycological mosaics. Species of *Parmelia* and *Xanthoria* are particularly used, mainly because they hold their shape and colour far longer than cut flowers and leaves. For similar reasons, *Cladonia* species are popular as a constituent of graveyard wreaths in Germany. At one time over 12,000 crates of these lichens were being shipped from Norway to Germany for this purpose in a single year. There is again considerable exploitation of wild populations to satisfy these demands. There are others, too. For example, lichens have been long been used in tabletop models and dioramas to represent trees and bushes and for this purpose are still available commercially for railway modellers. Several American dealers currently advertise lichens for modelling at around £6 for a 4-quart bag (a rather strange unit of measurement), without specifying species.

Cosmetics and clothing

Rather improbably, fungi have occasionally been used as cosmetics in various cultures around the world. The black spore masses of the rice-smut *Ustilago esculenta* were at one time sold in Japan as a form of mascara, used by actors as well as ladies, whilst the reddish-brown spores of the puffball-like *Podaxis pistillaris* were used as a face powder in south western Africa. Spores of the stilt puffball *Battarraea stevenii*, mixed to a paste, were similarly used as a cosmetic among the Topnaar people of the Namib desert, whilst the giant sclerotia of *Lentinus tuberregium* formed part of a mixture used as body paint in Nigeria. The bracket-like *Echinodontium tinctorium* gained its epithet and its popular name of 'Indian paint fungus' for its use (powdered and mixed with water or oil) as red-coloured war paint by native peoples in the American northwest.

The long, black, shiny rhizomorphs of *Polyporus rhizomorphus* have been woven to make belts in Gabon, whilst the similar but finer rhizomorphs of *Marasmius crinisequi* (the epithet means 'horse hair') have been used for jewellery strings in the Congo and Indonesia. Similar rhizomorphs, fashioned into fringed and beaded belts, were once said to have been used by Fijians, often as their sole article of clothing.

Jewellery in the form of brooches and even earrings has been made from the bracket fungus *Trametes versicolor*, commonly known as the 'many-zoned polypore' since it has concentric and often brightly coloured zones on the upper surface. As its tough fruitbodies dry readily without loss of colour and form, it is ideal for such decorative use.

In the former German duchy of Franconia, clothes were once made out of amadou beaten until soft and sewn together. In Hungary, caps and waistcoats were made out of large brackets of *Ganoderma*, the Rev. Miles Berkeley having exhibited such articles (bought for half a florin) at the Royal Horticultural Society in the 1870s. Caps were still being made out of fungal fruitbodies in Roumania one hundred years later, presumably for the tourist trade. The source was said to be *Ganoderma applanatum*, pre-treated by boiling in milk.

FUNGI AND WOOD-CRAFTS

Tunbridge Ware: fungi and marquetry

The manufacture of ornamental boxes and other objects using marquetry techniques known as 'Tunbridge Ware' was developed in the town of Tunbridge Wells in Kent in the early 17th century. A wide range of woods was used, but prominent amongst them was oak wood stained green or turquoise by the ascomycete *Chlorociboria aeruginascens*. This is a common species, producing deep greenish blue, cup-shaped fruitbodies which occur in swarms on rotting wood (Fig. 146). The green-stained wood is easily found in litter on the woodland floor, although the fruitbodies, which

FIG 146. The distinctive bright greenish fruitbodies of the discomycete *Chlorociboria aeruginascens*. Wood stained blue-green by the mycelium was formerly used in Tunbridge ware (P. Livermore).

FIG 147. An example of Tunbridge Ware, a once-popular form of marquetry, here used to decorate a box. The bluish-green colours are derived from wood stained by the fungus *Chlorociboria aeruginascens* (J. Cross).

develop in autumn, are much less frequent. The use of this fungus-stained wood is an attractive and distinctive feature of Tunbridge Ware which relied on natural colours rather than artificially lacquered or painted finishes (Fig. 147). However, by the early 20th century the industry was in decline, largely due to competition from cheaply coloured, mass-produced items. The development and history of Tunbridge Ware were more fully explored by Gill (1999).

Spalted wood: patterns of decay

Decayed timber often exhibits distinctive and conspicuous patterns of black or dark brown lines (Fig. 148). These zone lines are due to melanin produced at the boundaries between adjacent colonies of fungi, involving either the same or different species, and effectively demarcate territories held by individual wood-rotting fungi.

Such zone lines can be found in many different woods. They are common for example in beech where they are mostly caused by members of the

FIG 148. A bowl fashioned from spalted wood, in which the black zone lines, formed when fungal populations meet, make attractive patterns for ornaments (RBG Kew).

Xylariaceae, notably *Hypoxylon fragiforme*, *Kretzschmaria deusta*, and *Xylaria polymorpha*, or by bracket fungi such as *Trametes versicolor*. The patterns are commonly known as 'spalting' and the use of spalted wood for the production of decorative objects has a long history and is still of some commercial importance today. Spalting can occur within some six months of felling, depending on environmental conditions. As long as the decay is not too advanced, spalted wood can be readily worked for decorative, patterned effects.

Similar patterns are produced by species of *Cyttaria*, the edible, golfball-like ascomycetes which are found on galled branches of southern beech (*Nothofagus*) in the forests of South America. Sectioning branches infected by *Cyttaria* reveals attractive patterns created by the fungal hyphae and such branches are carved to make ornaments sold in local markets.

RECREATIONAL AND RELIGIOUS USES

A few fungi have a history of use as mild or strong intoxicants, taken either for pleasure or in magical ceremonies for purposes of divination. Species of *Psilocybe* and other 'magic mushrooms' are used as recreational drugs today, a vogue which started in the United States in the 1950s and has now spread around the world. Most other recreational and religious use of fungi is historic or extremely localised. Investigation and popularisation of the subject have been dominated by the works of R. Gordon Wasson, who was always keen to remind readers that 'my wife and I were solely responsible for the present development of what we were the first to call ethnomycology' (Wasson, 1980). It is a field where distinguishing facts from fancies is not always easy, particularly in the interpretation of historic texts, drawings, and artefacts. Spotting mushroom-shaped objects of religious import, as 'evident' in 9000-year-old rock drawings from Algeria (Gartz, 1996) or suggested in rock engravings at Stonehenge (Samorini, 2001a,b), is even easier than revealing signs of ancient astronauts.

Recreational and religious fungi include not only the psilocybin-containing toadstools, but also the fly agaric (*Amanita muscaria*), boletes in New Guinea, puffballs in Mexico, and a number of bracket fungi which are used as snuff. Other examples can be found in works such as those of Heim (1978), Gartz (1996) and Wasson (see below).

Fungal snuff

The preparation of snuff from the tough, hoof-shaped brackets of *Phellinus igniarius* is one of various uses to which fungi were once put by native North American peoples. The snuff was made from the ashes of the fungal fruitbodies and stored in finely crafted boxes and pouches made from a range of material such as wood, bone and leather. The ashes were added to finely chopped tobacco and also to chewing tobacco to increase its potency. As a result, fruitbodies of *Phellinus igniarius* were significant trade items, a practice that Blanchette (2001) found to be widespread amongst North American peoples. Berkeley in 1860 also mentioned the use of the same bracket fungus as snuff by 'natives in the northern region of Asia', whilst Britten (1877) claimed that the ashes of *Fomes fomentarius* were used as snuff by the Kamchatkans. Both brackets were also used for amadou.

Fungal intoxicants: Amanita muscaria

In Siberia, the fly agaric *Amanita muscaria* was once used as an intoxicant, more or less substituting for alcohol. The earliest reference is an account of a European visitor to western Siberia (near the River Ob) in 1658 who noted that the local tribesmen ate fly agarics and got 'drunk worse than on vodka'. Wasson reprinted many similar tales of fly agaric inebriation among the Yakuts, Ostyak, and other native Siberian peoples from travellers of the eighteenth, nineteenth, and early twentieth centuries. Drinking the urine of fly agaric eaters was said to be almost as effective as eating the fungus itself, though to us it might seem a rather desperate measure.

Several recent authors have elevated the former use of *Amanita muscaria* among Siberian native peoples to the status of a transcendental religion, but it seems the main object was to get very drunk indeed. Lesseps' 1790 journal of travels in Kamchatka noted that the natives' 'passion for strong liquors ... has led them to invent a drink, equally potent, which they extract from a red mushroom.' Invited to party 'the entertainment lasts for one, two, or three days, till the beverage is exhausted ... It is astonishing that there are not more examples of the fatal effects of this intemperance ... but experience does not correct them, and ... they return to their brutish practice. It is not from absolute sensuality, it is not from pleasure of drinking a liquor ... they seek merely in these orgies a state of oblivion, of stupefaction, of total brutishness, a cessation of existence ... which constitutes their only enjoyment, and supreme felicity'.

The suggestion that *Amanita muscaria* was once eaten by Vikings in order to go 'berserk' stems from a Swedish treatise of 1784 by Ödman, entitled (in translation) 'An attempt to explain the berserk-raging of ancient Nordic warriors through natural history'. Though the concept of Vikings eating hallucinogenic fungi to enhance their prowess makes an attractive story (still repeated today, e.g. as an early example of sports-doping by Delbeke, 2000), fly agaric rarely if ever induces aggressive behaviour and there seems to be no factual basis for Ödman's engaging idea.

The divine toadstool

Though the fly agaric was mostly used as a Siberian substitute for raw alcohol, several authors have claimed that it also formed part of shamanistic rites to reach worlds beyond everyday reality. Wasson (1980) also claimed it was used in this way in North America, by the Ojibway of the Algonkian nation, whilst Lowy (1972) suggested its past use in Central America, based on Mayan codices.

From Siberian travellers, there are sufficient contemporary accounts to substantiate the quasi-religious use of *Amanita muscaria*, but these are tempered by the equally prevalent observations that the shamans happily used brandy, vodka, or other strong spirits to achieve trance-like states. In other words, there was nothing particularly sacred or magical about the fly agaric. Any intoxicant would do.

Despite this, Wasson (1968) still claimed that *Amanita muscaria* was 'soma', the 'divine mushroom of immortality', mentioned in the ancient Vedic texts of the Hindus (Buddhist texts too, according to Crowley, 1996) and known to our earliest Indo-European ancestors. As such, according to Wasson, it was venerated in the pagan past and consequently demonised by the early Christians. The historically mycophobic peoples of northern Europe were those who rejected the fly agaric and all other 'toadstools' (a word linked with poison, serpents, and sin), whilst the mycophilic Slavs and Latins embraced the divine mushroom and all its kin. This apparently happened in the distant past 'for a reason that we cannot now tell' (Wasson *et al.*, 1978).

Wasson's dubious claims for the fly agaric were taken to yet more wonderful extremes by Allegro (1970) who maintained that Christianity itself was originally an orgiastic, pagan fertility cult based on *Amanita muscaria*. Allegro, a philologist and academic who worked on the Dead Sea scrolls, found coded messages in the language of the Bible revealing the true nature of early Christian belief and worship. Much of the early Christian vocabulary, it appears, related to the sexual symbolism of the sacred mushroom, and little if anything else. For this, he was dubbed 'the Liberace of Biblical scholarship', not least by mycologists who rather doubted the presence of the birch- and pine-associated fly agaric among the palm trees and deserts of the Holy Land.

Magic mushrooms and psilocybin

Since the 1960s, 'magic mushrooms' have become something of a totem for the counterculture. It all started with a popular article by Wasson (1957) in *Life* magazine which related the mind-altering experiences of shamanistic toadstool-eaters in Mexico. Wasson himself (1980) deplored the subsequent use of these fungi for recreational purposes by 'hippies ... oddballs ... the riffraff of our population', but his own capacity for self-advertising more or less guaranteed this would happen.

The knowledge that certain agarics contained psychoactive alkaloids spread, slowly at first, becoming widespread from the late 1970s onwards, when collecting magic mushrooms first became popular in Britain. The active ingredients, psilocybin and psilocin, were isolated by the Swiss chemist Albert Hofmann, who in 1943 had been the first to synthesise lysergic acid diethylamide (LSD) from ergot (*Claviceps purpurea*) and was consequently interested in hallucinogenic agents derived from fungi.

The species concerned are mostly small, dark-spored agarics in the genera *Psilocybe* and (less potently) *Panaeolus*. Most occur on dung or manure-enriched grassland, a few on wood chippings and composts. The best-known species in the British Isles is the liberty cap, *Psilocybe semilanceata*, which is common in enriched grassland, particularly upland sheep pastures. Currently, possession of wild 'magic mushrooms' is not illegal in England, but this changes as soon as they are processed (which may or may not include simple drying) whereupon they are regarded as a Class A drug on a par with heroin.

From a scientific point of view, magic mushrooms induce euphoria, hallucinations, anxiety attacks, and palpitations. From an enthusiast's point of view they are 'keys to dimensions surrounding us that ordinarily cannot be seen', bringing one 'closer to God, Jesus, Buddha, [and] Gaian consciousness' (Stamets, 1996).

Teonanácatl – the flesh of the gods

The Aztecs of Mexico once regarded magic mushrooms as the flesh of the gods, 'teonanácatl', and used them in shamanistic rites to communicate with deities. Biased accounts of such heathen practices involving 'wicked mushrooms' were given by Spanish conquistadors in the sixteenth century (extracts were compiled by Schleiffer, 1973). Wasson & Wasson (1957) publicised their continued use in secret ceremonies that were part-Aztec, part-Catholic. The principal fungi used in these rites are or were *Psilocybe* species, including *Psilocybe mexicana, P. cubensis* (Fig. 149), *P. aztecorum,* and *P. zapotectorum.* They are mainly eaten as part of a divination ceremony or 'velada' (vigil) by a 'curandero' (healer) who acts as an oracle, answering questions and dispensing wisdom.

Wasson & Wasson (1957) linked the modern *Psilocybe* ceremonies with strange stone artefacts of the Mayan period resembling toadstools, but with carved stems. These 'mushroom stones', found in Mexico and Guatemala, have been variously interpreted as phallic totems, land-markers, ceremonial seats, moulds for making latex balls (for the Mayan ball game), or devotional items connected with the teonanácatl rites. Several of these enigmatic artefacts were illustrated by Lowy (1971) and Wasson (1980).

FIG 149. The magic mushroom *Psilocybe cubensis,* once used in Mexican divination rites and now widely cultivated and sold in Britain as a recreational drug (RBG Kew).

Grave guardians and ceremonial offerings

More clearly fungal than the mushroom stones are the spirit guardians placed on the graves of shamans by the Tlingit and other native peoples of northwest America. These human and animal figures (illustrated and discussed by Blanchette *et al.*, 1992) were carved out of the large, woody brackets of *Fomitopsis officinalis*, the same fungus that was long considered a universal panacea in Europe. The fungus was reputed to have similar healing powers in North America, these being derived from supernatural forces.

Slightly more equivocal are the 4000-year-old clay artefacts excavated from Jomon period sites in Japan. These are simple, undecorated objects (illustrated in Kudo, 2000) which convincingly represent a range of agarics and may have been used as ceremonial food offerings. The stipitate polypore *Lignosus sacer* obtained its epithet 'sacer' (meaning 'sacred') since it was supposed to be an object of veneration and worship by local peoples in Guinea. Guzmán *et al.* (1975) gave details of a church in Mexico dedicated to 'Nuestro Senor del Honguito', in which an image of Christ drawn on the hymenium of the bracket *Ganoderma lobatum* was venerated.

FOLKLORE AND CURIOUS BELIEFS

As might be expected, the folklore of fungi is varied and diverse, with some beliefs being widespread, others decidedly local. Only a few can be sampled here. Further legends and usages concerning bracket fungi were collected by Thoen (1982); those involving gasteromycetes by Spooner & Læssøe (1994). Findlay (1982) published a popular review of fungal facts and fictions.

Toads, vipers, and slime

The mycophobia of the British, both Celts and Anglo-Saxons, is summed up by the word 'toadstool', applicable to any non-edible agaric and (in more modern times) to almost any agaric not in the genus *Agaricus*. Grove in 1888 suggested that 'the guilt lies mainly on the shoulders of the man who first bestowed on fungi the nickname 'toad-stools'. Give a dog a bad name, and you know the consequences. The toad has an evil reputation.' Indeed, in

Britain, toads were traditionally considered poisonous, to the extent that mountebanks selling patent medicines often employed a toad-eater (or toady) who would swallow a toad and take a draught of the medicine, to prove that it was effective. Former dialect words in English included the Scottish 'paddockstool', Berkshire 'toad's cheese', Dorset 'toad's meat', and the widespread 'toad's hat'. Venomous toadstools were believed 'to growe where olde rustie iron lieth, or rotten clouts, or neere to serpents dens', the serpents presumably conferring poison by association.

Slime may be the basis for the word 'mushroom', though its origin is obscure. The earliest record of its use in English dates to the fifteenth century, but whether 'mushroom' was derived from the French for moss (mousse), the Welsh for field (maes), the Latin for slime (mucus), the French for fly (mouche), or some other word entirely is unknown.

Wolves breaking wind

Mature puffballs release visible clouds of brown spores when squeezed or hit by raindrops. Our down-to-earth ancestors happily connected this with farting ('fist' in dialect), naming puffballs 'fist balls', 'woolfes fistes', 'bullfists', and so on. The French 'vesse-de-loup' and Latin 'lupi crepitus' are the same. Why wolves should be involved seems obscure. Nonetheless, this connection is maintained in the scientific name for the main genus of puffballs, *Lycoperdon*, which is derived from the Greek for 'wolf fart' (λυκος + περδομαι). The genus *Bovista* is similarly derived from the German for 'ox fart' (Bo + Fist). Fabre, writing in Victorian times, considered it undesirable to translate such scientific names 'bequeathed to us by earlier ages less reticent than ours', since they 'often retained the brutal frankness of words that set propriety at defiance'. This is wonderfully true of the following species.

Satan's member

The stinkhorn is common, evil-smelling, and unashamedly phallic, to the extent that its Latin name, *Phallus impudicus*, means 'rude or shameless penis'. It is not surprising, therefore, that its folklore and vernacular etymology have played on these associations. The very word 'stinkhorn' is based not only on the smell ('stink') but the shape, 'horn' (as in 'horny') having phallic connotations. Gerard's Herball of 1597 straightforwardly called the fungus 'the pricke mushroom', and other local English names included 'devil's horn' and 'satan's member'. It was once sold in Europe as an aphrodisiac and a related species was considered a semi-sacred phallic totem in New Guinea. Curiously, an unnamed Hawaiian stinkhorn is claimed genuinely to cause spontaneous female orgasm, an effect credited to 'hormonelike compounds present in the volatile portion of the spore mass' (Holliday & Soule, 2001).

Not surprisingly, genteel Victorians were not fond of the stinkhorn. Beatrix Potter, though a keen illustrator of macrofungi, 'could not find courage to draw it', whilst Charles Darwin's eldest daughter Etty, suitably attired in special hunting cloak and gloves, would scour her gardens and adjacent woods for stinkhorns. These were religiously collected and then burnt 'in deepest secrecy' for fear they would corrupt the morals of the maidservants, a practice charmingly described by Darwin's niece, Gwen Raverat (1952).

In mediæval times, the appearance of stinkhorns was unequivocal proof of witchcraft, and the unexpanded 'eggs' were locally known as 'devil's eggs' in England, 'Hexeneier' in Germany, or 'trolläg' in Sweden. Stinkhorns were also associated with the fingers of corpses, pushing up through the ground like B-movie zombies. One name for them in Germany was 'Leichenfinger' (corpse finger) or in Sweden 'ligsvamp' (corpse fungus). Some of the native peoples of Borneo combined both traditions by considering them the penises of dead heroes, soon to return in spirit form.

Witchcraft

As noted above, witches were once held responsible for the growth of 'obscene fungi' in honest people's gardens, Ramsbottom (1953) quoting this charge from a French court case as late as 1926. They were also frequently blamed for fairy rings, sometimes called 'hag tracks' (Chapter Eight). More curiously, witches were believed to produce butter in the shape of various gelatinous fungi, including the yellow *Tremella mesenterica* and the blackish-brown *Exidia glandulosa*, both of which were locally called 'witches' butter' in various parts of Britain. Stabbing, burning, or otherwise destroying these fungi were believed to harm the witch herself or to cause her to appear.

Gruffydd (1985) noted that the testimony against one Gwenllian David, accused of witchcraft at the Court of Great Sessions in Carmarthen, 1656, included the fact that witches' butter grew on her doorpost. A neighbour forced a red-hot knife through the fungus and left it there for a fortnight, during which time Gwenllian David 'lay sicke and cryed to take the knife out of her backe'.

Thunderbolts and shooting stars

There is a strange and widespread belief that fungi arise from fallen stars. In the British Isles, this belief was specifically connected to gelatinous material called 'shot-star' or 'star jelly' ('pwdre ser' or 'tripa'r ser' in Welsh), which was considered to represent the remains of meteors. A similar belief was held in Sweden and by settlers in New England. The material so named was mostly the cyanobacterium *Nostoc commune* which, during rainfall, rapidly expands from its dry crust-like state to seaweed-like, gelatinous blobs. The species is common in Britain and can cover large areas of ground. It was at one time grouped with the fungi and given various names in the genus *Tremella*. Bailey's Dictionary of 1747 defined 'nostock' as 'stinking, tawney jelly of a fallen planet, or the nocturnal solution of some plethorical and wanton star'. True gelatinous fungi, such as *Tremella mesenterica*, were also considered to be star-shot as were the plasmodial states of slime moulds, the remains of frogs, and almost anything else of a gelatinous nature.

In North America, puffballs were called ka-ka-toos or 'fallen stars' by the Blackfoot and ju'ba'pbich nakai or 'star excrement fungus' in parts of Mexico. The Inuit are said to consider most fungi 'the excrement of shooting stars'.

The association of fungi with thunderbolts and lightning is somewhat less strange, given the link with heavy rainfall. Wasson (1956) assembled associations from ancient Greece, modern France, North Africa, Afghanistan, Siberia, China, Madagascar, New Zealand, and Mexico, all leading inevitably to the prehistoric worldwide influence of the 'divine mushroom'. Most of Wasson's far-flung references, however, seem to be linked with storms and rainy seasons.

CHAPTER 17

Food and Technology

A
S WELL AS being directly used for food, fungi have traditionally been the agents of fermentation for beer, cider, wine, and bread in Britain and Europe, plus a remarkable range of fermented products in the Far East, Africa, and around the world. In the industrial age, fungi have been used commercially in the manufacture of many other food-related products, from citric and oxalic acids to glycerine, fats, and proteins. Marmite™ and Quorn™ are also examples of factory-processed fungal products, as are fungal pharmaceuticals and antibiotics (Chapter 15). In other areas of technology, fungi again have important roles to play as biocontrol agents for unwanted pathogens and as bioremediation agents for unwanted chemicals.

FUNGI FOR FOOD & DRINK

Wild fungi

Fungi, along with seafish and shellfish, are among the last commercial food-stuffs hunted and collected in the wild. The reason is quite straightforward. Although a number of saprotophic and parasitic macrofungi can successfully be cultivated, sought-after ectomycorrhizal species like boletes (porcini or ceps), chanterelles, and truffles are as yet extremely difficult or impossible to grow.

Apart from field mushrooms, collecting wild fungi has always been a minority interest in Britain, long notorious as one of Europe's few mycophobic nations (in company with Ireland, Belgium, and Holland). Nonetheless, in recent years there has been a greater willingness to sample new foods (Fig. 150) and an equal interest in collecting 'food for free'. A survey of the top twenty edible fungi collected in Britain for personal use by enthusiasts placed *Boletus edulis* (the cep) first, followed by *Macrolepiota procera* (parasol), *Agaricus campestris* (field mushroom), *Cantharellus cibarius* (chanterelle), *Lepista nuda* (wood blewit), *Coprinus comatus* (shaggy ink cap), *Calvatia gigantea* (giant puffball), *Agaricus arvensis* (horse mushroom), *Boletus badius* (bay bolete), and *Lepista saeva* (blewit). The next ten included morels, hedgehog fungi, and oyster caps.

In Scotland, apart from collecting for personal use, the wild fungus trade was worth around £400,000 per year in the 1990s and involved some 350 people. The main species collected were chanterelles (*Cantharellus cibarius*), ceps (*Boletus edulis*), and hedgehog fungi (*Hydnum repandum*), over half of which were exported from the UK. Less than 15% remained in

FIG 150. A wide range of tinned, bottled, and dried fungi are now widely available in delicatessens, supermarkets and speciality shops (RBG Kew).

Scotland, where they were sold to specialist greengrocers and restaurants. The total trade in UK-collected fungi is currently estimated at around £2,500,000 p.a.

Elsewhere, the trade is substantially higher. In Europe, major exporters include the Scandinavian countries, Baltic states, Spain, Eastern Europe, and the Balkans. In both Finland and Lithuania, for example, the value of edible fungi collected in native forests was estimated (in 1995) at around £10,000,000 per year, and in the Czech Republic considerably more at over £30,000,000 per year. Outside Europe, in the Pacific Northwest of the USA and Canada, around 2,000,000 kg p.a. of wild fungi were commercially harvested in the 1990s, the main groups being morels, chanterelles, matsutake, and boletes. Over 10,000 people were involved in the trade, as pickers, processers, and retailers, with the industry having a gross value of around £30,000,000 p.a.

Chanterelles and their allies

Chanterelles (*Cantharellus cibarius*), and their allies (principally *C. tubaeformis*, *C. aurora*, and *Craterellus cornucopioides*), are widely collected and marketed in Europe where they are found as ectomycorrhizal associates of forest trees. Their retail price ('fresh') varies, but is currently around £15–£30 per kilo. Globally, the trade in wild chanterelles and related species is estimated to be worth just over £1,000,000,000 per year. In North America, substantial quantities are collected in the Pacific Northwest mostly involving the species *C. formosus* and *C. subalbidus*. Turkey exported over 150 tons of chanterelles in 1990, mainly to Italy and Germany whilst, perhaps surprisingly, species like *C. rufopunctatus* from the savannah-like 'miombo' woodlands of central Africa, are exported in large quantities to Europe.

It was not always thus. Badham (1847) noted that 'the *Canth. cibarius* is very abundant about Rome, where it fetches, not being in great esteem, from twopence to twopence halfpenny a pound'. At that time the chanterelle was also eaten in Britain, though Badham suggested that 'the very existence of such a fungus at home is confined to the Freemasons who keep the secret!'. It was certainly a secret known only to a few. Britten (1877) remembered 'on one occasion encountering a woodman who was lost in wonderment at our having collected a basket of 'toadstools' . . . and when we told him that we were going to eat them, clearly thought our claim to a select apartment in the nearest lunatic asylum was absolutely indisputable'.

Boletes – ceps and porcini

Boletes, known as 'ceps' in France and 'porcini' in Italy, are also widely collected and some species are as sought after as chanterelles. The premium species is *Boletus edulis* (Fig. 151), but many other taxa of *Boletus* (including *Xerocomus*), *Leccinum*, and *Suillus* are also picked on a commercial scale. The global trade in these fungi is substantial. Turkey exported over 700 tons of boletes in 1990, and Arora (2000) noted that, by selling boletes to Italy, impoverished farmers in Bulgaria were earning enough to buy new tractors. In Britain, dried sliced boletes have long been available but, increasingly, 'fresh' specimens (some from as far afield as South Africa) can be found in supermarkets and delicatessens retailing at around £20–£50 per kilo.

FIG 151. Sometimes called the 'penny bun bolete', the cep *Boletus edulis* is one of the most popular wild, edible fungi in Europe (P. Roberts).

Morels

Morels (*Morchella* species) are among the largest of the ascomycetes and have long been valued as food. Unusually for larger fungi, they produce fruitbodies in the spring and in Victorian times were occasionally sold fresh in Covent Garden, though more generally obtained dried from Germany. Some species, notably *Morchella conica* and *M. elata*, are often associated with burnt ground, so much so that (according to Britten) 'the peasants of Branderburgh and some other parts of Germany ... set fire to the forests in order to obtain these fungi', an occurrence so prevalent that it was prohibited by law. A more recent example of the same practice has been reported from Oregon in the USA.

Morel hunting is a favourite and lucrative springtime occupation in the United States. Weber (1988) provided a first-hand account of the morel season in Michigan, which involves several thousand people, festivals and competitions, and is a major part of the local tourist economy. In the 1980s morel hunting was said to bring in over £1,000,000 p.a. to the Cadillac region alone. The species collected include *Morchella conica*, *M. esculenta* (Fig. 152), and *M. semilibera*.

FIG 152. The morel *Morchella esculenta* is a large, spring-fruiting species with a preference for chalky ground. It is a sought-after edible species (B. Spooner).

North America and Turkey are said to be the major exporters of morels into Europe. Turkey produced nearly 50 tons in 1989, whilst Pakistan exports around 50 tons each year. At one time morels were also exported from Afghanistan.

Since the 1980s, it has also been possible to cultivate morels on a commercial scale, and a patent has been taken out on the process in the USA.

Matsutake and the white gold rush

Tricholoma matsutake is a large, edible species, found as an ectomycorrhizal associate of pine in the Far East. It has long been harvested as a seasonal speciality in Japan, where it is particularly valued for the aroma of the young, fresh fruitbodies (there is no market for it dried). In 1950, over 6000 tons were harvested in Japan, but by 1984 this had fallen to just 180 tons, possibly because of pollution and changes in forest management. Part of this shortfall was taken up by substantial imports from Korea, China, and Tibet (where some villagers have been earning ten times the local salary by collecting the fungus, building 'matsutake mansions' on the proceeds). But part also was taken up by the importation of a related American species, *Tricholoma magnivelare*, the 'pine mushroom'. Altogether, global trade in *Tricholoma matsutake* and *T. magnivelare* is now estimated to be worth up to £3,500,000,000 per year.

With prices up to £30 per kilo being paid to collectors of *T. magnivelare*, the Japanese demand for the fungus has led to a 'white gold rush' in America. *Tricholoma magnivelare* is found from Alaska and the Yukon down to California and Mexico, with further populations running down from Quebec to the Great Smoky Mountains in Tennessee. Japanese Americans were collecting the species as far back as the 1930s, but the real boom started in the 1970s, when prices enabled some pickers to earn well over £500 per week in season. When this income rose to over £1000 per day in the late 1980s, turf wars broke out provoking headlines like 'Mushrooms, guns, and money' or 'Bloody war erupts in US wilds – over mushrooms'. Added to this is the problem that the pine-mushroom industry is now worth far more than the traditional timber industry, producing conflicts between itinerant pine-mushroom pickers and resident loggers. Arora (1999) has written an engaging, illustrated account of the itinerants' fiercely independent way of life. There is an additional conservation problem, since in America the most valuable button fruitbodies are often located by raking instead of being carefully hand-picked. This destroys the forest litter layers together with the mycelia of *T. magnivelare* and other ectomycorrhizal and saprotrophic species. As a result, there is now some regulation of collecting in parts of North America, including licensing (though the Texas ban on harvesting mushrooms more than six feet tall or three feet in diameter would seem less than effective).

Truffles and truffle-hunting

Truffles are ectomycorrhizal ascomycetous fungi which produce tuber-like fruitbodies underground, often at the interface between leaf-litter or humus layers and the harder, mineral-soil surface. Most of the edible species belong to the 'true truffles' in the genus *Tuber*, a few to the genus *Terfezia*. Since their spores are typically spread by the ingestion and defecation of animals (including insects, rodents, wild pigs, and the like – see Chapter Five), many truffles have enticing aromas when mature, some of which are also attractive to human beings.

Several species are collected commercially. The Piedmont or white truffle, *Tuber magnatum*, is the most pungent, sought-after and highly priced. It grows almost exclusively in northern and central Italy, with some small production in Slovenia and Croatia. Typical sites are on low hills (around 400–500 m) in open woodland, where it occurs as an ectomycorrhizal associate of oak and poplar, often in woodlands with walnut, and is collected in the autumn, between October and December. It is hunted with dogs, often (for no apparent reason) with two dogs, one of which locates the truffles, sits on the spot and barks, and is then replaced by the second dog which does the digging. Small spaniels seem to be favoured (Fig. 153). The headquarters of the white truffle trade is Alba, which holds an annual fair for the 'tartufo bianco' or 'tartufo di Alba'. Around 5–20 tons are produced each year and retail prices range from £1400–£1900 per kilo, making it one of the most expensive foodstuffs on earth. In 2000, Milanese shops were asking no less than £4000 per kilo, whilst the top auction price reached an astonishing £9800 per kilo (50% more than the price for gold).

The Périgord or black truffle, *Tuber melanosporum*, is perhaps the best-

FIG 153. A professional truffle hunter and dog in search of the Piedmont or white truffle *Tuber magnatum* in Italy (P. Roberts).

known, thanks to its connections with French haute cuisine. It grows on well-drained, rather dry, sunny, calcareous hillsides (around 200–1000 m) in southern France, Italy, Spain, Portugal, Slovenia, Croatia, and Serbia. Associated trees are typically species of oak, but also include hazel, hornbeam, limes, and even conifers. In Italy, it tends to occur in rather scrubby areas, often old, abandoned hill farms, and is hunted with dogs, since a considerable amount of ground needs to be covered. In France, trufflers tend to own their private, inherited patch of truffle woodland and *Tuber melanosporum* can therefore still be hunted for by pigs, which are not willing to travel fast or far. The pigs are specifically sows, since the truffle aroma is similar to boar pheromone, a remarkably effective attractant. As a consequence, sows hunt truffles naturally and the problem for the hunters is to prevent them from immediately eating their finds. Dogs have to be trained to collect truffles. *Tuber melanosporum* is collected between November and March, and hence is sometimes known as the winter truffle. Retail prices fluctuate, but are currently around £250–£320 per kilo. The main market for the Périgord truffle is France itself. At the beginning of the last century, some 1000 tons were produced in France each year, but this has now collapsed to just 20–40 tons, probably as a result of changes in upland management. Italy produces around 30–50 tons per year, some of which are eaten locally, some exported. Around 30 tons are produced annually in Spain, most of which are exported to France.

The summer truffle, *Tuber aestivum*, is far less pungent, far more widespread, and much less favoured (Fig. 154). It occurs in Britain and was once commercially hunted in southern England. Gilbert White, the celebrated naturalist of Selbourne in Hampshire, mentioned regular visits by truffle-hunters in his journals, as did his brother Henry in his diaries. A note of Gilbert White's for August 1767, for example, says 'Trufles . . . large & in plenty were taken by the trufle-hunters dogs Aug: 19 at Fyfield in a field of my Bro[r] Henry's, among the roots of a Grove of beeches.' Another, for 11–17th October 1789 says 'A trufle-hunter called on us, having in his pocket several large trufles found in the neighbourhood . . . Half a crown a pound was the price, which he asked for this commodity'. Half a crown a pound (27.5p per kilo) was a substantial sum of money in the eighteenth century.

FIG 154. A drawing of the truffle *Tuber aestivum*, once commercially hunted in England (E.Wakefield, RBG Kew).

Britten (1877) gave an account of a meeting with a truffle-hunter and his
dog in Buckinghamshire and reprinted a description of the breed of dog
concerned. The English truffle-dog was said to be white, black and white,
or black, and similar to a small poodle, though rather longer in the leg
(Fig. 155). In 1860 the truffle-hunters of Winterslow in Wiltshire petitioned
parliament for an exemption from dog licences, claiming that they were
'poor labouring men' dependent on truffling for which 'we do therefore keep
and use a small pudle sort of dog'. It was not recorded whether the petition
was successful. By 1891, Cooke noted that the truffle-dog was 'now almost
a rarity'.

Cooke also claimed that truffle hunting was formerly practised in Sussex
and Kent, whilst Rolfe & Rolfe (1925) reported that 'a few of the old truffle
hunters are still to be found in Sussex'. Pigs were apparently still used
in Sussex until about 1910, but truffle-dogs were more usual. Once located,
the Sussex trufflers used a 'spud' made of ash wood to dig up the truffles.

The English truffling trade had died out by the end of the 1930s. One of
the last local truffle-hunting families were the Olivers of Seven Points, and
Ramsbottom (1953) named Alfred Collins as the last of the professional
trufflers. Alfred, son of Eli Collins (also a truffler and possibly one of the
petitioners mentioned above), was based in Winterslow, Wiltshire, but
hunted as far afield as Somerset, Dorset, Oxfordshire, Berkshire, Surrey,
Sussex, and the Isle of Wight. He used truffle-dogs or terriers, often carried
poacher-style in pockets of a large coat, and a 'spike' to dig up truffles. Two

kinds of truffle were hunted, 'garlic' (*Tuber aestivum*) and the smaller, paler 'bud' (possibly *T. brumale*). His price was 4s 6d per pound (50p per kilo) and the truffles were despatched all over the country. He gave up truffling in 1940, but, according to his daughter (Moody, 1985), his spikes and other memorabilia are in Salisbury Museum.

Truffles, however, continue to occur in England and, indeed, north into Scotland. The main species, *Tuber aestivum*, is normally found between May and October, and is still collected commercially in Italy, where the annual production is around 3–10 tons, and in France which produces around 10–15 tons. It retails for around £50 per kilo.

In France and more recently in Italy, considerable effort has been expended on ways to cultivate truffles. Since the species concerned are ectomycorrhizal, this is not possible in the conventional manner. But, beginning in the nineteenth century, attempts were made to sow acorns or grow oaks and other saplings in appropriate truffle-producing sites (truffières), sometimes 'seeding' the ground with spores or impregnated soil. In more recent years, substantial forestry programmes have been initiated involving the inoculation of oak and hazel saplings with *Tuber* species and then planting them out in the hope of a harvest in future years. This has already produced results, not only in Europe, but in Australia and New Zealand, both of which have areas where the soil and climate are suitable for *Tuber melanosporum*. Tasmania now has six truffières in production, with over 20 more planted. New Zealand also has six productive truffières and harvested its first commercial crop in 1997. In the similar hope of success, an attempt has been made to establish the first British truffières, starting in Hertfordshire in 1999.

In North Africa and the Middle East through to Iran, a relative of the truffles, *Terfezia arenaria* or the desert truffle, is widely eaten and sold in local markets. It is an ectomycorrhizal species associated with members of the *Cistaceae*, and there are other species in the Kalahari and elsewhere. *Terfezia arenaria* was considered a particular delicacy by the ancient Romans and is one of the many contenders for the 'manna' of the bible. In Britain, the basidiomycetous false truffle *Melanogaster variegatus* was at one time sold in the markets of Bath, Somerset, and was known as the 'Bath truffle'. Rolfe & Rolfe (1925) also noted that 'gentlemen from Soho' collected the earthball *Scleroderma citrinum* as a substitute for truffles, notwithstanding the fact that it is poisonous. Perhaps not surprisingly, due to the high prices they command, this is not the only fraud involving truffles. Blackening cheaper white truffles with walnut juice to pass them off as more expensive species, and treating other dark-coloured fungi with artificial truffle flavour to fool inexperienced buyers are just two of many examples. Pegler *et al.* (1993) have provided a thorough, illustrated, taxonomic handbook on native British truffles and truffle-like fungi. Dubarry & Bucquet-Grenet (2001) have produced a nicely illustrated pocket guide to the ecology, history, and gastronomy of French and other European truffles.

Hedgehogs, lobsters, and other commercial species

Many other wild fungi are sold commercially, either 'fresh' or processed (dried, tinned, bottled, or frozen), and are frequently exported around the world.

In Britain, the traditional trade was almost entirely confined to the field mushroom (*Agaricus campestris*) and the horse mushroom (*A. arvensis*), both of which supplemented the shortfall in supplies of cultivated mushrooms. In times of glut, mushrooms were also made into a preserved sauce or ketchup. Berkeley in 1860 noted that an English 'ketchup-merchant' of his acquaintance had no less than 800 gallons on hand from local collections in a single season, with prices for ketchup mushrooms ranging from a penny to fivepence a pound (1p–4.5p per kilo). Rolfe & Rolfe (1925) reported that there was formerly some trade at Covent Garden in blewits (*Lepista saeva*) and parasols (*Macrolepiota procera*) for the same reason, but that this had 'fallen away or entirely disappeared' with the increase in mushroom cultivation. Blewits, however, continued to be sold in markets in the Midlands (from Gloucestershire to Nottinghamshire) up until more recent times. Britten (1877) noted that the polypore *Grifola frondosa* was 'sometimes sold in the market at Norwich under the name of 'morel' (to which it certainly has no claim), at prices varying from sixpence to eighteenpence according to size'. The same species was also said to be valued in Italy and is now commercially grown in Japan.

The trade in Britain today is quite different and owes nothing to tradition, but to a general interest in exotic and unusual foods. The species sold are a cosmopolitan mix of cultivated and (generally) imported wild fungi, typically given French, Japanese, Chinese, or American names. In continental Europe, however, the trade is more traditional and to a certain extent local, though many species are shipped throughout the continent or imported from America and elsewhere. Among the more popular are hedgehog fungi or 'pieds de mouton' (*Hydnum repandum*); the fairy-ring champignon or 'mousseron' (*Marasmius oreades*); the saffron milk cap (*Lactarius deliciosus*), a species particularly favoured in Catalonia where it is known as 'rovellons'; *Tricholoma portentosum*, known as 'fredolics' in Catalonia; the charcoal-burner or 'charbonnier' (*Russula cyanoxantha*); the cauliflower fungus (*Sparassis crispa*); grisettes (certain *Amanita* species); and many more. Even the honey fungus (*Armillaria mellea* agg.), characterised by Badham (1847) as 'a nauseous disagreeable fungus ... so repugnant to our notions of the savory, that few would make a second attempt, or get dangerously far in a first dish', is widely eaten, particularly in Poland, where it is available fresh or preserved in jars.

The same or equivalent species are marketed in North America, with the addition of the peculiar 'lobster fungus', actually fruitbodies of *Russula* and *Lactarius* species which are parasitised by an ascomycete, *Hypomyces lactifluorum*. This covers its host toadstools in conspicuous reddish-orange mycelium, completely replacing the gills (Fig. 156). The parasitised fruitbodies are widely collected and sold, a usage which appears to be traditional among native American peoples. It is even occasionally imported into Britain.

Elsewhere, there are some distinctly local specialities. In Chile and Argentina, species of the curious golfball-like ascomycete *Cyttaria* can be found growing on southern beech trees (*Nothofagus* species). Darwin noted that the inhabitants of Tierra del Fuego collected and ate them as part of their staple diet and they continue to be sold in markets in Chile today.

In Haiti, one or more *Psathyrella* species, toadstools related to ink caps, are collected and eaten as part of a national dish called 'riz noir' or 'riz djon-djon' (djon-djon being the creole word for mushroom). The fungi are sold fresh or dried and exported in the latter state to Haitian communities overseas. In Mexico and Central America the corn smut, *Ustilago maydis*, which forms large galls on sweet corn (*Zea mays*), is widely eaten as a delicacy

FIG 156. The so-called 'lobster fungus', fruitbodies of *Lactarius* infected with the ascomycete *Hypomyces lactifluorum*. They become bright reddish-orange and are a sought-after delicacy (S. Evans).

under the name 'cuitlacoche' and is sold fresh or tinned. A related smut, *Ustilago esculenta*, which galls wild rice (*Zizania aquatica*), is also eaten in China and the Far East.

Traditional collecting of wild fungi

An autumn visit to local markets in many continental European countries will often reveal an extraordinarily wide range of fungi on sale, not only the commercially marketed species noted above, but other less common, less favoured, or locally appreciated species (Fig. 157). In some countries, these markets are carefully licensed and controlled, so that only a limited range of permitted species can be offered for sale. Badham (1847) noted the appointment of an official 'Ispettore dei Funghi' in Rome, tasked to examine specimens brought in to market, tax those suitable for sale (a halfpenny on every ten pounds weight), and dispose of those which were rotten or

FIG 157. A market stall with a colourful display of edible fungi (S. Evans).

dangeous by throwing them into the Tiber. Similar inspectors are employed in Switzerland and elsewhere today.

In Finland, an historically mycophobic nation, the collection of edible wild fungi has been officially encouraged by the government, who instituted a programme to train 1650 advisers and 50,000 collectors between 1969 and 1983. Curiously, *Lactarius* species are amongst the most favoured by the Finns, including *Lactarius torminosus* (the epithet means 'griping' or 'fretting of the guts').

In Africa, the use of fungi varies from region to region and culture to culture. Over 60 species of fungi are said to be collected as edible in Malawi, but in parts of Nigeria and other areas fungi are often associated with dung and decay and are widely shunned. Rammeloo & Walleyn (1993) have published a survey of sub-Saharan edible fungi.

In various places, the large, ball-like sclerotia of certain bracket fungi have been used as a foodstuff, sliced and eaten as a 'native bread'. In Australia, this was known as 'blackfellow's bread', and a massive specimen (now in the Herbarium at Kew) was displayed at the Great Exhibition of 1851. A similar polypore sclerotium (of *Wolfiporia cocos*) was collected for food in Japan and also in North America, where it was given the name of 'tuckahoe' or Indian bread. This species, called 'fu ling', is still much used in China and the Far East as a traditional tonic for 'invigorating the spleen and tranquilising the mind'.

In Europe, the 'fungus stone', 'pietra fungeia', or 'lapis fungifer' was noted as a mediaeval marvel, associated with 'the mysteries of the Lynx' and believed to be the urine of wolves coagulated on mountain summits. When watered, this magical stone produced mushrooms and was much sought after by collectors of curiosities. Samuel Pepys much desired a specimen, whilst the Earl of Stafford actually possessed one. It is in fact the sclerotium of another polypore, *Polyporus tuberaster*, partly mixed with stones and earth.

Lichens have seldom been used for food (most are tough and bitter), but Iceland moss, *Cetraria islandica*, was once boiled in alkaline ashes and ground into a flour to 'constitute the basis of the food of the poor Icelander' (Lindsay, 1856). It is said that this was a useful ingredient of Scandinavian ship's biscuits, since even weevils would not eat it. Rock tripe (*Umbilicaria* species) was also used *in extremis*, as in Sir John Franklin's ill-fated expedition of 1819-22 to find the northwest passage, when his starving men ate lichen scraped from the rocks, as well as the leather from their boots, and possibly each other.

In the Far East, under less desperate conditions, another *Umbilicaria* species (*U. esculenta* – the name suggesting edibility) is favoured as a food in Hunan (China), Japan, and Korea. This is known as 'Iwa-take' or 'rock-mushroom', and similarly grows in rocky places, though usually on inaccessible cliffs where collecting is fraught with danger, commanding high market prices as a result. In the Middle East, *Sphaerothallia esculenta*, a desert lichen which blows in the wind like tumbleweed, is one of many organisms which have been claimed as the 'manna' of the bible. It can apparently be mixed with meal and baked as a bread, called 'schirsad' in Iran, and (according to Lindsay, 1856) 'has sometimes served as food for hordes of men and cattle in the arid steppes of various countries between Algiers and Tartary'. Also in the Middle East, it is said that the ancient Egyptians were fond of adding *Pseudevernia furfuracea* to flour for breadmaking. This is the species still used in perfumery today (Fig. 145A) and would have given an unusual flavour to the bread. The lichen had to be imported by ship from Greece, so was clearly not eaten out of desperation. It was also one of the many items used in mummy embalming, being used with myrrh and other ingredients to pack the body cavity.

Cultivated mushrooms

Worldwide, around 4,250,000 tons of mushrooms and other macrofungi are grown for food each year. Almost 40% of this production is devoted to *Agaricus bisporus* and *A. bitorquis*, the familiar cultivated mushrooms of the western world.

The deliberate growing of mushrooms (as opposed to the picking of field mushrooms, *Agaricus campestris*) is believed to have started in France some 350 years ago. Atkins (1979) quoted instructions given by De Bonnefons in 1650 for preparing 'a bed of Mules'or Asses' soyl' four fingers thick, casting upon it 'all the parings and offalls of such Mushrooms as have been dressed in your Kitchen, together with the water wherein they were washed', to obtain a 'very good' crop. More reliable methods, leading eventually to large scale commercial production, were rapidly developed, and in 1707

Tournefort gave the first scientific account of growing mushrooms in ridged beds for the Paris market.

French commercial cultivation was subsequently undertaken in disused mines in the former Seine department around Paris, the mines providing stable, year-round temperature and humidity. Robinson (1883) gave an English visitor's account of the 'great mushroom caves'. By 1918, over 300 commercial growers were based in these excavations, often working in conditions as difficult and dangerous as those suffered by the original miners. The mushrooms were grown on ridged beds of stable manure which was thrown down shafts and wheeled into place, sometimes along adits less than a metre high. Mushroom spawn (mycelium) was spread over the beds which were then cased (covered) with fine soil and kept moist with water. Fresh mushrooms appeared after some six weeks and continued to crop for up to eight months, after which the spent material was carted back to the surface and new beds made. Around 25 tons of mushrooms were produced each day, far more than in any other European country. Even today, *Agaricus bisporus* is still known in France as the 'champignon de Paris'.

This French system was copied on a limited scale in Britain, the most extensive underground workings being in the old bathstone quarries at Corsham, Wiltshire. Other subterranean farms were at Bradford-on-Avon, also in Wiltshire, Godstone in Surrey, and in a disused railway tunnel in Edinburgh. The Bradford-on-Avon caves are still in use for mushroom growing today. An alternative 'English method' was to grow mushrooms in sheds, glasshouses, or even in the open (when the beds were covered in protective litter).

The modern system of growing mushrooms in sheds on shelves or trays (also in bags or troughs) was first developed in the United States in the 1890s and mechanised by the Dutch in the 1970s. Van Griensven (1988) has provided a thorough account of modern, commercial mushroom production.

Some 65,000 tons of mushrooms were produced in the UK in 2000, worth around £120,000,000. Worldwide, the value of the industry has been estimated at around £2,800,000,000 per year. *Agaricus bisporus* (*A. brunnescens* in the USA) is the main commercial species, grown in several different strains. At the beginning of the last century, cultivated mushrooms were typically cream or brown and often scaly, but in 1927 a cluster of white, scaleless fruitbodies was found growing amidst brown specimens and all modern white mushrooms are said to originate from this strain. Today 'white strains', 'offwhite strains', hybrid 'white-offwhite strains', and the original 'brown strains' are grown for different purposes. The first and last are marketed fresh, the brown strains as 'chestnut' mushrooms in Britain and 'portabella' or 'crimini' mushrooms in the USA (all invented commercial names for strains previously considered unsaleable), whilst the offwhite and hybrid strains are typically grown for canning and for processing.

Oyster caps, shiitake, wood ears, and monkey heads

Many other species of fungi have long been cultivated in the Far East and have increasingly penetrated western markets since the 1980s. Of these, oyster caps (*Pleurotus* species) account for over 20% of the annual world market for cultivated macrofungi, with shiitake (*Lentinula edodes*) and wood-ears (*Auricularia cornea*) accounting for over 10% each. All of these are saprotrophic or parasitic species and can be grown on dead wood or waste products.

Oyster caps, *Pleurotus* species, are now widely cultivated and easily available in British supermarkets. *Pleurotus cornucopiae*, a whitish species, and *P. ostreatus*, a typically greyish or bluish-brown species, are both common on hardwood logs in the wild in Britain, but are also grown commercially. Pink varieties of the common tropical species *Pleurotus djamor* are also cultivated, as is the oriental, yellow species *P. citrinopileatus*. All oyster caps are fleshy, gilled fungi which normally occur on decaying wood and are said to be 'by far the easiest and least expensive [edible fungi] to grow' (Stamets, 1993). Like shiitake, they can be grown on logs, but are so tractable that they are easily cultivated on any of a wide range of compacted waste products containing cellulose, including sawdust, straw, sugar cane bagasse, cottonseed hulls, oil palm waste, banana leaves, and coffee waste. Unusually, growing *Pleurotus* species appears to have been a comparatively recent American innovation from the turn of the last century, rather than a long-established Asian tradition.

Growing shiitake (*Lentinula edodes*) is, however, a venerable occupation, having been practised in China and Japan for at least the last 1000 years. Shiitake is a gilled, fleshy fungus which grows wild in the cooler forests of

China, Japan, and Korea on logs and fallen branches of oak and 'shii' (*Castanopsis* species). Traditional cultivation consists of little more than encouraging this growth by felling logs of suitable size, drilling holes in them, and inserting wedges of wood mixed with mycelium from logs already supporting the fungus. This semi-natural, seasonal form of cultivation is still valued today, since it is said to produce the best quality shiitake which in turn fetch the highest prices.

China produced over 90,000 tons of shiitake in 1997, one third of which was exported. Most of this was undertaken by small rural farmers in the central highlands and it has been estimated that production on this scale requires the felling of some 100,000 trees each year, leading to massive deforestation. Methods of growing shiitake on compacted blocks of enriched sawdust have been developed which may be less destructive. These methods have also led to widespread cultivation of the fungus outside its natural range, not only in Asia but in Europe and North America. Since it currently retails (fresh) for around £10–25 per kilo in the west, shiitake-growing has been taken up by many small businesses, including some in Britain where it is now widely available fresh or dried in supermarkets.

Auricularia species are believed to be the first macrofungi deliberately grown for food, having been mentioned in a seventh century Chinese text. The main cultivated species, *Auricularia cornea* (synonym *A. polytricha*), sometimes known as the wood-ear, is a relative of the common British jew's ear fungus (*A. auricula-judae*) and is widely found throughout the tropics and subtropics on dead and decaying wood. Though *Auricularia* species are extensively grown in the Far East, Oei (1996) noted that 'taste and appearance may hamper [their] popularity in Western countries', a reference to their thin, rubbery texture and delicate or imperceptible taste. Curiously, they are sold into the non-oriental market in Britain by being finely ground to tealeaf size and added to 'woodland mushroom' instant soups. Formerly they had some medical reputation in Britain (Chapter 15) and still retain this reputation in the Far East. *Auricularia* species are commercially grown in China and Taiwan on logs or in plastic tubes filled with an enriched sawdust or cottonseed hull mix. Despite their long history of cultivation, wood ears were once commercially collected in the wild, particularly in New Zealand. Indeed in the late nineteenth and early twentieth century, *Auricularia* was

New Zealand's second largest cash export after sheep, with over 1800 tons shipped to China between 1872 and 1883.

Tremella fuciformis is another 'jelly fungus', though only distantly related to *Auricularia* species. It is sometimes marketed as silver ears or white jelly fungus and has a white, frondose, seaweed-like appearance (Fig. 158). Like all *Tremella* species, it is parasitic on other fungi, a fact overlooked in traditional cultivation methods on logs, where the species grew fitfully whenever its host (the ascomycete *Hypoxylon archeri*) happened to be present. Nowadays, it is grown in China as a mixed host-parasite culture on logs or in plastic tubes filled with an enriched sawdust or cottonseed hull mix.

The paddy straw mushroom, *Volvariella volvacea*, is a pink-spored agaric with a large basal volva, but no ring. Fruitbodies are occasionally found in

FIG 158. Sometimes sold as 'silver ears', *Tremella fuciformis* is an edible pantropical fungus, commercially cultivated in China (P. Roberts).

Britain, presumably as casual introductions, since it does not tolerate cold. The species is popular in south-east Asia, largely because it can be straight-forwardly grown outdoors as a low-tech, low-cost crop. Traditionally, straw from the rice harvest was piled up to form raised beds in paddy fields and the mushrooms grown on that, but a variety of other substrates can be used including cotton waste, banana leaves, and even weeded-out water hyacinth, *Eichhornia crassipes*.

The velvet shank, *Flammulina velutipes*, has been cultivated in Asia since the ninth century or earlier. It is a frost-resistant, winter-fruiting agaric called 'enokitake' (snow peak mushroom) in Japanese and found throughout the temperate north, including Britain where it fruits in clusters on dead wood, particularly elm. Unusually for fungi, the cultivated form bears little resemblance to wild collections. This is purely a matter of technique. *Flammulina velutipes* is typically grown in plastic bottles containing an enriched sawdust mix. When beginning to fruit, collars are attached to the bottles and lighting is lowered to obtain dense bundles of long-stemmed, small-capped fruitbodies (sometimes sold as 'golden needles').

Hericium erinaceus, the monkey head or lion's mane fungus, is a wood-rotting saprotroph producing large epaulet-like fruitbodies with a hymenium consisting of long, hanging spines (Fig. 163). It is a comparative newcomer to cultivation, but is quite easily grown on cellulose waste in a similar manner to *Pleurotus* species. The fungus occurs in England, particularly on old beech trees, but is scarce and legally protected under Schedule 8 of the Wildlife and Countryside Act 1981 (Chapter 18).

Several other fungi are cultivated for food on a comparatively small or local scale. The phalloid *Dictyophora indusiata* is widely cultivated in Asia, but (as a close relative of the stinkhorn) is unlikely to gain much acceptance in the west. The toadstools *Stropharia ruguso-annulata* (on mulch and in gardens) and *Agrocybe cylindracea* (on wood) are occasionally grown, as is the polypore *Grifola frondosa*, known as maitake in Japan. Blewits (*Lepista saeva* and *L. nuda*) are also now grown in Europe and generally marketed under the French name 'pied bleu'.

Stamets (1993) has provided an excellent, illustrated guide to the small-scale growing of edible fungi in the west. A further standard text was published by Chang & Miles (1989).

Yeasts and the brewing of beer

Brewing from fermented grains appears to be almost as old as human civilisation, having been known to the ancient Sumerians some 9000 years ago, when up to 40% of their grain harvest was set aside for the production of beer. The addition of hops, an essential part of beer as we know it today, followed much later, in mediaeval times.

Production starts with the 'malting' of barley (or, more rarely, wheat or other cereals) by germinating it in warm damp conditions, causing the release of amylolytic enzymes which enable pectolytic enzymes to convert the grain starch into sugars. The dried and finished malt (known as 'grist' when milled) is 'mashed' in water at temperatures up to 75°C and the sweet liquid or 'wort' extracted and boiled with hops. After cooling and filtering, the wort is inoculated ('pitched') with various strains of the yeast *Saccharomyces cerevisiae* (brewer's or baker's yeast) which ferment the sugars into alcohol and carbon dioxide. The resulting rough 'green beer' is then further conditioned in casks or bottles, sometimes with the addition of extra hops and sugars, where a slow, secondary fermentation takes place. This fermentation continues up to the point when the beer is ready for drinking, the slow release of carbon dioxide giving the beer its sparkle and head.

In Britain, traditional brewing uses strains of 'top-fermenting' yeasts which rise through the wort to produce a foamy surface crust. In continental Europe and North America, 'bottom-fermenting' strains are used, in which the yeast sinks. This style of brewing is typical of lager and the yeast strain used is sometimes treated as a separate species, *Saccharomyces carlsbergensis*.

In modern, mass-market 'beers', the secondary fermentation is arrested by pasteurisation, creating a sterile liquid which is easy to transport, long-lasting, and requires no skill to manage. This liquid is carbonated during bottling, canning, or (with draught beers) at the point of sale, to produce a fizzy, beer-flavoured drink. A textbook on modern, industrial brewing methods was published by Hardwick (1995) with a more recent review paper by Hartmeier & Reiss (2002).

Cider and perry making

Cider is intrinsically easier to make than beer, since it depends on fermenting the natural sugars present in apples using the natural yeasts on the fruit.

Apples are ground in a cider mill to form a thick 'cheese' which is then pressed in layers between straw or cloth to extract the juice. The yeasts present in the juice, principally *Saccharomyces* species, convert sugars into alcohol to form an initial rough cider; secondary bacterial fermentation then converts the sharp malic acids of the rough cider into milder lactic acids. Good quality ciders are still made from distinctive varieties of cider apples in the traditional cider counties (Cornwall, Devon, Somerset, Gloucestershire, Hereford, and Worcester) and from ordinary apples in Norfolk and south-East England. Other traditional cider centres include the Pays d'Auge area of Normandy and the Asturias region of Spain. As with beer, modern, mass-market 'cider' is a quite different drink made from apple concentrate, sugar, and various additives. It is pasteurised and then carbonated to produce a liquid that is bland, fizzy, and depressingly consistent.

Perry is made in a similar way to cider, but using perry pears, traditional varieties of which are still grown in small quantities, mainly in Gloucestershire, Hereford, and Worcester.

Wine, sake, and other fermented drinks

Wine is also made in a similar way to cider, the grapes being crushed to release the juice ('must') which is then naturally fermented by the yeasts, principally strains of *Saccharomyces cerevisiae*, growing with the fruit. A secondary, bacterial fermentation also takes place to convert malic acid into lactic acids. As with beer and cider, the whole process has long been industrialised, though with considerably more care. Mass-market wines are not normally carbonated, for example.

A mycologically interesting feature of certain sweet wines, principally Sauternes, is that the grapes are allowed to rot on the vine before harvesting. The rot, *Botrytis cinerea*, is the ubiquitous grey mould prevalent on soft fruits and other plant parts (Chapter Five) and normally regarded as a destructive pathogen. On grapes, however, initial attack by the 'noble rot' tends to shrivel the fruit and concentrate the sugars, many of which remain after fermentation.

The Japanese rice wine, sake, is made using a substantially different process. Rice is first fermented with the mould *Aspergillus oryzae*, to form a 'koji' starter (similar to soy sauce production, below). Further steamed rice is then added to the koji, together with water, and a traditional yeast mix containing *Saccharomyces cerevisiae*, to form a seed yeast stage or 'moto'. Further koji, water, and steamed rice are added in stages to form a complex 'moromi' or mash from which the sake is finally removed by filtration.

Toddy or palm wine is a sweet fermented drink made from the sap of various palms in West Africa, India, South-East Asia, and South America. It contains *Saccharomyces cerevisiae* and other yeasts which are naturally introduced as a by-product of the tapping procedure. Kanji is an Indian drink prepared from carrots and beetroots fermented by a mix of yeasts, said to include *Candida* species and *Hansenula anomala*. Pulque is a Mexican drink made from agave juice fermented with lactobacilli and *Saccharomyces* species. Closer to home, ginger beer is a mildly alcoholic beverage made from ginger, sugar, and water also fermented with lactobacilli and *Saccharomyces* species.

Yeasts and bread-baking

Different strains of brewer's yeast, the ubiquitous *Saccharomyces cerevisiae*, are also used in both traditional and industrial bread-baking. The leavening of bread with yeast is believed to have arisen anciently in Egypt, probably involving spontaneous yeast contamination during the mixing and baking process. Yeast fermentation in the dough releases carbon dioxide, causing loaves to rise and become porous. The yeast also produces complex by-products, including organic esters, alcohols, and carbonyls, which are responsible for much of the flavour of leavened bread. In India, papadams are traditionally made from gram flour fermented for a few hours before cooking. The fermentation medium usually comes from a previous batch and typically contains *Saccharomyces cerevisiae* and *Candida* species. In southern India, pancake-like idli are made from gram and rice flours. Principal fermenting agents for idli appear to be the yeasts *Torulopsis candida* and *Trichosporon pullulans*.

Fermented cheese and dairy products

If the idea of mouldy food seems unappetising, think for a moment of *Penicillium roquefortii* and *P. camembertii*. The first is the mould used not only in Roquefort cheese, but all blue cheeses including Stilton and Gorgonzola.

It not only produces a distinctive taste in the veins of blue mould, but is responsible for ripening the cheeses, releasing enzymes which soften the curd and helping produce ketones and acids which substantially contribute to flavour and texture. *Penicillium camembertii* is the white mould which covers the surface of Camembert and Brie cheeses. Like *P. roquefortii*, it releases enzymes into the cheese which are responsible for creating the distinctive creamy texture and taste. In addition to these moulds, various ascomycetous yeasts such as *Debaryomyces hansenii* and *Yarrowia lipolytica* may also be important in cheese starter cultures.

Saint Paulin, Bel Paese, and the pungent Limburger are examples of cheeses which are ripened using a combination of surface yeasts and bacteria. Similar combinations are found in fermented milk products, notably kefir which originated in the Caucasus and results from the dual action of various yeasts (*Candida kefyr* and *Saccharomyces unisporus* form part of a typical commercial recipe) and bacteria such as *Lactococcus lactis* and *Lactobacillus kefyr*. Koumiss, the fermented mare's milk popular in Russia, is a similar product using lactobacteria and the yeast *Kluyveromyces marxianus*. Both are considered to have tonic properties. Other more familiar milk products, like yoghurt, are fermented entirely by bacteria. Villi, a Finnish 'ropy milk' product, is ripened by the mould *Geotrichum candidum*.

Fermented meat and fish

A number of meat products, particularly sausages and hams, are ripened by moulds. These meats include some forms of salami, such as pepperoni, and Swiss hams such as Bauernspeck. Most of the moulds used with sausages are *Penicillium* species, particularly *P. nalgiovense*. Not surprisingly, these moulds are said to have a distinct effect on the taste.

Equally distinctive are the fermented fish products of Indo-China, Japan, and the East Indies. One example is bagoong, a salted fish paste from the Philippines which is fermented for up to a year using a mix of bacteria and yeasts, and is part of the staple diet in some areas. Slightly better known is katsuobushi, a hard, dry, fermented bonito tuna from Japan, mould-ripened with *Aspergillus glaucus*. Katsuobushi is a standard component of many standard soup stocks ('dashi') in Japanese cooking.

Soy sauce, tempeh, and other Far Eastern foods

In the Far East an extraordinarily wide range of fermented foods is produced, often on a large commercial scale. Amongst the best known in the West are soy sauce, miso, sufu, and tempeh, but Wang & Hesseltine (1986) provided notes on well over 100 different fermented products from China, Indo-China, Korea, Japan, and the East Indies. Nout & Aidoo (2002) have provided an update on Asian fungally fermented foods.

Soy sauce is traditionally made from soya beans cooked and mixed with variable proportions of wheat. The mix is fermented with a 'koji' starter consisting of the green moulds *Aspergillus oryzae* and *A. sojae* and is then further fermented in a brine solution (the 'moromi' mash) using a mix of lactobacteria and yeasts, including *Zygosaccharomyces rouxii*, *Candida versatilis*, and *C. etchellsii*. The pressed liquid from the moromi mash is the soy sauce itself, the whole process having taken some six months to complete. Modern industrial processes follow a similar path, but use selected, fast-acting fungus strains and production techniques which deliver a uniform product within a fortnight or so. Estimated annual production of soy sauce in China is around 1,700,000 tons with a further 1,200,000 tons produced in Japan. Soy sauce is also made in several other countries, including Malaysia and Indonesia where it is known as 'kecap', the origin of the English word for a spicy, savoury sauce.

Miso is a Japanese fermented paste, not too dissimilar from a thick soy sauce, but typically made with soya beans and rice, rather than wheat. The fermentation process involves the same fungal species. Several distinct varieties are made, varying in colour, saltiness, and sweetness, and the paste is mainly used as a basis for miso soups. Estimated annual production of miso is around 600,000 tons.

Sufu is a Chinese fermented bean curd sometimes called soya bean cheese. The basis is tofu, the rather bland, coagulated cubes of soya bean milk, which are treated with *Actinomucor elegans* or other zygomycetous moulds and then fermented in a mix of brine and alcohol. The popular hon-fang or red sufu is made with the addition of ang-kak (rice fermented with the yeast *Monascus purpureus*, used mainly for food colouring). Also popular is tsui-fang or 'drunken cheese', made with more than the usual amount of alcohol. The preparation of sufu combining bacterial as well as fungal fermentation resulting in 'a strong, offensive odour' is said to be 'a top secret in the industry' and is now becoming 'a lost art' (Wang & Fang, 1986). Estimated annual production of less offensive sufu is around 300,000 tons.

Tempeh is an Indonesian staple made from parboiled, pressed soya beans inoculated with *Rhizopus* moulds, particularly *R. oligosporus*. Mycelium of the mould grows rapidly through and over the soya beans, binding them together to form a tempeh cake which is sliced and fried, roasted, or added to soups. It is a major source of protein in the Indonesian diet. Oncom is a similar fermented cake made from peanuts and is a staple dish in western Java. Peanuts are first pressed for oil extraction, steamed, and then inoculated with the ascomycetous mould *Neurospora intermedia*. This grows over the peanut cake, producing a foodstuff similar to tempeh but coloured orange from the mould. Neither tempeh nor oncom have any keeping properties and must be eaten the same day they are prepared.

Gari, foo-foo, and other traditional foods

In the rain forests of equatorial West Africa, roots of cassava are pulped and fermented with bacteria and the ascomycetous yeast *Geotrichum candidum* to form a local staple known as gari. From experience in Cameroon, this closely resembles vinegar-flavoured tapioca, which indeed is more or less what it is. Foo-foo is a similar product from Nigeria and the Congo, probably involving lactobacteria and yeasts (*Candida* species).

Other local, fermented foods include the Hawaiian poi, a porridge-like preparation of taro prepared with lactobacteria and yeasts (including *Candida vini* and *Geotrichum candidum*); pozol, a simple dough of fermented maize eaten in southern Mexico, prepared with a wide and spontaneous mix of bacteria, yeasts, and moulds; kaanga-kopuwai, a Maori preparation of maize which turns the kernels 'slimy and distinctly aromatic'; and kanjika, a soured rice gruel eaten by the Dravidians of India.

In Mexico and elsewhere, beans from the tree *Theobroma cacao* are placed in pits or sweat boxes and naturally fermented for up to 12 days by a complex succession of yeasts including *Candida, Kluyveromyces, Saccharomyces,* and *Trichosporon* species which macerate the pulp and drain off the liquor. The fermented beans are the basis for xocalatl, a local speciality which, sweetened and marketed under the name 'chocolate', has become one of the world's most widely known and distinctive food products.

Hundreds more foods are fermented worldwide. Details of many of them can be found in an A-Z guide by Campbell-Platt (1987), with further substantial compilations by Steinkraus (1983) and Hesseltine & Wang (1986).

Kombucha, the Tibetan, Manchurian, or tea 'mushroom'

A peculiar Asian concoction which has long been made from cultures of sweetened tea has in recent years been touted as a universal New Age panacea, capable of curing cancer, AIDS, rheumatism and hair loss, whilst also prolonging life. Called kombucha (or kambucha), hongo, the Tibetan, Manchurian, or Japanese tea 'mushroom', it is not an individual organism, but a highly variable consortium of yeasts and bacteria which forms large, gelatinous, lobate growths in tea-based media. The constituents change from culture to culture, so it is unlikely that any two kombuchas are the same; but the consortia frequently include acetobacteria and yeasts like *Saccharomyces ludwigii*, *Schizosaccharomyces pombe*, and *Pichia fermentans*. The bacterial-fungal consortium is kept alive by continually subculturing in a mix of sugar, tea, and water, the excess fluid from which is drunk by the brave or demented. Ramsbottom (1936) mentioned it as 'tea cider', noted the presence of a bacterium and yeast (*S. ludwigii*), and commented that there had been a 'good deal of propaganda' regarding its 'reputed medicinal qualities.' More on kombucha, including a bibliography, can be found in Roussin (1996).

Marmite™ yeast extract

In the nineteenth century, a German chemist, Baron von Liebig, found that spent brewer's yeast could be made into an edible paste and in 1902 the Marmite Food Company was established at Burton-on-Trent, the heart of the British brewing industry, to develop yeast extract into a commercial product. Raw spent yeast from breweries, mixed with hop residues, is bitter and unpalatable, though sometimes used as an animal feed supplement. But after some refinements, the edible yeast extract Marmite™, with its distinctive savoury-salty taste, became popular as a vitamin source and dietary supplement in the 1920s and achieved more universal popularity in Britain during the Second World War. It is seldom eaten elsewhere but Vegemite™, an Australian yeast extract first produced in 1922 by Fred Walker & Co., is a similar product with an equally loyal following in its country of origin.

Quorn™ mycoprotein

Non-fermented food products from microfungi are rare. But since the 1980s, fungal protein has been commercially produced for human consumption from the mycelium of a non-pathogenic strain of the ascomycete *Fusarium venenatum* (originally misdetermined as *F. graminearum*).

Development of the process was initiated in Britain during the early 1960s, but it took twenty years before mycoprotein reached the supermarket shelves. Textured and flavoured, it is marketed as a meat-free health food, and as such provides an alternative to similar soya-based products (Trinci, 1992). Mycoprotein was launched in 1985 under the trade name Quorn™ and is now readily available as a range of fifty or more products, including meat-free burgers, sausages, and ready meals. By 1992, its UK retail value was £12,000,000 p.a., rising to over £100,000,000 p.a. by 2001.

Fungi as food additives: acids, vitamins and enzymes

Fungal fermentation processes are employed on a commercial scale to produce an extensive range of substances such as preservatives, vitamins, enzymes and other metabolites for the food industry. An example is citric acid, which is extensively used as an antioxidant, preservative, and flavour enhancer in a wide range of food products. It was once extracted from citrus fruits, but since 1923 has been commercially produced by fermentation of the mould *Aspergillus niger*, mainly using molasses as a substrate. Around 300,000 tons are produced each year.The production of vitamins, mainly as supplements for animal foodstuffs, is largely undertaken by chemical synthesis. However, since the 1970s riboflavin (vitamin B_2) has increasingly been manufactured from soybeans using a fermentation process involving the ascomycete *Ashbya gossypii*. Some commercial production of β-carotene (provitamin A), used as an anti-oxidant and orange food colouring, is also undertaken using the zygomycete *Blakeslea trispora*. A few polyunsaturated fatty acids (vitamin F group) are commercially produced using the zygomycete *Mortierella isabellina*, whilst other biosynthetic processes use a species of the marine *Thraustochytriales*.

Rennin, the milk-clotting enzyme used in cheesemaking, is now largely derived from zygomycetous *Mucor* species. Pectic enzymes from *Aspergillus niger* and other moulds are extensively used for clarifying fruit juices, whilst fungal amylases, typically derived from *Aspergillus oryzae*, are used in commercial baking. Bigelis & Lasure (1987) provided details of many other fungus-derived enzymes used in a variety of processes, from the manufacture of non-sugar sweeteners to the removal of 'flatulence factors' from soya bean products.

FUNGI AS BIOCONTROL AGENTS

Fungi are natural control agents for many pests and diseases, so the possibilities of exploiting them commercially have long been researched, to the point where a number of products are now on sale. In recent years, this research and development (though still minimal compared to R&D in the chemical industry) has increased as a result of the banning of dangerous chemicals (e.g. the pesticide, methyl bromide) and the growth of the 'organic food' sector. Fungal products may well provide replacement treatments.

Fungi to control weeds

Though plant pathogenic fungi can be economically devastating when they attack our crops, a few redeem themselves by attacking our weeds instead. These beneficial plant pathogens have been extensively researched and occasionally put into use as fungal biocontrol agents.

In many countries, the unintentional introduction of alien weeds has caused huge problems not only on arable farms, but also in pastures and grasslands. Freed from their natural checks and restraints, some of these invasive weeds have totally overgrown crops and native vegetation. In such cases, the careful introduction of the weeds' own host-specific pathogens, including fungi, can help bring them under control. This technique is generally known as the inoculative or 'classical' approach, the idea being that a single release of a tested pathogen will spread naturally and effectively through the weed population without further human interference. Host-specific rusts have been the main source of such inocula and have scored some success. The first to be tested was the rust *Puccinia chondrillina* which was introduced into Australia in 1971 to combat rush skeltonweed (*Chondrilla juncea*), a serious weed of cultivation introduced from Europe. The same fungus was introduced into the United States in 1975 for the same purpose. In Australia, the rust spread an encouraging 320 km in the first year, but proved an ineffective control which had little impact on the host population, mainly because several strains of the weed turned out to be rust-resistant. In America, however, infestation reductions of up to 87% were achieved in some areas. A further example was the 1973 release of blackberry rust, *Phragmidium violaceum*, in Chile to combat the spread of European brambles (*Rubus fruticosus* agg.), an objective which was achieved with some considerable success.

A different approach is the 'inundative' strategy, where pathogenic fungi are applied to weeds in much the same way as a conventional chemical herbicide. Several such 'mycoherbicides' have been tested and a very few have even been marketed commercially. DeVine®, for example, is a preparation containing the fungus-like blight *Phytophthora palmivora* marketed to Florida citrus growers to combat strangler vine (*Morrenia odorata*). The product was so successful, proving to be around 90% efficacious over a two to ten year period, that it was initially withdrawn for lack of repeat sales, though is currently available once more (Kilian *et al.*, 1997).

In Britain, concern about bracken (*Pteridium aquilinum*) as an invasive weed species, as well as its apparent status as a potential carcinogen, has led to research into bracken parasites as potential mycoherbicides. Among the most important of these are the ascomycetes *Ascochyta pteridis* and *Phoma aquilina*, two of the causal agents of a disease known as 'curl-tip'. Both have been investigated in Britain for bracken control, and *A. pteridis* has been assessed for its potential as a specific mycoherbicide. A wide range of further possibilities for weed control are being investigated worldwide (TeBeest, 1993; Evans *et al.*, 2001).

The whole subject of mycoherbicides achieved some notoriety in 2000 with the revelation that the British and American governments were quietly financing research into a fungus for use against opium poppies in Afghanistan. The species concerned, an ascomycete called *Pleospora papaveracea*, was being developed in a former soviet biological warfare plant in Uzbekistan (BBC, 1998). At the same time a form of the ascomycetous plant pathogen, *Fusarium oxysporum*, was being developed with UN funding for use against coca plants in Colombia (Kleiner, 2000). These revelations were generally presented in terms of a major scare story, with visions of lethally toxic fungi running out of control. One South American newspaper even dubbed *F. oxysporum* 'el hongo Frankenstein'. At present, however, it seems unlikely that many mycoherbicides – for weeds or for drugs – will go into full-scale production in the near future. Problems in bulk-growing plant pathogens, in storing them in viable condition, and in applying them at the right place and time are just the beginning. Successful mycoherbicides also have to compete with conventional chemical treatments in terms of cost, ease of use, and effectiveness, and all that adds up to a very tall order indeed.

Fungi to control fungi

There are basically two ways to utilise fungi themselves as a control for fungal diseases of crops. The first and more obvious method is to develop and deploy parasitic fungi to attack the plant pathogens. A commercial example of such a biofungicide is AQ10®, a preparation of the ascomycete *Ampelomyces quisqualis* a common parasite of powdery mildews. Tests on courgettes and cucumbers have shown substantial yield increases, with the added benefit of non-toxicity (as opposed to the traditional use of chemicals such as sulphur). The biofungicide Trichodex®, containing *Trichoderma harzianum*, is another commercial product said to be effective against the ubiquitous grey mould, *Botrytis cinerea*.

As well as these leaf sprays, soil-borne biofungicides have been developed to combat pathogens which attack plants through their root systems. Introducing the mycoparasitic ascomycete *Gliocladium virens* into soils has, for example, been shown significantly to reduce the incidence of damping-off by *Rhizoctonia solani* and *Pythium* species and a commercial product based on the fungus, Soilgard 12G®, is currently marketed in the United States.

A second and less obvious method of biocontrol is to use the natural antagonism of harmless fungal species to keep pathogenic species at bay. Many saprotrophic fungi growing on living leaf surfaces, for example, are antagonistic to other potential leaf colonisers, including some plant pathogens. As a result, these phylloplane fungi have potential use as biocontrols. A common phylloplane fungus, *Cladosporium herbarum*, has been shown to reduce *Botrytis* rots when sprayed onto soft fruits whilst spraying wheat with suspensions of phylloplane yeasts reduces leaf diseases. Aspire®, a commercial product based on the yeast *Candida oleophila*, is available in the United States as a treatment against post-harvest decay of pome and citrus fruits. Even without spraying, these phylloplane fungi may be providing some natural protection to plants. As a result, killing off the natural mycota by applying non-selective fungicides to crops may perversely increase rather than reduce the incidence of fungal disease.

In forestry, the harmless basidiomycete *Phlebiopsis gigantea* has been used on a commercial scale against the parasitic, wood-rotting polypore *Heterobasidion annosum*. *Heterobasidion* can quickly colonise the stumps of felled conifers, using them as a resource from which to attack living trees. But when fresh stumps are inoculated with *Phlebiopsis* (an aggressively territorial fungus), the *Heterobasidion* can gain no foothold. This form of biocontrol, pioneered in Thetford Forest, Norfolk, by Rishbeth (1961), was once widely used by the Forestry Commission, but has now fallen out of favour. It has, however, been adopted on a large scale in Finland and other Scandinavian countries where a spray-on suspension of propagules is marketed under the name Rotstop®.

Considerable research has been undertaken on the possibility of using other antagonistic species to keep parasitic, wood-rotting fungi in check. *Hypholoma fasciculare* (sulphur tuft), for example, may provide a possible biocontrol for use against *Armillaria* species (honey fungus).

The commercial use of fungi to control plant pathogens was reviewed by Whipps & Lumsden (2001) and a list of available products published by Butt *et al.* (2001).

Fungi to control insects and mites

Not surprisingly, entomopathogenic fungi (parasites of insects, mites, and other invertebrates) have been the subject of extensive research into their potential use as biocontrol agents for invertebrate pests.

Metarhizium anisopliae, an ascomycete anamorph (*Nectriaceae*), is one of the more successful control agents, with different strains attacking a range of pests including cockroaches, weevils, termites, whiteflies, and thrips. In the USA, a cockroach trap containing *M. anisopliae* spores is currently marketed under the trade-name Bio-Path® and a termiticide under the name Bio-Blast®, whilst in Germany a granular soil treatment called Biologic® containing *M. anisopliae* mycelium has been developed for use against the larvae of black vine weevils. Another anamorphic ascomycete, *Beauveria bassiana* (*Clavicipitaceae*), has an equally wide host range. Since the 1970s it has been mass-produced in Russia under the name Boverin® to control Colorado beetles and codling moths and it is extensively used in China where up to one million hectares of farmland and forest are treated each year against a variety of pests. In Britain, strains of the ascomycetous mould *Verticillium lecanii* are commercially available under the names Mycotal® (introduced in 1982) and Vertalec® (introduced in 1981) for greenhouse control of aphids and whiteflies respectively.

To date, however, only a few fungal pesticides have been marketed commercially compared to the vast range of chemical pesticides. In 1996, the cost of registering a pest control agent was around £250,000 in the USA alone, and fungal biocontrol agents have to compete with established chemical agents not only in performance, but in production costs, long-term storage, ease of use, and safety features. At present, it seems, many fungi have the potential to control pests, but only a few meet the criteria for commercial success (Butt *et al.*, 2001, provided a list of available products).

Fungi to control nematodes

Nematodes (eel-worms) cause considerable economic damage, either by attacking the roots of commercial crops, or by infesting cattle and other livestock. Worldwide crop losses due to nematodes are immense, estimated at around £50,000,000,000 per year. However, the nematodes have their own parasites and predators in the form of specialist fungi (Chapter Five). As with insect pathogens, these nematophagous fungi have been extensively researched as potential biocontrol agents, though with rather less success. Part of the problem is the difficulty of growing many of the fungal species, particularly the endoparasites, in vitro. Another difficulty is understanding the ecology of nematophagous fungi in soil and pasture and, as a consequence, tracking the precise effects of experimental applications. It may be that toxins extracted from nematophagous fungi will prove more successful than the fungi themselves, and a commercial product DiTera®, based on the anamorphic ascomycete *Myrothecium verrucaria*, is now available for nematode control.

FUNGI FOR BIOREMEDIATION

Rotting down poisonous wastes

As part of the natural process of decomposition, many fungi and bacteria break down complex chemicals into simpler compounds. When the initial chemicals are toxic, this breakdown can have a beneficial 'clean-up' effect and can be artificially enhanced by encouraging existing fungi to work harder or by introducing novel fungi to the chemical mix.

Crude oil spillages are obvious candidates for this bioremediation treatment. Some fungal species thrive on the hydrocarbons found in oils – including the kerosene used in aviation fuel (Chapter 14) – and under the right conditions are capable of degrading them into simpler and less polluting substances. The ascomycetous mould *Aspergillus terreus*, for example, has been found as a natural degrader of oil spills, occurring (together with *Fusarium solani*) in North American oil damaged sites and in the devastated oil fields of Kuwait following the Gulf War. On-site treatments such as tilling, fertilisation, and irrigation can help these natural degraders – bacteria as well as fungi – break down some or all of the pollutants (Morgan & Watkinson, 1993, provided a brief review of methods).

As well as helping the soil's natural mycota do its remedial work, researchers have also experimented with introducing novel fungal degraders to pollutants. Perhaps surprisingly, these fungal degraders include polypores and other wood-rotting basidiomycetes. But wood contains a wide range of oils, resins, gums, tannins, and other 'extractives' some of which are widely toxic, yet tolerated and even utilised by the wood-rotting fungi (Chapter Three). Lignin-degrading, white-rot basidiomycetes are amongst those which have been widely researched as potential biodegrading agents. The oyster fungus *Pleurotus ostreatus* has, for example, been shown to break down the aliphatic and aromatic hydrocarbons in crude oil and also the polychlorinated biphenyls (PCBs) in pesticides and other agents. The corticioid fungus *Phanerochaete chrysosporium* has been shown to break down PCBs, polycyclic aromatic hydrocarbons (PAHs) in creosote and other oils, some of the phenolic dyes in pulp-mill and textile effluents, and DDT pesticide residues. Some research has also been undertaken on biodegradation by brown-rot basidiomycetes.

Moulds (*Aspergillus* species) have been reported growing on gunpowder, but more remarkably some fungi can even degrade TNT. *Phanerochaete chrysosporium* is one of the species successfully tested, and trials have been made with fungi to clean naval dockyards of waste explosives on the ground.

Taking out toxic metals

As well as breaking down complex chemicals, many fungi are able to absorb and accumulate metals from the environment, and hence have a potential role in the bioremediation of toxic metal-rich effluents and contaminated sites. The mechanism is termed 'biosorption' and the metals involved include arsenic, cadmium, cobalt, copper, mercury, selenium, uranium, and zinc. Once taken up from soil or effluent, the metals can be recovered from the fungi and disposed of or recycled. Potentially useful species which have been studied include brewer's yeast, *Saccharomyces cerevisiae*, and the zygomycete *Rhizopus arrhizus*, both of which are capable of being cultured in bulk, an essential attribute for practical use. A list of these and other potential bioremediation fungi, mostly ascomycetes, was published by Singleton & Tobin (1996).

'Heterotrophic leaching' is another mechanism whereby fungi can remove metals from the environment. This can involve several different processes, the commonest of which utilises fungally produced organic acids (such as citric and gluconic acid from *Aspergillus niger*) to solubilise and leach out metals, which can then be recovered. The techniques could be used to recover metals from the ash left over from municipal incinerators or from various kinds of manufacturing and recycling scrap, such as old electronics and circuit boards. Fungi could also be used to leach out unwanted metals in contaminated sites and to recover valuable trace metals from waste or low-grade ores in the mining industry. Fungal bioconversion of low-grade coal could produce more versatile and valuable hydrocarbon fuels.

Reclaiming wasteland with mycorrhizas

Slag heaps, coal tips, and landfills were once left to their own devices, but are now routinely planted with birch, conifers, and other rapidly growing trees. Most of these trees are ectomycorrhizal, but their fungal associates are absent from reclaimed sites. To enable the trees to grow, seedlings are therefore deliberately inoculated with appropriate fungi before planting out. In Britain, favoured species are the earthball *Scleroderma citrinum* and the agaric *Paxillus involutus*, both common fungi capable of forming mycorrhizas with a wide range of hosts. Inoculation of tree seedlings can be achieved by the transfer of soil or roots from existing mycorrhizas, by sowing with spore-encapsulated seed, or by mixing soil with cultured mycelium. In America, the puffball-like *Pisolithus arhizus* has been widely used to form mycorrhizas with pines and other trees planted out in industrial waste sites and a commercial formulation called MycoRhiz® has been marketed for this purpose.

Radioactive fungi

Rather alarmingly, agaric fruitbodies are good bioindicators of radioactive contamination through deposition, including fallout from the atmospheric testing of nuclear bombs and plume deposits from the Chernobyl reactor disaster. Fungi are particularly receptive to the radioactive isotope caesium[137] (radiocaesium: [137]Cs) which is taken up by growing mycelium as a surrogate for potassium, which has similar physicochemical properties. Measuring radionuclides in agarics therefore provides an estimate of the contamination of the substrata (leaf litter, soil, wood, etc.) in which they grow, though take-up of ^{137}Cs varies substantially according to species, soil pH, and other factors. The subject was succinctly reviewed by Oolbekkink & Kuyper (1989) and in more detail by Reisinger (1994).

Investigation of a range of British agarics and other macrofungi following the Chernobyl accident, fortunately showed only modest levels of ^{137}Cs accumulation in fruitbodies (well below EU limits for food products). Even for people who habitually eat wild fungi in Britain, the extra intake of radioactivity resulting from Chernobyl was and is minimal (Barnett *et al.*, 2001). Much higher figures were obtained in central Europe and, of course, in Ukraine itself where contamination of edible fruitbodies exceeded safety limits.

CHAPTER 18

Conservation

T HE CONCEPT of conserving habitats and species has come a long way since its first official recognition in the 1940s when the Postmaster-General was considered the appropriate person to report on the subject and did so in the context of wartime reconstruction. Nowadays, conservation and natural history are intimately linked and it is the drive for conservation which funds and powers almost every kind of biodiversity research, from field trips to databasing, distribution mapping, and the description of new species.

Predictably, fungal conservation has come a very poor third to the conservation of animals and plants, reflecting not only public and political indifference but also (to a degree) some real problems about assessing risks to organisms whose ways of life are so cryptic and little-known.

Can we, for example, point to a fungus that is extinct? All too many animal and plant species have certainly died out in the last few centuries and one might presume the same to be true for fungi. But it would be difficult even to nominate a candidate species for this sad role, let alone prove that the nominated species really was extinct. Even in Britain, our local extinctions may not be forever. In 1999, the conspicuous scarlet corticioid fungus *Cytidia salicina* (Fig. 159) was refound on its willow host nearly 100 years after it was last seen and the stipitate stereoid fungus *Stereopsis vitellina* reappeared in the same site (Abernethy Forest, Scotland) where it was last found in 1900. There is therefore still hope for species

FIG 159. The scarlet, patch-forming fungus *Cytidia salicina* was not seen in Britain for nearly a century, but has now been refound in Tayside and the Kielder Forest. It grows on dead attached willow branches (E. Holden).

FIG 160. The earthstar-like 'pepperpot fungus' *Myriostoma coliforme* was originally described from East Anglia, but has not been seen in England for over a century. It still survives at one or two sites in the Channel Islands (S. Evans).

like *Myriostoma coliforme* (Fig. 160) and *Gomphus clavatus* (Fig. 161), neither of which have been seen in mainland Britain for more than 70 years.

Nonetheless, if evaluating the status of individual species is something of a problem to fungal conservationists, it is still clear that the disappearance of habitats – ancient woodlands, heaths and dunes, unimproved pastures and short turf grassland – presents a general threat to their indigenous communities, including the resident fungi. Moreover, as the preceding chapters have shown, fungi are an integral and essential part of every natural biosphere. Lose the fungi, and the whole ecosystem will swiftly collapse. For this reason, if no other, mycologists need to play an active role in conservation issues and happily this is increasingly recognised amongst the conservation community.

FIG 161. *Gomphus clavatus* looks rather like a mauve to pinkish chanterelle, but is more closely related to *Ramaria* species. It has not been recorded in Britain since 1927 (S. Evans).

FUNGI AS INDICATOR SPECIES

One increasingly important role for fungi is their use as 'indicator' species. These are species whose presence, absence, or shift in population tell us something more general and widespread about a given habitat. For example, certain species of plants and animals (particularly beetles) occur only in ancient woodlands. Their presence at a woodland site therefore indicates that the site is ancient (and hence generally species-rich), whilst their absence suggests it is more recent (and hence comparatively species-poor). There are other species which are intolerant of human disturbance or intolerant of various forms of pollution. Changes in their population can therefore indicate changes in the wider habitat, some of which (particularly those resulting from chemical and other pollutants) may otherwise go unnoticed.

Lichens and urban blight

The first and most important group of fungi to be recognised as indicator species were the lichens. As long ago as the nineteenth century, Crombie (1884) had attributed poor growth of lichens in Epping Forest to air pollution, noting that 'the smoke and fogs of London and its suburbs extend their deleterious influence ... to the Forest ... and we cannot be surprised that the result should be a great decrease in the numbers and change upon the condition of its lichens'. In the 1950s and 1960s, research indicated that sulphur dioxide from coal burning and similar processes was mainly responsible, and moreover that certain lichens were far more sensitive to pollution than others. Species of *Lobaria* and *Usnea*, for example, are highly intolerant, whilst *Lecanora conizaeoides* can cope with near-urban conditions. On this basis, Hawksworth & Rose (1970) established a scale for assessing sulphur dioxide pollution by recording the presence or absence of specified epiphytic lichens on mature trees. Depending on which species were present, ten different zones could be identified, ranging from heavily polluted to pure. This in turn enabled national and local maps to be made, showing the extent of industrial air pollution in England and Wales.

The composition of air pollutants, their manner of deposition, and the uptake and effect on different lichen species are complex, calling some of the results into question. Nonetheless, the shifts in lichen populations are real enough. Richardson (1992) has published a practical handbook for monitoring pollution using lichens and the subject has been extensively reviewed by Nash & Wirth (1988), and in the New Naturalist volume on lichens (Gilbert, 2000).

Lichens, polypores, and ancient forests

In Britain, epiphytic lichens can also provide some indication of the age and continuity of the woodlands in which they are found. Rose (1976) produced lists of ancient deciduous woodland indicator species which are slow colonisers, characteristic of undisturbed forest communities and absent from clear-felled sites and plantations. The original list, the Revised Index of Ecological Continuity (Rose, 1976), contained 30 indicator species and it was suggested that any site having 12 or more of these was likely to date back, in whole or part, to the original pre-mediaeval wildwood. Boconnoc Park, near Lostwithiel in Cornwall, has the highest known score, containing every one of the 30 RIEC species (Rose, 1976, provided data on over 100 woodland sites). Low scores, however, are less meaningful, since the lichen count may be reduced for reasons of climate, rainfall, pollution, and coppicing (the list depends on epiphytes growing on old trunks). Regional indices (collated in Hodgetts, 1992) allow for more accurate estimates to be made on a local scale. All have now been updated by Coppins & Coppins (2002).

Non-lichenised fungi may also serve as indicator species for ancient woodland, but little research has been undertaken into this in Britain. For agarics, the main problems are fitful fruiting periods (some may not even fruit annually) linked with difficulties in accurate determination (the notoriously complex *Cortinarius* group may be good indicators, if anyone could ever name them). At present, it is not possible to put forward an acceptable shortlist of ancient woodland agarics, though Orton (1986) suggested some possible indicator species for Caledonian pinewoods, including *Cortinarius caledoniensis*, *Pholiota graveolens*, *P. inopus*, *Russula decolorans*, *R. obscura*, and *Xeromphalina cauticinalis*.

On the continent, however, some considerable work has been done on non-lichenised fungi with less ephemeral fruitbodies as indicator species for

FIG 162. *Hydnellum aurantiacum* is one of the rarest British tooth fungi and may be confined to Caledonian pinewoods. All these stipitate tooth fungi are mycorrhizal and seem to be associated with ancient woodlands or old woodland banks (RBG Kew).

natural, old-growth forest systems. In Estonia, for example, a list of 44 species (plus five entire genera) has been drawn up and adopted as a standard method for assessing forest conservation sites. These are mainly wood-rotting bracket fungi (such as *Fomitopsis rosea*, *Ganoderma lucidum*, and *Phellinus chrysoloma*), wood-rotting hydnoid fungi (such as *Dentipellis fragilis* and *Hericium coralloides*), and ectomycorrhizal hydnoid fungi (the genera *Hydnellum*, *Phellodon*, and *Sarcodon*) (Fig. 162), but also include a few gasteromycetes (*Geastrum* species) and some rare ascomycetes (such as *Sarcosoma globosum*). To date, the best sites have up to 14 of these species (Parmasto, 2001). Similar work in Finland has identified 33 species of bracket fungi restricted to old growth forests (Kotiranta & Niemelä, 1993). In Sweden, a handsome illustrated guide book to old forest indicator species ('signalarter') has been published (Nitare, 2000). This details species of fungi typical of 20 woodland biotypes, and includes a number of agarics as well as bracket fungi, hydnoid and clavarioid fungi, gasteromycetes, and lichens.

Waxcaps and ancient grasslands

Old semi-natural grasslands typically have an associated mycota which is never found in grasslands that are recently disturbed or 'improved' by biocides, fertilisers, and resowing (Chapter Eight). This is obvious from the richness of autumn macrofungi in old lawns and unimproved pastures compared to their almost complete absence in modern grass monocultures.

Waxcaps (*Hygrocybe* species) are good indicators of ancient grasslands, along with a few other agaric genera (principally *Dermoloma*, *Porpoloma*, and some *Entoloma* (*Leptonia*) species), certain clavarioid fungi (*Clavaria* and *Ramariopsis* species), and the ascomycetous earthtongues (*Geoglossum* and *Trichoglossum* species). It seems to take at least ten years for the commonest *Hygrocybe* species to reappear in previously disturbed or 'improved' grassland and well over 30 years for the rarer species. For newly sown or recreated grassland, the time lags may be much longer.

Surveys suggest that the British Isles are particularly rich in ancient grasslands compared to most European countries (as detailed, for example, by McHugh *et al.*, 2001, for Ireland; Holden, 2000, for Scotland; and Rotheroe, 2001, for south Wales). These grasslands are not restricted to the remaining downlands and upland pastures, but are also found in old lawns, unspoilt churchyards, parks and commons. A popular leaflet championing grassland fungi has already been produced in Wales (Woods, 2001) with further leaflets and publicity planned throughout the British Isles.

THREATS TO FUNGI

An analysis of declining fungal species in Germany (quoted in Ing, 1996) suggested that 30% of species were deemed to be threatened by air pollution, 25% by agriculture, 24% by commercial forestry, and 21% by building and other developments. Though unlikely to be precise, this analysis does at least identify some of the main threats to fungi, not only in continental Europe, but also in Britain.

Air pollution

Sulphur dioxide pollution has historically been a widespread problem for lichens, since it can devastate vast areas without regard for nature reserves and protected sites. Building a coal or oil-fired power station in a 'clean' area (as was approved for Devon in the 1970s, despite formal objections by lichenologists) can cause a massive reduction in lichen biodiversity. Sensitive species, such as the bearded lichens *Usnea articulata* and *U. ceratina*, can be completely exterminated.

Evidence of decline had already been noted by Crombie (1884) for Epping Forest to the north-east of London (as quoted above), but by 1968-70 the 86 epiphytic lichens he recorded had dwindled still further to just 28 species. Laundon (1970) listed 71 species from the London area (within 16 km of Charing Cross) recorded between 1950 and 1970, down from more than 165 in the nineteenth century (a 57% extinction of species). By the 1960s, the pollution-tolerant *Lecanora conizaeoides*, a species discovered in Britain only in 1860, had became the commonest epiphytic lichen in lowland England, with the even-more tolerant *L. dispersa* the only lichen of any kind to survive in the City of London. A contemporary collection of papers on lichens and air pollution was published by Ferry *et al.* (1973).

The 1970s, however, saw the beginning of a remarkable lowering of sulphur dioxide levels, partly through anti-pollution regulations (the Clean Air Acts), partly through the collapse of old-fashioned, coal-fired, manufacturing industries. Between 1962 and 1996, SO_2 emissions dropped by 80% in the UK and, as a result, many lichens have since made a come-back, recolonising suburbs and cities. The gardens of Buckingham Palace, for example, supported just two lichen species in 1956, but 39 were recorded there in the 1990s. *Lecanora conizaeoides* has once more become something of a rarity in places like Richmond Park, where it was once the commonest species.

Acid rain

Following the decline in urban sulphur dioxide levels, pollution fears have switched instead to 'acid rain', a mix of chemicals (including sulphur dioxide and nitrogen dioxide) whose main effect is to lower the pH of the substrata on which it falls. When this includes living leaves, living lichens, soil and leaf litter, the results can be quite disastrous for organisms intolerant of acid conditions. In addition to altering the pH balance, acids can cause direct physical damage to both fungi and vegetation, as well as leaching aluminium and other toxic substances from substrata, inhibiting metabolic processes, and adversely influencing litter-degradation. Moreover, acid rain knows no boundaries and often falls a long way from its industrial sources.

Some lichen species have certainly suffered from acid rain deposition, particularly those with cyanobacterial photobionts, but the greater fears have been for ectomycorrhizal fungi and the forest systems they support. Visible damage to forests has been noted for some years in continental Europe together with a decline in many of their ectomycorrhizal associates. This has been particularly noticeable in the Netherlands, one of the few countries to have kept extensive long-term records of macrofungi and one of the first places to be concerned about their decline. Data on 185 ectomycorrhizal species showed over 80% of them decreasing between 1950 and 1990 (Nauta & Vellinga, 1993). A decrease of 50% in fruitbody production of the edible chanterelle *Cantharellus cibarius* was highlighted by Jansen & van Dobben (1987), with an even more dramatic decrease in the German Saarland based on the weight sold annually in the local market. The honey fungus *Armillaria mellea*, a non-mycorrhizal species also sold and eaten in the Saarland, showed no such decline. Nor did ectomycorrhizal fungi which prefer a low pH, such as *Paxillus involutus* and the earthball *Scleroderma citrinum*, both of which may actually have increased as a result of acid rain.

Acid rain also affects endophytic and phylloplane microfungi, promoting the growth of certain acid-tolerant species at the expense of the normal mycota. In the UK and elsewhere, for example, studies have shown that the conifer needle endophyte *Lophodermium piceae* is replaced by the more acid-tolerant *Rhizosphaera kalkhoffii* in polluted environments. This in turn may affect the overall tree or forest biota. Studies in Sweden, for example, have shown that needles colonised by *Rhizosphaera kalkhoffii* have a higher frequency of insect damage than those colonised by *Lophodermium piceae*.

Intensive farming and soil pollution

Fertilisers and consequent hypertrophication is a further widespread problem, certainly affecting us more in Britain than acid rain. Acidophilous lichens on farmland and hedgerow trees are 'often entirely decimated' (Gilbert, 1975) by fertiliser sprays and dust. Even the acidic standing sarsen stones on Marlborough Downs have lost their lichens in this way. Fertilisers also destroy the natural mycota of grasslands, replacing waxcaps (*Hygrocybe* species) and other fungi of 'unimproved' lawns and pastures with commonplace nitrophilic species, mainly members of such dung-loving genera as *Panaeolus, Coprinus, Psilocybe,* and *Stropharia.*

Increased nitrogen availability, through farm run-off and atmospheric deposition, also affects the woodland mycota. Indeed, this may be of equal or greater relevance to the observed decrease in ectomycorrhizal fungi than the effects of acid rain. Removal of nitrogen-enriched litter and humus layers appears to stimulate the production of fruitbodies by some (but not all) ectomycorrhizal fungi. In Britain, it is noticeable that nitrophilic toadstools such as *Clitocybe nebularis* and *Lepista inversa* are now extremely common in British woodlands, especially near the boundaries, where once they were considered quite unusual.

Habitat destruction

Habitat destruction is as great a threat to fungi as it is to most organisms. In the British Isles, the habitats most under threat include ancient grasslands (including old lawns and cemeteries), ancient woodlands, lowland heaths, dune systems, and old woodland pastures.

Part of the problem is an obsession with tidiness, disastrous for many fungi. Cleaning tombstones, monuments, and old walls destroys many lichens, some of them dating back to the time in which these artefacts were first erected. Lawns and amenity grasslands are also threatened, if managed by owners with a passion for chemicals – weed-killers, moss-killers, fungicides, and super-greening products.

Axing old trees and clearing up fallen wood obviously destroys wood-rotting fungi and epiphytic lichens. In 1995, some of the ancient trees in the Royal Estate of Windsor Great Park were felled for reasons of 'tidiness', an action only stopped by public protest. Older trees are also destroyed in the name of obsessive 'health and safety' precautions (similar to those decreeing the removal of urban horse chestnut trees for fear that passers-by might be injured by falling conkers).

The wholesale destruction of ancient woodlands, through clear-felling or underplanting with conifers, appears to have stopped, to the extent that in some places efforts are being made to rescue or recreate the former broad leaf communities. However, once destroyed, re-establishment of the ancient woodland mycota is a process that may take 400 years or more – even in areas adjacent to surviving ancient woodlands. In the United States, substantial measures have been taken to protect the vast but declining old-growth forests of the Pacific Northwest, including a considerable amount of research on the associated macrofungi (Molina *et al.*, 2001).

It is of some small comfort that habitat destruction is localised (unlike the threat from pollutants) and can theoretically be contained by the creation of protected areas and reserves, if these are of sufficent size and not too isolated. However, the level of protection in the UK, particularly for SSSIs, is widely regarded as 'inadequate', and they face a variety of threats ranging from road building, quarrying, and agriculture, to underfunding and inappropriate management. The last at least can be rectified, and a selection of papers on lichen habitat management has been published (Fletcher *et al.*, 2001), though as yet there is no similar volume for non-lichenised fungi.

Commercial collecting

Scare stories such as 'magical lure of easy cash brings out mushroom picking hordes' or 'mushroom pickers strip New Forest' have convinced many people in Britain that collecting fungi for food ('an obscure and harmless occupation') is a wicked and pernicious act, particularly if undertaken for cash. It has consequently led to bylaws banning collecting in certain areas, the production of 'mushroom-picking' codes of conduct, and even the heckling and barracking of fungus-loving chefs.

In fact, harvesting fruitbodies appears to be no more threatening to macrofungi than picking blackberries is to brambles. Experiments involving the continuous removal of fruitbodies from marked plots have shown no decline in productivity during a five-year period in Oregon (involving *Cantharellus* species), a seven-year period in the Netherlands, and a 13-year period in Switzerland (see Arnolds, 1995). An observed decline in chanterelles (*Cantharellus cibarius*) in the Netherlands occurred in non-harvested areas, and appeared to have been pollution-related (as noted above). However, real fears in collecting fungi for food concern damage to woodland litter layers through raking (a problem with *Tricholoma magnivelare* in the United States – see Chapter 17) and mass trampling by thousands of collectors (said to be a problem near urban centres in some mycophilic countries, like Italy). In addition, large scale collecting of fruitbodies may deprive fungus gnats and other invertebrates as well as some small mammals of their food source (though no study seems to have been undertaken into the consequent effects, if any, on invertebrate populations).

CONSERVING FUNGI

Conservation organisations

At present, there is no single organisation devoted to fungal conservation, nor is there likely to be. However, several organisations in the British Isles and overseas have an interest in fungal conservation. Many of them (such as the British Mycological Society) have a conservation officer or (as in conservation agencies such as Plantlife and English Nature) an officer dedicated to fungi or, all too often, to 'cryptogams' or 'lower plants' (categories indicative of low status and outmoded ideas, though hopefully this may change).

In the UK, an umbrella group, the Fungus Conservation Forum, was set up in 1999 to co-ordinate and exchange information on the conservation of fungi (though lichenised fungi are excluded). Its areas of focus are the identification and protection of important areas for fungi, the collation of fungal data and the development of a database for threatened fungi, the implementation of Biodiversity Action Plans for fungi (see below), and the management of sites for fungus conservation interest. It currently meets twice a year, is chaired by Plantlife, and includes representatives from the national conservation agencies (Countryside Council for Wales, English Nature, Northern Ireland Heritage & Environment Service, and Scottish Natural Heritage), the Royal Botanic Gardens Kew, the Joint Nature Conservation Committee, the Wildlife Trusts, National Trust, Woodland Trust, Forestry Commission, Royal Society for the Protection of Birds (which takes an interest in fungi on its many reserves), the British Mycological Society, and the Association of British Fungus Groups.

On a larger scale, the European Council for Conservation of Fungi (ECCF) was created at the ninth Congress of European Mycologists in Oslo in 1985. This had an initial brief 'to promote and coordinate studies and publications on the protection of fungi and to promote effective measures in this respect', though lichenised fungi were not included. The ECCF has subsequently met at regular intervals and published a series of collated reports on fungal conservation matters in various European countries (Jansen & Lawrynowicz, 1991; Arnolds & Kreisel, 1991; Perini, 1998).

Red Data Lists

Since the 1980s, most European countries and some local regions have produced Red Data Lists of endangered fungi, cataloguing species which are variously threatened, declining, or considered locally extinct. A provisional British Red Data List of non-lichenised fungi (Ing, 1992) is currently being revised, following criteria set by the International Union for Conservation of Nature – Species Survival Commission (IUCN, 2001). A Red Data List of British lichens has been published separately by Church et al. (1997). A provisional European Red Data List of non-lichenised fungi has also been produced (Ing, 1993) and the Council of Europe has published lists collated from various European countries (Koune, 2001). Thor (1995) provided a brief review of European lists for lichens.

In drawing up such lists, lichens have the advantage of being visible all year-round and are consequently comparatively well-documented and well-mapped. For non-lichenised fungi, however, Red Data Lists (in Britain and elsewhere) are necessarily arbitrary. In the UK, for example, a practical decision has been made to exclude most microfungi, specialist, and less conspicuous species, mainly because of the lack of sufficiently widespread expertise in identifying such species and consequent lack of distribution data. Under IUCN criteria, these species (unless obviously common) are all 'data deficient'. Local and national recording and mapping schemes are gradually filling in some of the missing data, but it will be a long haul before we know the full distribution of non-lichenised fungi in the British Isles and the extent to which species are or may be endangered. In the meantime, Red Data Lists are helping draw attention to fungi in the wider world of nature conservation and are providing at least some guidelines for assessing the value of sites and for setting conservation priorities.

Preserving habitats

The UK has over 6000 Sites of Special Scientific Interest (SSSIs), nearly 1000 local, national, and forest nature reserves, plus a bewildering assortment of national parks and other protected areas.

Lichens play a major role in helping to identify and establish these protected sites, largely because of their status as indicator species of ancient woodland. Non-lichenised fungi, in contrast, although now increasingly being taken into account when establishing and managing new reserves, have rarely played such a role. Historically, the main reason for this has been lack of sufficient data, both in terms of the species present and in terms of interpreting their role in the environment, their rarity, and their need for protection. This may change, however, with respect to waxcap grasslands, where *Hygrocybe* species and other non-lichenised fungi are proving to be good indicators of ancient, unimproved grassland. This includes not only semi-natural sites like Cwm Clydach in Breconshire, designated an SSSI based largely on its waxcaps, but also old undisturbed lawns, such as that at Llanerchaeron Mansion in mid Wales, proposed for SSSI status, and Down House in Kent, Darwin's former home. At present, however, not a single SSSI has been established based specifically on its fungi, although a very few sites have been protected through local initiatives. At Blyford in Suffolk, for example, a small area of roadside hedgebank, home to the rare stilt-puffball *Battarraea phalloides* (Fig. 128), was designated a Roadside Nature Reserve in the 1970s. Just 70 metres long, it is believed to be the smallest official nature reserve in Britain.

A provisional assessment of important sites for non-lichenised fungi in the UK has been produced by Evans *et al.* (2002), based on data received from national and local recorders. Some 520 sites were detailed, the criteria for inclusion being based mainly on the presence of Red Data List and other endangered fungi and on the availability of detailed records (all sites with more than 500 recorded species were included, for example). This initiative has followed similar work in the Netherlands which in turn has helped provide guidelines for managing particular sites. A proposal to identify important European areas for non-lichenised fungi was presented to the European Council for Conservation of Fungi in 2001.

Biodiversity Action Plan (BAP) species

In 1992, the international Convention of Biological Diversity was signed in Rio de Janeiro, calling for the creation and enforcement of national strategies and action plans to conserve, protect, and enhance biological diversity. As a result, the UK government set up a Biodiversity Steering Group which began to produce Biodiversity Action Plans (BAPs) to conserve both endangered species and endangered habitats. There are now over 400 BAPs for individual species, including some 50 for fungi (see Table 30 for a list of BAP fungi as of 2004). A few of these, such as the rare tooth fungus *Hericium erinaceus* (Fig. 163), are also protected under the Wildlife and Countryside Act 1981.

These BAP species receive funding through national and regional conservation agencies to compile distribution and other data, undertake taxonomic and ecological research, and formulate management plans for

FIG 163. Sometimes called the epaulette or pom-pom fungus, the edible *Hericium erinaceus* is now protected in the wild, but can quite easily be cultivated and is even marketed as a speciality food (B. Hughes).

FIG 164. The rare polypore *Piptoporus quercinus* is restricted to veteran oak trees. England, with its mediaeval deer parks and royal forests, may be a stronghold for the species (S. Evans).

long-term conservation. Fleming (2001) has provided a review of the BAP process with regard to fungi, including a list of some of the resulting projects.

Since most fungal species are considered 'data deficient' when it comes to distribution, mapping, and ecological requirements, BAP funding has proved quite useful in promoting field research. In this respect, *Hygrocybe calyptriformis*, the pink wax cap, provides an interesting example. It is a conspicuous and easily identified toadstool (Fig. 26), but when initially listed as a BAP species, it was known from just 46 sites throughout the UK. Following this listing, extensive waxcap grassland surveys were undertaken at local and regional levels, resulting in a further 200 UK sites being discovered (many in old cemeteries and lawns, both havens for unimproved grassland species). Another example is *Piptoporus quercinus*, the oak polypore, a rare British species growing only on ancient oaks and reported from just six sites in England (Fig. 164). Initial investigation aided by BAP funding has revealed an additional 16 sites for the species, and has identified enough habitat detail (including likely sites and time of fruiting) to encourage naturalists and mycologists to look for the species in their local patch.

TABLE 30. BAP species. List of British fungi for which Biodiversity Action Plans have been or are being formulated, as of 2004. The stipitate tooth fungi (*Bankera, Hydnellum, Phellodon,* and *Sarcodon* species) are treated as a single group with a shared action plan.

SPECIES	GROUP
Alectoria ochroleuca	lichen
Armillaria ectypa	toadstool
Arthothelium dictyosporum	lichen
Arthothelium macounii	lichen
Bacidia incompta	lichen
Bankera fuligineoalba	tooth fungus
Battarraea phalloides	stilt-puffball
Bellemerea alpina	lichen
Belonia calcicola	lichen
Biatoridium manasteriense	lichen
Boletus regius	bolete
Boletus satanas	bolete
Bryoria smithii	lichen

SPECIES	GROUP
Buellia asterella	lichen
Calicium corynellum	lichen
Caloplaca aractina	lichen
Caloplaca luteoalba	lichen
Caloplaca nivalis	lichen
Catapyrenium psoromoides	lichen
Chaenotheca phaeocephala	lichen
Cladonia botrytes	lichen
Cladonia mediterranea	lichen
Cladonia peziziformis	lichen
Collema dichotomum	lichen
Enterographa elaborata	lichen
Enterographa sorediata	lichen
Graphina pauciloculata	lichen
Gyalecta ulmi	lichen
Gyalideopsis scotica	lichen
Halecania rhypodiza	lichen
Hericium erinaceus	tooth fungus
Heterodermia leucomela	lichen
Hydnellum aurantiacum	tooth fungus
Hydnellum caeruleum	tooth fungus
Hydnellum concrescens	tooth fungus
Hydnellum ferrugineum	tooth fungus
Hydnellum peckii	tooth fungus
Hydnellum scrobiculatum	tooth fungus
Hydnellum spongiosipes	tooth fungus
Hygrocybe calyptriformis	toadstool
Hygrocybe spadicea	toadstool
Hypocreopsis rhododendri	pyrenomycete
Lecanactis hemisphaerica	lichen
Microglossum olivaceum	earth-tongue
Opegrapha paraxanthodes	lichen
Peltigera lepidophora	lichen
Pertusaria bryontha	lichen
Phellodon confluens	tooth fungus
Phellodon melaleucus	tooth fungus
Phellodon tomentosus	tooth fungus
Piptoporus quercinus	bracket
Poronia punctata	pyrenomycete
Pseudocyphellaria aurata	lichen

SPECIES	GROUP
Pseudocyphellaria norvegica	lichen
Sarcodon glaucopus	tooth fungus
Sarcodon imbricatus	tooth fungus
Sarcodon scabrosus	tooth fungus
Schismatomma graphidoides	lichen
Squamarina lentigera	lichen
Teloschistes chrysopthalmus	lichen
Thelenella modesta	lichen
Tulostoma niveum	stilt-puffball

Protected species

In the UK, 34 species of fungi are afforded some legal protection under the Wildlife & Countryside Act, 1981 (see Table 31). These species, listed in Schedule 8 of the Act, cannot legally be intentionally picked, destroyed, or offered for sale, though it seems enforcing these measures may not be easy (as in a case involving the bulldozing of a protected *Battarraea phalloides* site – Evans, 2002). Almost all the scheduled fungi are lichens, in part reflecting better knowledge about their distribution and rarity, in part reflecting the ease with which they can be damaged or destroyed.

TABLE 31. List of British fungi protected under Schedule 8 of The Wildlife And Countryside Act, 1981.

SPECIES	GROUP
Alectoria ochroleuca	lichen
Battarraea phalloides	stilt-puffball
Boletus regius	bolete
Bryoria furcellata	lichen
Buellia asterella	lichen
Caloplaca luteoalba	lichen
Caloplaca nivalis	ichen
Catapyrenium psoromoides	lichen
Catolechia wahlenbergii	lichen
Cladonia convoluta	lichen
Cladonia trassii (= C. stricta)	lichen
Collema dichotomum	lichen
Enterographa elaborata	lichen
Gyalecta ulmi	lichen

Hericium erinaceus	tooth fungus
Heterodermia leucomela	lichen
Heterodermia propagulifera	lichen
Lecanographa (Lecanactis) hemisphaerica	lichen
Lecanora achariana	lichen
Lecidea inops	lichen
Megalaria (Catillaria) laureri	lichen
Nephroma arcticum	lichen
Pannaria ignobilis	lichen
Parmelinopsis (Parmelia) minarum	lichen
Parmentaria chilensis	lichen
Peltigera lepidophora	lichen
Pertusaria bryontha	lichen
Physcia tribacioides	lichen
Piptoporus quercinus	bracket
Pseudocyphellaria lacerata	lichen
Psora rubiformis	lichen
Solenopsora liparina	lichen
Squamarina lentigera	lichen
Teloschistes flavicans	lichen

Ex-situ conservation and translocation

Conserving endangered species outside their natural habitat is always something of a desperate measure and reintroducing them to the wild is never easy. Very few fungi have ever been selected for such treatment, partly because so little is known about their ecological and other requirements, partly because such ex-situ conservation is expensive.

The Convention on Biological Diversity acknowledges that culture collections of micro-organisms, including fungi, may play an important role in the conservation of genetic resources. However, most institutes maintaining such collections face budget cuts and do not having the luxury of isolating and subculturing strains for free. For conservation purposes, of course, these strains need to be kept alive forever – not a word which funding agencies find attractive – though cryopreservation can help cut costs.

Where there is an immediate financial interest in maintaining a species, conservation and commerce can be happily combined. In Sicily, for example, there is a rare oyster cap, *Pleurotus nebrodensis*, which grows on the roots of the umbellifer *Cachrys ferulacea* on the slopes of Mount Etna and the Madonie

Mountains. It is edible and highly prized, but threatened by pickers looking for immature fruitbodies and damaging the associated plants. The answer has been a ban on collecting in the wild and the initiation of ex-situ cultivation to satisfy market demands.

Translocating fungi has rarely been attempted, except for lichens where a considerable degree of expertise has been built up. Hallingbäck (1990) and Scheidegger *et al.* (1995b) have reviewed attempts at re-establishing threatened species, many of which appear to have been successful. The latter gives details and illustrations of techniques applied in Switzerland for translocating endangered foliose lichens such as *Sticta sylvatica*, *Lobaria pulmonaria*, and *Parmotrema crinitum*, using adult thalli or diaspores. In Britain, a 20-year survey of translocations of the rare *Lobaria amplissima* in Lowther Park, Cumbria, was published by Gilbert (2002). This was occasioned by the felling (for inevitable health and safety reasons) of one of the few trees on which it was known to occur in the north of England. The translocations onto several other trees in the park appeared to have been generally successful, with some colonies lost but others growing well.

Responsible collecting

As well as the statute laws protecting endangered species in the UK, local bylaws often prohibit the collecting of fungi on nature reserves and other sites without express permission, and indeed it is a matter of common law that nothing – plants, animals, fungi, soil, or artefacts – can be removed from private land without the landowner's consent. Field mycologists should therefore always ask landowners for permission to collect specimens. Since the 1980s, an increase in the commercial harvesting of edible wild fungi has made a few larger landowners rather wary of collectors, but most are still happy to agree to data collecting by field mycologists.

English Nature and others have produced a leaflet providing a common-sense Code of Conduct for collectors, whether their intentions are scientific or culinary (Anon., 1998). The Scottish Wild Mushroom Forum have produced a similar code (Dyke, 2001), adapted and reproduced here.

COLLECTING FUNGI RESPONSIBLY

If you are going to collect fungi (for any purpose), it is important that you do so with consideration for the environment around you, since fungi are fundamentally important to the habitats in which they live.

When picking mushrooms or collecting other fungi, please consider the following points:

- Wildlife, especially insects, need fungi too, so only pick what you will use.
- Do not pick agarics until the cap has opened, and leave those that are past their best.
- The living mycelium of most fungi is below the surface. Take care not to damage or trample it, and not to disturb its surroundings.
- If collecting for food, scatter any trimmings discretely in the same area as the fungi came from.
- Some fungi are poisonous and others rare and should not be picked. If collecting for food, only pick what you know and take a field guide with you to identify edible fungi where you find them.
- Before you collect fungi at a nature reserve always seek advice from the manager, as special conditions may apply.

If you own or manage land:

- Be aware that your management activities may affect fungi.

If you wish to run a foray or collect for scientific purposes:

- Obtain permission from the landowner in writing.
- Give a record of what you have found to the landowner or manager and explain the significance of your findings.

Glossary

Acrasiomycota: a phylum of kingdom *Protozoa* containing the fungus-like cellular slime moulds.

actinomycete: one of the filamentous bacteria, superficially resembling fungi.

aero-aquatic: referring to fungi that grow under water but release their spores into the air.

aflatoxin: a toxic substance produced by the mould *Aspergillus flavus* and other species that grow on cereals and foodstuffs.

agaric: a general term for a mushroom or toadstool.

agaricoid: like a mushroom or toadstool in form.

ambrosia fungus: any species that grows in the tunnels of wood-boring beetles and provides food for larvae and adults.

anamorph: the asexual stage fruitbody of any fungus.

ascomycete: a member of the phylum *Ascomycota*.

Ascomycota: a major phylum of the kingdom *Fungi*, including the cup fungi, flask fungi, truffles and some yeasts.

ascospore: a sexual spore produced by an ascomycete.

ascus (-i): spore-producing unit of ascomycetes.

auricularioid: referring to the form of basidia (tubular and septate) found in the genus *Auricularia* and many *Urediniomycetes*.

basidiomycete: a member of the phylum *Basidiomycota*.

Basidiomycota: a major phylum of the kingdom Fungi, including agarics, puffballs, bracket fungi, corticioid fungi, club and coral fungi, jelly fungi, false truffles and some yeasts.

basidiospore: a sexual spore produced by a basidiomycete.

basidium (-ia): spore-producing unit of basidiomycetes.

biocontrol: control of pests and diseases by the use of their parasites or predators.

biodeterioration: degradation or damage to any material caused by the activities of fungi or other organisms.

bioindicator: an organism that can be used as an indicator of a specific habitat or environmental condition.

bioluminescence: the emission of light by

certain fungi and other organisms, through an oxidation process.

bioremediation: the use of fungi or other organisms to remove or reduce environmental pollutants.

biotroph: an obligate parasite that does not kill its host.

bird's-nest fungus: a basidiomycete that forms small, nest-like fruitbodies with egg-like peridioles.

bitunicate: applied to asci having a complex wall structure involving at least two membranes.

bolete: a member of the *Boletales* (*Basidiomycota*), whose fruitbodies have tubes rather than gills under the cap.

bracket fungus: a basidiomycete that forms a bracket, or shelf-like, fruitbody.

bryophilous: growing in association with bryophytes (mosses and liverworts).

bulbil: a discrete, multicellular propagule formed asexually from thin-walled hyphae and lacking any differentiation of tissues.

cep: a culinary (French) name for the edible *Boletus edulis*.

chanterelle: a popular name for the edible agaricoid basidiomycete *Cantharellus cibarius*.

chromistan: a member of the kingdom *Chromista*, some of which (e.g. oomycetes) are fungus-like.

chytrid: a member of the phylum *Chytridiomycota*.

Chytridiomycota: a phylum of the kingdom *Fungi*, including many freshwater microfungi, anaerobic rumen fungi, some soil microfungi and plant parasites.

class: a defined classification category at a level below 'phylum' and above 'order'. In fungi, a class always ends in '-etes', e.g. *Ascomycetes, Basidiomycetes*.

clavarioid: resembling the club fungi

(*Clavaria* and similar basidiomycete genera).

coelomycete: an anamorphic (asexual) fungus, typically belonging to the *Ascomycota*, which has a well-defined fruitbody.

commensal: living in close association with another organism, but not parasitic or dependent on it.

conidiophore: microscopical structure bearing conidia.

conidium (-ia): an asexually produced spore.

coprophilous (or coprophilic): dung-loving; referring to fungi that have an obligate association with dung.

coral fungus: the branched fruitbody of several basidiomycete genera, e.g. *Ramaria*.

corticioid: resembling the effused 'patch-forming' basidiomycetes (*Corticium* and similar genera).

crustose: referring to any lichenised fungus with a crust-like thallus.

cup fungus: any ascomycete that has a cup- or disc-shaped fruitbody.

cytolytic: cell-destroying; referring to toxins produced by some larger fungi that break down and destroy the walls of blood cells.

dermatotroph: a fungus or other organism living on the skin (e.g. ringworm).

diaspore: any reproductive unit formed by a fungus.

discomycete: a cup fungus.

downy mildew: a plant parasite belonging to the chromistan *Peronosporales*.

dry rot: a popular name for the rot of worked timber caused by the basidiomycete *Serpula lacrymans*.

earthstar: a popular name for a fruitbody of *Geastrum* species (*Basidiomycota*).

earthtongue: a popular name for a fruitbody of *Geoglossum*, *Microglossum* and *Trichoglossum* species (*Ascomycota*).

ectomycorrhiza (-s or -e): mycorrhiza in which hyphae externally wrap around root filaments without penetrating root cells.

endolith: a fungus (or other organism) living inside stones, stonework or rock surfaces.

endomycorrhiza (-s or -e): mycorrhiza in which hyphae penetrate root cells.

endophyte: a fungus or other microorganism that lives, usually symptom-free, within the tissue of living plants.

entomogenous: living, as either a parasite or saprobe, on insects.

entomopathogenic: parasitic on insects.

epiphytic: growing superficially on a plant host, as in many lichens.

epithet: the second element of a scientific name (e.g. '*muscaria*' in Amanita *muscaria*) which describes the species.

ergot: the sclerotium of *Claviceps purpurea* (*Ascomycota*), formed in the inflorescence of grasses, which is toxic but with some medicinal use.

fairy ring: a ring of fruitbodies formed by one of the larger fungi.

false truffle: a hypogeous fungus resembling a truffle but belonging to the *Basidiomycota*.

family: a defined classification category at a level below 'order' and above 'genus'. In fungi, a family always ends in '-aceae', e.g. *Agaricaceae*, *Pezizaceae*.

filamentous: thread-like, usually referring to hyphae. Most fungi are filamentous, but yeasts and a few other groups are not.

flagellum (-a): a whip-like process found in motile spores of chromistans and some other fungus-like organisms, used for swimming.

flask fungus: any ascomycete that has a flask-shaped fruitbody (e.g. pyrenomycetes).

fruitbody: the macro-structure of a fungus, producing the reproductive structures (e.g. mushroom, toadstool).

gall: abnormal growth of a plant, fungus or other host under the influence of another organism, involving enlargement or proliferation of host cells.

gasteroid: resembling a gasteromycete fruitbody.

gasteromycete: a basidiomycete producing spores inside its fruitbody rather than at the surface, e.g. puffballs, bird's nest fungi, false truffles, stinkhorns, earthstars. Once grouped together in the old, artificial class '*Gasteromycetes*'.

generalist: any species of fungus that has a broad habitat range.

genus (pl. genera): a defined classification category at a level below 'family' and above 'species', e.g. '*Amanita*' in Amanita *muscaria*, *A. phalloides*, etc.

gills: a common name for lamellae (the spore-producing surface in mushrooms, toadstools, etc.).

gleba: the spore-producing region found within some fungal fruitbodies, e.g. stinkhorns.

Glomeromycota: a phylum of the kingdom *Fungi* containing important VA-mycorrhizal species.

haustorium (-ia): a specialised branch formed by the hyphae of a parasitic fungus to penetrate host cells and absorb nutrients.

heterobasidiomycete: a basidiomycete in which the basidia have cross walls, or septa.

homobasidiomycete: a basidiomycete in which the basidia are not septate.

honey fungus: a popular name for several species of the toadstool genus *Armillaria*, some of which are important root parasites.

hydnoid: composed of conspicuous teeth or spines.

hygroscopic: reacting to atmospheric moisture, applied especially to fruitbodies that open to discharge spores in wet conditions, e.g. some earthstars.

hymenium (-ia): the fertile layer, bearing asci (in *Ascomycota*) or basidia (in *Basidiomycota*).

hyphae: the microscopic filaments that form the basic structure of fungal mycelia and fruitbodies.

Hyphochytriomycota: a small phylum of the kingdom *Chromista* containing microscopic fungi on algae and fungi in freshwater and soil.

hyphomycete: anamorphic (asexual) fungus in which organised fruitbodies are lacking.

hypogeous: subterranean; growing or developing below ground level, e.g. truffles.

Ingoldian: a term applied to hyphomycetes that develop and sporulate on submerged substrata, honouring Prof C T Ingold, who pioneered their study.

inkcap: a popular name for a toadstool of the genus *Coprinus*.

jelly fungus: a popular name for any member of the heterobasidiomycetes that has a gelatinous fruitbody.

keratinophilic: referring to fungi and other micro-organisms that are specially adapted to metabolise keratin.

kingdom: a defined classification category at a level above 'phylum' (e.g. *Fungi*, *Plantae*, *Protozoa*).

Labyrinthulomycota: a small phylum of the kingdom *Chromista* containing mostly microscopic marine fungi, including the thraustorchytrids.

lichen: a lichenised fungus.

lichenised: describing fungi with an algal or cyanobacterial associate, together forming a lichen.

lignicolous: growing in or on wood.

macrofungus: imprecise term for any fungus that produces large fruitbodies easily visible to the naked eye.

microfungus: imprecise term for any fungus that produces individually tiny or microscopic fruitbodies (though, like moulds, they may be visible in mass).

mildew: an imprecise term usually referring to a coating of mycelium, often with reference to leaf parasitic fungi or the diseases they cause.

morel: a popular name for the edible fruitbody of *Morchella* species (*Ascomycota*).

mould: a general term referring to the development of mycelium and spores of hyphomycetes and some other microfungi.

mushroom: a popular name for a member of the genus *Agaricus* or any edible agaric. In America, a term applied to almost any macrofungus.

mutualism: any mutually beneficial association between two or more organisms.

mycelium (-ia): mass of fungal hyphae (excluding the fruitbody), normally permeating the substrata, e.g. soil, rotten wood, leaf litter.

mycobiont: the fungus partner in a lichen.

mycology: the study of fungi.

mycophagy: the consumption of fungi for food.

mycophilic: fungus-loving (of peoples and cultures), regarding many fungi as edible.

mycophobic: fungus-hating (of peoples and cultures), regarding most fungi as poisonous.

mycorrhiza (-s or -e): an intimate mix of fungal hyphae and plant root forming a mutualistic relationship.

mycorrhizome: intimate association between fungus hyphae and the rhizome of ferns.

mycosis: a disease, usually of people or animals, caused by a fungus.

mycota: the fungal equivalent of 'flora' or 'fauna'; all the fungi living in a given area (e.g. the mycota of Surrey).

mycothallus (-i): intimate association between fungal hyphae and the thallus of a liverwort.

mycotoxin: a toxic metabolite produced by a fungus.

Myxomycota: a phylum of the *Protozoa* containing the fungus-like slime moulds.

myxomycete: a slime mould; a member of the phylum *Myxomycota*.

necrosis: death of plant or animal tissue caused by (e.g.) a parasitic fungus.

necrotroph: a parasitic fungus or other organism that causes the death of its host.

nitrophilic (or nitrophilous): growing in nitrate-rich substrata, e.g. dunged soil.

oomycete: a member of the fungus-like *Oomycota*.

Oomycota: a phylum of the kingdom *Chromista*.

order: a defined classification category at a level below 'class' and above 'family'. In fungi, an order always ends in '-ales', e.g. *Agaricales, Pezizales*.

ostiole: defined small opening on upper surface of fruitbodies, e.g. in puffballs.

pantropical: occurring throughout tropical regions worldwide.

parasite: an organism that takes its nutrients from a living host.

pathogen: a disease-causing organism.

pea-truffle: a popular name for the hypogeous fruitbody of a member of the *Glomerales* or *Endogonales*.

phalloid: relating to stinkhorns (*Phallus impudicus*) and similar fungi.

phoenicoid: growing on burnt ground.

photobiont: the algal (or cyanobacterial) partner in a lichen.

phylloplane: the surface of a plant leaf.

phylum (-a): a defined classification category at a level below 'kingdom' and above 'class'. In fungi, a phylum always ends in 'mycota', e.g. *Ascomycota, Basidiomycota*.

Plasmodiophoromycota: a phylum of kingdom *Protozoa* which comprises microscopic endoparasites of plants, algae and fungi some of which cause conspicuous galls.

plasmodium (-ia): amoeboid mass of protoplasm that produces the fruitbodies of slime moulds (myxomycetes).

plurivorous: able to grow and develop on a wide range of substrata.

polyphyletic: (of taxa) arising from more than one original ancestor, hence of mixed composition and not a natural taxonomic group.

poroid: having an hymenium formed of vertical tubes, each opening by a terminal pore (as in many bracket fungi and boletes).

powdery mildew: one of the plant parasitic *Erysiphaceae* (*Ascomycota*).

primordium: initial stage in fruitbody formation.

propagule: any unit of dispersal.

psychrophilic: cold-loving.

pteridicolous: growing on ferns and fern-allies (pteridophytes).

pyrenomycete: a flask fungus in the phylum *Ascomycota*.

resupinate: attached by the back surface to the substratum, as in many patch-forming fungi on wood.

rhizomorph: a cord-like strand of hyphae resembling a plant root.

rust: a member of the *Uredinales* (*Basidiomycota*) or the plant disease caused by a rust.

saprobe (or saprotroph): a fungus or other organism living on dead organic matter.

sclerotium (-a): a firm mass of hyphae, resembling a tuber, forming a non-growing resting stage.

secotioid: describing a fruitbody that resembles an agaric but never expands (as in the genus *Secotium* and similar fungi).

septum (-a): a cross-wall separating hyphal compartments.

slime mould: a popular name for a myxomycete.

smut: a member of the *Ustilaginales* (*Basidiomycota*) or the disease caused by it.

sooty mould: dark growth of hyphae on the surface of living leaves, formed particularly by the *Capnodiales*, *Chaetothyriales* and *Meliolales* (*Ascomycota*).

species: a defined classification category at a level below 'genus', e.g. *Amanita muscaria*.

sporangium (-ia): a structure, usually microscopical, containing asexual spores.

spore: a differentiated reproductive unit produced by fungi for dissemination or for resistance to adverse conditions.

sterigma (-ata): an extension of the basidium, typically apical and slender, which bears the basidiospore.

stinkhorn: a popular name for *Phallus impudicus* (*Basidiomycota*) and related fungi.

stroma (-ata): a mass or matric of sterile hyphae on or in which fungal fruitbodies are formed.

straminipile: a microorganism that bears tripartite tubular hairs, as found in most chromistans.

substrate: nutrition source for a fungus, e.g. cellulose, chitin, keratin.

substratum (-a): material on which a fungus grows, e.g. soil, wood.

symbiont: an organism that lives in mutualistic association with another.

synonym: a later, superfluous name for a species or other taxon.

taxon (pl. **taxa**): any defined classification unit, e.g. species, genus, family, etc.

taxonomy: the science of classification (e.g. naming and classifying fungi).

teleomorph: the sexual stage fruitbody of any fungus.

terricolous: living on the soil.

thallus: the vegetative body of a fungus, particularly a lichen. Also applied to plants such as liverworts where there is no division into roots, stem and leaves.

thermophilic: heat-loving.

toadstool: a popular name for a fruitbody of an agaric, especially a poisonous agaric.

truffle: an underground fruitbody of the genus *Tuber* (*Ascomycota*). Loosely applied to similar fruitbodies of other genera.

unitunicate: applied to asci having a simple wall structure, involving a single membrane.

VA-mycorrhiza: vesicular-arbuscular mycorrhiza; specific type of endomycorrhiza formed by members of the order *Glomerales* (*Glomeromycota*).

veil: a thin protective layer covering either the gills or the whole developing fruitbody (particularly in agarics).

volva: veil remains forming a persistent cup or ruptured sack at the base of a fruitbody, especially in the toadstool genera *Amanita* and *Volvariella*.

waxcap: a popular name for a toadstool in the genus *Hygrocybe*, characteristic of unimproved grassland.

xerophilic: referring to fungi that are specially adapted to thrive in extremely dry habitats.

xerotolerant: referring to fungi that are able to survive in extremely dry habitats.

zoospore: a flagellate and hence motile spore, as produced by most chromistans and protozoans.

zygomycete: a member of the phylum *Zygomycota*.

Zygomycota: a phylum of the kingdom *Fungi*, including many insect pathogens, mould-like plant parasites and a few truffle-like species.

References

Adams, M J (2002). Fungi. *Advances in Botanical Research* 36: 47–64.

Agerer, R (1987–1993). *Colour Atlas of Ectomycorrhizae*. Einhorn-Verlag Eduard Dietenberger.

Ainsworth, G C (1962). Longevity of *Schizophyllum commune*. II. *Nature, Lond.* 195: 1120–1121.

Ainsworth, G C (1981). *Introduction to the History of Plant Pathology*. Cambridge University Press.

Ainsworth, G C & Austwick, P K C (1973). *Fungal diseases of animals* (2nd Ed). Slough: CAB.

Alderman, D J (1976). Fungal diseases of marine animals. In Jones, E B G (ed), *Recent advances in aquatic mycology*. 223–260. London: Elek Science.

Al-Doory, Y & DiSalvo, A F (eds). *Blastomycosis*. New York: Plenum Press.

Allegro, J M (1970). *The sacred mushroom and the cross*. London: Hodder & Stoughton.

Allsopp, D & Seal, K J (1986). *Introduction to biodeterioration*. 136 pp. London: Edward Arnold.

Andrews, J H (1976). The pathology of marine algae. *Biol. Rev. Cambr. Phil. Society* 51: 211–253.

Anon. (1998). *The conservation of wild mushrooms*. Peterborough: English Nature.

Apinis, A E & Chesters, C G C (1964). *Ascomycetes* of some salt marshes and sand dunes. *Trans. Brit. Mycol. Soc.* 47: 419–435.

Aptroot, A (2001). Lichenized and saprobic fungal biodiversity of a single *Elaeocarpus* tree in Papua New Guinea, with the report of 200 species of ascomycetes associated with one tree. *Fungal Diversity* 6: 1–11.

Arnold, A E, Maynard, Z, Gilbert, G S, Coley, P D & Kursar, T A (2000). Are tropical endophytes hyperdiverse? *Ecology Letters* 3: 267–274.

Arnolds, E (1981). Ecology and Coenology of Macrofungi in Grasslands and moist Heathlands in Drenthe, the Netherlands. Part 1. Introduction and Synecology. *Bibliotheca Mycologica* 83.

Arnolds, E (1982). Ecology and Coenology of Macrofungi in Grasslands and moist Heathlands in Drenthe, the Netherlands. Part 2. Autecology. Part 3. Taxonomy. *Bibliotheca Mycologica* 90.

Arnolds, E (1988). Dynamics of macrofungi in two moist heathlands in Drenthe, the Netherlands. *Acta Bot. Neerl.* 37: 291–305.

Arnolds, E (1989). The influence of increased fertilization on the macro-fungi of a sheep meadow in Drenthe, the Netherlands. *Opera Botanica* 100: 7–21.

Arnolds, E (1992). Macrofungal communities outside forests. 113–149. In Winterhoff, W (ed), Fungi in vegetation science. *Handbook of vegetation science* 19. Kluwer.

Arnolds, E (1995). Conservation and management of natural populations of edible fungi. *Can. J. Bot.* 73 (Suppl. 1): S987–S998.

Arnolds, E & Kreisel, H (1992). *Conservation of fungi in Europe. Proceedings of the second meeting of the European Council for the Conservation of Fungi at Vilm, 13–18 September 1991.* Germany: Demminer Druck & Verlag.

Arora, D (2000). The global mushroom trade. [*Internet site*: www.wholeearthmag.com/ArticleBin/334.html]

Arx, J A von (1987). Plant pathogenic fungi. *Beih. Nova Hedwigia* 87: 1–288.

Atkins, F C (1979). Research and the mushroom grower. *Mushroom Science* 10 (II): 7–13.

Bacon, C W & White, J F (eds) (2000). *Microbial Endophytes*. Marcel Dekker.

Badham, C D (1847). *A Treatise on the Esculent Funguses of England*. London: Reeve Bros.

Badham, C D (1863). *A Treatise on the Esculent Funguses of England* (2nd Ed). London: Lovell Reeve.

Baker, G E, Dunn, P H & Sakai, W S (1979). Fungus communities associated with leaf surfaces of endemic vascular plants in Hawaii. *Mycologia* 71: 272–292.

Baker, K F (1970). Types of *Rhizoctonia* diseases and their occurrence. In Parmeter, J R (ed). *Rhizoctonia solani*, biology and pathology. 125–148. Berkeley: University of California Press.

Baker, T (1989). Fungal styptics. *Mycologist* 3: 19–20.

Baldwin, N A (1990). *Turfgrass Pests and Diseases* (3rd Ed). Sports Turf Research Institute.

Barnett, C L, Beresford, N A, Frankland, J C, Self, P L, Howard, B J, & Marriott, J V R (2001). Radiocaesium intake in Great Britain as a consequence of the consumption of wild fungi. *Mycologist* 15: 98–104.

Barron, G L (1992). Lignolytic and Cellulolytic Fungi as Predators and Parasites. 311–326. In Carroll, G C & Wicklow, D T (eds). *The Fungal Community. Its Organization and Role in the Ecosystem* (2nd Ed). Marcel Dekker.

Batra, L R, Batra, S W T & Bohart, G E (1973). The mycoflora of domesticated and wild bees (Apoidea). *Mycopath. Mycol. Applic.* 49: 13–44.

Bauer, R, Vánky, K, Begerow, D & Oberwinkler, F (1999). Ustilaginomycetes on *Selaginella*. *Mycologia* 91: 475–484.

Bazely, D R, Vicari, M, Emmerich, S, Filip L, Lin, D & Inman, A (1997). Interactions between herbivores and endophyte-infected *Festuca rubra* from the Scottish islands of St. Kilda, Benbecula and Rum. *J. Applied Ecology* 34: 847–860.

BBC (1998). Poppy-killing fungus developed [*Internet site*: http://news.bbc.co.uk/1/hi/uk/121735.stm]

Beaver, R A (1989). Insect-fungus relationships in the bark and ambrosia beetles. In Wilding, N et al. (eds), *Insect-fungus Interactions*. 121–143. London: Academic Press.

Bélanger, R R, Bushnell, W R, Dik, A J & Carver, T L W (2002). *The Powdery Mildews. A Comprehensive Treatise.* Minnesota: APS.

Benjamin, D R (1995). *Mushrooms: Poisons and Panaceas. A Handbook for Naturalists,*

Mycologists, and Physicians. New York: Freeman.

Bennell, A P & Henderson, D M (1985). Rusts and other fungal parasites as aids to pteridophyte taxonomy. *Proc. Roy. Soc. Edinburgh* 86B: 115–124.

Bennell, A P & Watling, R (1983). Mushroom poisonings in Scotland. *Bull. Brit. Mycol. Soc.* 17: 104–105.

Bennett, J W & Feibelman, T (2001). Fungal bacterial interactions. In Hock, B (ed), *The Mycota IX: Fungal associations.* 229–242. Berlin: Springer.

Berbee, M L & Taylor, J W (2001). Fungal molecular evolution: gene trees and geologic time. In McLaughlin, D J, McLaughlin, E G, & Lemke, P A (eds). *The Mycota VII (B): Systematics and evolution.* 229–245. Berlin: Springer Verlag.

Berkeley, M J (1844). Notices of British fungi. *Ann. Mag. Nat. Hist.* 13: 340–360.

Bessette, A R & Bessette, A E (2001). *The Rainbow Beneath My Feet. A Mushroom Dyer's Field Guide.* Syracuse University Press.

Bevan, R J & Greenhalgh, G N (1976). *Rhytisma acerinum* as a biological indicator of pollution. *Environmental Pollution* 10: 271–285

Bidartondo, M I & Bruns, T D (2002). Fine-level mycorrhizal specificity in the Monotropoideae (Ericaceae): specificity for fungal species groups. *Molec. Ecol.* 11: 557–569.

Bidartondo, M I, Bruns, T D, Weiss, M, Sérgio, C, & Read, D J (2003). Specialized cheating of the ectomycorrhizal symbiosis by an epiparasitic liverwort. *Proc. R. Soc. Lond. B.* 270: 835–842.

Bigelis, R & Lasure, L L (1987). Fungal enzymes and primary metabolites used in food processing. In Beuchat, L R (ed). *Food and beverage mycology* (2nd Ed). 473–516. New York: Van Nostrand Reinhold.

Bisby, G M & Ainsworth, G C (1943). The Numbers of Fungi. *Trans. Brit. Mycol. Soc.* 26: 16–19.

Bissett, J & Borkent, A. (1988). Ambrosia Galls: the significance of fungal nutrition in the evolution of the Cecidomyiidae (Diptera). In Pirozynski, K A & Hawksworth, D L (eds). *Coevolution of Fungi with Plants and Animals.* 203–225. Academic Press.

Blakeman, J P (ed) (1981). *Microbial Ecology of the Phylloplane.* Academic Press.

Blanchette, R A (1997). *Haploporus odorus:* a sacred fungus in traditional native American culture of the northern plains. *Mycologia* 89: 233–240.

Blanchette, R A & Shaw, C G (1978). Associations among bacteria, yeasts, and basidiomycetes during wood decay. *Phytopathology* 68: 631–643.

Blanchette, R, Compton, B D, Turner, N Y & Gilbertson, R L (1992). Nineteenth century shaman grove guardians are carved *Fomitopsis officinalis* sporophores. *Mycologia* 84: 119–124.

Boertmann, D (1995). The genus *Hygrocybe. Fungi of Northern Europe* 1: 1–184.

Boidin, J (1993). Les Aphyllophorales filicoles en Europe. *Bull. Féd. Myc. Dauphiné-Savoie* 129: 20–30.

Bond, T E T (1981). Macro-fungi on a garden lawn. *Bull. Brit. Mycol. Soc.* 15: 99–138.

Boullard, B (1957). La mycotrophie chez les Ptéridophytes. Sa frequence, ses caractères, sa signification. *Le Botaniste,* sér. XLI: 1–185.

Boullard, B (1979). Considerations sur la symbiose fongique chez les pteridophytes. *Syllogeus* 19: 1–59.

Boullard, B (1988). Observations on the Coevolution of Fungi with Hepatics. In Pirozynski, K A & Hawksworth, D L (eds), *Coevolution of Fungi with Plants and Animals*. 107–124. Academic Press.

Bowen, H (2000). *The flora of Dorset*. 373 pp. Newbury: NatureBureau.

Bramley, W G (1985). *A fungus flora of Yorkshire*. 277 pp. Yorkshire Nat. Union.

Brasier, C M (2000). Intercontinental Spread and Continuing Evolution of the Dutch Elm Disease Pathogens. In Dunn, C P (ed). *The Elms. Breeding, Conservation, and Disease Management*. 61–72. Kluwer Academic Publishers.

Braun, U (1995). The powdery mildews (*Erysiphales*) of Europe. Gustav Fischer.

Bravery, A F, Berry, R W, Carey, J K, & Cooper, D E (1987). *Recognising wood rot and insect damage in buildings*. 120 pp. Aylesbury: (DoE) Building Research Establishment.

Brinton, W T, Vastbinder, E F, Greene, J W, & Marx, J J (1987). An outbreak of organic toxic dust syndrome in a college fraternity. *J. Am. Med. Assoc.* 258: 1210–1212.

Britten, J (1877). *Popular British fungi*. London: The Bazaar.

Brooks, A & Halstead, A (1999). *Garden Pests and Diseases*. Mitchell Beazley.

Brown, J C (1958). Soil fungi of some British sand dunes in relation to soil type and succession. *J. Ecol.* 46: 641–664.

Bruns, T D (1984). Insect Mycophagy in the *Boletales*: Fungivore Diversity and the Mushroom Habitat. In Wheeler, Q. & Blackwell, M. (eds), *Fungus-insect relationships. Perspectives in Ecology and Evolution*. 91–129. New York: Columbia University Press.

Buczacki, S & Harris, K (1998). *Pests, Diseases & Disorders of Garden Plants*. Ed 2. Collins Photoguide. 640 pp. London: HarperCollins.

Buller, A H R (1909). *Researches on Fungi*. Vol. 1. Longmans, Green & Co.

Buller, A H R (1931). *Researches on Fungi*. Vol. IV. Longmans, Green & Co.

Buller, A H R (1933). The *Sphaerobolus* Gun and its Range. In *Researches on Fungi*. Vol 5. 279–370. Longmans, Green & Co.

Bultman, T L, White, J F, Bowdish, T I, Welch, A M & Johnston, J (1995). Mutualistic transfer of *Epichloë* spermatia by *Phorbia* flies. *Mycologia* 87: 182–189.

Burgeff, H (1938). Mycorrhiza. In Verdoorn (ed), *Manual of Pteridology*. 159–191. The Hague: Nijhoff.

Butt, T M, Jackson, C W, & Magan, N (2001). Introduction – fungal biological control agents: progress, problems and potential. In Butt, T M, Jackson, C W, & Magan, N (eds). *Fungi as biocontrol agents*. 1–8. Wallingford: CABI Publishing.

Buxton, P A (1960). British Diptera associated with fungi. III. Flies of all families reared from about 150 species of fungi. *Entomologist's Mon. Mag.* 96: 61–94.

Campbell, C K & White, G C (1989). Fungal infection in 'AIDS' patients. *Mycologist* 3: 7–9.

Campbell-Platt, G (1987). *Fermented foods of the world*. London: Butterworths.

Cannon, P F (1997). Diversity of the Phyllachoraceae with special reference to the tropics. In Hyde, K D (ed), *Biodiversity of Tropical Microfungi*. 255–278. Hong Kong University Press.

Cannon, P F, Hawksworth, D L & Sherwood-Pike, M A (1985). *The British Ascomycotina. An Annotated Checklist*. Slough: Commonwealth Agricultural Bureaux.

Canter, H M & Lund, J W G (1969). The parasitism of planktonic desmids by fungi. *Öst. bot. Z.* 116: 351–377.

Carpenter, S E & Trappe, J M (1985). Phoenicoid fungi: a proposed term for fungi that fruit after heat treatment of substrates. *Mycotaxon* 23: 203–206.

Carroll, G C (1992). Fungal mutualism. In Carroll, G C & Wicklow, D T (eds), *The fungal community. Its organization and role in the ecosystem.* 2nd ed. 327–354. Marcel Dekker.

Cavalier-Smith, T (1998). A revised six-kingdom system of life. *Biological Reviews* 73: 203–266.

Cavalier-Smith, T (2001). What are Fungi? In McLaughlin, D J et al. (eds). *The Mycota VII (A): Systematics and Evolution.* 3–37. Berlin: Springer-Verlag.

Cedano, M, Villaseñor, L & Guzmán-Dávalos, L (2001). Some *Aphyllophorales* tested for organic dyes. *Mycologist* 15: 81–85.

Chandler, P (1978). Associations with Plants. Fungi. In Stubbs, A & Chandler, P (eds), *A Dipterist's Handbook.* 199–228. Amateur Entomologists' Society.

Chang, S-T & Miles, P G (1989). *Edible mushrooms and their cultivation.* Boca Raton, Florida: CRC Press.

Cherrett, J M, Powell, R J, & Stradling, D J (1989). The mutualism between leaf-cutting ants and their fungus. In Wilding, N. et al. (eds), *Insect-fungus interactions.* 93–120. London: Academic Press.

Church, J M, Coppins, B J, Gilbert, O L, James, P W & Stewart, N F (1996). *Red Data Books of Britain and Ireland: lichens. Vol. 1: Britain.* JNCC.

Ciferri, O (1999). Microbial degradation of paintings. *Applied and Environmental Microbiology* 65: 879–885.

Clark, C C, Miller, J D, & Whitney, N J (1989). Toxicity of conifer needle endophytes to spruce budworm. *Mycol. Res.* 93: 508–512.

Clark, M C (ed) (1980). *A fungus flora of Warwickshire.* 272 pp. London: British Mycol. Soc.

Clay, K (1989). Clavicipitaceous endophytes of grasses: their potential as biocontrol agents. *Mycol. Res.* 92: 1–12.

Cooke, R (1977). *The biology of symbiotic fungi.* London: John Wiley & Sons.

Cooke, R C & Godfrey, B E S (1964). A key to the nematode-destroying fungi. *Trans. Brit. Mycol. Soc.* 47: 61–74.

Cooke, R C & Rayner, A D M (1984). *Ecology of saprophytic fungi.* London: Longman.

Cooke, R C & Whipps, J M (1993). *Ecophysiology of Fungi.* Blackwell.

Cooke, W B (1955). Subalpine fungi and snowbanks. *Ecology* 36: 124–130.

Cooper, M R & Johnson, A W (1998). *Poisonous plants and fungi.* 2nd ed. London: HMSO.

Coppins, A M & Coppins, B J (2002). *Indices of ecological continuity for woodland epiphytic lichen habitats in the British Isles.* British Lichen Society.

Coppins, B J (2002). *Checklist of Lichens of Great Britain and Ireland.* British Lichen Society.

Couch, H B (1995). *Diseases of Turfgrasses.* Ed 3. Florida: Krieger.

Crombie, J M (1884). On the lichen flora of Epping Forest, and the causes affecting its recent diminution. *Trans. Essex Field Club* IV, 9: 1–22.

Crowley, M (1996). The god who drank urine. *Fortean Studies* 3: 176–188.

Czeczuga, B (2000). Zoosporic fungi growing on freshwater molluscs. *Polish Journal of Environmental Studies* 9 (3): 151-156.

Dalpé, Y, Litten, W & Sigler, L (1989). *Scytalidium vaccinii* sp. nov. an ericoid endophyte of *Vaccinium angustifolium* roots. *Mycotaxon* 35: 371–377.

Dayal, R (1975). Key to phycomycetes predaceous or parasitic in nematodes or amoebae I. *Zoopagales. Sydowia* 27: 293–301.

De Hoog, G S & Guarro, J (1995). *Atlas of clinical fungi.* Baarn: CBS.

De Hoog, G S, Guarro, J, Gené, J, & Figueras, M J (2000). *Atlas of clinical fungi* (ed 2). Utrecht: CBS.

Dei-Cas, E (2000). *Pneumocystis* infections: the iceberg? *Medical Mycology* 38, Suppl. 1: 23–32.

Delbeke, F T (2000). From *Amanita muscaria* to somatotropine: the doping story. *Biology of Sport* 17: 81–86.

Dennis, R W G (1960). *British cup fungi and their allies.* 280 pp. London: Ray Society.

Dennis, R W G (1983). Fungi of *Ammophila arenaria* in Europe. *Revista de Biologia* 12: 15–48.

Dennis, R W G (1986). *Fungi of the Hebrides.* 383 pp. Kew: Royal Botanic Gardens.

Dennis, R W G (1995). *Fungi of South East England.* 295 pp. Kew: Royal Botanic Gardens.

Dick, M W (2001). *Straminipilous Fungi. Systematics of the Peronosporomycetes including accounts of the Marine Straminipilous Protists, the Plasmodiophorids and similar Organisms.* Kluwer Academic Publishers.

Dickinson, C H (1976). Fungi on the aerial surfaces of higher plants. In Dickinson, C H & Preece, T F (1976). *Microbiology of Aerial Plant Surfaces.* 293–324. Academic Press.

Dickinson, C H & Preece, T F (1976). *Microbiology of Aerial Plant Surfaces.* Academic Press.

Dickson, G & Leonard, A (1996). *Fungi of the New Forest.* 210 pp. London: British Mycological Society

Diederich, P. (1996). The lichenicolous heterobasidiomycetes. *Bibliotheca Lichenologica* 61: 1–198.

Dilcher, D L (1965). Epiphyllous fungi from Eocene deposits in Western Tennessee, USA. *Palaeontographica* 116B: 1–54.

Dix, N J & Webster, J. (1995). *Fungal Ecology.* London: Chapman & Hall.

Döbbeler, P (1978). Moosbewohnende Ascomyceten I. Die Pyrenocarpen, den Gametophyten besiedelnden Arten. *Mitt. Bot. München* 14: 1–360.

Dougoud, R (2001). Clé des discomycètes carbonicoles. *Documents mycologiques* 30, fasc. 120: 15–29.

Dubos, B & Bulit, J (1981). Filamentous fungi as biocontrol agents on aerial plant surfaces. In Blakeman, J P (ed). *Microbial Ecology of the Phylloplane.* 353–367. Academic Press.

Dunn, C P (ed) (2000). *The Elms. Breeding, Conservation, and Disease Management.* Kluwer Academic Publishers.

Dyke, A (2001). The Scottish Wild Mushroom Forum. In Moore, D, Nauta, M M, Evans, S E, & Rotheroe, M (eds). *Fungal conservation: issues and solutions.* 219–222. Cambridge University Press.

Eliasson, U & Lundquist, N (1979). Fimicolous myxomycetes. *Bot. Notiser* 132: 551–568.

Ellis, M B & Ellis, J P (1988). *Microfungi on Miscellaneous Substrates.* Croom Helm.

Ellis, M B & Ellis, J P (1997). *Microfungi on Land Plants. An Identification Handbook.* Ed 2. Slough: Richmond Publishing.

Emerson, R (1968). Thermophiles. In Ainsworth, G C & Sussman, A S (eds). *The Fungi. An Advanced Treatise. Vol. 3. The Fungal Population.* 105–128. Academic Press.

English, M P (1965). The saprophytic growth of non-keratinophilic fungi on keratinized substrata, and a comparison with keratinophilic fungi. *Trans. Brit. Mycol. Soc.* 48: 219–235.

Evans, H C, Greaves, M P, & Watson, A K (2001). Fungal biocontrol agents of weeds. In Butt, T M, Jackson, C W, & Magan, N (eds). *Fungi as biocontrol agents.* 169–192. Wallingford: CABI Publishing.

Evans, S (2002). Conservation corner. *Field Mycology* 3: 63–65.

Evans, S (2003). *Waxcap Grasslands – an*

assessment of English sites. English Nature Report 555.

Evans, S, Marren, P & Harper, M (2001). *Important Fungus Areas. A provisional assessment of the best sites for fungi in the United Kingdom.* Cumbria: Plantlife.

Fairman, C E (1920). *The ascomycetous fungi of human excreta.* Lyndonville, New York.

Fassatiová, O (1970). Micromycetes inhabiting the mines of Příbram (Czechoslovakia). *Česká Mykologie* 24: 162–165.

Felix, H (1988). Fungi on bryophytes, a review. *Botanica Helvetica* 98: 239–269.

Fell, J W (1986). Yeasts in oceanic regions. In Jones, E B G (ed), *Recent advances in aquatic mycology.* 93–124. London: Elek Science.

Ferry, B W, Baddeley, M S, & Hawksworth, D L (eds) (1973). *Air pollution and lichens.* London: Athlone Press.

Field, J I & Webster, J (1977). Traps of predaceous fungi attract nematodes. *Trans. Brit. Mycol. Soc.* 68: 467–469.

Findlay, W P K (1982). *Fungi: folklore, fiction, and fact.* Richmond, Surrey: Richmond Publishing.

Finlay, R D & Söderström, B (1992). Mycorrhiza and carbon flow to the soil. In Allen, M (ed), *Mycorrhiza functioning.* 134–160. London: Chapman & Hall.

Fischer, G W & Holton, C S (1957). *Biology and control of the smut fungi.* New York: Ronald Press.

Fisher, P J & Petrini, O (1990). A comparative study of fungal endophytes in xylem and bark of *Alnus* species in England and Switzerland. *Mycol. Res.* 94: 313–319.

Fisher, P J & Stradling, D J (2002). Laboratory studies with *Leucoagaricus* and attine ants. In Watling, R, Ainsworth, A M, Isaac, S, & Robinson, C H (eds). *Tropical mycology* Vol 1: 113–130. Wallingford, Oxford: CABI.

Fleming, L V (2001). Fungi and the UK Biodiversity Action Plan: the process explained. In Moore, D, Nauta, M M, Evans, S E, & Rotheroe, M (eds). *Fungal conservation: issues and solutions.* 209–218. Cambridge Univ. Press.

Fletcher, A (1975a). Key for the identification of British marine and maritime lichens I. Siliceous rocky shore species. *Lichenologist* 7: 1–52.

Fletcher, A (1975b). Key for the identification of British marine and maritime lichens II. Calcareous and terricolous species. *Lichenologist* 7: 73–115.

Fletcher, A, Wolseley, P, & Woods, R (eds) (2001). *Lichen habitat management.* Proceedings of a workshop held at Bangor, 3–6 September 1997. London: British Lichen Society.

Florian, M-L (1997). *Heritage eaters.* 164 pp. London: James & James.

Fogel, R & Trappe, J M (1978). Fungus Consumption (Mycophagy) by Small Animals. *Northwest Science* 52: 1–31.

Fokkema, N J & Van den Heuvel, J (eds) (1986). *Microbiology of the Phyllosphere.* Cambridge University Press.

Fox, R T V (ed) (1999). *Biology and control of honey fungus.* 222 pp. Andover: Intercept.

Francis, S & Waterhouse, G (1988). List of Peronosporaceae reported from the British Isles. *Trans. Brit. Mycol. Soc.* 91: 1–62.

Frankland, J C (1966). Succession of fungi on decaying petioles of *Pteridium aquilinum. J. Ecol.* 54: 41–63.

Frankland, J C (1969). Fungal decomposition of bracken petioles. *J. Ecol.* 57: 25–36.

Frankland, J C (1976). Decomposition of bracken litter. *Botanical Journal of the Linnean Society* 73: 133–143.

Fredrickson, J K & Onstott, T C (1996). Microbes deep inside the earth. *Scientific American* 275: 42–47.

Frisvad, J C, Filtenborg, O & Wicklow, D T (1987). Terverticillate penicillia isolated from underground seed caches and cheek pouches of banner-tailed kangaroo rats (*Dipodomys spectabilis*). *Can. J. Bot.* 65: 765–773.

Fuller, R M (1987). The changing extent and conservation interest of lowland grasslands in England and Wales: A review of grassland surveys 1930-84. *Biol. Cons.* 40: 281–300.

Galloway, D J & Aptroot, A (1995). Bipolar lichens: A review. *Cryptogamic Botany* 5: 184–191.

Garbaye, J (1994). Helper bacteria: a new dimension to the mycorrhizal symbiosis. Tansley Review No. 76. *New Phytologist* 128: 197–210.

Gardes, M & Bruns, T (1996). Community structure of ectomycorrhizal fungi in a *Pinus muricata* forest: above- and below-ground views. *Can. J. Bot.* 74: 1572–1583.

Gartz, J (1996). *Magic mushrooms around the world*. Los Angeles: LIS Publ.

Gaylarde, C C & Morton, L H G (1999). Deteriogenic biofilms on buildings and their control: a review. *Biofouling* 14: 59–74.

Gilbert, O L (1975). *Wildlife conservation and lichens*. Plymouth: Devon Trust for Nature Conservation.

Gilbert, O L (1993). The lichens of chalk grassland. *Lichenologist* 25: 379–414.

Gilbert, O L (1995). The conservation of chalk grassland lichens. *Cryptogamic Botany* 5: 232–238.

Gilbert, O L (2000). *Lichens*. New Naturalist 86. London: HarperCollins.

Gilbert, O L (2001). The lichen flora of coastal saline lagoons in England. *Lichenologist* 33: 409–417.

Gilbert, O L (2002). A transplant operation involving *Lobaria amplissima*; the first twenty years. *The Lichenologist* 34: 267–269.

Gill, M A (1999). *Tunbridge Ware*. Shire Publications.

Gimingham, C H (1972). *Ecology of heathlands*. London: Chapman & Hall.

Goh, T K & Hyde, K D (1996). Biodiversity of freshwater fungi. *J. Industrial Microbiology & Biotechnology* 17: 328–345.

Gravesen, S, Frisvad, J C, & Samson, R A (1994). *Microfungi*. 168 pp. Copenhagen: Munksgaard.

Gray, N F (1987). Nematophagous fungi with particular reference to their ecology. *Biol. Rev.* 62: 245–304.

Gregory, P H (1982). Fairy rings; free and tethered. *Bull. Brit. Mycol. Soc.* 16: 161–163.

Grove W B (1935–37). *British Stem and Leaf Fungi*. Cambridge University Press.

Gruffydd, E (1985). Witches' butter in Wales. *Bull. Brit. Mycol. Soc.* 19: 63–65.

Guého, E, Faergemann, J, Lyman, C, & Anaissie, E J (1994). *Malassezia* and *Trichosporon*: two emerging pathogenic basidiomycetous yeast-like fungi. *Journal of Medical and Veterinary Mycology* 32, Suppl. 1: 367–378.

Gumowski, P I, Latgé, J-P, & Paris, S (1991). Fungal allergy. In Arora, D K, Ajello, L & Mukerji, KG (eds). *Handbook of applied mycology*, Vol. 2: *Humans, animals, and insects*. 163–204. New York: Marcel Dekker, Inc.

Gupta, A K & Summerbell, R C (2000). Tinea capitis. *Medical Mycology* 38: 255–287.

Guzmán, G, Wasson, R G, & Herrera, T (1975). Una iglesia dedicada al culto de un hongo, "Nuestro Senor del Honguito", en Chignahuapan, Puebla. *Bol. Soc. Mex. Micol.* 9: 137–147.

Hallbauer, D K, Jahns, H M, & Beltmann, H A (1977). Morphological and anatomical observations on some precambrian plants from the Witwatersrand, South Africa. *Geol. Rundschau* 66: 477–491.

Hallingbäck, T (1990). Transplanting *Lobaria pulmonaria* to new localities and a review on the transplanting of lichens. *Windahlia* 18: 57–64.

Hamilton, A (2002). *Crytococcus neoformans* – the encapsulated menace. *Mycologist* 16: 125–126.

Hansson, L & Larsson, T-B. (1978). Vole diet in experimentally managed reforestation areas in northern Sweden. *Holarctic Ecology* 1: 16–26.

Hardwick, W A (1995) (ed). *Handbook of brewing*. New York: Dekker.

Harley, J L & Harley, E L (1987). A check-list of mycorrhiza in the British flora. *New Phytologist* 105: suppl., 1–102.

Harper, J E & Webster, J (1964). An experimental analysis of the coprophilous fungus succession. *Trans. Brit. Mycol. Soc.* 47: 511–530.

Harsh, N S K, Rai, B K, & Soni, V K (1999). Some ethnomycological studies from Madhya Pradesh, India. In Singh, J & Aneja, K R, *From ethnomycology to fungal biotechnology*. 19–31. New York: Plenum Press.

Hartmeier, W & Reiss, M (2002). Production of beer and wine. In Osiewacz, H D (ed). *The Mycota X: Industrial applications*. 49–65. Berlin: Springer Verlag.

Hastings, S & Mottram, J C (1917). Observations upon the edibility of fungi for rodents. *Trans. Brit. Mycol. Soc.* 5: 364–378.

Hatcher, P E (1995). Three-way interaction between plant pathogenic fungi, herbivorous insects and their hosts. *Biological Reviews* 70: 639–694.

Hawksworth, D L (1988). The variety of fungal-algal symbioses, their evolutionary significance, and the nature of lichens. *Bot. J. Linn. Soc.* 96: 3–20.

Hawksworth, D L (1991). The fungal dimension of biodiversity: magnitude, significance and conservation. *Mycol. Res.* 95: 641–655.

Hawksworth, D L (2001a). The magnitude of fungal diversity: the 1.5 million species estimate revisited. *Mycol. Res.* 105: 1422–1432.

Hawksworth, D L (2001b). Do lichens protect or damage stonework? *Mycol. Res.* 105: 386.

Hawksworth, D L (2003). The lichenicolous fungi of Great Britain and Ireland: an overview and annotated checklist. *Lichenologist* 35: 191–232.

Hawksworth, D L & Rose, F (1970). Qualitative scale for estimating sulphur dioxide air pollution in England and Wales using epiphytic lichens. *Nature* 227: 145–148.

Hay, R J, Clayton, Y M, DeSilva, N, Midgley, G, & Rossor, B (1996). Tinea capitis in south-east London – a new pattern of infection with public health implications. *Brit. J. Dermatol.* 135: 955–958

Heckman, D S, Geiser, D M, Eidell, B R, Stauffer, R L, Kardos, N L, & Hedges, S B (2001). Molecular evidence for the early colonization of land by fungi and plants. *Science* (New York) 293: 1129–1133.

Heim, R (1947). Sur quelques espèces nivales de macromycetes des Alpes françaises. *Rev. Mycol.* 12: 69–78.

Heim, R (1977). *Termites et Champignons. Les champignons termitophiles d'Afrique Noire et d'Asie méridionale*. Paris: Boubée.

Heim, R (1978). *Les champignons toxiques et hallucinogènes*. Paris: Boubée.

Henderson, D M (2000). *A Checklist of the Rust Fungi of the British Isles*. British Mycological Society.

Henrici, A (1996). Waxcap-grassland fungi. 1: *Hygrocybe, Camarophyllopsis* and *Dermoloma* in Britain. 2: Keys to Grassland Species of *Leptonia* s.l. British Mycological Society.

Hesseltine, C W & Wang, H L (eds) (1986). Indigenous fermented food of non-western origin. *Mycologia Memoir* 11. Berlin: J. Cramer.

Hibbett, D S, Grimaldi, D, & Donoghue, M J (1995). Cretaceous mushrooms in amber. *Nature* 377: 487.

Hibbett, D S, Pine, E M, Langer, E, Langer, G, & Donoghue, M J (1997). Evolution of gilled mushrooms and puffballs inferred from ribosomal DNA sequences. *Proc. Nat. Acad. Sci. USA* 94: 12002–12006.

Hildebrandt, U, Janetta, K, Ouziad, F, Renne, B, Nawrath, K, & Bothe, H (2001). Arbuscular mycorrhizal colonization of halophytes in Central European salt marshes. *Mycorrhiza* 10: 175–183.

Hingley, M R (1970). The Ascomycete Fungus, *Daldinia concentrica* as a habitat for animals. *J. Animal Ecology* 40: 17–32.

Hirst, J M (1952). An automatic volumetric spore trap. *Ann. Appl. Biol.* 39: 257–265.

Hobbs, C (1995). Medicinal mushrooms (2nd Ed). Santa Cruz: Botanica Press.

Hocking, A D (1993). Responses of xerophilic fungi to changes in water activity. In Jennings, D H (ed), *Stress tolerance of fungi*. 233–256. Marcel Dekker.

Hodgetts, N (1992). *Guidelines for selection of biological SSSIs: non-vascular plants.* Peterborough: JNCC.

Holden, L (2000). Conservation corner: Scottish waxcap survey. *Field Mycology* 1: 77.

Holliday, J C & Soule, N (2001). Spontaneous female orgasms triggered by the smell of a newly found tropical *Dictyophora* species. *Int. J. Med. Mushrooms* 3: 162.

Horn, B & Lichtwardt, R W (1981). Studies in the nutritional relationships of larval *Aedes aegypti* (Diptera: Culicidae) with *Smittium culisetae* (Trichomycetes). *Mycologia* 73: 724–740.

Horner, W E, Helbling, A, Salvaggio, J E, & Lehrer, S B (1995). Fungal Allergens. *Clin. Microbiol. Rev.* 8: 161-179

Howard, H J (1948). The Mycetozoa of sand-dunes and marshland. *South Eastern Naturalist* 53: 26–30.

Howard, D H & Miller, J D (eds) (1996). *The Mycota VI: Human and Animal Relationships.* Berlin: Springer Verlag.

Hughes, J (2002). Nightmare threat of the terror toadstools. *Western Daily Press*: 25th Jan. 2002.

Humphrey, J W, Ferris, R, Jukes, M R, & Peace, A J (2002). The potential contribution of conifer plantations to the UK Biodiversity Action Plan. *Bot. J. Scotland* 54: 49–62.

Hyde, K D & Pointing, S B (eds) (2000). *Marine mycology.* 377 pp. Hong Kong: Fungal Diversity Press.

Ikediugwu, F E W & Webster, J. (1970a). Antagonism between *Coprinus heptemerus* and other coprophilous fungi. *Trans. Brit. Mycol. Soc.* 54: 181–204.

Ikediugwu, F E W & Webster, J. (1970b). Hyphal interference in a range of coprophilous fungi. *Trans. Brit. Mycol. Soc.* 54: 205–210.

Ing, B (1974). Mouldy Myxomycetes. *Bull. Brit. Mycol. Soc.* 8: 25–30.

Ing, B (1993). Towards a Red List of endangered European macrofungi. In Pegler, D N *et al.* (eds). *Fungi of Europe.* 231–237. Kew: Royal Botanic Gardens.

Ing, B (1994a). European *Exobasidiales* and their galls. In Williams, M A J (ed) *Plant galls. Organisms, interactions, populations.* 67–76. Systematics Association Special Vol. 49.

Ing, B (1994b). The phytosociology of myxomycetes. Tansley Review No. 62. *New Phytologist* 126: 175–201.

Ing, B (1996). Red Data Lists and decline in fruiting of macromycetes in relation to pollution and loss of habitats. In Frankland, J, Magan, N, & Gadd, G M (eds). *Fungi and environmental change.* 61–69. Cambridge Univ. Press.

Ing, B (1998). Alpine myxomycetes in Scotland. *Bot. J. Scotland* 50: 47–53.

Ingold, C T (1953). *Dispersal in fungi.* 197 pp. Oxford University Press.

Ingold, C T (1971). *Fungal Spores: their Liberation and Dispersal.* Clarendon Press, Oxford.

Ingold, C T (1975). *Guide to Aquatic Hyphomycetes.* Freshwater Biological Association, Publication no. 30.

Ingold, C T & Chapman, B (1952). Aquatic ascomycetes: *Loramyces juncicola* Weston and *L. macrospora* n.sp. *Trans. Brit. Mycol. Soc.* 35: 268–272.

Ingram, D & Robertson, N (1999). *Plant disease. A natural history.* New Naturalist 85. London: HarperCollins.

IUCN (2001). *IUCN Red List categories and criteria, version 3.1.* Newbury: IUCN.

Jansen, A E & Lawrynwicz, M (eds) (1991). Conservation of Fungi and other Cryptogams in Europe. *Science Tracks* 18: 1–120.

Jansen, E J & van Dobben, H F (1987). Is decline of *Cantharellus cibarius* in the Netherlands due to air pollution? *Ambio* 16: 211–23.

Jansson, H-B & Poinar, G O (1986). Some possible fossil nematophagous fungi. *Trans. Brit. Mycol. Soc.* 87: 471–474.

Jennings, D H & Bravery, A F (eds) (1991). *Serpula lacrymans:* fundamental biology and control strategies. Chichester: John Wiley & Sons.

Johnson, T W & Sparrow, F K (1961). *Fungi in oceans and estuaries.* Weinheim: J. Cramer.

Jones, E B G (1973). Marine fungi: spore dispersal, settlement and colonization of timber. *Proc. 3rd Int. Congr. Marine Corros. Fouling:* 640–647.

Jones, A M & Jones, E B G (1993). Observations on the marine gasteromycete *Nia vibrissa. Mycol. Res.* 97: 1–6.

Jordal, J B & Gaarder, G (1993). Soppfloraen i en del naturbeitemarker og naturenger i Møre og Romsdal og Trøndelag. Fylkesmannen i Møre og Romsdal, Miljøvernavdelinga. Rapport nr. 9.

Kalgutkar, R M & Jansonius, J (2000). *Synopsis of fossil fungal spores, mycelia and fructifications.* American Association of Stratigraphic Palynolygists.

Kam, A P & Xu, J P (2002). Diversity of commensal yeasts within and among healthy hosts. *Diagnost. Microbiol. & Infect. Dis.* 43: 19–28.

Keller, S (1988). Arthropod-pathogenic Entomophthorales of Switzerland. I. *Conidiobolus, Entomophaga* and *Entomophthora. Sydowia* 40: 122–167.

Keller, S (1991). Arthropod-pathogenic Entomophthorales of Switzerland. II. *Erynia, Eryniopsis, Zoophthora* and *Tarichium. Sydowia* 43: 39–122.

Khan, A G & Belik, M (1995). Occurrence and ecological significance of mycorrhizal symbiosis in aquatic plants. In Varma, A & Hock, B (eds). *Mycorrhiza.* 627–666. Berlin: Springer Verlag.

Kilian, M, Hain, R, & Berg, D (1997). Biological herbicides – mycoherbicides. In Anke, T (ed), *Fungal biotechnology.* 51–64. London: Chapman & Hall.

Kirby, J J H. & Rayner, A D M (1988). Disturbance, decomposition and patchiness in thatch. *Proc. Royal Soc. Edinburgh* 94B: 145–153.

Kirk, P M (1981). New or interesting microfungi. III. A preliminary account of the microfungi colonizing *Laurus nobilis* leaf litter. *Trans. Brit. Mycol. Soc.* 77: 457–473.

Kirk, P M (1982). New or interesting

microfungi. V. Microfungi colonizing *Laurus nobilis* leaf litter. *Trans. Brit. Mycol. Soc.* 78: 293–303.

Kirk, P M (1983). New or interesting microfungi. X. Hyphomycetes on *Laurus nobilis* leaf litter. *Mycotaxon* 18: 259–298.

Kirk, P M (1984). New or interesting microfungi. XIII. Ascomycetes on *Laurus nobilis* leaf litter. *Mycotaxon* 19: 307–322.

Kirk, P M, Cannon, P F, David, J C & Stalpers, J A (eds) (2001). *Ainsworth & Bisby's Dictionary of the Fungi. Ninth Ed.* Wallingford: CABI Publishing.

Kirk, P M & Kirk, J P (1984). *Dimargaris*, a genus new to the British Isles. *Trans. Brit. Mycol. Soc.* 82: 551–553.

Kleiner, K (2000). Coca killer. *New Scientist* 2229: 5.

Kleiner, K (2001). The case of the killer blight. *New Scientist* 2294: 11.

Klironomos, J N & Hart, M M (2001). Animal nitrogen swap for plant carbon. *Nature*, 4 April: 651–652.

Kobayasi, Y & Shimizu, D (1983). Iconography of vegetable wasps and plant worms. Japan: Hoikusha Publishing.

Kohlmeyer, J (1985). Marine fungi (*Ascomycetes*) within and on tests of *Foraminifera. Marine Biol.* 90: 147–149.

Kohlmeyer, J & Kohlmeyer, E (1979). *Marine mycology*. 690 pp. New York: Academic Press.

Kohlmeyer, J & Volkmann-Kohlmeyer, B (1991). Illustrated key to the filamentous higher marine fungi. *Botanica Marina* 34: 1–61.

Koike, J, Oshima, T, Koike, K A, Taguchi, H, Tanaka, R, Nishimura, K, & Miyaji, M (1992). Survival rates of some terrestrial microorganisms under simulated space conditions. *Advances in Space Research* 12(4): 271–274.

Kotiranta, H & Niemelä, T (1993). *Uhanalaiset käävät Suomessa (Threatened*

polypores in Finland). Helsinki: Painatuskeskus Oy.

Koune, J-P. (2001). *Threatened mushrooms in Europe* (Nature and environment 122). 69 pp. Strasbourg: Council of Europe.

Køen, V & Cvak, L (eds) (1999). *Ergot: the genus* Claviceps. Amsterdam: Harwood Academic Publ.

Kudo, S (2000). Mushrooms of the Jomon Period. *Rep. Tottori Mycol. Inst.* 38: 46–57.

Kurup, V P, Shen, H D, & Banerjee, B (2000). Respiratory fungal allergy. *Microbes Infect.* 2: 1101-1110

Lachance, M-A, Starmer, W T, Rosa, C A, Bowles, J M, Stuart, J, Barker, F & Janzen, D H (2001). Biogeography of the yeasts of ephemeral flowers and their insects. *FEMS Yeast Research* 1: 1–8.

Laessøe, T & Spooner, B (1994). The uses of 'gasteromycetes'. *Mycologist* 8: 154–159.

Lagarde, J (1913). Biospeologica XXXII. Champignons (première série). *Archives de Zoologie Expérimentale et Générale* 53: 277–307.

Lagarde, J (1917). Biospeologica XXXVIII. Champignons (deuxième série). *Archives de Zoologie Expérimentale et Générale* 56: 279–314.

Lagarde, J (1922). Biospeologica XLVI. Champignons (troisième série). *Archives de Zoologie Expérimentale et Générale* 60: 593–625.

Lambley, P (2001). Management of lowland grassland for lichens. In Fletcher, A, Wolseley, P & Woods, R (eds). *Lichen Habitat Management*. Ch. 12:1–6. British Lichen Society.

Langley, D (1997). Exploiting the fungi: novel leads to new medicines. *Mycologist* 11: 165–167.

Large, E C (1940). *The Advance of the Fungi.* London: Cape.

Larsen, K (1971). Danish endocoprophilous

fungi, and their sequence of occurrence. *Botanisk Tidsskrift* 66: 1–32.

Laundon, J R (1970). London's lichens. *The London Naturalist* 49: 20–69.

Laundon, J R (1971). Lichen communities destroyed by psocids. *Lichenologist* 5: 177.

Lawrey, J D & Diederich, P. (2003). Lichenicolous fungi: interactions, evolution and biodiversity. *Bryologist* 106: 80–120.

Leatherdale, D (1958). A host catalogue of British entomogenous fungi. *Entomologist's Mon. Mag.* 94: 103–105

Leatherdale, D (1962). A host catalogue of British entomogenous fungi: first supplement. *Entomologist's Mon. Mag.* 97: 226–227.

Leatherdale, D (1965). A host catalogue of British entomogenous fungi: second supplement. *Entomologist's Mon. Mag.* 101: 163–164.

Leatherdale, D (1970). The arthropod hosts of entomogenous fungi in Britain. *Entomophaga* 15: 419–435.

Legg, A W (1991). The Fungi of Darlington West Cemetery. *The Mycologist* 5: 195–196.

Leith, I D & Fowler, D (1988). Urban distribution of *Rhytisma acerinum* (tar spot) on sycamore. *New Phytologist* 108: 175–181.

Lichtwardt, R W (1986). *The Trichomycetes. Fungal Associates of Arthropods.* Springer-Verlag.

Lindsay, W L (1856). *A popular history of British lichens.* London: Lovell Reeve.

Lisiewska, M (1992). Macrofungi on special substrates. In Winterhoff, W (ed). Fungi in vegetation science. *Handbook of vegetation science* 19. 151–182. Kluwer.

Lowy, B (1971). New records of mushroom stones from Guatemala. *Mycologia* 63: 983–993.

Lowy, B (1972). Mushroom symbolism in Maya codices. *Mycologia* 64: 816–821.

Lund, J W G (1957). Fungal diseases of planktonic algae. In Horton-Smith, C. (ed), *Biological Aspects of the Transmission of Disease.* 19–23. London: Oliver & Boyd.

Lundquist, N (1972). Nordic *Sordariaceae* s. lat. *Symb. Bot. Ups.* 20 (1): 1–374.

MacKinnon, J E (1969). Isolation of *Sporothrix schenckii* from nature and considerations on its pathogenicity and ecology. *Sabouraudia* 7: 38–45.

Magan, N (1997). Fungi in extreme environments. In Wicklow, D T & Söderström, B (eds). *The Mycota IV: Environmental and Microbial Relationships.* 99–114. Berlin: Springer Verlag.

Malloch, D & Blackwell, M (1992). Dispersal of Fungal Diaspores. In Carroll, G C & Wicklow, D T (eds). *The Fungal Community. Its Organization and Role in the Ecosystem.* 2nd ed. 147–171. Marcel Dekker

Margulis, L & Schwartz, K V (1982). *Five Kingdoms. An Illustrated Guide to the Phyla of Life on Earth.* San Francisco: W H Freeman.

Masters, M J (1976). Freshwater phycomycetes on algae. In Jones, E B G (ed). *Recent Advances in Aquatic Mycology.* 489–512. London: Elek Science.

Matossian, M K (1989). *Poisons of the past: molds, epidemics, and history.* 190 pp. Yale Univ. Press.

Matsumoto, T, Ajello, L, Matsuda, T, Szaniszlo, P J, & Walsh, T J (1994). Developments in hyalohyphomycosis and phaeohyphomycosis. *J. Medical and Veterinary Mycology* 32, Suppl. 1: 329–349.

McHugh, R, Mitchel, D, Wright, M, & Anderson, R (2001). The fungi of Irish grasslands and their value for nature conservation. *Biology & Environment* 101B: 225–243.

McIlveen, W D & Cole, H (1976). Spore dispersal of Endogonaceae by worms, ants, wasps and birds. *Can. J. Bot.* 54: 1486–1489.

Misra, J K & Lichtwardt, R W (2000). *Illustrated genera of Trichomycetes. Fungal Symbionts of Insects and other Arthropods.* Science Publishers, Inc.

Mitchell, D T, Sweeney, M & Kennedy, A (1992). Chitin degradation by *Hymenoscyphus ericae* and the influence of *H. ericae* on the growth of ectomycorrhizal fungi. In Read, D J *et al.* (eds), *Mycorrhizas in ecosystems.* 246–251. Wallingford: CAB International.

Mix, A J (1949). A monograph of the genus *Taphrina. University of Kansas Science Bull.* 33: 1–167.

Molina, R, Pilz, D, Smith, J, Dunham, S, Dreisbach, T, O'Dell, T, & Castellano, M (2001). Conservation and management of forest fungi in the Pacific Northwestern United States: an integrated ecosystem approach. In Moore, D, Nauta, M M, Evans, S E, & Rotheroe, M (eds). *Fungal conservation: issues and solutions.* 19–63. Cambridge University Press.

Monti, G, Marchetti, M, Gorreri, L, & Franchi, P (1992). *Funghi e cenosi di aree bruciate.* 149 pp. Pisa: Pacini Editore.

Moody, L (1985). The truffle hunters. *Hampshire,* Oct. 1985: 48–50.

Mordue, J E M & Ainsworth, G C (1984). *Ustilaginales* of the British Isles. *Mycol. Pap.* 154. Commonwealth Agricultural Bureaux.

Morgan, P & Watkinson, R (1993). Bioremediation of earth. *Mycologist* 7: 68–70.

Morrison-Gardiner, S. (2002). Dominant fungi from Australian coral reefs. *Fungal Diversity* 9: 105–121.

Moser, M (1949). Untersuchungen über den Einfluß von Waldbränden auf die Pilzvegetation I. *Sydowia* 3: 336–383.

Moser, J C, Perry, T J & Solheim, H (1989). Ascospores hyperphoretic on mites associated with *Ips typographus. Mycol. Res.* 93: 513–517.

Moss, S T (1979). Commensalism of the Trichomycetes. In Batra, L R (ed). *Insect-Fungus Symbiosis. Nutrition, Mutualism, and Commensalism.* 175–227. Allenheld, Osmun & Co.

Moss, S T & Descals, E (1986). A previously undescribed stage in the life cycle of Harpellales (Trichomycetes). *Mycologia* 78: 213–222.

Mottershead, D & Lucas, G (2000). The role of lichens in inhibiting erosion of a soluble rock. *Lichenologist* 32: 601–609.

Mountfort, D O & Orpin, C G (eds) (1994). *Anaerobic Fungi. Biology, Ecology, and Function.* Mycology Series 12. Marcel Dekker.

Murray, J S (1974). The fungal pathogens of oak. In Morris, M G & Perring, F H (eds), *The British Oak.* 235–249. Faringdon: E.W. Classey.

Nash, T H & Wirth, V (eds) (1988). Lichens, Bryophytes and Air Quality. *Bibliotheca Lichenologica* 30. Berlin-Stuttgart: J. Cramer.

Nauta, M & Vellinga, E C (1993). Distribution and decline of macrofungi in the Netherlands. In Pegler, D N *et al.* (eds). *Fungi of Europe.* 21–46. Kew: Royal Botanic Gardens.

Nicks, G (2002). Killer fungus alert: Danger mushrooms will eat your brains. (UK press clipping).

Nitare, J (1988). Jordtungor, en svampgrupp på tillbakegång i naturliga fodermarker. *Svensk bot. Tidskr.* 82: 341–368.

Nitare, J (ed) (2000). *Signalarter. Indikatorer på skyddsvärd skog. Flora över kryptogamer.* Sweden: Skogsstyrelsens Förlag.

Noble, M, de Tempe, J & Neergaard, P. (1958). *An Annotated List of Seed-borne Diseases.* Kew: Commonwealth Mycological Institute.

Nout, M J R & Aidoo, K E (2002). Asian fungal fermented food. In Osiewacz, H D (ed). *The Mycota X: Industrial applications.* 23–47. Berlin: Springer Verlag.

Novikova, N (2001). Review of the knowledge of microbial contamination of the Russian manned spacecraft. [*internet file:* industry.esa.int/ATTACHEMENTS/A114/novikova.pdf]

Oei, P (1996). *Mushroom cultivation with special emphasis on appropriate techniques for developing countries.* Leiden: Tool Publ.

Oldridge, S G, Pegler, D N, & Spooner, B M (1989). *Wild Mushroom and Toadstool Poisoning.* 23 pp. Kew: Royal Botanic Gardens.

Olsson, P A, Münzenberger, B, Mahmood, S, & Erland, S (2000). Molecular and anatomical evidence for a three-way association between *Pinus sylvestris* and the ectomycorrhizal fungi *Suillus bovinus* and *Gomphidius roseus. Mycol. Res.* 104: 1372–1378

Oolbekkink, G T & Kuyper, T W (1989). Radioactive caesium from Chernobyl. *Mycologist* 3: 3–6.

Orton, P D (1986). Fungi of northern pine and birch woods. *Bull. Brit. Mycol. Soc.* 20: 130–145.

Parmasto, E (2001). Fungi as indicators of primeval and old-growth forests deserving protection. In Moore, D, Nauta, M M, Evans, S.E. & Rotheroe, M (eds). *Fungal conservation: issues and solutions.* 81–88. Cambridge Univ. Press.

Patterson, K R (1996). Modelling the impact of disease-induced mortality in an exploited population: The outbreak of the fungal parasite *Ichthyophonus hoferi* in the North Sea herring (*Clupea harengus*). *Can. J. Fisheries & Aquatic Sci.* 53: 2870–2887.

Paviour-Smith, K (1960). The Fruiting-bodies of Macrofungi as Habitats for Beetles of the Family Ciidae (Coleoptera). *Oikos* 11: 43–71.

Peake, J F & James, P W (1967). Lichens and mollusca. *Lichenologist* 3: 425–428

Peden, N R & Pringle, S D (1982). Hallucinogenic fungi. *The Lancet*, 13 Feb.: 396–397.

Pegler, D N (1999). Taxonomy, nomenclature and description of *Armillaria.* In Fox, R T V (ed), *Biology and control of honey fungus.* 81–93. Andover: Intercept.

Pegler, D N, Spooner, B M & Young, T W K (1993). *British Truffles. A Revision of British Hypogeous Fungi.* Kew: Royal Botanic Gardens.

Penzig, O (1922). *Pflanzen-teratologie. Systematisch Geordnet.* Vol 3. Berlin: Borntraeger.

Perini, C (1998) (ed). *Conservation of fungi in Europe* (Proc. 4th Meeting ECCF). Univ. of Siena.

Petch, T (1921). Studies in entomogenous fungi. II. The genera *Hypocrella* and *Aschersonia. Annals Roy. Bot. Gard., Peradeniya* 7: 167–278.

Petch, T (1932). A list of the entomogenous fungi of Great Britain. *Trans. Brit. Mycol. Soc.* 17: 170–178.

Petersen, P M (1970). Danish fireplace fungi. An ecological investigation on fungi on burns. *Dansk Botanisk Arkiv* 27(3): 1–97.

Petrini, O. (1984). Endophytic fungi in British Ericaceae: a preliminary study. *Trans. Brit. Mycol. Soc.* 83: 510–512.

Petrini, O, Fisher, P J & Petrini, L E (1992). Fungal endophytes of bracken (*Pteridium aquilinum*), with some reflections on their use in biological control. *Sydowia* 44: 282–293.

Pilát, A (1927). Mykoflora dolù přibramských. *Sborn. Čes. Akad. zem.* 2: 445–533.

Pirozynski, K A & Hawksworth, D L (eds). *Coevolution of Fungi with Plants and Animals.* Academic Press.

Pitt, J I (1994). The current role of *Aspergillus*

and *Penicillium* in human and animal health. *J. Medical and Veterinary Mycology* 32, Suppl. 1: 17–32.

Pitt, J I (2000). Toxigenic fungi: which are important? *Medical Mycology* 38, Suppl. 1: 17–22.

Pitt, J I & Hocking, A D (1997). *Fungi and Food Spoilage*. Ed 2. London: Blackie

Poelt, J (1985). Über auf Moosen parastitierende Flechten. *Sydowia* 38: 241–254.

Pontón, J, Rüchel, R, Clemons, K V, Coleman, D C, Grillot, R, Guarro, J, Aldebert, D, Ambroise-Thomas, P, Cano, J, Carrillo-Muñoz, A J, Gené, J, Pinel, C, Stevens, D A, & Sullivan, D J (2000). Emerging pathogens. *Medical Mycology* 38, Suppl. 1: 225–236.

Preece, T F (2002). *A Checklist of the Downy Mildews* (Peronosporaceae) *of the British Isles*. British Mycological Society.

Preece, T F & Dickinson, C H (1971). *Ecology of Leaf Surface Micro-organisms*. Academic Press.

Preece, T F & Hick, A J (1994). British gall-causing rust fungi. In Williams, M A J (ed). *Plant galls. Organisms, interactions, populations*. 57–66. Systematics Association Special Vol. 49. Oxford: Clarendon Press.

Pugh, G J F (1965). Cellulolytic and keratinophilic fungi recorded on birds. *Sabouraudia* 4: 85–91.

Pugh, G J F (1966). Associations between birds' nests, their pH, and keratinophilic fungi. *Sabouraudia* 5: 49–53.

Pugh, G J F & Evans, M D (1970). Keratinophilic fungi associated with birds. I. Fungi isolated from feathers, nests and soils. *Trans. Brit. mycol. Soc.* 54: 233–240.

Rackham, O (1980). *Ancient Woodland*. London: Edward Arnold.

Rackham, O (1986). *The History of the Countryside*. London: J M Dent.

Raghukumar, S (1992). Bacterivory – a novel dual role for thraustochytrids in the sea. *Marine Biology* 113: 165–169.

Rai, B K, Ayachi, S S, & Rai, A (1993). A note on ethno-myco-medicines from Central India. *Mycologist* 7: 192–193.

Rald, E (1985). Vokshatte som indikatorarter for mykologisk vaerdifulde overdrevslokaliteter. *Svampe* 11: 1–9.

Ramel, G & Webster, J (1995). Abnormal wood blewit basidiocarps. *Mycologist* 9: 105.

Rammeloo, J & Walleyn, R (1993). *The edible fungi of Africa south of the Sahara*. Meise: National Botanic Garden, Belgium.

Ramsbottom, J (1936). The uses of fungi. *Ann. Rep. British Assoc. Advanc. Sci.* 1936: 189–218.

Ramsbottom, J (1953). *Mushrooms and Toadstools*. New Naturalist 7. London: Collins.

Rand, T G (2000). Diseases of animals. In Hyde, K D & Pointing, S B (eds), *Marine mycology*. 21–48. Hong Kong: Fungal Diversity Press.

Raverat, G (1952). *Period Piece. A Cambridge Childhood*. London: Faber & Faber.

Rayner, A D M & Boddy, L (1988). *Fungal decomposition of wood*. 587 pp. Chichester: John Wiley & Sons.

Rayner, A D M, Boddy, L, & Dawson, C G. (1987). Temporary parasitism of *Coriolus* spp. by *Lenzites betulina*: a strategy for domain capture in wood decay fungi. FEMS *Microbiology Ecology* 45: 53–58.

Rayner, A D M, Watling, R, & Frankland, J C (1985). Resource relations – an overview. In Moore *et al.* (eds), *Developmental biology of higher fungi*. Cambridge University Press

Rayner, R W (1979). The frequencies with which basidiomycete species, other than rusts and smuts, have been recorded on BMS forays. *Bull. Brit. Mycol. Soc.* 13: 110–125.

Read, D J (1974). *Pezizella ericae* sp. nov, the perfect state of a typical mycorrhizal endophyte of Ericaceae. *Trans. Brit. Mycol. Soc.* 63: 381–383.

Read, D J (1989). Mycorrhizas and nutrient recycling in sand dune ecosystems. In Gimingham, C H *et al.* (eds), Coastal Sand Dunes. 89–110. *Proc. Roy. Soc. Edinburgh*, B96.

Read, D J, Duckett, J G, Francis, R, Ligrone, R, & Russell, A (2000). Symbiotic fungal associations in 'lower' land plants. *Phil. Trans. R. Soc. Lond. B* 355: 815–831.

Read, H (2000). *Veteran trees: a guide to good management.* Peterborough: English Nature.

Redhead, S A (1981). Parasitism of bryophytes by agarics. *Can. J. Bot.* 59: 63–67.

Redhead, S A, Ammirati, J F, Walker, G R, Norvell, L L, & Puccio, M B (1994). *Squamanita contortipes,* the Rosetta Stone of a mycoparasitic agaric genus. *Can. J. Bot.* 72: 1812–1824.

Redlin, S C & Carris, L M (1996). *Endophytic Fungi in Grasses and Woody Plants. Systematics, Ecology, and Evolution.* Minnesota: APS Press.

Reisinger, A (1994). *Radiocäsium in Pilzen* (Bibl. Mycol. 155). Berlin: J. Cramer.

Retallack, G J (1994). Were the Ediacaran fossils lichens? *Paleobiology* 20: 523–544.

Rice, M & Beebee, D (1980). *Mushrooms for color.* Eureka, California: Mad River Press.

Richardson, D (1975). *The Vanishing Lichens. Their History, Biology and Importance.* Newton Abbot: David & Charles.

Richardson, D H S (1992). *Pollution Monitoring with Lichens.* Naturalists' Handbooks, 19. Slough: Richmond Publishing.

Richardson, M J (1972). Coprophilous *Ascomycetes* on different dung types. *Trans. Brit. Mycol. Soc.* 58: 37–48.

Richardson, M J (1979). An Annotated List of seed-borne diseases. 3rd Ed. *Phytopath. Paper 23.* CMI

Richardson, M J (2001). Diversity and occurrence of coprophilous fungi. *Mycological Research* 105: 387–402.

Richardson, M J & Watling, R. (1997). *Keys to fungi on dung.* 68 pp. British Mycological Society.

Rishbeth, J (1959). Dispersal of *Fomes annosus* Fr. and *Peniophora gigantea* (Fr.) Massee. *Trans. Brit. Mycol. Soc.* 42: 243–260.

Rishbeth, J (1961). Inoculation of pine stumps against infection by *Fomes annosus. Nature* 191: 826–827.

Ristaino, J B (1998). The importance of archival and herbarium materials in understanding the role of oospores in late blight epidemics of the past. *Phytopathology* 88: 1120–1130.

Robinson, W (1883). *Mushroom culture: its extension and improvement.* London: Routledge & Sons.

Rodwell, J S (1992). *British Plant Communities.* Vol. 3. *Grasslands and montane communities.* Cambridge University Press.

Rogerson, C T & Stephenson, S (1993). Myxomyceticolous Fungi. *Mycologia* 85: 456–469.

Rolfe, R T & Rolfe, F W (1925). *The Romance of the Fungus World. An Account of Fungus Life in its Numerous Guises, both Real and Legendary.* London: Chapman & Hall.

Rose, F (1974). The epiphytes of oak. In Morris, M G & Perring, F H (eds). *The British oak, its history and natural history.* 250–273. Faringdon: Classey.

Rose, F (1976). Lichenological indicators of age and environmental continuity in woodlands. In Brown, D H, Hawksworth, D L, & Bailey, R H (eds). *Lichenology: Progress and Problems.* 279–307. Systematics Association Special Vol. 8. London: Academic Press.

Rotheroe, M (1993). The macrofungi of British sand dunes. In Pegler, D N, Boddy, L, Ing. B & Kirk, P M (eds). Fungi of Europe. Investigation, Recording and Conservation. 121–137. Kew: Royal Botanic Gardens.

Rotheroe, M (2001). A preliminary survey of waxcap grassland indicator species in South Wales. In Moore, D, Nauta, M M, Evans, S E, & Rotheroe, M (eds). *Fungal conservation: issues and solutions.* 120–135. Cambridge University Press.

Roussin, M R (1996). Analyses of kombucha ferments: report on growers. http://w3.trib.com/~kombu/FAQ/mroussin2toc.html

Rubner, A (1996). Revision of predacious hyphomycetes in the *Dactylella – Monacrosporium* complex. *Studies in Mycology* 39: 1–134.

Rutter, G (2002). Fairy rings. *Field Mycology* 3: 56–60.

Ryvarden, L & Gilbertson, R L (1994). *European polypores*, Part 2. Oslo: Fungiflora.

Sagara, N (1978). The occurrence of fungi in association with wood mouse nests. *Trans. Mycol. Soc. Japan* 19: 201–24.

Sagara, N (1992). Experimental Disturbances and Epigeous Fungi. In Carroll, G C & Wicklow, D T (eds). *The Fungal Community. Its Organization and Role in the Ecosystem.* 427–454. Marcel Dekker.

Sagara, N, Honda, S, Kuroyanagi, E & Takayama, S (1981). The occurrence of *Hebeloma spoliatum* and *Hebeloma radicosum* on the dung-deposited burrows of *Urotrichus talpoides* (shrew mole). *Trans. Mycol. Soc. Japan* 22: 441–455.

Sagara, N, Kobayashi, S, Ota, H, Itsubo, T & Okabe, H (1989). Finding *Euroscaptor mizura* (*Mammalia: Insectivora*) and its nest from under *Hebeloma radicosum* (*Fungi: Agaricales*) in Ashiu, Kyoto, with a data of possible contiguous occurrences of three talpine species in this region. *Contrib. Biol. Lab. Kyoto Univ.* 27: 261–272.

Samorini, G (2001a). New data from the ethnomycology of psychoactive mushrooms. *Int. J. Med. Mushrooms* 3: 257–278.

Samorini, G (2001b). *Funghi allucinogeni: studi etnomicologici.* 247 pp. Italy: Telesterion.

Sampson, K & Western, J H (1941). *Diseases of British Grasses and Herbage Legumes.* Cambridge University Press.

Samson, R A, Evans, H C & Latgé, J-P (1988). *Atlas of entomopathogenic fungi.* Springer-Verlag.

Samson, R A, Hoekstra, E S, Frisvad, J C, & Filtenborg, O (eds) (2000). *Introduction to food- and airborne fungi* (6th Ed). Utrecht: CBS.

Samson, R A, Rombach, M C & Seifert, K A (1984). *Hirsutella guignardii* and *Stilbella kervillei,* two troglobiotic entomogenous hyphomycetes. *Persoonia* 12: 123–134.

Scheidegger, C, Frey, B, & Zoller, S (1995). Transplantation of symbiotic propagules and thallus fragments: methods for the conservation of threatened epiphytic lichen populations. In Scheidegger, C, Wolseley, P A, & Thor, G (eds)(1995a). *Conservation biology of lichenised fungi.* 41–62. Birmensdorf: EFWSL.

Schleiffer, H (1973). *Sacred narcotic plants of the New World Indians.* New York: Hafner Press.

Schmit, J P, Mueller, G M, & Courtecuisse, R (2002). Fungal diversity: estimates, predictions and future challenges. *International Mycological Congress 7, Book of Abstracts:* 35

Scott, P R & Bainbridge, A (eds) (1978). *Plant disease epidemiology.* Oxford: Blackwell Scientific Publications.

Seifert, K, Kendrick, B & Murase, G (1983). A

key to hyphomycetes on dung. University of Waterloo Biology Series No. 27.

Senn-Irlet, B (1988). Macromycetes in alpine snow-bed communities – mycocoenological investigations. *Acta Bot. Neerl.* 37: 251–263.

Sewell, G W F (1959a). Studies of fungi in a *Calluna*-heathland soil I. Vertical distribution in soil and on root surfaces. *Trans. Brit. Mycol. Soc.* 42: 343–353.

Sewell, G W F. (1959b). Studies of fungi in a *Calluna*-heathland soil II. By the complementary use of several isolation methods. *Trans. Brit. Mycol. Soc.* 42: 354–369

Sewell, G W F (1959c). The ecology of fungi in *Calluna*-heathland soils. *New Phytologist* 58: 5–15.

Shearer, C A (2001). The Distribution of Freshwater Filamentous Ascomycetes. In Misra, J K & Horn, B W (eds). *Trichomycetes and Other Fungal Groups.* 225–292. Science Publishers.

Sherwood, M A (1981). Convergent evolution in discomycetes from bark and wood. *J. Linn. Soc., Bot.* 82: 15–34.

Shivas, R G & Hyde, K D (1997). Biodiversity of plant pathogenic fungi in the tropics. In Hyde, K D (ed). *Biodiversity of tropical microfungi.* 47–56. Hong Kong University Press.

Singleton, I & Tobin, J M (1996). Fungal interactions with metals and radionuclides for environmental bioremediation. In Frankland, J C, Magan, N, & Gadd, G M (eds). *Fungi and environmental change.* 282–298. Cambridge Univ. Press.

Smiley, R W, Dernoeden, P H & Clarke, B B (1992). *Compendium of Turfgrass Diseases.* Ed 2. Minnesota: APS Press.

Smith, J D, Hackson, N, & Woodhouse, A R (1989). *Fungal diseases of amenity turf grasses* (3rd Ed). London: E & F N Spon.

Smith, J M B (1989). *Opportunistic mycoses of man and other animals.* Wallingford: CAB International.

Smith, K G V (1956). On the diptera associated with the stinkhorn (*Phallus impudicus* Pers) with notes on other insects and invertebrates found on this fungus. *Proc. R. Ent. Soc. A*, 31: 49–55.

Smith, S E & Read, D J (1997). *Mycorrhizal symbiosis* (2nd Ed). 605 pp. London: Academic Press.

Snowdon, A L (1990 & 1991). *A colour atlas of post-harvest diseases and disorders of fruits and vegetables, Vols.* 1 & 2. 718 pp. London: Wolfe.

Sparrow, F K (1960). *Aquatic Phycomycetes.* Ed 2. Ann Arbor: University of Michigan Press.

Spatafora, J W, Volkmann-Kohlmeyer, B, & Kohlmeyer, J (1998). Independent terrestrial origin of the *Halosphaeriales. Amer. J. Bot.* 85: 1569–1580.

Spooner, B M & Læssøe, T (1994). The folklore of 'Gasteromycetes'. *Mycologist* 8: 119–123.

Stamets, P (1993). *Growing gourmet and medicinal mushrooms.* Berkeley, California: Ten Speed Press.

Stamets, P (1996). *Psilocybin mushrooms of the world.* Berkeley, California: Ten Speed Press.

Steinkraus, K H (ed) (1983). *Handbook of indigenous fermented foods.* New York: Marcel Dekker.

Sterflinger, K (2000). Fungi as geologic agents. *Geomicrobiol. J.* 17: 97–124.

Sterflinger, K & Krumbein, W E (1997). Dematiaceous fungi as a major agent for biopitting on Mediterranean marbles and limestones. *Geomicrobiol. J.* 14: 219–230.

Stewart, W N and G W Rothwell (1993). *Paleobotany and the Evolution of Plants.* 2nd Ed. Cambridge University Press.

Sutton, B C (1974). Hyphomycetes on

cupules of *Castanea sativa*. *Trans. Brit. Mycol. Soc.* 64: 405–426.

Swanton, E W (1917). Economic and folk lore notes. *Trans. Brit. Mycol. Soc.* 5: 408–409.

Tansley, A G (1939). *The British Islands and their Vegetation*. Cambridge University Press.

Taylor, A F S & Alexander, I J (1989). Demography and population dynamics of ectomycorrhizas of Sitka spruce fertilised with N. *Agric. Ecosyst. & Environ.* 28: 493–496.

Taylor, T N & Taylor, E L (1997). The distribution and interactions of some Palaeozoic fungi. *Rev. Palaeobot. Palynology* 95: 83–94.

Taylor, T N, Hass, H & Kerp, H (1999). The oldest fossil ascomycetes. *Nature* 399: 648.

TeBeest, D O (1993). Biological control of weeds with fungal pathogens. In Jones, D G (ed), *Exploitation of microorganisms*. 1–17. London: Chapman & Hall.

Theodorou, M K, Zhu, W-Y, Rickers, A, Nielsen, B B, Gull, K, & Trinci, A P J (1996). Biochemistry and ecology of anaerobic fungi. In Howard, D H & Miller, J D (eds). *The Mycota VI: Human and Animal Relationships*. 265–295. Berlin: Springer Verlag.

Thoen, D (1982). Usages et légendes liés aux polypores. *Bull. Soc. Mycol. France* 98: 289–318.

Thor, G. (1995). Red Lists – aspects of their compilation and use in lichen conservation. In Scheidegger, C, Wolseley, P A, & Thor, G (eds), *Conservation biology of lichenised fungi*. 29–39. Birmensdorf: EFWSL.

Thorn, R G & Barron, G L (1984). Carnivorous mushrooms. *Science* 224: 76–78.

Thorn, R G & Barron, G L (1986).

Nematoctonus and the tribe *Resupinatae* in Ontario, Canada. *Mycotaxon* 25: 321–454.

Thornton, R H (1956). Fungi occurring in mixed oakwood and heath soil profiles. *Trans. Brit. Mycol. Soc.* 39: 485–494.

Trinci, A P J (1992). Myco-protein: A twenty-year overnight success story. *Mycol. Res.* 96: 1–13.

Trinci, A P J, Davies, D R, Gull, K, Lawrence, M I Nielsen, B B, Rickers, A & Theodorou, M K (1994). Anaerobic fungi in herbivorous animals. *Mycol. Res.* 98: 129–152.

Tucker, B E (1991). A review of the nonentomogenous Entomophthorales. *Mycotaxon* 13: 481–505.

Turnau, K (1984) Interactions between organisms isolated from burns. *K Nauk. Uniw. Jagiell. Pr. Bot.* 12: 145–170.

Turnbull, E (1995). Not only nuts in May . . . *Mycologist* 9: 82-83.

Tzean, S S & Liou, Y J (1993). Nematophagous resupinate basidiomycetous fungi. *Phytopathology* 83: 1015–1020.

Van Asselt, L (1999). Interactions between domestic mites and fungi. *Indoor and Built Environment* 8: 216–220.

van der Aa, H (1997). Confluent basidiocarps. *Mycologist* 11: 80–82.

van der Heijden, E W, de Vries F W & Kuyper, T W (1999). Mycorrhizal associations of *Salix repens* L. communities in succession of dune ecosystems I. Above-ground and below-ground views of ectomycorrhizal fungi in relation to soil chemistry. *Canadian J. Bot.* 77: 1821–1832.

Van Donk, E & Bruning, K (1992). Ecology of aquatic fungi in and on algae. In Reisser, W (ed). *Algae and Symbioses: Plants, Animals, Fungi, Viruses, Interactions Explored*. 567–592. Bristol: Biopress.

Van Griensven, L J L D (ed) (1988). *The*

cultivation of mushrooms. Rustington: Darlington Mushroom Labs.

Vánky, K (1994). European Smut Fungi. Gustav Fischer.

Vargas, S L, Ponce, C A, Hughes, W T et al. (1999). Association of primary Pneumocystis carinii infection and sudden infant death syndrome. Clin. Infect. Dis. 29: 1489–1493.

Vera, F W M (2000). Grazing ecology and forest history. CABI Publishing.

Vesterholt, J, Boertmann, D & Tranberg, H (1999). 1989–et usaedvanlig godt år for overdrevssvampe. Svampe 40: 36–44.

Visscher, H, Brinkhuis, H, Dilcher, D L, Elsik, W C, Eshet, Y, Looy, C V, Rampino, M R, & Traverse, A (1996). The terminal Paleozoic fungal event: Evidence of terrestrial ecosystem destabilization and collapse. Proc. Nat. Acad. Sci. USA 93: 2155–2158.

Vrålstad, T (2001). Molecular ecology of root-associated mycorrhizal and non-mycorrhizal ascomycetes. Ph.D. Thesis. University of Oslo.

Wainright, P O, Hinkl, G, Sogin, M L & Stickel, S K (1993). Monophyletic origins of the metazoa: an evolutionary link with Fungi. Science 260: 340–342.

Walleyn, R & Rammeloo, J (1994). The poisonous and useful fungi of Africa south of the Sahara: a literature survey. Meise: National Botanic Garden of Belgium

Walsh, G B (1975). Plants and the beetles associated with them. In Cooter, J & Cribb, P W (eds). A Coleopterist's Handbook. 2nd ed. 83–98. Amateur Entomologists' Society.

Wang, C J K & Zabel, R A (1990). Identification manual for fungi from utility poles in the eastern United States. 356 pp. Rockville: ATCC.

Wang, H L & Fang, S F (1986). History of Chinese fermented foods. In Hesseltine, C W & Wang, H L (eds). Indigenous

fermented food of non-Western origin (Mycologia Memoir 11). 23–35. Berlin: Cramer.

Wang, H L & Hesseltine, C W (1986). Glossary of indigenous fermented foods. In Hesseltine, C W & Wang, H L (eds). Indigenous fermented food of non-Western origin (Mycologia Memoir 11). 317–343. Berlin: Cramer.

Wardlow, C W (1972). Banana diseases including plantains and abaca. London: Longman.

Wasson, R G (1956). Lightning-bolts and mushrooms: an essay in early cultural exploration. In For Roman Jakobson. 605–612. Amsterdam: Mouton & Co.

Wasson, R G (1957). Seeking the magic mushroom. Life 49 (19): 100–120.

Wasson, R G (1968). Soma: divine mushroom of immortality. New York: Harcourt Brace Jovanovich Inc.

Wasson, R G (1980). The wondrous mushroom: mycolatry in Mesoamerica. New York: McGraw-Hill.

Wasson, R G, Hofmann, A, & Ruck, A P (1978). The road to Eleusis. New York: Harcourt Brace Jovanovich Inc.

Wasson, V P & Wasson, R G (1957). Mushrooms, Russia and history. (2 vols). New York: Pantheon Books.

Waterhouse, G M (1957). The larger fungi of lawns. Trans. Lincolnshire Nats' Union 14: 75–85.

Waterhouse, G M & Brady, B L (1982). Key to the species of Entomophthora sensu lato. Bull. Brit. Mycol. Soc. 16: 113–143.

Watling, R (1973). Identification of the Larger Fungi. 281 pp. Amersham: Hulton.

Watling, R (1974). Macrofungi in the oak woods of Britain. In Morris, M G & Perring, F H (eds), The British oak. 222–234. Faringdon: E W Classey.

Watling, R (1975). Prehistoric puff-balls. Bull. Brit. Mycol. Soc. 9: 112–114.

Watling, R (1984). Macrofungi of birchwoods. *Proc. Royal Soc. Edinburgh* 85B: 129–140.

Watling, R (1992a). *The fungus flora of Shetland.* 98 pp. Edinburgh: Royal Botanic Garden.

Watling, R (1992b). Macrofungi associated with British willows. *Proc. Royal Soc. Edinburgh* 98B: 135–147.

Watling, R (1995). *Children and toxic fungi.* Edinburgh: Royal Botanic Garden.

Watling, R, Eggeling, T., & Turnbull, E. (1999). *The fungus flora of Orkney.* 124 pp. Edinburgh: Royal Botanic Garden.

Watling, R & Rotheroe, M (1989). Macrofungi of sand dunes. In Gimingham, C H *et al.* (eds), Coastal sand dunes. 111–126. *Proc. Roy. Soc. Edinburgh,* B96.

Watson, E V (1955). *British Mosses and Liverworts.* Cambridge University Press.

Watson, R D, Minter, D W & McKelvie, A D (1984). Dense growth of deuteromycetes on and around bonded distillery warehouses in Scotland. *Bulletin of the British Mycological Society* 18: 57–58.

Webb, N (1986). *Heathlands.* New Naturalist 72. London: Collins.

Weber, N A (1979). Fungus-culturing by Ants. In Batra, L R (ed). *Insect-Fungus Symbiosis. Nutrition, Mutualism, and Commensalism.* 77–116. Allenheld, Osmun & Co.

Weber, N S (1988). *A morel hunter's companion.* Lansing, Michigan: TwoPeninsula Press.

Weber, R W S, Webster, J & Al-Gharabally, D H (1998a). *Puccinia distincta,* cause of the current daisy rust epidemic in Britain, in comparison with other rusts recorded on daisies, *P. obscura* and *P. lagenophorae.* *Mycol. Res.* 102: 1227–1232.

Weber, R W S, Webster, J , Wakley, G E & Al-Gharabally, D H (1998b). *Puccinia distincta,* cause of a devastating rust disease of daisies. *Mycologist* 12: 87–90.

Webster, J (1992). Anamorph-Teleomorph Relationships. In Bärlocher, F (ed). *The Ecology of Aquatic Hyphomycetes.* 99–117. Ecological Studies, Vol 94. Springer-Verlag.

Webster, J & Davey, R A (1984). Sigmoid conidial shape in aquatic fungi. *Trans. Brit. Mycol. Soc.* 83: 43–52.

Webster, J, Davey, R A, Smirnoff, N, Fricke, W, Hionde, P, Tomos, D & Turner, J C R (1995). Mannitol and hexoses are components of Buller's drop. *Mycol. Res.* 99: 833–838.

Webster, J & Descals, E (1981). Morphology, distribution, and ecology of conidial fungi in freshwater habitats. In Cole, G T & Kendrick, B (eds). *Biology of conidial fungi.* 295–355. Vol 1. Academic Press.

Weitzman, I (1991). Epidemiology of blastomycosis and coccidioidomycosis. In Arora, D K, Ajello, L & Mukerji, K G (eds). *Handbook of applied mycology,* Vol. 2: *Humans, animals, and insects.* 51–74. New York: Marcel Dekker.

Wheeler, Q & Blackwell, M (eds) (1984). *Fungus-Insect Relationships. Perspectives in Ecology and Evolution.* New York: Columbia University Press.

Whipps, J M & Lumsden, R D (2001). Commercial use of fungi as plant disease biological control agents: status and prospects. In Butt, T M, Jackson, C W, & Magan, N (eds). *Fungi as biocontrol agents.* 9–22. Wallingford: CABI Publishing.

Whittaker, R H (1969). New Concepts of Kingdoms of Organisms. *Science* 163: 150–160.

Wicklow, D & Malloch, D (1971). Studies in the genus *Thelebolus*: temperature optima for growth and ascocarp development. *Mycologia* 63: 118–131.

Wilding, N (ed) (1989). *Insect-fungus*

Interactions. 121–143. London: Academic Press.

Wilkins, W H & Patrick, S H M (1939). The ecology of the larger fungi. III. Constancy and frequency of grassland species with special reference to soil types. *Ann. Appl. Biol.* 26: 25–46.

Wilkins, W H & Patrick, S H M. (1940). The ecology of the larger fungi. IV. The seasonal frequency of grassland fungi with special reference to the influence of environmental factors. *Ann. Appl. Biol.* 27: 17–34.

Williams, M E & Rudolph, E D (1974). The role of lichens and associated fungi in the chemical weathering of rock. *Mycologia* 66: 648–660.

Wilson, M & Henderson, D M (1966). *British rust fungi*. Cambridge University Press.

Woese, C R, Kandler, O & Wheelis, M L (1990). Towards a natural system of organisms: Proposal for the domains Archaea, Bacteria, and Eucarya. *Proc. Nat. Acad. Sci., USA.* 87: 4576–4579.

Woods, R (2001). Ffwng glaswelltir /Grassland fungi. Cyngor Cefn Gwlad Cymru/Countryside Council For Wales.

Worsdall, W C (1915). *The Principles of Plant-Teratology*. Vol 1. Ray Society.

Zadoks, J C (1967). International dispersal of fungi. *Neth. J. Pl. Path.* 73, suppl. 1: 61–80.

Zak, B (1976a). Pure culture synthesis of bearberry mycorrhizae. *Can. J. Bot.* 54: 1297–1305.

Zhdanova, N N, Zakharchenko, V A, Vember, V V, & Nakonechnaya, L T (2000). Fungi from Chernobyl: mycobiota of the inner regions of the containment structures of the damaged nuclear reactor. *Mycol. Res.* 104: 1421–1426.

Index of Species

Index of Subjects